THE RESEARCH IMAGINATION

The idea that science is a blueprint for research and imagination gives research its life and purpose inspired this comprehensive explanation of research methodology. The authors' decades of experience have revealed that research is a craft requiring judgment and creativity, not simply memorization and application of the rules of science. Whether one is conducting an intimate one-on-one interview or a large-scale examination of an entire society, human imagination and scientific principles of inquiry go hand in hand. To that end, this book emphasizes scientific method but also acknowledges its critics. It covers a wide variety of data collection techniques but presents them as reinforcing, rather than competing with, one another, thus striking a balance between qualitative and quantitative methods. It is designed for students and instructors who want a comprehensive treatment of a variety of research techniques with special emphasis on qualitative approaches.

Professor Paul S. Gray (B.A. Politics, Princeton University; M.A. Education, Stanford University) received his Ph.D. in Sociology from Yale University and has taught at Boston College for thirty-two years. In addition to teaching, Gray also works as a business consultant, specializing in leadership development and corporate citizenship. Gray is the Faculty Chair of the Leadership for Change executive program associated with Boston College's Carroll School of Management. Gray has conducted research on topics as diverse as higher education in Massachusetts and labor unions in Africa. His research has been published in *Symbolic Interaction*, *Industrial Relations*, and the *Journal of African Studies*.

Professor John B. Williamson (B.S. Humanities and Science, Massachusetts Institute of Technology; Ph.D. Social Psychology, Harvard University) has taught at Boston College since 1969. He has written or co-written fifteen books and more than 100 journal articles and book chapters, and his writing has appeared in *American Sociological Review*, *American Journal of Sociology*, *Social Problems*, *Social Forces*, *Demography*, *International Social Security Review*, *The Gerontologist*, *Journal of Aging Studies*, *International Journal of Aging and Human Development*, *American Journal of Economics and Sociology*, and *Sociological Quarterly*. He is on the board of multiple journals and societies related to the study of sociology and aging. His current research concerns the comparative international study of social security systems.

Professor David A. Karp (B.A., Harvard University; Ph.D. Sociology, New York University) has taught sociology at Boston College for more than thirty years. Karp's 1996 work, *Speaking of Sadness*, was the 1996 winner of the Charles Horton Cooley Award from the Society for the Study of Symbolic Interaction. His most recent research uses qualitative methods to explore the moral boundaries of caring in emotional illness and conflict and seeks to discover the cultural resources people draw upon when confronted with this dilemma.

Professor John R. Dalphin (B.A., Holy Cross College; M.A. and Ph.D. Sociology, University of Massachusetts) has taught at Merrimack College for more than thirty years, teaching courses in population problems, research methodology, social class, and social inequality. He is also the author of *The Persistence of Social Inequality in America*, about the perpetuation of class inequality in America. Dalphin is a member of the American Sociological Association and the New England Sociological Association.

The Research Imagination

AN INTRODUCTION TO QUALITATIVE AND QUANTITATIVE METHODS

Paul S. Gray, BOSTON COLLEGE

John B. Williamson, BOSTON COLLEGE

David A. Karp, BOSTON COLLEGE

John R. Dalphin, MERRIMACK COLLEGE

with the collaboration of
Karen Bettez Halnon and James Carritte

CAMBRIDGE
UNIVERSITY PRESS

CAMBRIDGE UNIVERSITY PRESS
Cambridge, New York, Melbourne, Madrid, Cape Town, Singapore, São Paulo, Delhi

Cambridge University Press
32 Avenue of the Americas, New York, NY 10013-2473, USA

www.cambridge.org
Information on this title: www.cambridge.org/9780521879729

First published 2007

Printed in the United States of America

A catalog record for this publication is available from the British Library.

Library of Congress Cataloging in Publication Data

The Research imagination : an introduction to qualitative and quantitative methods /
Paul S. Gray . . . [et al.].
    p.   cm.
Includes bibliographical references and index.
ISBN 978-0-521-87972-9 (hardback) – ISBN 978-0-521-70555-4 (pbk.)
1. Social sciences – Research – Methodology.   2. Social sciences – Methodology.   3. Social
surveys – Methodology.   4. Research – Methodology.   I. Gray, Paul S., 1943–   II. Title.
H62.R4474   2007
001.4–dc22   2007002706

ISBN   978-0-521-87972-9 hardback
ISBN   978-0-521-70555-4 paperback

BRIEF CONTENTS

CONTENTS

PREFACE

Science is a blueprint for research; imagination gives research its life and purpose.

These ideas have inspired us to write this book about research methods. After decades of experience in planning and carrying out social research projects of all kinds, we are convinced that research is indeed a *craft* requiring judgment and creativity, not simply learning the rules of science and applying them. Whether one is doing the most intimate one-on-one interviewing or large-scale examinations of how entire societies make public policy, human imagination and scientific principles of inquiry go hand in hand. To that end, this book emphasizes scientific method but also acknowledges its critics. It covers a wide variety of data collection techniques but presents them as reinforcing, rather than competing with, one another.

A Balance between Qualitative and Quantitative Methods

This is a book for students and instructors who want a comprehensive treatment of a variety of research techniques but with special attention to qualitative approaches. We are committed to a balanced approach that gives a variety of qualitative methods full exposure alongside more mainstream quantitative strategies. Joe R. Feagin, a past president of the American Sociological Association, has commented on the almost exclusively quantitative emphasis of articles accepted for publication in leading sociology journals. He has advocated more realism in recognizing the methodological diversity within the discipline. Feagin (1999) also noted that many sociologists who study, for example, race, ethnicity, gender, class, and sexuality oppose a heavy emphasis on quantitative social research. In addition, he pointed out that introductory

sociology texts generally feature more qualitatively oriented studies because these are likely to be of more interest to students, as well as of immediate moral and practical importance to society.

In this book, we respond to Feagin's challenge. The separate chapters "Intensive Interviewing," "Observational Field Research," "Feminist Research," and "Historical Analysis" present the many qualitative approaches to data collection. At the same time, *The Research Imagination* gives ample attention to surveys, content analysis, aggregate data analysis, comparative research, and elementary and more advanced statistics. Throughout the text, the basic themes of scientific principles and human imagination that tie all research together are emphasized and reinforced.

This book is written by sociologists, but it is also appropriate for courses in other fields. Apt examples and student exercises are drawn from education, nursing, and social work. Separate chapters such as "Evaluation Research" and "Indexes and Scales" are applicable to a wide range of disciplines and professions. *The Research Imagination* is designed as a core text, but it can easily be supplemented with specialized readings on individual methods. Numerous suggestions for additional readings are offered following each chapter.

Responding to the Postmodern Critique

Since the turbulent 1960s, mainstream social investigation, especially experimentation and survey research, has had to contend with a humanistic critique (e.g., Phillips, 1971; Reinharz, 1984; Bruyn, 1986) that questioned its ability to capture fully the range and variety of human behavior. However, especially in the past twenty years, a new and more controversial genre of criticism has appeared. There has been a dramatic increase in postmodern and feminist scholarship (Rosenau, 1991; Harding and Hintikka, 2003; Law, 2004; Alexander, 2005) that either explicitly or implicitly challenges the very foundations of positivistic, scientific method: reliability, validity, objectivity, and representativeness. Of course, scientific method still embodies by far the most influential principles of social research, but we have responded to the postmodern critique by trying to understand terms like "objectivity" as less self-evident and all-encompassing than in the past.

So that students can take something constructive from the debate, *The Research Imagination* takes up the task of integrating postmodern methods into the overall examination of the research process. In colleges and universities all over the world, conventional canons of reliability and validity are being criticized in methods courses today; we try to show what these challenges are, where they originate, and how to cope with them. We decided not to present the battle of positivism versus postmodernism as a contest that seems to have no winner because the two sides often do not seem to agree on basic premises. Instead, we use ideas from each school of thought to comment constructively on the other – just as we also outline the strengths *and* weaknesses of both qualitative fieldwork and quantitative techniques. Our position is that positivists would benefit from some reflection on the impact and meaning of their own research and that postmodern researchers would do well to consider the prescriptive nature of, and at times the paucity of actual data in, their work.

What Is New in the Field?

Both the contemporary evolution of the literature on the various methods, as well as changes in the range of topics selected for research today have influenced the content of this volume. As new problems and research interests emerge, there is a shift in the methods that are best suited to study them as well as a need to improve existing methods. The methods literature has evolved to include wholly new elements such as action research, participatory evaluation research, and narrative analysis. At the same time, familiar research strategies such as participant observation and survey construction have been influenced by changes in technology via e-mail and the World Wide Web. The Internet telescopes space and time to the point at which even the definition of "field" work is changing, from having to travel to a natural setting to being in the setting virtually via computer. Finally, there has been increased emphasis on multimethod approaches in recent years (Jacobs, 2005). Because this text presents a variety of qualitative and quantitative methods as mutually reinforcing, rather than in opposition to each other, it is ideally suited to projects in which multiple methods are employed (Brewer and Hunter, 2006).

Twenty-five years ago the range of examples employed in methods texts reflected the social policy issues of the day – problems such as race relations, poverty, housing, crime, and drugs. Of course, these interests do remain, but they are augmented by an increasing emphasis on topics such as sexuality, aging, homelessness, violence against women, and child abuse. Methodologically, studies of children receive more attention today, as does research about women and research done by women. Also, the intense scrutiny regarding ethics in social research that first surfaced a generation ago has accelerated. Issues of informed consent and confidentiality have been made even more complex by Internet technology.

This text takes advantage of the widespread availability of the Internet, not just as a storehouse of information (in some cases supplanting books and articles) but also in providing students, as the consumers and creators of social science information, with interactive tools to push their projects forward. *The Research Imagination* is user-friendly for students who like using the Internet. For example, Chapters 7 and 14 include exercises that make use of newly available software. In most chapters, there are numerous references to online databases and methods source materials. These are academic and commercial Web sites, annotated bibliographies, and "how-to-do-it" tutorials. Almost all commercial links to data analysis software allow the reader to try out samples for a limited time. Students are encouraged to take advantage of these offers in order to determine which program best fits their needs and budget.

Teaching and Action Learning

We recognize the sheer volume and complexity of the material that is covered in most methods courses, so we show respect for the learning process by carefully building more complex ideas on the foundation of more basic concepts in the first three chapters and gradually elaborating ideas as we go. The writing in this text is accessible both to undergraduate and graduate-level audiences. Key terms and concepts are put in **BOLD CAPITAL LETTERS** and definitions in ***bold italics*** when first presented. Personal experiences of the authors as researchers are interspersed throughout. In most chapters, there are boxed inserts showing how prominent researchers have used the various techniques. The instructor should keep in mind that the chapters on individual methods may be assigned in any order. This book has a distinct applied focus, in that the material is presented to be useful! So, the real test of whether students have completely understood the concepts in *The Research Imagination* lies in their ability to design and carry out investigations of their own.

Graduate students who use this text will likely also be taking more advanced courses and will be involved in ongoing research projects. For these students, *The Research Imagination* can serve as a "text of record," in that it covers major developments in the literature on research of all kinds and includes an extensive bibliography that undergraduates may only sample, but that graduate students may use to review for general examinations in research techniques.

At the conclusion of each chapter, there are several regular features:

- A brief summary of chapter content
- Key terms that were **CAPITALIZED** throughout the chapter are listed separately as a guide to further study. These terms are also included in the index
- Suggested exercises testing what students have learned
- Readings illustrating the use of each method
- Readings about the method itself
- Complete references to sources (including Web sites) mentioned in the body of the text

Many of the homework or in-class exercises encourage students to enter the world of research. These optional exercises are designed to assist the instructor in making the reading come alive. *The Research Imagination* is written using an action learning pedagogy, an extremely effective technique that places emphasis on reflection as well as mastery of content. Using this approach, students can learn from their own experience in addition to what they learn from the text and outside readings. A Cambridge University Press Web site (www.cambridge.org/theresearchimagination) has been established as a companion to this text. It contains test banks, PowerPoint slides, exercises, and activities for classroom use.

The Plan of This Book

Chapters 1–4 may be considered introductory material – covering the scientific method, the interplay between social theory and methodology, research design, and measurement, respectively. These chapters provide a basic vocabulary for understanding the specific methods covered later in the text. Chapters 5–19 are designed to stand alone and may be assigned in any sequence, but they all convey the "research imagination" theme. Chapter 5 concerns ethics and politics in social research. It is placed relatively early in the text because an appreciation of important ethical dilemmas provides a context for, and informs the study of, topics like "Survey Research" (Chapter 7), "Observational Field Research" (Chapter 9), and "Experimental Research" (Chapter 12). Instructors and students especially interested in qualitative research might group together Chapters 8–11 ("Intensive Interviewing," "Observational Field

Research," "Feminist Methods," and "Historical Analysis"). A quantitative cluster may comprise "Survey Research," "Experimental Research," "Content Analysis," and "Aggregate Data Analysis," as well as "Basic Statistical Analysis" and "Multivariate Analysis and Statistical Significance" (Chapters 7, 12–14, 18, and 19). The readings on "Sampling," "Comparative Research Methods," "Evaluation Research," and "Indexes and Scales" (Chapters 6 and 15–17) present both quantitative and qualitative material.

Authors' Responsibilities

Paul S. Gray had overall editorial responsibility for all chapters. He is the author of Chapters 1–3 and 17 and co-author of Chapters 4, 7, 9–11, 16, and the Epilogue. John B. Williamson is the primary author of Chapters 18 and 19 and co-author of Chapters 4–8 and 12–16. David A. Karp is the co-author of Chapters 4, 9, 11–14, and the Epilogue. John R. Dalphin is the co-author of Chapters 5–7, 12, 13, 15, and 16. Collaborator James Carritte is the primary author of Chapter 7 and co-author of Chapters 14 and 15. Collaborator Karen Bettez Halnon is the primary author of Chapter 10. John M. Shandra is the co-author of Chapter 18. Tay K. McNamara is the co-author of Chapter 19. Stephen T. Barry contributed to Chapters 4, 7, 9, and 18. Richard S. Dorr contributed to Chapters 6–8, 12, and 13.

Acknowledgments

I thank our editor at Cambridge University Press, Ed Parsons, for his support and encouragement; Yuping Zhang, Shawn Guffey, Tracey Cullen, and Ami Jastrzemski for their excellent research and stimulating ideas; and Terry Smutylo for his thoughtful comments.

Paul S. Gray
Chestnut Hill, MA
February, 2007

REFERENCES

Alexander, Jeffrey C. 2005. *The Meanings of Social Life: A Cultural Sociology*. New York: Oxford.

Brewer, John, and Albert Hunter. 2006. *Foundations of Multimethod Research: Synthesizing Styles*. Thousand Oaks, CA: Sage.

Bruyn, Severyn T. 1986. *The Human Perspective in Sociology: The Methodology of Participant Observation*. New York: Irvington.

Feagin, Joe R. 1999. "Soul-Searching in Sociology." *Chronicle of Higher Education*, October 15: B-4.

Harding, Sandra, and Merrill B. Hintikka, eds. 2003. *Discovering Reality: Feminist Perspectives on Epistemology, Metaphysics, Methodology, and Philosophy of Science*. Boston: Kluwer.

Jacobs, Jerry. 2005. "Multiple Methods in ASR." *Footnotes* 33 (December): 9.

Law, John. 2004. *After Method: Mess in Social Science Research*. New York: Routledge.

Phillips, Derek L. 1971. *Knowledge from What? Theories and Methods in Social Research*. Boston: Houghton Mifflin.

Reinharz, Shulamit. 1984. *On Becoming a Social Scientist*. New Brunswick, NJ: Transaction.

Rosenau, Pauline. 1991. *Post-Modernism and the Social Sciences*. Princeton, NJ: Princeton University Press.

RESEARCH PROCESS

1

INTRODUCTION

What Is Social Research?

You are a curious person. That is why you are studying social research. You want to find out about the world, society, and human behavior. Research can be fun, but it is not just spinning out ideas from the comfort of an easy chair. Research is also a dynamic process that is more rigorous and complicated than many people realize. It is part perspiration and part inspiration. Learning the rules and principles of understanding that guide research is part of the challenge, but using our imagination and creativity is also essential for success. This book has been

1

written in that spirit, to provide a foundation from which you can make sense of the world.

This chapter focuses on the promise of social research, the goals of the scientific method, and the differences between science and common sense. The standards by which social researchers evaluate their own work and the work of others are also described.

Data Collection and Analysis

Systematic research in any field of inquiry involves two basic operations. The first is *to observe, measure, and record information* – in other words, DATA COLLECTION. The second is *to arrange and organize these data so that we may discover their significance, generalize about them, or tell what they mean*. This exercise is called DATA ANALYSIS. If you write down the weather in your hometown every day for one year, then that would be data collection. If you then divide this information into three categories: "fair," cloudy," and "stormy," then you will have performed a simple data analysis.

If, say, 70 percent of the days were either cloudy or stormy, it would be justifiable to conclude that the weather is not very pleasant where you live. A less superficial finding, and a practical recommendation, would be that a solar-powered electrical system would not be feasible there. No matter what interpretation is made, however, it must be "grounded"; that is, it must be related to, and follow logically from, the evidence collected. The conclusions of a reputable study are not merely the first thoughts or ideas that occur to the researcher; they are the ones supported and sustained by the data at hand.

ADDING TO KNOWLEDGE

The goal of social research is to add to what is already known about individuals in society and about the behavior and composition of human groups. This may be accomplished in three major ways: exploration, description, and explanation. EXPLORATION is *finding out about some previously unexamined phenomenon*. Often its purpose is to discover what is most significant or useful about the research setting, first by gaining a general overview. DESCRIPTION is *not-ing in meticulous detail how something or someone looks and acts*, both as a separate entity and in combination with other things or people. Finally, EXPLANATION is *telling why something or someone behaves as it does*.

As an example, let us take an issue from newspaper headlines. Suppose we are doing a study of terrorist organizations that train suicide bombers and this study will combine exploration, description, and explanation (Pape, 2005; Gambetta, 2006). After doing some reading on the subject, we would then carefully catalog these organizations and the behaviors associated with suicide missions. Perhaps we would decide that it is important to know what sorts of people belong to the groups, how they are recruited, and what they are taught to believe. If we are able, we might even interview members of terrorist organizations and the families of suicide bombers. We could also contact individuals and groups who are repelled by the suicide missions and who are trying to prevent them. If we gathered enough data, we might then be able to explain why people join violent terrorist organizations and how these groups inspire so much loyalty from their members.

Sources of Data

The data that are discovered and analyzed in social research may originate anywhere people interact. Some important sources of information about society are the home (Goodnow and Bowes, 2006), the workplace (Nippert-Eng, 1996; Hochschild, 2001), schools (Carter, 2005), and business corporations and other bureaucracies (Battelle, 2005). Other observation and listening posts may be voluntary associations – recreational and charitable groups (Mechling, 2001). In addition, data are generated from political parties, states, nations, and international organizations (Hatzfeld, Sontag, and Coverdale, 2006). Another fertile source of data is "everyday life" settings such as parks, streets, and other elements of the public realm (Lofland, 1998).

Researchers want to discover how these groups change and the extent to which they get along with one another. Thus, they might examine whether the increasing number of working women has influenced child-rearing practices in the United States. Or they might study the effect of the conservation movement on the enactment of laws to reduce air pollution. The area covered by an investigation may be relatively restricted or very broad. Thus, the research may concentrate on trying to understand the interplay between two people at a cocktail party or the conflict between a rich country and a poor one.

Social Significance

Over the past several decades, social researchers have become more visible to the public than ever before. It is not unusual to find sociologists, psychologists, or political analysts as guests on television and radio talk shows. This publicity reflects the importance of social science data in forming government policy, evaluating legislation, and even guiding judicial decisions. In fact, the social and psychological evidence contained in the plaintiffs' argument in the famous 1954 U.S. Supreme Court case *Brown v. Board of Education* helped usher in an era of civil rights legislation and an awakening of social concern. The data from social surveys helped justify the War on Poverty of the 1960s and the plans for affirmative action in employment that were developed in the 1970s. In the 1980s and 1990s, decisions to continue Project Head Start and Welfare to Work programs have often hinged on the recommendations of fact-finding research. Most recently, the courts have relied on the conclusions of researchers in making rulings that affect us all as citizens, for example, in deciding whether the death penalty is really a deterrent to crime.

What Is Methodology?

Because of the Internet and the explosion of knowledge that reaches us through the media and our educational institutions at all levels, our familiarity with findings and recommendations of social research has rapidly increased. For example, newspapers and magazines have popularized the work of Alfred Kinsey, who, as early as 1948, claimed that 13 percent of men and 5 percent of women in the United States were homosexuals (Kinsey, Pomeroy, and Martin,

1948/1998; Laumann and Michael, 2000).[1] More recently, a review of research over the past twenty years reported contradictory and ambiguous findings: Between 1 percent and 10 percent of Americans were found to be gay (Frankowski et al., 2004). How can we determine which findings are most reliable? We need to look at the methodology used to produce them!

Knowledge about the research process – about how studies are actually conducted – is much less widely disseminated than the research findings. It is easy to ignore some critical questions, such as

- What questions were these people asked, and who asked them?
- How many individuals provided the answers on which the researcher's conclusions were based?
- What categories were used for data analysis?

These are questions of **METHODOLOGY**; they explore *the principles, procedures, and strategies of research*. They are often thought to be too technical to sustain the interest of the public. This is unfortunate because the data that makes up any study, and the conclusions that are based on these data, are only as good as the methods of investigation that were used to obtain them. As one observer (Gottschalk, 1993:6–7) explained about data collected in 1991 that showed only a small percentage of gay Americans:

The surveys were conducted door to door, largely by female interviewers. Thirty percent of those polled refused to participate, and those that did were asked for their name, Social Security number and employer before being asked to reveal intimate details about their sexual behavior. The 1 percent "exclusively homosexual" figure also effectively rules out bisexual men as well as men who were involved with women before "coming out." Clearly, some men are going to be inclined to withhold some aspects of their sexuality from a strange woman who has just asked for his employer's name. But the questionable methodology has not been referred to in many of the media reports.

One of our goals is to increase the awareness of how research is done. After reading this book, you will have an understanding of the nature

[1] This debate is reviewed in Richard Lewontin's "Sex, Lies, and Social Science" (1995).

and complexities of the process. Even if you are not a future social worker, probation officer, educational specialist, or other professional-in-training, you will be able to critique research and to begin to recognize faulty conclusions that are based on poor evidence or that are unsupported by the data.

There are many different techniques for gathering information and a variety of procedures for analyzing data. These alternatives are explored in later chapters of the book. Researchers may contact a handful of people or thousands of people, in person or by sending a list of questions through the mail. They may use categories of analysis identical to those that have been used in previous studies, or they may use their imagination to develop a new set of concepts to make sense of the data collected. Research strategy is influenced by the questions that must be asked, the time and resources available to the researcher, and the purpose of the work, that is, whether it is primarily exploratory, descriptive, or explanatory. In most cases, several choices of technique are open to the researcher, regardless of the subject of the investigation. In her book *Tangled Lives: Daughters, Mothers, and the Crucible of Aging*, Rubin (2000) analyzed the process of growing old, the mother–daughter relationship, and the "sandwich generation" – those who feel obligated to care both for their own children and aging parents. She describes a pivotal period in her own life and conducts a series of intimate interviews and observations. Instead, she might have relied on census data showing the health, income, and family living arrangements of much larger numbers of elderly people. Her conclusions might have been less poignant and dramatic but no less informative and original.

The principles of research methodology are flexible. There are many more general guidelines and suggestions than specific dos and don'ts. Although the application of the principles of scientific knowledge to the investigation of human behavior has been subjected to criticism over the past twenty years (Harding, 1992; Lather, 1993; Law, 2004; Alexander, 2005), most social research remains self-consciously scientific. However, as you read the following explanation of the scientific method, keep in mind that science has not eliminated choice making, intuition, and imagination from social research. Rather, it has made us more aware of the necessity for choosing wisely our techniques of data collection and analysis.

THE SCIENTIFIC METHOD

The **SCIENTIFIC METHOD** is *a general model for inquiry in the physical and natural sciences, such as chemistry and biology, and in the social sciences, such as psychology and sociology*. It is, of course, possible to study human behavior within the framework of history, philosophy, or theology, but these disciplines do not use the language and procedures of science. When researchers claim to be scientists, they subject themselves and their work to scrutiny and judgment according to the standards and canons of scientific investigation. In this section, we will present these criteria, explain how the scientific method came to be applied to social research, and examine the differences between scientific and nonscientific research and modes of explanation.

The Research Cycle – Theory

A central goal of social science research is to make generalizations about human behavior. A general explanation is called a **THEORY** (see Figure 1.1). It is *a set of principles that tells why people do what they do* in a variety of contexts. Labeling theory, for example, addresses many kinds of deviant behavior, including both mental illness and criminality, by proposing that people act as society expects them to act (Shoemaker, 2006). For example, once the courts or the medical establishment label a person a "mental incompetent" or "felon," it is difficult to remove that label. The theory maintains that an individual who has been labeled will accept the label and behave in such a way as to deserve it.

A **HYPOTHESIS** is *a specific prediction that follows directly from a theory*. For example, we might predict that once people are negatively labeled, they will be more likely to get into trouble. However, fully elaborated theories are rarely created all at once. Often they begin as **HUNCHES**, *less formalized ideas or guesses that may eventually be refined into a theory.* One might suspect, for example, that the procedures for diagnosing and keeping records on mental patients hamper their reintegration into society after confinement. Or one might speculate that patients' knowledge of the diagnosis affects their self-concept. If these hunches are confirmed as data are collected, we might be encouraged to devise a more comprehensive theory along with specific hypotheses dealing with more kinds of labeling and deviance.

A good reason for conducting a scientific study is to find out whether an already existing theory makes sense in light of new observation. Therefore, when scientists do research, they are not merely adding to the storehouse of descriptive information about the world; they may also be making additions and corrections to theory. One such modification is called **VERIFICATION**. *A theory is verified when hypotheses that follow from the theory are supported, or the generalizations the theory makes are found to be accurate in several different settings.* Thus, labeling may be discovered outside the courts and mental hospitals (Rosenhan, 1973/2004), perhaps within the welfare system (Zucchino, 1999), or even on a Little League baseball team (Fine, 1987). Labeling theory may help us appreciate that welfare recipients and third-string, 8-year-old athletes can have something in common, namely, a relatively low level of self-confidence, as well as performance consistently below expectations. The theory explains these commonalities. One might conclude that the welfare system labels its clientele as inferior by making them wait for benefits, subjecting them to personal investigations, not paying them very much, and doing little to help them improve their position in life. The coach may constantly berate marginal ballplayers, subjecting them to humiliation or negative comparison with peers.

As labeling theory is verified in these and other examples, we move beyond the specific context of the welfare office or the baseball diamond to generalize about people everywhere. For the same purposes of generalization, scientific discoveries in atomic physics concerning

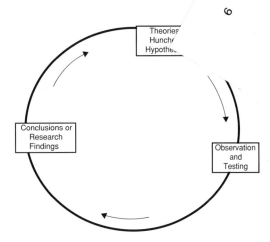

Figure 1.1. The research cycle.

the construction of matter are useful per se to the chemist, biologist, and astronomer. However, a theory does not have to be verified in order for research to be useful. It may be **DISCONFIRMED**: *found to be inaccurate, at least within a particular setting.* This is also valuable because it may lead to the reformulation of the theory.

Observation and Testing

In science, no theory may be either accepted or rejected without obtaining relevant information. This is accomplished during the field, or data collection, phase of research. The investigator uses data (1) to verify or disconfirm an already existing theory or hunch or (2) to establish, from observation, some new, general principle of behavior. The scientific method is shown as a circle in Figure 1.1 to illustrate that the research cycle may be entered at any point. One may begin with a theory or a hunch and then test it. Or one may begin with observation and construct theory bit by bit, much as a bricklayer adds to a wall.[2] In either case, the research process is, in reality, continuous. One study merely lays the groundwork for the next.

Conclusions and Findings

As Figure 1.1 implies, theory is never static in science; it changes constantly. The conclusions or **FINDINGS**, *what we have learned about the*

[2] See the discussion of induction and deduction in Chapter 2.

vorld as a result of the research, always carry implications for the endless process of theory creation and alteration. Theories are rarely completely proved or disproved. Often they are merely made more specific, in that the particular conditions under which they apply are stated explicitly. Therefore, findings influence theory by refining it, sharpening it, and making it a more precise tool of explanation.

The scientific method is a system for keeping track of the accumulation of theoretical generalizations and data in the physical and social sciences. This model for research is designed to be efficient. It makes us aware of theories that were disconfirmed, or of findings that were not fruitful for the creation of new theory, so that we are able to avoid the mistakes of previous investigators. The scientific method does not guarantee success; the results of many studies are inconclusive. Despite this, the scientific method has brought about unprecedented advances in medicine, space travel, and agricultural and manufacturing productivity.

These technological triumphs have led some to believe that there are scientific solutions to many of our problems of social disorganization: crime, political apathy, and the declining authority of school and church. Thus far, breakthroughs in the social sciences have been perhaps less dramatic than in the natural and physical sciences. Systematic research has, however, brought the world many fascinating and useful insights about human behavior.

A Short History of Social Science

As a basic model for asking questions about humankind and its environment, the scientific method is a relatively recent historic occurrence. The idea of the research cycle was first formalized in the eighteenth century, when the modem study of the natural sciences was initiated and the search for laws, axioms, and principles of the physical world was developed. To this end, the science laboratory was created. This work space, isolated from the outside world, served as a sanctuary where the scientist could test theories in a controlled setting. **EXPERIMENTATION** then,

as today, involved *keeping records of everything that occurred and repeating procedures again and again, perhaps each time changing only one small aspect of the environment* – temperature, space, light, or the amount of materials used in testing.

Early social thinkers were encouraged by the successes in physics, genetics, and medicine. They tried to develop laws and theories of human behavior, but the full significance of scientific methodology for social investigation was not to be immediately realized. The first pseudoscientific theorizers about society were really social philosophers, whose work held more in common with the speculations of classical Greek and Roman authors than with the experimenters in the new physical and natural sciences. The major reason for the comparative backwardness of social investigation until well into the nineteenth century was the tendency to avoid systematic observation. The first psychology laboratory was not established until 1879, in Germany.

Few investigators actually engaged in **FIELD-WORK** – *the examination of what people say and do in their own natural surroundings*. A rare exception was Alexis de Tocqueville, a French researcher whose analysis of the United States, *Democracy in America*, written in 1835, is still considered a classic in both political science and sociology. Its scope and careful attention to detail, combined with sensitivity to theory, were unique. Auguste Comte (1798–1857), the originator of the term *sociology*, set the tone for much of the pioneering social investigation. Comte imagined a "positivist" science of society that would study social reality as distinct from the perceptions and biases of those who studied it. We still use the term **POSITIVISM** today to refer to *the presumption that the principles of inquiry embedded in physical and natural sciences may productively be applied to the study of human behavior in society*. Ironically, Comte's writings were an armchair treatise on how society *ought* to be organized rather than a description of how it *was* structured, and why. Comte wanted social analysis to be separated from the theological and metaphysical explanations of an earlier era, but he did not actually subject his theories to the test of data collection.

A major turning point in the application of scientific techniques to the study of society was the publication of Charles Darwin's *Origin of Species* (1859/2003). Darwin, of course, became famous for his theory of evolution, but it is essential to realize that he was, first and foremost, an astute and thorough observer. The records he kept as a naturalist aboard the HMS *Beagle* as it made its voyage became both the inspiration and evidence for his theories. Darwin brought together and reconciled two major strands of nineteenth-century thought: the ideas of the natural sciences and those of human development and progress. Subsequently, such thinkers as Herbert Spencer (1820–1903) made the analogy between the growth of society and the evolution of the biological organisms that Darwin had described. This prepared the way for Emile Durkheim (1858–1917), Max Weber (1864–1920), and other theoreticians who were highly skilled in techniques of observation and cross-cultural comparison. Similar developments were occurring in psychology. The theories of Sigmund Freud (1856–1939) and his disciples were tested continually in the context of psychiatric treatment. Other psychologists began to study learning and perception following the studies of biology and physiology.

Social science entered the twentieth century with the traditions of laboratory and field research firmly established and with a degree of theoretical sophistication. However, in an age in which the prestige of physical science reached new heights because of its explanatory and predictive powers, social scientists were often preoccupied with trying to convince others that their disciplines were legitimate and that they were truly engaged in building a cumulative body of knowledge. During World War II, the power of newly perfected computers and data sorters was combined with improvements in survey research methods to produce an unprecedented growth in the number and influence of quantitative social research projects. Although by 1970 large-scale survey research was the most influential method for data collection (measured by the research dollars it attracted), the last few decades have seen a rebirth of interest in fieldwork and a greater diversity of methodological approaches.

The efforts to make all social research "scientific" have met with only partial success. Some still argue that despite their claims to scientific stature, disciplines such as political science, sociology, and social psychology cannot easily meet the standards of scientific investigation. Moreover, others take a philosophical position of **POSTPOSITIVISM** (Haack, 1993; Guba and Lincoln, 2005), which claims that *social scientists can never be certain that their techniques will allow them to see objective reality*. We will examine the postpositivism argument carefully in Chapter 10. Now, we will consider some of the technical demands of science and how science is distinguished from common sense. Are social scientists unjustifiably trying to share the spotlight with their more "exact" and well-respected cousins?

Common Sense and Social Science

When we search out bargains in the supermarket, describe how our favorite football team won the big game, or speculate about the causes of pollution or high taxes, we are attempting the same intellectual tasks that social researchers set for themselves: exploration, description, and explanation. These activities are as essential for human survival in society (for obtaining food, clothing, and shelter) as they are for leading a productive and satisfying existence. It is therefore not surprising that the public's reverence for physical science has exceeded its acceptance of social science. Biologists and physicists also describe and explain phenomena, but their subject matter has a mysterious quality. By contrast, many people believe they are familiar with and able to perform the same operations for which professional social researchers are paid a salary.

It is difficult for most of us to have our own ideas about the causes of cancer or the logistics of space travel, but it is relatively easy to feel expert about social life. If you doubt this, the next time you attend a gathering of friends or acquaintances, listen for "theories" about the causes of crime, poverty, prejudice, emotional problems, or political conflict. Many people believe that when it comes to social issues, one person's opinion is as good as another's. To support this contention, some individuals, who may think they understand science but who really do not, may cite the disagreements among sociologists, psychologists, and educators regarding fundamental social processes. However, genuine science is not merely opinion; it is opinion supported by data and connected to a body of theory.

The scientific method does not guarantee consensus in research findings, and this is no less true in the chemistry laboratory than in social analysis. Nevertheless, it does guide the attempt to move beyond the relatively restricted world of our own personal experience. If two social researchers disagree about the ethics of big business in America, it will not be because one has been a worker and the other a factory owner. They will both have made observations according to the canons of scientific research – viewing the world from unfamiliar perspectives, talking with people with whom they would never otherwise associate, and taking seriously and addressing directly many possible objections to their findings. These activities are rarely, if ever, done systematically in daily life. Therefore, COMMON SENSE is really *unsupported opinion, or attitudes inspired by insufficient and unreliable information.* We are not saying that a trained social researcher never makes an error in observation or judgment. Rather, the scientific method decreases the *probability* of error.

WHY COMMON SENSE FAILS US. "There's more crime in rich neighborhoods than in poor neighborhoods," said Uncle Ed, puffing on his cigar. "How do you know?" I asked. "Cause crooks aren't stupid," said he. "They know there's nothing to steal in poor neighborhoods!" In contrast to Uncle Ed's commonsense view of the world, the poor and racial minorities are victims of crime more often than any other segments of our society, and lower-class individuals are less safe from crime than members of the middle class. According to the U.S. Bureau of Justice Statistics, 44 of 1,000 black households and 28 of 1,000 white households experienced burglaries in 2004. Households with an annual income below $7,500 were burglarized at rates higher than those of households with larger incomes (Bureau of Justice Statistics, 2005). How is it that these unambiguous research findings appear so different from the layperson's conventional wisdom?

DISTANCE. First, most people *think* they are accurate observers. They are frequently deceived by the unfamiliar or the remote. Stand far enough away, and skimmed milk looks like heavy cream; in baseball, a scratch hit tonight will look like a line drive in tomorrow's box score. To the middle-class observer, poverty sometimes is seen as moral degeneracy and lack of education is seen as laziness. The roots of much prejudice and stereotyping may be found in overgeneralizations that people make from a distance. If Uncle Ed had lived in a poor neighborhood, he might have been better able to appreciate how dangerous it can be. His commonsense view of crime is neither an accurate description nor an accurate explanation; he is just too distant to see the problem clearly.

FAMILIARITY, NOT UNDERSTANDING. Second, we may be quite familiar with a phenomenon, yet not understand how it works. We ride in an elevator or we watch television, but we are powerless to fix these machines if they break down. Most of us do not know the principles of electricity by which they operate. Yet they are very much a part of our lives. We act as consumers without understanding the social economy, obey laws while ignorant of theories of social control, and try to learn from our teachers without necessarily appreciating the process of learning, and we may be the victims of crime without realizing what motivates the criminal. In sum, we are never quite as knowledgeable about society as we may think.

Human behavior is so diverse and complex that systematic research is required to determine the norms and social regularities of society.

Our personal experiences do not necessarily give us an accurate view of behavior in general because we rarely move beyond our own awareness. If the thief who is caught removing Uncle Ed's flat screen television turns out to be from a rundown neighborhood, it would be natural for Ed to see crime as a social problem through the prism of his personal involvement with it. It is easier for him to imagine millions of other victims who are also in his relatively comfortable position than to imagine victims who themselves are poor. His experience may reinforce the idea that criminals are economically desperate individuals, a generalization that ignores so-called respectable, or white-collar, crime in business or government.

A related point is that we often make assumptions about our immediate environment that other people, equally experienced, would not make. The movie industry appears differently to performers, producers, and technicians, depending in part on their function and status within it. Authoritarian parents may describe their family as being free of conflict whereas their outwardly compliant children view it as a prison. In short, our perception of society is usually limited and shaped by the demographic categories into which we fall, including our age, sex, income, ethnicity, religion, occupation, and educational level. Our economic behavior, our political attitudes, and our sense of what is normal psychologically – are all dependent in large measure on our membership in these kinds of social groupings.

The arena with which most of us are familiar is limited and relatively simple, when compared to the multiple realities that social researchers must understand if they are to obtain a comprehensive view of social relations. People often lack the skill, or the desire, to expand their horizons in a way that would let them appreciate the world as others see it.

EMOTIONS. Another reason that common sense fails us is that our everyday observations are colored by our emotions (Turner and Stets, 2005). Feelings are not bad in themselves, but their effect on our powers of judgment may go unrecognized. Some of us feel uncomfortable around people with disabilities; they may act in unexpected ways or appear different, and this makes us feel embarrassed and self-conscious. If we have to decide whether students with disabilities should attend classes with nondisabled children, we may find ourselves saying that their disabilities will prevent them from profiting from the experience. However, is it their lack of skill or our discomfort that prompts this assessment?

Many of us fail to recognize our negative reactions to others. People may profess love for humanity in general although they may actually have great difficulty relating to specific individuals who deviate from their norms of behavior. In addition, most of us find it difficult to overcome negative feelings toward others. Prejudice against African Americans, Jews, Italians, or any other racial or ethnic group will not necessarily be reduced by exposure to favorable evidence about them (Adams, Blumenfeld, and Castaneda, 2000). Through SELECTIVE OBSERVATION, *data that might disconfirm negative stereotypes can be screened out*. The data may prove to be too much of a challenge to the observer whose favorable self-image is intimately connected with a poor view of others. How many times, in polite conversation, do we say, "Well, let's drop the subject"? The feeling of being bored or otherwise dissatisfied with an encounter may result from having heard an argument that is threatening to one's ego or worldview.

Thus, our commonsense notions of how society works are often inaccurate or incomplete because we are either too distant from the data, or too close, or because our emotions act as a smokescreen. Despite these barriers to understanding, we may still believe that we are astute observers because we are rarely forced to recognize our mistakes. Prejudice, ignorance, and fear may be perpetuated generation after generation. People in everyday life are usually not held responsible for their opinions and may not always appreciate the far-reaching consequences of the domestic and foreign policies that they favor. It is much easier to advocate "bombing the enemy into the Stone Age" than to drop the bomb oneself or to cope with the human suffering that results from it.

Principles of Scientific Investigation

Although we may make many errors of omission and commission as we judge and observe, we may nonetheless function acceptably as private citizens in society. A scientist, however, is not allowed this luxury. Before research findings and procedures are scrutinized by outsiders, they are rigorously monitored by researchers themselves. A good scientist is a self-critic who wants to eliminate, or at least to reduce as much as possible, biased, prejudiced, or incomplete observation. Of course, this does not mean that creativity is lost in the process!

OBJECTIVITY. Some scientists assert that their work is objective, meaning that their own private values never intrude in determining their findings. In other words, the researcher's race, creed, color, or political beliefs have absolutely no significance in determining the outcome of a study. The canon of **OBJECTIVITY** maintains that, *ideally, any two researchers who study the same behaviors, processes, or phenomena should arrive at identical findings.*

Objectivity, so-called, is perhaps approached more closely in the physical science laboratory than in most social research because, in the laboratory, it is easier to control the environment for the collection of data. In all fields of systematic inquiry, however, objectivity remains an ideal. That most research reports in the natural sciences ignore the personal motives of investigators does not mean the reports really were completely objective. When a renowned biochemist lets us glimpse what goes on behind the scenes (Watson, 1969/1997), we discover that the background, personality, financial needs, and career interest of scientists do influence their work. The orderly accumulation of knowledge may be upset by professional rivalry and jealousy, sexism, or racism.

Recognizing that researchers in all fields, because they are human, cannot be wholly objective, many social scientists in recent years have given up chasing the ghost of objectivity. The investigator is not like a robot that works the same way in every case. Each person observing a social phenomenon will inevitably exercise some selective observation and memory. Even in choosing a topic for study, a researcher is indicating certain value biases; our perception of what constitutes a social problem may depend, to some degree, on our own position in society. Moreover, it is virtually impossible to keep from taking sides in studying some social phenomena (Becker, 1971). How would a study of the criminal justice system avoid adopting the perspective of the courts and police, or the criminal, or the innocent accused of crime? Can an analysis of the social welfare bureaucracy really be written from the point of view both of social workers and clients?

As the twenty-first century began, many researchers as well as philosophers of science were rethinking the issues surrounding objectivity (see Hammersley and Gomm, 1997). These writers have been influenced by the postmodern school of philosophy and sociology. Most of them believe that the people, events, and institutions that researchers study do have an existence "in reality," independent of the accounts of these phenomena that investigators create. But they also insist that the language used to construct these accounts becomes a part of that reality. Thus, the explanations developed in social research make the conventional canon of objectivity impossible to achieve. Even when a number of researchers agree to identical explanations of the same phenomenon, their arguments are socially constructed; that is, their accounts represent these phenomena from one or another point of view. Therefore, researchers are constantly "under the constraint of not producing an account that is at odds with the evidence available" according to established knowledge (Hammersley and Gomm, 1997:4.2). This constraint raises the likelihood of unconscious error resulting from the production of knowledge. According to this critique, researchers need to remain more skeptical than those working in other areas of social life because it is they who are primarily concerned with avoiding the danger of accepting as true what is in fact false.

Because objectivity is an elusive concept, some scholars believe that all investigation should stem from a clearly enunciated value position. They claim that little or no effort need be made to present opposing points of view. A Marxist who personally supports the aims of the Cuban Revolution may describe how that revolution has succeeded, deemphasizing its failures, based on the assumption that more conservative writers will take on the responsibility of pointing them out. On the basis of a similar assumption, an advocate of free enterprise as a principle of economic organization may concentrate on the beneficial effects of competition and give less attention to the problems of rampant materialism and unemployment that capitalism may create.

Most researchers, including the authors of this book, would not advocate abandoning the idea of objectivity. It remains a worthy goal because we do have control over many sources of bias and error (Kitcher, 2006). To test our theories fully, we must actively seek evidence that challenges them. One does not strengthen a theory by omitting, or dismissing as irrelevant, the data that do not support it.

To increase objectivity, researchers can solicit the views of all, not only those with whom they agree. By using a number of sources, they can verify the information they receive to guard against deliberate or unintentional misrepresentation of the facts. We cannot eliminate our feelings, but instead of ignoring their potential effect on our work, we can be explicit about our own biases and assumptions (Gubrium and Holstein, 2006). Such an explicit statement will be useful to those who evaluate our work. In addition, such **INTROSPECTION**, or *self-examination*, will help us to present as balanced and as complete a view of society as we can.

Finally, communication among social scientists is not precluded by the differences in their subjective orientation. Regardless of the variation in their backgrounds, two researchers may agree on a great deal of factual information. Our confidence in the report of a white policeman arresting a black suspect is increased when we discover that both black and white observers describe the scene similarly; our faith in the diagnosis of mental illness is strengthened when psychiatrists, psychologists, and social workers can achieve consensus. Even in cases in which two investigators differ regarding the sig-

nificance of a given event, they may still agree to disagree, in the sense that their argument is attributed to an honest difference of opinion, rather than to stupidity, bigotry, or mutual antipathy. This opens the way for scientists to learn from each other, although their research findings may sometimes be contradictory.

REPLICATION AND RELIABILITY. Another scientific ideal is **REPLICATION**. *Research should be conducted in such a way that those who question its outcomes can repeat it and obtain the same results. A measurement instrument, such as a test of intelligence or personality, that yields the same results when repeated* is said to have high **RELIABILITY**. Since scientific knowledge has to be cumulative, reliability is a cornerstone of science; one cannot build a coherent body of information without reliable measurement tools.

In the physical sciences, it is possible to replicate a study under conditions identical to the original. The laboratory environment may be monitored and controlled so that, for example, every time the two substances sodium and chlorine are combined in the proper amounts, we get table salt. In social research, by contrast, it is often difficult to recreate the original setting. Herbert Gans (1962) studied Italian American families in the West End of Boston. Today, the streets he walked are gone; the people he talked to are displaced. The entire area is a giant complex of government buildings, hospitals, and high-rise apartments. Gans's study thus could never be replicated.

Even when the buildings remain, the research environment may be altered. Suppose you study a nursing home and discover that the elderly residents are quite satisfied with their treatment. You might convey a relatively benign picture of convalescent care. Six months later another researcher visits the same place and finds the facilities in disrepair and patients lying in squalor, many of them demoralized and dissatisfied. What has happened? Either you were an unusually poor observer or some events have occurred that changed the setting dramatically, events over which the investigator had no control – for example, the owners of the home went bankrupt, the custodial staff staged a work stoppage, or supervisory personnel quit or were terminated. Any one of these happenings might affect the research conclusions in a major way.

In this example, and in any duplication of a study, the variation in results could be caused by differences in the conditions for observation rather than by a lack of objectivity in the original study. In many cases, researchers have little choice but to contend with these difficulties. Nevertheless, they are obligated to design their data collection procedures in such a way that replication is, at least, not precluded.

Studies that use highly reliable data collection tools are more easily replicated than those that depend on the questions that individual researchers devise "on the spot." For this reason, pencil-and-paper tests and printed schedules of questions have been developed to measure the skills, opinions, and attitudes of large numbers of people again and again. These instruments ensure that identical questions are asked each time a study is repeated, but they are still not perfect measures because it is difficult to control the environment in which the answers are being provided. People's opinions may be influenced by their health, life situation, or even the temperature or noise level in the room. Therefore, as with the goal of objectivity in social research, replication and reliability are scientific ideals worth trying to attain, but no instrument is perfectly reliable.

PRECISION. A fourth principle of science is **PRECISION** in measurement. In the laboratory, microscopes and scales have been developed to *an extremely fine tolerance*. We may know exactly how much of two chemical elements are present in the experimental environment. So precise are these measurement tools, in fact, that researchers may verify the existence of a compound by separating it into its component parts and recombining them at will.

Measurement is much more problematic in social science because in many ways the social world is more complex than the physical world. One can analyze a piece of paper blown about by the wind in terms of its velocity, weight, and the force of gravity, but people cannot literally be placed under a microscope to determine how and why they are swept along by crowd emotion. In spite of this limitation, we do have means available for checking on the quality of our measures. So, whereas social science can no more make the claim to perfect measurement than to perfect objectivity, we must again consider the problem to be one of degree.

VALIDITY. Social researchers are frequently interested in measuring complicated and abstract phenomena, such as happiness, alienation, community solidarity, political conservatism, the popularity of a president, and various psychological conditions. There is a great deal of disagreement regarding how best to measure these concepts because no unique, explicit, and comprehensive set of observable behaviors is indicative of each, to the exclusion of everything else. Moreover, the meaning of each of the concepts varies with its social context. The alienation suffered by white-collar workers is different from that experienced by poor, inner-city residents. The situational nature of these abstractions makes them more difficult to manipulate than concepts in the physical sciences such as height, density, distance, and pressure.

These problems with defining many of the concepts used in social research frequently create a dilemma: Are we really measuring what we claim to be measuring? Schizophrenia, a form of mental illness, is usually defined as disorientation in time, place, and person. A schizophrenic may suffer hallucinations or delusions and be highly distractible, losing a sense of emphasis and subordination in conversation and action. If we observe someone with these symptoms, how confident are we that we are measuring what we want to measure (Caplan, 1996)? Perhaps, instead of mental illness, we are merely seeing the temporary effects of LSD, Ecstasy, or some other mind-altering drug.

VALIDITY refers to *the fit between the concept that a researcher wants to examine and the evidence for that concept*. Increasing validity is another important goal of science. We want to make the fit between concept and evidence as exact as possible and to be aware of potential slippage between the two. In our last example, the longer we observe the various symptoms, the more valid representations of schizophrenia they become, in that the chances of the patient being in a temporary, drug-induced state diminish over time. As another example, a ballot cast for the incumbent president may not be the most valid measure of his popularity. Instead, it may indicate his opponent's unpopularity!

We need to pay careful attention to the manner in which complex concepts like schizophrenia and political popularity are defined in social research. If some important component of a concept is omitted from its definition, the investigator will have difficulty assessing how much of that concept is really there. At the same time, if the definition is too broad, we may create a less precise measure than we need. If social researchers are as explicit as possible about the definitions of the concepts they use and the situations to which they apply, it is possible to construct a cumulative body of knowledge about social reality. Ingenuity in devising concepts is a challenge in all sciences, particularly in the study of human behavior.

The Critical Perspective

Thus far, we have examined some canons of scientific inquiry: objectivity, replication, reliability, precision, and validity. These criteria are useful as a baseline for evaluating the scientific status of social research, but they do not fully capture its quality. There is, in addition, a particular attitude, a CRITICAL PERSPECTIVE, that social researchers share. To be critical is not necessarily to be negative about society, but it *entails looking beyond the obvious and into the many possible meanings and interpretations of human behavior*. It is driven by a restlessness of spirit and intense curiosity. The comparison between a researcher and a police detective is an apt one. The social scientist is like the lieutenant knocking at the door of the witness to a murder whom he has already questioned for an hour: "You know," he says earnestly, "you've been very helpful to me and I don't mean to trouble you again, but there's just one more thing that's been

nagging me, and if I don't get an ans\ be able to sleep tonight."

Scientists are constantly challengin ity of the knowledge they produce. They adopt a skeptical attitude that forces them to question the truth of the data being collected. They ask continually, "Are my data reliable and valid? What are the potential errors that might be intruding into my findings? What kinds of data will cause me to reevaluate my theoretical ideas?" Scientific understanding and explanation are not predicated on faith alone. The scientist considers theoretical speculation logical only when it is accompanied by supporting data. Scientists should never become so committed to a set of theoretical ideas that they are unwilling to modify them in the face of conflicting evidence. Although they may be disappointed when their own promising theories are challenged or disconfirmed, the canons of science dictate that researchers press on with their work.

Science is, in this regard, subversive. It cannot accept, without testing, the explanation of the status quo offered by the powers that be. The "official" reasons for war, economic recession, the high rates of crime, or poor national reading scores are merely part of the evidence. The social researcher is "compelled by what he is doing to fly in the face of what those around him take for granted," notes sociologist Peter Berger (1963:38). This imperative to "unmask the pretensions and the propaganda" by which humans cloak their actions is a logical outcome of research methodology. We do not stop once we learn people's explanations for their own behavior. On the contrary, we check out their explanations by talking to other people and by making our own observations. Using this strategy, what we discover through scientific investigation becomes both less obvious and more comparable from one setting to another.

Remaining Questions

What may we say about the scientific status of social research? Some attempts to understand the world, including theology, on the one hand, and common sense, on the other, are wholly nonscientific. By contrast, the modern practices of physics, biology, and chemistry are highly scientific. When speaking of social research, however, it seems fruitless to look at the issue of science in either/or terms. Some political science, psychology, and sociology studies are every bit as scientific as studies in the discipline of physics; others are no more scientific than most of what is today called *philosophy*. For most of the twentieth century, there was general agreement among the social sciences that the principles and goals of scientific inquiry were worthy. However, there has been great variation in the extent to which the canons of science are met in practice, and, at the beginning of the twenty-first century, as we will see in Chapter 10, there is even some significant resistance to the scientific model of inquiry within postmodern sociology.

It is legitimate to conclude that the application of the scientific method to the study of human behavior is more than a sterile exercise of aping the physical sciences. The scientific method represents a mechanism for the systematic reduction of error in the description and analysis of society. Through social science, we are held accountable for our theories and explanations, and we are compelled to consider their effect on the world. If our findings are incomplete or our recommendations unwise, then it is we, as social scientists, who are responsible.

SUMMARY

Social research is a dynamic process that involves the collection and analysis of data and the formation of conclusions based on those data. Its goal is to add to knowledge through the exploration, description, and explanation of social reality. The sources of data are diverse, from the interaction between two people to the behavior of states and nations. The recommendations of social researchers have in recent years become important in the formation of government policy, the evaluation of legislation, and the determination of judicial decisions.

Methodology is the study of the research process itself – the principles, procedures, and strategies for gathering information, analyzing it, and interpreting it. The conclusions of a study are only as good as the methods of investigation that were used to obtain them. Therefore, to be able to judge research critically, as well as to conduct it, we need a thorough knowledge of methodology.

The scientific method is a general model of inquiry in education research, political science, psychology, sociology, and other disciplines. Theories, general explanations for behavior, are continually being modified in light of new findings. This model was initiated in the physical and natural sciences. It has been adopted by the behavioral sciences with profitable results because it requires the systematic elimination or control of biased and inaccurate observation based on emotion or inadequate measuring tools. Principles of scientific investigation include the ideals of objectivity, reliability, precision, and validity. One must be able to replicate a scientific study and to assess whether it measures, in fact, what it was designed to measure, in theory. Scientists are self-critical and skeptical about the procedures they use and the data they obtain. They try to find as many explanations as possible for each phenomenon observed.

KEY TERMS

common sense
critical perspective
data analysis
data collection
description
disconfirmation
experimentation
explanation
exploration
fieldwork
findings
hunch
hypothesis
introspection
methodology
objectivity
positivism
postpositivism
precision
reliability
replication

scientific method
selective observation
theory
validity
verification

EXERCISES

1. Select one or more books or articles in which social research findings are presented and analyze each study from the standpoint of exploration, description, and explanation. Can you give examples of each research function? Did the researchers emphasize one function more than the others? How do you know?

2. We have suggested that the same form of social life might be investigated in a number of diverse empirical contexts. Try to list as many different settings or contexts as possible in which you could conceivably do a case study of alienation.

3. Attend a social gathering and note down five commonsense conclusions about social life from ordinary conversation. How would a scientific researcher attempt to verify each conclusion?

4. Imagine that you are about to embark on a study of the behavior of college students in their dormitories. Without specifying in great detail what you would study, write a short essay on the difficulties you might expect to face in meeting the three canons of the scientific method: objectivity, precision, and replication.

SUGGESTED READINGS

Gouldner, Alvin. 1962. "Anti-Minotaur: The Myth of a Value-Free Sociology." *Social Problems* 9 (Winter): 199–213.

A sharp, literate, and classic critique of sociological attempts at objectivity.

Hoover, Kenneth R., and Todd Donovan. 2000. *Elements of Social Scientific Thinking.* 7th ed. Belmont, CA: Wadsworth.

An excellent short introduction to study design and the scientific method.

Katzer, Jeffrey, Kenneth H. Cook, and Wayne W. Crouch. 1997. *Evaluating Information: A Guide for Users of Social Science Research.* 4th ed. New York: McGraw-Hill.

A highly readable introductory guide to measurement and the difference between research and common sense.

McDonald, Lynn. 1995. *The Early Origins of the Social Sciences.* Montreal: McGill-Queen's University Press.

A useful summary of the origins of the social sciences.

Myers-Lipton, Scott. 2006. *Social Solutions to Poverty.* Boulder, CO: Paradigm.

This volume contains an historical account of the influence of research scholarship on the idea of poverty reduction.

REFERENCES

Adams, Maurianne, Warren J. Blumenfeld, and Carmelita R. Castaneda, eds. 2000. *Readings for Diversity and Social Justice: An Anthology on Racism, Sexism, Anti-Semitism, Heterosexism, Classism, and Ableism.* New York: Routledge.

Alexander, Jeffrey C. 2005. *The Meanings of Social Life: A Cultural Sociology.* New York: Oxford University Press.

Battelle, John. 2005. *The Search: How Google and Its Rivals Rewrote the Rules of Business and Transformed Our Culture.* New York: Portfolio.

Becker, Howard S. 1971. "Whose Side Are We On?" In *Sociological Work,* 15–25. Howard S. Becker, ed. Chicago: Aldine.

Berger, Peter. 1963. *Invitation to Sociology.* New York: Doubleday.

Bureau of Justice Statistics. 2005. *Criminal Victimization 2004.* Washington, DC: U.S. Department of Justice, NCJ 210674.

Caplan, Paula J. 1996. *They Say You're Crazy: How the World's Most Powerful Psychiatrists Decide Who's Normal.* Reading, MA: Perseus Press.

Carter, Prudence L. 2005. *Keepin' It Real: School Success beyond Black and White.* New York: Oxford University Press.

Darwin, Charles. 1859/2003. *The Origin of Species.* New York: Signet.

de Tocqueville, Alexis. 1835/2003. *Democracy in America.* New York: Penguin.

Fine, Gary Alan. 1987. *With the Boys: Little League Baseball and Preadolescent Culture.* Chicago: University of Chicago Press.

Frankowski, Barbara L., et al. 1994. "Sexual Orientation and Adolescents." *Pediatrics* 113:6.

Gambetta, Diego, ed. 2006. *Making Sense of Suicide Missions.* New York: Oxford University Press.

Gans, Herbert. 1962. *The Urban Villagers.* New York: Free Press.

Goodnow, Jacqueline J., and Jennifer M. Bowes. 2006. *Men, Women, and Household Work.* New York: Oxford University Press.

Gottschalk, Kurt. 1993. *In These Times* (May 31): 6–7.

Guba, Egon G., and Yvonna S. Lincoln. 2005. "Paradigmatic Controversies, Contradictions and Emerging Confluences." In *Handbook of Qualitative Research*, 191–216. 3rd ed. Norman K. Denzin and Yvonna S. Lincoln, eds. Thousand Oaks, CA: Sage.

Gubrium, Jaber, and James A. Holstein. 2006. *The New Language of Qualitative Method.* New York: Oxford University Press.

Haack, Susan. 1993. "Science 'From a Feminist Perspective.'" *Philosophy* 67:5–18.

Hammersley, Martyn, and Roger Gomm. 1997. "Bias in Social Research." *Sociological Research Online* 2.
http://www.socresonline.org.uk/socresonline/2/1/2.html.

Harding, Sandra. 1991. "After the Neutrality Ideal: Science, Politics and 'Strong Objectivity.'" *Social Research* 59 (3): 568–587.

Hatzfeld, Jean, Susan Sontag, and Linda Coverdale. 2006. *Machete Season: The Killers in Rwanda Speak.* New York: Picador.

Hochschild, Arlie Russell. 2001. *The Time Bind: When Work Becomes Home and Home Becomes Work.* New York: Owl Books.

Kinsey, Alfred C., Wardell B. Pomeroy, and Clyde E. Martin. 1948/1998. *Sexual Behavior in the Human Male.* Bloomington: Indiana University Press.

Kitcher, Philip. 2006. *The Advancement of Science: Science without Legend, Objectivity without Illusions.* New York: Oxford University Press.

Lather, Patti. 1993. "Fertile Obsession: Validity after Poststructuralism." *Sociological Quarterly* 34 (4): 673–693.

Laumann, Edward O., and Robert T. Michael, eds. 2000. *Sex, Love, and Health in America.* Chicago: University of Chicago Press.

Law, John. 2004. *After Method: Mess in Social Science Research.* New York: Routledge.

Lewontin, Richard. 1995. "Sex, Lies, and Social Science." *New York Review of Books* (April 20): 24– 29.

Lofland, Lyn H. 1998. *The Public Realm: Exploring the City's Quintessential Social Territory.* Chicago: Aldine de Gruyter.

Mechling, Jay. 2001. *On My Honor: Boy Scouts and the Making of American Youth.* Chicago: University of Chicago Press.

Nippert-Eng, Christena E. 1996. *Home and Work: Negotiating Boundaries through Everyday Life.* Chicago: University of Chicago Press.

Pape, Robert. 2005. *Dying to Win: The Strategic Logic of Suicide Terrorism.* New York: Random House.

Rosenhan, David. L. 1973/2004. "On Being Sane in Insane Places." In *Social Deviance: Readings in Theory and Research*, 448–460. Henry N. Pontell, ed. Upper Saddle River, NJ: Prentice Hall.

Rubin, Lillian B. 2000. *Tangled Lives: Daughters, Mothers, and the Crucible of Aging.* Boston: Beacon Press.

Shoemaker, Donald J. 2006. *Theories of Delinquency: An Examination of Explanations of Delinquent Behavior.* New York: Oxford University Press.

Turner, Jonathan H., and Jan E. Stets. 2005. *The Sociology of Emotions.* New York: Cambridge University Press.

Watson, James D. 1969/1997. *The Double Helix: A Personal Account of the Discovery of the Structure of DNA.* London: Weidenfeld and Nicolson.

Zucchino, David. 1999. *Myth of the Welfare Queen.* New York: Touchstone.

THEORY AND METHOD

2

INTRODUCTION

In Chapter 1, the scientific method was described as a process that contains theory and the testing of hypotheses or hunches suggested by the theory. Indeed, in all of the various social science disciplines,[1] and no matter what method of data collection is employed, theory is used as a guide in the collection and analysis of data. Moreover, in many studies where the researcher does not begin with a thoroughly defined theory, we can create theory by searching through the data for recurring patterns of behavior.

The application of social theory to research is one of the prime areas for the use of the research imagination. This chapter explains the relationship between theory and methods in detail. It describes the various forms that theory may take. It compares and contrasts research that is

---

[1] Psychology, sociology, political science, anthropology, and economics.

designed to verify existing theory with studies that are designed to create new theory. Then, the source of research ideas or how researchers decide what to study is discussed. Finally, the idea of research as a "craft," or set of related skills that can be practiced and learned, is introduced.

THEORY AND SOCIAL RESEARCH

There are numerous options open to the investigator in choosing a theoretical perspective. Moreover, the many different kinds of social theory vary in terms of the specific concepts they contain, how complete or well articulated they are and in the way they are expressed on paper, with words or diagrams. An exhaustive review is beyond the scope of this book; however, in this chapter, some examples of theories that have been particularly influential in social research are offered to illustrate three key points about the relationship between theory and the research process:

- The scientific method is compatible with a variety of theoretical approaches to data.
- Creating and expanding theory itself are prime motives for research.
- The choice of theory is crucial because it may influence one's topic for investigation, as well as one's conclusions.

What Theory Looks Like

"Hunches," as described in the diagram of the scientific method (see Figure 1.1 in Chapter 1), are really theories in embryo form; they are speculations that have a relatively short life span. They may never actually be written down. By contrast, **SOCIAL THEORIES** are *more elaborate, general explanations of human behavior,* and they usually take a concrete form. Some of the formats used to express theory in social research are taxonomies, models, typologies, and paradigms. To show what theory actually looks like in practice, these expressions of theory will be examined in this chapter.

Taxonomies, models, and typologies are schemes for classifying data. Some of them are extremely lengthy and intricate. In practice, they represent conceptual frameworks that guide the analysis of data as they are being collected. To understand how these schemes work, consider what happens when the morning mail arrives at a bustling business office. It has to be sorted; perhaps it is distributed in boxes or pigeonholes, each one with a person's name on it or with the name of a department. In this analogy, the morning mail is the data. At first it is all jumbled and undifferentiated, but we can make sense of it by placing each piece in the proper box. Many theories approach the explanation of social reality in a similar way, by atomizing it, or breaking down observable phenomena systematically. Data are organized according to a diagram or to a list of categories, corresponding to a row of mailboxes. Thus, each bit of information gathered by the researcher, whether it is what someone says, how someone looks, or what someone has written, fits in somewhere in a well-articulated scheme.

If a taxonomy, model, or typology merely supplies labels for each of its conceptual "boxes," it is basically descriptive, rather than explanatory. It may be suggestive of theory, but it cannot stand as a complete presentation of theory. We can make only a few generalizations about the business office by looking at each pigeonhole separately. What makes these schemes more valuable theoretically is the explanation of how their various components relate to one another. Thus, each datum not only belongs in a certain category; it also carries implications for the rest of the data. It is useful to know how many letters go in each mailbox; it is perhaps more important to know why some mailboxes are always much fuller than the rest.

The foregoing generalizations are illustrated in the following examples.

TAXONOMIES. Perhaps the easiest of the classificatory schemes to understand is a **TAXONOMY**, or *list of categories*. An example depicted in Table 2.1 is the *Taxonomy of Educational Objectives* (Anderson, Krathwohl, and Bloom, 2000), used in research on teaching and teaming in schools. The authors created definitions of general concepts such as knowledge and intellectual ability and separated each into its component parts. They designed this to be an exhaustive list, in

Table 2.1. The Taxonomy of Educational Objectives

Knowledge
- Knowledge of specifics
  - Terminology
  - Specific facts
- Knowledge of ways and means of dealing with specifies
  - Conventions
  - Trends and sequences
  - Classifications and categories
  - Criteria
  - Methodology
- Knowledge of the universals and abstractions in a field
  - Principles and generalizations
  - Theories and structures

Intellectual Abilities and Skills
- Comprehension
- Translation
- Interpretation
- Extrapolation
- Application
- Analysis
  - Analysis of elements
  - Analysis of relationships
  - Analysis of organizational principles
- Synthesis
  - Production of a unique communication
  - Production of a plan or proposed set of operations
  - Derivation of a set of abstract relations
- Evaluation
  - Judgments in terms of external criteria

From Lorin W. Anderson, David R. Krathwohl. *A Taxonomy For Learning, Teaching, And Assessing: A Revision of Bloom's Taxonomy Of Educational Objectives, 1/e.* Published by Allyn & Bacon, Boston, MA. Copyright © 2001 by Pearson Education. By permission of the publisher.

that there are many occasions where students showed their "comprehension" of the lessons by making outlines of chapters, reciting what they had memorized, or putting the teacher's lectures into their own words. There might be fewer entries in other categories, that is, comparatively less opportunity for students to apply, to analyze, or to synthesize what they had learned. These data might help the teacher understand why some students appear uninterested in class or are discipline problems or why test scores are lower than expected. Because the taxonomy shows that there are many types of learning that the data indicated had been ignored, the researcher may suggest some specific changes in assignments and lectures to involve students more actively in learning.

Thus, taxonomies may point the way toward the explanation of human behavior and toward policy recommendations. Aside from the exhaustive description of knowledge and abilities, there is no real theory of learning expressed in the list of categories in Table 2.1. Nowhere in the scheme is it stated that the curriculum in each school subject must contain all types of knowledge or that tests must measure all kinds of intellectual ability. The taxonomy does not state that it is more difficult, or more desirable, to acquire one type of knowledge than another. It does not specify the degree of difficulty for each academic skill, nor does it specify that each must be acquired in a logical sequence or order. In fact, there is no particular relationship proposed between any of the elements in the taxonomy; they are merely labels. As the authors themselves note, researchers may use the categories "in very arbitrary fashion," out of sequence in the scheme, so long as their definitions remain intact (Anderson, Krathwohl, and Bloom, 2000:10–11).

Thus, the primary utility of taxonomies is for description. A complete list of objectives in any field, whether it be education, business, community organization, or medical treatment, is invaluable as a baseline against which to measure performance. Having commonly accepted definitions of concepts such as intellectual skill makes it easier to compare behavior in a variety of settings. This same list of categories could

other words, to contain every type of knowledge and every kind of intellectual ability and skill.

The taxonomy is an aid in sorting data. The researcher may, for instance, observe the work of a particular teacher for several weeks, placing each class exercise and homework assignment somewhere in the scheme. It may be discovered

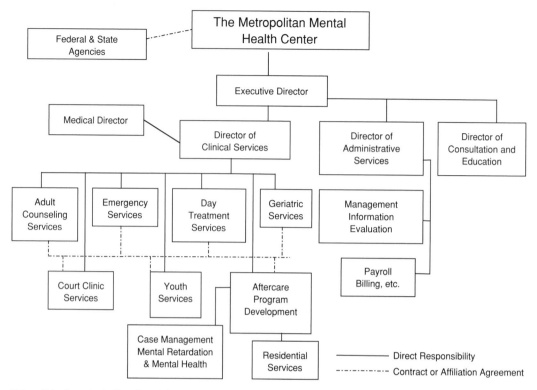

Figure 2.1. An organizational model.

be used to evaluate the curriculum in English, chemistry, sociology, history, or any other school subject. Finally, the taxonomy is useful for devising strategies of data collection. It tells us what the possible types of behavior are in a given setting; thus, we are encouraged to look for them, and, if some behaviors are not present, we can wonder why not.

MODELS. A **MODEL** is *a visual depiction of how something works. It is a prototype to which the real world is compared* as data are gathered. Some models are almost entirely descriptive, in that they are really labels arranged spatially in a diagram. Figure 2.1 is an organizational chart of a mental health clinic. It tells us who the principal actors in the bureaucracy are, and it specifies the lines of communication and authority between them. It also details the responsibilities of the various parts of the clinic. The administrative wing, on the right, relates to the departments that provide direct service, on the left, through the office of the executive director. The various clinical departments, for example, geri-

atric services and adult counseling, communicate with each other directly, although they all are the responsibility of the director of clinical services.

Like the taxonomy we have already examined, this model is suggestive of theory. We may, for instance, speculate that there could be friction between administrators and clinicians because they rarely, if ever, interact on a daily basis. In analyzing the role of the executive director, we may look for evidence of tension between administrative and clinical duties. Finally, the chart may lead us to investigate the difficulties of coordinating the several, diverse departments on the left of the diagram.

These hunches and insights may help us determine how the organization works, but the chart does not contain a real theory of group functioning or structure. It could not explain why two clinics, set up with substantially the same official positions and lines of authority, may differ greatly in their effectiveness and efficiency. The diagram, informative as it is, does not indicate how many employees work for the

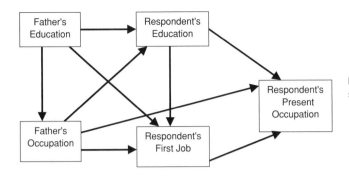

Figure 2.2. A model of the process of socioeconomic achievement.

clinic, the caseload, what sort of neighborhood it serves, or other details that may be theoretically relevant to the study of mental health care delivery.

By contrast, Figure 2.2 presents a model that is primarily explanatory. The components of Figure 2.2 are not parts of any single organization. Instead they are **VARIABLES** (*characteristics, attitudes, or behaviors that can be measured and that take on differing values*). These variables are used to explain part of the process of social class formation; namely, what leads a **RESPONDENT** (*person who is the subject of investigation*) into a particular occupation.

According to the model in Figure 2.2, a respondent's choice of employment is influenced by the nature of the first position that person obtained on entering the job market. Equally important, in theory, is the amount of education that the respondent has received. Two other variables are thought to be significant – the education and the occupation of the respondent's father. The model thus reflects the idea that a person's own educational history is greatly influenced by his or her parents. A father's occupation may influence his children's career patterns directly ("following in his footsteps") as well as indirectly, through the amount of education that they are given and the initial occupational goals that they are encouraged to set for themselves. There are many statistical procedures that may be used to verify the relationships among the variables in a model of this type.[2]

Figure 2.2 has much more explanatory power than Figure 2.1, the model of the mental health clinic. To create general explanations, however,

we often must sacrifice rich, descriptive detail. Both **DESCRIPTIVE** and **EXPLANATORY MODELS** are thus useful in the social sciences, but *the descriptive models are only aids to theory construction, whereas explanatory models are theory itself.*

TYPOLOGIES. A **TYPOLOGY** is *a device for analyzing all the logical combinations of at least two variables.* Figure 2.3 shows a simple descriptive typology for examining a population of college students according to the variables grade-point average and intelligence measured by an IQ (intelligent quotient) test. Nine student "types" are conceptualized in the cells, or boxes, in this table. A person classified as a "straight arrow" (type 1) is someone with both high grades and a high IQ. A "striver" (type 8) has fair grades but a low IQ. Two other types are "marginals," whose poor grades are perhaps more consistent with their low intelligence test scores, and "apathetics," who, despite superior IQs, have only fair grades.

This scheme lets us compare all students on a given campus; everyone may be placed somewhere in the typology. However, it has additional theoretical utility. We expect to find some people with average-tested intelligence in each of the three grade-point average categories (types 4, 5, and 6). The individuals whom we have labeled "underachievers" and "overachievers" (types 3 and 7) are probably more unusual, in that there is a great disparity between their tested intelligence and their grades in college. These are precisely the sorts of people we should examine closely if we want to understand fully the theoretical connection between natural talent and actual performance. Yet, without the typology,

2 More on this point in Chapter 19.

	Intelligence [IQ]		
	High	Average	Low
High	1 "Straight Arrows"	4 "Pluggers"	7 "Overachievers"
Average	2 "Apathetics"	5 "Normals"	8 "Strivers"
Low	3 "Underachievers"	6 "Slackers"	9 "Marginals"

Grade-Point Average

Figure 2.3. Typology of college students according to grades and IQ scores.

we might fail to isolate them, or we might concentrate exclusively on students whose IQ scores were more closely related to their grade-point averages.

PARADIGMS. Another sort of theorizing is of broader scope and not as easily diagrammed as those we have looked at so far. It is the application of a **PARADIGM**, or *coherent worldview*, to social life. In effect, when we follow a paradigm, we put on a pair of glasses *that colors all behavior with a particular interpretation.*

A classic example from social psychology is the work of Erving Goffman (1959), who has attempted to explain social interaction by uncovering its basic processes. The inspiration for Goffman's paradigm is Shakespeare's claim in *Hamlet* that "all the world's a stage and all the men and women merely players." He takes that notion seriously and offers evidence for it. In fact, Goffman's work is called **DRAMATURGI-CAL** because of *the close analogy between social life and what occurs "on stage." According to this paradigm, human beings are all "actors"* who, depending on the situation, must play a variety of roles for society, the "audience." People are constantly trying to convince their audiences

that their performances are genuine. Thus, Goffman forces us, as observers, to confront the manipulative, sometimes artificial quality of people's contacts with one another. If the "act" is successful, the audience gives people approval and confirms them in their roles. Only "backstage" in areas hidden from the public are people permitted a respite from their acting chores.

If we accept this paradigm, we see the basis of social reality continually shifting along the dimensions of managing impressions, putting our "best foot forward," and hiding imperfections. The categories Goffman develops to organize an enormous quantity of data provide strong insights into interpersonal relations. No one act is seen as being any more real or true than another. Acting per se is part of the human condition.

Another paradigm, one of the most influential in twentieth-century American social science, is the image of society associated with Talcott Parsons (1902–1979). It is known as **STRUCTURAL FUNCTIONALISM** in sociology and political science and as **SYSTEMS THEORY** in social work and business management. According to this paradigm, *every element of a society that exists over a period of time serves a distinctive function,* *helps to maintain the social system, and is supported by public consensus or agreement* (Parsons, Shils, and Smelser, 1962/2001; Alexander, 1998). Society is much like any living organism, claims Parsons, so that a change in any one social institution will result in corresponding changes in other elements of the system. Any alteration in the economic structure of a society, for example, will cause complementary changes in the political, religious, and educational spheres. Functionalists argue that any social system is always moving toward a state of equilibrium. In this paradigm, society is much like a rubber ball that may on occasion be squeezed out of shape but is always striving to return to its original form. The questions for functional analysis are therefore, What function is performed by each social element, and what would be the consequences for the social system as a whole if it were absent?

The explanations provided by functionalism are not very concrete. They seem abstract and general because they are meant to apply, at several levels of analysis, to families, business enterprises, ethnic groups, nations, and even the world system. Nonetheless, functionalism has been an attractive paradigm because it confirms the scientific notion of an orderly universe, in which there is a place and a reason for every element of society. It makes a very complicated world seem more intelligible by proposing that the relatively small social groups to which we belong operate according to the same principles as the larger society. Finally, although the paradigm of functionalism is relatively weak in providing specific explanations, it is extremely flexible. Like the dramaturgical perspective, there is scarcely a human action or attitude that cannot be fitted into the functionalist conceptual scheme and vocabulary.

A third key paradigm, which will be examined in detail in Chapter 10, is inspired by feminism. It sees research about women, and performed primarily *by* women, as contributing to the improvement of women's position in society.

Description and Explanation

Theory, as we have seen, takes many forms, but all help us to understand the world. To find out how something works, we must know its dimensions and the identity of its components, as well as the general principles of its operation. Therefore, in making use of theory, a balance must be struck between description and explanation. We must have both, but here is a dilemma: As we become wrapped up in the vivid description of a single event or person, it becomes difficult to generalize about other similar or related phenomena. Conversely, if we place less emphasis on description than on general explanation, theory tends to become a series of disembodied, self-evident propositions. Perhaps there is no foolproof solution to this dilemma, but the attempt to solve it is a constant challenge in social science.

The Verification and Discovery of Theory

Thus far some of the many ways that social theory may be expressed have been shown. However, the form that theory takes does not determine its place in the research cycle. We may begin with observation and gradually discover or create a model, a typology, or a general explanation for behavior. Or we may initiate research with the theory firmly in mind and through testing attempt to verify it. This section discusses the implications of these two approaches for the ongoing practice of research.

DEDUCTION. In the physical sciences, the typical research strategy is to *begin with a theory and then to subject it to observation*. This mode of inquiry is called **DEDUCTION**, and it has been most influential in the social sciences as well. We start with general principles and subsequently deduce whether they are sound. Deductive theory does not emerge immediately from the data; it is conceived beforehand and applied to the data.

To apply theory to data, the researcher formulates **HYPOTHESES**, *specific predictions that follow from the general theory*. Recall the model presented in Figure 2.2 showing the process of socioeconomic achievement. This model explains a person's present occupation by considering his or her first job and level of education, as well as his or her father's occupation and level of education. How could we develop hypotheses from this model? We would need to make some testable predictions based on its assumptions; for example:

- The less well educated a respondent's father, the less well educated the respondent
- The higher the status of a respondent's father's occupation, the higher the status of a respondent's occupation

The researcher, in fact, might produce a series of additional hypotheses that could be tested using a variety of deductive research methods.

Because the prediction of behavior is central to the process of deduction, it is difficult to begin that process with only a descriptive model or a very general paradigm. Each of the separate variables in a deductive theory must be carefully defined in advance, so that the researcher will recognize them when they appear in the real world, and so that they may be measured. We have to be as rigorous as possible because as we create measures and variables, we are in effect creating a yardstick against which everything we later observe will be compared. If our model suggests that a large organization will experience difficulty in communication among its parts, we had better be specific about what constitutes a large organization and what constitutes a barrier to communication. We need such reliable measures because we may have to examine as many as a hundred different groups to confirm or disconfirm our theory.

The more general, abstract, and purely descriptive the model or paradigm, the greater the problems of measurement and explanation, and the more difficult it is to use in deductive research. For this reason, models that specify the relationship among several well-defined variables are more easily adapted to the process of deduction.

INDUCTION. The major alternative mode of inquiry is **INDUCTION**. Its hallmark is *the discovery and building of new theory as research progresses*. The research cycle is begun with observation. From the data collected, a generalized understanding of behavior is gradually induced. Measurement of variables is as important to inductive research as it is to deductive research, but neither hypotheses nor measuring tools are developed in advance. Instead, the research problem emerges as a result of direct confrontation with a set of behaviors. The primary focus for study, the development of theory, and the production of an analysis may emerge at any point in inductive research, even toward the very end of the process. Induction is initially exploratory and vividly descriptive. Investigators must take in a vast amount of information because they have to develop categories for classifying data, based not on already existing theory but on the actual range and variety of data in the field.

No list of examples could do justice to the vast amount of excellent inductive research that has been conducted in the United States in recent years. Among the countless variety of topics that have been explored are inner-city life, the working poor, occupations, and leisure. Elijah Anderson (2003) uses induction to examine social class and street-corner life of the inner city. Mitchell Duneier (1999) describes the world of sidewalk booksellers. Jody Miller (2006) analyzes girls in gangs. Marvin Scott (2005) examined "The Racing Game." Cristina Rathbone (2005) vividly recounts the experience of women in prison. As downturns in the economy have placed particular strain on the working poor, a number of studies have focused on people who struggle to improve their position on the social ladder. These include Sharon Hays's (2004) analysis of the effect of welfare reform and Barbara Ehrenreich's (2001) account of her own adventures in taking a variety of low-paid jobs around the country.

There is a lively tradition of exploration of various stages of the life cycle. Recent studies that have continued in this vein are Milner's (2006) work on adolescent culture and identity and Dorothy and David Counts's (2001) examination of the on-the-road culture of senior citizens and their recreational vehicles. As you read further in this book, you will learn some of the methodological techniques that were employed to obtain data in these diverse contexts.

Although induction is usually identified only with the research goals of exploration and description, the explanation of social reality may also be created as research is being carried out (Glaser and Strauss, 1967; Strauss and Corbin, 1998). By generating hypotheses on a day-to-day basis, and discarding them when predictions are not verified by observation, we may create a theory. In a classic study, Becker (1953/1993) began to study marijuana use by looking at the history of people's experience with the drug and eventually formulated a theory of deviancy. Katherine Newman carefully observed and talked to young men and women who are part of the "working poor" in Harlem, primarily in the food industry. She found that they "do not need their values reengineered. They do not need lessons about the dignity of work." Newman (1999:297–298) concludes that they need jobs that pay a living wage.

These, and countless other inductive explanations, tend to be highly *valid*, particularly when they are based on lengthy fieldwork. Over many months the process of induction gradually eliminates the weaker alternative explanations for the behavior of the particular individuals observed. The chances become less and less that important variables remain hidden from the investigator. However, inductive explanation tends to be less *reliable* than it is valid. The measuring tools used in this mode of inquiry are developed on an ad hoc basis, and they are influenced to a considerable degree by the unique experience of individual researchers. Thus, if we use inductive, as opposed to deductive, research strategies, the chances are increased that another investigator may come to equally valid, yet different, conclusions. The theoretical explanations created by induction also may be less generalizable from one setting to another.[3]

Despite these difficulties, inductive research is no less scientific than the deductive approach. The tension over reliability and validity is felt by all researchers, no matter what their field of inquiry. We may have to sacrifice a little of one to improve the other. Indeed, the purely deduc-

tive strategy is often not followed to the letter, even in the physical and natural sciences. In all disciplines, the development of theory is necessarily both inductive and deductive. Scientists may begin with a theory, try to test it deductively with actual data, and find that it does not predict well. At that point, they may choose to modify the theory to make it more consistent with the data. When they do this, they are beginning to engage in an inductive process of inquiry.

THE DEVELOPMENT OF RESEARCH IDEAS

Even though the relationship between theory and research has been explained in this chapter, an important question remains: Where do research ideas come from? This is one of the keys to the research imagination!

Curiosity

Social researchers are generally intensely curious people. They want to know about those different from themselves, for example, an African society (Trefon, 2005); mental patients in a back ward (Knipfel, 2000); the very poor (Kozol, 1996); or the very rich (Herman, 1999). Often they begin to investigate some setting or group for little reason other than that they are intrigued by, or perplexed by, a set of behaviors. What is it like to be a woman in a motorcycle gang (Hopper and Moore, 1990)? Why can't "Johnny" read at the appropriate grade level (Spear-Swerling, 1997)? Why was the 2004 election so divisive (Sabato, 2006)? These are questions that have inspired social research. All scientists grapple with mystery. Social scientists, in particular, are attracted to those whose actions and motives are, at least at first glance, unclear or puzzling. Once they are attracted to a subject, the logic of science fuels their curiosity and their imagination. The scientific method disciplines the raw enthusiasm of the researcher but does not dampen it.

Pure and Applied Research

The investigator's curiosity is not confined to bizarre settings and to social problems of an

---

[3] For more details on this point, refer to Chapter 9.

immediate nature. Some science involves basic, or **PURE RESEARCH**, that is, finding the solution to *questions that are intellectually challenging but that may not have practical applications in the short run*. Pure research in social science is primarily devoted to expanding theoretical horizons; thus, the actual setting for data collection may be of secondary importance. If, for example, we are keenly interested in how people learn the grammatical structure of language, we might choose to gather data in an elementary school. There we would find out a great deal about how schools function, how teachers organize their time, and how young children dress and play. Any and all of this information might be of use to school administrators, teachers, and parents, but our concentration in this setting would be on data about language acquisition. In fact, we could probably discover similar processes of learning in another setting entirely, say, on a street corner, or in a home.

APPLIED RESEARCH, however, is inspired by the needs of social action. Its *findings and conclusions are applied immediately to solve a problem or to improve the effectiveness of an existing or proposed social program*. Are the agencies set up to help poor people serving their intended clientele? How many parking meters should be put on Main Street? How can hospital emergency rooms be made more efficient? These are examples of questions that inspire applied research. The answers to these questions may have theoretical significance, but the investigations were manifestly intended to help people. The results of basic research may offer practical assistance to the public sooner than expected, but its primary purpose is the accumulation of knowledge for its own sake.

Public Sociology

In practice, **PUBLIC SOCIOLOGY** appears to be a compromise between pure and applied research that seeks to effect social change and public policy (Agger, 2000). Practitioners of public sociology (e.g., Derber, 2000; Putnam, 2001) try *to communicate in language that resonates with the people, groups, and organizations that compose the nonacademic community, and to establish a*

dialogue with them. However, they also remain true to the theoretical insights of professional social science. A leading proponent of public sociology, Michael Burawoy (2005), makes the point that he is "unequivocally committed to the values and practice of professional sociology – its rigour, its science, its research programmes, its care to get things right, its concern with theoretical issues." The primary purpose of public sociology, in his view, is "promoting public discourse." However, he notes, "Without professional sociology there is no public sociology."

An excellent example of these principles is provided by Diane Vaughan (1996), whose academic investigation into the *Challenger* and *Columbia* space shuttle disasters has led to media exposure and numerous consulting opportunities. In the box on pages 27–28, Vaughan chronicles her foray into the realm of public sociology.

Already Existing Theory

In addition to researchers' basic curiosity and the problems they want to help solve, another major source of research ideas is the storehouse of theory that has been built and expanded by social science. These ideas channel the development of research. It is easy to see why this is so when we consider that deductive strategies for the collection of data have dominated the study of human behavior for the past sixty years. Even when we use the inductive approach to data, however, it is extremely difficult to enter the field with a clean slate. Ideally, induction begins with no theoretical preconceptions, but although researchers may not write down hypotheses or sketch models in advance, they still cannot fully erase the memory of a lecture, a book they have read, or the example of conceptual skill provided by another investigator whom they respect or admire.

In a book that is still widely read and discussed, Alvin Gouldner (1970) argued that in the latter decades of the twentieth century there was a reluctance to work at testing new ideas in the investigation of social life and a tendency to deal with the same old assumptions about society, merely applying them to new settings. Although we might agree with him concerning

How Theory Travels: A Most Public Public Sociology

The tragic disintegration of NASA Space Shuttle *Columbia* on February 1, 2003, sent me on an unexpected and remarkable eight-month journey in public sociology. Hours after the accident, I was deluged with press calls stemming from my study of the causes of the 1986 *Challenger* disaster. Recognizing the teaching opportunity and professional responsibility, I tried to respond to everyone.

I was teaching the theoretical explanation and key concepts of the book, linking them to data about *Challenger* and *Columbia* as changing press questions dictated. Because the investigation went on for months, these conversations became an ongoing exchange where the press brought me new information, and I gave a sociological interpretation. I noticed that the concepts of the book – the normalization of deviance, institutional failure, organization culture, structure, missed signals – began appearing in print early in the investigation and continued, whether I was quoted or not.

Two weeks after the accident, the publicity director at my publisher sent a copy of the *Challenger* book to retired Admiral Harold Gehman, who headed the Board investigating the *Columbia* accident. As the Admiral later told me, he read it mid-February, along with my jargon-free condensation published in a management journal. Persuaded of the relevance of the sociological analysis to *Columbia*, he sent copies of both to the Board. The Admiral and the Board members were experienced accident investigators, trained to look beyond technical causes to human factors, but the organizational focus and concepts of the book were new to them, helped make sense of their data and led them to other social science sources.

The Admiral believed that history was a scene-setter, not a cause. Citing examples from the *Challenger* case, I explained how historic decisions in NASA's political and budgetary environment changed the organization structure and culture, ultimately affecting risk decisions, thus contributing to both accidents. He was dubious [but as we collaborated] information and ideas flew fast and freely. Extraordinary investigative effort, data, analysis, and insights were integrated into my writing; sociological connections and concepts became integrated across the chapters of the Board's Report on the accident. It was based on their data but the outline of chapter topics paralleled my data and causal model. The Admiral, it turned out, was "delighted" with the result. The Board, too, accepted "History as Cause: *Columbia* and *Challenger*" as a chapter in the Report, along with its implications for the expanded causal model.

The new centrality of sociological ideas and the connection with the *Challenger* accident were not lost on the media. In press conferences, Admiral Gehman stressed the importance of the social causes. When he announced that I would testify before the Board in Houston, the field's leading journal, *Aviation Week and Space Technology*, headlined "*Columbia* Board Probes the Shuttle Program's Sociology." My testimony covered the causes of the *Challenger* accident, comparison with *Columbia*, and identification of systemic common institutional failures. The book's theory and concepts traveled farther as my testimony – like that of other witnesses – aired live on NASA TV and video-streamed into TV, radio, and Internet outlets.

The *New York Times* announced the equal weight the report would give to technical and social causes, identifying me as the source of the Board's approach. The language of sociology became commonplace in the press. The theory of the book traveled one more place that August week. An AP wire story, "NASA Finally Looks to Sociologist," revealed that NASA had invited me to headquarters to talk with top officials, who shifted from denial to acknowledgement that the systemic institutional failures that led to *Challenger* also caused *Columbia*.

Never did I foresee the extent of my involvement nor my impact. To give an idea of the extent of public and press interest in a sociological interpretation of the disaster's causes, I had been quoted in print 50 times by the end of May. [I was] elucidating principles that bring sociology alive, out of textbooks, academic monographs, and classrooms and into the public consciousness and policy debate. Sociology was the instigator of it all. The theory and concepts that explained *Challenger* led to these connections because they were an analogical fit with the *Columbia* data and made sense of what happened for journalists and the Board. My book and university affiliation gave me the opportunity to engage in ongoing dialogic teaching – akin to daily grass-roots activism – but with these two tribunals of power with authoritative voice . . . translating the ideas of the book into grist for critical public dialogue.

Excerpted with permission from Diane Vaughan. 2003. "How Theory Travels: A Most Public Sociology." *ASA Footnotes*, 31 (8) November/December.

the limitations of the theories bequeathed to us by previous generations of researchers, we must also recognize that science develops through the continual testing of already existing theoretical ideas (Kuhn, 1996).

Often the setting or subject for research is chosen because it appears to be ideal for testing a theory or a part of a theory. An extraordinary number of studies have stemmed from the work of Parsons, Shils, and Smelser (1962/2001). Investigators, starting with functionalist theories, have analyzed large-scale organizations, schools, and the military, as well as the general phenomenon of social stratification. Davis (1945/1993) concluded that our system of distinct social classes was of great value to society, in part because we need to reward people of talent and skill at a higher rate than those with less ability and ambition. The great disparity between rich and poor in America is desirable, according to this view, to motivate people to perform the important tasks of leadership in business and government.

Studies based on Parsons' paradigm have been challenged by those who see functionalism as inherently conservative and overly supportive of the status quo and the interests of the "establishment." Therefore, much research has been generated out of what social scientists see as the limitations of systems analysis. Marxists and other **CONFLICT THEORISTS** argue that

structural functionalism does not deal effectively with issues of social change and deviance (Harper, 2006). Their paradigm contrasts sharply with Parsons' because they see *change and conflict as continuous and natural, not disruptive of social order*. Whereas functionalists maintain that every society rests on the consensus of its members, their critics believe that *every society exhibits constraint of some of its members* (Ritzer and Goodman, 2003).

A change in theoretical position encourages changes in the kind of data that need to be acquired. Thus, as some researchers have moved away from the paradigm of functionalism, there has been increased emphasis on the investigation of groups that contribute to the disruption of the social system, for example, radical students and gays (Burawoy et al., 1991; Gamson, 1999). In addition, more attention has been devoted to power relations of dominance and subordination in the economy, law enforcement, among racial and ethnic groups, and between the sexes.

Training and Experience

Finally, in reviewing the sources of research ideas, we must consider the training and experience of the investigator. The nature of one's employment is important because a certain type of research may be expected in a particular department or agency. The priorities of the government bureaus that provide funding for the social sciences also influence the goals of the research and the settings chosen. Often the selection of a specific model or paradigm is influenced by one's colleagues and teachers at work or in the university.

These pressures can never be entirely eliminated, nor should they be. Science is a cooperative enterprise, and researchers often require some assistance in formulating research ideas. The choice of theories, models, and paradigms is crucial. It may, as we have seen, help determine the subject of an investigation. Even more significant is the effect of theory selection on research findings and conclusions. Whether a criminal is portrayed as a victim of society or as one who victimizes society may depend less on the crime committed than on whether the investigator was influenced by labeling theory or by functionalist theory.

To the layperson this may not sound very scientific, but the scientific method does not specify which theory is most appropriate or the form in which it should be presented. Because these choices are to be made by researchers, they need to be aware of the ways in which their prior training, and the expectations of others, influence the decisions they make. Data do not "speak for themselves." It is up to the researcher, using social theory, to demonstrate the significance of data. It is an awesome responsibility.

INTELLECTUAL CRAFTSMANSHIP

If by now you suspect that there are some dilemmas in research methods that cannot be resolved once and for all, you are right. To learn methodology and to do research itself requires a tolerance for ambiguity and living with some uncertainty. It is always possible that the data we collect may continually support our hypotheses but that our theory itself may be wrong. Or our stated hypotheses may be supported by the data, but for reasons simply unknown to us.

The canons of science are a basic blueprint, but to do good research, we must do more than follow their direction. The scientific method does not tell us whether to maximize descrip-tion or explanation in data analysis, nor does it tell us how much validity may be sacrificed to improve the reliability of a study. It does not guide us automatically to the theory that fits our data best or to the most effective technique of data collection. Weighing such decisions skillfully is only partly a science; it is also a craft that calls for research imagination. The researcher is both a scientist and craftsperson whose toolkit includes a vibrant imagination.

Noted sociologist C. Wright Mills (1959/2000: 215–223) explained that a true craftsman is someone who maintains the image of a completed product from start to finish, someone who knows everything that goes into it, even if some of the tasks are performed by others. It is in this sense that the skilled researcher practices a craft. Craftsmanship follows a plan devised by the worker. This plan, whether it is the pattern for carving a rocking chair or the design for examining a social problem, is of course shaped by the worker's imagination and prior experience. A researcher may use a theory that has been used before, in the same manner as the carpenter decides to make another chair like the one in his parlor. However, the plans of both are also highly individualistic and subject to modification as the work progresses. The result, therefore, reveals the personality and interests of the worker. The scientific canon of objectivity does not mean that research has to be uniform and colorless. The difference between ordinarily and finely crafted studies is comparable to the distinction between mass-produced and one-of-a-kind items. Despite the freedom to create which craftsmanship affords, there is, inevitably, some mechanical drudgery in some phases of the work. However, says Mills, the craftsman is "carried over these junctures by keen anticipation" of what the finished product will look like, and by pride at its completion.

Learning the Craft

In generations past, young apprentices received instruction in the workshop of a master. They first acquired some basic skills from books and perfected the essential "hands on" techniques by practicing continually. In teaching research methods, the authors of this book can perform some of the same functions. We will clarify the criteria that social scientists use in evaluating their work and the work of others. We will show you techniques for improving reliability and validity, and we will offer you helpful suggestions as you go, step by step, through the research process. When you finish, you will be acquainted with most of the tools in the researcher's "workshop."

Your ability to use these tools is indispensable for the collection of data about the world, but it will not, in itself, make you an imaginative craftsman or craftswoman. No rules or set of procedures will ever replace a keen imagination in producing a good study. Technique is important, but showing off methodological expertise for its own sake is pointless. The purpose of research is to produce findings that add to our knowledge.

Using Research Imagination

How, then, does one go about cultivating an "imagination"? Contrary, perhaps, to popular conception, creativity is not something that one either possesses or does not. One can acquire the knack of being an imaginative researcher by continually structuring one's thoughts and ideas. It takes work to develop this talent; how perceptive an observer you are will depend more on your own energy than on anything we can tell you.

In his essay on intellectual craftsmanship, Mills (1959/2000) suggested ways of channeling mental energy. He said that ideas and problems for research gradually take shape as social scientists "play around" with concepts. It is not uncommon to begin toying with an idea and wait, sometimes several years, before actually beginning to work on it. During the intervening period, the problem remains in the back of the mind, and each time one reads something, or has a relevant personal experience, a mental note is made. Part of intellectual craftsmanship is this continual reflection on ideas over time.

Mills, in fact, advocated that researchers keep a file, or journal, to serve as a reservoir for ideas. Entries in this file should continually reflect one's own life experiences. In this sense, to be a scientist does not mean separating our personal intellectual life from our career. Our private troubles, as workers, parents, consumers, and voters, are in reality public issues. We must appreciate this point and try to get others to understand it as well. In our journal we may keep memos to ourselves, excerpts from books, half-baked theories, snatches of conversations heard on the street, even our dreams. As the file begins to grow, it is useful to go through the entries, trying to see which pieces of information seem to have things in common. This periodic rearranging of data itself constitutes an exercise of the research imagination and frequently generates new ideas. We may find through such a continual reorganization that certain key concepts emerge and that many of our entries, previously seen as wholly independent and discrete, begin to fit into a larger mosaic.

One of the features of such a process is that we will eventually reach a point where we have generated more ideas than we could likely investigate in a lifetime. We find ourselves necessarily setting priorities among our several ideas. In Mills's own words, "Any working social scientist who is well on his way ought at times to have so many plans, which is to say ideas, that the question is always, which of them am I, ought I, to work on next?" (2000:198). A true craftsman or craftswoman, whether working in wood, clay, paint, or ideas, is never without something to do.

SUMMARY

The selection of an existing theory, or the construction of new theory, is as important to social research as the perfection of techniques for the collection of data. Theory may be suggested by taxonomies, models, typologies, and paradigms. Most theoretical forms are compatible with the scientific method. Creating and expanding theory are prime motives for research. The choice of theory is crucial because it may influence not only the topic of an investigation but the research findings as well. Existing theoretical models and paradigms exercise great influence over the research enterprise, but neither these formulations, nor any guidelines for gathering social data, can substitute for a creative imagination. The individual investigator as practitioner of a craft remains at the heart of the process.

KEY TERMS

applied research
conflict theory
deduction
descriptive model
dramaturgical paradigm
explanatory model
induction
model
paradigm
public sociology
pure research
respondent
social theories
structural functionalism
systems theory
taxonomy
typology
variable

EXERCISES

1. Choose some examples of research in the social sciences that attempt to offer theoretical explanation of some phenomena. For each, indicate whether the theoretical explanation is arrived at through an inductive or a deductive process. Then, say whether you feel the theories have been adequately verified by the data collected.

2. Using the same piece(s) of research as for exercise 1, try the following:

- Indicate the assumptions that you believe underlie the respective theories by creating a list of propositions that follow one another in sequence.
- If the theory is stated only in verbal terms, try to create a model similar to Figure 2.2 to illustrate the proposed causal connections between the variables in the theory.

3. From a textbook such as Shoemaker (2006), find two competing theories of delinquency. Indicate which theory you believe to be more reasonable and why. What type of data would you need to test each of your chosen theories?

4. On the basis of your personal observation, try to construct a classificatory scheme for describing the types of students on your campus.

5. Keep a journal in which you note aspects of your own everyday life that you believe have sociological, psychological, or political significance. After one week, reflect on the process of developing categories for making generalizations about your activities. Why are you selecting these categories? What have you left out, and why?

SUGGESTED READINGS

Blau, Judith, and Keri E. Iyall Smith, eds. 2006. *Public Sociologies Reader*. Lanham, MD: Rowman & Littlefield.

A variety of public sociology studies are summarized, along with commentary on this emerging method.

Ritzer, George, and Douglas J. Goodman. 2003. *Sociological Theory*. 6th ed. New York: McGraw-Hill.

Among the most clearly written theory texts.

Spradley, James P. 1979. *The Ethnographic Interview*. New York: Holt, Rinehart and Winston.

Numerous examples of different taxonomies and how they are constructed can be found on pages 132–154 of this book.

Stinchcombe, Arthur L. 1987. *Constructing Social Theories*. Chicago: University of Chicago Press.

This book compares and contrasts various types of theory and shows how they are created.

Vaughan, Diane. 1986/1996. *The Challenger Launch Decision: Risky Technology, Culture, and Deviance*. Chicago: University of Chicago Press.

A masterful sociological investigation of the accident that shocked the world and launched Vaughan's career in public sociology.

REFERENCES

Agger, Ben. 2000. *Public Sociology*. Lanham, MD: Rowman & Littlefield.

Alexander, Jeffrey C., ed. 1998. *Neofunctionalism and After*. New York: Blackwell.

Anderson, Elijah. 2003. *A Place on the Corner*. 2nd ed. Chicago: University of Chicago Press.

Anderson, Lorin W., and David R. Krathwohl, eds.; Benjamin S. Bloom. 2000. *Taxonomy for Learning, Teaching, and Assessing: A Revision of Bloom's Taxonomy of Educational Objectives*. New York: Longman.

Becker, Howard S. 1953/1993. *Becoming a Marihuana User*. New York: Irvington.

Burawoy, Michael. 2005. "Public Sociology: Populist Fad or Path to Renewal?" *British Journal of Sociology* 56 (3): 417–432.

Burawoy, Michael, et al. 1991. *Ethnography Unbound: Power and Resistance in the Modern Metropolis.* Berkeley: University of California Press.

Counts, Dorothy Ayers, and David Reese Counts. 2001. *Over the Next Hill: An Ethnography of RVing Seniors in North America.* Peterborough, Ontario: Broadview Press.

Davis, Kingsley. 1945/1993. *Some Principles of Stratification.* New York: Irvington.

Derber, Charles. 2000. *Corporation Nation: How Corporations Are Taking Over Our Lives and What We Can Do About It.* New York: St. Martin's-Griffin.

Duneier, Mitchell. 1999. *Sidewalk.* New York: Farrar Straus & Giroux.

Ehrenreich, Barbara. 2001. *Nickel and Dimed: Or (Not) Getting by in America.* New York: Metropolitan Books.

Gamson, Joshua. 1999. *Freaks Talk Back: Tabloid Talk Shows and Sexual Nonconformity.* Chicago: University of Chicago Press.

Glaser, Barney, and Anselm Strauss. 1967. *The Discovery of Grounded Theory.* Chicago: Aldine de Gruyter.

Goffman, Erving. 1959. *The Presentation of Self in Everyday Life.* New York: Doubleday.

Gouldner, Alvin W. 1970. *The Coming Crisis of Western Sociology.* New York: Basic Books.

Harper, Charles L. 2006. *Exploring Social Change: America and the World.* 5th ed. Upper Saddle River, NJ: Prentice Hall.

Hays, Sharon. 2004. *Flat Broke with Children: Women in the Age of Welfare Reform.* New York: Oxford University Press.

Herman, Andrew. 2000. *The "Better Angels" of Capitalism: Rhetoric, Narrative, and Moral Identity Among Men of the American Upper Class.* Boulder, CO: Westview.

Hopper, Columbus B., and Johnny Moore. 1990. "Women in Outlaw Motorcycle Gangs." *Journal of Contemporary Ethnography* 18 (4): 363–387.

Knipfel, Jim. 2000. *Slackjaw: A Memoir.* New York: Berkeley.

Kozol, Jonathan. 1996. *Amazing Grace: The Lives of Children and the Conscience of a Nation.* New York: Harper.

Kuhn, Thomas S. 1996. *The Structure of Scientific Revolutions.* 3rd ed. Chicago: University of Chicago Press.

Miller, Jody. 2006. *One of the Guys: Girls, Gangs, and Gender.* New York: Oxford University Press.

Mills, C. Wright. 1959/2000. *The Sociological Imagination, 40th Anniversary Ed.* New York: Oxford University Press.

Milner, Mu, Jr. 2006. *Freaks, Geeks, and Cool Kids: American Teenagers, Schools, and the Culture of Consumption.* New York: Routledge.

Newman, Katherine. 1999. *No Shame in My Game.* New York: Alfred A. Knopf and the Russell Sage Foundation.

Parsons, Talcott, Edward A. Shils, and Neil J. Smelser. 1962/2001. *Toward a General Theory of Action: Theoretical Foundations for the Social Sciences.* New Brunswick, NJ: Transaction.

Putnam, Robert D. 2001. *Bowling Alone: The Collapse and Revival of American Community.* New York: Simon & Schuster.

Rathbone, Cristina. 2005. *A World Apart: Women, Prison, and Life Behind Bars.* New York: Random House.

Ritzer, George, and Douglas J. Goodman. 2003. *Sociological Theory.* 6th ed. New York: McGraw-Hill.

Sabato, Larry J., ed. 2006. *Divided States of America: The Slash and Burn Politics of the 2004 Presidential Election.* New York: Pearson/Longman.

Scott, Marvin B. 2005. *The Racing Game.* Chicago: Aldine de Gruyter.

Shoemaker, Donald J. 2006 *Theories of Delinquency: An Examination of Explanations of Delinquent Behavior.* New York: Oxford University Press.

Spear-Swerling, Louise. 1997. *Off Track: When Poor Readers Become "Learning Disabled."* Boulder, CO: Westview.

Strauss, Anselm L., and Juliet M. Corbin. 1998. *Basics of Qualitative Research: Techniques and Procedures for Developing Grounded Theory.* 2nd ed. Thousand Oaks, CA: Sage.

Trefon, Theodore, ed. 2005. *Reinventing Order in the Congo: How People Respond to State Failure in Kinshasa.* London: Zed.

Vaughan, Diane. 2003. "How Theory Travels: A Most Public Public Sociology." *ASA Footnotes* 31 (8) November/December: 5, 11.

RESEARCH DESIGN

3

INTRODUCTION

The first two chapters have explained the elements of the scientific method and examined the connection between theory and the research process. After reading these chapters, you are now ready to look at how research is actually designed, step-by-step. RESEARCH DESIGN is *the overall process of using your imagination as well as the strategy and tactics of science to guide the collection and analysis of data.* Have you have ever wondered: "What is a proper problem to write about in my term paper?" This issue, selecting a topic for study, is the first and most crucial one to be addressed in social research. The dilemmas of research design are sometimes difficult to resolve. Professional social scientists with years of experience sometimes wonder if investigating a problem that happens to interest them personally will produce a worthy addition to knowledge in their field of inquiry.

A related and equally thorny issue to be explored in this chapter is whether it is legitimate, or desirable, to be wholly descriptive in one's work, rather than explanatory. In other words, should all research make some theoretical contribution? In addition, we will examine the question of how much information is needed to substantiate an argument. The old axiom that "the more we know, the more we realize our own ignorance" certainly applies in social research. Are there guidelines to help us determine when we should stop collecting data and begin to analyze it? Finally, this chapter will highlight the difficulties that may occur when a research topic demands more time, attention, and money than the social scientist can possibly give it. How does one match the available resources to one's research interests?

To answer such questions, we need to know more than the general canons and logic of the scientific method. This chapter explains the specific components of the research process to aid you in conducting your own investigations and also to convey what happens as professional social researchers actually begin to design a study. As you will see, their work invites, and even requires, the creative spark of the research imagination.

The Research Cookbook

Social investigation may be compared to the fine art of cooking. In the kitchen, creativity and skill each play a part in the preparation of a tasty meal, and things do not always turn out as expected. The first time you try to duplicate Grandma's prize recipe for homemade clam chowder it may look (and taste) like low tide at Coney Island. The more you practice, the better your results will be. The more relaxed you are, the more you feel like trying new combinations of ingredients. Grandma herself may seem like a magician, adding a "pinch of this" and a "dash of that." She may claim that intuition tells her when the oven is hot enough or when the baked apples are soft enough. However, most excellent cooks keep an extensive library of others' recipes, for information and inspiration. The following section presents the "ingredients" of the research enterprise and shows how they interact with one another. Knowing what goes into the mixture will not make you an instant success, but it is a good place to begin to learn. You will become more confident, and research will seem less a mystery, as you discover what others have done, and as you spend time doing it yourself.

MENUS AND RECIPES. Continuing the analogy, Table 3.1 compares and contrasts the various tasks of research design with the process of putting a meal on the table.

The simple act of BRAINSTORMING, *just letting our imagination flow*, is a good place to start, both for planning a meal and for research! As we think about our dinner guests and the meal we are about to prepare, our thoughts may wander to a range of menu choices. What would they most enjoy? Similarly, before we begin research we may ask, "What topics am I most interested in studying?" "What do people already know about that topic?" We are going to get lots of good ideas from brainstorming, but unless we move beyond it, we will remain rather unfocused; therefore, we may want to consider some specific possibilities! If in planning our meal, we eventually decide to serve chocolate cake for dessert, we have made a decision similar to the selection of a topic for research, a choice that focuses our energy and

Table 3.1. The Researcher as "Cook"

Preparing a meal...	Doing social investigation...
Deciding on the menu	Selecting a topic
Picking recipes	Conceptualizing a topic
Budgeting time, space, and money	Choosing a strategy for data collection
Shopping	Collecting data
Cooking	Processing and analyzing data
Inspecting	Interpreting and making inferences about data
Serving	Writing the final report

calls for some specific skills. In addition, as you can see from Table 3.1, the initial choice of dish (or topic) sets in motion a sequence of necessary and related activities.

Having decided on chocolate cake, we are immediately faced with a problem. Will the outside be milk chocolate or dark; will the inside be devil's food or yellow? Will the icing be smooth and creamy, thick and fudgy, or hard and sugary? Are we going to bake a cake with two large layers, several small layers, or a sheet cake with only one layer? To answer these questions, we may turn to a recipe that, in effect, refines the general concept "chocolate cake." This same process occurs in social research after we choose to study a general concept, for example, "alienation." We must then select a "recipe"; that is, we must make the concept more specific. In this case, one of the things we must do is decide whether the phenomenon we want to explain is alienation from work, alienation from loved ones, or alienation from the political system. A recipe gives the cook a list of ingredients to use and tells what amounts of each are required. In social research, a similar function is performed by OPERATIONAL DEFINITIONS. These are *lists of the specific components of each concept, or the actual evidence for each variable*. We may denote a politically alienated person as an adult who has never voted or supported a candidate of the two major parties.

There are many possible, valid operational definitions of a given variable, in the same sense that hundreds of different combinations of ingredients may still produce delicious chocolate cake. There are no absolute, one-and-for-all definitions of concepts or lists of evidence

for variables in social research. Conceptualization and operationalization are dependent, to a certain extent, on the purpose of the research. To return to our analogy, a large single-layer cake might be appropriate for a child's birthday party; a small, elegant, multilayered cake may be the perfect ending for a gourmet meal. If it is our concern about declining labor productivity in the United States that inspires our study of the topic of alienation, we are likely to examine the specific concept "alienation from work." We might define it by looking at three variables: evidence of employees' lack of pride in their work, absenteeism, and industrial sabotage. Each of these three dimensions of alienation from work also must be operationalized – for example, does absence from work because of illness count as "alienation"?

BUDGETING. In the realm of cooking, the recipe we select carries implications for the allocation of time, space, and money. We must set aside an hour or more if we have to follow a complex series of steps in the preparation of our dessert. If we must cook an entrée (say, a roast) in the oven, beginning at four o'clock, then we must arrange to bake the cake ahead of time. If we are planning a gala feast, we had better check to see whether we have exceeded our household budget for the month. If we are pressed for time, space, and money, we may elect to use a packaged mix in which the major ingredients have already been combined.

The comparison with social research strategy is an apt one because we may have only a few months to complete a study, a limited research staff, or a restricted budget. These considerations influence research design and may even preclude the selection of a topic that, though interesting, is too complex for an individual researcher. If we are planning to use a questionnaire as part of a social survey, we may save time and money by selecting an already completed instrument that has been used in a similar context by other researchers. We may even decide to avoid the collection of information ourselves and rely on data collected by others.

The choice of recipe and allocation of our resources affect the exercise of shopping for the ingredients for our cake. Shall we patronize an exclusive little store that sells delicious (but expensive) imported chocolate? Or, if we have more time than money, perhaps we can travel several miles to the supermarket in a neighboring community where a sale is in progress. Maybe it would be a good idea to obtain our ingredients at a wholesale outlet where we can get a substantial discount by buying in large quantities. Of course, we would need plenty of room to store cases of chocolate and fifty-pound sacks of flour.

The principle of shopping in the most desirable place for our ingredients applies as well to the research process. The setting for the collection of data is influenced by the concepts that interest us and the very real limits that restricted resources may impose. A single factory could be the ideal place to study alienation from work, but we also could investigate the same phenomenon in a large number of workplaces. Alienation from loved ones might be analyzed either in the context of therapeutic interviews or through using data from counseling agencies. Political alienation could be uncovered via public opinion polls or through in-depth examination of radical political movements. In each case, the choice of location may be affected by the nature of the topic, by the purposes of the investigation, and by what is possible, given the size of the research staff and available funding.

FROM KITCHEN TO TABLE. RAW DATA are *bits of information in the original form in which they were gathered*, for example, answers to questionnaires, field notes, or tape recordings. Just as the ingredients for a cake must be cooked, data need to be processed and refined before they are usable. Sometimes a computer software program can help us to place raw data into predetermined categories or to perform statistical operations. It is often assumed, in error, that this phase of the investigation requires little creativity on the part of the researcher. Many professionals will tell you that their excitement or enthusiasm does not diminish during the data processing portion. There is the anticipation of results (perhaps similar to the family peeking through the oven door and imagining how delicious the cake will be when it is done), and there is also the possibility that emergencies may require immediate attention. Sometimes these unexpected events are the results of unwitting errors such as mistakes inputting data into the computer. Often, however, strategy itself changes as the data are being processed. A cook may conclude that his two-layer cake would really be more impressive as a triple-decker, and, as we have noted, a researcher may decide to expand her analysis of data beyond what was originally planned.

When the cake is baked and frosted, the cook may give it a critical eye. Did it turn out as it was supposed to? Would it be better if the ingredients were modified slightly? At what other occasions would it be appropriate to serve? This inspection and critique are similar to what social scientists do when they interpret data and draw inferences from it. They ask what theories have been confirmed, disconfirmed, or created. What modifications in already existing theory are suggested? In what other contexts would a similar study be useful? These are questions that must be posed if scientific inquiry is to take place.

Once the cook has examined his own work, perhaps even made a note to revise the recipe the next time he bakes the cake, it is time to serve it. It is hoped that the diners at the table will confirm the cook's judgment. It may happen that a guest or family member offers a suggestion that, if followed, would make future cakes tastier. Serving the cake is analogous to preparing a final report of research, so that it may be evaluated by the scientist's peers and by the public.

Remember these parallels between cooking and research as we discuss each of the elements of research design in the sections that follow. Use the "cookbook" as a device to help you to recall the various components of social investigation and to appreciate how they are interrelated.

THE COMPONENTS OF RESEARCH

Let us suppose that as one requirement of the course in which this book is assigned, a student must conduct original research; that is, choose a topic and engage in inquiry to answer questions that follow from it. How would you go about completing this exercise successfully? You would indeed have to perform each of the tasks mentioned in the "research cookbook" (although not necessarily in the exact order presented).

Selecting a Topic

The **TOPIC** is *the subject about which you wish to generalize*. We have already explained that there are several sources of inspiration for good research ideas, but as a beginning exercise, it is perhaps most helpful to select a group, or an individual, or a set of behaviors and attitudes in which you have some personal interest. Perhaps you are concerned about the possibilities for employment after graduation, the changing and sometimes conflicting values of marriage and career, or the high prevalence of drug use among teenagers. Whichever topic you choose, your own curiosity will supply much of the energy needed to overcome research difficulties.

To initiate *exploratory* research, all you need to know is the subject for investigation. To move beyond exploration to description or explanation, you will need to begin specifying the **RESEARCH PROBLEM** – *the question or questions concerning your topic that you believe are most important to answer*. Let us assume that you have decided to investigate prevalence of drug use among teenagers. To begin to convert this general interest into a design for research, you might ask: "What intrigues me most about this topic?" Is it the threat that drugs pose to the lives and personal safety of the users, the connection between drug use and crime, or, in more specific terms, what happens to the intimate relation-

ships between drug users and their families and friends? You might be more curious about the "kingpins" and economic structure of the drug trade or perhaps the effect of youths' drug use on the completion of their education. In the latter case, an appropriate research problem would be to investigate the connection between drugs and dropout rates from schools in certain urban areas. This, in turn, may lead to a corollary issue: What, if anything, can schools do to deter or discourage drug use?

The formulation of a research problem narrows the topic to manageable proportions and suggests strategies for research design, particularly the possible variables to be used and settings for the collection of data. However, the fact that some particular questions have been asked does not determine how the abstractions "drug use," "teenage crime," and "school dropout" will be defined. This choice is still up to the researcher.

Sometimes the purpose of a study is as important as the topic in determining research design. We may discover the purpose of a piece of research by asking why and to whom it is useful to have the answers to the questions being asked. Sometimes there is no special motive for research other than to explore some phenomenon or to add to human knowledge in a particular area. In this situation, the investigator enjoys a great deal of latitude in defining concepts and operationalizing variables. However, on other occasions, particularly in deductive inquiry or in applied social science, the purpose of the investigation is much more focused, in that a specific hypothesis is being tested, or human behavior is being evaluated according to a predetermined set of standards. In these instances, the purpose of the study has a profound effect on research design. Indeed, we often cannot begin to choose the most appropriate measuring tools for the variables we are manipulating until we know why the data are being collected in the first place.

Conceptualizing a Topic

Once your topic has been chosen and a more specific research problem has been formulated,

Table 3.2. Alienation Poll

Survey question: "Now I want to read you some things some people have told us they have felt from time to time. Do you tend to feel or not feel . . . ?"

Item	2005	2004	2000	1999	1998
1. "The rich get richer and the poor get poorer."	75%	68%	69%	74%	72%
2. "What you think doesn't count much any more."	53%	51%	56%	68%	60%
3. "Most people with power try to take advantage of people like you."	60%	53%	59%	60%	58%
4. "The people running the country don't really care what happens to you."	53%	44%	53%	62%	54%
5. "You're left out of things going on around you."	35%	34%	39%	46%	33%

Adapted from the Harris Poll, November 8–13, 2005. $N = 1,011$ adults nationwide. Margin of error ± 3; percentage responding: "tend to feel," by year.

some **CONCEPTUALIZATION** is necessary. You will need *to discover*:

1. Which concepts are most appropriate to your topic?

2. Which variables follow from these concepts and how they are defined?

3. How do your variables relate to one another?

4. What are the specific sources of your data?

Ideally, in *inductive* scientific inquiry, each of these tasks is accomplished gradually, after research is initiated. The answers emerge as the investigator proceeds. By contrast, the more *deductive* the strategy for inquiry, the more likely it is that all four questions will be tackled at an early stage in research design, before the investigator goes into the field.

Concepts and Variables

A **CONCEPT** is *a general idea applicable to particular instances or examples of behavior*. More than one conceptual label may be applied to the same human behavior. When we see a police officer pushing someone against a wall and applying handcuffs, is that an instance of the concept "effective law enforcement" or the concept "police harassment?" Observers may legitimately disagree regarding the definition of complex concepts. It is relatively easy to spin out the meaning of the concept "chair" because we can point to several types of chairs, explain their use, and distinguish them from other types of furniture. What about a more complicated idea, such as "alienation"? We know that this abstraction exists, in some measure, but it has no obvious, observable referents. The researcher must isolate its component variables.

Let us say that your research topic is citizen apathy in the United States and that your research problem is to determine the extent to which Americans' sense of alienation increases or decreases over the years. How would you define alienation in such a way that the components of the definition could be measured?

Tables 3.2 and 3.3 show how the Harris Poll investigators did it (Harris Poll, 2006). They constructed an "alienation index" (see Table 3.3) that represents the general concept. It shows that, in any given year, significantly more than half the public feels "alienated," but the rate tends to fluctuate over time.[1]

The statements in Table 3.2 reflect five separate variables that the researchers believe comprise alienation, namely, perceptions of inequality (item 1); inefficacy (item 2); exploitation (item 3); invisibility (item 4); and isolation (item 5). The investigators could have included additional variables in their definition of the concept, "alienation." They might have asked people to assess the degree to which their work is valued ("It does not matter whether I do my best, or

---

[1] A detailed guide to index construction appears in Chapter 17.

Table 3.3. Mean of "Tend to Feel" Responses to Five Questions in Table 3.2, by Year

1998	1999	2000	2004	2005
55.4%	62%	55.2%	50%	55.2%

not") or the importance of their individual vote in national elections ("It is not that important to cast a ballot because a single vote is meaningless"). The indicators they *did* select, however, are so central to the idea of alienation in the context of looking for sources of citizen apathy that the addition of more components would be unlikely to influence the research findings. In addition, the five variables depicted in Table 3.2, taken together, present a valid approximation of alienation. We know this because it is most unlikely that a person tending to concur with all of the statements would, in fact, feel satisfied enough not to be alienated.

This example shows that a wise procedure, as you conceptualize any topic, is to choose or create definitions that are relatively simple and straightforward. These definitions should contain only a few variables, those that are most important. Each variable should be conceived in a way that allows it to be readily and precisely measured. The same principles apply in the selection or construction of theory (that is, the overall blueprint for relating each variable to the others). We may seek to explain the relationship between the rather high levels of alienation depicted in Table 3.2 and citizen apathy by hypothesizing that although alienation rises and falls, there is an underlying baseline of negative response to perceptions of citizen ineffectiveness and isolation that is expressed as apathy. To test this hypothesis, we would need to define "citizen apathy" as a concept, just as carefully as alienation was defined. Appropriate and readily measurable variables in this case might be the ratio between those eligible to register to vote and those actually registered; percentage of registered voters who cast ballots; or the number of uncontested elections at national, state, and local levels.[2]

The Role of the Literature in Research Design

In Chapter 2, we mentioned that the motivation for research may be theoretical, for example, to resolve arguments between competing theories or to add to theory. Even if your work is largely descriptive or only incidentally theoretical, you will need to immerse yourself in the existing literature relating to the topic you have selected. In the deductive model for research, conceptualizing any topic will be greatly influenced, even determined absolutely, by the existing literature. However, if you are following a model of inquiry that is primarily inductive, you will not begin data collection with concepts, definitions, or theories that are identical to those found in the literature. In either case, a review of previous efforts to understand similar or related phenomena is essential, even for the beginning researcher. To ignore the existing literature may lead to wasted effort on your part. Why spend time merely repeating what other investigators have already done? If you are aware of earlier studies of your topic, or related topics, you will be in a much better position to assess the significance of your own work and to convince others that it is important.

A glance through professional journals in social work or sociology, political science, or psychology may be somewhat intimidating to the apprentice researcher. You may be unfamiliar with many of the references cited or the techniques used to analyze data. Each academic and professional body of literature has its characteristic jargon, and this may serve as a barrier to understanding for the uninitiated. Work up the courage to take the plunge into the literature. You may be timid at first, but with practice, you will find that you can wade through it efficiently and with increasing confidence.

Remember that you do not have to know everything about the complexities of theory to

[2] The process of generating operational definitions for research variables is examined in more detail in Chapter 4.

Table 3.4. Type of Information Typically Used, by Data Collection Method and Book Chapter

Type of information	Methods technique and chapter number
• Moment-to-moment description of the incidents in which people participate	"Historical Analysis," Chapter 11
• The number of the characteristics of persons or events	"Surveys," Chapter 7; "Experimentation," Chapter 12; "Content Analysis," Chapter 13; "Aggregate Data Analysis," Chapter 14; "Statistics," Chapters 18–19
• People's feelings, perceptions, and the meanings they attach to events	"Intensive Interviewing," Chapter 8; "Observational Fieldwork," Chapter 9; "Feminist Methodology," Chapter 10

see contradictions in the literature. Ask yourself some basic questions about what you are reading, for example:

- Is the author trying to prove something to you as a reader? If so, what is it?
- Are there any gaps or inconsistencies in the author's argument?
- Are there any other studies that analyze the same or related phenomena in a different way?
- Which of the different ways of looking at your topic appeals to you most? Why?

Later, when you become more expert at reading the reports of others' work, you will be able to be more critical in your questioning of the author's methodology, the choice of data, and the quality of the inferences drawn from the data.

Types of Information

We have shown how a research topic might be selected and provided an illustration of the process of concept formation. Only one important step lies between conceptualization and the planning of strategies for the actual collection of data. That step is to figure out where to look for the information that is needed. If you have already chosen your topic, you know what you want to generalize *about*. But what will you be generalizing *from*? For any given research topic, there are numerous possible answers to this question.

The nature of the information that researchers need may itself help to determine the most appropriate methodology. If you were a sports reporter assigned to cover an important football game, you might go about it in any of several ways. You could record each play in sequence, telling the results of each one. You might compile lists of statistics from the game, including first downs, completed passes, yards gained, and scores for each team. Or you might ask the players what it felt like to be in the game to determine the meaning of victory or defeat for the participants themselves. Table 3.4 illustrates three of the most important types of information and pairs each one with a data collection strategy typically used to obtain it. We have also included chapter numbers showing the location of the detailed coverage.[3]

Let us examine the differences between these approaches, so that we can see how the nature of the data we need affects the selection of specific methods for gathering them. Incidents are discrete events; describing them from moment to moment gives us histories, or chains, of events. Social scientists use this kind of information not only to find out what happened in the distant past but also to re-create a wide variety of present-day phenomena. These include performances, such as the half-time shows at athletic contests (King and Springwood, 2001); social rituals, such as weddings (Ingraham, 1999); and work activity, such as the mass production of automobiles (Adler, 2001). Historical data often

---

[3] Chapters 15 and 17, "Comparative Analysis" and "Indexes and Scales," respectively, show that these techniques may be used to obtain all types of information.

take the form of a journal or log that provides a record of conversations or other interactions between people or rich accounts of what they were wearing, what they ate, how active they were, and so forth.

If we count the characteristics of persons or events, a different sort of picture is created. We might obtain data on numbers of civil and religious ceremonies or on how much food was consumed at each, rather than a moment-to-moment description of any single wedding or group of weddings. We may learn about auto production by, for example, tallying the number of cars completed each hour, rather than by following a single car on the assembly line from start to finish. Counting gives us two important descriptive statistics, frequency and distribution. A FREQUENCY *expresses how often a particular characteristic occurs*; a DISTRIBUTION is *the range and variation of its occurrence within a population*. Last year, for example, there might have been three thousand weddings in your town (frequency) but many more in some neighborhoods or among some ethnic groups than others (distribution). Often these kinds of data are generated when the researcher is more distant from the subjects of investigation than would be the case in obtaining histories firsthand. If we were researching the interaction of workers on the shop floor of a factory qualitatively, we could record the actual content of conversations as they occurred, if we could get close enough. However, even if we could not, we would learn a great deal about the work routine in the factory by simply counting the number of times people conversed (frequency) and noting who talked to whom (distribution).

This last example illustrates the need for another major type of information in some settings: the subjective perceptions of participants in social interaction. Counting the attributes of persons and things or writing a moment-to-moment description of events will not necessarily tell us what it is like to work on the assembly line, from the point of view of the worker. In the factory, most people adhere to formal and informal codes of conduct. However, even careful observation and recording of dialogue may not reveal whether a worker is com-

plying eagerly and willingly or out of the fear of losing his or her job. This is one reason we may need to uncover the subjective meaning of the prevailing rules and norms for the workers. Similarly, the behavior of a bride and groom at a wedding occurs within a cultural setting of which the participants are aware. Relationships between families, between the judge or clergy and the wedding party, or between children and adults are difficult to separate from the context of existing patterns of power and deference and standards of etiquette. The source of these standards of behavior is the larger society, and the researcher may need to know what the participants think of these standards before the participants' behavior can be fully explained.

These three types of information may be obtained using a variety of methodologies. A good rule of thumb is that social surveys, content analysis, and aggregate data analysis are usually the most effective methodologies for isolating the frequencies and distributions of characteristics within a population. Data about a large number of individuals and groups may be summarized in an efficient manner using these strategies. Although researcher and respondent may interact for only a few minutes in a survey, this is often enough time to enumerate just those characteristics that are important for the investigator to know. Generally, more lengthy and sustained contact with individuals or groups, or the use of written, historical materials, is required to obtain data about sequences of events. Prolonged observation and interviewing may be necessary to discover the subjective meaning of events for the people who participate in social interaction.

Whatever the topic of your own research, ask yourself which of these broad types of data will help you to understand it most effectively. The answer to this question depends, in part, on the level at which you are using or constructing theory. In many cases, you will have a number of options. A single critical event, such as the stock market crash of 1929, may profoundly affect a family, as well as a nation. In this example, as in many others, you would have a choice as a researcher. Would you prefer to spend your time examining the declining employment and

income figures for the entire United States during the 1930s to determine the effect of the stock
market crash? Or would you rather conduct a
series of in-depth personal interviews in which
you would observe and interact with individuals
who lived through the Great Depression? The
nature of the data you need might well determine whether yours is to be survey research,
content analysis, participant observation, or
some other mode of data collection.

Quantitative and Qualitative Techniques

A basic choice in research is the distinction between quantitative and qualitative data.
QUANTITATIVE DATA *use numbers to describe
what exists*. A major benefit of these data is that
they may be fed into a computer where they
can be counted, stored, and manipulated; however, numbers are often a poor substitute for
a researcher's vivid descriptions. **QUALITATIVE
DATA** *rely on words, especially nouns and adjectives that convey what exists*. Their main advantage is that they can capture subtleties of meaning and interpretation that numbers do not
convey. However, the use of numbers in quantitative research makes it more likely that studies
can be replicated and that the results of research
are *reliable* (see Chapter 1) because it is easier to
repeat the data collection procedures that generate numbers than exactly to re-create the conversations and observations that typically form
the basis of qualitative research.

These dilemmas may be illustrated in the
following example. Let us say that we wish
to generalize about the topic "growing old"
(Gubrium and Holstein, 2000). We might collect
quantitative data from retirement communities, recording each resident's age, health status,
and income. Or, we could collect other quantitative data looking at the *communities* themselves, noting their population density, how
much they charge for their services, the number
of employees, and so forth. However, qualitative
data may also be essential to understanding the
experience of growing old. We could use these
data to report on the appearance of its medical facilities, relations between staff and residents, the leisure-time activities that are made

available, and residents' relationships with their
families.

No matter which of these options is selected,
we will nonetheless be able to generalize about
growing old. Increasingly researchers are combining **MULTIPLE METHODS**, *using both quantitative and qualitative data collection*, in the
same study to reap the benefits of both and
minimize the deficiencies in each (Brewer and
Hunter, 2005).

Deciding where the data will come from is, in
part, a practical issue. It may be more expensive and time-consuming to select one type of
data, rather than another. To conduct qualitative personal, in-depth interviews of two hundred people requires a different set of resources
than does the continuous quantitative or qualitative observation of a group as it goes about
its business or the quantitative processing of
answers from a multiple-choice questionnaire.
If we are indeed to study growing old, the location of our data may depend on these practical considerations because we could probably
obtain data about the retirement communities
as a whole by doing some reading in a library and
by examining census data or publicity materials. However, we may have to undertake a more
lengthy project if we are to observe the behaviors
of the residents themselves or to discover their
attitudes.

Deciding on the source of data may be as
much a conceptual issue as a practical one. The
decision is often influenced, even determined,
by the theoretical concerns of researchers or the
level of human interaction that they feel most
comfortable explaining. In ascending order of
comprehensiveness, the major types of interaction examined in social science research occur
between two individuals, between an individual and a group, and between groups. The same
topic may be studied at each of these levels of
interaction. A social psychologist looking at the
issue of divorce is likely to be intrigued by the
conflict between individuals that leads to the
break up of marriage (Vaughan, 1990; Wallerstein, 1996). Qualitative interviews may be useful in obtaining such data. Another feature of
the social reality surrounding this issue might
be provided by a single case study of a divorced

person in the community. Alternatively, one might examine divorce at the group/group level, perhaps by studying the lobbying process to trace the effect of groups composed of separated men and women on changing divorce and child custody laws. Finally, we could use quantitative data to look at divorce rates in general; how long it takes for people, once divorced, to remarry; or how much income is lost as a result of divorce.

These examples all illustrate the point that sources of data are not necessarily the same as research topics. We may study big business in America by using data about corporate leaders (Useem, 2001) as well as data about corporations (Kanter, 1997); we may approach politics as a profession by examining politicians as personalities or by looking at their politicking; juvenile delinquency may be understood by collecting biographical information about youngsters with police records or by obtaining data about the quality of life in the neighborhoods in which they grew up. In short, people, the things they create, and the environment in which this activity occurs all may be legitimate sources of data. "Recipes" for social research do indeed differ. As this summary of the important issues researchers face in conceptualizing a topic concludes, you should have a clearer idea of what to look for as you begin your own research and where to begin looking for it. Now for the next question: How shall the data be gathered?

Strategies of Data Collection

There is no one best technique for gathering data, any more than there is one best theory for analyzing and drawing inferences from data. How would you go about selecting a strategy for collecting information about society? Your choice will depend on these five criteria, among others:

- How well formulated your theory is before you begin observation
- The level of social interaction you need or wish to observe
- The type of information you want to know
- The resources you have available for research
- The relative ease of access to individuals, groups, or institutions

There are several kinds of data collection in social research; each one is examined in detail in a subsequent chapter of this book. This chapter will define some of the most important ones and briefly note the general circumstances under which it is a good idea to use each.

PARTICIPANT OBSERVATION, or fieldwork, is qualitative research in which *social phenomena are observed firsthand in their natural setting. The researcher, or fieldworker, establishes continuing social relations with the individuals being studied* (see Chapter 9). The extent of actual participation may vary greatly, in that the researcher may or may not play an active part in events (Denzin and Lincoln, 2005). However, interviewing of respondents (see Chapter 8), when it does occur, is always part of the process of observation.

There is no logical reason why participant observation cannot be used to verify existing social theory. Yet it is used less frequently for this purpose than is survey research. Typically, fieldworkers contact only a small number of respondents, and this makes it difficult to generalize their findings to a much larger population. To increase the number of people observed or interviewed using participant observation might be prohibitively expensive. Moreover, because this technique relies to a great extent on the personal involvement between researcher and subjects, it is difficult to repeat the investigative procedure exactly. Thus social surveys are often used to verify existing theory because they can be replicated more easily and may be more reliable than participant observation.

The major strengths of qualitative observational techniques are that (1) they permit rich description, based on intimate personal involvement of the researcher in the everyday life of respondents; and (2) they provide explanations for human behavior that evolve gradually as theory is created inductively. Such theories are often verified using other techniques. Participant observation is, in some respects, ideal for the beginning researcher. Its small-scale, intensive approach is intrinsically interesting; it does not require mastery of complex statistical procedures. However, this data-gathering strategy does place a premium on interpersonal skills (e.g., being a good listener) and the intellectual capacity to make sense out of complex phenomena. Because questions are not usually developed in advance, many beginning researchers assume, erroneously, that little or no knowledge of theory is necessary to do an observational study. Actually, although inductive inquiry may require less sophistication to begin with, it places more of a burden on the individual researcher-in-training to develop theory than does the typical deductive survey.

By contrast, in the **SOCIAL SURVEY** (see Chapter 7), a quantitative technique, *interviewing is done with the aim of obtaining reports of social phenomena or attitudes apart from the natural setting in which they actually occur* (Nardi, 2005). In surveying, durable personal relations between researcher and subject are seldom necessary or possible. Contact between the two parties, when it occurs, is relatively brief. Whatever observation takes place entails minimum participation; in fact, it is possible to use a questionnaire sent through the mail. In this case, the investigator may never actually meet respondents face to face.

There is no necessary, logical relationship between survey research as a mode of investigation and either induction or deduction. Social surveys may be exploratory, descriptive, or explanatory, and there is no way to determine in advance just how much theoretical analysis must be done before, during, or following data collection. In the world of research practice, however, social survey procedures and deductive inquiry are often paired.

Because contact between researcher and respondent is typically short, survey work must rely on reaching large numbers of respondents to produce data. This exercise can be time-consuming and may also require many interviewers. Therefore, the nature of the contact with research subjects in survey work is often standardized by determining in advance the specific questions to be asked. This has the advantage of reducing wasted time, both during the interview and later in data analysis. It ensures that all subjects will be responding to the same issues. It also helps to eliminate the effects of the interviewer's personal interests on the research

results because all subjects are being asked the same questions. Because the questions are formulated in advance, survey research may more easily employ less expert, yet fully competent, interviewers. This is especially important because it would be quite expensive for highly qualified investigators to interview personally hundreds or thousands of respondents.

It is useful to devise questionnaires in advance, but it is also difficult to do so without some theoretical guide. For this reason, most social surveys, particularly large-scale ones, are initiated deductively. Because a questionnaire limits the nature and type of data that will be collected, a major function of surveys is to verify or test existing theories and hypotheses, rather than to discover theory. However, because they generate such a large quantity of information, some of it unexpected, social surveys may also inspire later inductive theory building. A certain degree of theoretical sensitivity in the researcher is required to begin a survey project involving more than a few dozen respondents. It is often helpful to obtain copies of the questionnaires used by other researchers, which you may alter slightly to suit your own needs. If this is not practical, try to create questions that use definitions of concepts, or variables, that are similar to those used in previous studies. In this way, you will increase the probability that your survey will be more than a descriptive exercise and that it will actually explain social behavior scientifically.

Another quantitative technique of data collection, **CONTENT ANALYSIS** (see Chapter 13) avoids the issue of personal involvement with research subjects and the problems of reliability associated with interviewing. It *concentrates on one aspect of human behavior, the manifest content of communication between individuals or groups* (Krippendorff, 2003). To measure and describe the words and pictures that make up human communication, content analysis does not rely on interviews, but on **ENUMERATION**, or the *counting of the number of times that specific types of communication occur* in a variety of settings. This enumeration does not necessarily involve firsthand observation of interaction (for example, in the screening of newspaper editorials). Observations may be carried out in a natural setting (as in the content analysis of leader/member relations in a small group). Either way, the categories used in the enumeration of data are determined in advance, and the counting exercise itself has minimal impact on what takes place.

Content analysis is a deductive technique that depends on some prior conceptual homework. You cannot begin to enumerate types of television commercials, for example, until you have developed a list of "types" or categories into which each advertisement might be placed. Once this sort of preliminary scheme is devised, content analysis may be used as part of either inductive or deductive investigation. We might ask, for example, whether there is an ideological bias in news coverage on prime-time television (Croteau and Hoynes, 2002). We can do this successfully, even without having formulated a theory of political influence that connects the content of the television news programs with the influence of national political or business leaders. However, we might begin with a relatively well-developed theory, such as the Marxist notion that the news media in a capitalist society attempt to influence the public to accept the leadership of the business elite. Then we might test this theory using content analysis of network television news broadcasts, looking for favorable images of big business and its representatives.

EXPERIMENTATION, a quantitative method, may involve face-to-face interaction between subjects and researchers, for example, observation, interviewing, enumeration of behaviors, or all three (see Chapter 12). The hallmark of the experimental method is that *the duration and nature of such contact are determined in advance and rigorously controlled by the researcher*. The individuals participating in an experiment may be asked to report how they feel or to say why they have acted in a particular manner, and what they do may be photographed or recorded with words or numbers. Social behavior is not, however, explained merely by citing people's subjective responses or the researcher's descriptions. For an experimenter, *the source of social explanation is the relationship between modifications made in the subjects' environment and subsequent changes in their behavior or reports of their behavior* (Campbell and Stanley, 2005). It is apparent, therefore, that the experimental environment must be one that can be manipulated by the researcher. For this reason (although a few ingenious designs have been created in natural settings) most experiments take place in the **LABORATORY**, *an artificial setting in which no encounters take place except those desired by the investigator*.

It is wise not to select experimentation as a strategy unless you have a theory in mind and have developed, on your own or from the literature, some specific hypotheses that follow from that theory. Experimental research is wholly deductive in nature. Each alteration in the laboratory environment is made for a reason, namely, to help you prove or disprove some theory or to test a hypothesis. Therefore, the meanings of concepts and the operational definition of the variables used in experimental research are determined in advance, not discovered as the research progresses.

In a famous experiment, Zimbardo (1972) wanted to test the theory that the behavior of prison guards and inmates is determined by the structure of the prison as an institution rather than by the personalities of the prisoners or their keepers. He simulated lockup conditions in the laboratory and carefully divided a homogeneous group of student subjects into "inmates" and "guards." He purposefully altered the environment by allowing rumors of a prison rebellion to spread. The student guards reacted with surprising brutality, providing data in support of the theory.[4] You could study the same topic – prisons – more inductively using either survey or participant observation techniques. In both cases, you would have less control over the research environment than Zimbardo; your work would take you outside the laboratory, perhaps for firsthand interviews with prison officials or inmates. Even if you did not confirm or disconfirm a particular theory or create a new theory of your own, you might nonetheless produce a valuable description of actual prison conditions.

---

[4] The ethics of this and other experiments that have the potential to cause emotional harm to research subjects is discussed in Chapter 5.

No mode of inquiry is easier than any other, but each does tap different strengths of the researcher. Your personal research and theoretical interests may influence your choice of method. A researcher setting out to investigate patterns of interaction in a relatively small social system, such as a bar or a voluntary organization, may find direct observation of behavior a wholly appropriate way to acquire data. It would certainly be more difficult to use participant observation when investigating the relations between the major institutions in a society. The problems faced by the researcher change as the level of research shifts. To the extent that a theory is more or less abstract and more or less verifiable by investigating small social groups or larger institutions, the theory you select will help to determine which techniques are appropriate for you to use in gathering data.

Spending Time and Resources Wisely

There is a story told in jest about a New England state in which the legislature, desperate for revenue and having already taxed every available resource, imposed a tax on air. One frugal Yankee, intent on saving as much money as possible, suffocated to death! This story has a message for us all as researchers. It is important to use time and money efficiently as we go about our work, but an underfunded study, or one that fails to take the time to contact as many respondents as it should, may be useless and even dangerous.

SAMPLING is one procedure that makes research manageable (see Chapter 6). When investigators take a sample, they *select a relatively small number of cases from the social whole*, for enumeration or observation. By sampling the behavior of several hundred families, we may discover the television-viewing habits of the entire nation (Nielsen Media Research, 2007). Sampling saves time and money, and if it is done correctly, it does not prevent us from making accurate generalizations about the population from which the sample is taken. If it is done poorly, sampling may have serious negative consequences. If a political survey does not sample the full variety of voter opinion, it may not

accurately predict the outcome of an election. If the true number of low-income households in a community is underestimated by a sample, federal or state aid may be restricted or reduced, causing hardship to the families concerned. As a beginning researcher, your own work may not have this sort of direct impact immediately, but it is still important to understand that your attempts to conserve resources may indeed affect the accuracy of your conclusions.

If investigators have only the time, funds, and staff to perform certain types of methodological procedures, they will be able to acquire only certain types of data. If you are doing a participant observation study of a single organization, you may indeed have enough time to call personally the respondents within the group who have relevant information to give you. If you are doing a social survey, which asks comparatively fewer questions of more people, or if you are performing a content analysis, you will need a sample of sufficient size to permit you to make generalizations about a much larger population or range of data.[5] To sample correctly, you may require the services of several co-workers or of sophisticated computer software. You can overcome some of these financial obstacles by performing a secondary analysis of another researcher's data. This procedure is generally less costly than working with **PRIMARY DATA**, *information that you have collected using your own resources*. In secondary analysis, *data may be manipulated in a manner different from the original research or used for another purpose* (see Chapter 14). These **SECONDARY DATA** may not, however, contain all of the variables you need, or they may not enable you to measure them in a manner appropriate to your own work.

Some data collection strategies will commit you to spending time and money over a period of months or even years. This is **LONGITUDINAL RESEARCH**, which involves *the gathering of information at different points in time*. The purpose of longitudinal research may be to monitor and to predict social change, to compare equivalent populations during different years,

---

[5] The procedures for determining sample size and selecting samples are explained in Chapter 6.

or to follow a particular group of people through time to see whether their behavior or attitudes have altered since the research began. To understand changes in consumer spending habits, for example, it is necessary to discover how families budget their income over several years. Surveys of middle-class families are taken periodically. Such **TREND STUDIES** note the amount of increase in disposable income, major purchases made, and plans for future purchases. We cannot predict trends with confidence unless we *gather information over a sufficient period of time.* Thus, this type of research can be quite costly.

A **COHORT STUDY** *looks at a more specific group of people as it changes over time.* For example, one "cohort" whose progress we might wish to follow is African Americans who first obtained employment as a result of the affirmative action legislation. We might sample them in selected occupations every five years to determine their income promotions, job satisfaction, and so forth. In a cohort study, the specific individuals in each sample differ, although they are all survivors of the original group being investigated (Duncan, Hofferth, and Stafford, 2004).

In a **PANEL STUDY**, one of the most elaborate longitudinal research designs, *the same respondents are followed through time and contacted again and again.* [6] An example of a panel study is the examination of the careers of gifted individuals initiated by the psychologist Lewis B. Terman (Goleman, 1980). In 1921, a sample of males and females, aged 3 to 19, with very high IQs was selected and interviewed. Their whereabouts were carefully tracked, so that they could be reinterviewed. Results have since been obtained for eleven points in time, so that the researchers have compared data from periods when the panel members were completing their education, when they embarked on careers or became parents, when they were nearing the end of their active work lives, and when they were well into retirement. Subjects were polled to determine their goals in life, whether these aspirations were met, and what careers these very intelligent people found to be most

rewarding. The Terman study, which began with a panel of 1,470 people, has proved to be a major undertaking; it is probably the longest survey ever conducted. Researchers have had to cope with attrition from the sample because of the death of panel members, people becoming annoyed with the questions they are asked, and those who move and cannot be traced. The project maintained an office and staff on the campus of Stanford University for nearly eighty years. By 1986, about 70 percent of the original 1922 sample still responded to researchers' requests for data (Holahan and Sears, 1995). Only two hundred of the original panel were still living in the year 2000 (Leslie, 2000).

Cost is only one factor in the selection of a strategy for data collection, but if it is your major stumbling block, remember that the cost of doing individual case studies, including in-depth interviewing or participant observation, is likely to be lower than for large-scale survey work. This is particularly significant for apprentice researchers, who typically spend a good deal of time working for little or no pay while they are learning the craft, and who in any event usually have more time than money to spend.

If you are using this chapter as a guide to doing your own research, you will have selected a topic and decided how to go about studying it by now. Consider all the mental and physical energy you have expended, and you have yet to collect even the first bit of information. Experienced researchers spend much of their time thinking about what they are going to do before they actually do it. There is a natural eagerness to go out into the field, but you were wise to prepare, to plan, to review the literature and your own resources. Now you are ready to collect data and to interpret them.

Collecting Data

In Chapters 7, 8, and 9, we will describe formats for acquiring raw data, using predetermined lists of questions, making tape recordings, or taking detailed notes on behavior that you observe in the field. Sometimes you need do no more than make a series of check marks, or write a series of numbers, on the printed page. On other

---

[6] Panel studies and other longitudinal survey designs are discussed in more detail in Chapter 7.

occasions you may take brief notes that can later be expanded to a rich description of events. In any case, the format for data collection should be tailored to the needs of the research. The theory you are testing or constructing, the variables you are examining, and your sources of information all will influence the specific form that your raw data take.

In experimental research the investigator knows when to stop collecting data, since the nature and amount of information required are specified in the research design. In social surveys that use only questionnaires to obtain information, the duration of the information-gathering phase of the project will be determined by the length of time required to contact all of the respondents in the sample. The more inductive the investigation, or the more observational techniques employed in data collection, the more ambiguous are the guidelines for bringing data collection to a halt.

Aside from the limitations imposed by our own resources, the data themselves may help us to decide when to wind down the process of accumulating evidence. Observational research may be an adventure in the early stages of data collection. After a time, however, it becomes more routine. The investigator becomes used to the research setting and notices more and more social behavior that, although interesting, is not particularly novel or puzzling. As more data are collected, more questions are answered, and eventually a **SATURATION** point is reached, at which *more data simply do not take the investigator any closer to the solution of the research problem*. This is a sure sign that data collection is nearing an end.

Analyzing and Processing Data

At this juncture it may be useful to recall the analogy between researcher and cook. The processing and analysis of data may be compared to cooking because even if two cooks use identical recipes, the results may differ depending on the cooking method, time, and temperature used. Similarly, raw data do not arrange themselves. The researcher groups them together and processes them in a variety of ways, to show what they mean and to facilitate their inter-

pretation. Raw data gathered about individuals and institutions may be lumped into categories and the results compared for each group. If we have asked a hundred people how they like their jobs, we may separate the findings for men and women if gender is a relevant variable; or we may divide the answers according to the social class of the respondents, their place of residence, their religion, and so forth. The categories for analysis are largely determined in advance in studies that are primarily deductive; they are allowed to emerge from the data themselves in studies that are basically inductive. Both in participant observation and social survey, however, surprising results are often obtained through imaginative data analysis.

DATA PROCESSING often consists of *translating raw information, which may appear in the form of words or descriptions, into letters or numbers* that can be manipulated by computer at high speed. This procedure is especially useful with large samples of respondents.[7] Statistical tests may be employed to compare or contrast two or more groupings of data. These tests may tell us whether men's job satisfaction is significantly different from women's or just how dissatisfied each group is. These procedures may indicate what happens to job satisfaction as socioeconomic status rises or whether the results for respondents in various parts of the country correlate well with the results for respondents who belong to different religious denominations. Most statistical tests will not yield reliable results when only a small number of respondents have been contacted. Therefore, data analysis with small samples may employ simpler summary measures: percentages, fractions, and ratios. Even with samples of only ten to twenty people, it is still useful to know that 80 percent of those polled prefer one candidate to another, that 60 percent of the members of a certain church committee are women, or that in a particular month divorces in your town outnumbered marriages by a margin of three to one. Note that data analysis may be presented in several different forms, including tables, charts, graphs, recorded dialogue with accompanying

---

[7] See Chapters 18 and 19 for discussion of quantitative data analysis.

comments from the investigator, or a critical essay.

Making Inferences and Recommendations

After data have been processed, they are used to draw inferences from behavior. This exercise is called **INTERPRETATION**. Suppose we find that divorces substantially outnumber marriages. What does this mean for the individuals directly involved, for the community, or for a society as a whole? These are the questions you should begin to think about after data have been collected and processed. Research conclusions or findings are not merely a rehash of the raw data; they should include an assessment of the significance of the data, in terms of the development of theory, the adoption of social policy, or both.

In a study in which deductive procedures have been followed, the results of hypothesis testing should be noted after the data have been processed. Do the data support existing theory, and if so, under what circumstances? How might other studies be designed in order to test the hypotheses still further? What new hypotheses are suggested by the results?

If the investigation has been inductive, this is the place to summarize the process of theory construction. What underlying principles of behavior might explain the data that were collected? In both cases, it is appropriate to spell out the policy implications of the findings and conclusions. If, for example, our findings indicate that divorces outnumber marriages, we might predict increases in the number of single-parent families, in the demand for housing space, and in the need for places where single adults may meet each other. These implications follow directly from the data, and may themselves suggest future research.

PUTTING IT ALL TOGETHER

The Final Report

Once research is completed, there remains the task of producing a **FINAL REPORT**, to show the world what has been done. This report cannot tell everything; it *summarizes how the investiga-tor has used his or her research imagination to craft each of the components of research*. Often the final report takes the form of a journal article, a paper read at a professional conference, or a fact-finding memorandum to be presented to the agency or organization sponsoring the research. For the student researcher, it may be a term paper! Whether done professionally or as part of a learning exercise, the final report should be an honest recapitulation of your own thoughts, activities, conclusions, recommendations, and suggestions for additional work by other investigators in the area of your interest. At a minimum, the final report should contain the following:

- A statement of the research problem
- A review of the literature relating to the problem
- A theoretical framework for explaining phenomena associated with the problem (developed either deductively from the literature and prior research or inductively from the present investigation)
- Identification of the major relevant variables (and in a deductive study, specification of the major relevant hypotheses)
- Explanation of the criteria used for measuring these variables, including a summary of the methodology used in the research and specific questions asked of respondents
- An indication of the sampling procedures used, if any, the setting for data collection, and the length of time required to complete the investigation
- An outline of the manner in which data were processed and analyzed, including statistical tests that were employed, if any
- The findings or conclusions, emphasizing those that contribute the most to knowledge, theoretically or descriptively; those that have potential for solving social problems; and those that are surprising or that violate conventional wisdom

This outline represents a workable guide for your term paper, as well as a summary of the key elements in most scholarly writing. Let us emphasize that it is a minimum; do not be afraid to add elements to your own final report.

As an apprentice researcher you may find it useful to record the process of learning that you experienced as the research progressed. Examples of such self-analysis include answers to the following questions:

- How did I come upon this particular research problem, and why is it important to me?
- Which prior research have I accepted, and which have I rejected, entirely or in part, and why?
- What problems did I encounter in theory construction, or in making additions to existing theory?
- What anticipated, or unanticipated, difficulties occurred during the data collection phase of the research?
- What were the limits to my ability to analyze data or to draw inferences from them? How might I proceed differently if I were to begin the same project again?

All social scientists, whether "newbies" or veterans, confront each of these questions as they go about their work. Unfortunately, in conventional research, reports of the "natural history" of the actual conduct of social investigation rarely accompany summaries of the findings. What one typically sees as a finished product is a document that presents only the hypotheses, data, and conclusions in a manner that conceals, rather than reveals, the difficulties and unexpected problems that arise during all social investigations. Many journal articles convey the impression that once we have defined a problem for study and chosen an appropriate data gathering technique, research proceeds trouble-free. Do not be deceived by research reports that fail to relate how projects actually take shape! There are always problems, and although personal experience is a good teacher, we may also learn much from the failures of other investigators – as well as from their successes.

The Ups and Downs of Research

Mistakes, as well as sudden inspirations, are part of the research process (Becker, 1998). Social scientists often have to contend with false leads and dead ends. It is quite common for research design to undergo a number of unanticipated turns and twists, pushing the investigator in new directions. Even the original questions that a particular study was designed to answer may change in subtle ways, or it may become apparent, after a project is well under way, that there are additional questions that need answering.

As research progresses, we may realize that new theoretical insights are called for, or that it is desirable to use data collection strategies quite different from those with which the study began. One may begin by looking at phenomena at one societal level (say, behavior between individuals) and soon realize that certain issues cannot be analyzed only at that level. Thinking about the conditions under which people misinterpret each other's communications, a researcher may find it necessary to examine the respondents' social values. This may lead to an investigation of the group affiliations of those being studied. One might, therefore, shift from one level of analysis to another, with the result that new types of data will be needed. A researcher operating from a deductive model of investigation may discover that the questionnaire so painstakingly devised to test a particular hypothesis is not getting at the information desired; perhaps some in-depth interviews with a selected sample of respondents would solve the problem. Each of these discoveries is an opportunity to make use of the research imagination.

Given the complex scheduling that is often necessary to coordinate a research project, it is no wonder that some social scientists have nightmares about natural disasters (snowstorms, earthquakes) that force delays in data collection. In fact, disasters can, and do, occur. Anticipated resources, in money or staff, may not be available, leading to a redesign of a project after it has begun. It may be impossible to gain access to the individuals from whom data are needed, whether they are inmates in a prison, business executives, or politicians. Or we may obtain access, only to discover that our presence has upset the status quo among respondents to the point where we cannot obtain reliable information about their usual behavior.

The lesson to be learned here is that you should not become discouraged if things do not go just as you planned. Whether your work is primarily deductive or inductive, there is still plenty of room for surprises, as well as the potential for "spinning your wheels" in frustration. Remember, however, that the same flexibility that allows for the possibility of error, and for the occurrence of the unexpected, also allows for creativity. Your individual effort and inspiration can make a difference in the outcome of research.

An Example: A Study of Undergraduate Life

The goal of this chapter has been to help you to grapple with the issues in research design. Your personal experiences will, of course, depend on your own resources, talents, and interests. It may be instructive, however, to describe the natural history of an ongoing project conducted by one of the authors and his colleagues – a project that took shape even as this chapter was being written. What follows is an illustration of how professional investigators deal with the issues we have been discussing in this chapter.

HOW WAS THE TOPIC SELECTED? The examination of undergraduate student life outlined here actually was inspired by a very ordinary event: lunchtime conversation among a group of professors. The discussion focused on the topic of university students, but it was not at all systematic or academic. Obviously, students are frequently the subject of faculty's interest and speculation. On this particular day, and given the curiosity of the group of professors who participated, certain puzzling themes emerged from the conversation. On the basis of gossip from secondhand sources, and on occasional, brief conversations with students outside the classroom, a disturbing vision of undergraduate student life was expressed. Many students reported that they had cheated on examinations and term papers; an anti-intellectual attitude was said to exist in some students. Their social life was described as centering not around regular or occasional dating in couples but around rituals of partying that sometimes occupied three or four nights a week. There was concern expressed about alcoholism and about general student alienation from peers, from the faculty, and from the university. Most of those present left the

table with a feeling of unease. They did not know how much of what they had heard, or spoken, was actually true. It was apparent that very little was known about how undergraduate university students view themselves, their schools, and their prospects for the future. Is college the place for learning and intellectual growth that so many university catalogs describe? Or is it experienced primarily as a ritual of necessary steps toward future employment, as a passage from late adolescence into adulthood, or simply as a place to "hang out"?

Later that day, and for the next few days, some of the professors met again to explore the idea of doing a systematic study to answer these questions. As a potential topic for research, undergraduate life had several attractions for these researchers. First, it was intrinsically interesting to them; because they share much of the university setting with students and interact with them constantly, it would be of concrete help to the professors to understand student behavior better. Moreover, the topic had wider social significance. Whatever was discovered might be useful to students and their parents, teachers, and administrators at many institutions of higher learning. As a result of these initial meetings, three of the professors decided to put something on paper, a proposal for research, mostly to get clear in their own minds just what they would be investigating, and why. At this point, they still had not specified the variables they would be using to assess student behavior and attitudes.

HOW WAS THE TOPIC CONCEPTUALIZED? The first step in isolating the variables for investigation was a brainstorming exercise, in which the researchers, individually and together, wrote down all of the possible, logical components of the concept, "student life." They produced a document in which the following eleven major variables were defined:

- The *classroom experience* and its impact on activities and attitudes outside the classroom
- *Student aspirations and values*, and in particular the extent of conformity or rebellion in relation to the larger society

- *Students' use of time*: How, with whom, and where do undergraduates spend time?
- *Students' use of space*: Where are students found; where do they like to be; how do they use the facilities of the university?
- *Social differentiation* in the student population: the subworlds of residence, race and ethnicity, income, sex, and age
- *Interpersonal relationships*: including friendships, dating, and shared sexuality
- The *use of student services* (counseling, health care, advisement, etc.): Who uses which services, and why?
- *Religion*: changes in spirituality, belief, and practice
- *Social control*: enacting and enforcing the formal and informal rules that restrict behavior
- *Extracurricular activities*: student government and organizations athletics
- *Leisure*: partying, playing, and recreation

Some categories in this list overlap (e.g., several of the variables are related to students' use of time). Moreover, although it covers much conceptual territory, the list is not exhaustive. One may imagine other variables, including students' relations with their families or with the community bordering on the university, which were not directly specified. The list is a preliminary one. There is a strong element of induction in the way these researchers are proceeding. The list of variables may be changed or whittled down and the definitions made specific, as the research progresses.

Conceptualization of the topic was influenced primarily by the investigators' own interests and their prior training and experience. A basic, deductive model of inquiry was rejected early on because there is no well-developed theory of student behavior and attitude formation. The topic was indeed broadly defined initially, in order not to miss relevant information about the influence on student life of changes in morality, sex roles, norms of student political activity, and career opportunities.

HOW WAS A STRATEGY FOR DATA COLLECTION SELECTED? Although previous studies suggested some effective strategies for obtaining specific kinds of information in the college setting (Kuh, 2004), the researchers decided to employ a variety of methods in this instance to cast as wide a net as possible for the collection of data and to capture the total college experience. They planned to obtain information about individual students via several techniques: participant observation of their daily routine, survey interviewing, and examination of records and documents.

The planning of this study of undergraduate life illustrates the point made earlier in this chapter that theory helps to determine the type of information required by investigators and that this, in turn, has an effect on the scope and costs of research. Initially, all levels of theory were explored in the attempt to explain student behavior and to suggest data collection strategies. If major social trends were thought to have affected student life within the university, then data would be needed about the larger society, for example, the availability of jobs and the income of families sending their children to college. If students' actions and attitudes were to be seen as a function of the structure and priorities of the college in which they enroll, then detailed data about the college would be called for, such as admissions practices, grading policies, disciplinary procedures, and the history of the college. The frequency and distribution of particular behaviors among the student population would have to be measured. Finally, if student behavior were conceptualized primarily in social psychological terms, that is, as exchange and communication among individuals, then detailed information about interpersonal episodes and encounters would comprise the data. The researchers would have to be near students when they felt pressure, pain, and anxiety; wondered about their futures; and experienced their pleasures. In fact, because of the wide range of theory that could potentially explain student behavior, there were no restrictions placed on data sources during the early planning of the project. Dormitories, student hangouts, cafeterias, classrooms, the libraries, and administrative offices of the university – all were potential valuable settings for the collection of data.

Up to this point, there had been little or no discussion among the researchers regarding financial support for the project. They estimated that such a wide-ranging study would take from three to five years to conduct. Such longitudinal research is expensive. Even if the professors involved donated their time and recruited graduate students to help out, the costs would be substantial. If its scope can be scaled down to the point where the research is manageable in practical terms, it will likely proceed with vigor and high hopes. At the same time, the extent of available research resources helps to determine what sorts of data may be collected, and this, in turn, has an impact on the theoretical significance of the project. We can say a great deal more about students and society as a whole after having conducted a five-year study employing several techniques of data collection than we can after having spent, say, one year only digging in university records or only talking to students or to administrators.

ISSUES OF DATA COLLECTION. Even as the project takes shape conceptually and financially, some concrete proposals for collecting data from students and from the university are being laid on the table. These are particularly interesting because of the ethical issues they raise. It has been suggested, for instance, that graduate students in social science departments be appointed as resident assistants in undergraduate dormitories. From this vantage point, they could note those aspects of student life that revolve around residence halls, leisure time, friendships, and so forth. This seems like a good idea, if students do not feel that they are being spied on. Suppose the graduate students discover some prohibited activity occurring in the dormitories. Are they obligated to report it to university authorities? This issue is especially vexing if the researchers are accepting financial aid from the university.

Another proposal involves a course that undergraduates could take for credit, called Student Life. Its manifest purposes would be to acquaint the class with the full range of student behavior and opportunities on campus and for students to study their own behavior and that of their peers in a systematic way. In addition, those enrolled in the course would be required to write papers about their own experiences. This seems to be an effective way to generate data about student aims and attitudes and to open up many of the themes of the research project for discussion among groups of undergraduates. Ethically, it raises the dilemma of students being "paid" (in course credits) for information. How reliable would these data be? Clearly, to be part of a scientific investigation, the information produced in the Student Life course would have to be cross-checked via other data sources, either observational or secondary.

A third proposal would use data obtained from university files. A sample of undergraduates might be selected at admission and followed through their four years at college. In this manner, their behavior and values could be matched with demographic factors such as their place of residence, ethnicity, and parents' income. A college may be willing to supply this sort of information for a bona fide research project, particularly if student records are kept confidential.[8] Should students be given the opportunity to refuse to participate?

These ethical issues have to be added to the equation, along with any financial limitations or conceptual problems, to determine whether to proceed with the project. The preliminary work previously described has been intriguing and even enlightening for the participants, but they need to answer many important questions of research design before substantial resources are expended or commitments made. We cannot say just how the proposed study of undergraduate life will turn out. If we could tell you, there would be no need to conduct the research in the first place! What we can predict with some certainty is that to be successful, the project will undergo changes in focus, in methodology, and in theory, as the research situation demands.

This example illustrates the complexity and diversity, as well as the promise, of social research. It also shows that there are countless conceptual recipes and that the ingredients of each may be combined in many ways and still

[8] See Chapter 5 for a review of ethical issues in research.

adhere to the principles of the scientific method. The "research cookbook" is full of imagination and creativity, but alas it is not foolproof. Do not become discouraged if your own work comes out "underdone" or "overdone" at first. It takes practice to draw all the possible valid inferences from a set of data or to avoid belaboring the obvious. With a little persistence, curiosity, and the wise use of time, many a study that seems hopelessly bogged down can be transformed into something useful.

SUMMARY

This chapter outlines the specific components of research, from selecting and conceptualizing a topic, to writing a final report in which the data collected on that topic have been processed, analyzed, and interpreted. Initially, social scientists specify a research problem – the questions concerning the topic that they believe are most important to answer. This problem is further refined by identifying the most appropriate variables and by defining them operationally so that they may be measured. Then, a theory showing how each of the variables relates to the others may be constructed inductively or be adapted from prior studies or from the literature. Practice is required to be able to evaluate the theoretical explanations in many professional journals, but if one's work is to become part of the accumulation of scientific knowledge, the effort is worth it.

Four major strategies of data collection are survey research, participant observation, content analysis, and experimentation. Selecting a particular strategy depends in part on how much inductive inquiry one is prepared to conduct, and on the level of social interaction one wishes to observe. The sources of available data and the type of information sought also affect selection of method because certain kinds of data are more easily obtained with surveys, for example, than with observational techniques.

No mode of inquiry is inherently easier than another; each taps different talents of the investigator and is compatible with different research interests. Resources (in money and staff) also play a part in the planning of any project because some research designs are inherently less expensive or typically take less time than others. It is wise to weigh the possible conceptual and methodological problems of studying a chosen topic carefully before actually going out into the field to minimize the unexpected, but inevitable, difficulties that can arise. Even in deductive social surveys, where the size of the sample to be contacted is known, and the questions to be asked are determined in advance, there are often difficulties in obtaining access to respondents or ethical dilemmas for the researcher to ponder.

Data, once collected, are in their "raw" state and must be processed to show what their significance is and to make interpretation easier. The conclusion of social science research ought to be more than a mere summary of the data gathered. It should include an assessment of the new information as it relates to theory, social policy, or both. The final written report of social investigation cannot restate everything that has occurred, but it should show how each of the components of research was crafted. It should be an honest recapitulation of the investigator's thoughts, activities, conclusions, and recommendations and suggestions for additional work by others.

KEY TERMS

brainstorming
cohort study
concept
conceptualization
content analysis
data processing
distribution
enumeration
experimentation
final report
frequency
interpretation
laboratory
longitudinal research
multiple methods

operational definition
panel study
participant observation
primary data
qualitative data
quantitative data
raw data
research design
research problem
sampling
saturation
secondary data
social survey
topic
trend study

EXERCISES

1. Review some of the professional journals in your field and select two articles for analysis according to the research cookbook. How did the authors of the articles imagine each of the seven essential components of social investigation listed in Table 3.1? In your opinion, which article reflects more research skill and insight, and why?

2. Using the same two articles as in question 1, indicate whether the primary motivation for each study was to add to theory or to solve some problem of social policy. How do you know?

3. Select one of the following three topics and describe how you would conceptualize it:

"Political Apathy in America"

"The Crisis in Health Care"

"Are Men and Women Equal?"

Hint: Begin by identifying the variables that might represent the concepts apathy, crisis, or equality.

4. Look through a newspaper or magazine and select five pictures that represent particular concepts. What concept do you think each picture represents? Give two different conceptual interpretations of each picture.

5. Locate three different sources of data for each of the following variables:

personal influence

success in school

racial discrimination

SUGGESTED READINGS AND SOURCES

Becker, Howard S. 1998. *Tricks of the Trade: How to Think About Your Research While You're Doing It.* Chicago: University of Chicago Press.

Excellent personal accounts of each step in the research process in a variety of studies from the researcher's point of view.

Burawoy, Michael, Joshua Gamson, and Alice Burton. 1991. *Ethnography Unbound: Power and Resistance in the Modern Metropolis.* Berkeley and Los Angeles: University of California Press.

This book is a compilation of qualitative studies by young researchers, many of whom are working in the field for the first time. Their accounts give us a glimpse into their own thinking as they try to develop research ideas and take on the researcher's role.

Duncan, Greg J., Sandra L. Hofferth, and Frank Stafford. 2004. *Evolution and Change in Family Income, Wealth, and Health: The Panel Study of Income Dynamics, 1968–2000 and Beyond.* Ann Arbor: Institute for Social Research, University of Michigan.

The Panel Study of Income Dynamics is a nationally representative, longitudinal study of nearly eight thousand American families, who have been followed in a panel since 1968. The PSID collects data on economic, health, and social behavior.

Leavitt, Fred. 2001. *Evaluating Scientific Research: Separating Fact from Fiction.* Upper Saddle River, NJ: Prentice Hall.

Chapter 4 is an excellent source on the issue of finding problems for study; Chapter 6 summarizes the major choices in study design that the researcher must make.

Leedy, Paul D., and Jeanne Ellis Ormrod. 2000. *Practical Research: Planning and Design.* Upper Saddle River, NJ: Prentice Hall.

A step-by-step guide to writing research reports based on quantitative or qualitative data.

Marshall, Katherine, and Gretchen B. Rossman. 2006. *Designing Qualitative Research.* 4th ed. Thousand Oaks, CA: Sage.

An accessible examination of the basics of qualitative study design.

Nielsen Media Research. 2007. http://www.nielsenmedia.com.

This Web site contains a description of the Nielsen sampling strategy for determining the television viewing habits of 262 million viewers.

Stern, Paul C., and Linda Kalof. 1996. *Evaluating Social Science Research.* 2nd ed. New York: Oxford University Press.

This book addresses the development of critical thinking skills in readers who are assessing the findings of research conducted using a variety of methodologies.

REFERENCES

Adler, William M. 2001. *Mollie's Job: A Story of Life and Work on the Global Assembly Line.* New York: Touchstone.

Becker, Howard S. 1998. *Tricks of the Trade: How to Think About Your Research While You're Doing It.* Chicago: University of Chicago Press.

Brewer, John, and Albert Hunter. 2005. *Foundations of Multimethod Research: Synthesizing Styles.* Thousand Oaks, CA: Sage.

Campbell, Donald T., and Julian C. Stanley. 2005. *Experimental and Quasi-Experimental Designs for Research.* Boston: Houghton Mifflin.

Croteau, David, and William Hoynes. 2002. *Media/ Society: Industries, Images, and Audiences.* 3rd ed. Thousand Oaks, CA: Pine Forge Press.

Denzin, Norman K., and Yvonna S. Lincoln, eds. 2005. *Handbook of Qualitative Research.* 3rd ed. Thousand Oaks, CA: Sage.

Duncan, Greg J., Sandra L. Hofferth, and Frank Stafford. 2004. *Evolution and Change in Family Income, Wealth, and Health: The Panel Study of Income Dynamics, 1968–2000 and Beyond.* Ann Arbor: Institute for Social Research, University of Michigan.

Goleman, Daniel. 1980. "1528 Little Geniuses and How They Grew." *Psychology Today* 13 (9): 28–53.

Gubrium, Jaber F., and James A. Holstein, eds. 2000. *Aging and Everyday Life.* Malden, MA: Blackwell.

Harris Poll. 2006. "Nation's Alienation Index up Significantly as More Feel Powerless and Isolated." *PR Newswire,* December 8, 2005. http://www.findarticles.com/p/articles/mi_m4PRN/is_2005_Dec_8/ai_n15926904.

Holahan, Carole K., and Robert R. Sears. 1995. *The Gifted Group in Later Maturity.* Stanford, CA: Stanford University Press.

Ingraham, Chrys. 1999. *White Weddings: Romancing Heterosexuality in Popular Culture.* New York: Routledge.

Kanter, Rosabeth Moss, ed. 1997. *Innovation: Breakthrough Thinking at 3M, DuPont, GE, Pfizer, and Rubbermaid.* New York: Harper.

King, C. Richard, and Charles F. Springwood. 2001. *Beyond the Cheers: Race as Spectacle in College Sport.* Albany: State University of New York Press.

Krippendorff, Klaus. 2003. *Content Analysis: An Introduction to Its Methodology.* 2nd ed. Thousand Oaks, CA: Sage.

Kuh, George D. 2000. *The National Survey of Student Engagement: Conceptual Framework and Overview of Psychometric Properties.* Bloomington: Indiana University. http://nsse.iub.edu/redirect.cfm?target.

Leslie, Mitchell. 2000. "The Vexing Legacy of Lewis Terman." *Stanford Magazine,* July–August.

Nardi, Peter M. 2005. *Doing Survey Research.* 2nd ed. Boston: Allyn & Bacon.

Nielsen Media Research. 2007. http://www.nielsenmedia.com.

Useem, Michael. 2001. *Leading Up: How to Lead Your Boss So You Both Win.* New York: Crown.

Vaughan, Diane. 1990. *Uncoupling: Turning Points in Intimate Relationships.* New York: Vintage.

Wallerstein, Judith S. 1996. *The Good Marriage: How and Why Love Lasts.* New York: Warner Books.

Zimbardo, Philip G. 1972. "Pathology of Imprisonment." *Society* 9 (April): 4–8.

MEASUREMENT

4

INTRODUCTION

Thus far we have examined the essentials of the scientific method, research process, and design. Only one more bit of background remains – a look at the measuring tools we employ in social investigation. **MEASUREMENT**, *the process of determining dimension, value, or degree*, is a critical component of research. We have to be thoughtful about the measures we use in all science.

To find the height of a man, the price of a piece of property, or the temperature outside on a winter day, we need measuring devices – yardsticks, calculators, thermometers – as well as units of measurement – inches, dollars, and degrees. Social scientists face many problems in selecting both the tools and the units of measurement. It is usually more difficult for us to agree about the dimensions, value, and degree of human behavior, attitudes, and ideas than about the physical description of people, the size of things, or the characteristics of the physical environment. However, it is essential that we try to perfect the tools and categories of measurement. If theories of human behavior are to be accepted as reasonable, and if we are to test these theories systematically, we must use measurement procedures that are clear and convincing.

There are many ways to gauge complex variables such as "violent crime," "freedom," "mental illness," or "political popularity." A craftsperson in the tool and die industry must often be accurate to one ten-thousandth of an inch in making the parts for a complex machine. By contrast, in the social sciences there is no absolute standard. The manner in which behavior and attitudes are measured will vary, depending on the purpose of the investigation and the research imagination of the investigator. How-

ever, measures in social research do share one attribute with their counterparts in industry: Measurement tools often must be customized and adapted to specialized situations. Thus in discussing problems of measurement, this chapter deals with the creation of new measures, as well as with those that have worked well in the past.

Another problem faced in all science is information loss during the process of measurement. As a child, you may have played the game "Telephone," in which an originally clear message was whispered from person to person until, by the end of the line, it had become unrecognizable. This is a danger we face continually in social research. Each time we process words, opinions, or pictures, we may be destroying some of the original evidence on which our findings must be based. Some loss is perhaps inevitable, but we need to guard against the disappearance of vital information caused by errors in recording, transmitting, conceptualizing, and storing data.

Keep these central issues – the choice of measuring device, standards for measurement, and the potential for information loss – in mind as we consider the following topics in this chapter: (1) the various levels of measurement, and what sort of data is appropriate to each; (2) operationalization – saying exactly how each variable we are using will be measured; (3) problems of reliability, or consistency, in our measures, and of validity, making sure that we are measuring the variables that we wish to measure; (4) sources of measurement error, particularly errors that may occur again and again unless their sources are found and eliminated; (5) difficulties in defining variables in research; and (6) suggestions for improving the quality of measurement in the social sciences.

LEVELS OF MEASUREMENT

There are four general levels of measurement – nominal, ordinal, interval, and ratio. Each level provides us with a different kind of information. We need to be aware of the advantages and limitations of each.

Nominal Measures

At the simplest level, *categories are generated so that we may determine whether the objects of investigation are the same or not*. These are called NOMINAL measures. "Male" and "female" are nominal categories, as are one's birthplace, religion, race, position on a team, eye color, and political affiliation. Indeed, the variety of nominal categories is immense. One criterion for nominal measures is that they must be MUTUALLY EXCLUSIVE; *a person is either a man or a woman*, has blue eyes or brown eyes, plays first base or shortstop, and so on. The other criterion for nominal categories is that they be EXHAUSTIVE, in that *every person or thing observed may be classified*. Suppose our variable is "state of birth," and it has fifty categories corresponding to the fifty states. As long as our sample includes only people who were born in the United States, who know the state they were born in, and who report it accurately, the criterion for a nominal level of measurement is met. If we add a fifty-first category designated as "other," our revised variable achieves the nominal level even if some of the respondents were born outside the country.

The best nominal measures isolate similarities and differences and are designed to minimize the number of ambiguous cases. Denoting "male" and "female" is quite adequate for almost all individuals, although it does not clearly separate out the transgendered from the rest of the population.

Ordinal Measures

In addition to distinguishing units as being the same or different from one another, we often wish to make statements about whether they possess "more" or "less" of a particular attribute.

This level of measurement is called ORDINAL because it *allows us to place people or things along a continuum from the greatest amount to the smallest amount* of the characteristic we are measuring. We may say that people are young, middle-aged, or old; thin, of average weight, or fat; and so on. It is possible to measure even more complex concepts using ordinal measures. If we were interested in describing citizens of a town in terms of their prestige in the community, we could include an item on a questionnaire that asked a group of judges to rank individuals accordingly. On the basis of these data, citizens might then be placed in the ordinal categories of "high," "medium," or "low" prestige. Other concepts that may be ranked in terms of their degree or intensity are athletic skill, intelligence, leadership, political liberalism, the tendency to conform, tolerance for pain, and sense of humor. It is easy to see why most variables used by social scientists are of the ordinal type.

Interval Measures

We can do more than categorize responses (at the nominal level) or rank order them (at the ordinal level). It is also often possible to *measure the distance between the rankings, so that we can know not only that one response is lower or higher than another, but how much lower or higher it is*. This is the INTERVAL level of measurement. In contrast with ordinal designations, the difference in interval rankings is expressed in units that have some absolute value and that remain constant from the bottom of the rankings to the top. Thus, the variable "temperature" may be expressed in intervals of degrees Fahrenheit, and a degree's difference is the same between 40 degrees Fahrenheit and 41 degrees Fahrenheit as between 80 degrees Fahrenheit and 81 degrees Fahrenheit. Obviously, if we are dealing with more complex variables, such as prejudice, conformity, or intelligence level, it becomes more difficult to specify the value of the units that separate one rank from another. The IQ (intelligence quotient) score is an attempt to measure aptitude at the interval level. Each IQ point has the same value.

Ratio Measures

The highest and most precise level of measurement is the **RATIO**. It *allows us to distinguish among persons or objects not only by adding and subtracting units of rank, as in the case of degrees or IQ points, but by using multiplication and division as well*. We may say that Mrs. A weighs *twice* as much as Mrs. B or that Mrs. X is *half* as old as Mrs. Y because ratio scales have a "true zero" point. Variables such as age, weight, and income do not have an arbitrary zero. A baby about to be born has no age; a penniless person may be completely without income; using a centrifuge, we may produce a state of "weightlessness." By contrast, we may measure prejudice with interval-level precision, using a questionnaire, but we would be hard-pressed to state that a respondent had no prejudice at all (the zero point on the scale). Similarly, we cannot say that a person with an IQ of 80 is half as intelligent as a person with an IQ of 160.

Precision and Accuracy

Regardless of the level of measurement employed, measures should always be accurate. They should also be as precise as possible, given the limitations of time and resources available for research. Let us examine these two interrelated ideas. In everyday language, to be accurate is also to be precise. We ask, "Precisely how tall are you?" and we expect an accurate answer, such as "five feet four inches tall." However, precision and accuracy, as they are considered in science, are not the same. When measures are **PRECISE**, they are *expressed in fine degrees*. Consider these two responses to the question, "What time is it?"

"A little after ten o'clock."

"Fourteen minutes and twenty seconds after ten."

The second answer is the more *precise* one. A building may be described as being 737 feet high, instead of simply as being tall; a crowd may be reported as containing 10,875 people, rather than being called a multitude; a person may be

noted as being born in Provo, Utah, rather than just west of the Rockies.

The highest possible degree of precision is not absolutely essential in all social research. Sometimes it will be sufficient to use ordinal categories, for example, to note that families in a particular neighborhood are "poor," rather than specifying their income, or that certain foodstuffs are "unaffordable," without stating their prices. Usually, however, it is important to reach as high a level of measurement as our data permit to reduce information loss and legitimately to apply the more powerful statistical techniques in data analysis. We may construct ordinal measures from interval or ratio scales, but we may not be able to reverse the process. Knowing the exact vote tally for candidates in an election, we might decide to label them "high," "medium," or "low" in popularity, but unless we are careful in preserving the original data and in recording the guidelines for the assignment of each candidate to the ordinal categories, the exact election figures may be lost forever.

Although it is generally important to be precise, the decision to use one level of measurement instead of another often depends on practical considerations, such as how precise we really need to be and whether appropriate measuring tools are available. This decision is one of the many that have to be made in the planning of research. Perhaps the energy and money required to increase precision would be better spent in broadening the scope of a study or in increasing the number of variables being considered.

ACCURACY differs from precision in that it is simply *the correspondence between our measure of some phenomenon and the actual thing, person, or event*. A totally accurate measure is a mirror image of the original. If my sleeve length is, in fact, 35 inches, and two tailors measure it, the more *accurate* result will be the one most closely approaching 35 inches. Precision and accuracy are logically related because the more precise a measuring tool is, the easier it may be to achieve absolute accuracy, but do not confuse these two ideas. Measures expressed in extremely precise terms can be grossly inaccurate. If a building described as being 726.5 feet tall is actually 710 feet high, we have an example of a precise, yet inaccurate, measure. It is important to recognize this distinction, because in evaluating reports issued by government or business or in watching television advertisements, we are often persuaded of the accuracy of numbers merely by the degree of precision with which they are expressed.

OPERATIONALIZATION

In Chapter 3, we noted that each variable in social investigation has to be defined in order for us to recognize and understand it when we see it in the data collection phase of research. This generalization holds true both for **QUANTITATIVE RESEARCH**, which *emphasizes ordinal measures and numbers*, as well as **QUALITATIVE RESEARCH**, which *may emphasize nominal measures*. The *process of arriving at a measure for a variable* is referred to as **OPERATIONALIZATION**. Let us examine this process in greater detail.

Example: Assessing Excellence in Education

When students are preparing to enter college, the actual choice-making process relies on a combination of subjective and objective factors (Karp, Holmstrom, and Gray, 2004). Let us imagine that we are trying to do an objective study of "excellence" in American college education. How could we define the variable in such a way that it could actually be used as a measuring tool to separate out the excellent schools from those which are merely good, average, or poor? A popular ranking of American colleges and universities is sponsored by *U.S. News and World Report*. One yearly edition (2006) contained the following overall ratings for major universities:

1. Harvard
2. Princeton
3. Yale
4. Pennsylvania
5. Duke
6. Stanford
7. California Institute of Technology
8. Massachusetts Institute of Technology
9. Columbia and Dartmouth (tie)

How was this ranking produced? The term "excellent" is a nominal measurement category that has no intrinsic meaning until we specify the **INDICATORS**, or *criteria*, used to assess it. The concept "academic excellence" has to be operationalized. The researchers use the following seven **DOMAINS**, or *general conceptual categories*: overall academic reputation, retention of students from year to year, resources available to faculty, selectivity in admitting students, financial resources, graduation rates, and alumni support (Morse and Flanigan, 2006). Then, within these domains, sixteen specific indicators of the concept "academic excellence" were identified. These included the following:

- The university's reputation according to college presidents, provosts, and deans of admission
- The proportion of entering freshman who graduate within six years
- The difference between the *actual* six-year graduation rate for entering classes and the *predicted* rate for the classes when they entered
- The proportion of freshman who return for sophomore year
- The proportion of courses with fewer than twenty students
- The proportion of courses with fifty or more students
- Average faculty pay and benefits
- The proportion of professors with the highest degree in their fields
- The student–faculty ratio
- The proportion of the faculty who work full time
- Scores attained by enrollees on the SAT or ACT tests
- The proportion of enrolled freshmen who graduated in the top 10 percent of their high school classes

- The acceptance rate (the ratio of students admitted to the number of applicants)
- The yield (the ratio of students who enroll to those admitted)
- The average spending per student on instruction, research, student services, etc.
- The percentage of alumni who contribute to the university

Obviously, in this case, the number of potential indicators are many. In assessing the *validity* of these measures, the researchers did *not* mention living accommodations, athletic facilities and programs, and advisement and counseling services, all of which may be legitimately construed as part of "excellence" in college education. A problem we always face in our efforts to operationalize a complex concept is that we can never be sure that the indicators named adequately reflect the presence or absence of the characteristic we wish to measure. To some degree the selection of appropriate indicators calls for guessing on the part of the researcher, particularly if there are few prior studies or a well-articulated theory that is being tested.

A second point is that in this example the overall ranking system rests on two pillars: quantitative measures, such as course enrollments and faculty salaries, and qualitative measures such as university officials' perceptions of reputation. Of these two types of data, the former tends to be more *reliable* because the method for measuring them remains relatively constant from year to year. Reputation or prestige of a university may change dramatically in response to some short-term negative publicity (for example, campus crime or academic dishonesty) that may temporarily skew the ratings. Moreover, because the actual deans and presidents who provide their opinions can change from year to year, the reputational data over time are in some sense dependent on their individual personalities and career experience.

Ideally, operational definitions must not be ambiguous; in this instance, they must state exactly the criteria for inclusion or exclusion from the category of "excellence." The *U.S. News and World Report* ratings are less reliable than they might be because the magazine has

reserved the right to "change [its] methodology from year to year" (Morse and Flanigan, 2001). For example, as a measure, the amount of money schools spend on education per student was criticized as invalid because there is no necessary and direct relationship between research funding and the overall quality of *undergraduate* education. The highest scores were typically assigned to the biggest spenders in the fields of engineering and medicine. For its 2001 rankings, *U.S. News and World Report* adjusted a school's research spending according to the ratio of its undergraduate to graduate students. One consequence was that many institutions that are strong in the sciences dropped in the ratings, although nothing had changed except the way the concept of "excellence" was measured!

Of course, you or any other observer are free to disagree with these measures and to use your research imagination to create and substitute ones you believe are more valid. But the operational definitions of all new variables must be at least as specific and explicit as those they replace. In this manner, the researcher's choice of measurement tools may be evaluated.

Example: Assessing Happiness

If we wish to examine the complex and sensitive concept "human happiness," the same principles apply. We may decide, for instance, that the ability to function successfully during the day, or a strong sense of self-esteem, or a feeling of general well-being are all reasonable indicators of happiness. How do we determine whether the individuals we observe show these capacities and attitudes, and to what degree? Our choice of measures is not restricted to nominal categories. We may, in fact, use ordinal measures to compare attitudes among individuals.

Many sources of data supply the indicators for variables in social research. They may be actual behaviors, written records, or attitudes expressed in interviews or on questionnaires. We may administer an attitude survey to a selected sample of people and use their responses to operationalize the concept "happiness." Then we may assign numbers to the responses that reflect the strength of the presence of the attitude

---

Table 4.1. Measures of Happiness

We have listed below two statements. Please circle the number that best describes how you feel about each of these statements. You may *strongly agree* (SA = 1), *agree* (A = 2), *be neutral* (N = 3), *disagree* (D = 4), or *strongly disagree* (SD = 5).

	SA	A	N	D	SD
I often feel depressed during the day.	1	2	3	4	5
Sometimes I wish I were someone else.	1	2	3	4	5

---

under investigation. The form and content of such questions may vary, but anyone who has ever answered an attitude survey has probably seen questions like those in Table 4.1. After these have been answered, we have a score for each question for each respondent that runs from 1 (for those we classify as least happy) to 5 (for those we classify as most happy). For certain purposes we may want to total the scores to get an overall index score of happiness.[1]

Behavioral Indicators

Because people sometimes say one thing and do another, it is important to compare self-reported indicators of attitudes with some other measure. Perhaps people are not as happy as they report. Generally, *what people do* is a more convincing indicator than what they *say* they do, and it is highly desirable to use such **BEHAVIORAL INDICATORS** when possible. One area where behavioral indicators have been useful is in detecting sexual abuse in children. Because children are themselves often reluctant to reveal that they have been abused, or may be confused themselves regarding what has happened to them, clinicians look for specific behavioral signs in addition to verbal reports that abuse has occurred (Kraizer, 2005). These indicators may include:

- Sudden reluctance to go someplace or be with someone
- Inappropriate displays of affection
- Sexual acting out

[1] See the discussion of indexing in Chapter 17.

- Sudden use of sexual terms or new names for body parts
- Uncomfortableness or rejection of typical family affection
- Sleep problems, including insomnia, nightmares, or refusal to sleep alone
- Regressive behaviors, including thumbsucking or bed-wetting
- Extreme clinginess or other signs of fearfulness
- Sudden change in personality
- Problems in school
- Unwillingness to participate in or change clothing for gym class at school
- Running away from home
- Bizarre or unusual sophistication pertaining to sexual behavior

In practice, the greater number of indicators present, the greater the likelihood that abuse has occurred. In this example, the term "sexual abuse of children" is actually a concept, and the list of indicators is an operationalization of that concept.

EVALUATING RELIABILITY AND VALIDITY

When we set out to measure a particular attribute, any differences among the people we study should reflect "true" differences on that attribute. If we were measuring mental health status, all the differences among individuals' scores on our mental health inventory (or on whatever measure we were using) would, ideally, reflect actual differences in their mental health. Or if we were measuring people's intelligence, any measured differences in the results of an IQ test would represent true differences in their intelligence. If this could be accomplished, we would have achieved a perfect state of measurement, maximum validity, and reliability. In a perfect state of measurement, differences among people would be entirely the result of the variable in which we were interested; they would not reflect "chance" variation (variation due to the effects of factors unknown to the investigator) or the process of investigation itself.

From Chapter 1 recall that **RELIABILITY** and **VALIDITY** are among the canons of scientific investigation. They are criteria used by social researchers in evaluating the quality of their measures. *A good measure is one that is consistent, that can be used over and over again with comparable results (reliability). A good measure reflects accurately what exists in the observable world, and only that part of the world that we have decided is important to measure (validity).* Scientific theories stand or fall in terms of our ability to make reliable and valid measurements. Disagreements over measures constitute a major element in scientific debate.

The Criterion of Reliability

We have already mentioned that the use of survey questionnaires has become increasingly popular over the past generation, in part because of their positive effect on reliability. With a properly administered questionnaire, one is assured that the identical questions are asked of each respondent, a necessity for consistency in social research. Asking the same questions, however, although necessary to maximize reliability, is no guarantee of it.

One factor known to affect reliability is the personal state of the subject when the data are collected. If one were to take college board examinations twice and receive somewhat different scores, part of the difference would probably reflect changes in one's mood, alertness, physical and emotional well-being, and anxiety. This would mean that the test had less-than-perfect reliability because of its sensitivity to these extraneous, or outside, factors. Variations in the environment and in data-gathering procedures themselves may also affect reliability

adversely. The weather, time of year, environment, or appearance or approach of an interviewer can all vary from one administration of a test or survey to the next. Although we cannot completely control these factors, if we know how they influence the data, we can measure them and correct for their influence as we analyze the data.

Because part of the change in results from one test to the next may reflect a true change in the subject, rather than just less-than-perfect reliability of the measure, it is extremely difficult to gauge reliability precisely by the so-called **TEST-RETEST** method of *comparing scores at time 1 and time 2.* This is a constant problem in measuring either change or reliability with no simple solution. Sometimes the confusion resolves itself, as when the test and the retest are close enough together in time that imputing significant change to the subject makes little or no sense. Sometimes the direction of change in scores unmistakably indicates a reliability problem, as when a person's IQ appears to drop twenty points within a week.

A second method of testing reliability is available when a survey instrument is fashioned from a number of subparts, all of which are expected to measure essentially the same thing. Such is the case with most **TEST BATTERIES**, *differing versions of tests* for intelligence, achievement, or aptitude in which a number of questions are designed to get at the same phenomenon. Reliability is tested by computing how closely the items tend to resemble one another in the results they produce. This is done in a variety of ways. *Each item can be correlated with every other item*[2] *and an average interitem correlation can be reported* as a **RELIABILITY COEFFICIENT**.

The Criterion of Validity

In practice, social scientists have concentrated much attention on problems of reliability and too little attention on matters of validity. The reason for this is quite simple. We know how to test and retest for reliability, but we feel at a loss to pin down validity with testing operations.

[2] See Chapter 18 for a discussion of correlation.

The "Bell Curve" Controversy – Debating Validity and Reliability

In their best-selling book, *The Bell Curve*, Herrnstein and Murray (1996) maintained that social inequality results from an essentially fair process that sorts people out according to their intelligence. Many observers (Fraser, 1995; Devlin, Fienberg, and Resnick, 1997) have been critical of their work from the standpoint of both validity and reliability. The critics charge that Herrnstein and Murray were not measuring what they intended to measure, that is, intelligence, and that they misused statistics to produce an unreliable result.

The "Bell Curve" Thesis

Herrnstein and Murray claimed that how well people did in life was determined mostly by how intelligent they were. Intelligence, they noted, is found among people in a distribution "shaped like a 'bell curve' with a few people at the lower end, a few people at the upper end, and most people clumped in the middle (Fischer et al., 1996). Wealth is distributed in the population according to this same principle; that is, people are rich primarily because they are smart, the poor are poor mostly because they lack intelligence, and the middle class occupies the position that it does because its members possess intelligence in the middle of the "bell curve" distribution. These conclusions lent support to laissez-faire, conservative political ideology. Basically, if innate intelligence determines whether people will rise or fall in social status, inequality is altogether natural and inevitable. It might be temporarily reduced by liberal economic policies (for example, progressive taxes designed to redistribute wealth), but such efforts, said the authors, do injustice to the more intelligent, talented people and hurt the national economy. Herrnstein and Murray argued that trying to alter the natural economic inequality stemming from the unequal distribution of intelligence was especially damaging at this point in history because current trends of globalization of trade and technological innovation depend so much on people of high intelligence

These ideas were not merely the authors' opinion but based on test data. According to Fischer et al. (1996) they relied on

their own analysis of . . . the National Longitudinal Study of Youth (NLSY), a massive survey of over ten thousand young Americans involving repeated interviews over more than a decade. The NLSY administered the Armed Forces Qualifying Test (AFQT) to its subjects in 1980. Herrnstein and Murray show that NLSY subjects who scored high on that test, which the authors treat as an "IQ" test, were usually doing well ten years later, and those who had low scores ended up poorly. This is proof, they argue, that intelligence largely determines life outcomes.

One of the most controversial notions in *The Bell Curve* is the purported connection between intelligence, race, and ethnicity. Racial inequality in America is well documented but is explained by the authors as a function of intelligence. They believe that blacks as well as Latinos are naturally not as intelligent as whites, so they tend to do less well economically.

Criticism of The Bell Curve

Fischer et al. (1996) summarize much of the criticism, noting that

The authors err in assuming that human talents can be reduced to a single, fixed, and essentially innate skill they label intelligence. They err in asserting that this trait largely determines how people end up in life . . . social milieux and social policy create inequal-ity . . . family, neighborhood, school, community – provide or withhold the means for attain-ing higher class positions in American society, in part by providing people with marketable skills. Much of what those milieux have to offer is, in turn, shaped by social policy. For example, the quality of health care that families provide and the quality of education that schools impart are strongly affected by government action. Second, social policy signif-icantly influences the rewards individuals receive for having attained their positions in society.

Skeptics also charged that Herrnstein and Murray "massaged" the Armed Forces Qualifying Test data so that it would support their position because the AFQT is designed to measure the effectiveness of the instruction given to armed forces per-sonnel. It measures what people have been taught and how much they can remember rather than the genetic intellectual attributes of the population. Many social scien-tists challenged the validity of Herrnstein and Murray's conclusions because "the AFQT score is only one factor among several that predict how well people do; of these factors, the social ones are more important than the test score" (Fischer et al., 1996).

By Herrnstein and Murray's own statistical estimate, only 5 to 10 percent of the differences in life outcomes among respondents . . . can be accounted for by differences among them in AFQT scores. Put another way, if we could magically give everyone identical IQs, we would still see 90 to 95 percent of the inequality we see today. (ibid.)

Finally, the critics tackled the racial argument made in *The Bell Curve* by showing that educational opportunity influences test scores to a much greater extent than race.

Whether it is Eastern European Jews in 1910 New York, the Irish in England, Koreans in Japan, or Afrikaaners in South Africa, being of lower caste or status makes people seem "dumb." The particular history of blacks and Mexicans in the United States fits the general pattern. *It is not that low intelligence leads to inferior status; it is that inferior status leads to low intelligence test scores* (Fischer et al., 1996).

The consensus among most social scientists who reviewed *The Bell Curve* was that the explanation for the pattern of test scores highlighted by Herrnstein and Murray was much less biological than social. Racial and ethnic groups that suffer from dis-crimination, poverty, or segregation usually do not do as well on standardized tests as their privileged counterparts. Moreover, as in the South African example, members of higher- and lower-status groups are often from the same race yet produce markedly differing test scores.

Part of the problem with judgments about valid-ity stems from complex terminology. Because validity cannot be tested directly, there have sprung up a variety of ways to test it indirectly. To add to the confusion, different authors some-times use a variety of terms to describe the same criterion. We may reduce the assortment of terms to four basic approaches – face, content, pragmatic, and construct validation.

FACE VALIDITY is the simplest type to under-stand, but it is also not very useful. It means that *the definition of the concept seems valid, "on the face of it,"* given prevailing cultural stan-dards. In 1964, U.S. Supreme Court Justice Potter Stewart tried to explain "hard-core" pornogra-phy, or what is obscene, by saying, "I shall not today attempt further to define the kinds of material I understand to be embraced . . . [b]ut

I know it when I see it."[3] In the years since those words were uttered, we have not come much closer to a once-and-for-all definition.

The essential problem with face validity is that it assumes, rather than proves, that the content of a measure is obvious. Can we ever be sure of the obvious? A good example of the dangers of such an assumption is afforded by the comprehension tests given to people at the conclusion of some commercial "speed reading" programs. Such tests are designed to prove that the course has increased reading speed several times without any loss of comprehension. A standard ploy over the years has been to give comprehension tests by having participants read passages about subjects of which they can be expected to have some prior knowledge (such as a basic point from American history or a biographical sketch of Abraham Lincoln). Another ploy is that the comprehension questions asked are often framed in a way so that common sense comes close to suggesting the answer. It has thus been shown that people reading fast and people reading at a slow, normal pace score about the same on these tests. In fact, people who have never seen or read the passages also get about the same comprehension scores as the other two groups. On the face of it, such a test clearly deals with the topic at hand, and it would appear to be a valid measure of comprehension even though it has virtually no power to discriminate between those who have taken the course and those who have not. It is only when we create and apply a scientific test (using a third group of persons who have not taken the course as a comparison or "control" group) that the "self-evident" logic behind the instrument falls apart.[4]

CONTENT VALIDITY is slightly more sophisticated. It *refers to how much a measure covers the entire range of meanings associated with the concept.* So, content validity depends on the plausibility of a measuring strategy in the eyes of researchers or their critics. The more complicated and disputable the concept, the more any judgment about the content validity of a measure is likely to reflect the predispositions, status, and role of the researcher. Consider the problem of measuring the quality of academic performance. If six different professors were to construct comprehensive examinations for introductory sociology students, there would be a great deal of divergence as to what was deemed important and worthy of emphasis on each of the exams. The exams might say more about the individuals who made them up than they do about students' knowledge of sociology per se. Each instructor would probably judge his or her own test to be most valid and would doubtless offer solid logic to back up this claim. Hence content validation is often less a real testing procedure than a method of justification and legitimation.

PRAGMATIC VALIDATION *judges a measure strictly according to its ability to predict.* A good intelligence test, for example, is one that predicts future success in school reasonably well. In a sense, so-called **PREDICTIVE VALIDITY** sidesteps the whole issue of measurement. Instead of worrying about the meaning of measures, a researcher can rest content with demonstrating that *"it predicts, so it must mean something."* Avoiding the more difficult validity questions can have serious, unanticipated ideological consequences. Some would argue that intelligence testing, for example, proceeds from and tends to reinforce the Social Darwinist theory – that ability varies widely from person to person and from group to group, and that success depends on the survival of the most able. However, let us consider this: Perhaps intelligence test scores *do* predict, but only because knowledge of their results constitutes a self-fulfilling prophecy.

The evolution of many diagnostic tests suggests that they have been somewhat tainted from the start. Some of the earliest instruments were validated by means of a pragmatic method called **CONCURRENT VALIDATION**, by which *a measure is judged according to its ability to distinguish between groups of people already considered to be different.* A test of psychosis should thus distinguish between people who have been institutionalized and labeled "psychotic" and

---

[3] *Jacobellis v. Ohio*, 378 U.S. 184, 197 (1964).
[4] This is actually an example of an experimental design, explained further in Chapter 12.

those who are "normal." Such a method automatically reinforces the status quo, be it wisdom or folly. In the case of intelligence test validation, one of the procedures used compared test results against teacher ratings of pupils. If a teacher believed a certain pupil to be dull-witted, a good test was defined as one that came to the same conclusion. To the extent that teachers' feelings about students affect the distribution of rewards (the "Pygmalion effect"), IQ tests based partly on the feelings of the teacher will necessarily correlate with grades, perseverance, and other teacher-influenced measures of performance (Rosenthal and Jacobson, 1992). There are simply too many reasons that a measure might predict behavior for us to consider predictive potency, by itself, to be a valid indicator.

Probably the most popular roundabout approach to the assessment of validity is CON-STRUCT VALIDATION. Here, *measures of concepts are judged to be valid if they relate to other concepts as anticipated in theory*. A complex concept such as "authoritarianism" may be defined, initially, by its relationship to other variables. Construct validation asks, in effect, whether these expected relations hold. We might expect that there will be a relationship between authoritarianism and voting behavior. We hypothesize that the more authoritarian individuals are likely to support political candidates who advocate a vigorous law-and-order position. If we were interested in validating a measure of authoritarianism, we might go to some community in the midst of a political campaign. We might choose a place in which the candidates for office clearly vary in their positions on law and order, take a random sample of residents, score them on authoritarianism, and finally ask them their preference with respect to the candidates running for office. If there is a high correspondence in the predicted direction between residents' scores on the authoritarianism scale and their choice of candidates, we might conclude that our technique does validly measure authoritarianism.

This is a valuable and increasingly accepted way of approaching the validation of indirect measures of phenomena. However, if relations do not hold as expected, does one blame the theory or the measures? Construct validation is a good deal more sophisticated than previous approaches, but it is still biased in favor of the assumptions of the researcher. A measure's failure to predict does not necessarily mean that the theory must be discarded. Typically, the researcher renews the search for a measure that does predict, but should such a measure be found, it is likely to be accepted as valid even though the chance still exists that the original theorizing was faulty.

Ironically, the most direct method of validation is one of the least often used. Much of the information essential to researchers is available from sources other than the subject. For this reason, much interview material can be CROSS-VALIDATED or *tested against independent but parallel sources of information*. Official records can be consulted to determine a person's age, marital status, ethnic background, political party affiliation, income, academic performance, consumption habits, and so forth. Unfortunately, to do so usually involves much more time and energy than are available. That this is so seldom done, even though the results are startlingly relevant and sometimes eye-opening, shows the low priority researchers and funding agencies have attached to studying validity. Some prominent social scientists have expressed the opinion that social research cannot progress much further until it attends more seriously to questions of measurement, especially validity.

Finally, it is often useful to distinguish between internal validity and external validity. Let us return to our earlier example of the researcher who has prepared a questionnaire to measure happiness. If we *question the ability of the questionnaire to make a valid assessment for the sample of respondents the researcher has interviewed*, we are calling into question the INTERNAL VALIDITY of the measure. If we *question the extent to which the results based on this sample can be generalized to other segments of the population*, we are calling into question the EXTERNAL VALIDITY of the measure.

If we have failed to draw a truly representative sample, external validity will be low; we will have no idea how generalizable our results are.

SOURCES OF MEASUREMENT ERROR

Measurement is part of research, from the way in which we conceptualize and operationalize variables to data processing. There is the possibility of error creeping into the measurement at each point along the way. There are three major sources of inaccurate measurement: random error, systematic error, and situational error.

Random Error

Manipulating social science variables is a multistage process, and *unknown, random factors may deceive us into believing that we have really measured what we set out to measure*. To understand such RANDOM ERROR, we might think of data as a combination of information and noise. The researcher's task is to collect data that are as rich in information as possible and somehow to separate the information from the noise, so that the message can come through clearly.

Mathematically, random error appears as unexplained variation. Social science deals with variation among individuals, groups, institutions, nations, and so forth. The data we collect consist of systematic variation (information) and random variation (noise). Systematic variation is that portion of the total that represents true differences; random variation is that portion attributable to measurement error. In practice, it is very difficult to separate these two types of validation. We often have *little or no idea how much of the variation in our observations is the result of true differences and how much derives from error in our measurement procedures*. At the end of any statistical analysis, we are left with what is called UNEXPLAINED VARIATION. This is produced both by relevant variables that have not been considered in our analysis and by measurement error, but we generally have no indication of the relative contribution of each to the unexplained variation.

Given the uncertainty of random error, how is research possible? The answer is that if errors are truly random, they will cancel each other out, especially if our sample of subjects or number of observations is large enough. We may estimate the effect of the variable as greater or lesser than it actually is, but our overall research findings should not be influenced, so long as there is no systematic inaccuracy.

Systematic Error

Inaccuracy of measurement that occurs repeatedly, and for the same reasons, is called SYSTEMATIC ERROR. Sometimes it is the result of improper research procedures, such as faulty conceptualization of a research problem, a poorly designed questionnaire, or the researcher's own BIASES or systematic distortion. These and other sources of systematic error are summarized in Table 4.2.

The respondent may also systematically generate inaccurate data. If, for example, an interviewer and a subject are of different races and the subject is highly prejudiced against the interviewer's race, this bias could affect the reliability of all of the subject's responses. Researchers must be ever vigilant for sources of systematic error. It is these that will compromise the results of an investigation.

Situational Error

SITUATIONAL ERRORS are ones that *occur not at random but as the result of particular personal characteristics of the subject(s) or other special circumstances that can influence the research encounter*, such as fatigue of respondents or unusual environmental distractions. It is, by definition, difficult to predict situational errors of measurement. If we could predict them, they would be, in some sense, systematic! Often we realize after the fact that situational errors have occurred and try to correct for them. Thus, we may prolong the data collection phase of research in order to add to or replace unreliable data.

Table 4.2. Measurement Errors at Various Stages of the Research Process

Phase of research	Typical error
Conceptualization	Problems of face validity
Choosing a strategy for data collection	Problems of reliability in the research instrument
Sampling	Problems of external validity
Data Collection	Problems of reliability and validity as a result of:
	Bias of researcher or respondent
	Poor rapport between researcher and subject(s)
	Faulty observation or recording of information
	Personal characteristics of the respondent, e.g., dishonesty or fatigue
	Special circumstances making the research encounter atypical (e.g., disasters, crises)
Data processing	Validity problems caused by analysis of imprecise or inaccurate data, or placing raw data into improper conceptual categories

From Table 4.2 we can see that certain kinds of systematic and situational errors are associated with particular phases of the research process. Let us explore this idea further as we examine several examples of errors.

Problems of Face Validity

If we have conceptualized variables in such a way that we are measuring them incompletely or are measuring phenomena other than those we think we are measuring, then all subsequent work will be subject to systematic error. Suppose that your objective is to assess the skill of baseball managers and that you select teams' win–loss records as an indicator of the variable "skill." Plainly, managers of teams with losing records will be systematically viewed as lacking in skill. Yet there are many possible reasons for losing (such as not enough player talent or injuries to key players) that are unrelated to managerial skill. There are also explanations for winning (easiness of schedule or abundance of skilled players, for example) that are unrelated to the variable we are examining, but the managers of winning teams will be systematically favored in the assessment. This is a problem of face validity. No matter how carefully the data collection and data processing phases of the research are executed, the result will probably

be inaccurate because of an initial conceptual mistake.

Problems of Reliability in the Research Instrument

No matter how deliberately a strategy for data collection is chosen, it is worthless if the exact information desired cannot be determined by respondents. Suppose a researcher is interested in the concept "alienation" and, in particular, whether workers experience this primarily as a feeling of powerlessness or of meaninglessness, a theoretical issue that has inspired much debate. The following item might be proposed for inclusion in a survey questionnaire[5]:

> When you experience anomie on the job, is it due to powerlessness or meaninglessness? (circle one)

This question can only be reliable if the respondent understands what "anomie" is and has some idea of the meaning and connotation of the words "powerlessness" and "meaninglessness." In the absence of such understanding, answers are likely to be no more than guesses. A

[5] The construction of survey questions is covered in Chapter 7.

questionnaire containing several items like this one will be systematically inaccurate in assessing both types of alienation and the extent of alienation in general. A more effective (and reliable) survey might ask subjects to respond to a series of statements by selecting answers from among the following:

strongly agree

agree

neutral

disagree

strongly disagree

Plausible statements might include:

In this job I usually tell people what to do, rather than people telling me.

Sometimes I don't know why I even bother coming to work in the morning.

Researcher Bias

The canons of the scientific method help to reduce bias by encouraging researchers to look for all relevant information, including that which runs counter to their own, preexisting beliefs. Experience has shown, however, that interviewer bias during data collection may lead to systematic error, even in studies that are conceptually evenhanded. Different results in surveys have been obtained depending on whether interviewers were male or female, religious or nonreligious, Jewish or Christian, liberal or conservative. Such errors have occurred not only in informal, oral interviews but also when identical questions were written down in advance but administered by different categories of researchers. Often the manner in which the question is read to the respondent, or the facial expression and body posture of the interviewer, can betray bias that leads to systematic error (Maynard, 2001).

Respondent Bias

Commonly held beliefs or ideologies may influence the answers that research subjects give. Derek Phillips (1971) presented an example from his own work illustrating how respondent bias may be built into a mental health survey. Puerto Ricans in New York scored consistently lower on measures of mental health than white, middle-class individuals. Not willing to accept this relationship at face value, Phillips did some further probing. He found that middle-class subjects attached stigma, or social undesirability, to the very characteristic of psychosomatic disturbances for which they were being tested. His middle-class subjects tended to avoid any admission of psychosomatic disturbance. They had reason to avoid telling the truth when that truth appeared damaging to them. In contrast, the Puerto Ricans in the sample felt neutral in revealing the information about themselves. Philips discovered that Puerto Ricans did not suffer disproportionately from mental health problems as had originally appeared to be the case. He concluded that his apparently scientific data served only to reflect differences of *attitude* toward psychosomatic symptoms – a far cry from the superficial finding about the relative incidence of mental health problems among different races and social classes (Santiago-Irizarry, 2001). Less industrious investigators might simply have asserted the face validity of their measure and presented conclusions with potentially racist implications.

Lying as a Source of Error

People do not always respond truthfully even to the simplest questions, and there may be an important pattern to what types of people lie and on which types of issues. It may be relevant to investigate how subjects define the situation and consequently how they respond when a stranger interviewing them asks what appears to be a routine question (Mishler, 1991). Even the most innocuous questions mean different things to different people. Though interviewers are probably accustomed to asking people their age, which kinds of people have gotten used to being asked and to answering such a question? Here, at least, there is reason to believe that we can validly measure a variable such as age in a questionnaire because we have the means to verify responses, thereby separating truth from untruth. But what if we are dealing with more complex issues?

We may find that welfare mothers respond differently from upper-income mothers to a series of questions about child care. How certain could we be that the variation in responses tells us something reliable and valid about differences either in the subjects' true feelings or in their true child-rearing practices? This is more than a statistical question. We have to know whether it is a difference in the true feelings of the two groups or only a difference in the way they approach being interviewed. The welfare mothers may have in common the experience that people who ask them questions are a threat to their well-being. Upper-income mothers probably have had quite different experiences in this regard. This could have a bearing on how the two groups respond to questionnaire items. Further, if the interviewers are middle class (or tend to be drawn from any one class), one group will feel more comfortable with them than the other group. This is one of the most consistent findings in social research.

In a famous study done many years ago, Richard LaPiere found some very compelling evidence that what people say on matters of race relations cannot necessarily be taken as a predictor of how they will behave (cited in Foddy, 1993). From 1930 to 1932, he and two Chinese associates traveled twice across the country seeking services or accommodations or both at hotels, motels, and restaurants. In 250 of 251 cases, they received service ranging from extremely warm to cordial to reserved. In some instances, LaPiere accompanied his Chinese friends; in others, he did not. After a lapse of six months, he sent a questionnaire to each of the establishments, asking whether or not it accommodated members of the Chinese race. The answer he received from 92 percent of the same people from whom he and his Chinese friends had recently received service was a flat "No." Instead of concluding that his subjects were liars, LaPiere judged that people typically respond to symbolic situations differently from the way they respond to real ones.

LaPiere's and others' studies provide us with concrete evidence that calls into question the simple, common assumption that attitudes are handy predictors of future behavior. The discrepancy between people's words and deeds has in fact been documented in a number of different contexts (Deutscher, Pestello, and Pestello, 1993). If some attitudes of respondents are stable enough to be used for purposes of prediction, many others are mainly rationalizations or are stated by respondents to test the feelings of other persons, including perhaps the interviewer. Thus, the measurement of attitudes is subject to systematic error.

Error Arising from Special Circumstances

Expressed attitudes are sometimes situational, generated out of the dynamics of group pressure, conversation, or the interaction in a particular interview. It is unwise to generalize from such data; the encounter with the researcher may be so untypical of a normal life situation that it acts as a barrier to explaining human behavior, rather than as a window on behavior. A subject who has just gone without sleep or nourishment for an extended period, in violation of normal routine, might appear to the investigator to be more irritable or muddleheaded than is really the case. If a woman receives a forty-item questionnaire in the mail and decides to answer it while her 15-year-old son and his friends are using her home as a rehearsal space for their rock band, her responses may differ considerably from those she might give in silence and solitude. Some environmental factors that may affect reliability are purely situational, for instance, an unusually cold or hot day. Others are systematic, in the sense that winter days are typically colder than fall days. We would expect some random error in a survey of consumer buying habits if some people had recently made unusually and unexpectedly large purchases. Unless we were looking for seasonal trends, we would wait until the end of the Christmas holiday season to sample consumers because December buying habits are systematically atypical.

Errors in Data Processing

Data processing is never subject to perfect quality control and, as Table 4.2 indicated, errors of omission and commission may occur after data have been collected. Experienced survey researchers have developed an assortment of techniques to minimize these faults and, properly applied, they can be quite effective.[6] However, so long as portions of the research effort are carried out by paid assistants, who have less of a stake than the primary investigators in keeping the data as uncontaminated as possible, large errors can be introduced at this stage, and they will quite often go undetected.

THE SITUATIONAL NATURE OF VARIABLES

Precise, reliable, and valid measurement lies at the very heart of any science. Precision is fundamental to scientific advancement because good measuring devices extend our ability to see, hear, feel, and generally get close to the people and objects we are studying. The better our measurement, the more critically we can test our ideas about the world. Our ability to resolve disputes over ideas or competing sets of ideas is in large part contingent on the accuracy of our measurements. Theological idea systems, for example, can compete with each other endlessly without any clear resolution because no one has figured out a way to observe (let alone measure) the divine.

If the "correctness" of any theory is to be properly evaluated, it is necessary for the researcher to obtain measures of all the variables contained in the theory. If, for example, a critical proposition in a particular theory is that the higher the level of anxiety among a group's members, the greater will be the cohesion in the group, we must have precise ways of measuring both anxiety and cohesion if we are to have any hope of accepting or rejecting the proposition. To discover the relationships between artistic expression and mental illness (MacGregor, 1992), teacher expectations and student performance (Rosenthal and Jacobson, 1992), and ethnicity and child-rearing practices (McGoldrick, Giordano, and Garcia-Preto, 1996), we must be able to measure the variables involved with a sufficient degree of precision.

A problem in social science is that the meaning of variables may change, depending on the

situation being observed. Most social phenomena are more like liquids than solids; that is, their shape depends on the circumstances in which they occur. In our discussion of measurement error, we noted how difficult it may be to measure attitudes. One reason for this is that attitudes may change according to the context in which they are expressed. People may not have the same feelings about race when they are among blacks as they do when they are among whites (Tatum, 1999). Adolescents' attitudes toward sex expressed in a discussion among their peers may differ from those they express in front of their parents (Adler, 1998). The differences do not necessarily indicate lying or concealment of the truth. These attitudes really do vary as people's definition of their social situation changes. Normally, we drink water as we need it and don't think twice about it. Were we suffering from dehydration after a week in the desert, however, even a sip of water could take on special significance.

Measurement in the Physical and Social Sciences

The variability of social phenomena goes beyond the issue of attitude measurement and has profound implications for the development of scientific explanation in sociology, psychology, political science, and related fields. Can we generate social laws similar to the kinds of laws that can be generated about the physical world? It is worth considering the relationships between scientific theorizing and the variability of social phenomena. We can begin by examining the nature and structure of a scientific explanation of the physical world. How would we explain the phenomenon of water boiling at lower temperatures on a mountaintop than at the seashore? We might construct the following explanation:

- The air surrounding the earth exerts atmospheric pressure on the surface of the earth.
- There is an inverse relationship between altitude and pressure; the higher the altitude, the less the atmospheric pressure.
- Water will boil at different temperatures depending on the magnitude of pressure

---

[6] See Chapter 7 for a discussion of some of these techniques.

applied to it; the lower the pressure, the lower the temperature at which water will boil.

Hence:

• Water boils at a lower temperature on a mountaintop than at the seashore.

The form of the explanation here is deductive. This is the model of explanation in the natural sciences. Let us consider the measurement conditions necessary to produce this type of explanation.

The logic of deductive explanation demands that each assertion, each element, each concept, each variable entering into the argument, have a stable, universal meaning. In our example, the meaning of such variables as *altitude*, *pressure*, and *temperature* will be understood and measured in the same way by all scientists. The meaning of the variables will not change each time the scientist goes to a different mountain or seashore to test the theory. But is this stability true of the variables in the realm of the social sciences?

Suppose we are interested in explaining why suicide rates are higher in Sweden than in the United States. We might explain it by saying that the welfare programs and state subsidies rob a person of initiative; that when persons are robbed of initiative, they are likely to get depressed; and that there is a much higher incidence of suicide among depressed persons. We might conclude logically that suicides will be higher in Sweden (historically, a welfare state) than in the United States. This explanation certainly has the *structure* of a deductive explanation. What makes this explanation quite different is the nature of the variables.

The major concepts in the suicide explanation – "initiative," "depression," and even "suicide" – do not have constant meanings. The meaning of initiative varies in different situations. Does initiative mean the same thing for a poverty-stricken person as for a millionaire? Will initiative have the same meaning in the United States as in other countries? The answer is no. Most concepts in social science allow for a variety of interpretations and meanings.

Lack of Consensus in Measurement

Because most of the concepts we deal with in social research are not real, in the sense of having obvious, single definitions or referents in the physical world, we need to be as exact as possible in saying how concepts are defined and measured. Consider the example of two reporters for a college newspaper who were asked to assess political opinion among undergraduates. One said that about 5 percent of the students were "conservatives"; the other said about 45 percent were conservatives. It is possible that one reporter is simply more skilled than the other, but the results differ so markedly that a problem of measurement is the more likely explanation for the discrepancy. The reporter with the lower figure may have used an extremely strict measure of conservatism, perhaps membership in a right-wing political organization. The higher percentage may have resulted from use of a less exclusive measure of conservatism, perhaps those students who favored a Republican in the last presidential election. The only way to resolve the dilemma of these divergent findings is through knowing the measures that were used in each case. In this example, and in countless others that could be drawn from the professional social science literature, there is little or no consensus in measurement. Lambert (1991) looked at psychotherapy research over a six-year period and found that only about 40 percent of measures were used more than *once*. In other specialties, up to 92 percent of measures were used only once.

Part of the reason for the failure to achieve consensus is the difficulty of establishing face validity for measures of abstract variables. The further removed from direct observation concepts are, the less agreement may be expected in devising measures. The differing theoretical positions of researchers, as well as the variety of uses to which data may be put, also account for the lack of consensus in social science measurement. A Marxist economist intent on showing flaws in the capitalist system may measure profits in such a way that they appear larger than when a conservative researcher measures them. The official government definition of unemployment has excluded those not looking for work and those not expecting to work in the future (Weiss and Fishelson, 1990). If the government included all individuals who were simply not employed at the time the data were collected, the official unemployment rate would be much higher.

IMPROVING THE QUALITY OF MEASUREMENT

The many problems entailed in producing quality measures of our concepts have caused quite a stir among social researchers. Long-overdue discussion and debate about the fundamental validity of our measures have occurred over the past twenty years. Postmodern and feminist critiques sometimes question the entire enterprise of social science measurement.[7] In the mainstream, there has been a growing effort to develop strategies to better cope with some of the problems outlined in this chapter. The most general outgrowth of this concern and intellectual exchange has been a renewed emphasis on the use of multiple measurement techniques.

Triangulation

The logic behind the use of multiple measurement techniques is elegantly simple. It is referred to as **TRIANGULATION**. Just as in trigonometry one can indirectly but precisely measure the location of a point by appropriate sightings from two other points, so also can one apply the method of triangulation to social measurement. All indirect measures have their own peculiar weaknesses. But by *concentrating on the point at which a series of independent, indirect, and perhaps weak indicators converge*, we can effectively minimize their separate errors and maximize their overall validity.

As an example of triangulation, let us look at the variable "teaching skill." How can we discover whether a particular teacher is "skilled"? We could ask his students, but they might be overly influenced by his friendly personality or lenient grading standards. We can increase the

likelihood of measuring skill, instead of these other factors, if we look for alternative sources of data about the same teacher. We might compare achievement test scores of students enrolled in his classes with the scores of students enrolled in other teachers' classes, or we might interview parents or school administrators. By itself, each individual source of data may be suspect; taken together, assuming results are consistent among them, they present a powerful argument that we have measured skill in a valid manner.

An important warning is necessary in discussing the logic of triangulation. We must continually bear in mind that the reason for using a number of measures is to better affirm their validity. The logic of triangulation gets short-circuited if the measures used are based on very similar types of data; that is, unless the data are diverse in nature, we will be doing nothing more than testing the reliability of our measures. That is far from the validity assertion we would like to make – that the techniques used are all measuring the dimensions of a particular variable.

Consider tests of the proposition that all bodies falling in a vacuum accelerate at an equal rate. If we dropped a one-pound steel ball and a two-pound steel ball and arrived at measures of acceleration very close to what we expect theoretically, there might still be those who would criticize the test by saying that the two objects had too much in common in the first place. If we drop a steel ball, a piece of wood, and a feather and find that the rates of acceleration are identical for each, there would be less reason to question the validity of our original proposition.

The key to triangulation, then, is independence among our various estimates. If a series of measurement estimates are all collected by the same method (say, a series of questionnaires), they may not be sufficiently independent to meet the logic required by triangulation. Each of these separate questionnaires could conceivably suffer from similar flaws, biases, or errors.

Using a Variety of Methods

Imagine that we are concerned with assessing worker attitudes in a company town. Suppose that we choose to assess workers' satisfaction

---

[7] For a detailed assessment, see Chapter 10.

with living and working conditions by using a questionnaire with twenty-five separate "satisfaction" questions. If 75 to 80 percent of the workers respond to each of the twenty-five questions by saying that they are quite satisfied, might we still have reason to doubt the validity of our data? In terms of the logic of triangulation, would we be twenty-five times as confident of the validity of our satisfaction measure as we would have been if we had used only one satisfaction question? If we add another twenty-five questions to our questionnaire and the results remain constant, will we double our faith in the validity of our findings on satisfaction? The answer is no. There are several reasons why we may fail to assess accurately the percentage of satisfied workers in the town; one is the possibility that workers fear reprisal by their superiors if they show discontent. Given this type of potential respondent bias toward showing satisfaction, we could multiply our questions ad infinitum and still be uncertain about our results.

Because it is possible to increase the validity of our satisfaction measure by collecting diverse types of data, we may decide to employ a number of independent data-gathering techniques. Along with our use of a questionnaire, we could also send a participant observer into the town and the factory. Suppose that over a period of time the observer hears little talk of dissatisfaction and sees few instances of conflict. Suppose, further, that we check migration patterns into and out of the town and find that few persons leave the town while many enter it. Beyond that, we carefully read the town newspaper and find few expressions of discontent. The larger the number of methodologically independent measures we use, the fewer doubts we will have about our assertions.

Unfortunately, it is too often the case in social science that researchers adopt a particular methodological approach and do virtually all of their work using that technique. This is to some degree the effect of graduate training in the various disciplines. Some schools or departments stress the development of quantitative, statistical skills. Others emphasize qualitative fieldwork. We have already pointed out that this patterning of training has implications for the selection of research problems and topics. In addition, the methodological empire-building we have been describing presents an obstacle to better measurement. If we are to treat the idea of triangulation seriously, it demands the use of multiple methods, including survey research techniques, participant observation, content analysis, experimentation, and historical research.

SUMMARY

Measurement is at the heart of any scientific discipline. The credibility and testability of any theory depends on adequate measurement tools. In social science, the major obstacles to be reckoned with in obtaining such tools are the abstract and situational nature of many of the variables with which we deal.

There are four levels of measurement: nominal, ordinal, interval, and ratio. They vary in complexity and in the degree of precision that they express. It is good to reach as high a level of measurement as our data permit; however, the choice of measure also depends on the purpose of the investigation and the nature of the phenomena being measured. We need to be as accurate as possible, that is, as close to the true value of what we are measuring as we can be.

The selection of appropriate indicators for our variables is called *operationalization*. Our operational definitions will be limited by theory and by the goals of the particular study, but they must in any case be exact: We must present clearly the criteria for evidence that each variable exists and to what extent it exists. A variety of abstract variables can be quantified so that they may be studied using ordinal measures.

Reliability may be assessed by the test-retest method of comparing results from different administrations of the same instrument, but it is often difficult to gauge the impact of the environment on score changes. Another technique for establishing reliability involves comparing results from various subparts of the same instrument. The validity of a given measure may be assessed by examining the extent to which it predicts behavior (pragmatic validation) or enables us to discriminate between individuals and groups already considered different (concurrent validation) or thought to differ according to theory (construct validation). When an instrument is checked against some outside source, this is called *external validity*.

The criteria for judging reliability and validity help us to measure how much error has crept into our investigative procedures. There are three main types of error: random, systematic, and situational. Random error is practically unavoidable, but it is generally correctable. In studies using large samples, random errors tend to cancel one another out. Situational and systematic errors tend to occur at specific stages of the research process. Some systematic errors result from faulty study design or researcher bias; others result from respondent bias. Situational error is caused by research encounters that are untypical of normal interaction among respondents. Some error takes the form of subjects' lying to the investigator. Lying is usually systematic and often is elicited by the subject's perception of the researcher's purpose or role. Some systematic error results from the complex nature of attitudinal variables; people do not always do as they say they do. For this reason, the use of behavioral indicators is desirable.

There is little consensus regarding the choice of measures in social science or how to use them. This is in part the result of the abstract nature of the variables, but it is also traceable to the differences in social science disciplines and in traditions of training. To improve our measures, we need to cooperate more across disciplinary lines and to employ a variety of independent corroborating measures of the same phenomena.

KEY TERMS

accuracy
behavioral indicator
bias
concurrent validation
construct validity
content validity
cross validation
domain
exhaustive measure

external validity
face validity
indicator
internal validity
interval measurement
mutually exclusive
nominal
operationalization
ordinal
pragmatic validation
precision
predictive validity
qualitative research
quantitative research
random error
ratio
reliability
reliability coefficient
situational error
systematic error
test batteries
test-retest reliability
triangulation
unexplained variation
validity

EXERCISES

1. Create lists of indicators for the following: *death*, *studiousness*, and *attractiveness* in a man or a woman.

2. Choose a variable or concept of particular interest to you and triangulate, that is, suggest as many concrete measurement strategies as you can. Try to explain how the different strategies affect or compensate for each other's weaknesses.

3. Recall the problem of face validity associated with measuring the skill of baseball managers according to their teams' win–loss records. Design a more valid set of measures for managerial skill.

4. Choose any research article of interest to you from a social science journal. How much attention does the author devote to assessing and evaluating the quality of the measures used in the research? Summarize the relevant discussion. If there is little or no attention given to the issue, criticize this absence.

5. How is class standing (your rank in class) computed at your school? What level of measurement is used: ordinal, interval, or ratio? What, if any, theoretical implications does the choice of measure carry?

SUGGESTED READINGS

Blalock, H. M., Jr. 1979. "Measurement and Conceptualization Problems: The Major Obstacle to Integrating Theory and Research." *American Sociological Review* 44 (December): 881–894.

An important, advanced-level summary of the problems of measurement in social science and a plea for us not to sidestep the difficult questions.

Campbell, Donald T., and Julian C. Stanley. 2005. *Experimental and Quasi-Experimental Designs for Research.* Boston: Houghton Mifflin.

An assessment of the validity of a number of experimental designs frequently used in the social sciences.

Hammersley, Martyn, and Roger Gomm. 1997. "Bias in Social Research." *Sociological Research Online* 2 (1).
http://www.socresonline.org.uk/2/1/2.html.

This article examines the ambiguity in the term "bias," the relationship between the notion of bias and the idea of science, accusations of bias in social and behavioral sciences, and the culpability of researchers.

Miller, Delbert C., and Neil J. Salkind. 2002. *Handbook of Research Design and Social Measurement.* 6th ed. Thousand Oaks, CA: Sage.

A single-volume encyclopedia of measures. Well worth looking at for information and inspiration.

Newman, Isadore, Carolyn R. Benz, and Carolyn Ridenour. 1999. *Qualitative-Quantitative Research Methodology: Exploring the Interactive Continuum.* Carbondale: Southern Illinois University Press.

This book conceives research as a holistic effort in scientific inquiry and rejects the artificial dichotomy between qualitative and quantitative research strategies. The authors argue that the two approaches are neither mutually exclusive nor interchangeable; rather, the actual relationship between the two paradigms is one of isolated events on a continuum of scientific inquiry.

Robinson, John P., Phillip R. Shaver, and Lawrence S. Wrightsman, eds. 1991. *Measures of Personality and Social Psychological Attitudes.* New York: Academic Press.

Reviews and evaluates the major measures of variables such as life satisfaction, happiness, and self-esteem.

Rosenthal, Robert, and Lenore Jacobson. 1992. *Pygmalion in the Classroom: Teacher Expectation and Pupils' Intellectual Development.* New York: Irvington.

Illustrates the frailty of many of our measures of student skill.

Schaeffer, Nora Cate. 1980. "Evaluating Race of Interviewer Effects in a National Survey." *Sociological Methods and Research* 8 (4) May: 400–419.

A treatment of the problem of systematic error. Also contains a useful bibliography.

REFERENCES

Adler, Patricia A. 1998. *Peer Power: Preadolescent Culture and Identity.* New Brunswick, NJ: Rutgers University Press.

Deutscher, Irwin, Fred P. Pestello, and Frances G. Pestello. 1993. *Sentiments and Acts.* Chicago: Aldine de Gruyter.

Devlin, Bernie, Stephen E. Fienberg, and Daniel P. Resnick, eds. 1997. *Intelligence, Genes, and Success: Scientists Respond to* The Bell Curve. New York: Copernicus Books.

Fischer, Claude S., et al. 1996. *Inequality by Design.* Princeton, NJ: Princeton University Press.

Foddy, William. 1993. *Constructing Questions for Interviews and Questionnaires.* New York: Cambridge University Press.

Fraser, Steven, ed. 1995. *The Bell Curve Wars: Race, Intelligence, and the Future of America.* New York: Basic Books.

Herrnstein, Richard J., and Charles Murray. 1996. *The Bell Curve: Intelligence and Class Structure in American Life.* New York: Free Press.

Karp, David A., Lynda Lytle Holmstrom, and Paul S. Gray. 2004. "Of Roots and Wings: Letting Go of the College-Bound Child." *Symbolic Interaction* 27 (3): 357–387.

Kraizer, Sherryll. 2004. "Sexual Abuse: Behavioral Indicators in Child." Coalition for Children, Inc.
http://www.safechild.org/childabuse1.htm#Behavioral%20Indicators%20in%20Child.

Lambert, Michael J. 1991. "Introduction to Psychotherapy Research." In *Psychotherapy Research:*

An International Review of Programmatic Studies, 1–23. L. Bentler and N. Crago, eds. Washington, DC: American Psychological Association.

MacGregor, John M. 1992. *The Discovery of the Art of the Insane*. Princeton, NJ: Princeton University Press.

Maynard, Douglas W., ed. 2001. *Standardization and Tacit Knowledge: Interaction and Practice in the Survey Interview*. New York: Wiley.

McGoldrick, Monica, Joe Giordano, and Nydia Garcia-Preto, eds. 1996. *Ethnicity and Family Therapy*. New York: Guilford Press.

Mishler, Elliot G. 1991. *Research Interviewing: Context and Narrative*. Cambridge, MA: Harvard University Press.

Morse, Robert J., and Samuel Flanigan. 2001. "How We Rank Colleges." In "America's Best Colleges 2001." *U.S. News and World Report*.

Morse, Robert J., and Samuel Flanigan. 2006. "Using the Rankings." In "America's Best Colleges 2006." *U.S. News and World Report*, August 28. See

http://www.usnews.com/usnews/rankguide/rghome.htm.

Phillips, Derek. 1971. *Knowledge from What?* Chicago: Rand McNally.

Rosenthal, Robert, and Lenore Jacobson. 1992. *Pygmalion in the Classroom: Teacher Expectation and Pupils' Intellectual Development*. New York: Irvington.

Santiago-Irizarry, Vilma. 2001. *Medicalizing Ethnicity: The Construction of Latino Identity in Psychiatric Settings*. Ithaca, NY: Cornell University Press.

Tatum, Beverly D. 1999. *Why Are All the Black Kids Sitting Together in the Cafeteria? And Other Conversations About Race*. New York: Basic Books.

U.S. News and World Report. 2006. "America's Best Colleges, 2006."

http://www.usnews.com/usnews/edu/college/rankings/ranknatudoc_brief.php.

Weiss, Yoram, and Gideon Fishelson, eds. 1990. *Advances in the Theory and Measurement of Unemployment*. New York: St. Martin's Press.

5

ETHICAL AND POLITICAL ISSUES

INTRODUCTION

The first four chapters of this book set the stage for learning about research by introducing you to a vocabulary that specifies the various parts of the process and presenting the basics of research design and measurement. These chapters are a foundation for investigating the social world. However, before the various methods are presented in detail, this chapter summarizes the ethical and political context for research.

Growing up, many of us have been taught to abide by the Golden Rule in church, school, and community. Social researchers, however virtuous they may be in a personal sense, are concerned about ethical behavior in a more specific context. Because of the public nature of science and the increasing visibility and accountability of researchers, they must pay attention to ethical principles or suffer the criticism of those who read their work and who provide them with data. As we will see in this chapter, in research, doing the "right thing" is not always easy or obvious!

Suppose that a team of politically moderate social scientists has received a research grant from the federal government to investigate political extremism on both the left and the right in America. The researchers will interview members of the Communist Party and the American Nazi Party to find out what their attitudes are on a variety of political and social issues. Because they know that their respondents may not give completely honest answers, the research team will use an alternative means of data collection as a check on the validity of the interview results. They will also hire and train research assistants to become members of the Communist Party and the American Nazi Party to observe the two groups from the inside without the groups knowing that they are being studied. These secret, or disguised, observational data will be compared with the interview data.

This hypothetical research example shows that ethical and political dilemmas enter into the process of conducting social research. Some of these questions relate directly to the ideal standard of objectivity that guides scientific research. How can social researchers minimize the effect of personal prejudices and biases on what they observe and on how they interpret what they observe? How can a group of politically moderate investigators examine political extremism without having their values color the conclusions of their study? The researchers should also consider the ultimate social use of their research findings. What role should the researchers play in determining this use? Research findings can be used either constructively or destructively. In our hypothetical situation, they could conceivably be used by the government to undermine politically extreme groups. Does the research team have any ethical or political responsibility with regard to this possibility?

Other ethical and political considerations for researchers are less directly related to objectivity. Are there ethical limits on the relationship between researchers and the individuals studied? In our hypothetical example, the second means of data collection involves the disguised entrance of research assistants into the political groups to be observed. The groups will not be asked for their permission to be studied. Does such a research tactic violate the ethics of social science research? In this chapter, the ethical and political issues that confront the social researcher are considered. However, before these issues are discussed, let us turn again to the question of objectivity.

OBJECTIVITY

Most social scientists have immediate intellectual and emotional reactions to the word **OBJECTIVITY**. To some, it is a straightforward term that refers to the scientific method and the belief that researchers should *remove the effect of their personal biases on their research* so that social reality may be uncovered. To others, the term refers to the disguise that social scientists often use to escape moral responsibility.

The Strict Position

A good starting point for unraveling this diversity of opinion is to examine the position taken by the classical sociologist Max Weber. Weber is generally considered to have strongly supported the traditional position that social scientists should rule out biases or **VALUE JUDGMENTS** in doing research. *Value judgments are our personal evaluations of the goodness or badness, rightness or wrongness of what we are investigating.* In other words, they depend on our personal belief and biases. According to Weber (Ringer, 1998), it is impossible to establish the ultimate validity or invalidity of such judgments on the basis of scientific investigation alone. Related to this point is Weber's argument that the goal of the social sciences is to understand "what is" and not "what ought to be." The latter, or normative, type of knowledge lies within the domain of social philosophy. Consider the researcher who studies same-sex couples. Weber would consider it appropriate to describe the experiences of individuals in same-sex relationships, to report on any negative treatment they might experience at work or in the community, but not to evaluate the moral correctness of being in a same-sex relationship.

Weber also makes the distinction between the conduct of science – the collection, analysis, and interpretation of data – and the selection of problems for study, which may be influenced by value judgments (Hammersley, 2000:33). The strict position on objectivity is that the value judgments of researchers should *not* enter into the conduct of science. However, even in the writings of Max Weber, he admits that it is difficult for social scientists to remove the effect their own values have on analysis and interpretation. He does say, however, that despite these difficulties, objectivity is a goal, or ideal, to aim for.

Those who agree would argue that although the ultimate correctness of value-based social goals cannot be established by scientific investigation, the means for achieving them *can* be determined. If, for example, the goal is to reduce poverty, the social sciences can be applied to explore the best ways to achieve it. The effect of researchers' values on the problems selected for investigation may not create any difficulty. An American immigrant might choose to study the assimilation process, or a person who is experiencing marital difficulties may want to study the dynamics of the American family system. The crucial consideration is for such researchers to

strive for objectivity in the collection, analysis, and interpretation of data. Weber (1958) encouraged social researchers to distinguish between their role as scientists and their role as private citizens. Such a segregation of roles would, in his view, increase the likelihood of objectivity in social science.

Criticism of Objectivity

Many objections to the plea for objectivity and a **VALUE-FREE SOCIAL SCIENCE** were raised in the late twentieth century. According to Gouldner (1973), the strict interpreters of Weber's ideas were narrow technicians who rejected the cultural and moral consequences of their work. Behind Gouldner's attack was his belief that the value-free notion had once allowed for the growth and independence of the social sciences but had outlived its usefulness. Eventually, objectivity became a dogma that was used too often as a rationalization allowing researchers to sell their goods to the highest bidder while ignoring the possible social consequences of their work. In Gouldner's view, this dogmatic approach also excluded the possibility of any social criticism developing from social science research.

Howard Becker also criticized the demand for rigorous objectivity. He maintained that we cannot separate our personal values from the research process (Galliher, 1995). Becker argued that researchers' biases influence which societal perspectives are emphasized in research. In his view, society is based on hierarchical relationships of *superordination* and *subordination*. The superordinates possess authority in a given situation; the subordinates are the "have-nots" in terms of authority. Wardens and prison guards are the superordinates in a penitentiary; the prisoners are the subordinates. Becker maintained that research generally does not include both perspectives. In fact, researchers encounter difficulty when they try to avoid the real conflicts present in many research settings.

A student of medical sociology may decide that he will take neither the point of view of the patient nor the hospital administration, but no matter what perspective he takes, his work either will take into account the attitudes of subordinates or it will not. If he fails to consider the questions patients raise, he will de facto be working on the side of the officials. If he does raise those questions seriously and does find, as he may, that there is some merit in them, he will then expose himself to the outrage of the officials. According to Becker, the researcher's own biases, examined or not, will likely influence the perspective that does become emphasized in his or her work (Hammersley, 2000).

The difference of opinion concerning objectivity, which we examined earlier in relation to the creation of knowledge,[1] is mirrored in the debate over objectivity in research ethics. One school of thought maintains that objectivity is achieved by removing the lenses of personal bias to view what really is going on in society. This is the traditional Weberian position. The other view is that objectivity is virtually impossible; it is being used as a shield for escaping moral responsibility. The solution to this seeming dilemma is to develop a balanced position, emphasizing both our desire to make scientific observations of society with a minimum of bias *and* the need for social responsibility. In this chapter, we will try to develop such an approach while looking at various ethical and political considerations at each major step of the research process. The major stages in study design to be considered are (1) formulation of the research question; (2) data collection; (3) analysis, interpretation, and presentation of research results; and (4) application of research results.

FORMULATION OF THE RESEARCH QUESTION

Ethical and political issues relating to objectivity appear at three points in the formulation of the research question: (1) in choosing the research topic and precisely posing the question to be pursued, (2) in choosing a theoretical model, and (3) in obtaining funds.

Topic Selection

Which slice of social reality will be cut out for examination? Some researchers would suggest

[1] See Chapter 2.

that the topic be important in one's field of study and personally interesting. Others would add that it should be relevant to the improvement of society (see, e.g., Chapter 10 for a discussion of the feminist approach to topic selection). Such topics are not always easy to come by, but let us assume that the researcher at least picks a topic of personal interest. Suppose that the general topic is crime. We imagine that the researcher has personal opinions and values related to the topic. As we have seen, some would argue that this situation does not, by any means, automatically rule out objective social research. However, such an appraisal becomes more difficult to accept when the precise research question is articulated. Will the general topic of crime be pursued from the perspective of the superordinates or the subordinates? What kind of crime will be studied: street crime (Lafree, 2000) or white-collar crime (Shichor, 2001)? Theft in the inner city by poor people (Scott, 2001)? Tax evasion by the rich (Lewis and Allison, 2001)? Illegal political contributions by the large corporations (Clawson, Neustadtl, and Weller, 1998)? Once again, from whose perspective will these more specific questions be pursued? Although the precise questions examined in research cannot always be attributed to the perspectives of the superordinates or the subordinates, many of them can. Even when they cannot, social researchers should see that their personal biases and values may affect how they conceptualize a research topic. The effect of bias can become apparent when one thinks about which questions and aspects of a topic are ignored and why. Perhaps the investigator should write down such thoughts about the conceptualization of the research topic and refer to them as the results are being interpreted and presented.

Choice of Theory

Closely related to the selection of a topic is the choice of a theoretical model that will help us to organize and interpret the data. Many theories make up the social sciences, but none has been proved beyond doubt. Many of the theories compete; for example, the functionalist and conflict theories. In Chapter 2, we learned that functionalists such as Talcott Parsons view society as a system made up of different parts, with each part contributing to the functioning of the system. Some functionalists believe that social classes in America, which differ widely in economic well-being and political power, are functional. Stratification, they say, operates as a reward system, encouraging people to work hard. The functionalists tend to view most realities in society as having some positive function. Otherwise, they say, these conditions would not exist in the first place. Researchers who adopt such a perspective are encouraged to predict that social change will be in the direction of maintaining the status quo.

The conflict model, on the other hand, views society from the standpoint of internal strains and competition rather than consensus. Researchers who favor this theoretical perspective are much more likely to predict revolutionary developments. A conflict theorist might expect the existence of relatively widespread poverty in our affluent society to lead to upheavals that would transform its nature. The choice of models is not confined to the functionalist and conflict theories. Social scientists have also tried to develop theories that achieve balance between the two.[2]

The theoretical model chosen to support a research question is important for determining what will be observed and how the observations will be interpreted. Do the personal biases of researchers affect their choice of theoretical model? Will conservatives choose the functionalist theory and radicals select the conflict theory? Or will researchers simply choose the theory that seems to explain the most? Quite often the answer may be that we opt for the theoretical perspective with which we are most comfortable. Indeed, how can anyone be sure that personal values have not played a role in the choice of a theoretical model? The solution here is similar to the one we suggested for the first problem area. Once again, researchers should try to become sensitized to the role played by their own values and be ready to discuss this issue during the interpretation and presentation of research results. They should also aspire to collecting data that are not contaminated by personal biases. How to accomplish this will be discussed later in this chapter.

Funding

Many social scientists depend on money from the government, private corporations, and private foundations to support their research. Obviously, such sources will support the research in which they are interested. Some social scientists point out that this interest is not always bad; the federal government, for example, supports research that is related to reducing poverty, crime, homelessness, and mental illness. Big businesses support research to determine the social and economic needs of the communities in which they are located. However, others note that the influence of the funding source explains why research that is likely to support the status quo is more often funded than research that might eventually lead to significant social change (Campbell, Daza, and Slaughter, 1999). A large corporation is more likely to fund research to find out how laborers can work more efficiently than it is to fund research aimed at discovering how workers might better organize themselves politically. Two researchers examined the literature on the effects of secondhand smoke on health from 1980 to 1995 (Barnes and Bero, 1998). They found that 80 percent of the studies that claimed that passive smoking was not harmful were conducted by investigators with ties to the tobacco industry. The National Institutes of Health (NIH, 2000) estimated that 25 percent of the institutional review boards set up by colleges and universities to monitor funded research deal routinely with potential conflicts of financial interest in research proposals.

Responding to "recent highly publicized instances of apparent financial conflicts of interest," the NIH invited public dialogue on the issue, noting:

Objectivity of researchers is an essential value in scientific research and the basis for public trust. Researchers should be led by their data, not by other interests that might undermine the scientific integrity of their work. Of course, success in research is likely to bring valued publications, grant

[2] See, for example, Anthony Giddens, *The Constitution of Society: Outline of the Theory of Structuration* (Berkeley: University of California Press).

renewals, career advancement, and the satisfaction of accomplishment . . . Any research links with industry raise the prospect that scientific advances will bring financial gain as well. The opportunity for investigators' personal financial gain or reward is not intrinsically unacceptable. However . . . concerns are raised when financial considerations may compromise or have the appearance of compromising an investigator's professional judgment and independence in the design, conduct, or publication of research. (NIH, 2000:399)

Whether the increased sensitivity to conflicts of interest will translate into laws and regulations prohibiting such practices remains to be seen. There is no regulatory requirement for institutional review boards to consider investigators' financial conflict of interest as they review proposed research. However, the rising public awareness and media scrutiny of the issue should encourage any researcher to take care in negotiating with the prospective sponsors of research. The key issue is not the identity of the sponsors or the source of the funds per se but the nature of the legal and implicit contract under which the funds are obtained. In brief, no matter who might be supporting a given research project, researchers should know what strings will be attached.

Broader issues are connected to the funding question. Who is going to use the knowledge developed by the research? How will the knowledge be used? Will the knowledge be used constructively or destructively? These issues will be discussed further as the application of research results is examined. As in all research, decisions at each step of the process affect decisions at later steps. One should not begin to worry about the application of research results only after the research is completed; rather, one should be concerned right from the outset.

DATA COLLECTION

Impartiality

The personal values of researchers can color the choice of topics and theoretical perspectives employed. Robert Rosenthal (1994) has also established that the investigator's personal stake

in the research can affect its outcome. His review of research errors made over thirty years reveals that in 70 percent of the cases the errors favored the researcher's hypothesis. Critics of positivistic science maintain that this impartiality is an unavoidable by-product of the construction of scientific knowledge. An alternative explanation is that the egos of individual social scientists may influence them to distort findings, to misinterpret equivocal findings, or to halt their inquiry prematurely when their preconceived hypotheses appear to be confirmed.

In spite of these unfortunate realities, the quest for objectivity in data collection still remains as an ideal for social scientists. A number of techniques have been devised that increase the likelihood that valid and reliable data will be obtained, with minimal contamination by personal bias. Modern sampling techniques enable investigators to include diverse segments of a population in a predictable manner so that their research truly represents the people being investigated.[3] Advances have been made in questionnaire construction so that "loaded" questions are less likely to appear in present-day surveys.[4] The point to be emphasized is that our data collection techniques should be used as impartially as possible. By using our theories and techniques impartially, we ought to be able to study all the things that need to be studied in such a way that we obtain all the facts we require, even though some of the questions that will be raised and some of the facts that will be produced run counter to our biases. Whatever side we are on, we must use our techniques impartially so that a belief to which we are especially sympathetic *could* be proved untrue (Becker, 1971).

One strategy for maximizing impartiality is to compare what different observers find when they examine the same social phenomena. In the hypothetical study of political extremism mentioned at the beginning of the chapter, it would make sense to have researchers of both radical and conservative political persuasions observe both groups. Another guideline is to make sure

[3] Sampling issues are covered in Chapter 6.
[4] Techniques for developing nonbiased survey questions are presented in Chapter 7.

that data gatherers are carefully trained to carry out precisely defined observational tasks. They should have no question about what is to be observed and how it is to be observed. A final recommendation is that observations be recorded as soon as possible to lessen the possibility that the biases of observers will alter their memory of what has been observed.

Confidentiality

Some respondents are reluctant to participate in research in part because they place a high premium on privacy and do not want their personal lives exposed by social scientists. To overcome this problem, researchers may offer promises of CONFIDENTIALITY or ANONYMITY. *If data are confidential, the identities of respondents are known to the researcher, but they are kept secret; if data are anonymous, it is impossible for anyone, including the researcher, to match particular responses with individual subjects.*

The question of ethics is relevant here. Obviously, if such promises are made, they should be kept. Confidentiality can be achieved in large-sample surveys by removing the identifying information about individual respondents from the questionnaires and substituting coded numbers. Sometimes the codebook that matches names and numbers is kept under lock and key. When a research project involves a small sample, it may not be possible to ensure confidentiality. In the famous community study *Small Town in Mass Society* (Vidich and Bensman, 1958), confidentiality was promised to community members. When the research findings were published, the identities of some respondents became apparent even though code names were used instead of the respondents' real names. This unfortunate result caused an uproar in the community. To assure true confidentiality, it may be necessary to do more than simply disguise the names of the people we have studied. If the group is small enough, identifying individuals such as "the Mayor" or "the CEO of a large chemical company" will be enough to expose their true identities.

In research of smaller scope (but no less devastating to those affected by it), a social work student was preparing her master's thesis and included a study of a family that had been part of her client caseload. Fifteen years later, the youngest son from this family was attending the same university. While he was doing a sociology assignment, he read this woman's thesis. The young man recognized the family to which she referred as his own and learned that he was actually the son of his father and eldest sister; he was a product of incest. The social worker did not change this family's special characteristics enough, making them recognizable (Sieber, 1992).

The laws protecting the confidence of attorneys, clergy, and psychotherapists do not at present apply to social researchers, although there has been some movement in the direction of protecting sources (Leo, 2001). In a well-publicized case, Rik Scarce, a graduate student at Washington State University, was doing research on animal liberation activists, and authorities demanded that he hand over information concerning an informant who became a suspect in a raid on a campus laboratory. Scarce would not cooperate and was imprisoned (Scarce, 1995).

The painful lesson to be learned from these examples is that it is ethically desirable not to offer confidentiality or anonymity when they cannot be delivered. Our inability to guarantee confidentiality does not necessarily reduce the possibility of cooperation of potential respondents. If we can demonstrate the social usefulness and significance of a research project, we may be able to gain cooperation without the guarantee of confidentiality. In fact, showing the social usefulness of a research project to respondents may be just as great an inducement as the promise of confidentiality.

Disguised Observation

Faced with the possibility of rejection by potential respondents, social researchers have sometimes used deception and manipulation in their work. One example of such deception is DISGUISED OBSERVATION, in which *the people who are being observed are unaware of it*. The setting might be the army, Alcoholics Anonymous, a street gang, or any other group of interest. The example at the beginning of the chapter included disguised observers of the Communist Party and the American Nazi Party. Some social scientists have argued that this method of observing is unethical because it invades the privacy of people who have not given their permission to be observed. They maintain that using such research approaches may alienate the larger society and threaten the acceptability of more straightforward research conducted by the broader social science community. Others have contended that such tactics should not be rejected automatically because they may be useful for advancing scientific knowledge in areas where other means of data collection are not feasible (Bulmer, 1982). Indeed, the intentional deception of research subjects has remained a regular, if not universally accepted, part of the researcher's toolkit (Baumrind, 1985).

A famous study, *Tearoom Trade* (Humphreys, 1975), raised the fundamental dilemma of the scientist's need to know versus the respondent's right to privacy. Humphreys was interested in the phenomenon of impersonal sex between male homosexuals. He observed numerous encounters among men in public restrooms (or "tearooms") with the subjects' consent but without their knowing he was a researcher. His role was to act as "watch queen," to warn of possible interruptions during the encounters. To find out more about the backgrounds of the men, he noted their automobile license numbers and traced some of their addresses. He then presented himself at their homes, suitably disguised, and introduced himself as a researcher, asking what appeared to be innocuous questions regarding the men's family life, socioeconomic status, physical health, and friendship networks. This study stirred up a major controversy. In his own defense, Humphreys argued that the behavior he had observed was important to know about, although the great majority of respondents would have wished it kept secret. He also kept all data strictly confidential. Disguised observation was justified in this case, Humphreys maintained, in order to obtain valid background data and also to minimize embarrassment to his research subjects. "Clearly," he writes, "I could not knock on the door of a suburban residence and say, 'Excuse me, I saw you engaging in a homosexual act in a tearoom last year, and I wonder if I might ask you a few questions.'"

These justifications notwithstanding, *Tearoom Trade* touched off a firestorm of controversy. The movement to establish a CODE OF ETHICS for sociologists in the United States was initiated after Humphreys' study appeared.[5] Many observers believed that the continued use of disguised observation in research would eventually turn the public against professional social science. As one study of ethics in psychology notes: "*A code of ethical standards 'professionalizes' an occupation by creating an implied social contract with the public that purports to balance professional privilege with responsibility*" (Koocher and Keith-Spiegel, 1998:27). However, critics are skeptical that codes of conduct really alter professional behavior or the power realities in society. Indeed, as the American Sociological Association's ethical provisions with regard to disguised research show, there is no outright ban on such research; in fact, it is acknowledged that deception may be necessary.

Ethics and Experimentation

Disguised observation is not the only research strategy that raises ethical questions concerning the relationship between social researchers and their subjects. Other deceptions and manipulations are sometimes used by psychologists, sociologists, social workers, and researchers in other fields, including education, nursing, and medicine. Newell (1994) describes a variety of these strategies:

- Evasion – systematically ignoring requests for information while pretending to respond to inquiries
- Suppression – deliberately leaving out or withholding relevant information
- Euphemism – substituting an agreeable response for a disagreeable one

[5] The Codes of Ethics of the American Sociological Association and the American Psychological Association may be accessed at the Web sites listed at the end of this chapter.

The Use of Deception in Research

American Sociological Association Code of Ethics, 12.05 (1997)

(a) Sociologists do not use deceptive techniques (1) unless they have determined that their use will not be harmful to research participants; is justified by the study's prospective scientific, educational, or applied value; and that equally effective alternative procedures that do not use deception are not feasible, and (2) unless they have obtained the approval of institutional review boards or, in the absence of such boards, with another authoritative body with expertise on the ethics of research.

(b) Sociologists never deceive research participants about significant aspects of the research that would affect their willingness to participate, such as physical risks, discomfort, or unpleasant emotional experiences.

(c) When deception is an integral feature of the design and conduct of research, sociologists attempt to correct any misconception that research participants may have no later than at the conclusion of the research.

(d) On rare occasions, sociologists may need to conceal their identity in order to undertake research that could not practicably be carried out were they to be known as researchers. Under such circumstances, sociologists undertake the research if it involves no more than minimal risk for the research participants and if they have obtained approval to proceed in this manner from an institutional review board or, in the absence of such boards, from another authoritative body with expertise on the ethics of research. Under such circumstances, confidentiality must be maintained.

- Exaggeration – making truth seem ridiculous by stating it in hyperbolic terms
- Changing the subject – direct evasion
- Disguise – masking the researcher's true feelings
- Gesturing – employing ambiguous body movements to create a misimpression
- Silence – saying nothing in a context in which such silence is likely to be taken in a certain way
- Inaction – not doing something in a context in which action would be important

At a minimum, these behaviors convey the impression that investigators do not respect those who participate in their research, but the potential effect of the strategies of deception can be much more serious. In a provocative example, Sieber (1992) cites CIA research on LSD in the 1960s. Investigators set up an elaborate laboratory in a brothel. As clients arrived, they were given beverages containing LSD. Men's behavior was then filmed from behind a two-way mirror.

One subject committed suicide while under the influence of LSD. His family was never told about the drugs he was given, and they were left puzzled by his death.

In a now notorious 1932 study, destitute African American men in Tuskegee, Alabama, were approached by doctors and researchers affiliated with the U.S. Public Health Service. They were given free medical care, having been told that a treatment had been found for "bad blood." Without knowledge or consent, these men were enrolled in an observational research study of untreated syphilis. This study ended forty years later in 1972, twenty years after penicillin was identified as an effective treatment for syphilis. The men were not told that penicillin would have helped them. This study has been called the "longest non-therapeutic experiment on human beings in medical history" (National Library of Medicine, 2001).

By today's standards the design of the Tuskegee experiment seems influenced by both racism and a deliberate attempt to deceive the research subjects without any obvious scientific gain that could justify the risks. As such, it represents an extreme instance of unethical research behavior rather than a negative example that could serve as a practical solution to the real predicament of contemporary investigators. The realities of the research environment are often so complex that the common-sense standard "tell the whole truth and nothing but the truth" seems inadequate. Consider, for instance, the psychologist who wants to test the effectiveness of a particular form of therapy. She decides without informing the subjects to treat only a selected group of mentally ill patients and to give the other patients no treatment. Is this fair to those who need help? Should all patients be informed of the purposes of the research – as well as of the methods to be used in conducting it – even if full disclosure may jeopardize the validity of the results?

Sometimes being *selected* to participate in experiments, not being *excluded* from treatment, will actually threaten the well-being of research subjects. A classic example is Stanley Milgram's (1973) experiment that had the apparent purpose of studying the effect of punishment on learning but that had the concealed purpose of investigating obedience to authority. Subject A enters a laboratory and meets subject B and the experimenter in charge of the research. Subject B is actually a member of the experimental team. The experimenter tells subject A to be the "teacher" in an experiment for studying the effect of punishment on learning. When subject B gives wrong answers, subject A is to give what he thinks are real electric shocks to subject B. They are not real shocks. The experiment begins. Subject B gives wrong answers and supposedly receives shocks of increasing voltage. Subject B screams and pleads that the experiment be stopped. When subject A asks the experimenter if he or she should stop, the experimenter replies in the negative. Subject A continues with the experiment. The real purpose of this study is to see whether subject A will follow the directions of the experimenter even though he thinks he is causing pain to subject B. Although the subject As were later given a **DEBRIEFING**, in which *the reason for the study was explained to*

them, several participants reported feeling acute anguish and subsequent mental depression over what they had done.

Some argue that such research strategies can add to scientific knowledge and therefore can be used in certain situations. Milgram defended the study by noting that the *results* of the experiments were not anticipated and that there is a difference between research *process* and outcome (Milgram, 1973). Several experiments, including Milgram's, are examined in more detail in Chapter 12. Now, most experimentation with human subjects is scrutinized more than in Milgram's day. The question is whether the ethical treatment of subjects should ever be sacrificed. Some have suggested that if more conscientious attention focused on this question at the outset of research, fewer studies employing deception and manipulation would be conducted. The question, however, is a relative one. The practices of deception and manipulation range from the fairly innocent to the outlandish. Some practices should obviously be avoided. When deception is employed, precautions should be taken. If the true purpose of an experiment is concealed, an explanation emphasizing the scientific merit of the research should be given afterward. When researchers decide that disguised observation is ethically tolerable in a particular research situation, special efforts should be made to ensure that the identities of the subjects will be protected. Perhaps the overall ethical guideline is that the people who are being studied should not be hurt by the research process.

Informed Consent

Reacting in part to the furor created by the Milgram experiments and by other studies that have used disguised observation, the federal government has issued guidelines requiring the **INFORMED CONSENT** of all human subjects in research projects receiving government funding.[6] Many academic departments and universities have also published informed consent

---

[6] Protection of Human Subjects, *Code of Federal Regulations*, title 45, pt. 46 (1994).

protocols (e.g., IRBMED, 2005). At a minimum, these typically require the following:

- The name of investigator(s) and their affiliation, as well as individuals and organizations sponsoring the research
- A description, in lay language, of the purpose for conducting the study, as well as all procedures to be followed, including duration of the study, frequency of contact with respondents, and whether interviews will be tape recorded
- A disclaimer stating that participants may decline to answer any questions or withdraw from participation altogether
- A description of all known or anticipated benefits arising from participation in the study as well as known or reasonably anticipated harm (e.g., physical, psychological, emotional, financial, and social risks)
- Details concerning financial or other remuneration of research subjects
- Procedures to ensure confidentiality of data and anonymity of participants
- A statement concerning the availability of research findings to participants
- Information on length of retention and security of data

Along with informed consent procedures, and prompted by federal regulations, universities receiving public funding for research have established **INSTITUTIONAL REVIEW BOARDS** (IRBs). Membership on these boards is drawn from the research community on each campus. Under statute, the IRBs *have the authority to screen all research involving human subjects in order to certify that the proposed research is ethical and will not cause harm*. In effect, the governmental agencies are involving each college and university in a self-policing function. On some campuses, research performed by students as part of a classroom exercise is exempt from review, but procedures do vary.

This bureaucratic solution to ethical dilemmas has its problems; researchers from the physical or biological sciences who sit on the IRB may be asked to evaluate the questionnaires and procedures used by sociologists, psychologists, teachers, or nurses (Chastain and Landrum, 1999). The complexities of encouraging

and enforcing ethical research behavior raise a troubling possibility that "ethics" may have different meanings for researchers in different fields of study.

Despite the development of IRBs, codes of conduct, and rules and regulations, it has been difficult to achieve the goal of genuinely informed consent (Thorne, 1980; Stanley, Sieber, and Melton, 1996). The guidelines do not really resolve the ethical dilemma because of the inherent and frequently apparent differences in status between researchers and subjects. Status disparities are especially important in research with students, incarcerated prisoners, the aged, the severely ill, the mentally or emotionally impaired, and, as we will see below, children. Even when individuals are not located in these vulnerable or marginal status categories, it is difficult to eliminate the possible effects of intimidation, which can induce a respondent to sign a consent form. Moreover, there is no real proof that a research subject actually understands the complicated theoretical rationale that may justify a particular study. People sometimes give their "consent" because they are embarrassed that they do not understand the explanation provided them. Plainly, the guidelines, while perhaps ethically desirable, are not a substitute for the researcher's own soul-searching and personal sense of fairness in the conduct of research.

It should be underscored that the issues of confidentiality, deception, and manipulation are relevant not only because of ethical considerations but also because of their effect on the possibility of objectivity. If respondents fear that their confidences will be broken or that they will be manipulated and deceived by social scientists, how can we expect to gain their trust and find out what is really going on in the segment of society with which we are concerned? How can we expect to collect objective evidence?

Research on Children

During the last decades of the twentieth century, there was a sea change in how we regard children in our society. Article 12 of the United Nations Convention on the Rights of the Child

A Sample Informed Consent Form

(revised from Newman, 1999)

Consent Form for Participation of Human Subjects in Research

Anywhere University

Project Title: Doing Homework in Small Groups

Investigator: Sandra A. Researcher, Department of Psychology, 514 High Hall, 617/555-0000

Description: The purpose of this research is to examine the patterns of task performance and social interaction that develop within small groups of students who are given common homework assignments. If you volunteer for this research study, you will be asked to participate in a series of group discussions and decisions. Groups will vary from four to ten persons and the assignments discussed will be appropriate to an introductory psychology course.

All other participants in the study will be fellow students completing the homework for their psychology course. The topics are neither embarrassing nor intended to be upsetting. You will first be asked to complete a questionnaire and then will discuss with other members of the group one to four of the homework assignments, which are related to items on the questionnaire. You may be asked some questions about your group work after it has been completed. The total time for your participation will be one hour.

The results of each individual's participation will be strictly confidential. The results of your participation will be recorded by identifying only your group. No names or individual identifying information will be maintained. With the exception of the researchers involved in running this study, nobody will be allowed to see or discuss any of the individual responses. Your responses will be combined with many others and reported in group form in a professional journal article.

The risks to you are minimal, although you may encounter other individuals attempting to change your mind on some issues during the group discussions. All participants will be asked to keep their comments constructive; however, the researchers are trained to step in to protect individuals from hostile or inappropriate comments made during discussions.

The overall nature of the study will be explained as soon as you have completed your session. A summary report and explanation of the results will be made available to you when the study is completed if you so request.

Authorization: I have read the above and understand the nature of this study and agree to participate. I understand that by agreeing to participate in this study I have not waived any legal or human rights. I also understand that I have the right to refuse to participate and that my right to withdraw from participation at any time during the study will be respected with no coercion or prejudice.

If you have any concerns about your treatment as a participant in this study, please call or write:

Professor John H. Vigilant

Director, Grants and Research, Anywhere University

Anywhere, Massachusetts 02400; telephone: 617/555-0001

This research project has been approved by the Anywhere University Institutional Review Board for the Protection of Human Subjects, protocol #_____.

Participant signature   Date

*Subjects should be given a copy of this form for their records.

assures to the child "who is capable of forming his or her own views the right to express those views freely ... due weight [given] in accordance with the age and maturity of the child." As social views have changed, so has the ethical positioning of children in research. Historically, studies of children regarded them only as subjects, rather than as active participants. Increasingly, research is conducted *with* children rather than *on* them. A heightened recognition of the importance of listening to children's views and wishes has emerged (Fraser et al., 2004).

One example of the new thinking occurs in informed consent for research on children. When the subject is a minor, permission from a responsible relative is needed; however, whenever a minor child is able to give consent, it should be obtained as well. This principle is not universally established by law, but it is contained in the informed consent regulations of many research organizations. In general, rules are established for medical and psychiatric research purposes, and they gradually filter into all research involving human subjects. It is very important to develop explanations that are not beyond the understanding of children; for instance, it is one thing to tell adults that they may withdraw from a study at any time, but children may become confused or intimidated. Guidelines should be presented in clear language, using visual aids if necessary. Before a study begins in which painful or sensitive material is likely to emerge, it is a good idea to gather information on local sources of help that are beyond the expertise of the researchers and have them available for the children if needed.

Confidentiality and anonymity must also be explained in a way that children can understand. The researcher present at the interview is rarely the only person to see the transcripts or listen to the tapes. It must be made clear to children who will have access to the data and what will happen to the data when the research is complete. The researcher is ultimately responsible to protect children, if they are considered to be "at risk of significant harm" (Corti, 2000). If there is only a remote chance for harm to occur, as would likely be the case in most interview studies, children should be so informed. However, in more sensitive studies the child needs to know what action may be taken in the event that "significant harm" occurs.

Because children are especially vulnerable, the researcher often has to negotiate access via **GATEKEEPERS** – parents, schools, voluntary organizations – who through their relationship with the child are assumed to have a protective role. The gatekeepers will *require information about the research, how consent will be obtained* from the children and responsible adults, *and the extent of confidentiality, before approving access* to children. Sometimes, in order to gain access, researchers may be asked to make changes to their data collection instruments or to require parents to take positive action, that is, elect for their child to "opt in" to the research (Corti, 2000). These ethical guidelines may create methodological problems for sampling and operationalization of concepts in the research design.

ANALYSIS, INTERPRETATION, AND PRESENTATION OF RESULTS

The Fudging Effect

There are unfortunately many well-documented cases of outright deception of the public by manufacturing, or "fudging," all or most of the data in medical and scientific research (Altman and Hernon, 1997). Full-blown use of phony data is probably more rare in the social sciences, but "trimming," or conveniently ignoring, certain parts of the data to make them fit the preconceived notions of the investigator occurs more often than we realize, according to some observers (Miller and Hersen, 1992). This phenomenon may occur because scientists often have a vested interest in the successful outcome of their own research. Self-interest is likely to discourage potential "whistle-blowers" from implicating their colleagues and themselves (Bell, 1992; Kevles, 2000; Cook and Bombardieri, 2005). Moreover, as noted in the discussion on sponsorship, there is a strong desire for recognition and fame, as well as for financial security.

Appraisals and Characterizations

Determining the facts and assessing the weight of the evidence are crucial to the goal of objectivity in our research. Regarding the determination of facts, Nagel (1979) discussed the role of value judgments. He made a subtle distinction between judgments that characterize and those that appraise. **APPRAISING JUDGMENTS** *express approval or disapproval of what is under investigation* and should be ruled out; **CHARACTERIZING JUDGMENTS** involve an *evaluation of the degree to which some state or condition exists in the phenomena under investigation and are important for analysis to proceed at all.* An investigator who is studying power relationships in the family must make a technical judgment about what kind of behavior is dominant and shows power and about what kind of behavior is submissive and shows a lack of power. This would be an appropriate characterizing value judgment. If the researcher proceeded to argue that either dominant or submissive behavior is good or bad, an improper appraising value judgment would be made. This distinction seems to clarify the desired role of value judgments in analyzing and interpreting data.

Assessing the weight of the evidence is also important. The process of reaching conclusions from the data can be affected by the values of the researcher in either the natural or the social sciences. To combat this difficulty, the researcher should state his or her values clearly. An increasing number of studies, most of them qualitative research, contain the authors' personal narratives acknowledging their own biases and preconceptions (see, e.g., Karp, 1996; Vaughan, 1997). However, we are not always fully aware of our precise values with respect to a particular research topic. In this situation, the worth of any claim we make to objectivity will be measured by the critical evaluation of others in the social science community. This fact, however, should not deter us from striving for openness in interpreting data nor from including evidence that contradicts what we might like to find out.

APPLICATION OF RESEARCH RESULTS

The written presentation of research results should discuss methods in enough detail so that others can replicate the work if they desire. If a complete report of the research is given, the claim to objectivity can be tested by those with different values, who may reach the same or different conclusions. Another aspect of the complete presentation of research results is discussion of both the positive and negative findings. Sometimes we are reluctant to discuss findings that do not confirm our hypotheses because we feel that they represent failure. What this attitude overlooks is that in the long run such findings may be even more significant from the standpoint of truly understanding social phenomena than the ones we are pleased with. Many of the great breakthroughs in knowledge developed from evidence that contradicted accepted explanations.

Co-optation or Potency?

The findings of social science quite often have implications for politics. Sometimes research data have a minimal effect on changing national and local policy: They are merely **CO-OPTED**, or *used to legitimate a policy position already decided upon* by government officials, Alternatively, if research findings are contrary to the ideological position of the decision makers, the research may be dismissed as invalid or of little consequence. When a President's Commission found evidence that pornography was not only harmless, but also potentially beneficial, its findings implicitly suggested that pornography ought to be legalized. The failure to act on the report was largely a function of the political undesirability of its findings (Hawkins, 1989). Similarly, although the commission appointed to investigate the causes of the 9/11 attack on the United States found "no credible evidence" that Saddam Hussein helped al-Qaida in the attack (Yen, 2004), the Bush administration continued to insist that he had.

However, social research may be potent and directly applicable to human problems. A survey on patterns of intimate behavior in a particular country can reveal whether or not the implementation of an educational program is likely to achieve a reduction in AIDS. Studies on black–white relations in America can tell us how to make an integrated workforce more productive. Research can help us to ascertain the dynamics of poverty and thus to take steps to reduce the extent of the problem.

Misuse of Information

All new knowledge can be manipulated for either constructive or destructive ends. We are all familiar with the example of nuclear energy, which can be used for bombs or as a diagnostic tool in medicine. On a somewhat less grandiose scale, the same can be said about social science knowledge. The analysis of black–white relations in America could be used by powerful racists to create backlash conditions that would wipe out what progress has been made in improving race relations. There is no question that the advertising industry has used social science knowledge to manipulate consumer behavior. The use of opinion poll information by our highest political leaders so that they may craft the most appealing message is often noted (Blaney and Benoit, 2001).

As mentioned earlier, the time to worry about the use of research findings is not at the end of the research process but at the outset, during the stage of problem formulation. Regarding the potentially destructive utilization of some research, two social scientists decades ago made this observation:

This is a knotty issue, and one which perhaps can only be resolved by an act of faith. If you believe that in the long run truth makes men free and more autonomous, then you are willing to run the risk that some people will use the facts you turn up and the interpretations you make to fight a rear guard action. If you don't believe us, if you believe instead that truth may or may not free men depending on the situation, even in the long run, then perhaps it is better to avoid these kinds of research subjects. (Rainwater and Pittman, 1967:361)

The message seems clear. If we feel that the knowledge gained from our research will be put to destructive purposes in the long run, we should not do the research in the first place. Many times, however, the situation is not so apparent, and we feel drawn to the act of faith.

In the more ambiguous cases, how can we guard against the destructive use of social science knowledge? Two courses of action appear. The first involves trying to form a standard for evaluating a proposed research project. Perhaps social researchers can commit themselves to doing research aimed at discovering the best means for achieving humane, as opposed to inhumane, goals. A second safeguard against the destructive use of social science knowledge is for researchers to press for the constructive use of their findings after the research is completed, thus blending their roles as scientists and as private citizens. The possible social uses of new knowledge could be communicated to the public at large, and researchers could comment upon them, particularly to groups that are in a position to implement decisions related to the knowledge.

Value judgments are indeed involved in such communication and comment, but as Gouldner argued, perhaps the technical competence possessed by social scientists provides a warrant for making such judgments within the area of their expertise (Hammersley, 2000). Even if one disagrees with Gouldner's assertion, social researchers are still as free to make value judgments as is anyone else. Moreover, if their technical competence does not give them a special mandate to say what ought to be, it does give them a unique responsibility to spell out the alternatives of what can be, so that the public may know and decide.

SUMMARY

Ethical and political considerations may affect the objectivity of social research. The traditional position regarding objectivity, exemplified by Max Weber, is that investigators should rule out their own value judgments and maintain a separation between their roles as researchers and as private citizens. Those who object to the traditional view argue that so-called value-free social science is too often a rationalization for uncritical research that supports the status quo and that ignores the possible social consequences of the findings. In discussing the various stages of the research process, this chapter attempts to find some middle ground between these differing conceptions of ethics and objectivity.

The choice of both topic and theory for one's work may be influenced by power relationships in society or by the lower-level politics of universities or other funding organizations. It is possible for the sources of funding to subvert the process of scientific inquiry altogether. The critical issue may not be the actual source of money but the explicit or implicit contract between the researcher and the funder. Sometimes the investigation is co-opted by government, business, or a private foundation, and research findings are used merely to justify policies already decided on. Nevertheless, social research frequently has had potent and lasting effects on public policy.

During data collection, the researcher should take steps to ensure impartiality and should protect the identity of research subjects who wish their privacy preserved. In no case should promises of anonymity or confidentiality be made if they cannot be kept. Debates have flourished over the ethical implications of disguised observation and human experimentation. There is rarely an unresolvable conflict between the scientist's "need to know" and the privacy and dignity of respondents. If attention is addressed to ethical dilemmas *before* research actually begins, many of the potential problems may be anticipated and their impact mitigated. The issues of confidentiality and exploitation of research subjects need to be addressed, not only because of ethical considerations but also because of their effect upon the validity of data. Federal guidelines have been issued in an attempt to eliminate abuses. A nagging difficulty is that we can never know whether the respondents' consent for observation or experimentation that has been given to researchers is really voluntary and fully informed. This problem is more acute in the case of research involving children and other vulnerable groups. Every attempt should be made to inform respondents, their parents, or other responsible adults concerning any potential danger from participating in research.

The fabrication of research results during data analysis and presentation occurs perhaps more frequently than we realize. The temptation to make the data fit desired outcomes is ever present. However, researchers rarely confront any conflict between their personal ambition and truthfulness on a conscious level. Rather, in many research contexts, the peculiar conditions of funding or the pressures of time exert continuous constraints on the researcher not to adhere fully to scientific norms. This pressure must be recognized and counteracted.

To prevent the misuse of information and to inject higher ethical standards into our work, we may have to deviate from the traditional Weberian view of value-free social science. We may, for example, commit ourselves to doing research that carries humane, as opposed to inhumane, goals, and we can inform the public of the wider social implications of our research findings.

KEY TERMS

anonymity
appraising judgments
characterizing judgments
code of ethics
confidentiality
co-optation
debriefing
disguised observation
gatekeepers
informed consent
institutional review boards
objectivity
value-free social science
value judgments

EXERCISES

1. Briefly describe three research situations in which the personal biases of the investigators may be a problem. What can be done to increase the likelihood of objectivity in each of these cases?

2. Briefly describe three research situations in which deception may have to be used. Why is this the case? What kind of deception would you use? In each situation, how would you defend your use of deception on ethical grounds?

3. In what ways could the Milgram experiment, described in this chapter, be improved on from the standpoint of treating human subjects in a humane way?

4. You are engaged in fieldwork with a volunteer group. Members suggest that the group participate in (a) a peaceful, though illegal, demonstration; (b) the theft of some documents from a university building; and (c) sabotage of college facilities. How would you, as a researcher, react to each of these suggestions?

5. Find out if there is an IRB or other committee that reviews human subjects research at your university. What problems of ethics has it uncovered? What rules apply to different types of research? What part can students have in contributing to the work of the committee?

SUGGESTED READINGS AND SOURCES

Bechtel, H. Kenneth, and Willie Pearson. 1985. "Deviant Scientists and Scientific Deviance." *Deviant Behavior* 6:237–252.

An examination of scientific fraud from three sociological perspectives on deviance. The authors present scientific fraud as an "elite occupational deviance" resulting from a "conflict between goals and the ability to achieve them." They claim that there has been a "reorientation away from the traditional values of disinterested inquiry."

Becker, Howard S. 1971. "Whose Side Are We On?" In *Sociological Work*, 15–25. Howard S. Becker, ed. Chicago: Aldine de Gruyter.

A concise, classic argument for social scientists to take sides in their research while still seeking to collect valid and reliable data.

Bell, Robert. 1992. *Impure Science: Fraud, Compromise, and Political Influence in Scientific Research.* New York: Wiley.

The author notes that money has a major influence on scientific investigation. Colleagues are resistant to reporting wrongdoing because the entire organization may lose credibility or funding. Often the whistle-blower is punished for speaking out.

Hamilton, James C. 1999. "The Ethics of Conducting Social Science Research on the Internet." *Chronicle of Higher Education* 46 (15): B6–B7.

A useful summary of the ethical issues raised by the increasing use of the Internet as a vehicle for social research.

Hammersley, Martyn. 2000. *Taking Sides in Social Research: Partisanship and Bias in Social Enquiry.* New York: Routledge.

An examination of the entire debate over bias and partisanship in research, including critiques of the positions of Weber, Mills, Becker, and Gouldner.

King, Nancy M. P., and Jane Stein, eds. 1999. *Beyond Regulations: Ethics in Human Subjects Research.* Chapel Hill: University of North Carolina Press.

A fascinating collection of articles on ethical issues, including the ethics of gender, science, and culture; roles, relationships, and obligations in fieldwork; the ethics of AIDS research; industry funding and corporate sponsorship of research; whether ethical standards are the same in developed and developing countries; and whether community consultation can substitute for informed consent.

Resnick, David. 1998. *The Ethics of Science: An Introduction.* New York: Routledge.

Addresses a variety of ethical questions arising from the logic of science and how it is conducted.

Reverby, Susan M., ed. 2000. *Tuskegee's Truth: Rethinking the Tuskegee Syphilis Study.* Chapel Hill: University of North Carolina Press.

A critique of the infamous research mentioned in this chapter.

Shamoo, Adil E., and David B. Resnik. 2006. *Responsible Conduct of Research.* New York: Oxford University Press.

An excellent, recent review of the issues.

Sieber, Joan E., and James M. Dubois, eds. 2005. *Using Our Best Judgment in Conducting Human Research.* Mahwah, NJ: Lawrence Erlbaum.

A very engaging collection of articles from Ethics and Behavior.

Weber, Max. 1917/1968. *The Methodology of the Social Sciences.* New York: Free Press.

The classic statement of the traditional position concerning the role of values in social science research.

Codes of Ethics

American Psychological Association. 2002. *Code of Ethics*.
  http://www.apa.org/ethics/code2002.html.

American Sociological Association. 2005. *Code of Ethics*.
  http://www.asanet.org/page.ww?section=Ethics&name=Ethics.

Applied Research Ethics National Association (ARENA). 2005.

  This group is interested in issues relating to the protection of human subjects, the humane care and treatment of animals, scientific misconduct, ethical decision making in health care, and other ethical issues pertaining to biomedical and behavioral research. Its Public Responsibility in Medicine and Research Web site is http://www.primr.org/index.html.

Indiana University Workshop on Teaching Research Ethics. 2005. *Teaching Research Ethics: Annotated Bibliography*.
  http://poynter.indiana.edu/Iforms/poynter-trebibindex.html.

  This Web site contains a comprehensive bibliography on the subject of research ethics, as well as a searchable database.

National Council on Ethics in Human Research (Canada). 2004.

  The mission of the council is to advance the protection and promotion of the well-being of human participants in research and to foster high ethical standards for the conduct of research involving humans. The Web site http://ncehr-cnerh.org/english/home.php *contains a comprehensive list of questions for obtaining informed consent and sample forms.*

National Library of Medicine. 2005. *Finding Aid to the Documents on the Origin and Development of the Tuskegee Syphilis Study, 1921–1973*.
  http://www.nlm.nih.gov/hmd/manuscripts/ead/tuskegee264.html.

  This Web site contains an extensive list of sources on the study of untreated syphilis among African American men in Tuskegee, Alabama.

Qualidata. 2005. ESRC Qualitative Data, Archival Resource Centre, Department of Sociology, University of Essex, Colchester, UK.

http://www.essex.ac.uk/qualidata/forms/children2.htm.

  This department's Web site contains much useful information on the ethics of research on children, especially the dilemma of informed consent with a young population.

REFERENCES

Altman, Ellen, and Peter Hernon, eds. 1997. *Research Misconduct: Issues, Implications, and Strategies*. Greenwich, CT: Ablex.

Barnes, Deborah E., and Lisa A. Bero. 1996. "Industry-funded Research and Conflict of Interest: An Analysis of Research Sponsored by the Tobacco Industry through the Center for Indoor Air Research." *Journal of Health, Politics, Policy and Law* 21 (3): 515.

Baumrind, Diana. 1985. "Research Using Intentional Deception." *American Psychologist* 40 (2): 165–174.

Becker, Howard S. 1971. "Whose Side Are We On?" In *Sociological Work*, 15–25. Howard S. Becker, ed. Chicago: Aldine de Gruyter.

Bell, Robert. 1992. *Impure Science: Fraud, Compromise, and Political Influence in Scientific Research*. New York: Wiley.

Blaney, Joseph R., and William L. Benoit. 2001. *The Clinton Scandals and the Politics of Image Restoration*. Westport, CT: Praeger.

Bulmer, Martin, ed. 1982. *Social Research Ethics: An Examination of the Merits of Covert Participant Observation*. New York: Holmes & Meier.

Campbell, Teresa Isabelle Daza, and Sheila Slaughter. 1999. "University-Industry Relationships: An Empirical View." In *Perspectives on Scholarly Misconduct in the Sciences*, 259–282. John M. Braxton, ed. Columbus: Ohio State University Press.

Chastain, Garvin, and R. Eric Landrum, eds. 1999. *Protecting Human Subjects: Departmental Subject Pools and Institutional Review Boards*. Washington, DC: American Psychological Association.

Clawson, Dan, Alan Neustadtl, and Mark Weller. 1998. *Dollars and Votes: How Business Campaign Contributions Subvert Democracy*. Philadelphia: Temple University Press.

Cook, Gareth, and Marcella Bombardieri. 2005. "MIT Professor Is Fired over Fabricated Data." *Boston Globe*, October 28, 268 (120).

Corti, Louise. 2000. *Legal and Ethical Issues in Interviewing Children: Advice for Researchers Archiving Data*. ESRC Qualitative Data Archival Resource Centre, Department of Sociology, University of Essex, Colchester, UK.
   http://www.essex.ac.uk/qualidata/forms/children2.htm.

Fraser, Sandy, et al., eds. 2004. *Doing Research with Children and Young People*. Thousand Oaks, CA: Sage.

Galliher, John F. 1995. "Chicago's Two Worlds of Deviance Research: Whose Side Are They On?" In *A Second Chicago School? The Development of Postwar American Sociology*, 164–187. Gary Alan Fine, ed. Chicago: University of Chicago Press.

Giddens, Anthony. 1986. *The Constitution of Society: Outline of the Theory of Structuration*. Berkeley: University of California Press.

Gouldner, Alvin, W. 1973. *For Sociology: Renewal and Critique in Sociology Today*. Hammondsworth, UK: Penguin.

Hammersley, Martyn. 2000. *Taking Sides in Social Research: Partisanship and Bias in Social Enquiry*. New York: Routledge.

Hawkins, Gordon. 1989. *Pornography in a Free Society*. New York: Cambridge University Press.

Humphreys, Laud. 1975. *Tearoom Trade*. Chicago: Aldine de Gruyter.

IRBMED. 2005. "Informed Consent Templates." University of Michigan Medical School.
   http://www.med.umich.edu/irbmed/ict.htm.

Karp, David A. 1996. *Speaking of Sadness: Depression, Disconnection, and the Meanings of Illness*. New York: Oxford University Press.

Kevles, Daniel J. 2000. *The Baltimore Case: A Trial of Politics, Science, and Character*. New York: W. W. Norton.

Koocher, Gerald P., and Patricia Keith-Spiegel. 1998. *Ethics in Psychology*. New York: Oxford University Press.

Lafree, Gary. 2000. *Losing Legitimacy: Street Crime and the Decline of Social Institutions in America*. Boulder, CO: Westview.

Leo, Richard A. 2001. "Trial and Tribulations: Courts, Ethnography, and the Need for an Evidentiary Privilege for Academic Researchers." In *Contemporary Field Research*, Chapter 12. 2nd ed. Robert M. Emerson, ed. Prospect Heights, IL: Waveland Press.

Lewis, Charles, and Bill Allison. 2001. *The Cheating of America: How Tax Avoidance and Evasion by the Super Rich Are Costing the Country Billions, and What You Can Do About It*. New York: William Morrow.

Milgram, Stanley. 1973. *Obedience to Authority*. New York: Harper & Row.

Miller, David J., and Michel Hersen, eds. 1992. *Research Fraud in the Behavioral and Biomedical Sciences*. New York: Wiley.

Nagel, Ernest. 1979. *The Structure of Science*. 2nd ed. Indianapolis, IN: Hackett.

National Institutes of Health (NIH). 2000. "Financial Conflicts of Interest and Research Objectivity: Issues for Investigators and Institutional Review Boards." *NIH Guide Archive*. Title 42, volume 1, parts 1–399. June 5.
   http://grants2.nih.gov/grants/guide/notice-files/NOT-OD-00-040.html.

National Library of Medicine. 2001. *Current Bibliographies in Medicine*, 99–3.
   http://www.nlm.nih.gov/pubs/cbm/hum_exp.html.

Newell, J. David. 1994. "The Case for Deception in Medical Experimentation." In *Ethical Issues in Scientific Research: An Anthology*, 141–154. Edward Erwin, Sidney Gendin, and Lowell Kleiman, eds. New York: Garland.

Newman, Robin M. 1999. "Subject Consent Form for Participation of Human Subjects in Research." *Institutional Review Board for the Protection of Human Subjects*. University of Wisconsin, River Falls.
   http://www.uwrf.edu/grants/sample~1.htm.

Rainwater, Lee, and David J. Pittman. 1967. "Ethical Problems in Studying a Politically Sensitive and Deviant Community." *Social Problems* 14 (Spring): 357–366.

Ringer, Fritz K. 1998. *Max Weber's Methodology: The Unification of the Cultural and Social Sciences*. Cambridge, MA: Harvard University Press.

Rosenthal, Robert. 1994. "Interpersonal Expectancy Effects: A 30-Year Perspective." *Current Directions in Psychological Science* 3:176–179.

Scarce, Rik. 1995. "Scholarly Ethics and Courtroom Antics: Where Researchers Stand in the Eyes of the Law." *American Sociologist* 26 (1): 87–113.

Scott, Yolanda M. 2001. *Fear of Crime among Inner-City African Americans.* New York: LFB Scholarly Publications.

Shichor, David. 2001. *Readings in White-Collar Crime.* Prospect Heights, IL: Waveland Press.

Sieber, Joan E. 1992. *Planning Ethically Responsible Research: A Guide for Students and Internal Review Boards.* Newbury Park, CA: Sage.

Stanley, Barbara H., Joan E. Sieber, and Gary B. Melton, eds. 1996. *Research Ethics – A Psychological Approach.* Lincoln: University of Nebraska Press.

Thorne, Barrie. 1980. "You Still Takin' Notes? Fieldwork and Problems of Informed Consent." *Social Problems* 27 (3) February: 284–297.

Vaughan, Diane. 1997. *The Challenger Launch Decision: Risky Technology, Culture, and Deviance at NASA.* Chicago: University of Chicago Press.

Vidich, Arthur J., and Joseph Bensman. 1958. *Small Town in Mass Society.* Princeton, NJ: Princeton University Press.

Weber, Max. 1958. *From Max Weber: Essays in Sociology.* Hans H. Gerth and C. Wright Mills, eds. New York: Oxford University Press.

Yen, Hope. 2004. "9/11 Commission: No Link between Al-Qaida and Saddam." Associated Press, June 16.

SAMPLING

6

INTRODUCTION

In this chapter, the detailed examination of the various methods tools and approaches in research that will be the focus for the remainder of this book begins, starting with **SAMPLING**, *the selection of a relatively small group of individuals from whom we obtain data in order to be able to generalize about a larger group.* Sampling demonstrates the idea that science is a blueprint for research because there are indeed some rules for proper sampling that are essential. However, as we will see, in many cases, research imagination is also an important ingredient in successful sampling.

Let us take a look at public opinion polls. Nowadays, the results of polls are readily available in newspapers, in magazines, and on television. Strategies have been developed to ensure that these polls can be completed affordably and yield accurate results. Most public opinion polls in America survey only 1,000 to 1,500 respondents. This is a surprisingly low number considering the population of the United States is more than 300 million. How can such a small number accurately reflect the opinions of these millions of people? It is a matter of good sampling.

Consider Table 6.1, which reports findings from a major ongoing poll of public satisfaction. Over a three-year period, the public appeared rather divided about "the way things were going," although there was a slight up tick in dissatisfaction. Only 1,003 adults were contacted; yet, they are taken to represent the opinions of the nation as a whole. The margin of error is plus or minus three. This means that the pollsters are saying that they could be wrong, but if they are, they have misrepresented the real opinions of hundreds of millions of adults by only 3 percent, up or down!

How can the pollsters make the claim that they have drawn a **REPRESENTATIVE SAMPLE**; that is, how can they be sure that the 1,003 persons they contacted will give *an accurate picture of the country as a whole*? How can they be so certain about the possible limits of error? A major objective of this chapter is to present a nontechnical introduction to these issues. It is as important to the consumers of social research as to the producers of the research to know the logic behind sampling, the alternative sampling methods available, and the relative precision that can be expected from each of these alternatives.

In social research, as in everyday life, when we sample, we gather information about a few cases and seek to make judgments about a much larger number of cases. Most people are much more expert at sampling methodology than they probably realize. We all engage in various forms of sampling. When we take a sip of milk from that carton that has been in the refrigerator for the past two weeks to determine whether it is sour or when we select a few plums at the market for close scrutiny before a two-pound purchase, we are carrying out a sampling procedure. When we pick up a book of poems in a bookstore and leaf through it, reading one poem at the beginning, another in the middle, and a third at the end, we are again sampling. In everyday life, we adapt our sampling procedure to the situation. We find that for some purposes a sample of one (for example, the one sip of milk) is more than adequate as evidence for the generalization we are interested in making; for other purposes, a more sophisticated sampling procedure is called for.

Sometimes our goal in sampling is to get a sense of the entire group from which we are drawing the sample, as in our three-poem example. At other times, our objective is to draw a sample with particular attributes in an effort to find the "best." This procedure can be seen in mate selection for marriage. Young adults usually go through a phase of their lives when they date many people with the intention of finding the best possible partner. Obviously, we cannot date all possible candidates for the position! Some people would like to try, but the exigencies of time and money rule out this alternative. In other words, in this crucial part of our lives, we are forced to sample from among the possibilities. Our final selection is hopefully the most attractive among these possibilities. The sampling process is in evidence to some extent when we choose a school to attend, look for a job, or pick a place to live. To the degree that we are free

Table 6.1. "In general, are you satisfied or dissatisfied with the way things are going in the United States at this time?"

Date	% Satisfied	% Dissatisfied	% Unsure
January 1–9, 2006	36	61	3
January 3–5, 2005	46	53	1
January 2–5, 2004	55	43	2
January 13–16, 2003	42	56	2

Gallup Poll, January 9–12, 2006. $N = 1,003$ adults nationwide. Margin of error ± 3 (Polling Report.Com, 2006).

to choose in these areas of our lives, we want the best, as defined by our personal likes and dislikes. The emphasis in these situations is not on finding the average or typical mate, school, job, or home; rather, we want a sample that will be disproportionately weighted in favor of our specific objective of finding the best.

Social scientists use sampling in their research because typically they do not have the time and money to study all the cases in the population of interest to them. Usually their aim is not to find the best case but to find a representative distribution of cases that will allow for generalizations about the average or typical. In other words, social researchers often want an unbiased sample so that on the basis of the cases considered they can generalize accurately to all the cases in the population.

It is generally assumed that results based on a total count are more reliable than results based on a sample. In fact, a well-designed sampling plan contributes to both the reliability and the validity of our research findings. Recall from Chapter 1 that reliability means being able to reproduce a study consistently and that validity means that we are measuring what we intend to measure. If we do our sampling carefully and in accordance with one of the standard sampling plans, it should be possible for another researcher to replicate our findings; this is an important aspect of reliability. Careful sampling ensures we have drawn our cases so that our sample accurately reflects the composition of the population of cases about which we wish to generalize; this contributes to the validity of

the generalizations we make on the basis of our sample.

It is a common misconception that sampling is relevant only to quantitative survey research. Although sampling procedures for use in quantitative research are more highly developed, sampling can play a important role in fieldwork. We will therefore consider sampling as it is employed in both major types of social investigation. Let us begin by examining a few basic sampling terms.

Populations

A sample is made up of some but not all instances, or cases, of some general category of people, things, or events. It is the specific group selected from all possible cases of interest in a particular research project. *The term used to describe all the possible cases of interest* is the **POPULATION**. The population for a particular study might be all adult women in the United States, all Christians living in China, or all students at State University. The population of interest varies, depending on the purpose of the research. *A particular subgroup within the population* is referred to as a **STRATUM**. All the male students at a college would make up one stratum, and all the female students would make up another stratum. Different strata within a particular population are usually formed on the basis of such characteristics as age, race, and sex. The characteristics of relevance for determining strata depend, of course, on the purpose of the study.

Any individual case in the population is called an ELEMENT of the population. For example, in a study of State University, students Fred and Suzie are two different elements of the population. Usually the elements are individual people, but they can also be poems, newspaper articles, families, plums, or even nations. Another key concept is the SAMPLING FRAME. Once a population has been defined for a particular study, it is necessary to *list all the elements so that a sample can be drawn from the population.* The sampling frame is such a list. The sampling frame at a college would probably be all the students registered at the school during the semester when the study was being conducted.

SAMPLING PLANS

There are two basic kinds of samples: probability and nonprobability. In a PROBABILITY SAMPLE, *every element of the population has a known, though not necessarily equal, chance of being selected for inclusion. Furthermore, every element has at least some chance (a nonzero chance) of being part of the sample. Neither of these conditions generally holds for* NONPROBABILITY SAMPLES. Probability sampling plans allow us to estimate *how closely our sample results approximate what we would have found out if we had considered the total population* (the MARGIN OF ERROR). This occurs because there are certain statistical regularities associated with probability sampling that are related to our knowing the chance that each element has of being included in a given sample. In contrast, such estimates of precision generally cannot be made with nonprobability samples because we do not know the chances that each element has of being selected for a particular sample. Nonprobability sampling is actually quite similar to the kind of sampling we do in our daily lives.

Nonprobability Sampling

Nonprobability sampling is particularly well suited for exploratory studies, where the focus is on the generation of theory and research ideas. It is also useful in observational and qualitative research. In this section, we will consider the three most important types of nonprobability sampling: accidental, quota, and purposive.

ACCIDENTAL SAMPLING. ACCIDENTAL SAMPLING, *interviewing whoever happens to stroll by*, comes closest to the familiar radio or television "eyewitness interview." An important event has occurred, such as the impeachment of a president or the guilty verdict in a long, well-publicized trial. The media coverage of the event switches to various reporters who stand on busy street corners and interview people as they pass by. The same kind of sampling is sometimes (but not frequently) done in social research. A survey of student attitudes at your school might be carried out by having interviewers stand at the main entrance to the student center and ask those who enter and leave how they feel about a number of issues. The assumption behind such a strategy is that by simply being in a particular location we should get a reasonably representative cross section of the population of interest. The obvious problem is that there is no assurance that this is going to be the case. Indeed, just as the people who congregate in Times Square may not represent a cross section of the American people, the group of students who frequent the student union may not represent a cross section of students at your school. There is no reliable basis for determining whether an accidental sample is representative. Therefore, we must be particularly cautious about generalizing from the data acquired through accidental sampling.

QUOTA SAMPLING. A QUOTA SAMPLE is one in which *interviewers are told to screen potential respondents in terms of desired characteristics.* A quota is sometimes established in accordance with the percentage of the population composed of a particular stratum and sometimes in accordance with the theoretical focus of the study. For a survey on attitudes about the possibility of a female president, the quota sampling plan might call for 50 percent of the interviews with women and 50 percent with men, or the plan might call for 50 percent of the interviews with white women and 50 percent with black women. The first example illustrates quotas based on the proportion of the population that the stratum represents; and the second sample illustrates quotas based on a study's theoretical focus, assuming that there were theoretical reasons for expecting the attitudes of black women to differ from those of white women. The main advantage of quota sampling over accidental sampling is the assurance that certain strata of the population will be included in the sample. However, the sampling done from the different strata in quota sampling is essentially accidental. The "eyewitness interview" is still being conducted, but interviewers are told to make sure to stop certain people. Interviewers are given a large degree of latitude in the quota sampling procedure, which can lead to problems. The tendency for interviewers to search for respondents in congested areas has already been mentioned. Another bias is that if interviewers are sent out into a neighborhood to interview householders, they are likely to skip houses that are not as physically appealing or houses that have a Beware of Dog sign in the yard. Possibilities such as these reduce the precision of estimates based on quota samples.

PURPOSIVE SAMPLING. PURPOSIVE SAMPLING is a general term for judgmental sampling in which *the researcher purposely selects certain groups or individuals for their relevance to the issue being studied*. This sampling method is often used in studies of deviance or other social phenomena that are too rare to be dealt with effectively using a representative cross section of the population. If, for example, we were interested in assessing whether there is an impact of pornography on sex crimes, we might decide to study the pornography consumption habits of those who are or have been in prison for sex crimes. If we were interested in monopolistic practices among large corporations, we might select a specific field such as the computer industry and attempt to interview top management at several of the major firms. While management at IBM might have very little to say about their own practices, the management of their competitors might have a good deal to say

about actions taken by IBM. In such situations, the researcher must often make do with whoever will grant an interview. Elaborate sampling procedures are out of the question. A major advantage of purposive sampling is that it is a way to ensure that we get at least some information from respondents who are hard to locate and crucial to the study. A major drawback with such samples is that there is little or no control over who is selected within the category. There is no assurance that those selected are in any way representative of some clearly specified population of more general interest.

Probability Sampling

A probability sample is one in which every element of the population has a known, nonzero chance of being selected for the sample. The probability of selection does not have to be equal for each element of the population. Since we know the chance each element has of being included in the sample, we are in a position to estimate how accurately results for the sample estimate the characteristics of the total population. We will consider the four most basic probability sampling plans: simple random sampling, systematic sampling, stratified random sampling, and cluster sampling.

RANDOM SAMPLING. Simple RANDOM SAMPLING is the most basic of the probability sampling plans, and the others involve some form of it. A simple random sample is one in which *each element of the population has an equal chance of being included*. Let us assume that the library at State University has 100 books on marine biology. Fred has to write a term paper on this subject, and he decides that he needs five sources for his bibliography. It is late in the semester and Fred does not have time to do a purposive sample of the library's best books on marine biology. As a compromise he decides to write down the names of all the books dealing with the topic on individual slips of paper. He places the slips of paper in a box and then shakes the box vigorously. After the slips of paper are well mixed, Fred picks five of them from the box and copies the book titles for his bibliography.

The bibliography represents a simple random sample of all the library books on marine biology because each book has been given an equal chance of being included in Fred's sample.

The requirement that every element of the population has an equal chance of being selected has an important implication: A complete listing of all population elements must be available. In other words, an adequate sampling frame must be located. (Notice that this requirement was not mentioned with respect to any of the nonprobability sampling plans.) Sometimes this requirement presents no major problem. In studies of college students, for example, a list of registered men and women often serves the purpose. In other research situations, however, a good sampling frame may be difficult to find.

When complete listings of a given population are not available, some researchers may be tempted to use incomplete sources that are ready at hand. This must be done with caution because use of an incomplete sampling frame can lead to biased results. Some survey research is conducted by telephone, and the telephone directory is used as the sampling frame. However, many homes either have no telephone or have an unlisted number. In some areas, fewer than 80 percent of the households have listed telephone numbers. Unlisted telephones may be located in upper-income households (which try to avoid being besieged with solicitations or checked out by would-be robbers) and in low-income households (which use the device to escape the pressure of creditors). Also, all the families that have moved into new homes in the past year are unlikely to be listed; in our mobile society, that can be a good-sized percentage of the population of a town. The findings of a study that has employed the telephone directory as its sampling frame may be biased if the sample underrepresents the very high income, the very low income, and the newly relocated households.

For a simple random sample, the choice of elements from the sampling frame must proceed in a manner that gives every element an equal chance of being chosen. The method used by Fred for his bibliography can be described as the "picking a name from the hat" approach.

This method is feasible when small samples are being selected. The process becomes awkward, however, when larger samples are chosen.

Let us assume that State University has 16,000 students and that we want to select a simple random sample of 400. The list of those currently registered has been obtained and will be used as our sampling frame. Tables of random numbers are commonly used for the process of selecting elements from a sample of this size.[1] These tables are composed of random numbers that range from one to as high a number as the total size of any sampling frame is likely to be. Such tables are found in the appendix of most statistics textbooks. To use a table of random numbers for selecting elements, one must first number all the elements in the sampling frame. In our case, each of the 16,000 students would be assigned a number, beginning with the number 1. If the first number picked from the table of random numbers is 379, the student who has been assigned the same number in the sampling frame would be selected for inclusion in our simple random sample. We would continue picking random numbers until we had selected 400 students for the sample.[2]

PROBABILITY THEORY. How do we know the extent to which our simple random sample reflects the larger population from which it has been drawn? To answer, we need to distinguish

[1] Suppose we were to put the number 1 on 100 gum balls, the number 2 on 100 gum balls, and so on up to the number 1,000, which we would also put on 100 gum balls. Then suppose we were to very thoroughly mix all these balls and put them into a large fish bowl. If we now select a very small fraction of these balls one at a time, recording the numbers as the balls are selected (e.g., 243, 71, 528), the resulting list of numbers could be used to construct a table of random numbers. This table would allow us to select numbers between 1 and 1,000 at random; with appropriate modifications in the procedures used, we could construct a table that would allow us to select numbers between one and a million or one and a billion at random. Some of the numbers in the specified range will be selected several times, and others will never be selected. In actual practice, computers are used to construct such tables. Programs such as those available at Research Randomizer http://www.randomizer.org/ can bypass the actual construction of a table and feed researchers the numbers, directly.

[2] Alternatively, we might first select the 400 random numbers between 1 and 16,000, put them in ascending order, and then count down an alphabetical list of all students selecting student numbers 7, 29, 36, 53, and so on, until the 400 students had been selected.

between the **PARAMETERS** of a population and the **STATISTICS** produced from a sample. A *parameter is a characteristic of the total population*. The percentage of all 16,000 students at State University who feel that undergraduates should have a responsibility in the hiring and firing of faculty members is a population parameter. A *statistic is a characteristic of a sample*. The corresponding percentage of students in our sample of 400 who hold this opinion is a sample statistic. The issue of accuracy may now be rephrased. How exactly do sample statistics reflect population parameters? Probability theory tells us that for a simple random sample such statistics as the sample mean fluctuate around population parameters in a known manner.[3] If many samples are drawn from the same population, the resulting *sample estimates cluster around the population parameter. The measure of this variation* is called the **STANDARD ERROR**. In general, the larger the sample size, the smaller the standard error of our estimate. That is, the larger our sample, the closer our sample estimate is likely to be to the true population value. Moreover, the logic of probability tells us that the more **HOMOGENEOUS** (*similar*) the elements in a population are, the more likely the sample reflects the true values within that population. This is the case since if all the elements in a population were identical, there would be no need for these random sampling strategies. Individuals picked by even the most accidental procedures would still be representative. However, as long as the sample size is large enough, it does not matter how heterogeneous the population is. The **CENTRAL LIMIT THEOREM** states that the distribution of sample means approaches a normal distribution as the sample size increases, regardless of the original distribution in the population.[4]

Probability theory allows us to estimate standard error, so long as we know the size of a given population and sample and can estimate how homogeneous the responses to our questions

$$s = \sqrt{\frac{p\,q}{N}}$$

Figure 6.1. Calculating standard error.

are. In the formula in Figure 6.1, N = sample size; p and q are population parameters such that ($q = 1 - p$); and s = standard error.

In our previous illustration, there was a sample of 400, and 80 percent of the students agreed with the proposition that undergraduates should be given responsibility in the hiring and firing of faculty.

Figure 6.2 shows that the standard error (s) is calculated to be 2. In other words, the true population parameter (that is, the result we would get were we to do a complete count of the attitudes of all the students) will generally be within two standard errors of our sample estimate if we use a sample of 400. Note that standard error will fall as sample size increases. Moreover, with a more heterogeneous population (say, one in which students were split 50/50 on the issue of hiring and firing faculty) we would have to increase sample size in order to maintain the same level of error.

In most studies the investigator is interested in not one but many questions. If each of these questions has a different split among the response categories, a case can be made for a different sample size for each question. The way this problem is usually handled is to select a sample size appropriate for a 50/50 split; this provides a conservative estimate of the sample size needed for all others. It is also quite possible that different levels of error are acceptable from one question to the next. If the question is how the respondent intends to vote, we would not want to accept more than a 2 percent error if the

$$s = \sqrt{\frac{80 \times 20}{400}}$$

$$s = 2$$

Figure 6.2. Calculating standard error for a specific sample.

---

[3] For a more complete discussion of this issue, consult any introductory statistics textbook.

[4] As sample sizes decrease, the distribution of the original data must be reasonably normal for this assumption to hold.

expected split were 52/48. However, if the split were 90/10, we could predict the election outcome with a much smaller sample and we would be willing to tolerate a much greater error in our estimate. One way to deal with this problem is to select the question that is of greatest importance and use the sample size that corresponds to the acceptable level of error for this question. Another alternative is to select the question for which the acceptable level of error is lowest and choose the sample size that corresponds to this question. For most studies, however, neither of these alternatives is possible because the investigator does not have a clear idea of what level of error is acceptable. The acceptable level will in large measure depend on aspects of the statistical analysis that are difficult to anticipate prior to the data collection.

SYSTEMATIC SAMPLING. A SYSTEMATIC SAMPLE is similar to a simple random sample. It also initially requires an adequate sampling frame. *A random starting point is selected* on this list *and every "nth" name or unit is selected* from that point on.

If we decided to select a systematic sample of 400 students from the list of those currently registered at State University, we would first obtain a SELECTION INTERVAL by *dividing the population size* (16,000) *by the desired sample size* (400). In this case, the selection interval is forty, which means that every fortieth student would be selected from the sampling frame for the systematic sample. To ensure that each student has an equal chance of being selected, the starting point for the selection process must be randomly chosen. In other words, the first student would be selected from somewhere in the first interval of forty on the list, and the "somewhere" is determined randomly. Let us assume that the numbers 1 through 40 are thrown into a hat and the number 5 is selected. The initial student selected for our systematic sample would be the fifth student on the list of those currently registered at State University. The selection interval would then be applied by adding 40 to 5, so that the forty-fifth student on the list would be selected next. This process would continue until we had chosen 400 students for the sample.

The principal advantage of systematic sampling over simple random sampling is the relative ease in executing the selection process. Only one act of randomization is required (selecting a random starting point) with systematic sampling, whereas simple random sampling requires the random selection of every element to be included in the sample. We do not have to refer back and forth constantly between the sampling frame and a table of random numbers. One disadvantage of systematic sampling is that it may be subject to bias if there is PERIODICITY, that is, if *the sampling frame that is used has a regular, recurring pattern or cycle.* Consider a research situation where the sampling frame is a list of street addresses for housing units (the population elements are housing units rather than individual people). Imagine that the selection interval is ten and that the randomly chosen starting point for the selection of elements is also ten. If city blocks containing ten housing units apiece are being studied, this might mean that one of the corner housing units on every block would be selected for the systematic sample. It is possible that corner housing units tend to be inhabited by people with higher incomes because they may have larger lots or better views and consequently command higher rentals. The same problem could occur if we did a systematic sample of newspapers with a selection interval of seven. This could result in a sample that contained only Sunday newspapers. It should be clear from these examples that if systematic sampling is used, the sampling frame should be checked beforehand for the possibility of such cyclical bias.

STRATIFIED SAMPLING. STRATIFIED RANDOM SAMPLING is another form of probability sampling. It involves *dividing the population into two or more strata and then taking either a simple random sample or a systematic sample from each stratum.* (Notice that quota sampling is very similar to this procedure. The difference is that accidental samples are taken from different strata in quota sampling.)

The hypothetical behavior of Suzie offers an illustration of stratified random sampling. She has just met Fred outside the library, and he has related to her how he handled the problem of researching the literature for his paper on marine biology. We recall that Fred in his inventive way has done a simple random sample of 5 books from the 100 that are in the library. Suzie is in the same class and is faced with a similar time pressure, but she knows intuitively that there is something shaky about Fred's procedure. She is certain that some of the books on marine biology are more important than others. Her suspicion is that the hardbound books are more scholarly than the paperbacks, and therefore she wants to make sure that at least some are included in her bibliography. There are sixty hardbound books and forty paperback books on marine biology in the library. Suzie writes down the names of all sixty hardbound books on individual slips of paper and places them in one box. She does the same for all forty paperback books, and she places these slips in a different box. She shakes up both boxes thoroughly and then picks out three slips of paper from the first box and two slips of paper from the second box. Suzie copies the selected book titles for her bibliography, which represents a stratified random sample of all the library books on marine biology.

Social scientists often use stratified random sampling in their research. It is necessary, of course, to have an adequate sampling frame to implement a stratified random sample. The sampling frame must be divided into separate lists for each stratum. The next step is to take a simple random or systematic sample from each of the lists. As with quota sampling, the strata are selected on the basis of variables relevant in the context of a particular research project.

An important reason for selecting a stratified random sample is that if it is chosen correctly, it should yield more precise results than a simple random sample. The trick is to form strata that are internally homogeneous yet different from one another. In a survey of American attitudes toward United States foreign policy in the Middle East, it would be appropriate to consider stratified sampling by religion or ethnicity to ensure that there would be specified proportions of Jewish and Arab Americans in the sample. If strata are formed that are internally homogeneous yet

different from one another, the amount of sampling error is less than with a simple random sample of the same size. That is, the sampling error (as estimated using the standard error) is smaller for a stratified random sample than for a simple random sample. This means that the precision of a stratified random sample can be greater than that of a simple random sample.

The general procedure in stratified random sampling is to *sample from each stratum according to its percentage in the total population*. If a particular stratum makes up 20 percent of a given population and the designated sampling size is 500, a selection of 100 elements from that stratum should be made. This is called **PRO-PORTIONATE SAMPLING**. There are, however, research situations where it becomes apparent that a proportionate sample will result in very small numbers of elements for particular strata. In such cases, **DISPROPORTIONATE SAMPLING**, in which *the strata are not sampled according to their percentages in the population*, is more appropriate. The goal in disproportionate sampling is to select enough elements from each stratum so that a fairly detailed statistical analysis of each stratum can be carried out.

In a study of the student body at State University, the population might be stratified by subject major. Some majors have very few students (e.g., physics), and for some purposes, it would make sense to sample from them in larger numbers than their proportion of the entire student body warrants. When a disproportionate sample is selected, all of the elements of the population no longer have an equal chance of being included in the sample. Remember that the crucial aspect to probability sampling is that we have to know what the chance is of each element being selected. In this case, we might decide to give physics majors twice the chance they would have of being selected for a simple random sample. When our goal is to estimate a population characteristic (e.g., mean income) based on a disproportionate sample, the *results for each stratum must be weighted according to the percentage of the total population that the stratum represents*. Since physics majors have been given twice the chance of being included as have students with other majors, their responses must be weighted by a **CORRECTION FACTOR** of one-half when information about the total student body is calculated. If physics majors had been given four times the normal chance of being included in the sample, the correction factor would have been one-fourth.

CLUSTER SAMPLING. One potential difficulty with all the probability sampling plans discussed so far is the requirement of ascertaining an adequate sampling frame. In some cases, an actual list of the elements of the population is not readily available. It is not too difficult to find a sampling frame for the student population of a university. It would be difficult, however, to find a good sampling frame for all students who are currently enrolled in all of the universities, colleges, and junior colleges throughout the United States.

CLUSTER SAMPLING can sometimes be used in situations where it would be impractical or impossible to obtain a complete list of all the elements in the population. Cluster sampling *involves an initial stage wherein sampling is done from groups of elements that are called clusters.* A simple, systematic, or stratified random sample of clusters is selected from a total list of such groups. Once a sample of clusters has been picked, a simple, systematic, or stratified random sample of individual elements is obtained from the chosen clusters. In the case at hand, one might first sample from a list of colleges (clusters of students) in the United States that could be derived from a publication such as "America's Best Colleges, 2006" (*U.S. News & World Report*, 2006). A sample stratified by size of institution might be very appropriate. The final stage of sampling would entail the selection of a simple, systematic, or stratified random sample of individual students from the chosen colleges. We might, for example, decide to carry out a stratified random sample of students at each college according to their subject major.

A key advantage of cluster sampling is that initially a complete listing of all the elements in the population is not necessary. Only a listing of the relevant clusters is required. One disadvantage of cluster sampling is that the accuracy of estimates based on such samples is less than

that for other probability samples of the same size. One way to deal with this problem is to use a larger sample size. In cluster sampling, interviewers are sent to a few randomly chosen areas, and they interview a substantial number of people in each. In contrast, a simple random sample might result in a situation where interviewers are dispatched to many more locations, and they might interview only one person in each. The obvious advantage of cluster sampling is a savings of time and money.

MULTISTAGE CLUSTER SAMPLING. Let us look at another example that involves more stages of sampling from clusters than the previous illustration and that also shows the advantage of cluster sampling in saving time and money when interviewers are used. Imagine that we are interested in conducting a survey of the entire college student population in the United States. Because a list of the entire student population would be very difficult to obtain, we decide to use **MULTISTAGE CLUSTER SAMPLING** *on an area basis* (see Figure 6.3).

We might begin by using states to obtain our sampling clusters, since lists of every college in each state are not difficult to find. Suppose we select a simple random sample of seven states from among the fifty states. This is the first stage of our cluster sampling procedure. (Incidentally, when selecting the states, we should take into account the varying population sizes through a weighting process that makes the probability of selection for any given state proportionate to the relative population size of that state compared with the others.[5]) Figure 6.3 assumes that Texas is one of the states selected at random.

Many states contain dozens of universities, colleges, and junior colleges, so the second stage of sampling would be designed to produce even more manageable cluster sizes. Using the probability sampling procedure previously described, from each of the seven states we might select five cities or towns, indicated by the dots in Figure 6.3, stage 2. However, it may still be difficult

[5] This procedure is called PPS, or probability proportionate to size. To actually demonstrate it would get us into more sophisticated sampling designs than would be appropriate to consider here.

Stage 1
Random Selection of States

Stage 2
Random Selection of Cities and Towns within States

Texas

Stage 3
Random Selection of Colleges within Cities and Towns

Stage 4
Random Selection of Students within Colleges

Figure 6.3. Multistage cluster sampling.

to identify the student population living in these cities and towns for the purpose of assigning individuals to interviewers. Therefore, we could proceed to a third stage where we would select specific colleges within each city or town (Figure 6.3, stage 3). If we select three colleges within each of the five cities and towns, within each of the seven states, by using probability sampling methods, we would have a total of 105 colleges in our sample. The final phase of a multistage sampling plan is shown in Figure 6.3, stage 4. If we select 15 students from each school, our total national sample size will be 1,575. From this example is should be apparent that the cost of

interviewing would be considerably lower for a national multistage cluster sample than it would be for any other probability sampling plan at the national level (if, indeed, other probability sampling plans could be carried out at that level). In any event, when a multistage cluster sampling procedure is used, a relatively small number of interviewers is needed to cover the entire sample.

Combining Sampling Plans

To this point, we have discussed probability and nonprobability sampling as if the choice were to use one or the other. In actual practice, the two are often combined. When we employ both probability and nonprobability stages in our design, the final sample is always a non-probability sample. Despite this, it is common for such well-known public opinion organizations as Harris and Gallup to combine sampling plans. The design for a national sample typically combines probability cluster sampling at the initial stages (e.g., county or census tract[6]) with quota sampling at the final stage. When probability sampling is combined with quota sampling in such a way that the interviewer has relatively little freedom of choice with respect to where to obtain respondents, the resulting sample can be a close approximation to a probability sample. The success of such organizations as Gallup and Harris in forecasting national elections is evidence of the accuracy that is possible with a sampling design that combines probability and nonprobability procedures. It is also evidence for the productive use of the research imagination.

Polling Research

In the pure form of probability sampling, people with certain demographic traits or attitudes are no more likely than anyone else to be included in the sample. However, in practice, many pollsters do eliminate individuals with certain characteristics from their samples: people living in institutions such as prisons and nursing homes; those in temporary residences such as college dormitories; the homeless and military personnel are frequently excluded from surveys because of difficulty contacting these groups. The most efficient and cost-effective method for contacting respondents in polling is a technique called **RANDOM DIGIT DIALING** (RDD). In RDD, *computers are used to generate phone numbers at random* from all working residential telephone exchanges in the United States. A subset of these numbers is then dialed and interviewers conduct a survey over the telephone.[7] Of course, some people will not be home to take the call;

their numbers are later redialed automatically. As cell phones and VOIP (voice over Internet protocol) become more popular, researchers are deprived of a comprehensive sampling frame because phone numbers for these devices tend to be unlisted.

PROBLEMS AND ISSUES IN SAMPLING

In this section, three key issues in sampling that need further attention will be discussed. These are (1) selection of sample size, (2) non-sampling error, and (3) sampling in qualitative research.

Sample Size

One question most frequently asked of the sampling expert is, How large must my sample be? This question is crucial because sample size has a major impact on the amount of time and money that must go into the data collection phase of the research. At a minimum, simple random samples need to contain between thirty-five and forty elements to fall within the scope of probability theory. Generally, it is wise to select a sample of at least 100 elements of a population. The implication is that if the population under investigation is small (say, less than 150), elaborate sampling procedures are probably inappropriate.

In principal, we do know the mathematical relationship between sample size, heterogeneity, and error (see Figure 6.1), but in most real-life situations, the researcher does not have all the information for a precise statement of the necessary sample size. We can only state the exact sample size required by a particular study if the following three conditions are met:

- We must be able to identify a specific population parameter that is the primary focus of the study (for example, the answer to a question asking how the respondent intends to vote in November).
- We must be able to make a reasonable estimate of the split on the question (for example, 50/50 or 90/10 on a question with two choices).

---

[6] An officially recognized geographic area. See Chapter 14 for more information about census tracts.

[7] For more about telephone surveys, see Chapter 7.

Table 6.2. Sample Sizes Required for Various Margins of Error, by Confidence Level (Population = 10,000)

Margin of error +/-	1%	2%	3%	4%	5%
95% Confidence Level	4,899	2,088	1,000	579	375
99% Confidence Level	6,247	2,938	1,561	942	624

- We must be able to specify how precise a result is desired (for example, will an error of 1, 2, or 5 percent be tolerable?). If these conditions have been satisfied and simple random sampling has been used, then a formula such as the one in Figure 6.1 will specify the sample size that will be needed.

Confidence Levels

As Table 6.2 shows, the larger the sample, the smaller the margin of error, and the more accurate will be estimates based on the sample. However, the increase in accuracy with increased sample size does reach a point of diminishing returns. We need much more of an increase in sample size to reduce the margin of error from 2 to 1 percent than from 5 to 4 percent.

Table 6.2 also indicates that a larger sample is required for a 99 percent **CONFIDENCE LEVEL** than for a 95 percent level. What does this mean? *If we use the 95 percent confidence level, we can be sure that 95 of 100 samples of the specified size will be within the specified percent error of the population parameter.* These estimates are given for a question with a 50/50 split, but they can be used with other splits because the error is greatest for the 50/50 split; that is, the sample sizes specified are large enough for items with more extreme splits.

The sample size estimates in Table 6.2 are based on a population of 10,000. Approximately the same size sample would be needed to estimate the opinions of the adult population of one state (or even one large city) with the same degree of precision. Typically, Harris and Gallup polls use cluster samples of between 1,200 and 1,500 respondents to reflect the opinions of the adult population of the United States. Increasing the number of respondents does decrease the margin of error slightly. However, the addi-

tional cost may be enormous for a very small decrease in margin of error.

With a stratified random sample, smaller sample sizes are needed for a specified level of precision. For such samples, the estimates presented in Table 6.2 can be used because they are conservative. For cluster sampling, a larger sample size is needed for a specified level of error than for a simple random sample. Thus, Table 6.2 would not be appropriate for use with a cluster sample. Davis, Smith, and Marsden (2005) estimate that a national cluster sample of 1,500 cases is roughly equivalent in accuracy to a simple random sample of 1,000 cases. It is usually impossible to meet the conditions necessary for making a precise estimate of the needed sample size. In such situations, the researcher is forced to fall back on the experience of others. If the topic of the research or the population being sampled is of great interest and if it has not been studied before, it is quite possible that even a study based on a small sample (and, consequently, of relatively low accuracy) will be of general interest. However, if the topic has been repeatedly studied using large national samples, then possibly there will be little interest in the proposed study unless it too is based on a large national sample.

Nonsampling Error

SAMPLING ERROR is a general term referring to *those differences between sample statistics and the corresponding population parameters that are unavoidable but measurable* and that arise as the result of probability sampling methods. In most social research, however, there are many *other factors that tend to reduce the accuracy of estimates based on sample results*. These are called **NONSAMPLING ERRORS**. The formal term **BIAS** is also used to refer to the *distortion caused by the various sources of nonsampling error*.

Poor Sampling Frame

One source of bias is the failure to choose an adequate sampling frame. A classic illustration of this error occurred in the 1936 presidential election. Two major polls were conducted that year to predict the election outcome. One was conducted by George Gallup and the American Institute of Public Opinion. Gallup polled just over 3,000 people, asking which candidate they were supporting. Gallup predicted that Franklin Delano Roosevelt, a Democrat, would win the presidency.

Another much larger poll was conducted by the *Literary Digest*, which sent out an astounding 10 million ballot surveys. Over 2 million people responded. *The Literary Digest* predicted that the Republican, Alf Landon, would win with a 57 percent margin. In fact, he won only two states. Roosevelt was elected president with 61 percent of the vote. What had gone wrong? First, telephone directories and lists of automobile owners and club members were used as the sampling frame. However, only 40 percent of the homes in the United States had telephones at the time. Only a slim majority of families owned a car. This meant that the sample did not accurately represent the voting public. It was biased in the direction of higher socioeconomic groupings, which traditionally vote Republican. Moreover, there appears to have been a **SELF-SELECTION BIAS** among the more than 2 million adults who returned the questionnaires. They were likely more interested in the outcome of the election than the 8 million who did not return their surveys (Squire, 1988). By contrast, Gallup used quota sampling techniques to develop detailed quota categories for whites, blacks, males, females, and rural and urban populations. Thus, his sample was much more broadly representative than the one used by the Literary Digest. The self-selection bias was eliminated because Gallup used interviewers rather than self-returned questionnaires.

Nonresponse

A significant potential source of sampling bias that may lead to inaccurate research findings is **NONRESPONSE**. In surveys of many types (door-to-door, mail, or telephone), there may be a difference between those persons who respond and those who do not. The potential differences are greatest in mail surveys (such as the *Literary Digest* poll), where the opportunity to *refuse cooperation with the survey* is almost completely unrestricted. Nonresponse, however, is a problem with all methodologies. When door-to-door interviewing is used, people who are very active are less likely to be at home than nonactive people. Consequently, a good survey will allow for several return visits to the not-at-homes. The return visits will be more successful if they are staggered over various times of day and different days of the week. One technique for dealing with the nonresponse problem is to ask those people who are at home during the initial call how many nights of the previous week they had been at home. Those who were not usually at home but happened to be there when the interviewer called are weighted more heavily in the data analysis stage of research than the people who are always at home.

Bias in Panels

A special biasing factor occurs in panel studies wherein the same respondents are interviewed repeatedly over time on the same topic or different topics. The original composition of the panel may be representative of the population of interest, but over a period of time, people leave the panel (because of moving, death, or lack of interest). Unless some provision is made to assess the change in makeup of the panel and to compensate for this change, the results will be skewed. We need to ask whether there is anything special about those who do leave; if a particular segment of the panel (say, women) are systematically more likely to leave than are men, bias will occur. Another potential problem is that some panel members may become "expert respondents" during the course of their association with the study. They may thoroughly research the various topics covered in the questionnaires (which are frequently self-administered) and then try to give the "right" answers. Thus, membership on a panel may encourage some respondents to become less than representative of their counterparts in the population of interest. In order to circumvent this possibility, panel studies are sometimes supplemented by concurrent studies of "fresh" respondents to determine whether there is serious bias caused by membership on a panel.

Internet Polling

Self-selection polls are popular on the Internet. Many Web sites contain "snap poll" links to test the attitudes of the public on political issues of the day, popular culture, and consumer buying habits. These polls can generate much debate, and people seem to enjoy comparing their own opinions to those of other poll participants. However, the results of these Internet polls are very unreliable because the samples are not scientifically selected. Not everyone has access to the Internet, and most of those who do will not find the link to the poll. Moreover, they may choose not to answer it, or conversely, they may answer any number of times. Internet users tend to be disproportionately male, and more affluent and well-educated than the general population (Kehoe and Pitkow, 1996). For this reason, the most reliable research conducted by e-mail or the World Wide Web tends to be studies of Internet users themselves (Smith, 1997; Tse, 1998). Even in these cases, the absence of complete or reliable sampling frames has the potential to compromise Internet research. Only about 62 percent of American households had computers in the year 2003 (United States Census, 2003).

Can scientific and representative polls be conducted on the Internet? Harris Poll Online uses a hybrid sampling strategy that has been necessitated by the emerging technology. Internet users register to become survey participants.[8] Harris then collects demographic and lifestyle information about these individuals. This information is entered into a database from which samples are drawn to represent the general population. Selected individuals are then asked, through e-mail, to participate in each survey, using individual passwords. Software monitors their participation and will not allow

participants to log on more than once. With this sampling procedure, it is still possible that the findings may be more representative of Internet users than the general public.

Bias in Respondent Selection

Even when a probability sample has been selected scientifically to maximize similarities between those interviewed and the entire population of interest, there are a variety of sources of bias that the interviewer may introduce into the sampling procedure. One is the possibility that interviewers will cut corners on sampling and either not do all of the work assigned or fabricate responses. This is particularly likely when they are being paid by the interview rather than by the hour. Another danger is that interviewers will attempt to save time or money on return visits or calls by substituting respondents. Suppose a cluster sample calls for contacting every seventh house, but the interviewer finds that people are not at home. Is it legitimate to use the sixth or eighth house instead? Absolutely not! Similarly, if you are using a computer program or a table of random numbers to generate a telephone sample, you *must* make every possible attempt to contact the exact people or households to which you are directed by the table. If a researcher fails to adhere to the proper procedures for administering a probability sample – whether it is a simple random, stratified, or cluster sample – the accuracy of the results will be highly questionable. The laws of statistical probability work only when they are followed precisely.

Unfortunately, while chance error due to sampling fluctuation can be estimated, there is no simple formula for estimating the magnitude of the various sources of nonsampling error and bias. The best the researcher can do is be aware of these sources of error and attempt to keep them to a minimum.

SAMPLING IN QUALITATIVE RESEARCH

We have seen that a major reason for sampling in survey research studies is to ensure that the people from whom we gather our data are representative of the larger population about

---

[8] Visit the Harris Web site at http://www.harrispollonline.com/.

whom we seek to generalize. One might suppose that sampling procedures are unnecessary in qualitative research or fieldwork. Those doing field research typically observe only one case – one organization, one community, a single area of a city, or a discrete set of events. Since participant observers rarely seek systematic information from a large number of people, they do not ordinarily randomly select people to interview nor do they typically devise quota or purposive samples before entering the field. Nevertheless, sampling procedures are used in qualitative investigations. Participant observers must fashion sampling procedures to be certain that observations made in some setting are representative of what generally goes on in the setting. To see how and why field researchers might sample "times," "places," "roles," or "statuses," we will imagine an investigation of a large city hospital.

Time Sampling

After a few weeks of preliminary observation, the researcher recognizes that activities in the hospital vary at different times during the day. Perhaps more automobile accident cases show up in the emergency room in the early hours of the morning, or certain types of operations are scheduled in the afternoon. The researcher begins to sense that there are times when doctors are not easily accessible and that this might alter the functioning of the organization. In short, as in virtually all contexts, there is an ebb and flow to activity. To get a total picture of a setting, one must avoid doing all the observational work at the same time each day. Field researchers will often sample times for doing their observation to ensure that their image of the organization is not based solely on the kinds of activities occurring during a particular time interval. It would be possible for the researcher to break the twenty-four-hour day into discrete time units and let the times of observation be dictated by a random sampling of these time units.

Place Sampling

Activities and events also vary in different places within an organization. Imagine the biased picture of the hospital obtained if a field researcher restricted all observation to the emergency room. The activities of doctors, nurses, patients, and administrators observed in this particular area of the hospital are likely to be quite different from those in other areas. Our researcher correctly decides, therefore, that it is necessary to witness activities in different places within the hospital. One strategy might simply be to make a list of various strategic locations (e.g., the emergency room, the nurses' station, the admitting office, the cafeteria, the waiting rooms) and to systematically do observations in each. It might be reasonable in some studies to combine time sampling and place sampling. Researchers must, of course, use good judgment with regard to place sampling. They might discover after a short period of observation in a particular place that they have likely seen all the essential activities that go on there. Our researcher would be foolish to spend hours observing clothes drying in the hospital laundry room simply because a regimented sampling plan demanded it.

Event Sampling

Related to time and place sampling is event sampling (Strauss and Corbin, 1998). In any organization are routine, special, and unexpected events. In organizations such as hospitals, the vast majority of happenings are routine – meetings at specific times, meal serving, visiting hours, doctors' rounds, and so on. Although special events occur infrequently, they may still be anticipated. If one learns, for example, that an examining board responsible for continuing the hospital's accreditation will be visiting, one surely would want to observe how this special event alters the routine operation of the organization. Once researchers have gained the trust of people in the setting, they may even ask to be called if unexpected events are in the process of occurring. It is possible to make a list of routine events and selectively sample each. Although it is more difficult to plan observations of special and unexpected events, researchers will want to make a determined effort to observe them. Past research experience suggests that a great deal is learned about the functioning of any social system by observing its responses to special events.

Status, Role, and Relationship Sampling

Finally, there will be occasions when a qualitative researcher wants to discover the behavior of, or to interview, specific types of people in an organization. People in unique positions within an organization or setting will have quite different perspectives on it. Field researchers rarely try to interview a large number of people systematically in a particular setting. They might determine, as the research progresses and theoretical ideas begin to take shape, that people occupying certain statuses in the organization can supply them with important information. So, they may choose to sample statuses and roles. In the hospital setting, the researcher might want to observe the behavior of, or talk to, individuals who serve specific functions. If the researcher wanted to find out the kinds of changes that have occurred over time in the hospital, it might be reasonable to sample some of the "old-timers" there. As an extension of status and role sampling, a field researcher might even be interested in sampling social relationships. The researcher might decide that it is theoretically important to observe a sampling of interactions between doctors new to the job and nurses who have long service on the staff.

Sampling and the Creation of Theory

An important point emerges from our examination of the sampling procedures frequently employed in qualitative research: The basis for sampling in many qualitative studies is not to make statistical estimates of population parameters based on sample data but to make theoretical generalizations. Certainly, any social scientist wants to ensure that observations made of people, events, and places are typical. At the same time, the qualitative researcher would rarely be concerned with having observed every type of event, only those that are most related to emerging theoretical ideas. It is not a criterion of such sampling that the elements of the sample closely approximate the characteristics of some known universe.

In survey research, sampling procedures are chosen only once – at the beginning of the investigation. By contrast, in qualitative research, sampling is often a creative, ongoing practice. As theoretical ideas develop during the researcher's observations, it may become necessary to sample features of the situation that were not anticipated earlier. It is then that a quota or purposive sample may be decided on, primarily to help the fieldworker understand a particular setting.

Snowball Sampling

Reputational, or SNOWBALL SAMPLING, is one of the most widely used nonprobability sampling techniques in qualitative research. It is especially helpful when a complete or reliable sampling frame is unavailable or when access to appropriate subjects for interviewing and observation is difficult. Examples of groups that are typically closed to more conventional sampling strategies include people who engage in deviant behavior; secret societies; highly specialized, or "insider," interest groups; and networks that form or come together quickly or temporarily. To initiate a snowball sampling plan, the researcher might locate a single individual who possesses the needed characteristics, and at the conclusion of an interview say:

> Well, it has been great meeting with you and I do appreciate the time you have given me. I am wondering if there are any other people who share your interests/experience and who you think may be interested in meeting with me?

If individuals appear reluctant to offer any specific names to the researcher "on the spot," they may be asked to contact these additional people themselves to determine whether the researcher could meet with them. Once potential new respondents in the "snowball" have indicated their interest or agreed to be contacted by the researcher, the odds that new interviews will ultimately occur are greatly increased. Of course, snowball sampling is not an effective technique for ensuring a broadly representative sample. On the one hand, reputational referrals tend to follow the patterns of established networks, friendships, and acquaintanceships with like-minded individuals who may not reflect the true diversity needed by the researcher. On the other hand, snowball sampling is an invaluable tool for gaining access to informed and experienced people who may provide in-depth information available nowhere else.

SUMMARY

In social research as in daily life, we *sample*; that is, we must make generalizations about the world on the basis of examining relatively few cases. The major difference is that a researcher consciously takes precautions to ensure that the sample is as representative and unbiased as possible. This chapter is a nontechnical introduction to the logic and rules of sampling for both quantitative survey research and qualitative fieldwork.

There are two basic kinds of sampling techniques. One is nonprobability sampling (e.g., accidental, quota, and purposive). Nonprobability sampling plans require substantial judgment on the part of the researcher. The other type is probability sampling, which reduces the chances of bias by limiting the role of the researcher in the process of selecting the elements for the sample. In simple random, stratified, and cluster sampling, each element in the population of interest has a known, nonzero chance of being selected. The accuracy of probability samples is measured by the standard error, which, in general, decreases as sample size increases. The more homogeneous the original population, the smaller the error is likely to be. Stratified sampling procedures use this principle, in that the sample is separated into different segments, which are internally homogeneous. The result is more accuracy than would be obtained with a simple random sample. Cluster sampling is also a modification and expansion of the logic of random sampling and is especially useful where it would be difficult or impossible to obtain an adequate sampling frame. As a general rule, one should use the most precise sampling plan that time and resources permit. Probability and quota sampling procedures may be combined and produce good results, as long as the interviewer's freedom to select individual respondents is limited.

Three major issues in sampling are size, non-sampling error, and sampling in qualitative research. It is usually difficult to determine exactly how large a sample ought to be, and it is impossible unless specific population parameters are identifiable and unless the distribution of responses to given questions may be estimated with reasonable accuracy. If these conditions are met, we may project the sample sizes necessary for obtaining varying degrees of precision and confidence in our findings. For some purposes, a tolerated error of 3 or 4 percent is all that is necessary. In other cases (as in forecasting election results), a tolerated error as high as 3 percent would be useless. The sample size needs to be increased to raise confidence limits and lower tolerated error, but there is a point of diminishing returns, above which it may not be helpful to contact more respondents.

Probability sampling plans make use of mathematical principles to reduce bias and increase representativeness. However, nonsampling errors may still occur as the result of a poor sampling frame, nonresponse of subjects, or bias in the administration of the sample after it has been selected. The researcher should be aware of these and other sources of error and attempt to minimize them.

Because there are many research situations where the use of probability samples is impossible or impractical, sampling in fieldwork is receiving renewed attention. Often some form of judgment sampling is used that is open to modification as the research progresses. The sampling of places, events, and people's roles and statuses at different points in time achieves greater representativeness. It also aids in the construction through induction of social, political, and psychological theory, by demonstrating principles of behavior based on carefully selected individual cases. Because fieldwork is often predicated on the personal relationships constructed between the researcher and networks of people being studied, snowball sampling can be an invaluable technique for penetrating groups of similarly situated individuals.

KEY TERMS

accidental sampling
bias

central limit theorem
cluster sampling
confidence level
correction factor
disproportionate sampling
distribution
element
generalization
homogeneous
margin of error
multistage cluster sampling
nonprobability sample
nonresponse
nonsampling error
parameter
periodicity
population
probability sample
proportionate sampling
purposive sampling
qualitative research
quota sample
random digit dialing
random sampling
representative sample
sampling
sampling error
sampling frame
selection interval
self-selection bias
snowball sampling
standard error
statistic
stratified random sampling
stratum
systematic sample

EXERCISES

1. Describe the sampling you do in your everyday life with respect to dating and marriage, selecting a school to attend, or buying a car. What kind of sampling do you do? How good a sample do you choose? Is the issue of accuracy relevant to your sampling? Why?

2. Select one observational or qualitative study from the literature and critique its sampling procedure. Does the author of the study you chose deal with issues of sampling reliability and validity? If so, how?

3. Suggest appropriate items, locations, events, roles, and statuses to sample when doing participant observation of:

an airport

a factory

a city park

a doctor's waiting room

a bar

4. Visit A. C. Nielsen's Web site at http://www.nielsenmedia.com and click on "Inside TV Ratings." The national media ratings, which influence advertising as well as the production and cancellation of television series, are based on samples of 5,000 households. Investigate this procedure. Does it give us a reliable and valid picture of America's taste in television programming? Is it fair that 5,000 families carry so much weight in determining what programs we all can see?

5. A survey is being conducted to determine the favorite popular music performer among college students, and you are asked to select a sample of 100 undergraduates at your school. Compare sampling plans for accidental, quota, and simple random samples. After you have described the differences between them, speculate on the likely differences in results of the survey depending on which sampling plan is used.

SUGGESTED READINGS AND SOURCES

Dillman, Don A. 2006. *Mail and Internet Surveys: The Tailored Design Method – 2007 Update*. 2nd ed. New York: Wiley.

> *This book contains an excellent section on limiting error arising from coverage and sampling in Internet-based research.*

Kelley, D. Lynn. 1999. *Measurement Made Accessible: A Research Approach Using Qualitative, Quantitative, and Quality Improvement Methods*. Thousand Oaks, CA: Corwin Press.

> *This resource contains a discussion of sampling in qualitative research along with a comparison with probability sampling in quantitative studies.*

Levy, Paul S., and Stanley Lemeshow. 1999. *Sampling of Populations: Methods and Applications*. 3rd ed. New York: Wiley.

> *This comprehensive, relatively advanced-level text covers the major probability sampling designs and other key topics in survey methodology, including nonresponse issues and telephone sampling. A knowledge of basic statistics is helpful in maximizing your learning from this book.*

Lohr, Sharon L. 2006. *Sampling: Design and Analysis*. 2nd ed. Pacific Grove, CA: Duxbury Press.

> *Designed for students who have taken an introductory statistics course, this book uses a step-by-step approach to explain whether a sample is valid and how to design and analyze many different forms of sample surveys. A companion CD-ROM contains data sets and a computer program, providing support for exercises and projects.*

Slonim, Morris J. 1960. *Sampling in a Nutshell*. New York: Simon & Schuster.

> *A classic nontechnical introduction to sampling, this book is written in a humorous vein and contains a number of illustrations.*

Thompson, Steven K. 2002. *Sampling*. 2nd ed. New York: Wiley-Interscience.

> *An excellent and authoritative resource on sampling.*

Other Resources

Audience Dialogue. 2003. Know Your Audience: Chapter 2, Sampling.

> http://audiencedialogue.org/kya2.html.

> *This Web site contains a step-by-step guide to developing a variety of sampling plans, including multistage cluster sampling.*

Creative Research Systems. 2003. Sample Size Calculator.

> http://www.surveysystem.com/sscalc.htm.

> *This Web site will calculate the sample size you need if you provide input on population size, confidence limits, and tolerated error.*

Polling Report.Com. 2006.

> http://www.pollingreport.com.

> *This Web site contains the results for a wide variety of national public opinion polls, along with information on sample sizes.*

Research Randomizer. 2006.

> http://www.randomizer.org/.

> *Research Randomizer generates numbers that produces customized sets of random numbers. It is designed to assist researchers and students who want an easy way to perform random sampling. It can be used in many situations, including psychological experimentation, medical trials, and survey research.*

REFERENCES

Davis, James A., Tom W. Smith, and Peter V. Marsden. 2005. *General Social Surveys, 1972–2004 Cumulative File*. ICPSR04295-v1. Chicago: National Opinion Research Center.

Kehoe, Colleen M., and James E. Pitkow. 2000. "Surveying the Territory: GVU's Five WWW User Surveys." *World Wide Web Journal* 1 (3).

Polling Report.Com. 2006. *Gallup Poll*.
http://www.pollingreport.com/right.htm.

Smith, Christine B. 1997. "Casting the Net: Surveying and Internet Population." *Journal of Computer Mediated Communication* 3:1.

Squire, Peverill. 1988. "Why the 1936 Literary Digest Poll Failed." *Public Opinion Quarterly* 52: 125.

Strauss, Anselm L., and Juliet M. Corbin. 1998. *Basics of Qualitative Research: Techniques and Procedures for Developing Grounded Theory*. Thousand Oaks, CA: Sage.

Tse, Alan C. 1998. "Comparing the Response Rate, Response Speed and Response Quality of Two Methods of Sending Questionnaires: E-mail vs. Mail." *Journal of the Market Research Society* 40 (4): 353–361.

U.S. Census Bureau. 2003. *Computer and Internet Use in the United States*. "Presence of a Computer and the Internet for Households, by Selected Characteristics." Table 1A, October.
http://www.census.gov/population/www/socdemo/computer/2003.html.

U.S. News & World Report. 2006. "America's Best Colleges 2006."
http://www.usnews.com/usnews/rankguide/rghome.htm.

7

SURVEY RESEARCH

INTRODUCTION

Having learned about sampling in the preceding chapter, we are now ready to examine social surveys, a quantitative technique. Surveys are the most common form of research in the social sciences. We are all regularly exposed to surveys in one form or another. We may be stopped on the street or in a shopping mall by interviewers who ask our opinions on current issues or our preferences for consumer items. We are telephoned by surveyors who ask how we intend to vote in an upcoming election or why we chose one airline over another. We receive a variety of questionnaires in the mail – from government agencies, business corporations, and community organizations. Newspapers report the latest public opinion polls; the major television networks employ their own pollsters. All these are forms of survey research: systematic attempts to collect information, mostly from individuals, to describe and explain the beliefs, attitudes, values, and behavior of selected groups of people. Nearly every topic of interest in the social sciences has been studied through surveys, and the broad adaptability of this research method is one of its greatest strengths.

The characteristic of surveys that best illustrates their value and explains their extensive use is their ability to produce a representative distribution, or cross section, of the "target" population, whether that population is the entire American voting public or the people who stayed at a certain hotel during a given month. So, surveys are most often coupled with probability sampling techniques.[1] Because the value of a survey depends on the representativeness of the group surveyed, the sampling plan and its execution

are almost as crucial to final success as are the planning and execution of the overall survey.[2] This means that anyone conducting a survey should begin by thoroughly reviewing all issues and options related to sampling.

A major difference between the survey and other research methods lies in the number of persons from whom data are usually collected. Surveys generally use much larger samples of subjects than are used in research involving intensive interviews, experiments, or observational studies. For example, the University of Michigan Health and Retirement Study biennially surveys more than 22,000 adults older than the age of 50,[3] and the National Educational Longitudinal Study of 1988 collected data from more than 26,000 students in 1988, with follow-up studies in 1990, 1992, 1994, and 2000.[4] Also, through its *Current Population Survey*, the U.S. Bureau of the Census conducts a monthly survey of approximately 50,000 households to arrive at an accurate description of current labor force characteristics, such as the unemployment rate.[5] Despite these examples of massive studies, the standard, accepted sample size for contemporary national surveys is about 1,500 cases, and in carefully designed and well-executed surveys, much smaller samples can and do regularly produce surprisingly accurate results.

After the size and type of sample have been determined, several other decisions must be made before a survey can be conducted. How much personal contact will be necessary to

---

[1] See Chapter 6 for a review of probability sampling.

[2] Some surveys, instead of sampling, study all members of their target populations. The U.S. Census's counting of the population is an example.

[3] See http://www.umich.edu/~hrswww/ for more information.

[4] See http://nces.ed.gov/surveys/nels88/ for more information.

[5] See http://www.bls.census.gov/cps/ for information.

gather the data? Must each of the subjects be contacted in person? And, if so, how much time and expense are involved? Would it be all right to contact the subjects by mail or telephone or over the Internet? The savings in time and expense can be enormous, but the data will not be as accurate or as detailed, and the tendency of subjects to refuse to provide data may be higher. Can the objectives of the research be met with a single survey? Or must several surveys be conducted at different times in order for changes and trends to be measured and analyzed? These overriding design issues must be resolved before a researcher can construct a questionnaire or establish specific tactics for data collection.

A survey research project may be thought of as a sequence of major steps to be carried out. These steps include formulating research objectives, deciding how to collect the data, constructing the questionnaire, choosing a sampling method, preparing the collected data for processing and analysis, and processing and analyzing the data. Because sampling techniques and methods of data analysis have been treated in detail in other chapters, the discussion that follows will concentrate on the other major considerations and issues involved in survey design and execution.

SURVEY DESIGN

As we emphasized in earlier chapters, no research method flows from one discrete step to the next by a totally rational and trouble-free process because no researcher can anticipate all possible contingencies. There is room for the research imagination in all types of data collection. But research methods do differ in their degree of rigor; in one method, the stages of planning, data collection, and data analysis may be more distinct than in another. Compared with other research techniques, surveys are fairly rigid and structured when they are being administered; each step builds on what has gone before and necessarily inherits all the limitations of preceding plans and procedures. If a researcher has a brilliant insight in the middle of a survey interview, it is probably too late at that point to formulate and to test a new hypothesis. So, in survey research the planning stages are crucial because the worth and relevance of the survey's results depend on them.

Formulating Objectives and Hypotheses

Although the survey method has wide applicability, one can never assume that a survey will be an appropriate research strategy until the overall aims of the study have been fully laid out. The formulation of objectives must precede the choice of research method. It's good to begin by asking yourself, "What do I need to know, and why do I need to know it?" Surveys call for research imagination primarily at this early stage of their development; although most survey research projects start with very general questions, those questions must then be narrowed, focused, and justified.

Motivated simply by curiosity, a researcher might begin a study about the degree of public support for certain local and national politicians, both incumbents and challengers. She may then anticipate possible results and try to imagine what related popular sentiments might produce one or another election outcome. Does the project aim simply to describe the current popularity levels of a group of politicians, or does it also aim to discover the reasons behind them? What are the general issues that concern people and that affect their attitudes toward the candidates? Are politicians being judged on style or performance, on local or national issues, on action or rhetoric, on work or visibility, on their own records or the general tide of events during their tenure in office? These research questions could be studied in a number of different ways.

A survey could be conducted in which a researcher first asked a sample of people to name some politicians they like and some whom they dislike and then probed for detailed reasons behind the stated preferences. The data thus collected might reveal a great deal about what people believe to be true about political figures and might help to explain the figures' relative levels of popularity. Another researcher might approach the same set of questions by relying on other kinds of data, such as politicians' legislative voting records, campaign speeches and campaign literature, measured against the length of their political careers and the percentage of votes they have polled in each election. Whether the result of these strategies proves more or less useful or illuminating than the findings produced by a survey would depend largely on the priorities of the individual researcher and on the nature of the specific questions asked.

Before you decide that the survey method is necessary and suitable for your research project, thoroughly review all the existing literature (books and articles) written by other researchers on the same general topic. Many of the points of interest to you may have been resolved by previous studies. Or, relevant survey data may already exist which you could obtain and use for your own purposes. Only after you have reviewed and exhausted these possibilities should you embark on a fresh survey of your own. Although a review of past research might occasionally produce satisfactory answers to your queries, it is far more probable that reading the results of others' work will help you to clarify exactly what questions, of the many that will probably occur to you, are most worth pursuing.

Another procedure helpful in the formulation of survey objectives is the **PILOT STUDY**: a *tentative examination*, often using relatively unstructured interviews, *of a handful of subjects who are similar to those who will be the target of the later survey*. Pilot studies, like rehearsals, are intended to allow the researcher to try out various possibilities before deciding which ones to adopt. Such studies can often stimulate new lines of inquiry, prompted by the reactions or unsolicited responses of the subjects. They can also suggest new types of data that should be collected, point up and resolve ambiguities in the way that questions are being asked, indicate changes needed in the order of topics covered, and help to eliminate fruitless lines of inquiry. If a study of migration to cities were planned, the pilot phase might involve in-depth, intensive interviews with migrants in several different areas. It might serve as a guide to the sampling of those who have moved and to uncovering reasons for migrating that had not occurred to the researcher. Any investigator who is thinking about doing an extensive survey should consi-

der the pilot study as an opportunity to discover and correct mistakes before they become serious or difficult to remedy.

Choosing a Time Frame

After you have formulated a research question, and if you have decided that a survey is the most appropriate method for collecting data, you must determine whether all necessary data can be collected at once or whether it must be collected by means of surveys conducted at different times.

CROSS-SECTIONAL DESIGN. A *single, unrepeated survey*, referred to as a **CROSS-SECTIONAL DESIGN**, has the virtue of producing prompt results; such a study can often be completed within a few months or weeks, or even within hours.[6] The cross-sectional design is most appropriate for making inferences about the characteristics of the population from which you drew your sample and about the degree of association between those characteristics.

Suppose a team of researchers interested in exploring the fear of crime in American cities chooses six cities of different sizes, carefully selects samples of households within each one, hires interviewers, and conducts a survey in each city. When the data have been collected and analyzed, the researchers may generalize about the extent and distribution of fear of crime in each city and about the variations in levels of fear within the population of each, and they may make comparisons among the cities. Using a cross-sectional survey design, they may draw an elaborate picture of fears of violence and victimization at one moment in the history of six American cities. Through detailed examination of variations in fear levels within and among cities, they may even be able to suggest the sources or causes of those fears. Other questions, however, will remain largely unanswered. The cross-sectional survey design is sometimes referred to as the "snapshot approach" because

[6] Television news services and polling organizations sometimes sponsor "overnight polls" immediately after major political speeches or events. Usually, such surveys are conducted by telephone, and the results are available within hours.

although the single survey can provide a momentary, representative portrait of a population, it cannot trace the processes of change.

LONGITUDINAL DESIGN. The more suitable procedure for studying the processes of change is the **LONGITUDINAL SURVEY DESIGN** in which *a survey is repeated several times in order to measure the rate and degree of change occurring in patterns of response*. As noted in Chapter 3, one type of longitudinal design, the **TREND STUDY**, consists of *several successive surveys, each based on a different sample of subjects*. Each sample is independently drawn, at regular intervals, from the same general population. Gallup polls are conducted in this way, and comparisons of the results of several different polls can be quite useful for analyzing trends. A single poll indicating that 62 percent of the American people expect the economy to get worse before it gets better would probably be interpreted pessimistically. However, if a trend analysis indicated that only three months earlier 82 percent of those polled felt the economy was going to turn downward, the later finding might be interpreted more optimistically.

Although our ability to study processes of change is greatly enhanced by the trend study, one major limitation of this design seriously reduces the reliability of measured differences that appear between surveys based on separate samples. In such studies changes in patterns of response from one survey to the next arise in part from real shifts in behavior or sentiments and in part from sampling variations. Neither the amount of sampling error in a survey nor its effects on the figures that the survey produces can be assumed to be equal or constant from one survey to the next. Suppose a trend study of attitudes toward capital punishment showed an increase from 60 percent supporting capital punishment in 1995 to 75 percent supporting the same policy in 2005. How reliably can we conclude from these figures that support for capital punishment had increased in a decade? The answer depends on the amount of sampling error that occurred in each survey. It is entirely conceivable that sampling fluctuations deflated the 1995 figure and inflated the

2005 figure and produced an apparent difference larger than any shift that may have actually occurred. Indeed, in trend studies the analyst's attention tends to be drawn to shifts that are abnormally large or small. Unfortunately, these deviations, which may be the most interesting results, are often heavily influenced by sampling error.

PANEL STUDIES. The **PANEL STUDY** is a longitudinal design devised specifically to minimize the effects of sampling error. A sample, or panel, is chosen, and that *same group of respondents is resurveyed at selected intervals*.[7] Thus, the later responses of any subject or category of subjects, or of the sample as a whole, can be directly compared to responses given at an earlier time. The measures of change that are produced by such a design are highly reliable.

Besides eliminating the problem of variation between successive surveys due to sampling error, the panel study has another distinct advantage over other longitudinal survey designs: the sheer volume of information that can be collected from each respondent. The time during which a volunteer subject can be expected to remain cooperative and attentive is limited, and a researcher usually devotes a great deal of that time to collecting necessary background information (e.g., age, race, gender, income, and education). Thus, the limits of comprehensive coverage of relevant topics are fixed by the average respondent's tolerance and attention span. In panel studies, however, there is no need to repeat background questions after the initial interview, so subsequent contacts with subjects can focus progressively more attention on issues at the heart of the inquiry. Moreover, the data accumulated in the successive interviews, when considered as the overall record of an extended investigation, are more detailed and comprehensive than could ever be produced from a single contact. Because of its usefulness for predicting outcomes and because of the relative detail and accuracy with which it re-creates patterns of persuasion and decision

---

[7] See the description of the Terman Study of the Gifted in Chapter 3.

making, the panel study has become a standard tool in the study of voting behavior.[8]

Panel studies are not without their disadvantages and limitations. The sheer cost of repeatedly conducting the same survey creates pressure on the researcher to restrict the size of the initial sample, and as a consequence, the sample's representativeness is restricted as well. This problem is magnified by the inevitable loss of some subjects before the study has been completed. Remember that the longer the study design, the more probable it is that some respondents will lose interest, move without leaving a forwarding address, or die. Some of the problems typical of panel studies are found in the Survey Research Center's Study of Income Dynamics, which initially interviewed individuals in nearly 5,000 households in 1968 and now biennially interviews individuals in nearly 7,000 households.[9] The study has yielded detailed information about economic and demographic behavior as well as social, psychological, health, and lifestyle characteristics of the respondents and that information has been applied to many research questions. Although a great effort has been made to avoid sample loss, after twenty years, only about 50 percent of those members in the original sample remained (Fitzgerald, Gottschalk, and Moffitt, 1998).

Planning a Sampling Strategy

The strengths and weaknesses of alternative sampling methods have already been discussed in detail in Chapter 6. These are of central importance to survey research. In general, probability sampling is desirable, but quota sampling is widely used by commercial pollsters because it is less expensive than other options. The choice of a sampling strategy is most often determined by (1) available funds, (2) the numerical and geographical scope of the survey, (3) the availability of an adequate sampling frame, and (4) the method chosen for collecting the data.

When data are collected by mail or by telephone, it is often possible to do simple random sampling, or even stratified sampling, for no more than the cost of a less complex sampling method. If data are collected through personal interviews, however, methods that involve individually selecting and contacting each subject can consume large amounts of time and money. Funds thus devoted to locating subjects are no longer available for other aspects of the research, and the increased cost per interview may seriously restrict the size of the final sample. These concerns become more and more critical as the geographical dispersion of the target population increases. If the Social Security Administration were to draw a simple random sample of Social Security recipients for personal interviewing, the travel costs involved in locating subjects would far exceed all other expenses. Therefore, national surveys rely on complex, multistage combinations of stratified, quota, and cluster sampling techniques.

The type of probability sample most widely used in survey research is cluster sampling, in which a sample of groups (clusters) is drawn before individuals within them are identified and selected. If, in a given survey, clusters are represented by neighborhoods, travel time and expense may be minimized because interviews could be conducted in concentrated areas, not in households scattered throughout the city. As the area to be covered increases, so also does the potential savings to be derived from the use of a multistage cluster design.

Whatever type of sampling strategy you choose, it must involve vigorous and successful efforts to contact and gain the cooperation of as many members of the sample as possible. Nonresponse is a plague that can ruin any sample, and it must be minimized. Individuals not at home during a door-to-door survey should be followed up by telephone, by mail, or in person. More than one callback is often necessary for that small percentage of subjects who are most difficult to reach, until arrangements are

---

[8] See, for example, Heath and Taylor (1999) and Fournier et al. (2001).

[9] The Panel Study of Income Dynamics (PSID) is conducted by the Survey Research Center of the University of Michigan. Data, information, and a bibliography of the many studies employing PSID data are available at the PSID Web site, http://www.isr.umich.edu/src/psid/. The number of households has increased as the PSID has continued to follow children in the study as they establish households of their own and as families have been added to reflect the changing demographics of American society.

finally made to complete the interview. Similar and equally persistent efforts are necessary in phone or mail surveys.

Despite the researcher's best efforts, surveys nearly always fall short of the ideal of 100 percent cooperation, although some do achieve response rates of 80 percent or better. So, the question inevitably arises: At what point can a rate of response be considered adequate? Unfortunately, there is no simple or direct answer to this question. A low response rate can occur for many reasons and does not necessarily render the sample unrepresentative. It does, however, cast a shadow over the results of the research, and it transfers the burden of proof to the researcher to demonstrate that the sample remains representative and unbiased despite the low rate of response. For this reason, whenever adequate data are available, it is wise to compare the characteristics of respondents to those of nonrespondents. If the two groups from the sample can be shown to be similar in important respects, confidence in the representativeness of the respondents is greatly enhanced.

Choosing a Data-Gathering Technique

Researchers may collect data from subjects through face-to-face interviews, telephone contacts, or self-administered questionnaires. All three approaches allow the same options for the kinds of information that can be gathered. What varies is the degree of personal contact used to obtain the data.

SELF-ADMINISTERED QUESTIONNAIRES. SELF-ADMINISTERED QUESTIONNAIRES are written in two general forms, paper-based and computer-based. Paper-based self-administered questionnaires, whether distributed to a captive audience (as in a classroom) or through the mail, are often the least costly data-gathering technique, for *no interviewers are needed*. This technique has the added advantage of allowing respondents as much time as they require to consider each question carefully before answering. There is no pressure to produce an immediate reply, as there often is perceived to be in an interview, and there is not likely to be any

embarrassment regarding sensitive questions. Some respondents feel more comfortable about expressing their honest reactions to questions on sensitive topics (such as sex, politics, or religion) on a questionnaire than they do in an interview. These advantages, particularly the relatively low cost involved, make the self-administered questionnaire one of the most popular methods of social research.

The major disadvantage of paper-based self-administered questionnaires is their tendency to inspire only a low degree of enthusiasm and involvement in potential respondents. Unstructured questions that require serious consideration (e.g., "What do you think the government ought to be doing about public education?") seldom get more than perfunctory replies. Hence, these questionnaires rely heavily on items that offer predetermined response alternatives and thus can seldom probe issues in any real depth. Worse yet, the most typical reaction to a mail survey is to throw it away! The rate of response to mail questionnaires is considerably lower than that for either face-to-face or telephone interviews. Although homogeneous populations tend to be fairly responsive, when a cross section of the population is surveyed by mail, return rates of 10 percent or less are common.

The prevailing low rates of return for paper-based self-administered questionnaires may stem from subjects' unwillingness or inability to reply. A skilled interviewer can help almost any subject through a set of questions, but approximately 14 percent of the adults in the American workforce have very limited reading proficiencies (U.S. Department of Education, National Center for Education Statistics, 2003)[10] and thus would likely have difficulty completing even simple self-administered questionnaires. Complex questionnaires would certainly pose a strong challenge to even larger numbers of the workforce as well as the population in general. The most carefully selected sample is unlikely to

[10] The data are from the National Adult Literacy Study. Rather than classifying adults as simply literate or illiterate, the study measured literacy proficiencies along three scales. The National Center for Educational Statistics Web site can be found at http//:nces.ed.gov.

remain cross-sectionally representative if only a small fraction of those sampled choose to reply.

The self-administered questionnaire also transfers a great deal of control from the researcher to the subject. If some subjects fill out their questionnaires hastily or without reflection, or if some subjects seek the aid of friends or family members, the researcher has no way of detecting or controlling these disturbing influences – no way even of estimating their effects.

As information technologies have become important in virtually all aspects of scientific research, so too have they become a part of survey research administration. In recent years, computer-based systems have aided the process of survey research, including self-administered questionnaires. One recent technological development in self-administered survey research is the use of the Internet or personal computers to allow respondents to read and respond to the survey. These computer surveys are often much easier to follow than paper-based surveys because the computer can be programmed to prohibit ineligible responses and to present to respondents only those questions that are relevant to them. To use the Internet, survey researchers can establish Web sites to display the survey instrument. To ensure privacy and restrict the survey to those chosen in the sample, an identification number can be assigned to each of the potential respondents. A CD-ROM containing the survey can be provided to those selected in the sample, who then take the survey on their own computers and return the CD to the researcher after the survey is complete. One problem with Internet- and computer-based surveys is that that those technologies are not always available to all potential respondents. Unless the population of interest has access to the technology, the survey results may be invalid. Having kiosks or a survey administration center available where people may come to take the survey is one way around this problem.

Another development in the use of self-administered surveys, **AUDIO COMPUTER-ASSISTED SELF-INTERVIEWING** (ACASI) tech-

nology, *allows survey participants to listen to a digitally recorded interview over headphones and enter responses through a number on a computer keyboard*. The respondent can also read the survey on the computer screen simultaneously. ACASI offers survey researchers some important advantages over other forms of self-administered or face-to-face surveys. First, because it is audio-based, respondents with literacy deficiencies are able to participate with greater success than they could with paper-based or text-based computer surveys. Second, some evidence indicates that respondents are more likely to volunteer sensitive information with ACASI surveys than with face-to-face surveys (Turner et al., 1998). Third, as with all **COMPUTER-ASSISTED INTERVIEWING** (CAI), the researcher is able to program the computer to ask the respondent only relevant questions (so-called skip patterns) and to have those *responses entered directly into a database* for later analysis. The National Health and Nutrition Survey, which is conducted by the National Center for Health Statistics at the Centers for Disease Control and Prevention, uses ACASI technology for part of its survey.[11]

FACE-TO-FACE INTERVIEWS. In general, the best data-gathering technique for survey research, if the interviewers are well trained and the substantial expense involved can be met, is the **FACE-TO-FACE INTERVIEW**. Face-to-face interviews allow the researcher to collect data from a much larger percentage of those sampled than is usually possible with self-administered questionnaires. Subjects tend to be more impressed with the seriousness of a study when *the researcher contacts them personally* than when they receive a form letter and questionnaire through the mail. Personal contact may make an interview seem far less routine and standardized, and it is also far more difficult for a subject to refuse an interviewer in person than it is to relegate a questionnaire to the wastebasket.

---

[11] See http://www.cdc.gov/nchs/nhanes.htm for more information and for links to other National Center for Health Statistics studies.

The presence of an interviewer can also improve the quality, as well as the quantity, of responses from each subject. If a subject does not understand a question, the interviewer can clarify its meaning. If a respondent's answer seems not to fit the intent of the question, the alert interviewer will seek clarification through the use of a **PROBE** – asking, *for example, "Could you explain exactly what you mean by that?"* Such probes can both clarify and add depth to the information the respondent is providing. A trained interviewer also heightens the validity of the data by detecting and weeding out insincere respondents and obviously false replies.

In recent years, some face-to-face interviewers have begun doing **COMPUTER-ASSISTED PERSONAL INTERVIEWING** (CAPI). When using CAPI *the interviewer reads the survey from a computer* (usually a laptop) *and then enters the responses directly during the interview*. Because the data are entered during the interview, they do not have to be entered again after the interview is completed, thus saving a step in the research process. The in-home interviews of the Bureau of Labor Statistics' *Current Population Survey* are now carried out using CAPI.[12]

TELEPHONE SURVEYS. Less expensive than face-to-face interviews, telephone surveys avoid many of the problems that can arise when mailed questionnaires are used and, within certain limits, can meet a variety of research needs effectively. Telephone interviews generally cost less than half as much as the same number of face-to-face interviews, and the availability of toll-free telephone service has further reduced costs while extending the useful range of the telephone survey. Researchers with very limited resources often find it within their means to conduct regional, statewide, or even national surveys by telephone. Because in a telephone survey all contacts can be made from a single location, the researcher is better able to monitor the quality of work done by hired interviewers.

Early telephone surveys developed an unfortunate reputation for sampling bias because

some categories of respondents tended not to have telephones, while others tended to have unlisted numbers. The potential for such bias greatly diminished over the years. The telephone has become so standard an item that the poor are no longer necessarily underrepresented (except, perhaps, in rural areas). In fact, in some inner-city neighborhoods plagued with high crime rates, potential subjects of face-to-face interviews may pretend that they are not home or refuse to let the interviewer in because they fear strangers. The biases incurred by this refusal to cooperate may often be far greater than the bias created by missing those individuals who have no phone. As a result, phone surveys can sometimes better represent the poor than door-to-door surveys.

Another potential source of bias in telephone surveys is that so many people have unlisted phone numbers. This problem has actually increased in recent years because of the prevalence of cell phones for which there are no central directories to serve as sampling frames (see Chapter 6). If there is a relationship between having an unlisted telephone number and demographic variables or opinions about the issues being researched, then relying only on listed telephone numbers may introduce a bias into the results. Researchers get around this problem and reach people who have unlisted telephone numbers through the technique known as **RANDOM-DIGIT DIALING**. If the researcher knows the exchanges (the first three numbers) in the areas under study, the last four digits can be chosen by a random method, and *all telephone numbers, listed or unlisted, will have an equal chance of being dialed*.

A limitation of telephone surveys is the length of time involved in a telephone interview. A contact that will run more than fifteen or twenty minutes may be refused or prematurely terminated by the subject. This reduces the amount of information that can be gathered to between one-third and one-half of the data usually collected in a face-to-face interview. Questions must also be kept fairly simple because no written lists or illustrations can be displayed as aids to the subject's understanding. On balance,

---

[12] See http://www.bls.census.gov/cps/ for more information.

however, if the topic of your research is relatively brief and straightforward, the telephone survey may prove an accurate, representative, and cost-effective option.

One potential problem with telephone surveys that may not be easily resolved is the widespread usage of call-screening devices such as caller identification systems and answering machines. These technologies have made the task of contacting respondents more difficult and that difficulty will likely increase.

While call-screening devices have interfered with telephone respondents, other new technologies have benefited the administration of telephone surveys in recent years. First, through the use of COMPUTER-ASSISTED TELEPHONE INTERVIEWING (CATI), the process of administering and tabulating telephone surveys is much easier than with paper or booklet surveys. With CATI, *interviewers read the survey to the respondent from a computer screen and enter responses directly* similar to how CAPI is used for face-to-face interviewing. CATI is now commonly used by large telephone survey organizations.

Another recent innovation in telephone survey administration is TELEPHONE AUDIO COMPUTER-ASSISTED SELF-INTERVIEWING technology, T-ACASI. Recall from the section on self-administered questionnaires on page 128 that ACASI technology allows surveys to be *administered over computers with digitally recorded audio files*. T-ACASI systems work similarly, but the survey is conducted over the telephone rather than in front of a computer screen. T-ACASI systems can be programmed to accept audio responses or telephone keypad responses. An important potential of T-ACASI is that it will encourage respondents to reveal more sensitive information than they would to live interviewers. Certainly, if research efforts prove that respondents reliably volunteer more sensitive information to T-ACASI systems than to live interviewers, then those systems will be a great benefit to health survey research.[13] Another potential benefit of T-ACASI systems

is that they standardize the administration of phone surveys. With these systems, every respondent hears the questions asked with the same emphasis and intonation. Such consistency should eliminate potential interviewer bias in survey administration.

Formulating Questionnaire Items

All three data-gathering techniques (through the mail, face-to-face, and by telephone) are based on a set of questions to which subjects are asked to reply. The generation of measures for concepts – specifically, the transformation of research objectives into carefully chosen questions – is one of the most important steps in the survey research process. It is also a critical opportunity to employ the research imagination. In this section, the types of questions most often used in surveys and the general rules for determining the form in which these questions are to be presented to the subject will be considered.

QUESTION CONTENT. In general, the content of specific questionnaire items should be determined by the goals of the research project. Questions should be as direct and as relevant to research objectives as possible. There are four types of data that are most often sought in surveys: (1) information about the respondents' backgrounds, (2) information about their activities (past and present behavior and experiences), (3) information about their knowledge, and (4) information about their sentiments (opinions, values, attitudes, and feelings).

Background questions are designed to elicit respondents' personal history and current situation (sex, race, income, religion, marital status, age, education, ethnic group, and so on). Usually, these data are gathered to check the representativeness of the sample and to enable the researcher to make statistical comparisons of DEMOGRAPHIC CATEGORIES (*men/women, old/young, etc.*) with regard to variations in their patterns of response to other questionnaire items. Though these questions are both necessary and basic, some subjects may feel that they are embarrassing or too personal. This

[13] The University of Massachusetts Tobacco Study of 2000/2001 used T-ACASI in an effort to determine whether it would improve the reporting of smoking behavior among youth.

reaction can be minimized if the researcher words the questions carefully and waits to ask them until a degree of understanding and rapport has been established with the respondent. It is often helpful for the interviewer to explain why the questions need to be asked and to remind the subject that all responses will be kept in confidence.

By the same token, questions about a person's activities and experiences can seem too personal unless the respondent sees them as justified. Instead of apologizing for questions, or unduly calling attention to their somewhat personal nature, you may find it most effective to simply phrase and organize them in ways that make their relevance to the stated purposes of your research apparent. A subject should never have to wonder, let alone ask, what bearing a question has on the objectives of the research.

Along with the appearance of relevance, questions should always be as specific as possible. The following item is designed to elicit information about respondents' voting behavior:

How often do you vote in national elections?

1. Always

2. Often

3. Seldom

4. Never

The question is worded clearly, but it is very general. A more specific question would ask:

Did you vote in last month's national election?

1. Yes

2. No

The more specific question could then be followed by another:

In how many of the last five national elections have you voted? (Indicate the number, from 1 to 5, in which you cast a ballot.)

What are the advantages of the second scheme? First, because it is a general precept of American civics that every responsible adult citizen ought to vote, many more people feel they should vote than actually do. The first question almost invites the occasional voter to magnify his or her civic image by liberally interpreting the word often. The second scheme, however, first ties honest respondents (as most are) to the memory of their most recent vote or nonvote, and then poses a more general question in a way that elicits from the respondent a very definite answer. Also, asking about the last five national elections, instead of asking about national elections in general, reflects a more reasonable view of the limits of the respondent's memory. Moreover, the responses that will result from the second scheme will convey a great deal more information: The percentage of people who say they voted in three or more of the last five national elections is a much more meaningful, definite, and interpretable finding than the percentage of people who say that they vote "often" in such elections.

Questions about a person's sentiments are probably the most common items found on questionnaires. Views about the future of the nation's economy, attitudes toward abortion, beliefs about the poor, opinions regarding law enforcement and the court system, evaluations of the president's performance, and similar public and private sentiments are the staples of survey research. However, such questions can be misused or overused if the objectives of the research are not kept in mind constantly while the individual questions are being framed. Before you decide to ask an attitude question, be certain that you are really most interested in what the subject feels. Beginning researchers sometimes mistakenly ask a person's opinion when the research design would be better served by asking what a person knows or how a person acts. As a rule, questions should be framed so that data do not become more subjective than they need to be. Remember also that subjects are less likely, consciously or unconsciously, to misrepresent facts about their behavior than they are to idealize their inner and unverifiable attitudes and preferences. Questions concerning attitudes are most effective when they are related to concrete realities by being combined with questions concerning behavior.

Questions concerning knowledge are asked sometimes for their own sake and sometimes for use as FILTER QUESTIONS to *determine which respondents have sufficient information on an issue to provide meaningful opinions.* Consider the following question that was asked in the General Social Survey (Davis, Smith, and Marsden, 2005):

Have you heard or read about the recent U.S. Supreme Court decision concerning abortion?

1. Yes

2. No

This question, aside from its intrinsic content, could have been used to screen people before deciding to ask them whether they agree or disagree with the position of the U.S. Supreme Court regarding abortion. Surprisingly, many respondents will automatically agree or disagree with things they know nothing about rather than admit ignorance on an issue. Questions should be carefully worded to avoid the implicit assumption that "everyone knows and should have an opinion," thus making it easier for respondents to gracefully withhold uninformed comment.

Sometimes, rather than merely testing knowledge, a question can convey information to provide the respondent with a context for expressing an opinion. Consider the following example (Davis, Smith, and Marsden, 2005):

The U.S. Supreme Court has ruled that no state or local government can require the reading of the Lord's Prayer or Bible verses in the public schools. What are your views on this? Do you approve or disapprove of the Court's ruling?

1. Approve

2. Disapprove

3. No opinion/neutral

This question has the advantage of assuring that all respondents will share a minimum factual background, which improves their competency to answer.

The content of questions should never be treated as obvious or predetermined. Content is as much a function of what the subject perceives as what the researcher intends. So, in deciding exactly what to ask respondents, always keep in mind: (1) your own intentions, (2) the impression a question is likely to make on subjects, and (3) the response motivations (particularly the desire to appear knowledgeable and to express the "right" opinions) your questions are likely to arouse.

MULTIPLE INDICATORS. Questionnaire items should be thought of as indicators of the concepts that underlie the research design. As such, they can at best only roughly reproduce the ideas the researcher has in mind. This is especially true of items that deal with matters of subjective disposition and of items that measure complex and abstract concepts. Because of this, questionnaires frequently contain several closely related items that are intended to measure a complex or subtle concept from different angles and in slightly different ways.

Let us look again at *anomie*, a sense of isolation in a world without guiding values. Though the concept of anomie may be clear, ways of measuring it are not so clear. As a composite measure of anomie, survey researchers usually devise a series of related questions (multiple indicators) such as those in Table 7.1.

It is unlikely that any one of these questions alone could serve as a valid and reliable indicator of anomie because several factors probably affect each person's response to each question. The overall pattern of responses to the group of related questions may be substantially more accurate and dependable as an indicator of anomie. Thus, the use of a series of related questions to produce multiple measures of a single concept has become a regular and important part of effective questionnaire construction.

STRUCTURED VERSUS UNSTRUCTURED QUESTIONS. Two kinds of questions are used in questionnaires: STRUCTURED (CLOSED-ENDED) QUESTIONS AND UNSTRUCTURED (OPEN-ENDED) QUESTIONS. *Structured questions provide a set of fixed alternatives from which the*

> **Table 7.1.** Multiple Indicators
>
> **Please indicate whether you agree or disagree with each of the following statements:**
>
> Sometimes I can't help wondering whether anything is worthwhile anymore.
>   a. Agree
>   b. Disagree
>
> To make money, there are no right and wrong ways anymore, only easy ways and hard ways.
>   a. Agree
>   b. Disagree
>
> Nowadays a person pretty much has to live for today and let tomorrow take care of itself.
>   a. Agree
>   b. Disagree
>
> It's hardly fair to bring a child into the world with the ways things look for the future.
>   a. Agree
>   b. Disagree
>
> Most people don't really care what happens to the next fellow.
>   a. Agree
>   b. Disagree
>
> Adapted from Davis, Smith, and Marsden (2005).

respondent must choose a reply. The following example is adapted from Davis, Smith, and Marsden (2005):

> Would you favor or oppose a law that would require a person to obtain a police permit before he or she could buy a gun?
>
> 1. Favor
>
> 2. Oppose
>
> 3. Don't know

Structured questions are relatively easy to answer, and the responses are easy to code and record as data. If the researchers know what they want from the question and can anticipate most or all of the ways in which respondents will be inclined to answer, structured questions are both efficient and appropriate. *Unstructured questions permit respondents to answer as they see fit, and encourage free and lengthy discussion*:

> What, in your view, would be the major advantages or disadvantages of a strict gun-control law?

Substantial space must be left for the respondent to write an answer to the questions or for the interviewer to record as much of what the respondent says as possible.

Unstructured questions are most useful when researchers expect an issue to provoke a wide range of responses or when responses are likely to be quite detailed. However, such questions should not be mistaken for, or substituted for, the kind of involved exploration and probing that characterizes intensive interviews – a wholly different research method.[14] Neither should they be expected to produce revealing or provocative in-depth responses. In fact, heavy use of unstructured questions can lead to great disappointment, in that respondents will

[14] See Chapter 8.

frequently either neglect to respond to such items or provide only brief, superficial answers.

In interviews, when open-ended questions fit more naturally into the conversational atmosphere, they can be quite useful as general introductions to subjects that the interviewer will later probe with more specific, structured queries. In this situation, the unstructured question helps to create a proper context for a line of inquiry to follow by encouraging the respondent to sort out ideas and feelings and to establish a clear frame of reference.

QUESTION WORDING. Questions should be worded in the most concise and direct way possible, avoiding both technical jargon and patronizing overelaboration. The meaning of every question must be clear to all respondents. Never assume that vocabulary common among social scientists will have meaning for any other group, let alone for all the individuals represented in a cross section. Let us examine the following questionnaire item:

> Do you favor or oppose the current effort to reduce taxes by making government more accountable and less wasteful?
>
> 1. Favor
> 2. Oppose
> 3. No opinion

The wording of this question violates several important standards of research practice. First, it is **LOADED**. It is so *biased* that a respondent would find it difficult to oppose a "tax revolt" in these terms. Questions are loaded or slanted whenever their wording even subtly suggests that one response is preferable to another. The question is also **DOUBLE-BARRELED**: It *presents the subject with more than a single issue to respond to*. In this case, people who favor making government "more accountable and less wasteful" (laudable goals that no responsible citizen could oppose!) but who do not favor tax cuts are placed in a dilemma by the wording. Complex questions, often requiring involved responses do not fit well within the limits of survey techniques, especially the limits of the self-administered questionnaire. If complex issues are to be studied by means of a survey, they must first be broken down into a series of one-dimensional questions.

Slanting can also occur, despite neutral wording of the question, if the fixed responses presented to the subject do not cover the entire range of potential replies. Here is an example:

> How many politicians do you think are a little bit corrupt?
>
> 1. All
> 2. Most
> 3. A few
> 4. None

Although the range of possible reactions seems to be covered, how should someone reply who believes that the great majority of politicians are much more than "a little bit" corrupt? The researcher has put the respondent into the strange position where the reply "none" is most logical and truthful but least likely to convey what the subject intends.

As mentioned in Chapter 4, the responses to any closed-ended question must be mutually exclusive and exhaustive. In addition, a respondent should not be able to skim through a questionnaire, blissfully agreeing or disagreeing with everything in sight. Instead, "agree–disagree," "yes–no," or "favor–oppose" choices should be interspersed with other sets of response options that restate the substance of the question.

Look at the following item:

> What connection, if any, exists between your present job and your college education?
>
> 1. I work at the specific career for which I was trained.
> 2. The work I do is related to my major field.
> 3. Though not directly related to my major field, the work I do draws on my college education.
> 4. My work is unrelated to my college education.

Now compare the wording of that question with the wording of the one that follows:

Table 7.2. Balancing Agree–Disagree Items

1. A working mother can establish just as warm and secure relationship with her children as a mother who does not work.
   a. Strongly agree   b. Agree   c. No opinion   d. Disagree   e. Strongly disagree

2. A preschool child is likely to suffer if his mother works.
   a. Strongly agree   b. Agree   c. No opinion   d. Disagree   e. Strongly disagree

3. It is better for everyone involved if the man is the achiever outside the home and woman takes care of the home and family.
   a. Strongly agree   b. Agree   c. No opinion   d. Disagree   e. Strongly disagree

4. It is just as important for the wife to have a career of her own as it is for the husband to have one.
   a. Strongly agree   b. Agree   c. No opinion   d. Disagree   e. Strongly disagree

---

Adapted from Davis, Smith, and Marsden (2005).

How related is your present work to the education you received in college?

1. Closely related

2. Somewhat related

3. Unrelated

Although both questions have similar intent, the first version repeats the substance of the question in the responses. This helps to elicit more specific and informative data by directing the respondent to consider the question more carefully. The "contentful" response format also counteracts the tendency of some subjects to respond agreeably or disagreeably (according to their general dispositions, irrespective of the issues being addressed) in a patterned and unreflective way.

Another strategy that counters yea-saying (a pattern of agreement) and nay-saying (a pattern of disagreement) is the use of contradictory questionnaire items. As Table 7.2 illustrates, the respondent cannot simply agree or disagree with all statements without demonstrating gross inconsistency.

Constructing the Questionnaire

The principles of questionnaire construction remain fairly constant, regardless of whether the questionnaire is being prepared for self-administration or as a "schedule" to guide the inter-action between interviewer and subject. Both form and content must be considered, especially when subjects have only the printed questionnaire as a guide. Seemingly minor details regarding the organization, phrasing, and order of the questionnaire items and the recording of responses can make the difference between a successful research effort and a quagmire of confusion and frustration.

INTRODUCTION. Every questionnaire should have an introduction that explains what the study is about in a way that captures the attention of potential respondents, impresses them with the importance of the study and their participation in it, and assures them that all data will be handled in a way that protects their identity. If the study can be linked to a sponsor known and trusted by members of the target population, identification of the sponsor in the introduction can have dramatic results on the rate of response. Presenting a survey as a "class project," for example, is generally less effective than identifying it with the college or university in which that class project is being conducted.

The serious tone of the introduction will encourage potential subjects to treat the questionnaire seriously and to respond to the items conscientiously. The tone of the introduction must also be neutral. If controversial issues are to be covered in the questionnaire, nothing in the introduction should give the respondent the impression that the researcher advocates a particular attitude or is interested in eliciting a particular set of opinions. On the contrary, subjects must be impressed with the researcher's sincere desire that they express their own ideas, lest they instead express views intended to be agreeable to the researcher.

INSTRUCTIONS. Instructions prepared by the researcher for an interviewer may be quite elaborate, with several pages of general guidelines separate from the interview schedule and with many specific directions and reminders interspersed throughout the schedule. The guidelines for a self-administered questionnaire should be much simpler. They should include a clear explanation of how responses are to be indicated: by checking, by circling, or by other means. The respondent's attention should be drawn to any questions that require or allow more than one response. Also, if the questionnaire contains some items that pertain only to a subset of the respondents, the rest should be explicitly directed to omit the items to which they are not expected to respond. In the absence of explicit instructions, subjects will often improvise, but improvisation does not promote uniform, interpretable data.

SEQUENCE OF QUESTIONS. Because questionnaires are useless unless subjects are willing to fill them out, the researcher's initial aim must be to capture the potential respondent's attention. In an interview situation, where there is the additional necessity of developing rapport, or a personal connection, between interviewer and respondent, opening questions should also be general, nonthreatening, and easy to respond to.

The body of the questionnaire should consist of questions on a progression of topics, following some logical pattern that the respondent is likely to recognize and that will promote an orderly interchange between interviewer and subject. Sometimes the very nature of the material to be covered by the questionnaire suggests the best method of organization; at other times, only trial and error can determine what pattern will most effectively produce rapport and easy communi-

cation. If necessary, alternate schemes can be evaluated when pretesting (see p. 138) the questionnaire to iron out any minor problems it may contain.

When dealing with questions on the same subtopic, most researchers prefer to organize their queries from the more general items to the more specific. A series of questions on "issues of the day" might begin with a general item:

> What, in your view, are the most important issues facing the American people today?

This might then be followed by a more specific "issues inventory":

> Here is a list of ten issues and concerns currently facing the United States.
> We would like to know which of these you consider the most important and which seem to you the least important.
> (A list of the ten issues would then follow.)

The interviewer might then guide the respondent to rank all issues from 1 (most important) to 10 (least important). If the general question is intended to encourage the respondent to identify important issues other than those listed in the inventory, it must precede the more specific one. Otherwise, the answer to the general question will tend to mirror the issues identified on the researcher's list and will likely generate redundant data.

Finally, sensitive questions should be reserved for the end of the questionnaire. By this time, the subject is accustomed to replying and probably feels at ease with the interviewer. Careful wording, which makes personal questions seem less obtrusive and offensive, can greatly increase the rate of response. Let us compare these two items:

> Unemployment has been steadily increasing in the United States for the past two years. During this time have you yourself been affected by this growing problem?
> At any time during the past two years have you lost a job or been laid off?

The second question would probably stimulate a less open and frank exchange than the first.

Surveys, unlike cross-examinations, do not seek a confession. They must respect, appreciate, and foster the goodwill of those respondents kind enough to give their time and share their experiences.

LAYOUT AND RESPONSE FORMAT. For a self-administered questionnaire, the layout of questions and response alternatives on the page or screen can seriously affect the ease, accuracy, and completeness with which subjects respond. Issues surrounding the layout and formatting of self-administered questionnaires differ depending on whether the survey is computer or paper based. Computer-based surveys, whether audio or text based, can be constructed in a way that makes them very clear for the respondent to follow. The correct mode of response is made clear at the beginning of the survey and remains consistent throughout, and respondents do not have to worry about following instructions to skip to other sections of the survey because the computer presents all relevant questions in their proper order.

For paper-based surveys the issues of layout and response format are more complex. Questions should be spread out evenly on the page, with sufficient blank space between them for subjects to note easily where one item ends and another begins and to enable subjects to comment fully on all questions. This is especially important for items with subparts, for items with special instructions, and for filter items that are to be answered by only some of the respondents. Careful layout helps to minimize two problems: (1) subjects' failure to respond to questions intended for them and (2) subjects' tendency to respond inappropriately to questions because they have misunderstood them or because they did not realize that the questions were not intended for them.

The mode for indicating responses on paper-based surveys should be made clear to respondents at the outset. It is helpful to include a sample question with the appropriate response clearly and properly marked. The absence of explicit instructions will lead subjects to improvise often in strange and undecipherable ways.

Respondents can be directed to record their answers in a variety of ways:

Please indicate your gender.

| ___X___ Male | ☑ Male | ① Male |
| ___X___ Female | ☑ Female | ② Female |

The third alternative, circling a number that stands for the correct response, has the advantage of indicating simultaneously what the subject's response is and how that response is to be coded for data processing. This eliminates an error-prone intermediate step in the transfer of responses to a data file.

When a *filter*, or **CONTINGENCY QUESTION,** is used to identify a subgroup of respondents for further questioning on paper-based surveys, explicit instructions should direct subjects to the next item they are supposed to answer. Using a page of a different color can help to isolate a series of questions intended for a specific category of respondents. Figure 7.1 shows the use of arrows and special indentation and verbal instructions in the layout of a page.

Schemes in which one set of questions applies to one group of subjects and a different set applies to the remainder are common in interview surveys, but they are considerably more difficult to build into self-administered questionnaires. As the contingency scheme becomes more complex, the chances increase for confusion on the part of the respondent. However, the difference between a successful contingency questioning scheme and an unsuccessful one can be the physical layout.

When you design any type of questionnaire, it is wise to assume the worst – that many respondents will rush through it, more motivated to simply finish than to be thorough and accurate. If you word the questions and design the layout to politely but effectively focus the respondent's attention, the resulting data will be useful and informative.

Response formats on interview schedules are usually similar to those on self-administered questionnaires, although issues of style are not as crucial when a trained interviewer is

25. Did you vote in the 2004 presidential elections?

   a. No (*Skip to Question 28.*)

   b. Yes

             26. Did you vote for Bush, Kerry, or some other candidate?

                  a. Bush

                  b. Kerry

                  c. Other (please specify for whom you voted):

                  _____

             27. How strongly did you prefer the candidate for whom you voted

                to other candidates?

                  a. Very strongly   c. Weakly

                  b. Strongly   d. Very weakly

             Please skip to Question 29

28. If you had cast a ballot in 2004, which candidate would have been your choice?

   a. Bush

   b. Kerry

   c. Other (please specify): _____

   d. No preference

Figure 7.1. Layout of contingency items.

recording the answers. Sensitive or personal questions, however, do pose a special problem for the interviewer. To minimize uneasiness or embarrassment in subjects completing personal interviews, the response choices to questions such as "Could you indicate which of the following income ranges your earnings for last year fell into?" are often printed on a card that the interviewer hands to the subject when asking the question. The respondent can simply indicate to the interviewer the appropriate category (by its code number) without actually talking about the sensitive topic.

PRETESTING. No amount of care and planning can ensure that the questionnaire will have the intended effect in all respects. For this reason, the assumptions and judgments that go into questionnaire design should be tested before the actual survey begins. A **PRETEST** involves *drawing a very small sample of subjects, conducting interviews or administering a questionnaire, and noting all the problems that arise* for the interviewers and for the subjects. The subjects should be encouraged to comment freely about the questions themselves, as well as about the issues they address. In effect, an interview takes place within and about that interview. The pretest often suggests necessary or desirable changes in wording, format, or layout; identifies ineffective questions that should be deleted; and sometimes uncovers new issues to which additional questions should be addressed. If hired interviewers are being used, the researcher should also solicit their reactions during the pretesting phase.

SURVEY EXECUTION

After the plans have been formulated and the pretest has been conducted, a number of problems may arise in carrying out your survey. In this section, the major difficulties associated with implementing research using either self-administered questionnaires or interviews are considered.

The Self-Administered Survey

The main problem associated with self-administered surveys that are not completed at a central location such as a kiosk is their characteristically low rate of return. Questionnaires received by mail are often mistaken for "junk mail" and ignored or discarded. Several techniques can be used to make mail surveys more appealing, thereby increasing the rate of response.

The introductory letter that accompanies the questionnaire should emphasize the importance of the research and appeal to the altruism of potential respondents. Such an appeal is realistic and, as many researchers have discovered, proves more effective than the suggestion that the subject has something to gain by participating. The inclusion of a "reward" – a pen or a small amount of money – also improves the rate of response, probably because it is a token of the researcher's sincere appreciation rather than because of its actual value.

The longer the questionnaire, the lower the response rate tends to be. So, mail surveys, whether paper-based or on a CD, must be restricted to essential questions. Perhaps because they seem less impersonal, pre-stamped, individually typed return envelopes produce higher return rates than do business-reply envelopes. Surveys that involve some personal contact, either at the outset or in later follow-ups with nonrespondents, show markedly better returns than those that rely exclusively on the mail.

Finally, and most important, mail surveys require aggressive and unrelenting follow-up. Second and third mailings can often prod listless subjects into responding to and returning the questionnaire. Telephoning can be an effective way of reminding people that they have not completed their questionnaires. If reminders have been sent and have received no response, a personal call can sometimes result in a successful telephone interview. Thorough follow-up campaigns can often increase the rate of response to a mail survey by as much as 50 percent.

Even if all these techniques for increasing the rate of response in a mail survey are employed, it is unlikely that more than 70 percent of the questionnaires will be returned. When between a third and two-thirds of the subjects in a sample do not respond, the researcher should attempt to evaluate the possibility that this process of "self-selection" has introduced sample bias. Suppose a mail survey is sent to a random sample of students at your college, and 60 percent of the subjects return completed questionnaires. Information from the survey about the respondents' age, race, sex, and major can be compared to similar data about the composition of the entire student body. If this comparison shows no startling differences between the 60 percent of the sample who replied and the student body as a whole, we could probably be justified in concluding that the respondents are representative of the entire group (although other important differences between respondents and nonrespondents may be undiscovered).

The Interview Survey

Most personal interview surveys, depending on the size of the sample, require a team of interviewers so that no one person is burdened with an unwieldy or unduly protracted task. Whether the interviews are conducted by hired assistants or by a team of cooperating researchers (as in a class project), it is essential that the interviewers be consistent in their understanding of the questions and in their manner of approaching and dealing with respondents. To ensure consistency and similarity among interviewers requires not only extensive discussion, common training, and practice but also coordination and control by the chief investigator, who supervises the entire operation. The following discussion explores some of the major considerations and techniques that a chief investigator should emphasize and that interviewers should bear in mind and follow.

PREPARATION. All interviewers must become thoroughly familiar with both the objectives of the study and the item-by-item content of the interview schedule. The interviewer should use the exact wording that has been set down for every question; however, he or she should not seem to be reading! A good survey interview is ideally a scripted, but conversational, encounter between interviewer and subject, during which both feel at ease. For the interviewer, as for an actor, this means appearing spontaneous and at ease while rigidly adhering to the questions as asked. No one achieves this balance of ease and control without being thoroughly immersed in the intent of the research and in its execution.

Hired interviewers must be thoroughly prepared for their tasks; otherwise, their limited involvement in the overall project may lead to errors and misunderstandings that could undermine the quality of the data. Interviewers who are aware of the overall sampling strategy, for example, are more likely to resist the temptation to avoid approaching valid but inconvenient potential subjects (such as those who live on dark streets, who work at odd hours, or who live three flights up). Interviewers need to be impressed with the importance of proceeding consistently and following instructions. Group training of interviewers helps to ensure this consistency. Finally, interviewers, even more than respondents, must be convinced of the significance of the research project.

A manual of interviewer specifications, gleaned from past experience and from the results of the pretest, should accompany the questionnaire. The manual should provide item-by-item instructions about what to do when faced with any conceivable problem. Typically included are suggestions for clarifying a question by explaining the meaning or its wording if a subject does not seem to understand it or asks for an explanation. The manual may also contain helpful probes that the interviewer can use to encourage the respondent who initially expresses no opinion on a question or who responds with "I don't know." To accommodate the variable statuses of respondents

(for example, widows, single parents, the unemployed, members of minority groups), some slight rewording of questions may be necessary; in such cases the manual should specify exactly how the wording is to be modified.

DEVELOPING RAPPORT. Rapport between subject and interviewer depends on many factors, including familiarity with the role being enacted. Because subjects are seldom experienced in the role of survey respondent, the interviewer must orient them and place them at ease. First, dress in a manner appropriate to the neighborhood in which you are conducting the interview, yet one that reflects the professional nature of your work. Establish your own identity. Show whatever credentials you have to avoid being mistaken for a salesperson, a bill collector, or a potential burglar. If possible, interviewers should be matched with the average traits of their subjects to facilitate recognition and communication.

Once the interview is under way, convey a nonjudgmental attitude toward the subject and toward the subject's responses. With a series of nods or brief verbal expressions of encouragement ("yes," "uh-huh"), you can let the subject know that you are eager to hear and record whatever opinions are offered. However, you must be careful not to inadvertently encourage the respondent to offer pleasing replies; offer the same level of encouragement whether you like or dislike what you hear.

PROVIDING A UNIFORM STIMULUS. For statistical comparisons between the responses of different groups of subjects to have any meaning whatsoever, the researcher must be able to assume that they all were asked the same questions in the same way. This requirement dictates that all interviewers adhere to the exact order and wording of questions as they appear in the interview schedule. It also demands a degree of control over the tone of voice in which an interviewer asks a question since changes in inflection can substantially alter the subject's interpretation of a question even though the wording is followed exactly. The question, "Do you sometimes drink more than you should?" would produce more admissions if the word "sometimes" were emphasized than it would if the word "drink" were emphasized. Practice and discipline help an interviewer to establish an appropriate tone and to maintain it from one interview to the next.

PROBING. In most instances, questionnaires that have been carefully designed and pretested will pose little problem for subjects. Questions should be asked slowly and clearly; any misunderstanding can usually be dealt with by repeating the item.

Because surveys may solicit a wide range of opinions and feelings from subjects, it is not always sufficient for a question to be clear; a question must also stimulate and encourage respondents to express their personal views freely and fully. One of the major advantages of the personal interview is the opportunity it gives the interviewer to immediately evaluate the completeness of the responses. When confronted with reticent subjects who, out of shyness or lack of confidence in the worth or accuracy of their own views, claim to have no opinion or offer only short and unrevealing relies to open-ended questions, the skillful interviewer will use a variety of neutral probes to encourage fuller and more relevant replies. Often a momentary pause can convey your expectation that the respondent ought to have more to say. Simply repeating the subject's reply may bring forth a good deal of elaboration. Brief, nonloaded questions – "Could you explain that a bit more?" "Could you elaborate?" "Any other reasons?" "Why do you say that?" "Any other ideas on that?" – can be very productive. Although some subjects occasionally have no opinion to offer, many others simply need a little time to work out their ideas on an issue or a little encouragement to overcome their hesitation about offering their opinions. Lack of assertiveness on the part of a subject should never be taken for lack of a point of view, and the artful use of probes may help to compensate for the subject's reticence.

RECORDING RESPONSES. Most survey interviews involve a mix of closed-ended and open-ended questions. Recording the replies to closed-ended questions is usually simple and straightforward, but recording the replies to open-ended questions can be challenging. You should make every attempt to record responses verbatim, writing or typing key words instead of whole sentences if necessary, but returning to complete the record after the interview is over. Start to record as soon as the subject begins to reply, looking up occasionally to maintain some eye contact. Try to avoid distracting the subject or holding up the interview with your note taking, so that the conversational atmosphere will not be lost. When you use probes, put them in parentheses in the record or in a comment box on the computer to distinguish your remarks from those of the subject. Finally, when the interview is complete, conduct a careful, item-by-item review to make sure you have recorded everything that was said and to aid in preparing a written summary of your overall impressions of the interview. In the summary, you should comment on the subject's general attitude and cooperativeness, describe the setting of and circumstances surrounding the interview, and express your personal feelings about its quality and tone.

Preparing the Data for Processing

Even modest surveys generate enormous amounts of data. A fifty-item questionnaire, completed by a sample of 500 people, will result in 25,000 separate pieces of information that must be checked, recorded, and made relatively easy to handle. Before the data can be processed and analyzed, it must be represented in a form that statistical computer programs can read. This requirement is satisfied by *quantifying the data – transforming them into a series of numerical codes that can be read, stored, manipulated, and summarized statistically* by the computer. This process of **CODING** typically proceeds through several stages, from precoding the questionnaire through "cleaning" the data after it has been entered into the computer.

PRECODING. Whenever possible, the best way to organize the processing of data is to begin before the survey is actually carried out. **PRECODING**, a procedure that applies only to closed-ended questions, involves two operations: (1) *attaching a numerical code to each response alternative* and (2) *designating a location for every questionnaire item*, where the coded response to that item will eventually be stored in a computer **DATA FILE**, an *organized collection of data*. With paper-and-pencil surveys, codes may be printed next to each possible response on the questionnaire, and the appropriate code is circled when the respondent answers the question. Also, the location of the column(s) where each coded response will later be entered into the data file may also be printed unobtrusively on the questionnaire. With computer-assisted surveys, however, the data are entered automatically to their correct location in a data file.

CODING. With traditional paper-based surveys, as soon as the interview is finished or the completed questionnaire returns by mail, it should be reviewed for completeness and edited to make sure that all questions have been answered properly. Sometimes spaces left blank on the questionnaire can be filled in on the basis of information provided on other questions. A person who fails to indicate his or her employment status but who lists an income of $0 can safely be categorized as having no paid job. If a person has skipped or refused to answer certain questions, the editor should enter a "missing value code," a number that signifies the absence of valid data and that the computer will later be instructed to treat separately from other codes. When the editing is finished, there should be some code entered into every address in the data file. Computer-based surveys generally prompt the respondent or interviewer if a question has been omitted or answered incorrectly and therefore overcome many of the problems associated with missing or invalid responses.

Open-ended items cannot be precoded; coding can occur only after the data have been collected. The categories into which responses are to be coded must be established by closely examining what the respondents actually had to say. This procedure is almost identical to the one described in Chapter 13 on content analysis (to which the reader may refer for more detail). In brief, the researcher reviews a sample of the verbal responses to an open-ended question and decides how many different kinds (categories) of responses exist. Each category must then be defined and illustrated with a concrete example, and a numerical code attached

to it. Once this coding scheme has been settled, the full set of verbal responses can be reviewed one at a time and recorded as a compact series of numbers. Since a great deal of judgment is often involved in this translation of words into numbers, accepted practice dictates that at least two people independently code the entire set of responses and their judgments be compared so that differences can be resolved and consistency of coding can be achieved.

PREPARING A CODEBOOK. As soon as all decisions about coding have been made, a **CODEBOOK** should be prepared to serve as both a guide to and a record of the coding process. The codebook *contains instructions for the transfer of all data from the questionnaires to the data file*. For every questionnaire item, the codebook contains the location (usually a column number) in the data file assigned to that item, the exact wording of the question, each legitimate response, the numerical code for each legitimate response, and the code used to signify missing data. It may be sufficient to state the code used to signify missing data only once, to be followed consistently throughout the transfer of data from the questionnaire to the data file. A common practice is to indicate missing data with the largest number that will fit in the cell(s) corresponding to that item (i.e., the number 9 or a series of 9s). The codebook will also indicate the location of the **IDENTIFICATION NUMBER** of each survey respondent; *a numbering system is typically used in order to preserve anonymity*.

ENTERING THE DATA. A number of methods can be used to enter survey data into the computer. In general, data from computer-assisted interviewing programs are stored in a computer as the survey is conducted. This is because most necessary background coding information for closed-ended questions, including variable names, value labels, and so on, is entered into a computer when the survey is constructed and the program is set up to record responses to a data file linked to that information. All that remains for the researcher to do is establish codes for open-ended questions and enter those into the computer. Once the data have been entered, they can then be analyzed with any statistical analysis package such as SPSS or SAS. For most paper-based survey types, it is necessary to create a data file manually from the raw survey data.[15] Researchers can create these files by using statistical software programs such as SPSS, database programs such as Microsoft Access, spreadsheet programs such as Excel, or through integrated survey analysis software packages. Also, they can create ASCII[16] files that can be read by software programs such as SPSS or SAS.

A Hypothetical Survey

In the example that follows, portions of a pre-coded questionnaire and codebook for a hypothetical survey are presented (see Appendixes A and B). The codebook is set up so that the data can be entered into a spreadsheet program such as Excel or a data editor in SPSS. The purpose of the survey is to discover the social and political priorities of a cross section of American adults.

Appendix A presents the part of the pre-coded questionnaire. When the questionnaire is edited, the proper code for each response selected by the subject is to be entered in the space provided in the right-hand margin. To the left of each space and enclosed in parentheses is the number of the column into which the particular response code is to be recorded in the spreadsheet or data editor.

Appendix B includes the codebook entries that correspond to the survey questions in Appendix A. The codebook entry for question 1a contains all relevant information about the numerical codes in which the data will now appear. There is no need to continue entering the same codes for the series of questions 1b through 1i because they follow the same format. Following the series of questions about government spending, the survey then gathers some

demographic information. Of course, while we have presented only a small number of variables in our hypothetical survey, it is important to remember that many surveys gather data on far more variables.

DATA ANALYSIS

After researchers have completed the work of administering and coding the surveys and entering the data into a computer, the process of data analysis can begin. In this section, checking the data to verify that they have been accurately recorded is discussed first, followed by the statistical analysis of the data.

Code Checking and Cleaning

Quality control is an important part of the survey research process. Questionnaires must be carefully edited. All coding of unstructured material must be checked for reliability, and verification, item-by-item and digit-by-digit, must be conducted each time the data are transferred from questionnaires to data files. With proper verification procedures, error rates can be kept below 1 percent; without them, errors can occur and accumulate every time the data are recorded or transferred. Because these random errors (sometimes exceeding 10 or even 20 percent) tend to destroy data patterns and make the results of statistical tests inconclusive, the difference between the success and failure of a well-designed study can often depend on the adequacy of procedures for quality control.

The last step in verification involves checking for incorrect data entry. This step can be considered the beginning of the data analysis phase of our research. It is when we begin to look at our data file and see whether there are obvious inconsistencies that will interfere with the statistical analysis that will come later. If, for example, the proper codes for the variable gender are 1 (for males), 2 (for females), and 9 (for missing data), the appearance of any other number, a 7 for instance, indicates a mistake that must be traced and corrected. Logical checks can also be conducted; all those subjects coded on one variable as not being employed should be coded as "not appropriate" on another variable that purports to measure job satisfaction.

---

[15] Another type of data entry system, Optical Mark Recognition (OMR), also enters data directly from the survey form to a previously established computer data file. When OMR is used, survey respondents mark the survey form in a prescribed manner, and the OMR device scans the surveys to identify the responses. If the respondents have correctly completed the survey, the OMR can directly transfer the results to a file that can be read by a statistical program such as SPSS.

[16] ASCII (American Standard Code for Information Interchange) is a common form of computer text file storage. Text can be entered numerically or alphabetically in an ordinary word processor and read by a wide variety of computer programs.

Statistical computer packages such as SPSS or SAS include programs that are designed to perform this type of data checking. Data should be cleaned immediately by *tracking down and eliminating all such errors*. Once DATA CLEANING is completed, the data are ready to be statistically analyzed.

Statistical Analysis

Typically, researchers start their statistical analysis by examining the data one variable at a time (univariate analysis). Many researchers will then follow the univariate analysis with an effort to look at the association between dependent variables of interest and various independent variables using bivariate statistical methods such as contingency tables and correlation coefficients (see Chapter 18). Bivariate analysis is often followed by multivariate analysis in which an effort is made to assess the impact of several independent variables on a dependent variable of interest in statistical models such as multiple regression or path analysis (see Chapter 19).

The kinds of analysis researchers undertake depends on the goals of their research and the types of data they have collected. Different statistical procedures carry different assumptions about whether our independent and dependent variables are measured on nominal, ordinal, interval scales or ratio scales (see Chapter 4). Violating the assumptions of the procedure about these levels of measurement generally casts doubt on the results. For example, if the researcher plans to use multiple regression in the analysis of the data, then the dependent variables of interest must be measured at the interval or ratio level. Often the researcher will find that his or her options for statistical analysis are limited because the level of measurement issue was not adequately considered when certain key variables were operationalized.

Secondary Analysis

Survey research can be an expensive undertaking. If the survey uses a large and complex sample, the costs can quickly reach into the tens of thousands of dollars. Consequently, the costs of data collection now stand as the major barrier limiting the number of students and professionals who can afford to conduct major surveys without the support of government or other funding agencies. However, researchers are overcoming this final cost obstacle by engaging in SECONDARY ANALYSIS, building research projects around the analysis or *reanalysis of data originally collected by someone else*. Sometimes, as in the case of the General Social Survey, the data may have been purposely collected with the intent of providing it to the research community for analysis. In other cases, the data may have been collected for and already analyzed by researchers, but new information or scientific interest may lead someone to reanalyze the data. In still other cases, the data may have been collected for one purpose but use variables of interest to another researcher.

Suppose you want to isolate factors that predispose people toward racial prejudice, and you find an already existing study of factors affecting voting behavior, in which a scale of racial prejudice was developed as one of the many variables under investigation. You can obtain the existing data and conduct a reanalysis in which prejudice becomes the most important variable. Or, you might examine variables from the General Social Survey and try to construct a scale of racial prejudice and then conduct an analysis.[17] In either of these ways, you entirely avoid the cost of data collection by producing a new set of findings using old data.

Secondary analysis may be performed by taking information from sources other than surveys, but survey data are increasingly likely candidates for secondary analysis because of the quantity of such data and because of their availability in an inexpensive and well-organized form. For example, data collected by the U.S. Bureau of the Census (http://www.census.gov) are distributed for secondary analysis, and social scientists from a variety of disciplines use this abundant source. In addition to its low cost, secondary analysis has several other advantages that make it a useful research tool. Analysis of available records may often be the only way

---

[17] Please refer to Chapter 17 on index and scale construction.

to obtain quantitative data about the past. As more and more survey data accumulate, trend studies comparing responses to similar survey questions asked over the course of many years become more practical and valuable for testing or creating theory. Also, secondary analysis can often be the basis for an important pilot study. Before embarking on an extensive and costly project, researchers may use secondary analyses of other research to assess the soundness of their research design, to pretest the plausibility of their hypotheses, and to determine the strengths and weaknesses of proposed indicators and question wordings. To accomplish any of these purposes, it may be necessary to reanalyze a single survey or a combination of surveys, to treat several surveys as replications of each other and compare their results, or to compare several different indicators used within the same survey.

Despite these virtues, secondary analysis is not without its pitfalls. Researchers using secondary data must be certain that the procedures for sampling, data collection, and data entry used in other studies were sound. This is unlikely to be a problem where the data were collected by prominent research organizations but may be a concern with older studies or data from less sophisticated research teams. Furthermore, the older the research you wish to reanalyze, the less likely it is that the original researcher provided thorough documentation of procedures used in anticipation of later interest in the data. There may be no codebook or no account of how the sampling was done. These limitations, the inevitable drawbacks that accompany the use of someone else's data, mean that researchers must be cautious in interpreting results and should not try to extend limited data to cover a broad, but only partially tested, set of research questions.

DATA BANKS. A number of **DATA BANKS** have arisen as repositories of survey data. Although some data are free, data banks usually make their holdings available for a fee. Data are usually obtained on CD-ROM or through the Internet. Sometimes specific tables of data can be requested, and the data bank will process the data for a minimal payment. Some of the largest data banks in the United States are listed at the end of this chapter.

THE STRENGTHS AND LIMITATIONS OF SURVEY RESEARCH

We have already referred briefly to some of the strengths of the survey method. First, it is a method uniquely capable of generating a broad range of data about the characteristics of large populations. Since this coverage is usually accomplished by using carefully designed methods of scientific sampling and since the data being sought are usually provided, without charge, by the goodwill of voluntary subjects, the method is also a cost-efficient approach to large-scale research.

Surveys are also flexible and adaptable in terms of the variety of subjects and research problems that can be studied in this way. Only a limited range of either individual or group behavior is sufficiently public for a researcher to study it directly. Of the types of behavior that could be considered public and accessible, many are episodic, sporadic, and unpredictable, thus making it inconvenient and costly to search them out, wait for them to occur, and record them. In contrast to these serious difficulties of observation, there is almost no type of behavior – public or private, regular or intermittent – that cannot be talked about. In a very real sense, surveys substitute talk for action, and this thereby greatly extends their range of applicability. Unfortunately, they also substitute reports of behavior for direct, empirical observation of it.

The problem of accepting self-reports as true has already been discussed in detail in Chapter 4. Briefly, the motives behind what people report (and what they fail to report) about themselves are more complex than any pure desire to provide the researcher with an accurate account. The motives of avoiding painful or embarrassing self-revelation and of highlighting personal qualities that may lead to respect or prestige make it difficult to assume that survey respondents' reports about either their actions or their attitudes are, in all cases, accurate.

Ideally, self-reports should be limited to those topics about which the average respondent can be assumed to have enough knowledge or insight to speak. For example, although people consistently report that they are worried about privacy on the Internet, and 93 percent of consumers say it is "very important" that Web sites disclose their privacy practices, only a tiny percentage of consumers ever actually read privacy policies that are posted on the Web (Goldman, 2003). Equally problematic are questions that ask the respondent to provide a self-diagnosis. It cannot be assumed that subjects are sufficiently aware of their own personalities, beliefs, or dispositions to describe themselves accurately on a questionnaire. Introspectiveness and self-awareness are themselves highly variable human traits that greatly affect respondents' abilities to analyze themselves. For these reasons, the self-reporting method should not be relied on exclusively in situations in which other, more direct methods of observation and measurement are available.

A simultaneous limitation and strength of the survey method is that it is typically deductive, theoretically, and that it relies on sticking to a preplanned research design. On the one hand, designing and finalizing a questionnaire before contacting subjects in the field means that the researcher must anticipate problems in the research design, and that flaws that might appear during the data collection stage cannot easily be altered. On the other hand, this rigid consistency about procedure can produce remarkably uniform and reliable results. A properly executed survey strives to maximize the comparability of data collected, and this strategy in turn increases the chances for clear and fruitful analysis.

An awareness of the breadth of the applications of the survey method should encourage you to experiment with many different ways of asking questions and with a variety of subjects. At the same time, keeping in mind the limitations of self-reports should lead you to design your questionnaire carefully and to consider whether available, supplementary methods of data collection might be combined with the survey to enhance the overall effectiveness of the research (Brewer and Hunter, 2006).

SUMMARY

Survey research is a procedure for systematically collecting information about the attitudes, beliefs, background, experiences, and behavior of a sample of people by using interviews and questionnaires. This chapter has concentrated on six critical aspects of the survey research process: (1) planning the survey, (2) formulating questions, (3) constructing a questionnaire, (4) executing the self-administered survey, (5) interviewing, and (6) preparing the data for processing. The survey is the most frequently used research technique in social science; most topics of any interest to social researchers have been studied in this way. The survey method is not only flexible and adaptable to a number of research purposes; it is also capable of producing, from a relatively small sample, results that can be generalized to a much larger population of interest.

Careful and thoughtful planning are crucial to successful survey research; the likelihood that any survey will produce data of interest and value to the social researcher is largely determined before any data are collected. A well-planned design, nonetheless, requires skillful execution and careful attention to every detail if the aims of the project are to be realized.

Survey research, like other methods, has its limitations and is not a solution for every research problem. Perhaps the greatest weakness of the method is its total dependence on the respondents – on their memory, their interest, their clarity of self-perception, their frankness, and their honesty. Although deliberate deception is rare, many factors determine how and what people report about their attitudes, beliefs, and behavior, and these factors affect the quality of the data generated in surveys. Consequently, every element, however minor, that goes into the construction of a questionnaire must be carefully designed to serve the aims of the project while minimizing the opportunities for error. The content, wording, sequence, and structure of questions as well as the overall layout of the questionnaire are crucial to the success of any survey.

KEY TERMS

audio computer-assisted self-interview (ACASI)
closed-ended questions
computer-assisted interviewing (CAI)
computer-assisted personal interviewing (CAPI)
computer-assisted telephone interviewing (CATI)
codebook
coding
contingency question
cross-sectional design
data banks
data cleaning
data file
demographic categories
double-barreled question
filter questions
identification number
loaded question
longitudinal survey design
open-ended questions
panel study
pilot study
precoding
pretest
probe
random-digit dialing
secondary analysis
self-administered questionnaire
structured question
telephone audio computer-assisted self-interviewing (T-ACASI)
trend study
unstructured questions

EXERCISES

1. Two students should work on this exercise together. Work up a brief list of questions on a topic of interest to both of you. Each student should select five people to interview by means of these questions. One will conduct face-to-face interviews and the other will carry out telephone interviews. (Determine who will use which data collection technique by flipping a coin.) After the interviews are completed, compare notes on your interviewing experiences.

2. Two students should work separately on this exercise. Design a very brief questionnaire asking what people consider to be the main problems facing the leaders of the United States. One questionnaire should ask the question without suggesting any answers; the other should contain a list of possible answers to be shown to the respondents. Administer each questionnaire to ten classmates. Compare the answers received. What implications are there for questionnaire design? Which question format is preferable? Why? In what situations might each format be more effective than the other?

3. Think of a topic about which you want to find out information through a questionnaire. Construct three structured and three unstructured questions for the topic. Ask another student in the class to respond to these questions. Then ask the student to offer constructive criticism of the questions.

4. Think of survey research situations in which it would be most appropriate to use each of the following data collection techniques: a self-administered questionnaire, a face-to-face interview, and a telephone interview. Compare your answers with others in class.

5. Suppose you wish to obtain data on the ethnic backgrounds of wealthy people. You must represent the entire United States with your research. How will you go about the study if:

   a. you have an extremely limited budget?

   b. you have an unlimited budget?

SUGGESTED READINGS

Readings about the Method

Asher, Herbert. 2004. *Polling and the Public: What Every Citizen Should Know*. 6th ed. Washington, DC: CQ Press.

   Although, as its title suggests, the book focuses primarily on opinion polls, much of the discussion is useful for all survey research. Asher demonstrates clearly how and why polls sometimes fail to capture true public opinion.

Czaja, Ron, and Johnny Blair. 2005. *Designing Surveys: A Guide to Decisions and Procedures*. 2nd ed. Thousand Oaks, CA: Sage.

   This volume contains timely information on Web-based and telephone surveys, comparing and contrasting these new developments with more traditional modes of survey execution.

Dillman, Don. 2006. *Mail and Internet Surveys: The Tailored Design Method – 2007 Update.* 2nd ed. New York: Wiley.

> Dillman has long been an important figure in the field of survey research. This textbook offers practical insights into the design and implementation of surveys as well as useful suggestions for improving response rates. Dillman also discusses the expanding role of technology in survey administration.

Fink, Arlene. 2006. *How to Conduct Surveys.* 3rd ed. Thousand Oaks, CA: Sage.

> This is a step-by-step guide for students, including useful advice on which topics are best researched using surveys, how to code open-ended questions, questionnaire formatting, and pilot testing.

Peterson, Robert A. 2000. *Constructing Effective Questionnaires.* Thousand Oaks, CA: Sage.

> This book focuses exclusively on the questionnaire development phase of survey research. It offers a more detailed discussion than is usually found in introductory survey research textbooks.

Rea, Louis M., and Richard Parker. 2005. *Designing and Conducting Survey Research: A Comprehensive Guide.* San Francisco: Jossey-Bass.

> A clear and useful introduction to the process of survey research, accessible to first-time survey researchers. Part 1 addresses the development and administration of surveys. Part 2, "Ensuring Scientific Accuracy," discusses sampling theory. Part 3 covers the analysis and presentation of survey results. An interesting feature of the book is that it presents itemized cost analyses of survey and focus group research.

Weisberg, Herbert F. 2005. *The Total Survey Error Approach.* Chicago: University of Chicago Press.

> This is a thorough treatment of survey research design, focusing on the many sources of error and what can be done to reduce or eliminate them.

Readings Illustrating the Method

Essinger, Robert M. 2000. "Partisan Absolution? Exploring the Depths of Forgiving." *International Journal of Public Opinion Research* 12:245–258.

> Have you ever wondered why people seem so forgiving of the mistakes or improprieties of those who share their political leanings and so unforgiving of those who do not? Using data from

the General Social Survey and public opinion polls about the Clinton-Lewinsky affair, Essinger shows how partisanship affects the absolution that citizens accord politicians. Then, drawing from social interaction and reference group theory, he reports an experiment confirming that loyalty is an important factor influencing the forgiveness of impropriety.

Inglehart, Ronald. 1997. *Modernization and Postmodernization: Cultural, Economic, and Political Change in 43 Societies.* Princeton, NJ: Princeton University Press.

> The World Values Survey is an internationally collaborative survey research project designed to measure values, attitudes, and opinions of residents of sixty-five nations. Using data from an early wave of the World Values Survey, Inglehart analyzes the political and cultural changes that accompany economic development.[18]

International Journal of Public Opinion Research. Serial.

> An Oxford University Press publication for the World Association for Public Opinion Research, the IJPOR publishes empirical articles that employ survey data in testing hypotheses as well as articles about the methodology of survey research. Recent and past issues of the IJPOR are available on the World Wide Web at http://www3.oup.co.uk/intpor/.

Jacobs, Lawrence R., and Robert Y. Shapiro. 2000. *Politicians Don't Pander: Political Manipulation and the Loss of Democratic Responsiveness.* Chicago: University of Chicago Press.

> This book argues that politicians of both major American parties are less responsive to public opinion now than they were in the past. Rather than craft legislative positions that respond to public opinion, Lawrence and Shapiro contend that politicians generally use public opinion research to help them identify strategies for manufacturing popular support for their preferred policies.

Kelley, Jonathan, and Nan Dirk De Graaf. 1997. "National Context, Parental Socialization, and

---

[18] See the World Values Survey Web site http://wvs.isr.umich.edu/ for updated information about recent surveys, methodology, and the availability of the research for secondary analysis.

Religious Belief: Results from 15 Nations." *American Sociological Review* 62:639–659.

This study examined how a nation's religious environment influences the religious beliefs of its citizens. Do citizens in religious nations differ in the intensity and nature of their religious beliefs from citizens of secular nations? To explore this issue, the authors used survey data from the International Social Survey Programme (ISSP) for nearly 18,000 respondents from fifteen countries.

Public Opinion Quarterly. Serial.

A publication of the American Society for Public Opinion Research, this journal also publishes empirical articles that employ survey data in testing hypotheses as well as articles about the methodology of survey research. A notable feature is a section called "The Polls – Trends" that provides background information and analysis of the trend in public opinion for an important political, economic, or social issue.

Rasinski, Kenneth A., et al. 2002. "America Recovers: A Follow-Up to a National Study of Public Response to the September 11th Terrorist Attacks." Chicago: National Opinion Research Corporation.

The author and his associates at the National Opinion Research Corporation initiated a series of poll studies of the public's reaction to 9/11.

Data Banks and Internet Resources

The Inter-University Consortium for Political and Social Research (ICPSR) holds a vast collection of social science data including survey data. Access it at http://www.icpsr.umich.edu/index.html. *Although much of the data is available to subscribers only, some is available without cost, including the General Social Survey and data sets from the National Center for Health Statistics.*

Louis Harris Data Archive at the Howard W. Odum Institute for Research in Social Science at the University of North Carolina at Chapel Hill holds data from more than 1,200 Louis Harris and Associates polls as well as other surveys. The center offers a free search of Harris data with results available online. http://www.irss.unc.edu/data_archive/home.asp.

The Public Opinion section of the University of Michigan's Document Center Web site http://www.lib.umich.edu/govdocs/stpolisc.html#opinion *lists many organizations that publish information using survey data.*

Roper Public Opinion Research Center, Yale University. The Roper Center maintains a large archive of survey studies that are available to researchers for a fee at http://www.ropercenter.uconn.edu/.

The Survey Research Center at Princeton University Web site http://www.princeton.edu/~abelson/index.html *has links to research resources, including "Poll and Survey Findings and Data," university and private research sites, software vendors, and professional associations.*

University of Illinois Survey Research Laboratory Web site http://www.srl.uic.edu/ *is a good place to find links to survey research–related journals, organizations, codes of ethics, software, and data archives.*

REFERENCES

Brewer, John, and Albert Hunter. 2006. *Foundations of Multimethod Research: Synthesizing Styles.* Thousand Oaks, CA: Sage.

Davis, James A., Tom W. Smith, and Peter V. Marsden. 2005. *General Social Surveys, 1972–2004 Cumulative File.* ICPSR04295-v1. Chicago: National Opinion Research Center.

Fitzgerald, John, Peter Gottschalk, and Robert Moffitt. 1998. "An Analysis of Sample Attrition in Panel Data: The Michigan Panel Study of Income Dynamics." National Bureau of Economic Research Working Paper No. T0220. Cambridge, MA: National Bureau of Economic Research.

Fournier, Patrick, et al. 2001. "Validation of Time-of-Voting-Decision Recall." *Public Opinion Quarterly* 65 (1): 95–107.

Goldman, Eric. 2003. "Does Online Privacy 'Really' Matter? 'No' According to Consumers." *Circle ID* (September 12).
    http://www.circleid.com/.

Heath, Anthony, and Bridget Taylor. 1999. "British National Sentiment." *British Journal of Political Science* 29:155–175.

Turner, Charles F., et al. 1998. "Adolescent Sexual Behavior, Drug Use, and Violence: Increased Reporting with Computer Survey Technology." *Science* 280:867–873.

U.S. Department of Education, National Center for Educational Statistics. 2003. *A First Look at the Literacy of America's Adults in the 21st Century.* Washington, DC: NCES.

INTENSIVE INTERVIEWING

8

INTRODUCTION

In the last chapter on survey research, the focus was on asking the right questions and getting them put down on the printed page (or the Web-based medium) in a clear and concise way. Much of the research imagination employed in survey research occurs *before* data are actually collected and is apparent in the overall design of a survey, the operationalization of variables, and the wording of the specific questions to be asked. In this chapter, the focus is on intensive interviewing, a technique in which, by contrast, appropriate questions are often determined *as data are being collected*. This means that creativity and spontaneous decision making are integrated at every step of the research process. In this up-close, conversational technique, clarity of communication is a mutual effort between the researcher and those being studied.

Interviewing is increasingly well established as a methodological alternative that can help us explore what to ask and how to ask it. Sometimes such information is used only to formulate structured questionnaires for surveys, but interviews are also immensely valuable in their own right. There are many research challenges for which intensive interviewing is *the* ideal investigative technique. Let us look at one example. Beyond a few memoirs (Delong and Petrini, 2001; A. C. Gray, 2003), not much is known sociologically about female crime-fighters – private investigators, police detectives, and FBI agents. We do know that relatively few women engage in these traditionally male-dominated occupations. How could we study them? Would they agree to be contacted? What types of questions would we ask? If the women did agree to participate in our research, would they be cooperative or would they be evasive or deliberately misleading in their responses? In what setting should they be studied?

We can quickly dismiss the possibility of sending a task force armed with questionnaires to interview a random sample of female crime-fighters. The logistical problems alone could be overwhelming; imagine arranging for a large number of interviewers to obtain access to the places where they work. Of even greater con-

sequence could be the difficulty of anticipating what the most productive lines of questioning would be. Women who engage in an unusual occupation could mean that, as respondents, they would be unpredictable and their reactions to specific questions would vary greatly; so how could the primary investigators devise a standard set of questions that would be productive in each interview and easy for hired-hand interviewers to administer?

Which data-gathering method might meet the researchers' needs for this purpose better than traditional survey research? We know that participant observation has been useful in studies of occupational groups (see Chapter 9), but remaining inconspicuous or maintaining courage in the face of danger require specialized training that most researchers do not possess. It might be difficult (not to mention, dangerous) to follow the female detectives around as they work. We would also have to confront the reality that much of their work is undercover. Even simple observational research might compromise secrecy or confidentiality. Crime-fighters out of uniform are not a group that can be easily and unobtrusively observed. In this case, we have the added complication that they are female but working within a male milieu. So, observing them as they work alongside their male counterparts would only give us part of the picture, in any case. It becomes apparent that information will have to be obtained by interviewing the female crime-fighters themselves.

The methodology of **INTENSIVE**, or **IN-DEPTH** or *conversational*, **INTERVIEWING** is appropriate for this particular challenge. Any number of people could be contacted, but the size of the sample is usually limited compared to survey research because the interviews are conducted very differently. For the interviewer, preparation is as intensive as the encounters themselves. Researchers using intensive interviewing need to gird themselves for any contingency by compiling a list of alternative reactions to possible developments during their conversations. The objective is to encourage spontaneity in the respondents' comments (Kvale, 1996), while minimizing the possibility that the interviewers will be so taken aback by a remark or turn of events that the momentum of the interview will be permanently disrupted.

The process of preparation begins by devising a list of avenues for questioning that the researcher believes might be productive. However, during the course of an actual interview, using a specific question is guided by the progress of that interview. If the interviewee is especially responsive, or unresponsive to a particular question, the researcher can **PROBE** extensively via *supplementary questions* (some prepared in advance, others devised on the spot). Questions evoking minimal response are sometimes rephrased; if they still bare little fruit, they will usually be put aside for another meeting. In short, these interviews are *customized* to each respondent and interviewing situation. These contacts are dependent on the **RAPPORT** – *mutuality of trust and sense of reciprocity* – that develops between researchers and respondents during their transition from strangers to confidants of sorts. The quality of this evolving relationship between interviewer and interviewee is the cornerstone of the intensive interviewing method.

The intensive interviewing technique offers an opportunity to probe extensively for sensitive information from potentially evasive individuals, tailoring each interview so the interviewee feels as comfortable as possible and is encouraged to provide candid self-reports. The format is generally flexible. The interviews can be conducted in any setting that is mutually agreeable. The manner and demeanor of the interviewer are governed not only by the study objectives and the cumulative information flow but also by a continuing assessment of what it will take to make or keep the interviewee most responsive. Although some standardized questions may be asked of every respondent, the interviewer takes account of each respondent's individuality in deciding what to ask, as well as when and how to ask it. Intensive interviewing places a premium on the interviewer's ability to make quick judgments concerning what to say or do next at any given point in the interview. This factor, more than anything else, determines its ultimate value.

Most intensive interviews are lengthy, with two or three hours not an uncommon duration, or there may be multiple meetings with the same respondent. This provides an opportunity for the good intensive interviewer to nurture the relationship, enhancing the development of a conversational, give-and-take rapport, and the likelihood of frank revelations. Indeed, an interview does resemble a social conversation in form and tone, but one that is "orchestrated." At least one of the parties in the exchange has a predetermined and serious purpose (Stewart and Cash, 2000). It is really a *deliberate* dialogue (Maso and Webster, 1995).

The mood of the intensive interviewer goes a long way toward encouraging rapport with the respondent. The interviewer must appear enthusiastic about the interview and about the prospect of being allowed to converse with the subject. Patience is an important attribute, as is the confidence that comes with advance preparation. Interviewees may expect interviewers to know certain facts, and failure to do one's homework may result in a loss of interviewer credibility.

APPLICATIONS OF INTENSIVE INTERVIEWING

Respondents who can be studied through intensive interviews, when other data-gathering methods would probably fail, include senior officials in nonprofit organizations and business and famous entertainment figures (Cieri and Peeps, 2001; Watson, 2001; Zucker, 2002). These people may be too geographically dispersed to facilitate carrying out observational studies. They may perceive themselves as too busy or too important to participate in a standardized survey research interview with a hired-hand interviewer. The ability of the intensive interviewer to accommodate their schedules and to converse knowledgeably about the study and its purposes usually are highly persuasive aids in obtaining cooperation. The elite are not the only population segment that is particularly appropriate for intensive interviewing. This methodology should be strongly considered for any category of respondent that is highly likely to be unwilling or unable to participate in other forms of research investigation, including convicted criminals (Scully and Marolla, 1999), the elderly (Hansen and Platz, 1995), and battered women (Chatzifotiou, 2000) to name a few.

In-depth interviews have been extremely useful in studies of private troubles that people are intensely curious about but do not understand in detail. Examples of such calamities include mental illness, drug addiction, divorce, and death and dying. David Karp, one of the authors of this textbook, interviewed fifty men and women suffering from depression. In the conclusion of *Speaking of Sadness* (1996:202), he says:

The ultimate test of a study's worth is that the findings ring true to people and let them see things in new ways. In this case, I hope those personally familiar with depression recognize themselves in the words of my respondents and feel that my analysis illuminates their life situations.

The intensive interview technique highlights the words of the respondents, which can be reproduced as part of the author's analysis with poignant effect. One of Karp's interviewees was asked to describe what depression was like (1996:29):

A sense of being trapped, or being caged, sort of like an animal, like a tiger pacing in a cage. That's sort of how I feel. I feel like I'm in a cage and I'm trapped, and I can't get out and it's night time and the daylight's never going to come. Because if the daylight came, I could figure out how to get out of the cage, but I can't . . . Sometimes I feel like I'm being smothered in that I can't breathe. I am being suffocated . . . And it's like falling down a well, like I'm free-falling. That's what it is. And I have nowhere to grab onto to stop it. And I don't know what will happen when I land.

Lee Vigilant (2001) interviewed forty heroin users and former addicts in his attempt to identify the processes involved in becoming addicted and reducing or eliminating dependence on heroin through the use of the drug methadone. Diane Vaughan (1990) used interviews to understand the process of estrangement that leads to marital breakup. Elisabeth Kübler-Ross (1997) produced a wealth of data from perhaps the most difficult group to interview – dying people – through intensive interviews in her study on death and dying. In each of these studies, and countless others that use in-depth interviewing, the words of the people interviewed form the centerpiece for the authors', and the reader's, understanding.

We have shown that the characteristics of the intensive interview – being personal and encouraging respondents' introspection – can give us insight into the troubling and unfamiliar parts of life. However, these same qualities can also make familiar experiences seem rich and fascinating. In-depth interviewing lets us see ourselves in a new way. Martha McMahon (1995) interviewed fifty-nine middle- and working-class mothers for her study published in the book *Engendering Motherhood*. The average length of each encounter was 2.5 hours, and the interview schedule contained standardized, semistructured, and open-ended questions. McMahon's goal was to uncover the changes in outlook and identity that occur through the process of mothering. She describes her book as "a story based on what participants in the study told me about their lives" (1995:v).

Analyzing the interview data brought McMahon to a deeper understanding of motherhood as "symbolizing the special social bonds of connectedness" (1995:vi), responsibility, and personal growth. The notion of *engendering* is a process ideally captured through in-depth interviews because it is gradual and largely unconscious and thus requires the interviewer's encouraging respondents to be pensive and reflective:

Why does anyone ever want to have children? . . . It wasn't a *decision*, it wasn't a question. We didn't try to decide to have a child or not to have a child . . . It was taken as given. (1995:53)

I had thought a mother had to be certain things . . . One of them was that a mother had to be unhappy – my impression of a mother was that she was self-sacrificing and that she was unhappy. And I discovered it does not have to be the case . . . I thought I would have to become self-sacrificing and unhappy . . . I found I didn't have to change myself . . . I learned and I grew and the changes did

The World of Topless Dancers

Intensive Interviewing may also give us entrée into subcultures that lie outside the mainstream. Thompson and Harred (1999) were curious about the processes by which people considered to be deviant manage the negative reputation, or *stigma*, associated with their deviant status. They decided to investigate one occupational group, topless dancers. Data were collected during nine months of interviewing. Research was done at seven topless bars in a major city in the Southwest (in the "heart of the Bible Belt"). Over forty dancers were studied. Some of the best information was obtained through casual conversation, but there were also more formal interviews. The majority of these encounters took place between 11 a.m. and 6 p.m. because the subject clubs specialized in "daytime entertainment," targeting a business crowd. The club owners permitted a female graduate student backstage to interview dancers in their dressing rooms. The authors also interviewed waitresses, bartenders, and club managers. All dancers were female, ranging in age from 19 to 41; the majority was white.

Stigma is an attribute that sets people apart and discredits them or disqualifies them from full social acceptance. People are most likely to be stigmatized because of their occupation if it is viewed as deviant by other members of society. An occupation will be seen as deviant if it is illegal or considered to be immoral. Stripping and dancing are viewed as unusually low-status occupations; many people consider them promiscuous. All of the dancers admitted they felt stigmatized, at least by some groups of people, because of their occupation. To manage the stigma, some of the women divided their social world by only letting a select few know what they did, and allowing others to believe they were waitresses. Others rationalized and neutralized their activities by claiming that there was "no victim, no crime," or that the people who condemned them were hypocrites.

happen, but I didn't have to force myself unto any kind of mold. (1995:87)

Sometimes I get irritated when I come home from work...Some days I'm really irritated and some days I'm all right. I guess it depends on how my oldest [two children] get on when they come from daycare. If they start screaming right away, then my night is ruined. It's their mood, not mine [that counts]. (1995:218).

[When I see other women of my age who have full-time jobs or careers but no children] I guess it makes me remember when I had more time on my hands and not as much responsibility. But that doesn't make me feel I'd like to return there...I really feel that where I am now is better than I was...I imagine they have more free time, more money to do traveling and stuff with, but I don't think they are happier. I see myself as being happier. I see them as still searching. (1995:223)

In these quotes from four different respondents, we see self-examination and the devel-opment of insight that the women are able to share with us. Thus, the skillful interviewer can assist respondents to become more self-aware while informing the reader at the same time.

In the preceding section we have indicated that intensive interviewing is applicable to a variety of investigations. Whether intensive interviewing is employed as the sole data-gathering mode or used in combination with other methods depends on a number of considerations to be discussed later. For the moment, let us turn from the applied aspects to the more theoretical implications of this methodological tool.

DISTINCTIVE CHARACTERISTICS OF INTENSIVE INTERVIEWS

Interviews involve direct interaction between two parties – the interviewer seeking information from the interviewee. As in any interaction, the ultimate value of the interview depends on a number of considerations:

1. *Commitment*: the degree of interest in both parties in making the interaction mutually beneficial

2. *Meaning*: the ability of each party to recognize the true intent of the other's actions and statements

3. *Flexibility*: the extent to which the course or content of the interaction may be adapted to meet the needs of both parties

4. *Assimilation*: the ways in which the two parties digest and interpret the ongoing interaction

Using these four criteria, we may contrast intensive interviews with **STRUCTURED INTERVIEWS**. Structured interviews *utilize a questionnaire with precisely worded questions*, appearing in a certain sequence, and administered by an interviewer who has no authority to change or amend either the wording or the order of these questions (except in clearly prescribed ways, as discussed in Chapter 7). Most survey research studies employ structured questionnaires.

Commitment and Reciprocity

Throughout any interaction each party consciously or unconsciously makes a series of decisions concerning the presentation of self to the other. Each is constantly deciding how much to reveal and what impression to make. The benefits each party feels as the interaction progresses will govern the extent and nature of continued personal commitment to the interaction (P. S. Gray, 1980).

Theoretically, as the interaction proceeds, each party derives sufficient rewards from the relationship for it to continue; if the relationship fails to provide these rewards, it will be terminated either mutually or unilaterally. The emerging rapport between the two parties may be one source of satisfaction. Receipt of valued information (sometimes as formalized as a promised copy of the study report) may be another. Gratification at being the object of another's interest is sometimes sufficient reward. We are not just referring to getting interviewees to participate. This is not usually a severe problem, and cash payments are frequently useful incentives in difficult cases. It is the *quality* of participation that is crucial – the motivation and ability of interviewees to provide introspective and candid responses throughout the interview.

An intensive interviewer may frequently praise the effort of the respondent, contributing to the latter's self-esteem. Interviewers may reveal facts about themselves that will not influence the respondent's opinions but will make the interaction an exchange of information rather than a one-way flow:

INTERVIEWEE: It's important to get out of the house once in a while. I love my kids, but they really get on your nerves.

INTERVIEWER: I can understand. I have kids of my own.

Reinforcement of self-worth and a sense of **RECIPROCITY**, or "*giving back*," are but two of several techniques for enhancing respondent commitment through the interview.

Most interviews are forced interactions on the part of at least one participant. The initial contact between interviewer and interviewee is usually an arbitrary meeting of two strangers. A structured survey interview is unlikely to progress much beyond its initial formality. However, intensive interviews are normally conducted in ways that encourage and nurture the development of rapport. In other words, the interviewer is relatively free to guide the emerging relationship into directions that offer the best chance for mutual reward. It is therefore useful, where possible, to pay attention to the "fit" between interviewer and subject. It may be necessary to change interviewers if the match seems to be a problem in a given study. It is easier to interview people of lower socioeconomic status than oneself, and it is preferable to match race and ethnicity. In general, the sex of the interviewer does not matter unless sensitive issues are being discussed, such as sexual abuse or rape (Weiss, 1995).

Shared Meanings

Even if interviewees are highly motivated to provide detailed and accurate responses, their ability to do so is at least partly dependent on their interpretation of the questions. Will a given question mean to the respondent exactly what it meant to the person who prepared it? This problem increases with the level of abstraction in the question. If a question refers to "success in life," will a given respondent interpret "success" as being measured by level of affluence, esteem from one's peers, occupational status, or some other indicator? To provide a detailed definition of success for respondents' benefit might be helpful, but a survey questionnaire filled with definitions can be boring and fatiguing to interviewees. In an intensive interview, the appropriate working definition of "success" from *both* interviewer's and interviewee's perspective can emerge via conversation.

A related consideration is whether respondents' answers will mean to researchers what the respondents intended. Most structured interviews include a few open-ended questions that ask respondents to answer in their own words (for example, "What do you think are the most important pros and cons of capital punishment?"). The people who analyze the answers to these questions are generally not the ones who conducted the interviews. Considering the various possible meanings or nuances of each comment, these analysts may not be able to interpret correctly the intended meaning of people they have never met.

Many survey research questions appear to get at the heart of a concept (sometimes termed *face validity*) without really doing so. What could be more concise or direct than the question, "Are you prejudiced against minority individuals or groups?" The wording of the question, however, is so loaded to almost demand a "no" response. Leaving terms such as "prejudiced" and "minority" open to respondent definition invites a different interpretation of the question from interviewee to interviewee. Forcing a "yes" or "no" response prevents an interviewee from indicating a degree of prejudice

that is something less than total. If this question had been pretested among several respondents under mock survey research conditions, it would indeed have yielded answers; interviewees would have forced themselves in one direction or another (more likely the less damning one). However, we should not always interpret the answering of a question as evidence that the question has been clearly stated in the questionnaire or understood by the respondent.

Intensive interviewing, if conducted properly, can go much further in ensuring against misinterpretation of meaning by either interviewer or interviewee. Unlike survey interview encounters, intensive interviews offer ample opportunity for researchers to search for contradictions in the responses and to use these as a rationale to probe for deeper clarification. If a respondent describes himself as being extremely thrifty, but the interviewer notices lavish furnishings in the home, the credibility of the respondent's remarks may be called into question. The interviewer might interject a comment to challenge the interviewee such as

> You're very fortunate to have such a beautifully furnished home while being able to save a lot of money at the same time [or while operating on a limited budget].

The respondent might reply that the furnishings were inherited, that he dislikes them, and that he intends to change homes in the near future; or he might say:

> What I meant before was that I think it's important to save systematically, but I don't believe in living like a monk.

Moreover, if the interviewee asks for clarification, the researcher can give it, unlike the survey interviewer who is generally warned not to change or amend a question in any way. If the intensive interviewer suspects even the opportunity for misinterpretation, it is a simple matter to ask subjects to repeat a question in their own words. Some intensive interviewers deliberately phrase the same question in different ways from respondent to respondent, either to make certain that the nature of the answer is not being biased by the way in which the question is asked or to customize the wording to the characteristics of the interviewee. (A question on occupational aspirations, for example, would probably be asked differently of a middle-aged physicist than of a junior high school student.)

Intensive interviewing emphasizes the direct interchange between a single respondent (or sometimes a pair or small group of respondents) and an individual researcher who is often the director of the study. The interviewer, in addition to gathering information, is actually conducting an analysis during the course of the interaction and should be particularly capable of knowing when and how to clarify meaning. The following hypothetical exchange would not be unusual:

> INTERVIEWER: Do you consider this neighborhood a good place in which to live?
>
> RESPONDENT: Do you mean generally or for me in particular?
>
> INTERVIEWER: Well, why don't you discuss it generally at first and then for you in particular?
>
> RESPONDENT: Generally speaking, it's a dump. It used to be nice but then it started going downhill.
>
> INTERVIEWER: What do you mean by "downhill"?
>
> RESPONDENT: Well, it started with parlors. And then we have lots of drug pushers in town. They hooked our kids on dope.
>
> INTERVIEWER: Parlors?
>
> RESPONDENT: Betting parlors. Bookie joints. Aren't you from around here?
>
> INTERVIEWER: No, but I'm enjoying getting the inside story from you.
>
> RESPONDENT: Well, these are places where you can go make a bet, like on the horses. They're illegal, and they operate in the backs of stores. Everyone has been in there at one time or another. I've lost a lot of money there lately. The police know about them, but they look the other way. I think it's the money from the parlors that financed the dope dealers in the first place.

This brief example illustrates how both interviewee and interviewer obtained clarifications, which might not have been possible in a structured interview.

Although each interviewee in an intensive interview study is likely to be asked a variety of questions tailored to his or her own knowledge or experience, there may be some questions that must be asked of all respondents. In these instances, the emphasis is on *equivalence of meaning*. The objective is for a question to have the same meaning to each interviewee, even though it may have to be phrased differently from interview to interview to achieve this goal. Suppose we were interested in this question:

> If some people in your community suggested that a book written by a socialist and advocating socialist policies be taken out of your public library, would you favor removing the book or not?

For some respondents, we might be able to ask the question in its present form, but for others, it would not be safe to assume that they understood what we meant by the term "socialist." Some might even interpret the word removing to mean "borrowing." Faced with these dilemmas, the intensive interviewer would not hesitate to reword the question. Here is a possible rewording:

> Suppose a person who favored government ownership of all the railroads and all major industries such as the steel industry, the auto industry, and so on had written a book that was in your public library, advocating government ownership of the railroads and major industries. If some people in your community suggested that the library get rid of the book, would you agree that it would be a good idea to make the library get rid of the book, or wouldn't you agree?

This revision might seem overly simplified, redundant, and even patronizing to some respondents, but it would be used only in those cases where it promised to communicate a meaning equivalent to the original question and to do it more easily than the original question would have.

Flexibility

In an intensive interview, as in any conversation, the participants may sometimes be unaware of exactly what direction the exchange will take until they are in the middle of it. They each have certain objectives, but the way they pursue them hinges on the flow of conversation. In a sense it is like a chess game, where a given move depends on what the other player has just done and affects what the other player will do next. The researchers who studied topless dancers prepared a list of discussion areas but also were equipped with a number of alternative questions for use if various contingencies occurred. They could not foresee all possible eventualities, but they prepared as best they could. Most important, they were not restricted in the actual interviewing by either the wording or the sequence of the initial list of questions.

The flexible format of intensive interviews is important for a number of reasons. Whenever the interviewee mentions anything of particular note, the interviewer has the opportunity to probe immediately for additional information. This display of interest on the part of the interviewer also helps to solidify the relationship with the interviewee. In some intensive interviews, the respondent will introduce a topic that the interviewer intended to discuss later. The interviewer may switch topics immediately to capitalize on the momentum provided by the interviewee. This tactic also reaffirms the interviewer's interest in the respondent's comments. When switching topics, the good interviewer will take care not to interrupt an important train of thought of the interviewee. Sometimes instead of risking such an interruption, the interviewer will say, "That's interesting. I'd like to pursue that in greater depth soon" and will then proceed with the original topic.

Intensive interviewing offers many options for investigators in terms of what to say as well as when and how to say it. These options make it possible for the interview to approach the continuity and momentum characteristic of a productive conversation. One way in which intensive interviewing generally differs from normal conversation is the way in which both interviewer and interviewee assimilate the results.

Assimilation

Typically, the interviewee's assimilation of what transpires in an intensive interview revolves largely around trust and gratification. It is natural for a respondent to have initial reservations or fears concerning the "real" intentions or objectives of the interviewer. As the interview progresses, if the researcher is performing well, the evolving conversation reassures the respondent that the interviewer's intent is to learn and share, not to exploit.

At the outset, the respondent may regard the interview as an imposition or a chore, particularly if the interviewer has not been careful in explaining the significance of the study and of participating in it. The many potential sources of gratification from an intensive interview should become apparent to the respondent as the ongoing give-and-take is digested. The amount of genuine interest shown by the interviewer is probably the most important element in determining how much benefit the interviewee perceives. For the interviewee, assimilation is one key to producing useful results. Such assimilation takes place both within and between interviews.

For the researcher, assimilation *is* the result. What the interviewer gleans represents the essence of the findings (sometimes supplemented by a few structured questions). The interviewer must constantly be aware of the implications of an interviewee's comments. While taking notes on the interviewee's replies, the interviewer has to be simultaneously alert for any inconsistencies in the respondent's "story," mindful of how this respondent differs from others, cognizant of whether the objectives of the study are being met by the cumulative flow of information, ready to formulate or test hypotheses, and, finally, prepared with what to say next.

Interviewing and Induction

Between interviews, the researcher may take advantage of a key benefit of intensive interviewing: the sequential nature of the contacts with respondents and the opportunity to use the process of induction (discussed in Chapter 2). The following steps reiterate the main elements of induction as research progresses:

1. Formulate a rough definition of the phenomenon you want to explain.

2. Devise a preliminary explanation of that phenomenon.

3. Examine only one case in light of your proposed explanation. Try to determine whether the facts of that one case can be accounted for by the preliminary analysis.

4. If the explanation fits the facts of that one case, turn to other cases to see whether it still fits. If the explanation does not fit that one case, either reformulate the original theoretical explanation or redefine the phenomenon that you want to explain.

5. Keep examining a number of cases in sequence, reformulating the theory each time that a new case cannot be explained by the existing theory.

6. Continue this process of examining cases, redefining phenomena, and reformulating hypotheses until you are satisfied that you have formulated an explanation that will not be contradicted by additional data.

Sequential interviewing has other advantages. The researcher does not have to formulate arbitrary answer categories before the interviewing but can derive the answer categories from the cumulative responses given. By further refining these categories as the interviewing progresses, the researcher better describes the full range of respondent opinion.[1]

Interviewing, Reliability, and Validity

Sequential interviewing allows the researcher to make it progressively more difficult for respon-

dents to give answers that appear to be contrived to win the approval of the interviewer. Suppose we were using intensive interviewing to conduct a study of attitudes toward gay rights among the students at a major college. If the question "Do you think there should be laws against marriage between members of the same sex?" elicited negative responses from the first six students interviewed, we might begin to suspect that they were giving answers contrived to demonstrate their supposedly liberal attitudes. We might revise the question to minimize the possibility that one response could appear more socially attractive than another: "Some people feel there should be laws against marriage between members of the same sex; others feel there should not be laws against marriage between members of the same sex. Which way do you feel?" If sentiment continues to run in the same direction as before, we might try an even stronger inducement to "shake" ensuing respondents from this answer: "Many people suggest that there are good reasons for maintaining laws against marriage between members of the same sex. Would you agree with these people?"

We do not advocate the wholesale slanting of research questions, but this measure may sometimes be strategically employed for the special purpose of determining whether respondents are indulging in answer "shading," as previously described. This tactic must be followed with the greatest of care to prevent the deliberately slanted question from compromising the objectivity of the overall interview. Even when there is a strong suspicion that responses are not completely candid, intentional slanting of questions is a last resort, to be used only after other measures have been exhausted (for example, presenting two possible opinions, stating that each opinion may be widely held, and asking which comes closer to the respondent's view).

The sequential nature of intensive interviewing partially offsets one of the strongest criticisms of this method. In studies of large populations, users of research generally feel that large samples produce highly reliable results, which come close to reflecting the beliefs of the entire population. Intensive interviewing,

---

[1] For a complete discussion of induction in fieldwork, see Chapter 9.

which normally uses relatively small samples, is seldom mentioned in the same breath with the word "reliability" unless the total population is not much larger than the sample. But, by combining data gathering with a continuing analysis as the study progresses, and by varying many elements of the study (e.g., the order in which the questions are asked, the way in which a given question may be posed, and safeguards against biased questions or less-than-candid responses), intensive interviewers believe that they usually come up with results in which a high degree of confidence may be placed. The word **STABILITY** is sometimes used to describe *the cumulative results of sequential intensive interviewing that incorporates test after test to challenge the emerging results.*

In short, when the cumulative results of an intensive interview study continue to fall within a given range with interview after interview, despite attempts by the researcher to identify deviations from this range, the researcher senses the sort of stability that can inspire a high degree of confidence. In studies involving matters other than easily observable phenomena, this kind of confidence can be just as important as the statistical reliability attributed to survey research.

The flexibility of intensive interviewing and the researcher's opportunity to revisit interview content, either during a given interview or subsequent meetings, generally has a positive effect on validity. As time goes by, developing rapport with the interviewee decreases the likelihood that the researcher is not measuring what she or he intends to measure. However, there are instances when it is difficult to use interviewing tactics alone to assure validity. Scully and Marolla (1999) interviewed 114 convicted rapists in a prison setting. Because the prisoners had a reputation for "conning," or bending the truth to make themselves appear less to blame, the researchers compared prisoners' accounts with factual research from the police and court files. They also looked at how the criminal's story changed from his first police interrogation to the present. They compared victim's accounts of the crime with that of the rapist. (There was usually a big difference.) This example illustrates the powerful synergy that can result from combining intensive interviews with other forms of data collection. The interviewer who enters the conversation well prepared with factual data from other sources will conduct a much stronger and more authoritative interview.

CONDUCTING AN INTERVIEW

A more concrete examination of intensive interviewing procedures follows. Up to this point, differences between intensive and structured interviews have been emphasized. However, some elements fall along the continuum between these two.

Degrees of Structure

Interviews are usually characterized as one of three types:

- **STRUCTURED OR STANDARDIZED**: *All questions are asked exactly the same way and usually in the same order for all respondents.*
- **NONSCHEDULE STANDARDIZED**: *All questions are asked of each respondent, but they may be asked in different ways and in different sequences.*
- **UNSTRUCTURED OR NONSTANDARDIZED**: *No standardized schedule of questions is used.*

There are variations involving combinations of these types. **SEMISTRUCTURED INTERVIEWS** *include questions that are asked of all respondents (either in a structured or nonscheduled form) as well as other, unstructured questions.* Semistructured interviewing was used in the study of motherhood cited earlier. This is a popular form of intensive interviewing because it provides some data that are comparable for all respondents (for example, age, marital status, and level of affluence) and other data derived from questions tailored to the unique experiences and perspectives of each individual.

Access to Respondents

In discussing the procedures of intensive interviewing, we will employ a hypothetical case. Suppose we are about to begin a study of upper-middle-class suburbanites' attitudes toward active involvement in political campaigns, whether as candidates themselves or on behalf of others.

Our first problem is to get these people to submit to intensive interviews. We wish to interview them at length in their homes – half adult female household heads and half adult male household heads – and we cannot afford to pay them for their trouble. Why should they have the slightest inclination to participate in the study?

Ordinarily, we might seek the public endorsement of a respected and well-known local organization to help establish our credibility, but because of the nature of our topic, we cannot risk any respondent's thinking that we represent a group with a specific political agenda. We write a letter to the chief of police, with details of the manner in which we intend to go about our study. We state that our objective is to determine what motivates an individual to become politically active and what some of the implications of the research may be, both for the person and for the community. We guarantee that no participant will be identified with specific responses in the report. The ultimate beneficiaries, we state, will be people and organizations wishing to nurture a healthy political system within the community. We formally request permission to conduct the study as outlined in the letter, verify that interviewers will have appropriate identification, and follow up the letter with a personal visit to the police station. We are granted permission to go door to door to conduct the study.

We now send letters to a sample of homes (selected randomly if the study is a large one or, perhaps, selected to reflect widely disparate neighborhood conditions if we will be conducting only a few interviews). In the letters, we explain the broad purpose of our research, and, if applicable, identify its sponsors. We do need to reveal sponsorship in order to be truthful and ethical, but in this case, if funding for our study comes from a specific source, it is likely a nonpartisan research, academic, or public interest organization. This will decrease the likelihood that people will determine whether to participate based solely on the identity of the sponsoring group.

Now comes some hard and delicate work – actually obtaining respondent cooperation. We visit a few homes that have received our letter and ask for an appointment to conduct an interview, stating that it may last as long as two or three hours. Most of the people we approach perceive themselves as being very busy. Some are suspicious of us and our motives. We emphasize that their participation is extremely important to us because we have selected only a few households to represent the entire community. We also stress that the information they provide will not be linked to them personally. We offer to make a synopsis of the results available to them. We assure them that our intent is not to inconvenience or to exploit them but simply to collect information, at their convenience, that will benefit many people in working toward a healthy and viable political system in the community. When they express concern over the length of the interview, we explain that it can be divided into more than one session and suggest that they start the interview to see if they find it as interesting as most people do.

In other words, we attempt to induce participation (1) by capitalizing on the fact that an intensive interview approaches the sort of sociable conversation enjoyed by most people. It is not, strictly speaking, a social occasion, but it tends in that direction and can be a positive experience for people who take pleasure in being asked their opinion. (2) In presenting ourselves as interviewers, we hope to be viewed by the people we approach as what Goffman (1966:129) called **OPENING PERSONS –** *individuals such as newspaper reporters who, because of their roles, are implicitly granted the license to approach strangers* without causing the suspicion and rejection that often accompanies such confrontations. Thus, intensive interviewers may be accommodated because of their uniquely perceived role as people whose job is to talk to strangers.

We do *not* advocate that an interviewer plead with potential interviewees to "help me do my job." This borders on the unethical and is also a sign of weakness that could influence interviewees' later comments.

Preparation

Preparation for the actual interviews consists of two key elements. First, we obtain all available background information on local political organizations, residents' voting behavior and party affiliations, elective positions in the area, and other pertinent factors. Sources might include published material (for example, newspaper articles or editorials, voting records, voting registration lists, and books and Web sites containing information on the history of the community), and brochures or material made available by local political or other organizations. We speak with a few community or civic leaders. We also speak with leaders of specific political organizations.

This first type of preparation leads directly to the second type – formulation of a tentative guide for conducting the interviews. Despite the generally open-ended nature of intensive interviews, they do involve an equivalent to a questionnaire, called an **INTERVIEW GUIDE**, which *lists specific issues to be brought to an interviewee's attention*. It contains items that might be appropriate for a given interview, including:

- Specific questions or topics that promise to be fruitful, along with a rough outline for the ordered placement
- Some contingency questions that presuppose a certain comment or answer on the respondent's part
- Any hypotheses already formulated for testing

Most researchers follow the rule of thumb that interviews should commence with some general questions that are relatively easy to answer; with these as background, the topics and questions become progressively more specific and probing.

Through this intensive preparation, we obtain a "feel" for the community in general and for its political activity patterns in particular. It reduces the chances that we will appear completely shocked or unknowledgeable in the face of an interviewee's responses. Our investigation emerges from abstraction to reality. Our sense of personal involvement and commitment is heightened, and we gain confidence in our ability to cope with any unexpected complications that may arise during the interviews.

Execution

We arrive at the home of the first respondent and introduce ourselves. We restate the purpose of the study and mention any pertinent ethical considerations. We might say something like:

> Hello, I'm _____. We spoke the other day about the study I'm conducting on political involvement. Thank you for giving me the opportunity to ask you some questions. I'm particularly interested in people's impressions on what political life and organizations are like, how political organizations function, what purposes they serve, why people participate in them, and anything else you can tell me about your impressions of political activity and political organizations. As I said the other day, I can promise that your name will never be linked with anything you say; you will remain completely anonymous. I'd like to tape-record our conversation, although I don't want your name to appear on the tape. Taping our discussion means that I don't have to take a lot of notes, which speeds up the process and ensures that I have an accurate record of what we say. No one except me will hear the tape.

This introduction has suggested the range of topics to be discussed. The word "impressions" is important because interviewees often leap to the assumption that they are inappropriate respondents if they do not participate frequently in the phenomenon under study. Tape-recording the interview, in addition to providing a permanent record of the exchange, will enable us to evaluate our interviewing technique after the interview is completed.

Nowhere in the introduction did we refer to the interview as an "interview." Since some people equate "interview" with "interrogation," it is important at the outset to present the exchange as a conversation, or discussion, between two "participants."

The researchers decided to hold the interviews in people's homes. But there is no assurance that this would be the best setting. In fact, it is likely that the respondents may be distracted by events around them (including telephone calls or the needs of family members) or by the very presence of onlookers in the form of other residents of the home. The intensive interviewer should be prepared to change the setting of the interviews. If the suburbanites are bothered by the home environment, we might request that interviews be held elsewhere, such as an anteroom in the town hall or library.

Once the interview begins, we follow the predetermined topic outline until it seems natural to deviate from it. Let us say we have decided to conduct semistructured interviews, in which we will ask each person about involvement in political activities, parties, and organizations. These questions are relatively easy to answer, so we ask them at the beginning. The interviewee is reassured that participation in the discussion will not be a difficult task, and we now have knowledge about the respondent that later may be used as a frame of reference.

From this point, the course of the interview and the questions that are asked will depend largely on input from the respondent. As in every conversation, the participants may use many devices in manipulating the interchange to achieve a given purpose. It is the task of the interviewer to facilitate the accomplishment of both parties' objectives. As an example of the various intents that may motivate interviewer and interviewee input, a hypothetical dialogue is presented in Figure 8.1. Beside each comment is a statement of the underlying intent.

In addition to the many conversational devices that may be employed by either party, this example shows how the interviewer may seize on just one word ("club") to propel the interview in a related and useful but slightly different direction. The perceived importance of having a common goal, which might or might not be covered later in the interview, emerged at this point and provided important insights into the respondent's real outlook on political involvement.

Some of the conversational techniques that may be used by an intensive interviewer to maximize information obtained in the execution of the interview include the following:

- Repetition or restatement (exemplified earlier)
- Expressing ignorance to elicit information
- Expressing interest or support as a reward (exemplified earlier)
- Encouraging expanded response (exemplified earlier; also simple nodding)
- Legitimizing alternative responses – stating that some people feel one way while others feel another way, to reduce interviewee's fears of sanctions on a given opinion
- Introducing transitions – announcing a change in topic to avoid catching interviewee by surprise or making interviewee feel like an "outsider"
- Summarizing – giving frequent summaries of the conversational highlights up to the time of the summary, in order to keep interviewee involved in the total conversation and to ensure that interviewer and interviewee are on the same "wavelength" as to the results
- Challenging answers – tactfully bringing up apparent inconsistencies in responses and seeking clarification
- Purging irrelevant responses – allowing respondent to become "talked out" concerning an irrelevant tack with which respondent seems preoccupied
- Granting vacation – allowing respondent to indulge in irrelevancies for a short period, in order to build up interviewee energy for the next conversational tasks
- Revealing self-information – interviewer's mentioning of certain facts about self – facts that flow naturally into the conversation that will not change interviewee's responses or train of thought

Denzin (1978) conducted a study of mental patients, examining changes in their attitudes as they moved in and out of hospitals. One respondent, when asked if she "would be against a daughter of hers marrying a man who had been

Conversation	Intent
IR: Let's talk for a moment about the reasons why someone might become active in campaigning for a political candidate.	*Definition of purpose.*
IE: (Silence)	*Encouragement to proceed.*
IR: What are some of the reasons why someone might join this kind of activity?	*Restatement of purpose into question.*
IE: Well, you want to be of service to the community.	*Indication of opinion in response to direct question.*
IR: Uh-huh.	*Encouragement to proceed.*
IE: I mean you become politically active because you think your candidate will help other people.	*Restatement and expansion of earlier response.*
IR: I understand.	*Indication that no further restatement is needed; encouragement to proceed in another direction.*
IE: And of course you enjoy belonging to a club too.	*Additional opinion response to earlier question.*
IR: Club?	*Echo statement to elicit more information.*
IE: Well, I'd never be a candidate, so I think of political activity as being a member of an organization that is sort of like a club and having a common goal – at least the ones I'd want to join.	*Expanded definition in response to echo request.*
IR: So, there are some you'd want to join and others you wouldn't want to join.	*Restatement of IE's comment to elicit more information.*
IE: Sure. I'd rather work for a school committee member than for a mayoral candidate, because I feel a school committee member can make more of a difference.	*Clarification of former statement in response to IR's restatement.*
IR: What are some of the ways in which a school committee member can make more of a difference than a mayor?	*Probe for additional related information.*
IE: Well, there are many ways to make a difference.	*Evasion of question, perhaps because earlier response is difficult to substantiate or because the topic is too sensitive, or because IE is tired of discussing topic.*
IR: That's interesting. What are some of the ways in which you think the school committee members themselves might feel they make an important difference?	*Initial support, so as not to alienate IE. Refocus on previous topic, approaching question from different perspective.*
IE: Well, that's what I meant by a common goal. They have the ultimate goal of helping kids – or at least they should have.	*Partial amplification of previous response and indication of possible skepticism, which may provide yet another avenue for questioning.*

IR = interviewer; IE = interviewee.

Figure 8.1. Interview dialogue and intent.

to see a psychiatrist about a mental problem," answered initially, "I know I shouldn't say this but I don't want any daughter of mine marrying a man who has been through what I have been." When the question was repeated, the woman replied, "No, I guess I wouldn't be against this!" (Denzin, 1978:129). The persistence of the interviewing revealed what appeared to be the difference between a hasty judgment and a more considered opinion.

Sensitive Topics: Emotionality

Intensive interviews may be useful in probing into sensitive areas. If a respondent appears to evade a question because it is too personal, the interviewer may wait until rapport has grown and may then ask the question in a different way. If a question about the interviewee's family relationships elicits no response, the interviewer may later pose a more general question about family ties in today's society and then ask how the respondent's family contrasts with other families in this respect. Only the most highly trained and perceptive researchers can succeed in employing this technique without arousing the suspicion or ire of the interviewee. There are some sensitive subjects for which the anonymity provided by mail questionnaires may encourage more candid responses than many intensive interviewers can generate.

Occasionally, there may be unanticipated, emotional responses to a line of questioning. Consider the following exchange:

> INTERVIEWER: So, how's it going to feel when your youngest child goes off to college?
>
> INTERVIEWEE: Well, it's going to be tough [becoming teary]. I guess my husband and I always have had problems in our marriage [is sobbing] and maybe now there won't be much of a reason for us to stay together! [crying uncontrollably]

In this situation, the interviewer should not ignore the respondent's outburst and loss of control; maintaining rapport may require extending emotional support (Stewart and Cash, 2000). Appropriate responses would be

> It's okay to cry.
>
> Take your time.
>
> Want to break for a few minutes?

In some cases, it may be advisable to cut short the interview and to reschedule the remaining questions.

There are other interview topics that touch on predictably vulnerable issues. One major advantage of mastering the skills of intensive interviewing is that we can approach such issues with depth and sensitivity.

Guidelines for Questioning

As we noted earlier in this chapter, preparation for questioning includes the development of an interview guide. How many and which topics are covered with each person depend on several factors, including the nature of respondents and their experience as well as time constraints. The list of topics in the interview guide is usually quite extensive and is typically organized into general categories (see the example of the battered women's interview). Of course, most interviews are not conducted under emotional duress, but they still may be a daunting experience for respondents.

Throughout the interview, the researcher should be on the lookout for any indications of fatigue or disinterest on the part of the interviewee. It may be necessary to halt the interview and resume it at a later point. Sometimes it is important to allow the respondent to ramble on about a seemingly irrelevant point to provide a "vacation" from the topic at hand. The good intensive interviewer will develop several techniques for recognizing and dealing with respondent restlessness or boredom.

Recording Information

Recording information may strongly influence the tempo of the interview, the nature of the responses, and the quality of the analysis. Consequently, the interviewer must weigh several factors before deciding on the recording method to be used in a given study.

Using Intensive Interviewing to Screen for Domestic Violence

The American Medical Association (AMA) and many other professional organizations advocate routine screening for domestic violence of all women patients in hospital settings. The AMA recommends starting with a statement such as, "Because abuse and violence are so common in women's lives, we screen for it routinely."[2] Questions may be asked in a number of domains, for example:

1. Questions that tell victims they are not alone:
   - Many patients tell me they have been hurt by their partners. Is this happening to you?
   - Sometimes people who are as jealous as you've described may use physical force. Is this happening in your situation?
   - Has your partner ever hit or threatened you?

2. Questions based on your observations:
   - You seem frightened of your partner. Has he/she ever hurt you?
   - Your partner seemed not to want to let me speak with you alone. I'm concerned that he/she might want to control what you might tell me. Do you think that is happening?
   - I noticed you check with your partner before you answer any questions. Are you afraid you might get hurt if you said the "wrong thing"?
   - The receptionist noticed you and your partner arguing in the parking lot, and saw you get shoved up against the car. I'm concerned for your safety.
   - I noticed you have several bruises. How did they happen? Did someone hit you?

3. Questions about physical abuse:
   - Are you in a relationship where you get hit, punched, kicked, or hurt in any way?
   - Do arguments ever end in your partner pushing, shoving, or slapping you?
   - Has your partner ever used a fist or weapon to hurt or threaten you?

4. Questions about the relationship:
   - Is your partner short-tempered with you or the children? Does he/she become abusive when he/she gets angry?
   - You mentioned your partner drinks a lot. Has he/she ever threatened you when he/she was drunk?
   - Who controls the finances in your relationship? Does your partner insist on having all possessions in his/her name?

5. Questions about sexual abuse:
   - Has your partner ever forced you to have sex when you didn't want to?
   - Does your partner force you to engage in sex that makes you uncomfortable?
   - Does your partner ignore your decisions regarding safe sex or contraception?

---

[2] While most victims of domestic violence are women in relationships with men, a significant proportion are men and women in gay or lesbian relationships, and it is also important to ask these patients about domestic violence (DV). You can say, "Because so many people experience abuse and violence from their partners, I've begun to screen for it routinely." Using gender-neutral statements like this can communicate to patients both that you are knowledgeable about DV and that you don't assume that everyone is heterosexual (New York State, 2004).

6. Specific questions about emotional abuse, threats or intimidation:

- Does your partner ever call you names or put you down?
- When your partner gets angry, does he/she ever throw things? Threaten you? Destroy things you care about, like family photographs or clothes? Hurt your pets?
- Does your partner ever threaten to hurt you when you disagree about something?
- Does your partner accuse you of having affairs? Check up on you?
- Do you have to ask your partner's permission to do things you want to do? Are you comfortable making decisions about daily activities, or are you afraid to do so?
- Does your partner try to control who you can be friends with, or keep you from having friends?

AVOID asking:

Labeling questions. (Many victims do not see themselves in those labels.)

- Are you being battered? abused?
- Are you the victim of domestic violence?

"Why didn't you . . . ?" questions. (They sound accusatory and blaming.)

- Why didn't you come to the hospital sooner?
- Why didn't you just leave the first time he/she hit you?
- Why didn't you call the police?

"Why don't you . . . ?" questions. (They sound like you know what is best for the victim, and your suggestions may have safety implications of which you are unaware.)

- Why don't you go to the shelter?
- Why don't you tell him/her you won't put up with it any more?

Adapted from New York State Office for the Prevention of Domestic Violence (2004).

The recording method should enable the interviewer to transcribe all substantive communication from the interviewee. Some interviewers simply write notes as copiously as they can, believing that exhaustive recording of the interviewee's comments is the best path. Others prefer to record only the main points of the respondent, sacrificing some recording in favor of being more heavily involved in the interaction. Many interviewers do not rely exclusively on an audio recorder; in fact, inarticulate respondents or noisy background conditions may require interviewers to go back over a tape to hear each word slowly and distinctly, before attempting an analysis. The interviewer must decide (sometimes in advance, but often after the first few meetings) how much note taking will be necessary and whether to supplement notes with tape recordings. Some intensive interviewers compromise by taking written notes in every interview but taping only a portion to obtain verbatim quotes that may add "flavor" to findings based on the handwritten notes. Some balance between note taking and taping usually is best. In some cases, tape recordings are not feasible because of anonymity concerns that voices of respondents may be recognizable (Scully and Marolla, 1999). Videotaping is highly desirable to pick up nonverbal cues that go unnoticed on audiotapes. However, videos typically present more problems of anonymity than either taking notes by hand or audiotaping.

Interviewing Children

As indicated in Chapter 5, there is increasing interest in involving children in research. Interviewing young people raises some important methodological issues. Children are highly suggestible, and one must always question the credibility of a young child's self-report (Zwiers and Morrissette, 1999). Grieg and Taylor (1999), who have interviewed preschoolers and primary schoolchildren, recommend that the researcher should dress in casual clothing. Before the interview, it is beneficial to play and to use toys with the child, so that a trusting relationship is built. One can also "enter" the children's world through the use of stories, puppets, sand, and drawings. Grieg and Taylor also advise that drawings can serve as nonverbal cues to help the researcher gain insight into the workings of the child's mind. For example, the intensity of line pressure or shading may indicate anxiety, and sexualized body parts could indicate abuse. One should always speak slowly to small children, and use simple words (Grieg and Taylor, 1999).

As part of a study of class and gender in schools' work-experience programs, Mackenzie (2005) engaged thirty-nine high school students in semistructured group and individual interviews. Students were assured of confidentiality and given the opportunity to opt out of the experience. Group interviews were selected as a strategy to reflect the social context of young people's understanding of the topic for study and "to map as nearly as possible the discourse young people use among their peers when talking of gender, class and work." Single-sex groups were used to facilitate analysis of any differences between the sexes and to provide freedom from any constraints that might have operated in the presence of the opposite sex. Mackenzie found that the presence of the interviewer constrained the conversation to some extent. However, in the groups, the discussion quickly became the property of the children, and the researcher intervened only to introduce a new topic or to encourage a quieter member to contribute. "The young people soon abandoned the register they were accustomed to using with adults in school as they warmed up to enthusiastic and sometimes heated exchange on issues which were of great concern to them."

As examples of research with children become more numerous, techniques for sustaining higher levels of reliability and validity in data derived from children will undoubtedly be even further improved.

The smooth flow of the interview should be facilitated by the recording method. Some intensive interviewers take notes on a series of cards, each of which is devoted to one of the general categories from the outline in the interview guide. This technique allows quick referral to previous comments on a given topic, thus ensuring that the respondent is being consistent and preventing interviewee boredom that might arise if the same topic were inadvertently covered twice. Other interviewers do the same sort of organizing on sheets of paper, on which they include several categories to minimize paper shuffling, which they feel can disrupt the interview flow.

The method of recording information should facilitate ongoing analysis of the responses. During the interview, the interviewer should identify implications, develop hunches and hypotheses, and formulate directions for the remainder of the particular interview and for future meetings. Audio- and videotapes are used only after the interview – one of the principal limitations of relying on a machine instead of taking detailed notes. Some intensive interviewers employ symbols, forms of shorthand, or other special notations to indicate a variety of factors, including a potential hypothesis; a question that should be asked immediately or later in the interview; whether a given respondent comment was the result of an interviewer probe; at what point in the interview a particular communication occurred (if recording is being done by category rather than in simple sequential form); and even the footage point on a recorded tape at which a given comment occurred.

The relatively unstructured nature of intensive interviews may suggest that the recording of information from them should also be done in an unstructured way, but this is not necessarily so. Using a notepad or a laptop computer, the researcher can list the general categories of interview content. Another section of notes may be devoted to the responses to what has been asked. There might also be a place for the variety of theoretical ideas that are being inductively or deductively produced. An interviewer might even change the color of a pen or pencil at several junctures during the interview, to identify the approximate points at which certain communication occurred. Of course, if the computer is used to store data taken from interviews, appropriate shifts in font and typeface color can be used to denote key points in each interview or the various categories of notes.

Remaining in Control

Without being abrasive or authoritarian, the researcher in the hypothetical interview (Figure 8.1) maintained in control and guided the respondent into productive conversation. When the interviewee gave evasive or superficial answers, the interviewer strategically pursued the line of questioning to obtain more meaningful responses. The interviewer maintained a steady PACE, or *tempo*, not allowing the conversation to get bogged down with repetitions and not skipping over important points. Pacing is important: It is not desirable for an interview to gain momentum and then to deteriorate because the tempo has suddenly become too slow or too fast. The desired momentum is one that permits a steady and productive flow of conversation. If *either* of the participants speaks

for a long time without some input from the other, the interview is suffering from a lack of control.

However, if the interview consists of a series of rapid-fire inputs between interviewer and interviewee, this is a sign that the researcher is failing to get responses of sufficient length to obtain relevant information. A good rule of thumb is that a sixty-minute in-depth interview should average between two and four inputs per minute (including inputs of both parties). More frequent exchanges defeat the in-depth, conversational purpose of intensive interviewing; if an interview transcript looks similar to a survey transcript, the encounter is simply not "intensive" enough!

Appropriate use of **PREEMPTIVE TECH-NIQUES** – *measures taken to prevent the respondent from taking certain conversational directions* – can greatly enhance the efficiency and control of interviews. Many interviewees want to avoid revealing anything about themselves, so they speak about "people in general." The interviewer can preempt this tendency by saying to the interviewee at the outset that "It is important that you answer only for yourself; we'll be asking other people how *they* feel." Respondents sometimes like to see themselves as exceptions to norms – exceptions that make them unsuitable to answer a given question. The interviewer can preempt this avoidance technique by explaining that opinions or impressions are needed from *all* respondents and that the analysis can take note of the exceptional circumstance.

Avoiding Overrapport

We have already stated that the quality of the emerging relationship between researcher and respondent is the key to how productive the intensive interview will be. This does not mean that the two will become close friends, and in fact there is a danger of **OVERRAPPORT** – *inappropriate familiarity that could compromise the researcher's detached perspective*. Seidman (2006) argues that, while friendly relationships can be useful in the interview process, it is wise to err on the side of formality. In most types of intensive interviewing, it is important for the researcher to nurture rapport with the other party within the framework of professionalism and neutrality.[3]

The best avenue for creating and sustaining a productive relationship with respondents is to ensure that they receive sufficient rewards from the relationship without their feeling that these gratifications are artificial. It is a good idea, for example, to praise the interviewee's contributions occasionally but not to the point where such praise is overdone. Sometimes it is the timing, rather than the amount, of praise that is most important.

One of the attractions intensive interviewing has for respondents is that it gives them an opportunity to reveal in a nonjudgmental environment the multiple identities they perceive themselves as having. A woman who may know she is criticized by neighbors for "going off and leaving her child" with a babysitter while she pursues a career need fear no recriminations on this subject from a skilled intensive interviewer. In this sense, the interaction with the researcher may offer benefits not available in most day-to-day encounters. As we observed in the interviews of mothers conducted by McMahon (1995) the intensive interviewer, who accepts without judgment the various self-identities revealed by the respondent, is promoting development of strong rapport with the other party and perhaps, also, greater self-acceptance on the part of the interviewee.

Nonverbal Signs

At one point in the hypothetical dialogue offered in Figure 8.1, the interviewee remained silent at a time when it might have been appropriate to say something. This was a nonverbal message for the researcher. The interviewer interpreted the silence as a signal to proceed because the respondent needed more inputs. When in doubt about the meaning of such signals, it is best to take the positive approach and to proceed.

Nonverbal communication is an important part of any conversation and, therefore, of any intensive interview. Many signals may be given by either party, involving tone of voice, eye contact, body position, gestures, facial expressions, and pauses. (Even the point at which one person interrupts another can be meaningful.) Nonverbal signs offer interviewers many ways in which to manipulate an encounter while not appearing to do so (Gorden, 1998). Because the same devices are available to interviewees, it behooves researchers to be constantly aware of any nonverbal communication in which the other party engages. Burgess and Holmstrom (1974:144–145) illustrated how a rape victim used nonverbal means to indicate her feelings of distress during an intensive interview:

Laura, age 13, wouldn't say anything. She sat holding a little pink coin purse. Then she bent over and picked up a short screw from the floor that her mother had dropped. She took the screw and kept hitting, with some force, the purse with the screw. First she drew lines across the purse; then she really stabbed it, making holes in the purse.

Researchers should be acutely aware of the nonverbal messages they are giving off. One of the easiest ways to undermine rapport between interviewer and interviewee is for the former to look or act in a manner outside the bounds of acceptability. In most suburban communities, for example, a stranger entering a private home is implicitly expected to present a neat appearance and not to be dressed too informally. Although someone interviewing on a Saturday might find the respondent clothed in faded, torn jeans while doing household chores, the interviewer should not attempt to duplicate this appearance, as it may be interpreted as a lack of respect for the person whose home is being entered. Neither should the interviewer be so well dressed that the respondent will feel uncomfortable by comparison. Interviewers should maintain their own identities without overemphasizing differences between themselves and interviewees.

LIMITATIONS OF INTENSIVE INTERVIEWING

We turn now to a review of the most significant limitations of the intensive interviewing method. Although it is possible to minimize

---

[3] An exception to this rule-of-thumb is so-called "experiential research" (Reinharz, 1984) and other feminist interviewing techniques, which are covered in Chapter 10.

some of these problems, it is ironic that many of them are the unavoidable consequences of characteristics that represent the greatest strengths of the method.

First, it is difficult to generalize about entire populations from studies based on intensive interviewing. This is not to say that generalizations cannot be made; the problem is that we usually have no way to assess the accuracy of these generalizations. One source of difficulty is the sampling procedure. Intensive interviewing studies are generally based on small, nonprobability samples. Typically, no effort is made to obtain a random sample of some clearly definable population. Use of a sample of as many as fifty respondents is rare. Even if probability selection procedures are used, with such small samples the error involved in making any statistical generalizations from the sample to the relevant population would be too large to be useful. It would not help us much to know that 50 percent plus or minus 30 percent (that is, between 20 percent and 80 percent) of those in the population of interest oppose gun-control legislation, favor abortion on demand, or believe that the United States should have a female president. One reason for the small sample is that the interviewing is usually done by one or two people on a limited budget. Another is that the data are not easily adapted to quantitative statistical analysis. So, even if the number of respondents approaches the several hundred that are common in survey research studies, it becomes very difficult to analyze the data qualitatively.

Another threat to generalizability is the lack of standardization in the interviewing procedure. The way in which a question is asked differs from one interview to the next. The goal is to ask each respondent the question in a way that gets the most complete and accurate information possible on the issues of interest, but we have no way of knowing that the alternative ways the question was asked compare in meaning.

The amount of emphasis placed on a question is not standardized from one interview to the next. Typically, there will be a whole series of questions asked of a specific respondent and not asked of any other. Even for questions asked

of all or most respondents, the length of the responses will vary considerably. This inconsistency is due partly to differences among subjects with respect to how much they would volunteer in response to the same question asked in exactly the same way. The same general question may elicit eight-word answers from some respondents and 800-word replies from others.

The lack of standardization in the data collection process makes it difficult to replicate an intensive interview study. Suppose we try to repeat such a study and come up with different conclusions. It will be difficult to pinpoint the reason for the discrepancy. Problems in replicating the sampling and interviewing procedures of the original study mean that the reliability of the method is low relative to the reliability of survey research. There is generally no way to make statistical estimates of the reliability of the results of an intensive interview study.

Intensive interviewing is highly vulnerable to interviewer bias. Bias may occur in any form of data gathering based on interviewing, but it poses a much greater threat to the validity of in-depth interview data than to the questionnaire data used in survey research. Although interviewers are always instructed to avoid communicating their own views on the issues, they always give off some cues that can be used by the respondent as a basis for at least guessing where they stand on a variety of questions. This is particularly true in intensive interviewing, which is informal and conversational. Even if interviewers are successful in avoiding verbal cues, there are many ways to communicate nonverbally of which they may not be fully aware and over which they do not have full control. In a long encounter, it is likely that interviewers will unintentionally communicate a great deal about themselves, their values, and their attitudes. This communication has an effect on the opinions expressed by interviewees. The wish to give socially desirable answers or to please the interviewer is a problem in any kind of interviewing but especially in intensive interviewing.

The researcher's flexibility in casting questions and probing issues is another potential source of bias. In the simplest case, the interviewer can ask leading or loaded questions, which make it more likely that the respondent will choose one answer over others. Taped interviews can be checked for evidence of this kind of responding, but since usually only the researcher (who is also the interviewer) reviews these tapes, it is not very likely that any bias present will be detected. By the time the results are prepared for publication, any such bias will be all but impossible to determine. Even if audiotapes are reexamined thoroughly, body language that might have indicated researcher bias, or respondents' reaction to it, goes undetected.

The quality of the data collected using the intensive interviewing approach depends very heavily on the skills of the interviewer. In this sense, it is similar to participant observation research (see Chapter 9), which relies to a great extent on the acumen of the observer. In survey work, competent interviewers are important, but the skills required are much narrower and are easier to teach. One reason that intensive interviewing studies are typically based on small samples is the difficulty of finding good intensive interviewers or of adequately training new ones.

One of the supposed advantages of in-depth interviews is that they provide more accurate responses on sensitive issues than do survey questionnaires, but we cannot always rely on this to happen. In fact, with some respondents the more formal survey encounter (or the anonymous mailed questionnaire) may yield the more honest responses. Unfortunately, there are no clear guidelines available to tell us which substantive issues, or which conditions, make intensive interviewing most effective.

Finally, standardization in data analysis procedures is lacking. In contrast to the typical quantitative research study, it is possible for two data analysts to come up with very different interpretations of a single body of data generated from intensive interviews. Because of the lack of any systematic procedures for analyzing such data, it would be very difficult to decide which interpretation was more valid; however,

the situation does not arise very often because usually the interviewer and the data analyst are the same person.[4] This dependence on the judgments of one investigator (or perhaps two) in data interpretation leaves the door open for the researcher's theoretical perspective and personal ideology to influence substantially the reported findings of the study.

Even though all these salient criticisms of intensive interviewing have been raised, for some purposes, it remains the most effective and appropriate method of data collection. A skillful application of the research imagination will tell us when to make use of this technique. It should be clear from the list of shortcomings, as well as the review of advantages that preceded it in this chapter, that its weakest attributes tend to be generalizability and reliability and that its greatest strengths are found in the validity and richness of data obtained and the personal accounts and stories that are often missed by more quantitative approaches to data.

CURRENT DEVELOPMENTS IN THE TECHNIQUE

Telephone Intensive Interviewing

Intensive interviewing has typically involved face-to-face encounters and the associated expense of this form of data gathering. However, special-purpose intensive interviews may also be conducted successfully by telephone. The quality of these telephone contacts is highly dependent on the complexity of the research objectives; their scope must be somewhat limited for relatively brief telephone intensive interviews to work well. One advantage of the telephone intensive interview, in addition to financial savings, is that some people who perceive themselves as too busy to grant a personal audience will agree to a telephone contact lasting the same amount of time. A disadvantage is that telephone interviewing removes the ability

---

[4] In larger studies where two or more analysts are used, they should be trained as a team. Individuals aside from the interviewer who are charged with transcribing the interviews should also be included on this team.

of the interviewer to use and interpret visual cues, including facial expression, that accompany face-to-face conversation.

Using E-mail

As computer communication spreads, practitioners have begun to experiment with interviewing using e-mail and the World Wide Web. These technologies allow the researcher to contact subjects who may otherwise be hard to reach because of distance or scheduling. E-mail can be used as an electronic version of mailed surveys (see Chapter 7), but it can also be used in "interviewing," that is, using written questions and answers exchanged between the interviewer and subject, with follow-up questioning undertaken through ongoing correspondence. Like face-to-face interviewing, the approach can form an ongoing social relationship. However, rapport is mediated through formal letter writing, and in using e-mail the feedback between letter writers is usually not instantaneous and therefore not spontaneous (Selwyn and Robson, 1998). The method allows for very inexpensive interviewing to be undertaken, and, because of the speed with which electronic mail can be delivered, it can be relatively fast and convenient (especially for the researcher, who can store and collate the messages in electronic form). However, because of the nature of the communication, e-mail interviewing can stretch the discussion out over time if respondents do not check their e-mail frequently.

Using the World Wide Web

Software has been developed that allows cost-effective interviewing in real time over the World Wide Web.[5] Although the methods are similar, the online interview and the e-mail interview differ in that the real-time responses cannot be subjected to detailed, considered revision. However, doing the interview in real time allows the researcher to maintain the spontaneity of an in-person or telephone interview. The immediacy of a real-time interview provides a key advantage over interviews by e-mail correspondence because it demonstrates greater attention and commitment on the part of the interviewer to their communication partner. It also places the technical burden on the researcher to set up the interactive technology, reducing the effort required by respondents. Information gained from the interview can be incorporated directly into qualitative data management packages.[6] It is possible for the researcher to customize the pages used in the real-time interview to meet the needs of respondents by the inclusion of animated graphics, background images, fonts, and highlighted text.

Chen and Hinton (1999:4.4) outline a number of criteria that should be applied in deciding whether Web-based interviewing is appropriate:

- Are interviewees able to access the technology required?
- Are interviewees amenable to the use of the technology, as opposed to an alternative method?
- Will the interview examine noncontroversial material that does not require a private, or secure, form of communication?
- Is the status of the interviewee such that the use of an impersonal interviewing method would not be offensive?
- Does the interviewer have the skills required to use the technology?
- Is observation of the interviewee not important for the analysis of data collected?

Potential problems with using this promising technology include information loss and sampling difficulties. Face-to-face interviews are an intensely personal activity. Interviewers use a range of senses as their data collection tools. The lack of physical presence in the online interview precludes non-language-based communication. In addition, because it is dependent on written rather than spoken language, some of the subtleties of oral communication are lost.

---

[5] This discussion draws substantially on Chen and Hinton (1999).

[6] Chapter 9 contains descriptions of qualitative data management software programs that are appropriate for fieldwork and intensive interviewing.

Finally, this technology is usable only by individuals who are computer-literate and have access to appropriate hardware. This reality may mean that representative samples, or even good quota samples, are impossible to obtain. It also may influence the range of topics that may be studied using real-time interviewing.

SUMMARY

Intensive interviewing attempts to round out the image of respondents, rather than reducing them to an atomized set of background characteristics and specific attitudes. It explores their underlying motives and personal experiences; it illuminates the troubling and unfamiliar parts of life as well as more familiar, everyday behavior. In-depth interviews differ from survey interviews in that they are less structured. They allow the interviewer flexibility in questioning the respondent – flexibility that enables the interviewer to encourage respondents' introspection. The researcher can ask for or give immediate clarification in cases of misunderstandings, probe for additional detail on interesting comments volunteered by the interviewee, and defer or rephrase sensitive questions. There is thus a smaller chance that the interviewer and the interviewee will misunderstand one another in an intensive interview than in the structured interaction used in survey research.

Effectiveness is predicated on the interviewer's ability to know what to ask, when and how to ask it, and how to conduct a continuing and cumulative analysis of the entire process. One advantage of the sequential nature of intensive interviews is that the investigator is usually equipped to conduct analysis while asking questions; this ability enables the researcher to challenge and adjust or refute hunches as the study progresses and more interviews are conducted. Compared with survey research, there is less danger of imposing a set of irrelevant categories on the interviewee or of casting the question in a form that does not correspond to the respondent's view of how the world works.

If both parties obtain sufficient rewards from the relationship as time passes, the interview will proceed; otherwise, it will terminate. Thus, the intensive interview should be more of an information exchange than a one-way flow of data and of rewards or benefits to the researcher alone. Whatever method is used to record the interview, it should not upset the smooth flow of the conversation.

In a sense the interviewer is the data-gathering tool in an intensive interview study (as is the fieldworker in an observational study), in contrast to the questionnaire, which is the data-gathering tool in a structured interview survey. Intensive interviewers usually employ no questionnaires, although they do use interview guides, which may include a few structured questions to be asked of every respondent (a semistructured interview). Intensive interviewing is sometimes employed in exploratory studies, in which the researcher wants to obtain a "feel" for what to ask and how to ask it in a large survey research study. In other studies, it may be the only method of data collection.

Like all research techniques, intensive interviewing has its limitations. The data generated do not lend themselves to quantitative analysis and do not permit statistical inferences to be made about the population from which the respondents were drawn. The method is highly dependent on the capabilities of the interviewer. The lack of standardization in sampling, interviewing, and data analysis makes it difficult to determine the generalizability of the results. This lack of standardization also increases the chance that the researcher's theoretical perspective and personal ideology will have a substantial effect on the outcome of the study.

Intensive interviewing is a technique that is highly useful in obtaining information in a relatively short time from potentially elusive or inaccessible respondents. The method permits direct solicitation and collection of information from subjects, rather than the development of inferences based only on observation. Those studied may be located in a relatively confined area or spread throughout the world. Current directions involve the increased use of the telephone, e-mail, and the World Wide Web for intensive interviews.

EXERCISES

1. Discuss the ethical considerations and potential methodological pitfalls of conducting intensive interviews among dying patients in a hospital. Develop a list of fifteen interview questions to ask them. *On Death and Dying*, by Kübler-Ross (1997), will be helpful. How would you counter the patients' tendency to give the "right" answers to please the interviewer?

2. Read *The Overworked American: The Unexpected Decline of Leisure* (Schor, 1993). Prepare a list of fifteen interview questions about the decline of leisure at work or at home. Conduct an interview with a person you do not know; gain access to this person using the procedures outlined in this chapter.

3. Select two pages of dialogue from the interview you have done for exercise 2. Analyze each entry from the interviewer and the respondent according to the treatment in Figure 8.1 in this chapter. What have you learned about the *purpose* of your own questions?

4. Read *The Life Story Interview*, by Atkinson (1998); develop a list of fifteen questions and conduct a life history interview with a person 60 years old or older.

5. Read Zwiers and Morrissette (1999), and, using a topic of your choice, design a fifteen-question interview for a child under the age of 12. Then, gain access using the procedures described in this chapter and conduct the interview. What special problems of interviewing children did you encounter?

SUGGESTED READINGS

Readings about the Method

Atkinson, Robert. 1998. *The Life Story Interview.* Thousand Oaks, CA: Sage.

> *A variation on the intensive interview technique that elicits an individual's life story.*

Gubrium, Jaber F., and James A. Holstein. 2001. *Handbook of Interview Research.* Thousand Oaks, CA: Sage.

> *An authoritative summary of interviewing skills, theory, and process.*

O'Connor, Henrietta, and Clare Madge. 2001. "Cyber-Mothers: Online Synchronous Interviewing using Conferencing Software." *Sociological Research Online* 5 (4).
http://www.socresonline.org.uk/5/4/o'connor.html.

> *This article describes "virtual synchronous" interviews conducted online and introduces the use of a software conferencing technique – Hotline Connect.*

Rubin, Herbert J., and Irene Rubin. 2005. *Qualitative Interviewing: The Art of Hearing Data.* 2nd ed. Thousand Oaks, CA: Sage.

> *A comprehensive, easy-to-read review of the technique.*

Weiss, Robert S. 1995. *Learning from Strangers: The Art and Method of Qualitative Interview Studies.* New York: Free Press.

> *This is one of the best general sources on interviewing, especially the logistics of preparing for the encounter and gaining access. The author also includes a useful section on how to excerpt raw data from interviews into a final report.*

Wengraf, Tom. 2001. *Qualitative Research Interviewing: Semi-Structured, Biographical and Narrative Methods.* Thousand Oaks, CA: Sage.

> *An informative review of qualitative interviewing practice, reflecting the contemporary interest in narrative discourse.*

Zwiers, Michael L., and Patrick J. Morrissette. 1999. *Effective Interviewing of Children.* Philadelphia: Accelerated Development.

An excellent practical resource about interviewing children, this book tells how to dress, speak, and frame questions and includes a discussion of informed consent with children.

Readings Illustrating the Method

Carter, Prudence L. 2005. *Keepin' It Real: School Success Beyond Black and White.* New York: Oxford University Press.

After interviewing high school students of varied ethnic backgrounds, Carter refutes commonsense beliefs about teenage behavior and racial difference. She identifies "multicultural navigators," teens who are culturally aware and who maintain high ambition.

Jensen, Vickie. 1997. *Saltwater Women at Work: In Their Own Words.* Vancouver, BC: Douglas and McIntyre.

Interviews with an unusual occupational group – female mariners who work on boats of all sizes, from water taxis to deep-sea freighters.

Karp, David A. 1996. *Speaking of Sadness: Depression, Disconnection, and the Meanings of Illness.* New York: Oxford University Press.

In-depth interviews with people who suffer from depression. Also contains a useful chapter on qualitative sampling.

Kübler-Ross, Elisabeth. 1997. *On Death and Dying.* New York: Scribner.

This study of dying patients in a hospital used intensive interviewing as the sole data-gathering technique. On the basis of these interviews, Kübler-Ross developed a theory that people who are terminally ill go through a process of dying that has five identifiable stages. She found nonverbal communication between the interviewer and interviewee to be very important. The emerging relationship and its importance in eliciting information are well illustrated in this study.

McMahon, Martha. 1995. *Engendering Motherhood: Identity and Self-Transformation in Women's Lives.* New York: Guilford Press.

In-depth interviews concerning personal identity and motherhood.

Projects A, Work Projects Administration. 2004. *Slave Narratives: A Folk History of Slavery in the United States from Interviews with Former Slaves.* Whitefish, MT: Kessinger.

During the Great Depression, the Works Progress Administration sponsored an interviewing project that contacted former slaves who were still living. This volume contains fascinating first-person accounts recalled from memory.

Schwartz, Pepper. 1995. *Love between Equals: How Peer Marriage Really Works.* New York: Free Press.

A lively study based on interviews with 100 couples.

Terkel, Studs. 1997. *The Good War: An Oral History of World War Two.* New York: New Press.

———. 1997. *Working: People Talk about What They Do All Day and How They Feel About What They Do.* New York: New Press.

———. 2000. *Hard Times: An Oral History of the Great Depression.* New York: New Press.

———. 2004. *Hope Dies Last: Keeping the Faith in Troubled Times.* New York: New Press.

———. 2005. *Race: How Blacks and Whites Think and Feel about the American Obsession.* New York: New Press.

Five works from one of the master interviewers of our time. Terkel's technique relies on asking the right questions, maintaining excellent rapport, and selecting quotes that distill the essence of the phenomena he is analyzing. He does not typically perform much independent analysis, but lets respondents speak for themselves.

Vaughan, Diane. 1990. *Uncoupling: Turning Points in Intimate Relationships.* New York: Vintage.

Eloquent personal revelations about the process of disengagement that leads to the dissolution of marriage.

REFERENCES

Burgess, Ann W., and Lynda Lytle Holmstrom. 1974. *Rape: Victims of Crisis.* Bowie, MD: Brady.

Chatzifotiou, Sevaste. 2000. "Conducting Qualitative Research on Wife Abuse: Dealing with the Issue of Anxiety." *Sociological Research Online* 5 (2).
    http://www.socresonline.org.uk/5/2/chatzifotiou.html.

Chen, Peter, and Samuel M. Hinton. 1999. "Real-time Interviewing Using the World Wide Web." *Sociological Research Online* 4 (3).
    http://www.socresonline.org.uk/4/3/chen.html.

Cieri, Marie, and Claire Peeps, eds. 2001. *Activists Speak Out: Reflections on the Pursuit of Change in America*. New York: St. Martin's Press.

Delong, Candace, and Elisa Petrini. 2001. *Special Agent: My Life on the Front Lines as a Woman in the FBI*. New York: Hyperion.

Denzin, Norman K. 1978. *The Research Act: A Theoretical Introduction to Sociological Methods*. 2nd ed. New York: McGraw-Hill.

Goffman, Erving. 1966. *Behavior in Public Places*. New York: Free Press.

Gorden, Raymond L. 1998. *Basic Interviewing Skills*. Prospect Heights, IL: Waveland Press.

Gray, Amy C. 2003. *Spygirl*. New York: Villard.

Gray, Paul S. 1980. "Exchange and Access in Field Work." *Urban Life* 9 (3) October: 309–331.

Grieg, Anne, and Jayne Taylor. 1999. *Doing Research with Children*. Thousand Oaks, CA: Sage.

Hansen, Eigil Boll, and Merete Platz. 1995. "*The Living Conditions of the 80–100 Year-Olds: An Interview Survey among the Elderly in 75 Danish Municipalities.*" Institute of Local Government Studies (AFK), Denmark.
http://www.akf.dk/eng/weak_eld.htm.

Karp, David A. 1996. *Speaking of Sadness: Depression, Disconnection, and the Meanings of Illness*. New York: Oxford University Press.

Kübler-Ross, Elisabeth. 1997. *On Death and Dying*. New York: Scribner.

Kvale, Steiner. 1996. *Interviews: An Introduction to Qualitative Research Interviewing*. Thousand Oaks, CA: Sage.

Mackenzie, Jeannie. 2005. "Group-Interviewing of Pupils: One Experience." *Scottish Council for Research in Education*.
http://www.scre.ac.uk/tpr/observations/obs10/obs10mackenzie.html.

Maso, Objee, and Fred Webster, eds. 1995. *The Deliberate Dialogue*. Brussels: VubPress.

McMahon, Martha. 1995. *Engendering Motherhood: Identity and Self-Transformation in Women's Lives*. New York: Guilford Press.

New York State Office for the Prevention of Domestic Violence. 2004. *Medical and Legal Protocol for Dealing with Victims of Domestic Violence*. Albany, NY.
http://www.opdv.state.ny.us/health_humsvc/health/protocol/protocol.pdf.

Reinharz, Shulamit. 1984. *On Becoming a Social Scientist*. New Brunswick, NJ: Transaction.

Schor, Juliet. 1993. *Overworked American: The Unexpected Decline of Leisure*. New York: Basic Books.

Scully, Diana, and Joseph Marolla. 1999. "Convicted Rapists' Vocabulary of Motive: Excuses and Justifications." In *Social Deviance: Readings in Theory and Research*, 150–158. Henry N. Pontell, ed. Upper Saddle River, NJ: Prentice Hall.

Seidman, Irving. 2006. *Interviewing as Qualitative Research: A Guide for Researchers in Education and the Social Sciences*. 3rd ed. New York: Teachers College Press.

Selwyn, Neil, and Kate Robinson. 1998. "Using E-mail as a Research Tool." *Social Research Update* 21 (Summer).
http://www.soc.surrey.ac.uk/sru/SRU21.html.

Stewart, Charles J., and William B. Cash, Jr. 2000. *Interviewing Principles and Practices*. Boston: McGraw-Hill.

Thompson, William E., and Jackie L. Harred. 1999. "Topless Dancers: Managing Stigma in a Deviant Occupation." In *Social Deviance: Readings in Theory and Research*, 277–287. Henry N. Pontell, ed. Upper Saddle River, NJ: Prentice Hall.

Vaughan, Diane. 1990. *Uncoupling: Turning Points in Intimate Relationships*. New York: Vintage.

Vigilant, Lee G. 2001. "*Liquid Handcuffs.*" PhD Dissertation, Department of Sociology, Boston College.

Watson, Lucinda. 2001. *How They Achieved: Stories of Personal Achievement and Business Success*. New York: Wiley.

Weiss, Robert S. 1995. *Learning from Strangers: The Art and Method of Qualitative Interview Studies*. New York: Free Press.

Zucker, Carole. 2002. *Conversations with Actors on Film, Television, and Stage Performance*. Westport, CT: Heinemann.

Zwiers, Michael L., and Patrick J. Morrissette. 1999. *Effective Interviewing of Children*. Philadelphia: Accelerated Development.

OBSERVATIONAL FIELD RESEARCH

9

INTRODUCTION

In contrast to most survey research and *all* experimental research, in this chapter we concentrate on techniques that are almost always inductive, where theory is primarily generated *from* data. Rather than using data to confirm or support existing theory, researchers use *observational field research*, or **PARTICIPANT OBSERVATION**, to discover theory. They try to gain an understanding of human action and social process by entering, as far as possible, the worlds of those whose behaviors they are trying to understand. Participant observation lets us see the world as others see it – "in their own terms." When we do that we learn how they achieve a coherent, ordered existence. Participant observation is, therefore, based on the presumption that by studying people in the natural settings where they live and work, social scientists will maximize the ability to grasp the motives, values, beliefs, concerns, troubles, and interests that underlie human behavior.

The Chicago School and Beyond

The famous researcher Robert Park is quoted as having issued the following methodological directive to his students:

You have been told to go grubbing in the library, thereby accumulating a mass of notes and a liberal coating of grime. You have been told to choose problems wherever you can find musty stacks of routine records based on trivial schedules prepared by tired bureaucrats and filled out by reluctant applicants for aid or fussy do-gooders or indifferent clerks. This is called "getting your hands dirty in real research." Those who counsel you are wise and honorable; the reasons they offer are of great value. But one more thing is needful: first-hand observation. Go and sit in the lounges of the luxury hotels and on the doorsteps of the flophouses; sit on the Gold Coast settees and on the slum shakedowns; sit in Orchestra Hall and in the Star and Garter burlesque. In short . . . go get the seats of your pants dirty in real research. (Crabtree, 2003:48)

In the United States, this perspective began in the 1920s at the sociology department of the University of Chicago and with the efforts of Robert Park and Ernest Burgess. Both Park and Burgess emphasized the importance of using the city of Chicago as a laboratory to study human nature and society. Their students employed mixed methods: formal and informal interviews, casual conversation, observation, and collection of historical archives, newspaper articles, and police and court records. Originally, Park and Burgess taught that one should seek the subjective point of view of the actor by abandoning the detached observation of the journalist and striving for empathy and an imaginative participation in the lives of others. As the "Chicago School" evolved during the remainder of the twentieth century, views on outright subjectivity changed (Platt, 1998). Nowadays the guiding principle of research inspired by the Chicago School is that investigators should personally participate in the activities and social worlds of their subjects while maintaining some degree of objectivity and detachment in their role and analysis.[1] To do all this successfully is surely a test of one's research imagination!

Observational research has long been used in anthropology;[2] thus there is justification if the term conjures up the image of a social scientist living with some preliterate tribe, perhaps for several years. The investigator who becomes a member of a relatively unfamiliar American subculture is, in a real sense, doing anthropology. The classic Chicago School studies, *The Hobo* (N. Anderson, 1923), *The Gang* (Thrasher, 1927), and *The Jack Roller* (Shaw, 1930), illustrate this approach, as do countless more recent works, including "Researching Crack Dealers: Dilemmas and Contradictions" (Jacobs, 1998), *Down on Their Luck: A Study of Homeless People* (Snow and Anderson, 1993); *Engineering Culture: Control and Commitment in a High-Tech Corporation* (Kunda, 2006), and *Body and Soul: Notebooks of an Apprentice Boxer* (Wacquant, 2003).

---

[1] As we will see when we examine feminist social research in Chapter 10, not all qualitative fieldworkers share the perspective of the Chicago School regarding the quest for objectivity.

[2] For a more complete description of the uses of anthropological field research, see Chapter 15.

These studies all imply a "spatialized" notion of the "field" as being distant and separate from "home" (Coffey and Atkinson, 1996:59). We may not have to travel as far as an anthropologist would,[3] but when we arrive at the research setting, whether it is a street corner or a complex organization, the Chicago School approach denotes an immersion in that setting for a period of several weeks to years, after which we may return to "normal" life. As the twenty-first century begins, this perspective is being challenged by technology. Researchers still try to establish a reasonable degree of distance between the realms of home and field setting, but people from "home" can easily reach the researcher by e-mail, fax, pager, or cellular phone. Thus, fieldwork may not necessarily mean traveling to a place inhabited by "exotic others"; and it may not be as isolating as in the past.[4] Continual movement in and out of the field poses challenges of concentration for contemporary field researchers, but it also may be more compatible with the complex and competing demands of twenty-first-century professional life (Caputo, 2000).

Examples from the Literature

Three classic works using participant observation include *Street Corner Society*, whose author, William F. Whyte (1943/1995), spent more than two years living in Boston's North End; Herbert Gans's study *The Levittowners* (1982), in which the researcher moved into a new suburban community to understand the quality of life there; and *Tally's Corner*, by Eliot Liebow (1967), which contains his observations of the black street-corner men with whom he spent more than a year. However, observational fieldwork[5]

has transcended the focus on community studies that was part of its Chicago School roots. The range of subjects includes subcultures, for example, alcoholics (Denzin, 1993), the chronically ill (Charmaz, 1993), preadolescents (Adler, 1998), teens in high school (Best, 2000), and religious sects (Rochford, 1985); organizations, such as schools (Eder, 1995); fast food restaurants (Leidner, 1993); and even pornographic bookstores (Karp, 1973). Occupational groups make up another major area of this genre of inquiry, for example, elite lawyers (Granfield, 1992), psychiatrists (Luhrmann, 2001), truckers (Ouellet, 1994), restaurant workers (Fine, 1996), and women's professional golfers (Crosset, 1995).

Promise and Problems

Fieldwork, concentrating as it does on subjective experience, is inherently person oriented. Typically, relatively small groups or well-defined social settings are studied through observation, so that the researcher can establish and maintain firsthand contact with subjects and their actions. Fieldworkers assume that the nature of social, political, and psychological reality is enormously problematic. For them, the way people assign meaning to the objects, events, or situations that they confront daily must be the major concern of scientific investigation. Ideally, qualitative fieldwork should be highly valid because the lengthy engagement in the field tends to reduce the likelihood that researchers are measuring something other than what they intended to measure. There are, however, significant questions about its *reliability*, in part because those who engage in participant observation do not produce studies whose data are presented in quantitative form. Rather, the data consist of *qualitative descriptions of events and statements from the individuals involved*. These descriptions are called ETHNOGRAPHIES.

It is difficult not to sympathize with the goal of providing rich, ethnographic analyses

---

[3] Of course, merely because you are in the field does not mean you are conducting fieldwork. Wolcott (1995:66) noted that he spent one year each in five foreign countries, but only conducted fieldwork three times.

[4] For example, when one of the authors was in the field in Ghana, West Africa (Gray, 1980), it took six weeks for a "snail mail" exchange to occur between him and his thesis supervisors. Today, that same communication would be instantaneous!

[5] The terms *field research* and *fieldwork* are sometimes used in a comprehensive, generic fashion to include any methodology requiring researchers to collect data from individuals in nonlaboratory settings. Given this definition,

survey research and field experimentation could, for example, be labeled field research techniques. To avoid confusion, the terms *field research* and *fieldwork* are being used in a more limited way in this chapter, that is, interchangeably with "observational research."

of one or another culture. However, historically, advocates of participant observation have been much more diligent in making claims for the benefits of their methodology than they have in explaining just how field research gets done. Although it is certainly useful to read the results of observational studies, we are nevertheless left to wonder how to undertake this type of research ourselves. What must be done to gain access to those being studied? What exactly should be observed? How should one behave in the field? Just how much participation is allowed? Which data are important and which unimportant? What kind of identity should a researcher adopt in the field and how long must be spent there?

The standard response to such questions is that they cannot be answered definitively. Observation is indeed the primary and indispensable tactic distinguishing the technique, but field researchers must proceed with a highly varied methodological toolkit, choosing the research strategy that best suits their purpose and circumstances at any given point in the study. Hence, unobtrusive measurement, life histories, documentary and historical analyses, statistical enumeration, in-depth interviews, imaginative role taking, and *personal introspection* (AUTOETHNOGRAPHY) are all important complements of direct observation in the fieldworker's repertoire. Any method of inquiry that can enrich researchers' insight into the social life they are observing, and in which they may be participating, is appropriate.

Perhaps the most comprehensive definition of observational fieldwork is that it aims at a thorough and systematic collection, classification, and reporting of events in a natural setting, as well as the specification of the relations between those events. Thus, while fieldworkers set out to narrate and describe a "slice of social life," they must make their description more than a journalistic account. By employing or fashioning concepts and propositions to order the data they collect, researchers try to illuminate the underlying structure of human organization. If successful, they do a good deal more than simply use abstract categories to describe the events observed; they add a new dimension to our understanding of a social setting or set of events.

They break through the facade of conventional explanation to account for social labels, stereotypes, cultural taboos, fear, ignorance, indifference, or avoidance in the settings they examine. Observational researchers may give us a fresh perspective on our own social positions as well as contribute to the formulation of social theory. All these related aims of observational field research provide the criteria according to which such research ought to be evaluated.

General definitions of fieldwork are helpful because they give us a feel for the nature of the technique. It is one thing, however, to be told that the aim of participant observation is discovery of substantive theory and quite another to know when this task has been adequately accomplished. The idea that field researchers should take the role of those whom they are studying and thereby see the world from their standpoint is sensible in the abstract, but it does not serve as a clear guideline for researchers in the field. The novice field researcher can be perplexed when given advice such as

> Don't worry about clearly defining the research problem too early. The focus of the research should emerge as the investigator becomes involved in the context of the observation. (Taylor and Bogdan, 1998)

> Try to be sensitive to the underlying dimensions of the behaviors being studied. Be flexible and responsive to changes in the setting investigated. Try to be complete in noting observations and descriptions of persons, places, and events. (Strauss and Corbin, 1998)

Yet, this is just the sort of advice we might offer to our own students as they prepare for the field.

Our discussion to this point makes it quite apparent that one of the most striking aspects of observational field research is the absence of standardized operating procedures.[6] Since all cultures have their own distinctive char-

---

[6] The general description of the research process offered here does not extend to those cases in which researchers do quite structured observation. In some instances, researchers decide in an a priori fashion what data are necessary to test their ideas and then construct standard coding categories for their collection. See Chapter 13, "Content Analysis," for examples.

acteristics, different demands are placed on researchers in observing them. A set of rules for doing good field research would be rather like a teachers' manual; although we are surely better off with a discussion of teaching techniques that have worked for other people than with nothing at all, we can never carry out the actual practice with only the manual in hand. Both teaching and field research are instances of complex and sensitive human interaction, and neither can be reduced to a simple set of techniques. The objective sought by the fieldworker, a deep understanding of the meaning of social action, cannot be realized by mechanically and unfeelingly using a simple set of instructions.

Although the field research process cannot be rationalized or mechanized, there *are* benchmarks along the path that observational fieldwork "typically" follows. As we proceed through this chapter, we will examine these and also offer some practical suggestions based on the accumulated successes and failures of many field research projects.

DOING FIELDWORK

Beginning with some general notions and perhaps some tentative hypotheses, field researchers observe a set of behaviors in detail. They then begin to formulate a series of *questions* and *guesses* – HUNCHES – about the meaning of those observations. As more data accumulate, some hunches are supported, others eliminated. It is hoped that some general analytical structure begins to suggest itself. Hunches become more formal hypotheses; inquiry begins to center around these hypotheses; and tentative conclusions begin to solidify. Truly skilled fieldworkers begin to refine their propositions through a vigorous search for NEGATIVE CASES – *phenomena that do not seem to fit into their developing structure of explanation*. In other words, theoretical propositions are not only generated in the field but, insofar as possible, are tested in the field as well.

In sum, fieldworkers do not begin with all their propositions formulated. They follow a long, sometimes difficult path that begins with a sense of something problematic to be investigated,

and they try gradually and inductively to formulate a more sharply defined theoretical model for explaining the events at hand. Within this general process, there are a number of stages through which the research passes.

Beginning the Research: A Question and a Research Site

Field research begins with these basic elements: a general area of inquiry, a problem that calls for explanation, and a potential site where a phenomenon of interest may be observed. When we speak of an area of interest, we mean that in the broadest sense. A researcher might initially be curious about the culture of college students, the way that power is exercised in a community, or the possible alienation of workers in large organizations. Whatever area of interest is chosen, researchers do well to begin by asking themselves what they know and do not know about the area. For example, if one has an interest in social movements, is it general, or in reference to a particular group? Does it come from firsthand experience or from books and lectures on the topic? Or, perhaps social movements have been a prominent part of the recent social scenery? What unanswered questions have been raised through these previous intellectual experiences?

These preliminary thoughts are important for three reasons. First, they should help in pinpointing a manageable area for further inquiry. Second, they may help to specify what is already known about the area of inquiry and therefore suggest the issues needing further investigation to round out personal knowledge of the subject. Finally, some serious reflection on what motivates the choice of one sociological topic instead of another will be an invaluable base from which one may continually assess and reassess potential sources of bias as data are collected and analyzed. This introspective questioning will also help in making researchers' personal sentiments explicit to an audience – and so better allow readers to assess for themselves the validity of the findings.

Most methodologists would argue that the choice of a research site should follow this general problem-formation process. Although some formulation must precede the choice of a setting, the very logic of naturalistic inquiry demands that these preliminary conceptualizations not become so elaborate and compelling that they become self-fulfilling prophecies. There is the danger of leaping from the choice of a generic problem area to the assumption that a particular research setting is indeed a species of that genus. For example, we know that privacy on the Internet is a potential problem (Privacy Rights Clearinghouse, 2007) and that there are individuals called "hackers" who try to gain unauthorized access to Web sites and computers. Suppose that a researcher is interested in studying the "hacking" phenomenon. He or she should not set out with the absolutely rigid idea that hackers make up a social movement with all the characteristics that have come to be associated with such phenomena. This is a matter to be investigated.

It is a sound principle of qualitative research (though perhaps not a widely practiced one) that one's initial interest should be with situations and settings more than with concepts and theories. If we start with the idea that hackers make up a social movement, it is likely that we will uncover a good deal of evidence that they do. If we stick to the more open-ended guiding question "How can hackers best be understood sociologically?", the self-fulfilling prophecy risk is reduced. Put simply, researchers must consciously avoid switching from inquiry to rhetorical demonstration.

The choice of a context for investigation is rarely made without some kind of rationale; somehow we expect the context chosen to inform us about some feature of social life. We must have some set of questions, explicit or not, that leads us to a particular setting for observation. Even researchers who claim to be purely inductive, or exploratory, or merely curious about behavior in one place or another must have some prior idea about that place. "An open mind is not an empty head" (Dey, 1995); they know enough about it to be curious. Rather than pretending, therefore, that we have absolutely no a priori assumptions in such cases, we ought to make our assumptions explicit and put them to work. If we make our assumptions clear,

we can submit them to testing. If we hide our assumptions, they are potential obstacles to a full understanding of the situation under investigation.

We begin to perceive a complex relationship between our initial questions about a phenomenon, the choice of a research setting to answer these questions, and the data collected in the setting. Later, collected data may cause us to ask some questions more insistently, reject other questions as unimportant, and create the need for answers to previously unformed questions. As a research strategy, then, fieldwork ideally allows us to create a balance between theory and data. We must not develop such an investment in one set of questions or theoretical ideas that we become blind to events in a setting unrelated to these questions or ideas. We must be prepared to accept the possibility that our original questions or ideas about a setting are irrelevant to an understanding of it.

Mitchell Duneier (1999:10) points out that "one of the greatest strengths of firsthand observation is also its greatest weakness." That is, in participant observation we become involved in people's lives, so we can understand their world from their point of view. At the same time, however, all of the rich and vivid detail we encounter has the potential to "distract us from the forces that are less visible to the people we observe but which influence and sustain the behaviors" (Duneier:10). Here, Duneier is referring to the economic, cultural, and political factors that surely influence the lives of the people he is studying, although they may be unaware of them. As we begin to use field data to develop a more macrolevel insight into the people who we observe, we risk imposing our own "outsider's" understanding on their world.

Duneier is one of the most effective ethnographers working today and a worthy heir to the Chicago School tradition. His book, *Sidewalk*, is about the world of New York City vendors who sell books and other merchandise to passersby. The following excerpts give the flavor of his rich observations, as well as the theorizing developed from it. Duneier also shares with the reader his basic methodology and some personal reflections:

Observations, Theory Development, and Field Roles in *Sidewalk*

Description:

Hakim Hasan is a book vendor and street intellectual at the busy intersection of Eighth Street, Greenwich Avenue, and the Avenue of the Americas . . . He is a sturdy and stocky five-foot-seven African American, forty-two years old. In the winter, he wears Timberland boots, jeans, a hooded sweatshirt, a down vest, and a Banana Republic baseball cap. One Thursday . . . an African-American man in his mid-thirties came up to Hakim's table and asked for a copy of Alice Walker's book *The Same River Twice* . . . Hakim was all sold out, but said he would get some more in stock soon. "When you get some, you let me know," said the man, who worked delivering groceries. "I'll let you know." "Because, you see, not only that," said the man, "I've got a friend that loves to read." "Male or female?" asked Hakim. "Female. She's like this: when she gets a book in her hand, in another hour it's finished. In other words – like, with me, I'll read maybe . . . five chapters, then I'll put it down 'cause I gotta do something, then maybe I'll come back to it. But with her, she gets into it and goes through the whole book like that. Boom. And she puts it on the shelf and it's just like brand-new. Like, when it's her birthday or what-have-you, I buy her books, because that's one of the things that she likes. I bought the book *Waiting to Exhale* in paperback, right? Listen to this: when I approached her with the book, the movie was coming out and she said, 'You late! I been read that book!'"

Hakim doesn't just name titles. He knows the contents. I have observed the range and depth of his erudition . . . and have seen him show great patience with uneducated people who are struggling with basic ideas and don't know much about books. He might sit for hours without having a single customer step up to his table; other times the table becomes a social center where men and women debate into the night . . .

Theory Development:

Not long after we met, I asked Hakim how he saw his role. "I'm a public character," he told me . . . Hakim's insight would figure in a central way in the manner in which I would come to see the sidewalk life of this neighborhood . . . The social structure of sidewalk life hangs partly on what can be called self-appointed public characters. A public character is anyone who is in frequent contact with a wide circle of people and who is sufficiently interested to make himself a public character. A public character need have no special talents or wisdom to fulfill his function – although he often does. He just needs to be present, and there need to be enough of his counterparts. His main qualification is that he is public, that he talks to lots of different people. In this way, news travels that is of sidewalk interest . . .

The people making lives on Sixth Avenue depend on one another for social support. The group life upon which their survival is contingent is crucial to those who do not rely on religious institutions or social service agencies. For some of these people, the informal economic life is a substitute for illegal ways of supporting excessive drug use. For others, informal modes of self-help enable them to do things most citizens seek to achieve by working: to support families, others in their community, or themselves. For still others, the informal economy provides a forum where they can advise, mentor, and encourage one another to strive to live in accordance with standards of moral worth. Yet the stories of these sidewalks cannot ultimately serve as sociological romance, celebrating how people on the streets "resist" the larger structures of society. The social order these relationships carve out of what seems to be pure chaos, powerful as its effects are, still cannot control many acts that affront the sensibilities of local residents and passersby.

How can we comprehend types of behavior such as sidewalk sleeping, urinating in public, selling stolen goods, and entangling passersby in unwanted conversations?

Research Role:

I gained entrée to this social world when I became a browser and customer at Hakim's table in 1992. Through my relationship with him, I came to know others in the area. He introduced me to unhoused and formerly unhoused people who scavenge and sell on the street, as well as other vendors who compete with him for sidewalk space and access to customers. These relations then led me to panhandlers, some of whom also sometimes scavenge and vend. Once I was in the network, contacts and introductions took place across the various spheres. Eventually, I worked as a general assistant – watching vendors' merchandise while they went on errands, buying up merchandise offered in their absence, assisting on scavenging missions through trash and recycling bins, and "going for coffee." Then I worked full-time as a magazine vendor and scavenger during the summer of 1996, again for three days a week during the summer of 1997 and during part of the fall of 1997. I also made daily visits to the blocks during the summer of 1998, often for hours at a time, and worked full-time as a vendor for two weeks in March 1999, when my research came to an end.

Although in race, class, and status I am very different from the men I write about, I was myself eventually treated by them as a fixture of the blocks, occasionally referred to as a "scholar" or "professor," which is my occupation. My designation was Mitch. This seemed to have a variety of changing meanings, including: a naïve white man who could himself be exploited for "loans" of small change and dollar bills; a Jew who was going to make a lot of money off the stories of people working the streets; a white writer who was trying to "state the truth about what was going on."

My continual presence as a vendor provided me with opportunities to observe life among the people working and/or living on the sidewalk, including their interactions with passersby. This enabled me to draw many of my conclusions about what happens on the sidewalk from incidents I myself witnessed, rather than deriving them from interviews. Often I simply asked questions while participating and observing. Sometimes, when I wanted to understand how the local political system had shaped these blocks, I did my interviews at the offices of Business Improvement Districts, politicians, and influential attorneys. I also questioned police officers, pedestrians, local residents, and the like. I carried out more than twenty interviews with people working the sidewalk in which I explicitly asked them to tell me their "story." These sessions, held on street corners, in coffee shops, and on subway platforms, lasted between two and six hours. I paid the interviewees fifty dollars when their sessions were over, as compensation for time they could have spent selling or panhandling.

Gaining Access

Once a site is chosen for study, researchers must face the **GATEKEEPERS**, or *guardians, of that social arena* to obtain entry. Some settings provide virtually free access, while others are nearly impenetrable. In some places, the fieldworkers may be readily admitted with the full understanding of their hosts that they are researchers. Access to other settings may require the researcher to conceal both motives and profession. In still other instances, observation may be done so unobtrusively that the issue of motives never arises.

The degree of difficulty faced by researchers in gaining access to settings and to people in those settings seems to be a function of two dimensions. First, just how public is the setting? Are involvement and membership in the setting clearly restricted, or is the setting open to anyone who chooses to be there? Fully public settings – such as bars, museums, and department stores – pose few problems of access. In other cases, membership and participation are clearly restricted or, at least, monitored, as in private country clubs or labor union organizations. We could, of course, envision any setting as lying somewhere along this public/private continuum.

Second, and perhaps of greater importance, do the participants in the setting perceive the need to keep part or all of their activity (perhaps even their very membership) secret? To choose an example at the extreme end of the continuum, it would be nearly impossible for an outsider to study, firsthand, certain features of organized crime.

Given these two dimensions, we could conceive of situations in which access to the setting itself would pose no problem but in which it would be difficult to talk to participants directly. This might be the case for the researcher trying to study behavior in X-rated video stores. As a general rule, we can expect to have the fewest problems of access to those settings that are most public and in which people do not engage in secretive activities.

Few settings of interest to the observational researcher pose such difficult problems as those experienced by Laud Humphreys (1975) in his study of impersonal homosexual encounters in public restrooms (see Chapter 5). Many community studies have been conducted without raising the suspicions of the "locals" to the point they felt the need to question the researcher's motives extensively. In many observational studies, it is not even necessary for researchers to identify themselves. Studies of bars, waiting rooms, subways, and the like pose few dramatic problems. Sometimes investigators take advantage of a role they normally occupy or adopt a specialized role for the sake of research. Howard Becker (1997) put his musical talents to work to study the professional musi-

cian. Joan Emerson (1970/2006), a nurse, studied problems of maintaining reality definitions in gynecological examinations. Patricia Adler (1998) did participant observation among elementary school pupils who were her own children's classmates.

Taking a Role

In conducting fieldwork, researchers must often put aside their academic or other everyday life roles and assume new roles that fit into the worlds they are interested in studying. Their perspectives on these settings and the kinds of information they can learn about them are greatly influenced by the character of the research roles they choose (Adler and Adler, 1987). Raymond Gold (1969/2006) summarized the array of possibilities into four basic roles that the fieldworker can assume: **COMPLETE OBSERVER, OBSERVER-AS-PARTICIPANT, PARTICIPANT-AS-OBSERVER**, and **COMPLETE PARTICIPANT**. The specification of these four conceptual roles results from Gold's response to two basic questions: (1) How involved should researchers become in the ongoing activity? (2) To what extent, if any, should researchers conceal their intentions?

Complete observers remain relatively or totally detached from the situation studied. They can operate from behind a one-way mirror, at the listening end of a tape recorder, or from some concealed observational vantage point. However, most of the time complete observers are visible in the setting but identified to gatekeepers in advance as researchers who will not be participating. If people ask why the "strangers" are there, they will freely admit to being observers; if encouraged to participate in the setting in any way other than "being there," they will decline.

Complete participants remain totally disguised to the people in the setting with whom they interact on a day-to-day basis. They become almost fully immersed, both behaviorally and emotionally. This posture can present a number of problems; over time the researcher may identify more with the goals of other people in the setting than with the goals of the research!

Being Sane in Insane Places: A Case of Disguised Observation

David L. Rosenhan (1999) was interested in exploring the question of how sanity exists. He arranged for eight male and female associates to pose as "pseudopatients" in twelve different hospitals. If the pseudopatients' sanity were discovered, this would serve as evidence that a sane individual can be distinguished from the insane in the context in which he is found. All pseudopatients had the same complaints, and all were admitted with diagnoses of schizophrenia. Besides this, each person presented the true events of their own personal history. Once admitted to the ward, the pseudopatients behaved as they normally would, and had no further schizophrenic complaints. Despite the absence of symptoms, none of the pseudopatients were ever discovered. They were hospitalized for periods of seven to fifty-two days. Interestingly, although the true identities of the pseudopatients were concealed from everyone in the ward setting, truly insane patients recognized that the pseudopatients were not ill, and confronted them. The patients recognized normality when staff did not!

Rosenhan explained the inability of the staff to spot the imposters by noting the power of the label, *schizophrenic*, as well as the reluctance of doctors to admit that they might have made a misdiagnosis. He found that diagnoses of sanity and insanity are less substantive and more subjective than previously realized. In this case disguised observation produced some valuable findings which could not have been obtained using more open research roles.

In the field of anthropology, *overinvolvement of complete participants* is termed **GOING NATIVE**. It is discouraged in part because of the risk that researchers may become reluctant to criticize those with whom they are working and interacting or to ask the difficult or uncomfortable questions which the logic of discovery often demands. Therefore, investigators taking this role have to be on guard that their full participation does not prevent them from maintaining an independent working agenda for the development of research ideas.

The two remaining roles differ according to the amount of emphasis placed on detached observation as opposed to active participation. *The participant-as-observer tends to become quite involved effectively and to downplay or conceal the role as researcher*, as in Humphreys's case (1975). Humphreys did not engage in the homosexual acts occurring in the "tearoom," but he did serve as "watch queen," or lookout, an ancillary role in the setting. This role is an ambiguous one to negotiate, and sometimes research subjects will have a difficult time figuring out just what the researcher can and can-

not do in the setting. Aspects of the researcher's true purpose are still concealed or revealed only selectively.

By contrast, the *observer-as-participant is completely open about research objectives and approaches people in the setting on that basis*. However, when encouraged to participate substantively in the routine of the setting, the researcher in this role may agree to some requests. A good example of this role is Gary Alan Fine and Kent Sandstrom's (1988) research with children. The adult participant-observer attempting to understand a children's culture cannot pass unnoticed as a member of that group. Yet, there is a measure of participation possible as children learn to trust the researcher as a friend or leader.

The choice of any one of these roles depends on both the situation and the nature of the information sought. Roles tending toward the covert, participatory end of the spectrum are generally chosen by researchers when respondents or informants consider the sharing of their knowledge potentially dangerous to themselves or outsiders (Berk and Adams, 2001) or when the

Nickel and Dimed: A Case of the Participant-as-Observer

In research inspired by the welfare reform laws that drove 12 million women into the labor market, Barbara Ehrenreich (2001) was curious about their chances of survival in unskilled jobs paying $6 to $7 per hour. She tried to make a living earning about $300 a week by working as a waitress in Key West, Florida, as a cleaning woman and a nursing home aide in Portland, Maine, and in a Wal-Mart in Minneapolis, Minnesota.

Ehrenreich has a PhD, but she decided not to make use of her training or qualifications in securing employment. In this sense, her work was disguised observation. However, since she performed as would any other worker in these settings, it was not a case of outright deception. Ehrenreich was not a *complete participant* in that she allowed herself $1,000 in start-up money, a car, and her laptop computer. Although she stayed in trailer parks and isolated, inexpensive housing, she maintained "an acceptable level of safety and privacy."

During the job application process, Ehrenreich endured routine drug screenings and bogus "personality tests" with trick questions such as "Some people work better when they're a little bit high." Once hired, she put up with constant surveillance and being harangued for minor rule violations like serving a second roll and butter to a customer.

Despite the advantages of her race, education, good health, and lack of children, Ehrenreich's income barely covered her month's expenses. Many of her co-workers slept in their cars because they could not afford rent. She concludes that many of her fellow workers were in fact the borderline homeless, but society does not regard them as "poor" because, after all, they have jobs. America's prosperity, in her view, has been attained on the backs of the lowest paid. Based on her experience, hard work fails to live up to its reputation as the ticket out of poverty.

information is highly ego involved – buried under a protective layer of rationalization such that direct methods of information seeking could well elicit faulty data.

The choice of a covert role always raises serious ethical questions. Is the information sought in any sense public? If it is strictly private, then what justification can the researcher give for "stealing" it? Whose interests must researchers protect? Do they owe anything to the subjects who have made the research possible? In general, are there any limits to the investigator's right of inquiry? These are, if not unanswerable, at least thorny questions that continue to spark lively professional debate (Miller, 2001). As noted in Chapter 5, some researchers frown on *any* disguised observation in principle. It may be contended that most social researcher participation in field settings does not in fact harm anyone and that if it ever threatened to do so, most investigators would take steps to provide a remedy. However, laudable personal moral-

ity and good intentions are no assurance that researchers can anticipate all the effects of their participation. If people are harmed unwittingly, it may be impossible to reverse the damage. All research with human subjects must be carefully considered for its value, impact, and its potential to exploit.

As we mentioned in Chapter 5, institutional review boards (IRBs) have been created on the campuses of colleges and universities accepting federal funding. These boards have oversight concerning research design in both social and natural sciences. Although various types of disguised observation have a long tradition in social science, it is increasingly difficult to obtain approval to use them in a regulated environment. This problem is of course complicated by the highly inductive nature of most fieldwork. A researcher's role does not necessarily remain static. At different points during the project, and in the company of different respondents, different roles may be demanded. However, once our research design is "approved" by an IRB in its original form, does that mean that researchers must seek approval for every change in their own roles that is called for by changing conditions in the field? This is the cutting edge of ethical debate in the practice of fieldwork.

Ideally, the specific role taken by the investigator should be tempered to the individual personalities involved and the situations in which researcher and respondent mutually find themselves. Each researcher can identify his or her own most effective role and then adapt it according to the problem at hand. Some researchers will find that their contacts in the field allow them to raise questions aggressively and vigorously, but others may see the need, at least at the outset, to remain more reserved. One thing is clear: Whenever research involves interaction between subjects and investigators, there is no such thing as total, bland unobtrusiveness. In effect, the ideal of "naturalistic" inquiry can never be fully realized. Subjects always place researchers in some meaningful frame or context and relate to them accordingly. Researchers who maintain a mechanically objective detachment may create an uncomfortable ambiguity that forces subjects to interpret their actions as best they can, possibly resulting in behavior toward the researcher that is atypical of them and harmful to the research goals.

Participant-observers should try to understand and take into account the identity that their subjects attribute to them (Tewksbury and Gagne, 2001). How do a researcher's race, sex, ethnicity, physical appearance, known affiliations, and other attributes affect respondents' behavior? Does the researcher pose any kind of threat to the group or to any particular individuals or factions? Is he or she being manipulated to serve the overt or hidden interests of anyone? How do subjects interpret the researcher's intentions? What kinds of rewards might especially cooperative subjects be anticipating? Serious consideration of these and related questions can help social scientists to see their already collected data in proper perspective and may also suggest useful strategies for future data collection.

The more interaction occurring between researcher and subjects in naturalistic observation, the more the broader cultural context in which the research is done will affect research roles. Thus, there are a number of reports dedicated to the experience of women as fieldworkers because, as they are collecting data, they are also reacting to the culturally sensitive gender relations prevailing in their settings (Whitehead and Conway, 1986; Warren and Hackney, 2000). Diane Wolf (1996:7) concludes that women's issues in fieldwork revolve around the issue of power. Unequal hierarchies, or levels of control, are often maintained, perpetuated, created, and re-created during and after fieldwork.

Virtually all organizations are characterized by an elaborate stratification system such that certain individuals or groups have more power and authority than others. Researchers whose roles are too closely identified with one or another of these strata (subgroups) are likely to lose access to other groups in the setting (Gray, 1980). It is hoped that fieldworkers can thus sidestep the sometimes fatal problem of exclusive identification with one or another faction (Berk and Adams, 2001). Groups pursued, persecuted, or stigmatized by public authorities or private moralizers are, in general, least likely to accept an inquisitive outsider seeking their friendship and admission to their worlds of private knowledge. Researchers who encounter difficulties in foreign countries holding a poor image of the "Yanqui" are likely to find similar sentiments among many groups in the United States. Many community and minority groups have become increasingly suspicious of, if not openly hostile to, sociological "snoopers." We can no longer assume that social research will be unquestioningly accepted as a legitimate enterprise.

Some Practical Suggestions

What these tales of failures and mistrust signify is that researchers' conduct during the first few days and weeks in the field may be an enormously significant factor in determining the eventual success or failure of their studies. If observers are initially viewed with distrust and suspicion by those whom they seek to study and they do not handle the situation well, this may spell the end of their work before it really begins. So, the most appropriate way to summarize the issues we have been considering is in the form of some tactical guidance. If any recommendation offered below seems inappropriate for the situation being studied, it should be discarded. In the abstract, both common sense and previous research experience lead to the following suggestions:

1. Whenever possible, level with respondents about what you are doing. This does not mean that you must engage in a detailed exposition of any developing theoretical ideas you might have. But when people ask, it will be useful for you to offer a standard explanation of your work. Generally, honesty is the best policy.[7]

2. For the first few weeks in the field, it is best to adopt, if possible, a fairly passive research role. After all, your first task as a field researcher is to get a feeling for the context you are studying. If you begin active research before you know the "rules" of a particular setting or culture, you run the risk of unwittingly engaging in behaviors that members of the setting may find objectionable.

3. As a corollary to our second suggestion, it is probably not a good idea to conduct any in-depth interviews with informants at the beginning of your work. You simply do not know as yet what to ask. Of course, this does not mean that you should discourage people from talking to you if they seem eager to do so.

4. At least initially, it is unwise to get into the position of offering advice. Many people have the conception of social scientists as therapeutic agents who can solve personal or organizational problems. You are primarily an investigator, not a therapist. If people insist on telling you their problems, listen sympathetically, for what you are being told may constitute valuable data.

5. Do not be afraid to answer questions if the situation calls for it, but do not assume the role of the expert on anything. Make it plain to people that they are the experts and that you are there to learn from them.

6. Do not let people force you into one or another particular role. Your subjects should not be able to decide for you what you should and should not be observing. If you do not make plain that your job as a researcher is to investigate all features of the situation, you may find yourself observing only a limited number of events.

7. Do not become closely aligned with one or another group in the setting you are studying, at least not until you are confident that your decision to do so will not keep you from making valuable contacts with other groups. If you become viewed as a partisan during internal political battles, it will likely be impossible for you to observe certain segments of the organization.

Data Collection and Note Taking

At this point, we will make the happy assumption that you have successfully gained access to a setting. Of course, you have been collecting data all along – preliminary thoughts about the broad area of concern, considerations of the best context in which to do observation, and experiences in making initial contacts with people in the chosen setting all constitute relevant data. Once you have gained access to a particular setting, the collection and continual interpretation of data become your most preoccupying research tasks. Because the essential advantage of participant observation is that it allows you constantly to integrate the processes of data collection *and* analysis, you will need some guidelines concerning the nature of the data that ought to be collected and the content of the notes you should keep.

The secret of successful systematic and analytical participant observation that aims at objectivity lies in keeping accurate and detailed field notes. The first and perhaps only

---

[7] If you feel that it is impossible to tell the truth or, even further, that you must actually disguise your research identity, you should take a particularly careful look at the ethical implications of your research.

unequivocal rule about the content of field notes is that they must be complete. Researchers do not go into the field with a well-formulated problem or an explicit set of hypotheses to be tested; they simply cannot foretell which data ultimately will be important. For that reason, researchers who fail to be complete in their note taking may very well miss a good deal of information that later on turns out to be important. Let us assume that you have begun to observe behavior in some reasonably well-defined organizational setting. Especially during the first few weeks of fieldwork, the following kinds of descriptions and explanations of data ought to find their way into your field notes.

Descriptions

First, strive to produce a complete description of the setting under investigation. It should provide enough information so that anyone reading it will have a clear picture of, and a "feeling" for, that setting. To accomplish this task, you must develop an eye for detail. Let us suppose you have begun to investigate a small religious group, such as the devotees of Krishna. You would likely begin the research by visiting their temple. In the description of that setting, you will want to note a number of details – the colors of the walls, the general condition of the place, the kinds of objects to be found there. If you see that there is a bulletin board in the setting, do not simply note its existence. Make some assessment of the kinds of important information found there. Write down the titles of the magazines lying around on a table. After all, the things that people read are often good unobtrusive indicators of their interests, beliefs, or ideological outlook. In short, your description of the setting should include anything that informs a reader about the nature of the setting or the people who use it. One useful strategy is to draw maps of the setting. What might the spatial arrangement of furniture, for instance, say about the quality of interactions occurring in that setting?

Second, you should include complete descriptions of individuals. These descriptions should accurately portray to any reader what your subjects are like. Again, such a task requires developing an eye for detail. Note the distribution of males and females, individuals' racial groups and their ages. Try to be aware, as well, of less visible but important indicators of status. How are people dressed? What proportion of people wear wedding rings? Do people have noticeable accents? Do they have tattoos or other body markings such as scars? It might be useful in some settings to get an indication of people's physical health: Are their teeth in good condition? Is their skin condition good? Are they as a group disproportionately underweight or overweight? The collation of these details is an example of **THICK DESCRIPTION** (Geertz, 2001), *highly specific, rich content from field observation and experience*.

Compiling a *really* complete description may seem overwhelming. It would, of course, be impossible to note every possible description about the setting and the people in it. You have to be selective to some degree. Full descriptions of people and places need not be accomplished during the first or second visit to the setting. You can keep adding to your description on subsequent visits. Beyond that, it should become clear after a time that some people are more "important" than others in the group to be studied. When you discover who the influential members of the group are, you may want to give a more detailed description of them. In this sense, descriptions will be cumulative.

Along with descriptions of people and places, notes should be filled with quotations. Include both conversations you have and those you overhear. Once again, the challenge is not to record every exchange that occurs, but to convey to the reader a good sense of the general content and tone of the conversations in the context studied. It is not absolutely necessary to remember the exact words of a conversation, but it is essential to retain the integrity of its substance. You should also work to re-create phonetically the dialects that individuals may use. If individuals have a distinctive way of speaking, try to capture it. If someone says, "Duya wanna gow-out?", record it that way instead of "Do you want to go out?" If a group has its own slang or specialized vocabulary, it is your job to learn to understand it and ultimately to present it to others. Keep in mind that a good deal of communication is nonverbal. Part of your descriptive task is, therefore, to note nonverbal gestures, postures, and facial expressions.

Go out of your way to record anything that you find inexplicable or unusual. The data that you simply cannot understand may turn out to be among the most significant. If you cannot make sense out of a conversation or an event, perhaps an important aspect of the meaning fabric of the setting is eluding you. The essential task of field researchers is to arrive at some understanding of the meaning structures of the individuals being studied. You should, therefore, note these inexplicable conversations and events and keep them in mind as you continue to collect data. Try to orient your data gathering to lead you ultimately to understand these puzzling phenomena.

Explanations

Along with providing accurate description, it is the continual task of field researchers to formulate tentative explanations of the things they see. A critical element of the note-taking process is statements of your own personal feelings, hunches, and hypotheses. Include in your notes any guesses you have about why individuals are acting as they are. Try continuously to weave observations into some kind of theoretical or explanatory structure. If at any point during the observations you feel that you are seeing a theme that may emerge as the focus of your work, you *must* get it down in the notes. Force yourself to be speculative. Do not worry about the quality or correctness of the explanation offered. Remember that the notes do not constitute a finished product; they are raw data for your eyes only – not a term paper! Include even brief theoretical ideas, such as the following:

> There may be some kind of link in this organization between the status of persons and the conflict and hostility I am seeing.

You may want to expand several theoretical ideas into a larger memo for your own use. **THEORETICAL MEMOS** include *a portion of the data already collected for the purpose of generating theoretical ideas*. Aside from the actual collection of data, the ongoing attempt at theorizing is the most important activity in which you can engage. As you go along, continue to refine these ideas. The product of this continuous refinement is called **GROUNDED THEORY** (Charmaz, 2006). Using your theoretical memos, *retain the ideas that keep making sense for the context you are studying and discard or rework those that seem inadequate as explanations*. As induction proceeds, the range of data you need to collect will narrow (Agar, 1996). Thus, the longer you remain in the field, the deeper and more focused your work becomes. As you amend, expand, assess, and reassess theoretical ideas in your notes, you are actually writing substantial portions of the final research report.

Remember that the process of inductive theory building and using grounded theory represents an "ideal type" method. That is, your ultimate goal may be to generate theory purely from observation, but in practice you may not actually begin with a completely "clean slate," having made no prior theoretical assumptions. It would be difficult, if not impossible, to prevent yourself from thinking about the theoretical ideas in books or articles you have read before entering the field. So you may need to track these ideas in your notes and explain how your observations contributed to the alteration of theory as the research proceeds.

Keep **METHODOLOGICAL NOTES**. These are *a recording of, and commentary on, the success or failure of the data-gathering approaches you have used*. Your own feelings and the reactions of your subjects as you attempt to explore various features of their lives can be used as an index of the quality of the data obtained. Resistance can be a valuable clue that more is going on than meets the eye. When subjects suddenly become reluctant to communicate, is it because you have touched on a particularly sensitive area that they would sooner bury than uncover? Or does it have something to do with the way they were approached? Might you have broken an informal norm by asking someone in a group to comment on the activities or character of another group member? If so, what might this imply about the maintenance of group solidarity? Much can be learned about a group by analyzing how and why the members expose or conceal knowledge about themselves.

A final word about recording field notes. It will often be impossible for you to take notes as action occurs before you. In such cases, look for opportunities to jot down key phrases so that you may later recapture the proceedings in full. Further, it is essential that you sit down to record complete notes as soon as possible after the actual observations are made. Memory tends to flag quickly unless stimulated by the active attempt to reconstruct events.

Leaving the Field

By the time you are ready to leave the setting in which you have been collecting data, you will likely have become reasonably fluent in balancing all of the tasks that are necessary for successful field investigation. Exactly how do you know that the time for making an exit has arrived? The answer lies in the process of induction. As you use it continually to monitor the data you are taking in, assimilating and trying to categorize information that contributes to the development of a coherent picture, you are gradually approaching a state of **SATURATION**. That is, *there will come a point where new information does not surprise you*. People are behaving in relatively predictable ways in the setting, and there is very little if anything that seems beyond your understanding or ability to place within an appropriate framework. You will know when saturation has been reached because you will find it difficult to develop a day-to-day plan for operating in the field that places you in a position to refute what you believe you know about the setting. At that point it is indeed time to leave.

It is important to plan an exit strategy for a number of reasons (Rossman and Rallis, 1998). Fieldwork is very time consuming, and during the period of your research, it is likely to tap most of your energy. You are about to switch from being "on" in the constant presence of respondents to a more solitary routine of reflection and writing. You will need to prepare for these changes by tying up any loose ends and mak-

ing sure that any promises you have made to respondents are kept.

Over the duration of your involvement in the field, you will get to know a variety of respondents well. Your **KEY INFORMANTS**, *those who have been especially helpful and welcoming to you*, are likely to take on the status of friends, or at least close acquaintances. These are people who will miss you and whose feelings may suffer when your impending exit serves to remind them of your primary identity as a researcher. If you have paid attention to the ethics of doing fieldwork, and if your research role involved a measure of participation in the setting, people have come to rely on you to do the work that your role demanded, even if it was simply to offer a sympathetic ear or relief from their boredom. In effect, your contribution to the research setting became part of the research bargain through which your access, entry, and successful functioning in the field were accomplished. **RECIPROCITY** is the term used to refer to your *"payback," or contribution as a participant in the field* (Wax, 1986). As you think about your exit, you will want to make sure that your part of the "bargain" has been upheld.

Finally, observers have often remarked that leave-taking presents an opportunity to learn more about the setting and the people in it, even though you may believe that saturation in a more formal sense has been reached. It may be an ideal time for respondents to express their feelings toward you. Perhaps individuals with whom you have not been that close during your stay in the field will reveal their thoughts to you, or their wish that they had gotten to know you better. Even those who might have appeared suspicious or wary of you may now be more open, recognizing that you are about to leave and soon will not be in a position to do them any harm.

Formulating an Analysis

From our account of what goes into good field notes, you may infer that a number of activities are carried out simultaneously in fieldwork. Methodological problems are addressed as data are being collected, and data analysis accompanies both of these operations. However, for the purposes of our discussion here, we can divide the fieldwork process into three phases, in terms of time and energy expended by the researcher. We have already looked at two of them: first, gaining access to the setting and beginning one's observations, and second, reconstructing past events and seriously collecting data. The third and last phase of field research is the actual data analysis.

At this point, let us assume that you have left the field altogether. Analysis has already begun in that you have developed grounded theory to the point where a substantial number of theoretical notes and memos have been accumulated. By now you have a pretty good idea of the various theoretical directions that the final research report might take. The time has come, however, to decide on the theoretical framework that will best allow you to make sense of the data. Given this task, what procedures might be most helpful in producing a comprehensive analysis?

It is not possible to offer a definitive set of criteria. Two fieldworkers exercising the research imagination and independently entering the same social situation might emerge with two quite different, equally cogent analyses of data collected. It may simply be that the two researchers saw quite different features of social life illuminated in the context studied. Any one context may display a number of generic forms of human behavior. The heart of an analysis, therefore, involves the researcher's application of a small number of well-selected concepts to show his or her reader the dimensions of social life reflected in the data. If successful, an analysis will cause us to see connections between pieces of data that might at first seem wholly discrete. In addition, what is uncovered through an analysis of the collected data may challenge or confirm some already existing theory or specify a new one.

Jarrett and Burton (1999) used a combination of participant observation and interviewing to analyze poor African American families. They were motivated to conduct this research because the traditional, quantitative demographic categories – "intact" versus "nonintact" (single-parent) families – did not seem to capture the true variety of family structure within the community. They found that the following four qualitative variables could be used effectively to characterize family life: (1) extended family networks, (2) socioeconomic structure of these extended family networks, (3) the pace of change in these networks, and (4) the age structure of family members. These variables all turned out to be more important than the simple dichotomous measure (intact vs. nonintact) typically used in quantitative studies. This example shows the possibilities of using fieldwork to produce a rich analysis that carries practical implications because it is important to be able to predict the resiliency of families, regardless of whether they are intact.

Conceptual Categories

The beginnings of an analysis must be generated by means of a search for descriptive categories that will help us arrange good portions of the collected data. Standard concepts such as social class, ideology, identity, status, role, deviance, stigma, pathology, socialization, and informal organization may provide a core for initial data classification. Sometimes these categories alone are sufficient to an analysis because they are flexible enough to be molded around the events at hand. The unique linking of such concepts can be a creative and theoretically informative expression of the researcher's imagination. In other instances, the nature of the setting and the data collected call for the development of new conceptual categories.

Before one can create new ideas from data or synthesize standard concepts in a novel way, data must be divided into their logical components. Lofland et al. (2006) suggest six classes for the initial ordering of observational data: *acts, activities, meanings, participation, relationships,* and *settings.* Each class further suggests a series of questions to be asked of the data: What are the basic types of acts and activities that go on? What is the typical frequency of each activity, and what is its duration? How do actors define the situation? What does their action mean to them, and what kinds of collective norms dictate their choice of action? How deeply does each participant get involved?

Decent and *Street* Families – an Example of Concept Formation

The conceptual categories in Elijah Anderson's work, *Code of the Street* (1999), emerged inductively after much information had been collected. In the following excerpt, he makes the distinction between *decent families* and *street families*:

The decent family and the street family ... represent two poles of value orientation ... The labels "decent" and "street," which the residents themselves use, amount to evaluative judgments that confer status on local residents ... Individuals of either orientation may coexist in the same extended family ... There is also a great deal of "code-switching": a person may behave according to either set of rules, depending on the situation. Decent people, especially young people ... often share many of the middle-class values of the wider white society but know that the open display of such values carries little weight on the street: it doesn't provide the emblems that say, "I can take care of myself." Hence such people develop a repertoire of behaviors that do provide that security. Those strongly associated with the street, who have less exposure to the wider society, may have difficulty code-switching; imbued with the code of the street, they either don't know the rules for decent behavior or may see little value in displaying such knowledge.

At the extreme of the street-oriented group are those who make up the criminal element. People in this class are profound casualties of the social and economic system, and they tend to embrace the street code wholeheartedly. They tend to lack not only a decent education – though some are highly intelligent – but also an outlook that would allow them to see far beyond their immediate circumstances. Rather, many pride themselves on living the "thug life," actively defying not simply the wider social conventions but the law itself. They sometimes model themselves after successful local drug dealers and rap artists like Tupac Shakur and Snoop Doggy Dogg, and they take heart from professional athletes who confront the system and stand up for themselves. In their view, policemen, public officials, and corporate heads are unworthy of respect and hold little moral authority. Highly alienated and embittered, they exude generalized contempt for the wider scheme of things and for a system they are sure has nothing but contempt for them ... They tend to approach all persons and situations as part of life's obstacles, as things to subdue or to "get over." To get over, individuals develop an effective "hustle" or "game plan," setting themselves up in a position to prevail by being "slick" and outsmarting others. In line with this, one must always be wary of one's counterparts, to assume that they are involved with you only for what they can get out of the situation ... In these circumstances, violence is quite prevalent – in families, in schools, and in the streets – becoming a way of public life that is effectively governed by the code of the street ... [But] the family one emerges from is distinct from the "family" one finds in the streets. For street-oriented people especially, the family outside competes with blood relatives for an individual's loyalties and commitments. Nevertheless, blood relatives always come first. The folklore of the street says, in effect, that if I will fight and "take up for" my friend, then you know what I will do for my own brother, cousin, nephew, aunt, sister, or mother – and vice versa. Blood is thicker than mud.

In decent families there is almost always a real concern with and a certain amount of hope for the future ... This means working hard, saving money for material things, and raising children – any "child you touch" – to try to make something out of themselves. Decent families tend to accept mainstream values more fully than street families ... to instill "backbone" and a sense of responsibility ... Decent parents are much more able and willing than street-oriented ones to ally themselves with outside institutions such as schools and churches. They value hard work and self-reliance and are willing to sacrifice for their children ... Rather than dwelling on the hardships and inequities facing them, many such decent people . . . often see their difficult situation as a test from God and derive great support from their faith and church community . . .

Intact nuclear families, although in the minority in the impoverished inner city, provide powerful role models. Typically, husband and wife work at low-paying jobs, sometimes juggling more than one such job each. They may be aided financially by the contributions of a teenage child who works part-time. Such families . . . are often vigilant in their desire to keep the children away from the streets. In public such an intact family makes a striking picture as the man may take pains to show he is in complete control – with the woman and the children following his lead. On the inner-city streets this appearance helps him play his role as protector, and he may exhibit exaggerated concern for his family, particularly when other males are near. His actions and words, including loud and deep-voiced assertions to get his small children in line, let strangers know: "This is my family, and I am in charge."

From *Code of the Street: Decency, Violence, and the Moral Life of the Inner City* by Elijah Anderson. Copyright © 1999 by Elijah Anderson. Used by permission of W. W. Norton & Company, Inc.

Are some participating more than others? Who relates to whom, and how? Who avoids whom, and why? Is there a chain of communication or command? Which individuals appear to be central? Finally, what are the distinctive characteristics of the setting and to what extent do they affect or limit what takes place, how it takes place, and who gets involved? How might the participants and their actions be different in another setting?

Data Coding

The organizing categories suggested by the Loflands are helpful, but they will not solve the problems of the researcher who has collected a large volume of field notes. Researchers must also somehow take into account the specific kinds of data they have gathered. A usual procedure engaged in by fieldworkers to get a closer picture is to somehow *code* their data. Although there are many ways to code qualitative data, for example, using computer software, color categories, or cutting and pasting, all represent variations of an essentially similar process (Coffey and Atkinson, 1996).

Coding in qualitative analysis is not the same as quantitative coding.

Quantitative coding requires preconceived, logically deduced codes into which the data are placed. Qualitative coding, in contrast, means creating categories from interpretation of the data. Rather than relying on preconceived categories and standardized procedures, qualitative coding has its own distinctive structure, logic and purpose. (Charmaz, 2001)

We will look briefly at a coding procedure that may serve as a basis for any specific variation demanded by a researcher's own data. The first step in coding qualitative data is to generate as many descriptive categories as possible. To accomplish this, researchers should carefully read through their data and write down each new category that is suggested. We could imagine the data collected from observing a religious community yielding the following categories: description of setting, description of individuals, eating habits, treatment of outsiders, internal conflict, proselytizing activities, value expressions, economic considerations, street behavior, conversion process, and patterns of leadership. Production of a hundred or more categories through this first close inspection of the data would not be unlikely.

After such initial categories have been produced, we begin to work with them more carefully. We may decide that some of the categories need to be further divided into even more subcategories and that a number of others need to be collapsed into one broader category. We arrange and rearrange the categories until we are satisfied that they are reasonably discrete and comprehensive. Then we simply assign each of the developed categories a number, a color, or a label. Next, we again examine the data in the field notes, indicating by number the category or categories into which each piece of data fits. We will find, of course, that one verbal statement, one story, or one event might properly be coded into a number of different categories.

Before the widespread use of computers, researchers used to turn to a pair of scissors and a pile of index cards to make the data more manageable. Nowadays we can keep one file copy of notes intact and move copies of the data from category to category until we find the right placement for each. If a specific piece of data fits in more than one category, we can make as many copies of that data specimen as we need and insert them in the categories to which they apply.[8] After reviewing all the data assigned to each category, we may choose to refine the list of categories even further. At the very least, this coding procedure will give us a clear idea of the areas in which we have the most data. Returning to our example of studying a religious group, it would certainly say something if we were able to uncover fifty pieces of data on, say, the conversion process, and only a couple on eating habits. The sheer volume of data on one or another feature of the context being studied will be very likely to influence the organization and content of the final report.

From Analysis to Theory

We have described the process of formulating an analysis largely in technical, procedural terms. Everything suggested to this point is preliminary to the actual writing of the analysis. Frequently, the work of writing the data analysis in a coherent fashion causes a reevaluation of old ideas and leads to the formulation of new ones. The process of writing allows the researcher to see the possible solutions to theoretical problems more clearly. New insights reflect on the initial organization and statement of thoughts that may have first appeared in field notes. These may

at first have been terribly jumbled and inarticulately framed, but they now assume new vigor and demand amplification. An analysis is not produced in a predictable, linear fashion. There is a reciprocal relationship among ideas, such that one suggests others, which in turn reflect on and change the original idea, and so on. These are the hallmarks of the creative process.

Categorization alone will not produce a striking, convincing, compelling analysis. An analysis will be successful if the researcher can, through the use of the procedures described and complemented by personal awareness, uncover in the data an overriding pattern or story line that provides new insight into the situation investigated. This pattern may be expressed as a typology[9] or as a principle of behavior that has relevance in a variety of settings. Such key linkages are at the heart of a developing theoretical perspective. Of course, different observers can look at the same set of events and come up with very different typologies. A psychiatrist and a city planner could analyze the same problem and produce quite different interpretations and suggestions. This is inherent in the nature of analysis because the description of a phenomenon is dependent on the choice of conceptual categories, and any system of categories is somewhat arbitrary and artificial. Just as wave theory and particle theory produce different interpretations of the nature of light, a functionalist and a Marxist analysis of any phenomenon will differ. Therefore, one's analysis is not likely to produce a final, definitive interpretation. It is important that it add something to the ongoing practical and intellectual discussion surrounding a phenomenon.

LIMITATIONS OF OBSERVATIONAL FIELD RESEARCH

In this chapter, we have discussed the theoretical basis for fieldwork, some areas in which it has traditionally been done, and the nature of the fieldwork process. We have also considered, where appropriate, some practical guidelines for those who may eventually do field research.

---

[8] The development of computer software that can accomplish the process of storing and retrieving coded qualitative data is discussed later on in this chapter.

[9] See Chapter 2.

Now, let us look at some of the limitations of the observational method.

Qualitative techniques cannot be used as a substitute for quantitative research. Rather, as we have so often suggested, structured and unstructured methods ought to be used in conjunction with one another. The in-depth understanding provided through field research constitutes an important contribution to our knowledge. At the same time, we must recognize that qualitative research does not easily allow a researcher to produce reliable measurements of phenomena and consequently is of limited utility in definitively testing quantitative propositions. In addition to this general limitation, we can list the following related weaknesses of field research:

1. The method is not applicable to the investigation of large social settings. The context studied must be small enough to be covered exhaustively by one or a few investigators.

2. The participant observer is most likely to be involved in a *single case analysis*, or **CASE STUDY** (Gerring, 2007). As a result, making generalizations about a variety of phenomena on the basis of isolated field studies is always problematic.

3. There are few safeguards against the interference of the particular biases, attitudes, and assumptions of the researcher who does field research.

4. The likelihood of the researcher's selective perception and memory biasing the results of the study is very great.

5. There is the related problem of selectivity in data collection. In any social situation, there are literally thousands of possible pieces of data. No one researcher can account for every aspect of a situation. The field researcher inevitably pulls out only a segment of the data that exist, and the question inevitably arises whether the selected data are really representative of the whole.

6. The mere presence of the researcher may change that system or group being studied into something different from what it would be were he or she not present. It is impossible to observe human beings without both influencing their behavior and being influenced by them.

7. Because there is no set procedure defining the field research process, it is difficult for one researcher to explain to another exactly how the work was done. It is, therefore, virtually impossible to replicate the findings of a particular field study.

Taken together, these problems add up to a major, severe criticism of field research. Aside from our own private feelings and experiences, there is no way easily to assess the reliability and validity of the interpretations made by the researcher. We are forced to presume that investigators have been careful in their data collection and interpretation. However, as long as data are collected and presented by one or a few researchers with their own distinctive talents, faults, and foibles, skepticism concerning the validity of their rendering of the phenomena studied will remain.

Qualitative field researchers often respond to these criticisms by suggesting that the cost of imprecision is more than compensated for by the in-depth, authentic quality of the data produced. They can live with the limitation of research on human behavior that we often cannot formulate our explanations with "definitive concepts" whose terms are unambiguous and whose empirical referents are precise. Instead, they see the positive features of using **SENSITIZING CONCEPTS** (van den Hoonaard, 1997), *constructs derived from the research participants' perspective that employ their language and expression* to unlock the mysteries underlying the empirical world.

Such a position has a certain plausibility, in that it is important to respect the way our respondents see their own world, but it can easily become an umbrella protecting shoddy research practices. In reviewing the substantive contributions of fieldworkers, one is immediately struck by the failure of most to review conscientiously the validity and reliability of their data and the inferences made from that data. There have been many discussions of the relative merits of fieldwork and of the special problems in evaluating qualitative data (Becker, 1969/2006; Becker and Geer, 1969; Hammersley, 1992, 1998), but one finds few research reports in which the authors self-consciously consider these questions.[10] Field researchers need to work harder at explicating the procedural and analytical processes through which they produce their data and interpretations. To better evaluate the quality of data presented to us, we need to know more than we are normally told about the researcher's sampling procedures[11] and more information about the basis for data selectivity. We should have a fuller sense of the researcher's biases and assumptions and the procedures used in developing the analysis produced. Field researchers must, in short, be more responsible for specifying the methods used in seeing what they have seen.

Fieldwork was the centerpiece of the practice of social research in the United States until 1940, but for the next twenty-five years, the use of observational field techniques declined considerably. This decline was related to the simultaneous and rapid growth of quantitative methods. Survey research in particular rose in popularity as it allowed investigators to reach large numbers of people, increase the accuracy of generalizations made from collected data, replicate the findings of earlier studies, and test theoretical ideas with more precision. Quantitative techniques such as survey research correctly remain central methodological tools today. Since the mid-1960s, however, there has been a reemergence, a rebirth, of the use of qualitative fieldwork (Adler and Adler, 1987). Many studies relying on qualitative methods have appeared, as well as a growing volume of books describing the underlying logic of observational work and the strategies found useful in its execution. This change has been brought about in part by the recognition that other techniques alone cannot provide the rich insight and information

that come when scientists involve themselves directly in the worlds of those they study.

NEW DEVELOPMENTS IN QUALITATIVE FIELDWORK

Cyberspace as a Field Setting

The widespread availability of computers and the use of cyberspace have created "virtual communities." Rheingold (1993:5) defines these communities as "social aggregations that emerge from the Net when enough people carry on those public discussions long enough, with sufficient human feeling, to form webs of personal relationships." Using participant observation to study these relationships in Web-based interest groups and chat rooms is not possible. The researcher and subjects may never meet face to face, but they can establish a sustained connection in the context of data collection. Of course, the issues of disguised observation, access, confidentiality, bias, and personal involvement that have been discussed in this chapter do not disappear merely because one is operating in cyberspace.

Smyres (1999) studied anorexia among young women by signing on to an online chat community. She spent approximately sixty hours exploring all areas of the Web site and reading posts from users on a daily basis. She gained extensive knowledge of the community. Much of this information was obtained by simply following links within the site. She also read comments from more than sixty Web site reviewers and examined newspaper articles about it. This research is an example of *complete observation* because Smyres simply added her name to the list of site subscribers, obtained a username and password, and was free to log on at any time. "It was easy to remain anonymous. Quite simply, no one even knew I was there..." (Smyres, 1999:1). However, the anonymity of the Web-based contacts in the chat community provided the researcher with access to intimate communication not typically available to complete observers in other venues of data collection:

Please help me. I know i am on the way to anorexia, but i cant stop myself. I know I am fat, and i WANT

[10] We could, of course, raise the same questions about the effectiveness of quantitative researchers' checks against invalidity and bias. Those using structured techniques might more fully and satisfactorily resolve the questions addressed here, but the absence of "transparency" about their work remains a special problem for field research specialists. Adler and Adler (1987) note that the Chicago School emerged at a period when reflections on and codification of sociological methods were basically nonexistent. Perhaps we are still paying the price today.

[11] For a discussion of sampling procedures in qualitative research, see Chapter 6.

to be annorexic. I know it is very harmful, but i cannot lose any weight. I need some more alternitives before really am in trouble. Please Please help me. ScorpioSistah (Smyres, 1999:1)

Of course, Web-based ethnography may include a measure of researcher participation. Professor John Suler (1999) joined the Palace, an online visual chat group with a subscription charge. He was quite deliberate regarding his research role, devoting some time to the selection of a screen name for himself and developing a strategy for divulging personal information to members of the group. He decided to be honest regarding his role as a researcher. Suler reported that it took him nearly a month of daily "attendance" to feel as though he "belonged." He also noted that through participant observation, he came to understand the community of "Palatians" far sooner than he would have if he had conducted interview or survey research. Based on these examples, it is apparent that in the coming decades we will be comparing Internet-based participatory research with other, more well-established modes of data collection in order to ferret out their strengths and weaknesses.

Computer-Assisted Qualitative Data Analysis

In the wake of the revolution in personal computing and software development, a variety of programs for processing qualitative data have become available (QSR, 2005; AEA, 2007). The more advanced programs enable a combination of editable text and multimedia capabilities. They use hypertext and hypermedia technology to move nimbly between text, pictures, and movies (Bauer and Gaskell, 2000). The programs are flexible in that they allow the researcher to edit, visually code, and link documents as they are created and to change and to reformulate coding categories in field notes as research proceeds inductively. Most programs also allow the researcher to write short comments on the data (theoretical memos) and to link these memos either to segments of field notes or to other memos.

INDEXING is a basic function of computer programs that perform qualitative analysis. *An electronic index stores together all the words or phrases from field notes that are coded in similar categories.* The computer remembers the location of all passages that share the same code label. Thus, the software allows the researcher to retrieve a list of all relevant quotations and observations instantaneously. For example, if there are seventy-five different passages referring to domestic violence in our data, the computer can provide us with a list of these references. Text segments may be retrieved according to a virtually limitless set of variables, such as the age, gender, or profession of an interviewee. This capability lets us systematically compare the behavior of men and women or individuals in different occupations. Most of the sophisticated programs allow the assignment of several coding categories to the same set of data without recopying the material. For example, examine the following excerpt from an interview:

INTERVIEWER: Did you and your son agree about choosing a college?

PARENT: Like I wanted him to apply to Notre Dame, I wanted him to apply to a few of these big schools because I think it would be a wonderful education. We could afford the education. It is national recognition. I think it would be *fun* to be there in that kind of environment. But . . . he feels that it would be absolutely *impossible* to play sports and [also] it is too far away from home.

This excerpt could simultaneously be coded as an instance of "parent/child disagreement" *and* "reasons for attending a college." To accomplish this task, the researcher highlights the passage on the computer and uses the program to indicate how it is to be labeled and where it is to be stored.

It may seem that electronic coding and retrieval is simply a mechanization of widely used manual indexing techniques but that it does not change their underlying logic. However, several software programs actually go beyond the indexing function and are "not only regarded as an instrument for data archiving and management but also as a tool for data analysis" (Kelle, 1997:3.4). They do this by allowing the researcher to arrange the coding categories he or she has created into hierarchies or to "nest" one set of categories inside another. In this way, the coding categories can form chains of causal relationships or loops of understanding that resemble the construction of formal theory. These chains and loops can be expressed visually in diagrams that look like the theoretical models we examined in Chapter 2.

Observers have expressed concern about the more advanced and complex coding and retrieval techniques that approach "theory building." They perceive a threat to the genre of research presented in this chapter because the technology allows the investigator not to be as intimately involved in the continual process of recoding, and in the construction of models of understanding, as was the case in the precomputer era (Coffey, Holbrook, and Atkinson, 1996). Because the computer-based analysis of qualitative data makes it look more "scientific," it may be a strategic means to convince funding agencies that research is rigorous (Kelle, 1997:1.4). Of course, one of the challenges imposed by the sophisticated technology is for researchers not to forget the meaning of grounded theory. For explanation of human behavior to remain "grounded" in the field experience, the role of the researcher as evaluator of the data must remain paramount.

Qualitative Data and the Postmodern Critique

As we have noted, fieldwork relies on generating theory inductively from observation. This process calls for researchers to be ever sensitive to what people are telling them and "tuned in" to situations they encounter. In that sense, it has been appealing to feminist and postmodern scholars who are wary of imposing the researcher's own understanding onto the "reality" of other people's experience.[12] However, we

should not forget that inductive fieldwork, as traditionally practiced, is nonetheless positivistic; its ultimate goal is to generate formal theories from observations that are no less valid than the theories used deductively in quantitative research (Glaser and Strauss, 1967). In response to the postmodern critique of positivistic science, some creative approaches to fieldwork and qualitative methods have been developed (Clarke, 2005; Charmaz, 2006; Gubrium and Holstein, 2006). In these approaches, there is much more genuine collaboration between researchers and the people they are studying. Even the term "research subject" is discouraged because it denotes a boundary that "objectifies" others and therefore impedes genuine empathy and understanding. These newer approaches expose and critique the idea that qualitative researchers working in the field receive special training in theory building that sets them apart from the people they want to study. They challenge the notion that one can master the techniques presented in this chapter without thinking that one can understand people's lives in some more fundamental way than those who are actually living them.

SUMMARY

Observational field research is based on the assumption that we may understand peoples' motives, values, beliefs, and interests by studying them in their natural environment. Participant observation techniques have been applied in a wide variety of organizational settings, in deviant subcultures, and across many occupations. An important characteristic of this method is the absence of standard operating procedures. Data collection and the formulation of research questions and analysis are highly variable in practice. This chapter has attempted to provide some general guidelines. Ideally, fieldwork is an inductive, emerging enterprise; however, even in the choice of settings, the effects of the researcher's previous thinking and training may be apparent. The goal is to remain uncommitted to a given set of ideas or group of informants long enough to discover the full range of behavior in a particular setting, its

---

[12] Please refer to Chapter 10, "Feminist Methods," for further explanation of this position.

significance for the participants, and its potential relevance to other settings.

To gain access to fieldwork settings, the researcher must take on a role somewhere along the continuum from complete observer to complete participant. The role eventually selected may depend on the response of the subjects and on how public or private the setting is. Researchers also have to decide whether any of their activities are to be concealed, a controversial ethical issue raised by naturalistic inquiry. The more interaction that occurs between researcher and subjects, the more the role taken by the researcher has to be adapted to the individual personalities and situations involved. There is, however, no such thing as total unobtrusiveness. Adopting a research role satisfactory to one group of respondents may necessitate cutting oneself off from contact with others in the same setting. In general, fieldworkers should be as honest as possible about what they are doing. They should let their research role evolve gradually and should avoid being used by respondents for their own purposes.

The route to successful, systematic, and analytical participant observation lies in keeping accurate and complete field notes. These are essential not only for validity but also for maximizing theoretical flexibility. Notes should contain both description and explanation. They should be filled with dialogue, personal feelings, hunches, and speculative hypotheses. Data analysis ideally is initiated as notes are being drafted and expanded during fieldwork. However, the real analytical homework may not come until the researcher has left the field. Analysis may consist of ordering one's data using standard concepts or of creating new ideas or combinations of ideas. A complete analysis requires an exhaustive inventory of data so that they may be coded into relevant categories. Coding itself is not analysis. We need to explain and assess the significance of coding categories before we can construct theories of human behavior.

Despite its acknowledged strengths, particularly in the production of rich, descriptive data, fieldwork has a variety of limitations in the areas of reliability and generalizability, in its vulnerability to researcher bias, and in the risk that participant observers will, by their presence, contaminate the research setting. Nevertheless, there has been a resurgence of interest in fieldwork as a data-gathering technique. This renewed attention has coincided with calls for social scientists who do observational research to be more thorough in their reporting of methodological procedures. The need for thoroughness and transparency in the research process is likely to accelerate as postmodern approaches to qualitative analysis become more prevalent and as computer technology becomes a standard data manipulation tool in qualitative studies.

KEY TERMS

autoethnography
case study
complete observer
complete participant
ethnography
gatekeeper
going native
grounded theory
hunch
indexing
key informant
methodological notes
negative cases
observer-as-participant
participant-as-observer
participant observation
saturation
sensitizing concept
theoretical memo

EXERCISES

1. Choose some relatively familiar context such as your dormitory room or a classroom and spend two hours doing careful observation. Consider some of the elements of good observation mentioned in the chapter. Write a brief essay indicating the things, events, or processes observed that you had previously taken for granted during your normal involvement in the setting.

2. Assume that you are about to embark on an observational study of a weight-loss support group.

Briefly indicate some of the methodological problems you might have. Do you speculate that there might be problems of access? Will there be difficulties in talking to group members? Might your own values intrude in your findings?

3. Kai Erikson (1967) established two rules concerning the ethicality of observational work. First, researchers must never deliberately misrepresent their identities to enter a private domain where they would otherwise have no legitimate access. Second, investigators must never misrepresent their research intentions. Write an essay indicating whether you think these rules are too restrictive. Will it be possible to follow these two rules and still study most social groups? (Refer to Miller and Tewksbury [2001] for examples of challenging research settings.)

4. Read an article presenting data acquired through participant observation. (You may find good articles in one of the journals listed below in "Readings Illustrating the Method.") After reading the article, answer the following questions:

   a. How fully did the author describe his or her methodology?

   b. What additional discussion could have been included to give you a clearer idea of the procedures used?

   c. Did the analysis conform well to the data presented?

   d. What questions do you have about the reliability and validity of the findings?

   e. Could the subject studied be investigated using methods other than participant observation? If so, indicate the methods that could have been used.

5. Read Adler (1998) and design a qualitative study of preadolescents. What is your topic? In what setting would you study the children? What problems of access do you anticipate in the setting and what can you do about them?

SUGGESTED READINGS

Readings about the Method

Bochner, Arthur P., and Carolyn Ellis, eds. 2001. *Ethnographically Speaking: Autoethnography, Literature and Aesthetics*. Lanham, MD: Rowman & Littlefield.

This volume presents the newer explorations of the literary turn in ethnographic work, including personal narrative, ethnographic performance, and the blending of social science and the arts.

Caputo, Virginia. 2000. "At 'Home' and 'Away': Reconfiguring the Field for Late Twentieth-Century Anthropology." In *Constructing the Field: Ethnographic Fieldwork in the Contemporary World*, 19–31. Vered Amit, ed. London: Routledge.

A useful discussion of the "fit" between fieldwork sites and one's personal life. It tries to answer the question: "Do we have to travel faraway to do fieldwork?"

Charmaz, Kathy. 2006. *Constructing Grounded Theory*. Thousand Oaks, CA: Sage.

An authoritative source on inductive theory building, this book also examines the relationship between grounded theory and postmodern and feminist approaches to data.

Clarke, Adele E. 2005. *Situational Analysis: Grounded Theory After the Postmodern Turn*. Thousand Oaks, CA: Sage.

This book is a reworking of the more positivistic version of grounded theory pioneered by Anselm Strauss, in light of the rise of postmodern theory.

Emerson, Robert, Rachel I. Fretz, and Linda L. Shaw. 1995. *Writing Ethnographic Fieldnotes*. Chicago: University of Chicago Press.

A good source for learning what goes into field notes, coding, and writing theoretical memos.

Fine, Gary Alan, and Joseph R. Gusfield, eds. 1995. *A Second Chicago School?: The Development of a Postwar American Sociology*. Chicago: University of Chicago Press.

This book chronicles the evolution of the Chicago School of qualitative research in the twentieth century.

Geering, John. 2007. *Case Study Research*. New York: Cambridge University Press.

A comprehensive examination of the logic of the case study approach, with emphasis on research problems for which case studies are particularly useful.

Goodall, H. Lloyd. 2000. *Writing the New Ethnography*. Walnut Creek, CA: Altamira Press.

This book is a primer on qualitative writing in the social sciences. Its focus is on turning qualitative data and field notes into final reports.

Gray, Paul S. 1980. "Exchange and Access in Fieldwork." *Urban Life* 9 (3) October: 309–331.

This article describes the barriers to access encountered by the author as he studied a labor organization. It is a natural history of participant observation that explains how the investigator's announced role changed over time and describes techniques for inspiring the trust of respondents as participation increases.

Holmes, Robyn M. 1998. *Fieldwork with Children.* Thousand Oaks, CA: Sage.

A good source on using qualitative methods with young people.

Kelle, Udo, ed. 1995. *Computer-Aided Qualitative Data Analysis: Theory, Methods and Practice.* Thousand Oaks, CA: Sage.

A resource for understanding both the logic and pragmatic details of computer applications in qualitative studies.

Kelle, Udo. 1997. "Theory Building in Qualitative Research and Computer Programs for the Management of Textual Data." *Sociological Research Online* 2 (2).

http://www.socresonline.org.uk/2/2/1.html.

This article is a comprehensive review of the relationship between the use of software packages for qualitative data analysis and the practice of research. Kelle evaluates the claim that the introduction of the computer has negatively affected the process of induction in data analysis. There is also a useful section giving examples of coding field notes in multiple categories, as well as an extensive bibliography on computer applications in fieldwork.

Lofland, John, et al. 2006. *Analyzing Social Settings: A Guide to Qualitative Observation and Analysis.* 4th ed. Belmont, CA: Wadsworth.

The author first offers a broad description of the purposes and goals of qualitative analysis. He then establishes guidelines for collecting and analyzing observational data. Lofland's discussion should serve as a useful introduction to observational techniques for the student entering the field for the first time.

Macphail, Ann. 2004. "Athlete and Researcher: Undertaking and Pursuing an Ethnographic Study in a Sports Club." *Qualitative Research* 4 (2): 227–245.

The author was an active athlete in a sports club while at the same time conducting ethnographic research. She examines role relationships and the maintenance of the balance between distance and involvement

Maxwell, Joseph A. 2005. *Qualitative Research Design: An Interactive Approach.* 2nd ed. Thousand Oaks, CA: Sage.

A clear, step-by-step guide to planning qualitative research. This book provides an example of a dissertation proposal for research using qualitative methods.

Miller, J. Mitchell, and Richard Tewksbury, eds. 2001. *Extreme Methods: Innovative Approaches to Social Science Research.* Boston: Allyn & Bacon.

This volume contains commentary on doing fieldwork in a variety of unusual groups and risky settings, including active burglars, drug dealers, juvenile and motorcycle gangs, pornographers, strippers, and witches.

Perecman, Ellen, and Sara R. Curran, eds. 2006. *A Handbook for Social Science Field Research.* Thousand Oaks, CA: Sage.

This book contains excellent bibliographic sources on research design of field studies.

Spradley, James P. 1997. *The Ethnographic Interview.* New York: Harcourt.

Chapters 5 through 12 are among the best on analysis of field data. The author offers concrete suggestions for making sense out of an array of information.

Suler, John. 2000. *The Psychology of Cyberspace.* Home page and table of contents.

http://www.rider.edu/users/suler/psycyber/psycyber.html.

The purpose of this online hypertext book is to explore the psychological dimensions of environments created by computers and online networks. One large section, "Life at the Palace," focuses on a chat community.

Taylor, Steven J., and Robert Bogdan. 1998. *Introduction to Qualitative Research Methods: A Guidebook and Resource.* 3rd ed. New York: Wiley.

One of the best "how to do it" books on all aspects of qualitative research.

Whyte, William Foote. 1943/1995. *Street Corner Society*. Chicago: University of Chicago Press.

Whyte's book stands as a classic example of observational field research. It is also one of the few qualitative studies in which the researcher gives an in-depth description of how the study proceeded. To get a feeling for some of the typical problems any researcher doing participant observation is likely to experience, read the appendix. It is an honest, sensitive statement on the practical, intellectual, and ethical issues Whyte had to face as he did his research. It is fascinating and informative reading.

Other Resources

Cybersociology. 1999.

http://www.socio.demon.co.uk/magazine/6/issue6.html.

Cybersociology is a nonprofit, multidisciplinary Webzine dedicated to the critical discussion of the Internet, cyberspace, cyberculture, and life online. Issue 6 contains many useful links on Internet-based ethnography.

QSR International. 2005.

http://www.qsr.com.au/.

This Web site contains information about the NUD*IST software program for qualitative data.

Qual-Software. 2006. The CAQDAS Project.

http://www.jiscmail.ac.uk/lists/qual-software.html.

This Web site was set up to increase awareness and debate about Computer Assisted Qualitative Data Analysis Software. It is an e-mail discussion forum for users of CAQDAS.

Samik-Ibrahim, Rahmat M. 2005. Grounded Theory References.

http://www.vlsm.org/rms46/citations-gtm.html.

This site provides comprehensive resources and commentary on the topic of grounded theory.

Readings Illustrating the Method

The references for this chapter and for Chapter 1 contain numerous examples of observational research.

Becker, Howard S. 1997. *Outsiders: Studies in the Sociology of Deviance.* New York: Simon & Schuster.

Through his research on two separate subcultures – marijuana smokers and jazz musicians – Becker develops the theoretical idea of labeling to explain how and why certain persons embark on a "deviant career."

Beitz, Charles A. Jr., and John R. Hook. 1998. "The Culture Of Military Organizations: A Participant-Observer Case Study Of Cultural Diversity." *Public Administration and Management: An Interactive Journal* 3 (3).

http://www.pamij.com/beitz.html.

A well-written and comprehensive qualitative analysis of military culture. This article uses an unusual methodology of "retroactive" participant observation. That is, the authors, former career military officers, rely on their reflections and experience to create the concepts they use in their analysis. This piece is also unusual in that it takes the reader, step by step, through the process in which the authors engaged to develop their conceptual categories.

Burawoy, Michael, et al. 2000. *Global Ethnography: Forces, Connections, and Imaginations in a Postmodern World.* Berkeley and Los Angeles: University of California Press.

This volume is a collection of ethnography projects written by members of Michael Burawoy's dissertation seminar. Like his previous work (1991), this book is helpful to those learning about fieldwork because, in addition to presenting their research findings, the student authors share their personal experiences in applying the method. However, this volume differs in that the research topics all have a global focus; it is an attempt to expand ethnography theoretically beyond the realms of social psychology or a single organizational setting, into a worldwide milieu of international social movements, corporations, migration, and trade.

Burawoy, Michael, Joshua Gamson, and Alice Burton. 1991. *Ethnography Unbound: Power and Resistance in the Modern Metropolis.* Berkeley and Los Angeles: University of California Press.

A collection of ethnographic studies of community and social change organizations, including unions and occupational and environmental groups. This book will interest those learning ethnographic method because the contributors freely explain their personal involvement in the organizations they are researching as well as their skepticism concerning validity and reliability issues. This work directly confronts the issue of political bias in fieldwork.

Correll, Shelley. 1995. "The Ethnography of an Electronic Bar: The Lesbian Café." *Journal of Contemporary Ethnography* 24 (3) October: 270–298.

An example of Internet-based ethnography.

Griggs, Claudine. 2005. *Journal of a Sex Change.* New York: Palgrave.

A classic example of autoethnography, this book chronicles a compelling journey from male to female.

Hays, Sharon. 2004. *Flat Broke with Children: Women in the Age of Welfare Reform.* New York: Oxford University Press.

A three-year study of women on welfare, this book demonstrates the connection between individual experience and larger public issues.

Liebow, Eliot. 1967. *Tally's Corner.* Boston: Little, Brown.

In this lively, well-written, and classic study, Liebow analyzes the lives of black street-corner men in Washington, DC. His data are used to construct a convincing argument that their behavior is explicable in terms of the obstacles they face in trying to realize the "middle-class" values of achievement and success. From a methodological point of view, the reader will want to consider the threats to validity in a study in which a white researcher interacts with black persons. This is one of the several dilemmas Liebow discusses in his appendix.

The journals *Qualitative Sociology, Ethnography,* and *Qualitative Inquiry* are excellent sources of fieldwork-based research and commentary about the method.

REFERENCES

Adler, Patricia A. 1998. *Peer Power: Preadolescent Culture and Identity.* New Brunswick, NJ:. Rutgers University Press.

Adler, Patricia A., and Peter Adler. 1987. *Membership Roles in Field Research.* Newbury Park, CA: Sage.

AEA (American Evaluation Association). 2007. "Qualitative Software."
http://www.eval.org/Resources/QDA.htm. Fairhaven, MA.

Agar, Michael H. 1996. *The Professional Stranger: An Informal Introduction to Ethnography.* 2nd ed. New York: Academic Press.

Anderson, Elijah. 1999. *Code of the Street: Decency, Violence, and the Moral Life of the Inner City.* New York: W. W. Norton.

Anderson, Nels. *The Hobo.* Chicago: University of Chicago Press.

Bauer, Martin W., and George G. Gaskell. 2000. *Qualitative Researching with Text, Image and Sound.* Thousand Oaks, CA: Sage.

Becker, Howard S. 1969/2006. "Problems of Inference and Proof in Participant Observation." In *Sociological Methods: A Sourcebook*, 398–414. Norman K. Denzin, ed. New Brunswick, NJ: Transaction.

_____. 1997. *Outsiders: Studies in the Sociology of Deviance.* New York: Simon & Schuster.

Becker, Howard S., and Blanche Geer. 1969. "Participant Observation and Interviewing: A Comparison." In *Issues in Participant Observation*, 322–331. George J. McCall and J. L. Simmons, eds. Reading, MA: Addison-Wesley.

Berk, Richard A., and Joseph M. Adams. 2001. "Establishing Rapport with Deviant Groups." In *Extreme Methods: Innovative Approaches to Social Science Research*, 58–71. J. Mitchell Miller and Richard Tewksbury, eds. Boston: Allyn & Bacon.

Best, Amy L. 2000. *Prom Night: Youth, Schools, and Popular Culture.* New York: Routledge.

Caputo, Virginia. 2000. "At 'Home' and 'Away': Reconfiguring the Field for Late Twentieth-Century Anthropology." In *Constructing the Field: Ethnographic Fieldwork in the Contemporary World*, 19–31. Vered Amit, ed. London: Routledge.

Charmaz, Kathy. 1993. *Good Days, Bad Days: The Self in Chronic Illness and Time.* New Brunswick, NJ: Rutgers University Press.

_____. 2001. "The Grounded Theory Method:" In *Contemporary Field Research: A Collection of Writings*, 109–126. Robert M. Emerson, ed. Prospect Heights, IL: Waveland Press.

———. 2006. *Constructing Grounded Theory*. Thousand Oaks, CA: Sage.

Clarke, Adele E. 2005. *Situational Analysis: Grounded Theory after the Postmodern Turn*. Thousand Oaks, CA: Sage.

Coffey, Amanda, and Paul Atkinson. 1996. *Making Sense of Qualitative Data*. Thousand Oaks, CA: Sage.

Coffey, Amanda, Beverley Holbrook, and Paul Atkinson. 1996. "Qualitative Data Analysis: Technologies and Representations." *Sociological Research Online* 1 (1).

http://www.socresonline.org.uk/1/1/4.html#top.

Crabtree, Andy. 2003. *Designing Collaborative Systems: A Practical Guide to Ethnography*. New York: Springer.

Crosset, Todd W. 1995. *Outsiders in the Clubhouse: The World of Women's Professional Golf*. Albany: State University of New York Press.

Denzin, Norman K. 1996. *The Alcoholic Society: Addiction and Recovery of the Self*. New Brunswick, NJ: Transaction.

Dey, Ian. 1995. "Reducing Fragmentation in Qualitative Research." In *Computer-Aided Qualitative Data Analysis: Theory, Methods and Practice*, 69–79. Udo Kelle, ed. London: Sage.

Duneier, Mitchell. 1999. *Sidewalk*. New York: Farrar, Straus and Giroux.

Eder, Donna. 1995. *School Talk: Gender and Adolescent Culture*. New Brunswick, NJ: Rutgers University Press.

Ehrenreich, Barbara. 2001. *Nickel and Dimed: On (Not) Getting By in Boom-Time America*. New York: Metropolitan Books.

Emerson, Joan. 1970/2006. "Behavior in Private Places: Sustaining Definitions of Reality in Gynecological Examinations." In *The Production of Reality: Essays and Readings on Social Interaction*, 4th ed., 201–214. Jodi O'Brien, ed. Thousand Oaks, CA: Pine Forge Press.

Erikson, Kai. 1967. "A Comment on Disguised Observation in Sociology." *Social Problems* 14: 366–373.

Fine, Gary Alan. 1996. *Kitchens: The Culture of Restaurant Work*. Berkeley and Los Angeles: University of California Press.

Fine, Gary Alan, and Kent L. Sandstrom. 1988. *Knowing Children: Participant Observation with Minors*. Newbury Park, CA: Sage.

Gans, Herbert J. 1982. *The Levittowners: Ways of Life and Politics in a New Suburban Community*. New York: Columbia University Press.

Geertz, Clifford. 2001. "Thick Description: Toward an Interpretive Theory of Culture." In *Contemporary Field Research: Perspectives and Formulations*, 37–59. 2nd ed. Robert M. Emerson, ed. Prospect Heights, IL: Waveland Press.

Gerring, John. 2007. *Case Study Research*. New York: Cambridge University Press.

Glaser, Barney G., and Anselm Strauss. 1967. *Discovery of Grounded Theory: Strategies for Qualitative Research*. New Brunswick, NJ: Aldine/Transaction.

Gold, Raymond L. 1969/2006. "Roles in Sociological Field Observations." In *Sociological Methods: A Sourcebook*, 370–380. Norman K. Denzin, ed. New Brunswick, NJ: Transaction.

Granfield, Robert. 1992. *Making Elite Lawyers: Visions of Law at Harvard and Beyond*. New York: Routledge.

Gray, Paul S. 1980. "Exchange and Access in Fieldwork." *Urban Life* 9 (3) October: 309–331.

———. 1981. *Unions and Leaders in Ghana: A Model of Labor and Development*. New York: Conch Books.

Gubrium, Jaber F., and James A. Holstein. 2006. *The New Language of Qualitative Method*. New York: Oxford University Press.

Hammersley, Martyn. 1992. *What's Wrong with Ethnography? Methodological Explorations*. New York: Routledge.

———. 1998. *Reading Ethnographic Research: A Critical Guide*. Reading, MA: Addison-Wesley.

Humphreys, Laud. 1975. *Tearoom Trade: Impersonal Sex in Public Places*. Chicago: Aldine de Gruyter.

Jacobs, Bruce. 1998. "Researching Crack Dealers: Dilemmas and Contradictions." In *Ethnography at the Edge: Crime, Deviance, and Field Research*, 160–177. Jeff Ferrell and Mark S. Hamm, eds. Boston: Northeastern University Press.

Jarrett, Robert L., and Linda M. Burton. 1999. "Dynamic Dimensions of Family Structure in Low Income African American Families: Emergent

Themes in Qualitative Research." *Journal of Comparative Family Studies* 30 (2): 177–184.

Karp, David A. 1973. "Hiding in Pornographic Bookstores: A Reevaluation of the Nature of Urban Anonymity." *Urban Life and Culture* 1 (January): 427–451.

Kelle, Udo. 1997. "Theory Building in Qualitative Research and Computer Programs for the Management of Textual Data." *Sociological Research Online* 2 (2).
   http://www.socresonline.org.uk/2/2/1.html.

Kunda, Gideon. 2006. *Engineering Culture: Control and Commitment in a High-Tech Corporation.* Philadelphia: Temple University Press.

Leidner, Robin. 1993. *Fast Food, Fast Talk: Service Work and the Routinization of Everyday Life.* Berkeley and Los Angeles: University of California Press.

Liebow, Eliot. 1967. *Tally's Corner.* Boston: Little, Brown.

Lofland, John, et al. 2006. *Analyzing Social Settings: A Guide to Qualitative Observation and Analysis.* 4th ed. Belmont, CA: Wadsworth.

Luhrmann, T. M. 2001. *Of Two Minds: An Anthropologist Looks at American Psychiatry.* New York: Vintage.

Miller, J. Mitchell. 2001. "Covert Participant Observation: Reconsidering the Least Used Method." In *Extreme Methods: Innovative Approaches to Social Science Research*, 13–20. J. Mitchell Miller and Richard Tewksbury, eds. Boston: Allyn & Bacon.

Ouellet, Lawrence J. 1994. *Pedal to the Metal: The Work Life of Truckers.* Philadelphia: Temple University Press.

Platt, Jennifer. 1995. "Chicago Methods: Reputations and Realities." In *The Tradition of the Chicago School of Sociology*, 89–104. Luigi Tomasi, ed. Aldershot, Hampshire, UK: Ashgate.

Privacy Rights Clearinghouse. 2007. "A Chronology of Data Breaches."
   http://www.privacyrights.org/ar/
   ChronDataBreaches.htm (February 12).

Rheingold, Howard. 1993. *The Virtual Community.* New York: Harper.

Rochford, E. Burke. 1985. *Hare Krishna in America.* New Brunswick, NJ: Rutgers University Press.

Rosenhan, David L. 1999. "On Being Sane in Insane Places." In *Social Deviance: Readings in Theory and Research*, 398–412. Henry N. Pontell, ed. Upper Saddle River, NJ: Prentice Hall.

Rossman, Gretchen B., and Sharon F. Rallis. 1997. *Learning in the Field: An Introduction to Qualitative Research.* Thousand Oaks, CA: Sage.

Shaw, Clifford. 1930. *The Jack-Roller: A Delinquent Boy's Own Story.* Chicago: University of Chicago Press.

Smyres, Kerrie Michelle. 1999. "Virtual Corporeality: Adolescent Girls and Their Bodies in Cyberspace." *Cybersociology* 6. Research Methodology Online.
   http://www.cybersociology.com/files/6_3_
   girlsandbodiesonline.html.

Snow, David A., and Leon Anderson. 1997. *Down on Their Luck: A Study of Homeless Street People.* Berkeley and Los Angeles: University of California Press.

Strauss, Anselm L., and Juliet M. Corbin. 1998. *Basics of Qualitative Research: Techniques and Procedures for Developing Grounded Theory.* 2nd ed. Thousand Oaks, CA: Sage.

Suler, John. 1999. "One of Us: Participant Observation at the Palace."
   http://www.rider.edu/users/suler/psycyber/
   partobs.html.

Taylor, Steven J., and Robert Bogdan. 1998. *Introduction to Qualitative Research Methods: A Guidebook and Resource.* 3rd ed. New York: Wiley.

Tewksbury, Richard, and Patricia Gagne. 2001. "Assumed and Presumed Identities: Problems of Self-Presentation in Field Research." In *Extreme Methods: Innovative Approaches to Social Science Research*, 72–93. J. Mitchell Miller and Richard Tewksbury, eds. Boston: Allyn & Bacon.

Thrasher, Frederick M. 1927. *The Gang.* Chicago: University of Chicago Press.

Van den Hoonaard, Will C. 1997. *Working with Sensitizing Concepts: Analytical Field Research.* Thousand Oaks, CA: Sage.

Wacquant, Loic. 2003. *Body and Soul: Notebooks of an Apprentice Boxer.* New York: Oxford University Press.

Warren, Carol A. B., and Jennifer Kay Hackney. 2000. *Gender Issues in Ethnography.* 2nd ed. Thousand Oaks, CA: Corwin Press.

Wax, Rosalie H. 1986. *Doing Fieldwork: Warnings and Advice.* Chicago: University of Chicago Press.

Whitehead, Tony Larry, and Mary Ellen Conaway, eds. 1986. *Self, Sex, and Gender in Cross-Cultural Fieldwork.* Urbana: University of Illinois Press.

Whyte, William Foote. 1943/1955. *Street Corner Society.* Chicago: University of Chicago Press.

Wolcott, Harry F. 1995. *The Art of Fieldwork.* Walnut Creek, CA: Altamira Press.

Wolf, Diane L., ed. 1996. *Feminist Dilemmas in Fieldwork.* Boulder, CO: Westview Press.

FEMINIST METHODS

10

INTRODUCTION

In earlier chapters, three often-used research techniques, quantitative social surveys, qualitative interviewing, and participant observation, have been presented. Although quantitative and qualitative approaches differ from each other in many ways, in practice most of them do share a commitment to mainstream social science. The foci of this chapter, by contrast, are feminist methods that are based in a fundamental *critique* of conventional social science, its methods, and the roots of the knowledge on which it is based. Today, feminist methods represent a prime example of the research imagination, literally imagining a less conventional purpose for research. Feminists claim that **PATRIARCHAL**, or *male-centered*, perspectives and concerns have historically dominated mainstream research. They believe that their methods are more likely to produce valid findings or truthful and inclusive accounts of social experience.

Although some feminist research tools are new, many others are identical to the surveys and interviews you have already read about. **FEMINIST METHODS,** therefore, are not so much a specific toolkit as they are *a distinctive perspective or understanding of research practices*. So, in this chapter, before the methods or techniques themselves can be specified, considerable attention must be devoted to feminist theory because the perspective that informs feminist method is embedded in theory.

From the feminist perspective, all knowledge is "socially located and situated" and thus partial or incomplete. That is, one's position in the social system of gender and class relations influences how research is conducted and, ultimately, one's research findings. Feminist methods, it is claimed, emerged precisely because of the insufficiency of so-called good science, as traditionally defined. Many feminists have made the point that conventional science *claims* to be universal, that is, to apply to both genders; however, positivist (allegedly value-neutral and truth

producing) science has historically excluded, distorted and mismeasured women's experience.

Australian scholar Dale Spender (in Reinharz, 1992:7–8) provides a general explanation of the need for feminist alternatives:

Feminist knowledge is based on the premise that the experience of all human beings is valid and must not be excluded from our understandings, whereas patriarchal knowledge is based on the premise that the experience of only half of the human population needs to be taken into account and the resulting version can be imposed on the other half. This is why patriarchal knowledge and the methods of producing it are a fundamental part of women's oppression, and why patriarchal knowledge must be challenged – and overruled.

So, feminist methods are not only about correcting inadequacies in scientific truth telling but also, in the process, about emancipating or liberating women from scientific practices that continue to oppress them. **FEMINIST METHODOLOGY**, *the explicitly methodological discussion that emerges from the feminist critique*, has as its central goals to create fuller accounts of women's experiences and to make them visible (DeVault, 1996:31). To reach these goals, feminist researchers must challenge established canons in their disciplines or adopt a feminist attitude toward science, variously described as "feminist distrust" (Reinharz, 1985); "resisting the discipline" (Kitzinger, 1990); "strategic heresy" (Star, 1979); "rational skepticism of handed-down doctrine" (Lerner, 1976); and "resistant reading" (Fetterley, 1978). Feminists who use these methods are, like members of other political groups, impassioned about what they study. As such, feminist methods are *explicitly concerned with social activism as a part of or as a by-product of research*, or with the **EMANCIPATORY POTENTIAL OF FEMINIST RESEARCH**.

One delicate and important issue for the use of feminist methods in research is to avoid allowing political passion to obscure or distort social scientific vision – in other words, to avoid a biased feminist vision. If used properly, DeVault (1996:30) says that sociologists who "are committed to both feminism and social science," will "use the tools of the discipline to 'talk back' to sociology in a spirited critique aimed at improving the ways we know society." Similarly, Celia Kitzinger (in Reinharz, 1992:13) asserts her "passionate...commitment both to feminism and psychology" when she explains:

For me, being both a feminist and a psychologist means to be responsible to other feminists for my psychology, and equally to be responsible to other psychologists for my feminism.

However, an important claim by FEMINIST EPISTEMOLOGISTS, *those who theorize about how and what we know about, and as women*, is that the political bias of feminism is a grounds for, not an impediment to, approaching more objective accounts of social life.

Multiple Disciplines and Methodologies

Feminist methods are used in multiple academic disciplines (e.g., sociology, psychology, anthropology, history, political science, economics, geography, communications, theology, and science) and draw on multiple theoretical perspectives. Within the social sciences, many approaches can be found among the feminist works of Marxist anthropologist Gale Rubin, object relations theorist Nancy Chodorow, phenomenologist Louise Levesque-Lopman, postpositivist Zillah Eisenstein, symbolic interactionists Mary Jo Deegan and Michael R. Hill, personal construct theorists Susan Volentine and Stanley Brodsky, economic theorist Laura Olsen, and ethnomethodologists Wendy McKenna and Sarah Kessler (Reinharz, 1992:246).

Another important point is that feminist methods are *plural, not singular*. Reinharz (1992:4) stresses the PLURALITY OF FEMINIST METHODS in the introduction of her book:

...this book is entitled *Feminist Methods in Social Research* with an emphasis on plural. It demonstrates the fact that feminist have used all existing methods and have invented some new ones as well. Instead of orthodoxy, feminist research practices must be recognized as a plurality. Rather than there

being a "woman's way of knowing," or a "feminist way of doing research," there are women's *ways* of knowing.

Reinharz (1992:244) explains that sometimes feminist researchers use conventional methods with no modification whatsoever. In other cases, methods are "modified to meet the demands of feminist research or when conventional methods are inadequate." A plurality of feminist methods can be found, for example, among survey and experimental methods (Eichler, 1988), interview research (Oakley, 1981), inductive fieldwork (Reinharz, 1979), oral history (Gluck and Patai, 1991), experimental ethnography (Gordon, 1988), action research (Smail, Shyte, and Kelly, 1982), and multiple methods (Chesler, 1972; Herman and Hirschman, 1981; Weitzman, 1985). Reinharz (1992:243) emphasizes disciplinary and methodological inclusiveness: "Feminist research is amoeba-like; it goes everywhere, in every direction. It reaches into all the disciplines and uses all the methods, sometimes singly and sometimes in combinations." DeVault (1996:29) similarly advocates the plurality of feminist methods, while highlighting their political spirit:

Feminist methodologists do not use or prescribe any single research method; rather, they are united through various efforts to include women's lives and concerns in accounts of society, to minimize the harms of research, and to support changes that will improve women's status.

Although some authors (Klein, 1983; Stanley and Wise, 1983; Smith, 1987) advocate distinctive feminist methods, or alternatives to conventional research methodologies (Collins, 1989; DeVault, 1990; Fonow and Cook, 1991), scholars such as Haraway (1988) and Harding (1987) argue that to prescribe distinctive methods would result in an oppressive hierarchy among feminists, cover up differences among feminist researchers, and thus, contradict the very heart of feminist methodology. Clegg (1975) claims that specific methods are unnecessary for feminist research as long as research questions and interpretations of results are feminist. Still other authors, such as Francesca Cancian, advocate adopting a "'social practice' or 'social construction' perspective on science" that employs conventional research methods:

Science, in this perspective, is a social activity of particular groups, and scientific methods and findings are heavily influenced by the groups' values, position in the social structure, and historical circumstances. (1992:624)

Finally, the common claim that feminist methods can include all methods is a tenuous one, given that most feminist research is qualitative in orientation. In her review of the literature, DeVault (1996:36) pointed out that "(e)xplicit discussion of how feminism might modify quantitative practice seems relatively difficult to find." Moreover, some feminist theorists explicitly claim that survey research methods are antithetical to escaping the constraints of "objectifying knowledges" that they make subjects disappear, that they do not adequately convey the localized realities of women, or that they do not treat "the everyday/everynight" worlds of women as a serious social scientific problem (Smith, 1990a). Gorelick (1991:461) criticizes large-scale survey research by claiming: "In 'hired hand research' low-level research staff may find myriad ways of cutting short their work, constituting a 'labor problem' in the truth factory." In a similarly critical spirit, Graham (1983) details several ways survey methods are in and of themselves a source of gender bias.

Although the claims of inclusiveness may be problematic in one sense, the opposite claim, that feminist methods are distinctive, may be problematic in another sense. For instance, feminist methodologists assert that not all research that is "feminist" would qualify as social research grounded in feminist methods. How then can one distinguish between the two types of research? Reinharz (1992:6) uses three criteria:

1. Research self-identified as feminist by the feminist researcher

2. Research published in "journals that publish only feminist research, or in books that identify themselves as such"

3. Research "that has received awards from organizations that give awards to people who do feminist research"

The first criterion has the advantage, Reinharz (1992:7) says, of "avoid[ing] deducing what feminist research is from the standpoint of personal definition. This approach rejects the notion of an overall authority that decides what constitutes 'feminist,' consistent with the anti-hierarchical nature of many feminist organizations and much feminist spirit." Reinharz's criteria, to say the least, are ambiguous and conflate the two very categories she aims to distinguish. How does one – especially one who is concerned with accuracy – assume that self-identification (rather than objective criteria), publication in a feminist journal (rather than a feminist methods journal), or receiving an award for feminist research (rather than uniquely feminist methods) can denote feminist methods?

Understandably then, what makes feminist methods distinctive is feminist theorizing about research practices more than the specific type of data collection methods used. However, it is difficult to reduce feminist methodology to orthodoxy because feminists share a common commitment to the plurality of women's experiences, and to giving multiple "voices" to women.[1] Rather than prescription, Smith (1990a: 206) offers an open and discretionary invitation: "The techniques of analysis and the concepts are there for your use. Feel free." Thus, to use feminist methods, and to learn about them successfully, is to do so with a spirit of openness to and tolerance of difference and diversity but does not reconcile definitional problems associated with such openness.

A final point is that using feminist methods does not mean that one simply replaces conventional methods with new ones. Reinharz (1992:243) explains that one must learn the ordinary disciplinary methods, even if learning results in criticism:

The researcher has to learn the disciplinary methods, rules of logic, statistical procedures, procedures for "writing up" research projects, and whatever else is relevant to the field in which she wishes to work. She may learn them only to criticize them, but she has to learn them nonetheless.

[1] For example, Smith (1990a:206) disclaims any strict policy for correct use of methods when she concludes: "The technical practices are not an orthodoxy; they are not required, nor is the concept of ideology."

Thus, the feminist method is not a shortcut to learning or a way to circumvent the standard learning processes in various disciplines. If used responsibly and properly, feminist methods are more work intensive as an elaboration of, or as a well-informed departure from, conventional learning.

PATRIARCHAL SCIENCE

The use of feminist methods raises awareness of the ways women's experiences have been ignored and distorted in scientific research and of the importance of working toward more inclusive social sciences. Therefore, we offer a brief discussion of patriarchal science and its omission and distortion of women's experiences.

Psychology and medicine have been and continue to be especially fertile grounds for feminist criticism of the treatment of women, both theoretically and in clinical practice. For example, during the first two decades of the twentieth century, numerous psychological studies were published linking menstruation with deterioration in women's performance, reminiscent of nineteenth-century nerve theories positing women's natural defects linked to their reproductive cycles, and Hippocratic notions of "wandering wombs" as a primary source of women's illnesses (Thompson and Bullough, 1999). Tuana's (1988:147) detailed survey of reproductive theories from Aristotle to the sociobiology theory of the 1970s shows how "adherence to a belief in the inferiority of the female creative principle biased scientific perception of the nature of women's role in human generation." She shows how biases of female weakness, passivity, and natural defect provided institutional and intellectual legitimacy to numerous theories of biological inferiority. French feminist Luce Irigaray's (1985a, 1985b) re-readings of psychoanalysis show further how patriarchal bias defines women without a sexuality of their own and how psychoanalytic practice has undermined and distorted the subjectivity of patients.

Jeffrey Masson (1984, 1988) provides a tour de force critique of how psychoanalysis and other conventional psychology theories and clinical practices have harmed women physically, psychological, socially, and spiritually. Among many works with similar thematic content are Phyllis Chesler's (1972) now classic, radical exposure of how psychiatric theorizing and practice have encouraged punitive sanctions for women who transgress socially constructed sex roles, and Dorothy Smith's (1990c) critical examination of how women's mental health statistics obscure oppressive realities that lead to psychiatric "symptoms." Also influential has been Carol Gilligan's (1982) critique of the patriarchal bias in Lawrence Kohlberg's theory of the moral development of children, which was based on male sampling. Gilligan argues that when girls are considered in such studies they do not lack moral development but express it with a "different voice." An array of other psychology critiques show how psychology researchers use male subjects more frequently than female subjects, use males to generalize to the entire population, and often cite one-sex studies to substantiate arguments about sex differences.

Sociology is not immune to sexist and patriarchal biases. For example, how many times does the sociologist with the perspective that social reality is a social construction routinely quote W. I. Thomas: "If men [sic] define situations as real, they are real in their consequences" or quote Peter Berger and Thomas Luckmann, Erving Goffman, Charles Horton Cooley, George Herbert Mead, Karl Marx, Emile Durkheim, or Max Weber, and while doing so, wonder about the presence or absence of women in their authoritative writings? Each time, for the feminist with a raised consciousness of women's omission from social scientific knowledge, one must stop, explain, and qualify the socially situated knowledge claims of the "fathers" of the sociological discipline.

If gender were added as a serious variable in the analysis:

- Would the processes of externalization, objectivation, and internalization be the same in Berger and Luckmann's (1966/1990) social construction of reality?
- How would the social psychology of stigma vary if women's gender-related shame were added to Goffman's (1963/1986) account?

- Or, in *The Presentation of Self in Everyday Life* is the presentation of self as general or gender-neutral as Goffman's (1959/1973) work suggests?
- How might Cooley's (1902/1964) "looking glass self" change if women's socially situated experiences, such as greater empathy socialization, were taken into account?
- And, how, for example, might the internalized "male gaze" make Mead's (1934/1967) conceptualization of the spectator-judge "me" and the spontaneous-actor-judged "I" problematic?

And certainly not exhaustively, we might ask, how might the very foundational insights about modernism, industrial life, capitalism, rationality, and social control be different if women's experiences were incorporated as real, valid, and worthy of inclusion in the works of the fathers of the discipline of sociology? How might those accounts be altered if women researchers authored them, or if they included as important considerations the active voices and experiences of black women, poor women, Native American women, lesbian and bisexual women, working women, or "wives" and mothers? Feminist research challenges the most fundamental bases of our intellectual understandings and the tools used in creating them, as Acker, Barry, and Esseveld (1991:136) explain:

Exploration, in our usage, means an open and critical process in which all the intellectual tools we have inherited from a male dominated intellectual tradition are brought into question, including ideas about the basic nature of human beings, the nature of social life, the taken-for-granted world-view of traditional science, what concepts and questions might help illuminate our shared conditions, and how we should go about developing such knowledge.

In 1980, the American Sociological Association's Committee on the Status of Women in Sociology described five parts of the research process where sexist bias frequently occurs. These are summarized in the box on page 217.

Institutional recognition of sexist bias throughout the research design process helps to make the emancipatory work of feminist researchers legitimate. However, recognition of widespread bias is merely a first step. FEMINIST CONSCIOUSNESS-RAISING, or *to experience a heightened awareness of the depth and pervasiveness of sexism in society,* is, for Catherine MacKinnon (1983), the basis of feminist methodology. The necessary process of raising awareness may in itself be discouraging for many social scientists, as philosopher Sandra Lee Bartky's (1990) work strongly suggests. In her account, feminist consciousness is a way of experiencing the world involving painful anger, anxiety, and suspicion but also certainty and hope. Toward the end of the chapter, we will discuss feminist research practices that aim toward more inclusive social sciences. For now, we turn to a deeper consideration of problems inherent in scientific research as explained by feminist epistemologists.

BASICS OF FEMINIST EPISTEMOLOGY

There are many sociohistorical events that provide the context for the emergence of FEMINIST EPISTEMOLOGY, or *theorizing about women's socially constructed and socially situated knowledge.* Among them are the collapse of European colonial empires during the 1950s, the Civil Rights Movements in the United States during the 1960s, the 1968 university student walkout strikes in Paris, anti-Vietnam protests, and the women's movement during the 1970s (Mann and Kelley, 1997:392). "Third Wave" feminism involved women demanding not only the right to become makers and administrators of knowledge but also the right to criticize and correct the oppression embedded in the production of knowledge. These movements, conflicts, and protests shared the following common themes:

- Crises in the faith in institutional legitimacy
- Struggles for inclusion
- Demands for recognition of differences
- Refusal to accept the "truths" generated by conventional science

Feminist epistemology is grounded in these historical events and political issues. It denotes

Sources of Sexist Bias in the Research Process

1. *Research Problem Selection and Formulation*

   - gender-blind social theory
   - significant topics ignored
   - selective treatment of topics
   - a research problem formulated for men or women only
   - a research model thought to apply to men and women only
   - inadequate exploration of topics which transcend sex-stereotypes
   - pejorative labeling or conceptualization

2. *Review of Previous Research*

   - failure to mention that samples are single-sex or have highly imbalanced sex-ratios
   - failure to observe methodological weaknesses in previous research

3. *Selection of Population and Sample*

   - women or men are arbitrarily excluded from sample
   - inadequate justification for exclusion of men and women from sample

4. *Validity Issues*

   - biased question wording in surveys
   - scales validated on a single sex
   - cross-sex interviewing

5. *Interpretation of Research Results*

   - over-generalization of single-sex studies
   - improper titles which don't reveal single-sex nature of research
   - inferences unwarranted by data

Connie Miller and Corrinna Treitel. 1991. *Feminist Research Methods: An Annotated Bibliography*. (New York: Greenwood Press), pp. 36–37.

a more general shift in intellectual knowledge, during the 1960s to the present day, in three broad areas of social thought:

- Deconstruction
- Postmodernism
- Poststructuralism

DECONSTRUCTION aims *to decenter or "dismantle truths,"* to "generate skepticism" about taken for granted beliefs in social scientific discourses, to challenge "the function of knowledge in legitimating power relations," and to "refute the very rules used to justify knowledge" (Collins, 2001:53–54). **POSTMODERNISM**, the most extreme of these perspectives, *proclaims the death of objectively verifiable knowl-* *edge, and material reality, and tends to treat social life as a series of sign systems or discourses* without referents in reality as we once knew it. It is a direct challenge to positivistic social science. **POSTSTRUCTURALISM** represents not an abandonment of the search for "truth," or "social reality," but a deconstructive and self-reflexive approach to them. Poststructuralism *emphasizes a radical shift from objectivity to subjectivity,* from reality to social constructed reality, from unbiased knowledge to socially situated knowledges, from singularity to plurality, and from "partial knowledge presented as generally true" to admittedly "partial knowledge" (DeVault, 1996:41). Feminist theory as well as method are derived from the foregoing basic assumptions and approaches.

FEMINIST STANDPOINT THEORY

FEMINIST STANDPOINT THEORY *focuses on* the socially located and situated nature of knowledge, and the *unique perspectives on social reality that are taken by members of oppressed groups, especially women*. Standpoint theory draws on postmodernism's "powerful critique of existing knowledges and the hierarchical power relations they defend" (Collins, 2001:41).

In the works of sociologist Dorothy Smith, sociologist Patricia Hill Collins…and philosopher Sandra Harding, the concept of essentialized, universalized woman disappeared in the lens of standpoint thinking to reappear as a situated woman with experiences and knowledge specific to her in the material division of labor and the racial stratification system. This carries with it the view that all knowledge claims are socially located and that some social locations, especially those at the bottom of social and economic hierarchies, are better than others as starting points for seeking knowledge not only about those particular women but others as well. (Olesen, 2000:222)

This section focuses on two essential concepts in standpoint theory that bear on research methods, marginality and "outsider within" status, and summarizes the work of the three most influential standpoint theorists, Collins, Smith, and Harding.

"Outsider Within" Status

Black feminist sociologist Patricia Hill Collins (1991:35) says that "Afro-American women have long been privy to some of the most intimate secrets of white society." Using the example of black women who nurtured white children, who served and were "honorary members of their 'white families,'" Collins says that they were both in, but not of, those families, just as more generally black women scholars are in, but not of, predominantly white academe. These caregivers and black scholars occupy positions of **MARGINALITY**; that is, they are *both close and far, strangers to what they know or come to know intimately*. Collins calls this social location – *being between worlds, with both intimacy and distance* – "**OUTSIDER WITHIN**" **STATUS**. She

says it can be beneficial because it specially equips one to see the connections between the everyday subjective world and larger or more macro structural arrangements.

Collins argues that those who are really (authentically) marginal are better able to see the world through a sociological lens. Collins's work, and the work of other feminist standpoint theorists, poses a question with the potential of turning sociological practice on its head. Have social scientists in practice – even if professing to adopt a sociological perspective – actually done so? In the following selection, Collins explains the marginality of black women sociologists and how it equips them with a keener and more self-reflexive view of the sociological enterprise.

This more intense sociological marginality, according to Collins, ironically gives black women sociologists a privileged sociological perspective. This perspective not only allows them to see through and beyond social phenomena (or to see more keenly subjectively *and* objectively) but also to see through and beyond existing theoretical accounts of social life. Moreover, as black women move to the center of sociological analysis, Collins claims, they will improve the discipline by "reaffirming human subjectivity and intentionality" (Collins, 1991:52). Next, the distinctive standpoint of black feminist thought and its contributions to black women and sociology is discussed.

Patricia Hill Collins's Black Feminist Thought

Black feminist standpoint theory (Collins, 1991) begins with the idea "that it is impossible to separate the structure and thematic content of thought from the historical and material conditions shaping the lives of its producers" (1991:37). A second assumption is that "Black women possess a unique standpoint on, or perspective of, their experiences and that there will be certain commonalities of perception shared by Black women as a group" (ibid.). Third, the "diversity and class, region, age, and sexual orientation" among black women produces varying or nuanced expressions of those common perceptions. A final assumption is that black

The Marginality of Black Female Researchers

Remaining in sociology by doing normal scientific investigations may . . . be less complicated for traditional sociologists than for Afro-American women. Unlike Black women,
learners from backgrounds where the insider information and experiences of sociology are more familiar may be less likely to see the taken-for-granted assumptions
of sociology and may be more prone to apply their creativity to "normal science." In
other words, the transition from student status to that of practitioner engaged in finding significant facts that sociological paradigms deem important, matching facts with
existing theories, and furthering paradigmatic development itself may proceed more
smoothly for white middle-class males than for working-class Black females. The latter group [that has not been allowed to take an active role in shaping and reshaping
sociological knowledge] is much more inclined to be struck by the mismatch of its own
experiences and the paradigms of sociology itself. Moreover, those Black women with
a strong foundation in Black women's culture (e.g., those that recognize the value of
self-definition and self-evaluation, and that have a concrete understanding of sister-
hood and motherhood) may be more apt to take a critical posture toward the entire
sociological enterprise. In brief, where traditional sociologists may see sociology as
"normal" and define their role as furthering knowledge about a normal world with
taken-for-granted assumptions, outsiders within are likely to see anomalies.

Reproduced with permission from Patricia Hill Collins. 1991. "Learning from the Outsider Within."
In *Beyond Methodology: Feminist Scholarship as Lived Research*, 50–51. Mary Margaret Fonow
and Judith A. Cook, eds. (Bloomington and Indianapolis: Indiana University Press). Bracketed
expression added.

female intellectuals are needed to "produce
facts and theories about Black female experience that will clarify a Black woman's standpoint
for Black women" (ibid.). That is, black women
(presumably nonacademic, nonsocial scientist
black women) may not necessarily understand
the thematic or theoretical complexity of their
socially situated knowledges; hence, the value
of black female intellectuals.

Thematically, there are three main ingredients
in Collins's black feminist thought (1991:35):

- The necessity for changing self-definition and
  self-valuation of black women
- The interlocking nature of oppressions
- The importance of redefining African American women's culture.

Collins aims to replace externally defined, controlling, and stereotypical knowledge of black
women with "authentic Black female images."
This involves both correcting stereotypical
images and asserting and reassigning valuation

to maligned and ridiculed images of black
women, such as sassiness or assertiveness.
Therefore, Collins proposes that "Black women
create their own standards for evaluating Afro-
American womanhood and value their crea-
tions" (1991:39). Thus, Collins's work centers on
black women's "self-definition, self-valuation,
and the necessity for a Black female-centered
analysis" (1991:40), which resists dehumaniz-
ing black women through white male positivistic science that has devalued and distorted the
"subjectivities of the oppressed" or has treated
black women as "objects lacking full human subjectivity." Collins says further that work about
black women by black women intellectuals
that provides more authentic images of black
women's experience has the benefit of coun-
tering the damaging effect of previous research,
"internalized psychological oppression" (ibid.).

Collins emphasizes that it is not only necessary to challenge black women's oppression but also the **INTERLOCKING NATURE OF**

OPPRESSIONS. This does not mean merely to "add Black women's oppression and stir" into existing theoretical models such as Marxism that emphasize class oppression. Rather, "Black feminists aim to develop new theoretical interpretations of the interaction [*between various modes of oppression*] itself"[2] to provide a more "holistic analysis of oppression" (1991:40–41), Collins concludes.

A third theme in Collins's black feminist thought is redefining African American women's culture. In this reconceptualization, culture is an ongoing and constantly changing "ideological frame of reference" that depends on shifting material conditions. The importance of focusing on black woman's culture[3] is first, that it may illuminate a greater complexity in "the relationship between oppressed people's consciousness of oppression and the actions they take" than is "suggested in existing theory" (1991:45). Collins argues, for example, that oppressed persons, black women in particular, "may overtly conform to society roles laid out for them, yet covertly oppose these roles in numerous spheres, an opposition shaped by the consciousness of being on the bottom" (ibid.). Black women's culture is also important, Collins says, because "it points to the problematic nature of existing conceptualizations of the term 'activism.'" An understanding of black women's culture carries with it the more general insight that activism may be contained within more general and "multiple structures of domination" or that willful human action may be contained as a possibility within structural constraint. So, black women's culture offers an "analytical model" for "exploring the relationship between oppression, consciousness, and activism" (1991:46).

The general methodological project of black feminist thought is to produce **WEBBED ACCOUNTS**, or what Mann and Kelley (1997:398) succinctly paraphrase as

a more developed picture of the social world [that] can be generated by "pivoting" from the interpreta-

tions and knowledge of one group to the interpretations of the next group. *By understanding perspectives of many groups, knowledge of social reality can become more complete*. Thus, social knowledge is constructed in a quiltlike fashion whereby the many and diverse social realities are interwoven to form a more complete fabric of the whole.[Bold italics added.]

While webbed accounts are useful for Collins to account more adequately for black women's experiences, this model of weaving together partial experiences is also helpful to other feminist researchers who similarly aim to provide adequate and holistic accounts of white women's experiences. Dorothy Smith's "institutional ethnography" is a case in point. Smith (1987) makes the nonintuitive, inductively grounded case that the day-to-day, localized activities in the home between children and their mothers shape activities in children's classrooms. This shows the relevance of domestic activities, considered irrelevant in previous research, to reveal a knowledge gap created by that value-laden bias and to work toward assembling left out, yet necessary, pieces of a "quilt" "which remains to be attached to other pieces in the creation of the whole pattern." Dorothy Smith's work aims to examine the "everyday/everynight world" of women researchers, that is, to make the lived worlds between which women travel relevant to social scientific analysis.

Dorothy Smith: Women's Standpoint

Sociologist Dorothy Smith's critique is rooted in her everyday experience of trying to falsely "bracket," or artificially separate, the social worlds in which she uneasily traveled, between the "objective" social world of social science and the "subjective" world of single mothering. It was out of Smith's experience of "knowing" that this was a false dichotomy that she developed a more elaborate criticism of scientific objectivity.

The standpoint of women situates the inquirer at the site of her bodily existence and in the local actualities of her working world. It is a standpoint that positions inquiry but has no specific content. Those

---

[2] Parenthetical comment added.
[3] That is not a monolithic culture, but a collection of socially constructed black women's cultures.

who undertake inquiry from this standpoint begin always from women's experience as it is for women. We are authoritative speakers of our experience. (Smith, 1990a:28)

In *The Conceptual Practices of Power*, Smith says that women's experience, if seriously and scientifically considered, constitutes a "radical critique of sociology." Her focus is "on the socially organized and organizing practices... that constitute objectified knowledge, the kind of knowledge that bureaucracies produce and sociologists depend on (census data, labor statistics, demographic information, epidemiological data, and so forth)" (Smith 1990a:4). Such survey research practices, she claims, "convert what people experience directly in their everyday/everynight world into forms of knowledge in which people as subjects disappear and in which their perspectives on their own experience are transposed and subdued." More specifically, Smith aims to escape participation in the "fathertongue," or in modes of research that make women disappear as subjects in their real lives, by working "toward a different method of thinking and knowing the society we live" (Smith 1990a:6).[4]

To achieve this goal requires broadening areas of relevant sociological inquiry beyond areas that are inconsistent with women's experience of the world, such as industrial sociology, social stratification, and political sociology. The shift toward newly relevant areas of inquiry would include the predominant women's "worlds of household, children and neighbor," which are "the primary grounds," Smith says, "for most women's lives" (1990a:13).

Smith also says that research for and about women's lives must begin with the lives of women researchers (1990a:13). The reason for beginning there is embedded in a twofold problem. First, "There is...a disjunction between how women experience the world and the theoretical schemes by which society's self-

consciousness is inscribed." Smith says that women's lives, everyday realities, and experiences do not match conventional male-biased conceptual schemes and theoretical constructs. A second interrelated issue is that "the worlds of women are not equally represented in objectified bodies of knowledge," in particular, the domestic world – the world of housework, children, and home life in general. These two difficulties are related to each other in a special way. The effect of the second interacting with the first is to compel women to think of their world in the same concepts and terms as men think of their lives. Hence, the established forms of consciousness alienate women from their own experience.

For Smith (1990a:14–15), sociological theorizing from a male perspective on the social world, and based on its selectivity of issues, is a form of ideological governance.[5] Here, Smith's work focuses on **RELATIONS OF RULING**. By "ruling" she means the "*total complex of activities, differentiated into many spheres, by which our kind of society is ruled, managed, and administered*." This complex includes the activities of sociologists who "participate in ruling." Clarifying further, she explains:

The governing of our kind of society is done in abstract concepts and symbols, and sociology helps create them by transposing the actualities of people's lives and experience into the conceptual currency with which they can be governed.

Smith says that sociologists are trained to subsume or ignore "the actualities of ourselves and of other people," or inconsistencies between lived experiences and prefabricated conceptual schemes.

All of the foregoing components of standpoint theory are directly relevant to research methods because methods used in the practice of objectivity are at the center of the problem:

The ethic of objectivity and the methods used in its practice are concerned primarily with the separation of knowers from what they know and in particular with the separation of what is known from

---

[4] Smith's critique of ideological practices offers "an alternative, reflexive, and materialist method of developing a systematic consciousness of our own society through which we can become conscious both of the social organization and relations of the objectified knowledges of the ruling institutions and of our tacit and unconscious complicity in them when we speak the fathertongue" (1990a:7).

[5] Male-dominated social science selects issues based on what is deemed administratively relevant rather than on what is "significant first in the experience of those who live them" (Smith, ibid.).

knowers' interests, "biases," and so forth, that are not authorized by the discipline. In the social sciences the pursuit of objectivity makes it possible for people to be paid to pursue a knowledge to which they are otherwise indifferent. What they feel and think about society can be kept out of what they are professionally or academically interested in. Correlatively, if they are interested in exploring a topic sociologically, they must find ways of converting their private interest into an objectified, unbiased form. (Smith, 1990a:16)

The result is that women researchers experience a **BIFURCATION OF CONSCIOUSNESS**, or *split awareness*. As Smith (1990a:20) explains:

The bifurcation of consciousness becomes for us a daily chasm to be crossed, on the one side of which is this special conceptual activity of thought, research, teaching, and administration, and on the other the world of localized activities oriented toward particular others, keeping things clean, managing somehow the house and household and the children – the world in which the particularities of persons in their full organic immediacy (feeding, cleaning up the vomit, changing the diapers) are inscapable. Even if this isn't something that currently preoccupies us, as it no longer preoccupies me, our present is given shape by a past that was thus.

Smith elaborates further how women's gender-specific experiences bear on the actualities of doing sociological work and of pursuing professional careers as sociologists:

How are we to manage career and children? . . . How is domestic work to be done? How is career time to be coordinated with family caring time? How is the remorseless structure of the children's school schedule to be coordinated with the equally exigent scheduling of professional and managerial work? Rarely are these problems solved by the full sharing of responsibilities between women and men. (Smith, 1990a:20)

Smith's alternative is not indulgent subjectivism, wherein she says we might not "escape the circles of our own heads," but to take "direct experience" as a starting point "and to return to it as a constant 'test' of the adequacy of systematic knowledge." In other words, sociology must "begin from where we are." This gender-specific experience of the world, she says, must become an integral part of sociological knowledge.

Sandra Harding's Critique of Scientific Objectivity

Sandra Harding's feminist standpoint epistemology goes beyond Collins's fundamental critique of social location with respect to sociological practice, to call into question the more general fabric of Western science. "*Whose Science? Whose Knowledge?*" she asks in the provocative title of her book. Harding aims not only to decenter (or, not take for granted) patriarchal bias in science but also to "decenter white, middle class, heterosexual, Western women in . . . feminist thought and yet still generate . . . analyses from the perspective of women's lives" (Harding, 1991:13). Moreover, akin to Collins's view concerning the "interlocking nature of oppressions," she says that gender is a relation, not a thing, and is socially defined according to other relations such as class and race. She explains at greater length, providing concrete examples of the importance of recognizing multiple "cultural configurations of womanhood":

Gender relations in any particular historical situation are always constructed by the entire array of hierarchical social relations in which "woman" and "man" participates. The femininity prescribed for the plantation owner's wife was exactly what was forbidden for the black slave woman. The forms of femininity required of Aryan women in Nazi Germany were exactly what was forbidden – in fact eliminated – for women who were Jews, Gypsies, or members of other "inferior races."

Harding's work focuses on "a call for better science." In Harding's view, science is "politics by other means" and should be understood as a social problem:

From a sociological perspective, it is virtually irresistible to regard contemporary science as fundamentally a social problem . . . How the monster actually got created – and gets nourished and reproduced day after day – retreats into the shadows, as if there are not personal or institutional practices that we can hold responsible for the shape of the sciences and the kind of social order with which they have been in partnership. (Harding, 1991:1)

Even though her critique sounds negative, Harding's aim is not to reduce all science to "bad" science. She emphasizes: "Western science contains both progressive and regressive tendencies" (Harding, 1991:3). Her work exposes the regressive tendencies of science; however, she favors the development of more adequate and objective *social* sciences, all sciences being social in her view. In other words, Harding (1991: 14) aims to develop a framework to "enable us to understand sciences-in-society and the consequent society-in-sciences."

Harding (1991:11–12) says that "scientific knowledge is always, in every respect, socially situated," or the site for political struggles. She offers a fundamental critique of positivist objectivity, saying there is no such thing as, nor could there ever be, impartial or disinterested knowledge:

Neither the knower nor the knowledge they produce are or could be impartial, disinterested, value-neutral.... The challenge is to articulate how it is that knowledge has a socially situated character denied to it by the convention[al] view, and to work through the transformations that this conception of knowledge requires of conventional notions such as objectivity, relativism, rationality, and reflexivity.

This most crucial point is made at length with the analogy of a scientific striptease:

We cannot "strip nature bare" to "reveal her secrets", as conventional views have held, for no matter how long the striptease continues or how rigorous its choreography, we will always find under each "veil" only nature-as-conceptualized-within-cultural projects; we will always (but not only) find more veils. Moreover, the very attempt to strip nature bare weaves more veils, it turns out. Nature-as-an-object-of-knowledge simulates culture, and science is part of the cultural activity that continually produces nature-as-an-object of knowledge in culturally specific forms. (Harding, 1991:12)

Bias cannot be and should not be cleansed from scientific research, Harding claims. In making this claim, she separates herself from the feminist empiricism of work such as Carol Gilligan's, mentioned earlier in this chapter. When Gilligan

(1982) examined girls' gender-specific moral development, she was attempting to cleanse science of bias, sexist bias in particular, to produce a less partial and more objective account. Harding does acknowledge that some bias in science is regressive (or socially harmful), but she claims that other bias, such as feminist bias, can be progressive (or socially useful).

Harding (1991) highlights several reasons for the superiority of feminist research that begins with women's lives. The first is that women's lives can be used as the basis for asking scientific questions, as well as "sources of scientific evidence, and checks against the validity of knowledge claims" (Harding, 1991: 123). Second, echoing Collins and Smith, as summarized above, Harding says that "marginal intellectuals" can "enrich sociological discourse":

Women are valuable "strangers" to the social order ... The stranger brings with her research just the combination of nearness and remoteness, concern and indifference, that are central to maximizing objectivity ... the stranger can see patterns of belief and behavior that are hard for those immersed in the culture to detect. Women are just such outsiders to the dominant institutions in our society. (1991:124)

In contrast, she says, "Men in the dominant groups are 'natives' whose life patterns and ways of thinking fit all to closely the dominant institutions and conceptual schemes" (1991:124). To bring women to the "center of analysis may reveal views of reality obscured by more orthodox approaches."

In Harding's view, there are several other important arguments for the *superiority* of feminist research:

Because women are oppressed, they have fewer interests in ignorance.

This situation can lead potentially, Harding says, to more careful and accurate knowledge.

Scientific narratives are told from the perspective of the "winners" of the "battle of the sexes." (1991:126)

Feminist research can therefore lead to less partial, more inclusive, and more objective accounts of social reality.

> Feminist research is superior to patriarchal research because it provides women's perspective and begins with the lives of women.

This means that it is superior to accounts of women's lives from the perspective of "ruling" or dominant groups.

And finally, feminist research that focuses on women's lives and work can make visible and explain how women have transformed "natural objects into cultural ones" or how women's gender-specific work produces men and other women on a daily basis and "processes children, food, all bodies, balky machines, social relations" (1991:131). Harding says that this is "the right time in history" for challenges to the "sex/gender system" (1991:132).

One of the most significant implications of Harding's work is that while she provides a detailed and often scathing critique of science and its regressive tendencies, she does not abandon objectivity. Rather, she says we must dispense with WEAK OBJECTIVITY *based in the myths of value-free objectivity, impartial and disinterested science* (1991:138ff.). "Weak objectivity," she argues, must be replaced with STRONG OBJECTIVITY. At the center of strong objectivity is the explicit value of REFLEXIVITY; scientists must *position themselves as an object of inquiry*:

> *The notion of "strong objectivity" conceptualizes the value of putting the subject or agent of knowledge in the same critical, causal plane as the object of her or his inquiry*. It permits us to see the scientific as well as the moral and political advantages of this way of trying to achieve a reciprocal relationship between the agent and object of knowledge.[Bold italics added.] (1991:161)

What distinguishes strong objectivity from weak objectivity is that it admits to cultural values and interests of researchers and aims to develop a mechanism for identifying them. Reflexive standpoint, Harding says, must *not* be regarded as an impediment to science (or as a descent into radical relativism or as a valuation

of intuition – both of which she discounts) but as a valuable and necessary scientific resource. Harding explains the necessity of explicit socially situated science and scientists that gaze back on themselves as the only plausible means of "obtaining greater objectivity":

> A notion of strong reflexivity would require that the objects of inquiry be conceptualized as gazing back in all their cultural particularity and that the researcher, through theory and methods, stand behind them, gazing back at his (or her) own socially situated research project in all its cultural particularity and its relationships to other projects of his culture ... (1991:163)

In sum, Harding asks for more honest, modest, explicitly socially situated research practices; and as such, a more authentic knowledge-producing science.[6]

FEMINIST METHODOLOGY

Now that we have drawn on the major ideas of some leading feminist methodologists and theorists, we can identify several concrete guidelines for the use of feminist methods:

- Closing the gap between sociology and women's lives
- Making women's invisible experiences visible
- Offering a view from below
- Encouraging feminist activism as the product of research
- Producing webbed accounts
- Putting women researchers in the research
- Collaboration with research subjects
- Acceptance of alternative sources of women's knowledge claims
- Minimizing the harms of social research

Grassroots Sociology

Perhaps the most fundamental guideline that emerges from feminist methodology is that sociology must begin to close the gap between "the

---

[6] The influence of these ideas can be seen in the development of action research and participatory evaluation research (see Chapter 16 and the section on activism in this chapter) as well as innovative forms of fieldwork (see Chapter 9).

world we put together in the texts of the discipline and the actualities of our and others' lives" (Smith, 1990b:3). An alternative feminist sociology must be a "grassroots" sociology that employs "'being with people' as a method for critical research" (Smith, 1990b:4). Being with people means "listening" and "hearing." These techniques do not involve just hearing and listening to what people say, but becoming attuned to how people feel. They "do not have anything to do with mere sound" or "the surface features of talk." Smith (1990b:5) explains further:

Listening is that kind of practice – a tuning-in of a capacity to find, hear, and create a shape, an order, an organization that is already there. It depends upon having learned...how to listen for social organization in what people say, because they are not, of course, going to tell you about what is in what they say but don't know how to talk about.

Smith (1990b:5) asks that sociology live up to its "promise," for researchers truly to take the role of "the other" and to glean both subjective intimacy and objective meaning.

Smith (1990b:6) provides even more concrete direction on "listening and hearing," using inductively grounded, empathetic, and micro- and macrolevel methods:

The sociological work begins with "hanging out with people" and "listening" to them. Here is where the first research questions are posed. Research is then developed to explore how macro social processes, [e.g.] the policies of large-scale corporations, the ongoing organization and reorganization of an industry in relation to its workers, and the like shape people's lives. The object is not to investigate their lives, but to find out how what is going on in the large-scale organization is consequential for them. For example, under the cover of corporate talk of the use of attrition as a gentle approach to labor-force reduction, women reported increasingly intensified and insulting surveillance of their work; under the guise of affirmative action, white men were laid off and black men and white women were brought in to do jobs that had been downgraded. Investigation picks up from the site of pain and goes after any sources that will yield knowledge for people of what is going on, including corporations themselves, but also what people know in their lives and what organizations working at the grassroots level know, through their membership, about what is going on.

Thus, the first requisite in the use of feminist methods is that research must begin with the localized and lived realities of the women studied, fully incorporate their lived experiences through empathetic understanding, and make connections between those subjective realities and the broader objective or sociostructural meanings contained within them.

Making Women's Invisible Experiences Visible

Another principle for conducting feminist research concerns topic selection. As we have seen, one of its goals is to make women's invisible experiences visible, which involves conducting research in areas of social life previously treated as nonexistent or, at the very least, unimportant to social research. Areas for likely inclusion are the everyday domestic activities of women, for example, child care, day care, housecleaning, mothering, hired domestic labor, or home economics. Exemplary works of feminist research include Judith Rollins's (1985) participant observation study of domestics, Mary Romero's (1992) study of Latina domestics, and Majorie DeVault's (1991) study of domestic food preparation. Other significant research that aims to make women's domestic experiences visible are Christine Bose's (1991) study of how household composition and resources affected the distribution of women's paid work in the United States at the turn of the twentieth century; Sally Hacker's (1990) discussion of the experiences and traditional roles of farm women in relation to agribusiness; Myra Ferree's (1990:174) study of "how factory-employed women in Germany work with, through, and around domestic/public distinctions"; and Heidi Hartmann's analysis of the relationship between housework and the family "as the locus of gender, class, and political struggle" (1987:109).

While it is important to make women's domestic lives visible in and through feminist research, any facet of women's experience – within or outside of the domestic sphere – contributes to the visibility of women in social life and in social scientific discourse. The central goal for many feminist researchers, however, is to specify women's overlooked or devalued experiences.

A View from Below

A related strategy for feminist research is to situate research "from below," that is, from the perspective of oppressed groups, including women. For example, quoting Rollins, Sherry Gorelick (1991:470–471) explains how a "view from below" – in this case, the view domestics had of their employers – was not only different but also more insightful precisely because of a power relation:

Domestics were able to describe in precise detail the personalities, habits, moods, and tastes of the women they had worked for. (The descriptions employers gave were, by comparison, less complex and insightful – not, it seemed to me, because employers were any less capable of analyzing personalities but rather because they had less need to study the nuances of their domestics) .... The domestics I interviewed knew the importance of knowledge of the powerful to those without power.

Providing a view from below does not mean merely to include the perspective of women or other oppressed groups but to give their perspectives major emphasis in the research. Subsequent written accounts should give primacy and concreteness to the real "voices" of women who are research subjects. Abstract analysis should be tailored around those voices.

Feminist Activism as Product of Research

Any feminist work that challenges patriarchal knowledge is a form of activism; it challenges ideological systems that oppress women (Smith, 1990a). However, many feminist research designs are planned with a social action component. **ACTION RESEARCH** is *a data collection strategy that includes advocacy and intervention.*[7] Reinharz (1992:175) says that feminists such as Patti Lather "believe research is feminist

[7] See Chapter 16 section titled "Action Research."

only if it is linked to action ... In her view, feminist action research must be oriented to social and individual change because feminism represents repudiation of the status quo."

Some specific examples of feminist action research are Barbara Smail, Judith Whyte, and Alison Kelly's (1982) work that aimed to increase girl students' interests in physical science and technology, and to initiate institutional supports; Catherine MacKinnon's (1975) research on men's sexual harassment of women at work; Lenore Weitzman's (1985) research on the devastating effect of divorce on women; Lenore Walker's (1989) and Angela Browne's (1987) research on battered women who kill in self-defense; and the Boston Women's Health Book Collective (1976) project *Our Bodies, Ourselves* aimed to demystify women's bodies and to educate girls and women of a broad readership. In all of these cases, concrete social changes – legal, economic, political, or social – were results of research. However, feminist action researchers add more concrete and immediate goals for their research. Maria Mies (1978:122–126) argues for replacing value-neutral science with "conscious partiality," for researchers to side with the oppressed and to take part in their struggles, and for developing research designed to raise consciousness of oppression and oppressive relationships. In this spirit, many feminist action researchers aim to produce concrete improvements in the lives of research subjects as a material consequence of academic research. Reinharz (1992:175) discusses some of these contributions:

Feminism's mandate for change is as broad as saving life itself. It does this by working to prevent "lovers" from battering heterosexual, lesbian, and bi-sexual women; to prevent abortion restrictions from butchering women; to prevent individuals and organizations from sexually enslaving girls and women; to prevent families from committing infanticide; physicians and pharmaceutical companies from physically endangering women; and men from raping women, to name only a few examples.

So, a key goal of feminist methodology is to use research to bring about a change in both intellectual understanding and public policy concerning women. As such, feminist research is empirical, theoretical, and practical.

Webbed Accounts

Another guideline for feminist research is that any study should contribute so far as possible to webbed accounts of women's lives. Feminist methodologists understand that the multiple experiences of women are more important to a generalized understanding than any individual woman's experience. What these experiences have in common is that women's lives have not been adequately included or portrayed in social scientific knowledge. However, feminist writers such as Sandra Harding (1993), Patricia Hill Collins (1990), bell hooks (1989), Donna Haraway (1988), Gloria Anzaldua (1987), Chrys Ingraham (1994), and many others have pointed out that the present state of scholarship on women's lives is still biased in its overrepresentation of heterosexual, middle- and upper-class, and white women's lives. The feminist researcher, then, should be modest in generalizing findings about the particular women's lives examined in any piece of work, but if possible, weave connections, contrasts, and comparisons with other women's lives.

Putting Women Researchers in the Research

An important task for feminist methodology is to put women researchers in the research. A variety of inclusive strategies follows. In all cases, the goal is to strip the research of the false "veils" of objectivity, distance, or neutrality:

- Use first-person authorship when writing accounts.
- Use full names of authors when citing research (as in the departure from convention in this chapter).
- In written accounts, be open and *self-reflexive* about your social locations and perspectives coming into the research project, how they related to and affected the research process, and how they changed throughout the research. This does not mean self-indulgent

subjectivism, as Smith cautioned earlier, but tempered and useful information for readers in assessing the worthiness of your work. Stanley and Wise (1981), writing on this subject, say that all feminist research must include a detailed description of the process of research, and an explanation of how and why the researcher(s) came to know what they know.

- As a researcher conducting a "study," share your impressions, theories, and conceptual leads with research subjects and ask for feedback. Use this feedback to test and modify your ideas.

Collaboration with Research Subjects

Collaboration with research subjects is a characteristically feminist method. The benefits of working with the people you are studying include the following:

- It reduces – but never completely eliminates – the objectifying relationship between researcher and research subject.
- It has the potential to increase trust and rapport by democratizing the researcher–researched relationship.
- It has the potential to increase the research subject's interest and commitment to the research project and questions, and thus can also maximize information yielded from a study.
- It provides one – but not the only – validity check on the adequacy and accuracy of the researcher's conceptualizations and theories.

In general, reducing or eliminating detached, hierarchal relations between researcher and researched can aid in avoiding false results due to lying and other distortions (Klein, 1983).

Finally, if the research is truly collaborative, the research subjects should be provided direct or, at the very least, easy access to the final written products of the research, for which, again, the researcher could openly solicit feedback. This may be a more or less difficult task or choice, depending on the level of accessibility of the written account(s), the eventual content and conceptualizations in the written account(s), and the resources of the researcher.

Exemplary research aimed at collaboration is Ann Oakley's (1981) use of two-way interviews between researcher and researched, which also included multiple written accounts by research assistants. Oakley's aim was to liberate multiple voices and to demonstrate the plurality of perspectives. This general guideline for feminist research is based on the idea that we need to treat those whose are researched as subjects (not objects), and so it is important to bring them into the research as *active* subjects.

Acceptance of Alternative Sources of Women's Knowledge Claims

Empathy, intuition, and knowledge based on emotion are treated as adequate grounds for knowledge in some, but certainly not all, feminist research. For example, Kathleen R. Gilbert's *The Emotional Nature of Qualitative Research* introduces the idea of an "emotion-focused research." For Gilbert, to empathize with research subjects, one cannot do so as "a purely intellectual exercise, but as a process of exploration and discovery that is felt deeply – that is, research is experienced both intellectually and emotionally" (Gilbert, 2000:9). Rather than treating the researcher's emotions as an impediment to achieving objectivity, they are regarded as a useful source of information and for aiding the reader in assessing a work with respect to the social situation of the researcher. These alternative sources of women's knowledge claims would likely be used by most feminist researchers under careful scrutiny, subject to the validity standards of any other kind of data. Although many who use feminist methods acknowledge the emotional dimensions of research for themselves and research subjects, it would be mistaken to reduce feminist research or "women's ways of knowing" to emotion-centered or even emotion-focused approaches.

Minimizing the Harms of Social Research

A final guideline for feminist research is the goal of correcting for the past and present harms social scientific research has perpetrated

on women. Feminist research aims to cultivate research practices that are liberating for both women researchers and subjects of research. Two strategies for minimizing harms of social research, which overlap with previous discussion, are the following:

- Bring the voices of those researched as fully as possible into the research process and eventual written account. This can be accomplished in part through collaboration with research subjects and acceptance of alternative knowledge claims.
- Respect and care for the feelings of those who are researched. Take thoughtful measures to guard against exploiting research subjects. Be honest in explaining the goals and processes of research involvement, and make regular inquiries with research subjects about their feelings and attitudes concerning the research process, end the process in ways that give research subjects respect and consideration, and perhaps also a willingness to befriend research subjects during and after the research process.[8]

Because these approaches grate against conventional "objective" and objectifying practices, the feminist researcher must be diligent in the research account to show how she struggled to maintain the necessary balance of subjectivity and objectivity.

ISSUES AND CRITICISMS

Are Feminist Methods Exclusionary?

Feminist research draws on many perspectives, uses multiple methods, crosses numerous disciplines, centers the voices of women who are research subjects and collaborators, employs webbed accounts, and aims to theorize the interlocking nature of oppressions. All of which suggest inclusion. However, feminist methodology could be criticized on the grounds that it *excludes*. For instance, one might claim

---

[8] However, it is important to guard against "going native," or overly identifying with them. See Chapter 9.

that feminist methods exclude nonfeminists. This charge is valid but is assuredly a criticism feminist methodologists are willing to live with. It could be further criticized, for example, that Collins excludes by privileging a black feminist standpoint. The critic might ask: Should only those with working class roots or who have experienced poverty conduct Marxist research? Should all scholars on gay and lesbian life live gay or lesbian lifestyles? Or, more generally the critic might wonder: Can researchers only conduct research on an experience or social location from which they already have biographical intimacy?

This question is especially acute with regard to marginality and oppression. Most feminist researchers claim that empathetic understanding, based in social location, is what is essential in determining if a researcher is appropriate to perform any given study. They note that such empathy is much easier for researchers who are marginalized by conventional research practices that do not represent their lived experiences and who are at the same time in some way "below" on rankings of social stratification. So, are nonmarginal researchers excluded? Perhaps, but perhaps not! Everyone experiences marginality to some extent, and most of us could draw on experiences in which we felt marginal (as an actor draws on experience to play a role). We could visit marginalizing places or groups or develop marginality through reading critical theory, deconstructive or poststructuralist materials, or other works that exhibit and thus teach critical distance by example.

Can Men Do Feminist Research?

As suggested throughout this chapter, the application of feminist methods to research is accomplished with a specifically feminist vision and perspective, or grounding in feminist theory. A part of the theoretical debate concerns whether *men* can use feminist methods. Although some feminists say that men can advocate feminism but cannot *be* feminist, many other feminist methodologists agree that men *can* employ feminist methods so long as they are feminists. For

example, Shulamit Reinharz (1992:16) includes male researchers in her exemplary collection of feminist methods but notes in her wide survey that she found few instances.

The question whether men can use feminist methods raises other questions still open to debate, such as Are wealthy, heterosexual, or white women, albeit privileged members of an oppressed group, more removed from the experience of welfare mothers, African American women, or lesbian women than, say, a male social researcher who is African American, gay, or who has working-class roots? This is not to suggest that it is impossible for wealthy, white, or heterosexual men to use feminist methods but, rather, that those privileged social locations raise methodological problems (and cumulative problems, if these positions are combined) that impede seeing through and beyond the social lenses attached to positions of privilege. It is likely that the degree of alienation that women researchers experience (Smith, 1987, 1990a) would not apply to male researchers – and, in particular, white, wealthy, or heterosexual men – who lead conventional lives outside academe. The case for the inclusion of male researchers is stronger in the work of Collins (1991), who focuses more generally on marginal location as key. In that case, male researchers would be required to have or to otherwise acquire an experience of marginality but with the understanding that all experiences of marginality are not the same. It may be that it is one's own actual and personal social location that holds the key to greater understanding of the relations of the ruling, not that the knowledge producer is herself a woman.

Although Smith (1990b) rejects the notion that a feminist approach to research can be taken only by women, she does suggest that women may be more qualified to undertake it. Because women (as their roles have been socially constructed in the past and present) are not as "bound to the wheel of rationality as men [are]," notes Smith, women intellectuals "are at this time free to work with and free to put forward as systematic bases of inquiry, methods of knowing that have been repressed" (1990b:5).

The central point is that all researchers are not equally equipped with social location or with the kind of lived experience at the center of feminist research. Men can engage in research practices that are informed by the feminist critiques of science and can borrow many of the techniques from feminist methodology, but it is much less likely that they can produce research based in women's experience, simply because it is not their experience. Therefore, men can use the insights of feminist theory and methodology to produce more modest and less oppressive research of their own, from their own social locations. If this more direct and consistent invitation were extended to men – with a willingness to limit the all-inclusive spirit among feminist methodologists – there would be less ambiguity, more understanding, and a greater likelihood of heightened interest in feminist methods among men.

Do Most Feminists Avoid Feminist Methods?

The likely and eligible candidates for using feminist methods are feminists. However, this raises a most important and practical question, posed by Cancian (1992:629): "Why do most feminists avoid these methods in practice, even though they applaud them in principle?" She offers three primary explanations:

1. "Resistance to rigid, dogmatic stance on the 'correct' feminist methodology."

This explanation does not have much empirical basis in the literature on feminist methodology, given its persistent, pluralistic spirit (as discussed earlier). However, ironically, some feminists may avoid feminist methods because they focus so intensely and insistently on women's domestic lives.

2. "Many researchers are uneasy with feminist methodology because it seems to undermine scientific standards of objectivity."

This second explanation seems much more valid, in that feminist methodology and epistemology do directly confront and challenge mainstream standards of objectivity. To conduct feminist research is to explicitly challenge at least some of the conventional rules of scientific practice.

3. "Concerns about being punished by the power and prestige system of academia."

Whether a feminist chooses to adopt feminist methods will depend on her level of commitment. Because feminist methodology challenges what is at the center of academe, women who adopt an explicitly defiant "feminist attitude" toward research will likely incur some costs in concrete areas such as the journals in which they can publish their work, the level of collegial praise for work, research funding, and even tenure and promotion.[9] However, those who are committed to feminist research, nonetheless, can benefit from integration in feminist groups, organizations, conferences, and other forms of social and research support.

Why Bother Using Feminist Methods?

A positivist scientist who believes in the possibility of reaching unbiased and universal truths will undoubtedly find little value in these techniques. However, what about other social scientists who are less convinced about value-neutral science? For example, what about researchers who recognize that all knowledge is partial and socially situated, and whose research practices are marked by induction, self-reflexivity, empathy, giving voice to research subjects, and respect for research subjects? In that case, the researcher might claim that they are already, in effect, using feminist methods (that is, as long as such researchers self-identify as feminists). Although these researchers may likely benefit from and agree with much written by feminist methodologists and epistemologists, they may find it unnecessary to identify their work as "feminist methods research." If they find little clear advantage, they will refrain from doing it.

---

[9] Although certainly it is not an entirely satisfactory answer, any type of deconstructive work carries with it the risk of devaluation within academe to the extent that the academic establishment still prizes and rewards adherence to the canons of value-neutral, impartial, truth-producing science.

EXAMPLES OF FEMINIST RESEARCH

Several collections of research employing feminist methods are recommended, for example, Reinharz (1992), Harding (1987), and Fonow and Cook (1986). Two detailed examples from work self-identified and widely cited by others as using feminist methods are provided. These examples also illustrate the feminist epistemology and methodology themes discussed in this chapter. In each case, we quote extensively from the works to convey not only their substance, but also the voices of women in them. In the final section, we review several new or innovative feminist methods.

Increasing Validity with Feminist Methods

Joan Acker, Kate Barry, and Johanna Esseveld's research emphasizes subjectivity rather than objectivity as a way to increase validity. It may serve as a model to contrast with conventional social scientific approaches. The authors chose as their research problem "the relation between changes in consciousness and changes in the structural situation of individuals" (1991:133). The group they chose to study were "women who were at the end of their period of intensive mothering" (1991:136–137). They used qualitative data collection methods, including tape-recorded and transcribed interviews. To increase validity, the researchers let the respondents explain their worlds as they saw them. An additional factor in their attempt to maximize validity was that the researchers were women who shared similar experiences. As feminists and researchers, they also enhanced validity through balancing empathetic listening and hearing, as well as regular analytic discussion of the research process. Validity was further assured through having respondents read and listen to interviews and comment on the accuracy of the researchers' interpretations and written reports. Finally, validity was based in, and fully depended on, the trust of the research subjects, which was cultivated through the research process in general. An excerpt from the authors' discussion of validity follows. It not only describes these methods, but also reflects the open, self-reflexive spirit characteristic of accounts of feminist methods.

Perhaps the most likely critical response to the passage on page 232 would concern the validity of the information. That is, did the respondents really tell the truth? Are their accounts truly valid? In their discussion of validity, the authors offer three criteria for the "adequacy of interpretation." The first criterion is *"that the active voice of the subject should be heard in the account*[10] . . . seeing persons as active agents in their own lives, we will not view them as totally determined or lacking in comprehension of the social world" (1991:35). Trust in the subject, and the subject's subjectivity, are central to feminist methods. This kind of trust requires a shift away from the traditional scientific trust in objectifying the subject. However, Dorothy Smith (1987:92), who similarly attributes much agency and voice to research subjects, cautions that "The everyday world is not fully understandable within its own scope. It is organized by social relations not fully apparent in it nor contained in it."

A second criterion of validity offered by Acker et al. is that *the theoretical analysis must be able to account for the investigator as well as for those who are investigated*. The interpretation must locate the researcher in the social structure and also provide a reconstruction of the social relations that produce the research. In other words, the researcher's account should explain the researcher's relationship to the study and the people in it. It should also provide a self-reflexive account of the sociohistorical context of the study itself: "For example," the researchers ask, "what are the social relations that produce this research situation and the enterprise of research itself? What makes it possible to raise this research problem at this time, in this place, in this society" (1991:145–146).

A third criterion of validity discussed by the authors is that "*the reconstruction should reveal the underlying social relations that eventuate in the daily lives we are studying*" (1991:146). In other words, the written account must consider

---

[10] Emphases in the excerpt and in cited passages from Acker, Barry, and Esseveld (1991) is added.

A Feminist Research Account

Our research problem demanded that we try to understand reality from the perspective of the people experiencing it. Since we directly asked [the women] about their experience, we did not have the problem of developing indicators of concepts. Rather, we wanted to maximize direct communication in their own terms. We assumed that our study participants would have a better chance of telling us about their worlds as they saw them if their active participation in defining the dialogue was encouraged . . . we are confident that in most of our interviews the interviewees felt comfortable about stating their own case.

In qualitative work, the accuracy of listening and hearing may be as important as the openness of telling. The fact that we, the interviewers, were women who have been married, divorced, and had children (one of us had a baby after the study began) increased the validity of our data. We did not have to go through the process of getting to know the special perspectives and nuances of meaning of those we were studying – a process that is often identified as necessary if the qualitative researcher wants to avoid errors that simply come from ignorance . . . We were studying people who had experiences very similar to ours, although of course there were important differences (the most important one being our status as researchers) and we were thus sensitive to problems and issues that might otherwise have been invisible.

We think it was also important that we were feminists. Our feminist analysis of women's oppression, which constituted much of the theory informing our work, also increased our sensitivity and awareness in the interview process, and contributed to the emergence of an empathetic atmosphere in the interaction process. A faithful account is best pursued, we are arguing in research such as ours where changing consciousness is the central question, through the close and sympathetic involvement with the informant rather than through distancing and objectifying. At the same time such closeness may create certain kinds of blindness in the researcher. One protection we developed against this was in the ongoing process of analysis in the research group. Our analytic discussions, of necessity, forced us to distance ourselves from our subjects.

We have confirmation of the accuracy of our findings from those women we interviewed. We received feedback from many of them in both individual and group discussions. Some read their interviews or listened to their tapes. We also discussed our written material with many and in those discussions our findings and our interpretations were confirmed.

Unless a relationship of trust is developed, we can have no confidence that our research on women's lives and consciousness accurately represents what is significant to them in their everyday lives, and thus has validity in that sense. This is particularly true if we are trying to understand their lives in their totality, as ongoing processes in which the person plays an active part. Certain survey data becomes, then, even more suspect. We have difficulty in assessing the validity of even the most factual data, to say nothing of data about opinions and attitudes. Even "in depth" interviews present problems of interpretation, as the above discussion indicates.

Reproduced with permission from Joan Acker, Kate Barry, and Johanna Esseveld. 1991. "Truth and Objectivity." In *Beyond Methodology: Feminist Scholarship as Lived* Research, 146–147, 149. Mary Margaret Fonow and Judith A. Cook, eds. (Bloomington and Indianapolis: Indiana University Press).

the everyday life worlds, or the very local and intimate details of everyday life, as a significant context for understanding the subjects of study. Although the authors recognize the practical difficulties of achieving this goal, it should be pursued as far as possible.

Example: A Feminist Reinterpretation of the Bible

Although feminist methods focus on the social sciences, they may be applied in the humanities as well. An example of how feminist methods are used in a reinterpretation of the Bible can be found in *A Feminist Companion to Reading the Bible: Approaches, Methods, and Strategies* (Brenner and Fontaine, 2001:12–14).

In this book of edited essays, the authors address a "gap of credibility," or patriarchal bias, in biblical interpretations. They "examine the state of [biblical] methodologies as they pertain to bias, including gender bias, in interpretation, and strategies used to unmask and overturn bias." Like others employing feminist methods, Athalya Brenner and Carole Fontaine aim not only to listen "for ancient voices of various timbre" but also to discover and recover "one's *own* voice as a[n] interpreter engaged in the circular activity of reading and making meaning." Further characteristic of feminist methods, the authors "give explicit space to . . . the 'day-to-day'-ness of their work as feminist scholars who study the biblical record."

NEWER FEMINIST METHODS

In her chapter "Original Feminist Research Methods," Reinharz (1992:214–239) discusses a variety of original methods that were created because they were required by the knowledge that researchers sought. One of her first examples is psychologist Sandra Lipsitz's Bem Sex-Role Inventory: a paper-and-pencil instrument that distinguishes among masculine, feminine, and androgynous individuals but treats masculinity and femininity as two dimensions and presents both as positive (rather than the conventional format of masculinity as positive and

femininity as its absence). Other examples of uniquely or innovative feminist methods discussed by Reinharz are consciousness raising; the creation of an anonymous computer-based group diary for a Graduate Women's Forum for the purpose of documenting incidents of sexism in a sociology department; the performance of written articles treated as theater; genealogies of female friendship; multiple-person stream-of-conscious narratives; the use of nonauthorial voice in oral history; using intuition and writing associatively (as in Susan Griffin's "conversation between two or more parts of the self"); "deep identification" with women studied (as a methodological principle revived in view of the "renewed critique of distancing, neutrality, and objectivity"); and Robbie Pfeufer Kahn's book reviewing by reading of photographs. In the review (of her two books about birth), she "reads" the photographs and projects herself into various roles – the male physician looking at and holding the birthing woman, the child being born, the other people in the room – including the role of the reader gazing at the photographs.

Feminist methods can also be used in the classroom to revive the usual objectifying techniques for studying women's lives. For example, one author of this chapter teaches the course Women and Madness and assigns students to write first-person narratives of their madness. The assignment does not simply ask students to research a so-called madwoman (her biography, her sociohistorical situation, and medical [including psychiatric] or theological knowledges of her "disorder") but also to convey what they researched as a *first-person* account. Accounts can take many forms (diaries, series of notes, poetry, journals, letters, captioned photo albums) and include emotional responses and reactions. This feminist and sociological technique aims at enhancing the ability of students to empathize with the women studied or to lessen the distance between objective and subjective knowledges. It also aims at filling in historical gaps in voices of women, unrecorded or distorted in patriarchal accounts of their "sicknesses," through deep scholarly and artistic identification.

A "Decentered" Understanding of Scripture

Fontaine's contribution, "The Abusive Bible," provides an analysis of "how what has been *left out* of the Bible – the unedited voices of real women and children and a deity who saves them, regardless of their gender – works to the disadvantage of members of those groups" (Brenner and Fontaine, 2001:102). Showing the abusive impact of biblical stories beyond the text, she explains, for example, how women often blame themselves for victimization, or attribute harms such as rape and death to God's punishment for sins committed. Such concrete interpretations are the effects of biblical stories that depict a violent and vicious God approving of child sacrifice, rape, and genocide, and that distort the ordinary pattern of father–daughter incest.

Fontaine's analysis focuses on three pragmatic effects of biblical scripture: gendered authority, role reversal, and the appropriation of fertility. Addressing gendered authority, Fontaine (ibid.:104) explains how "the image of God as patriarchal father has a nasty, deforming effect on our theological portrait of the deity; and its legitimation of male power has had drastic effects on the lives of real women and children, even unto this very day." God, as measure of man perfected, provides an aggressive, violent, and abusive authority over women and a model for heterosexual relations in everyday life.

Fontaine (ibid.:105) explains that a second pragmatic effect of biblical scripture is role reversal, or the "lessening of women's visible role in the creation of life." "Powers that have to do with women's biological 'creativity' are transferred wholesale to the father-god, who is now considered to be the one who opens and closes the womb and brings forth healthy children to birth."

A third pragmatic effect of the Bible is the male appropriation of fertility:

Think of the Genesis narratives where the first humans are created: what a shocking reversal! Instead of the natural order of men (and women!) emerging from the bodies of women, a fact verified by simple observation, we are told as a religious datum of the highest order that the first woman emerged from the body of a male – assisted, of course, by the father-god. (ibid.:105).

The pragmatic effect of such patriarchal biblical stories is that the father-god and the paternity it portrays has "had concrete effects on restricting the lives of women," such as stricter sexual standards for women, and a man's ownership claim to his wife's reproduction (ibid.:107).

SUMMARY

The body of work labeled feminist methods emerged because of patriarchal biases in the production of scientific knowledge that has historically excluded or distorted the experiences of women. It emerged in the sociohistorical contexts of poststructuralism, deconstruction, and postmodernism, as well as a variety of social and political movements, including Third Wave feminism, that challenged the truths of conventional science. Feminists not only criticized the processes of knowledge-production but also demanded the right to become makers and administrators of knowledge. In the place of objectifying, universalizing, falsely asserted value-neutral science, feminist standpoint theorists have claimed that the likelihood of actually achieving objectivity lies in a new kind of science that is explicitly partial, politicized, and self-reflexive. Feminist epistemologists have further asserted that women's marginal position in academe provides them with privileged standpoints for understanding and conveying the experiences of women, for employing the sociological perspective, and for perceiving and correcting the inadequacies in existing theories. Feminist methodologists have provided concrete feminist critiques of the use of conventional research techniques, modified their use, and have created some alternative feminist tools for research.

Although feminists have provided lengthy and compelling critiques of the positioning and techniques of positivistic science, the all-inclusive, nonhierarchal spirit of their work has resulted, perhaps unwittingly, in a lack of clear definition of what exactly constitutes the existence and proper use of feminist methods. In particular, it is difficult to distinguish feminist methods (beyond commitment to feminism) from the use of research methods by those social scientists who share a commitment to self-reflexivity, empathy, giving voice to research subjects (the oppressed in particular), action research, and reducing the harms of research. Despite the amorphous quality of feminist methods, social scientists may benefit from discussions about them in that they may cultivate a raised awareness of the socially situated and socially located nature of science, the harms that have resulted from denying those realities, and a desire to produce more modest, consciously contextual accounts of social life.

KEY TERMS

action research
bifurcation of consciousness
deconstruction
emancipatory potential of feminist research
feminist consciousness raising
feminist epistemologists
feminist epistemology
feminist methodology
feminist methods
feminist standpoint theory
interlocking nature of oppressions
marginality
"outsider within" status
patriarchal
plurality of feminist methods
postmodernism
poststructuralism
relations of ruling
strong objectivity
weak objectivity
webbed accounts

EXERCISES

1. Have a class discussion, the goal of which is to select a research question about women's lives and or experiences. Divide into two groups. Group 1 develops a survey research project that is based in feminist methodology. Group 2 develops a participant observation research project based in feminist methodology. Both groups are developing research projects on the same question. Compare and evaluate the two projects in terms of how well they will incorporate women's voices. As a longer class exercise, groups 1 and 2 could conduct the projects and then compare the findings in terms of objectivity and validity.

2. In small groups, discuss the possibility of "women's ways of knowing." What are the specific ways women know themselves and others and experience the world around them that are not the same as men? How can one make such arguments without overgeneralizing about all men or all women? If there are women's ways of knowing, what are the politics (power issues, possible academic costs) of asserting the "truth" of them? For best results, the groups might be divided by gender, and then compare the results with the class as a whole.

3. Your class is working on a research project called "The Experience of Single Mothers Managing Day Care Arrangements and Professional Responsibilities: A Case in Role Conflict." Break up into small groups divided by gender (men's groups and women's groups). Working independently, each group should develop a general research design and state detailed hypotheses about the nature of single mother role conflict, based in their experience as men or as women. After a designated period of time (determined by the teacher), meet in a large group and compare and contrast the results. Does this exercise demonstrate the usefulness of "women's ways of knowing"? Do women without children in the groups have greater sensitivity and insight than men in the groups?

4. In small groups discuss whether naturally "marginal" persons are in fact better prepared to conduct feminist research and sociological research. If marginality were assumed to be a requirement of research, and the researcher was stably socially situated as white, wealthy, heterosexual male, to what extent can that researcher produce valid and objective research accounts? Can that person learn marginality? If so, how? Give concrete examples. What are other sources of marginality (beyond race, class, gender, and sexual orientation) not considered in feminist methodology?

5. Many people argue that we now live in a period of postfeminism, in which many women situate themselves as being beyond, or beyond needing, a feminist movement. Discuss how this might affect the future of feminist methods, given that a raised feminist consciousness and perspective are basic requirements for using feminist methods. Is it possible to develop "postfeminism feminist methods"? If so, what might they be like? Or, does postfeminism erase the need for feminist methods?

SUGGESTED READINGS

Cancian, Francesca M. 1992. "Feminist Science: Methodologies that Challenge Inequality." *Gender and Society* 6 (4) December: 623–642.

  A good statement on the connection between feminist methods and social change.

Collins, Patricia Hill. 1992. *Black Feminist Thought: Knowledge, Consciousness, and the Politics of Empowerment*. Boston: Unwin Hyman.

  The classic exposition of black feminist theory.

Denzin, Norman K., and Yvonna S. Lincoln. 2003. *The Landscape of Qualitative Research*. 2nd ed. Thousand Oaks, CA: Sage.

  This volume contains some excellent analysis relating feminist research to qualitative methods in general.

Elliot, Jane. 2005. *Using Narrative in Social Research*. Thousand Oaks, CA: Sage.

  A rich source of information on narrative analysis, a well-used technique in feminist research. Of particular interest is the author's discussion of quantitative as well as qualitative approaches to narrative.

Fonow, Mary Margaret, and Judith A. Cook, eds. 1991. *Beyond Methodology: Feminist Scholarship as Lived Research*. Bloomington and Indianapolis: Indiana University Press.

  A frequently cited, excellent edited volume.

Friedan, Betty. 1963/2001. *The Feminine Mystique*. New York: W. W. Norton.

  One of the most influential feminist writings.

Gilligan, Carol. 1982. *In a Different Voice: Psychological Theory and Women's Development*. Cambridge, MA: Harvard University Press.

  This book makes the case for distinctly female modes of thought.

Harding, Sandra, ed. 1991. *Whose Science? Whose Knowledge?* Ithaca, NY: Cornell University Press.

  Harding is a masterful critic of mainstream science.

Hesse-Biber, Sharlene Nagy, and Michelle L. Yaiser. 2003. *Feminist Perspectives on Social Research*. New York: Oxford University Press.

  A review of the feminist perspective on research across a range of topics, including race, class, gender, and sexuality.

Hesse-Biber, Sharlene Nagy, and Patricia L. Levy. 2006. *Feminist Research Practice: A Primer*. Thousand Oaks, CA: Sage.

  A hands-on guide to conducting feminist research.

McNiff, Jean, and Jack Whitehead. 2006. *All You Need to Know About Action Research*. Thousand Oaks, CA: Sage.

  A good primer on doing action research with a focus on verification of knowledge.

Smith, Dorothy E. 1987. *The Everyday World as Problematic: A Feminist Sociology*. Boston: Northeastern University Press.

  The foundations of standpoint analysis.

Whitworth, Sandra. 2004. *Men, Militarism, and UN Peacekeeping: A Gendered Analysis*. Boulder, CO: Lynne Rienner.

  This study uses a feminist perspective to investigate United Nations' military intervention. The author claims that peacekeeping efforts have failed because they do not challenge traditional understandings of the military.

REFERENCES

Acker, Joan, Kate Barry, and Johanna Esseveld. 1991. "Truth and Objectivity." In *Beyond Methodology: Feminist Scholarship as Lived Research*, 133–153. Mary Margaret Fonow and Judith A. Cook, eds. Bloomington and Indianapolis: Indiana University Press.

Anzaldua, Gloria. 1987. *Borderlanda/La Frontera: The New Mestiza*. San Francisco: Aunt Lute.

Bartky, Sandra Lee. 1990. *Femininity and Domination: Studies in the Phenomenology of Oppression*. New York: Routledge.

Berger, Peter L., and Thomas Luckmann. 1966/1990. *The Social Construction of Reality: A Treatise in the Sociology of Knowledge*. New York: Anchor Books.

Bose, Christine E. 1991. "Household Resources and U.S. Women's Work: Factors Affecting Gainful Employment at the Turn of the Century." In *Beyond Methodology: Feminist Scholarship as Lived Research*, 197–225. Mary Margaret Fonow and Judith A. Cook, eds. Bloomington and Indianapolis: Indiana University Press.

Boston Women's Health Book Collective. 1976. *Our Bodies, Ourselves: A Book by and for Women*. New York: Simon & Schuster.

Brenner, Athalya, and Carole Fontaine. 2001. *A Feminist Companion to Reading the Bible: Approaches, Methods and Strategies*. Sheffield, UK: Sheffield Academic Press.

Browne, Angela. 1987. *When Battered Women Kill*. New York: Free Press.

Cancian, Francesca M. 1992. "Feminist Science: Methodologies that Challenge Inequality." *Gender and Society* 6 (4) December: 623–642.

Chesler, Phyllis. 1972. *Women and Madness*. New York: Avon.

Clegg, Sue. 1975. "Feminist Methodology – Fact or Fiction?" *Quality and Quantity* 19:83–87.

Collins, Patricia Hill. 1990. *Black Feminist Thought: Knowledge, Consciousness, and the Politics of Empowerment*. New York: Routledge, Chapman & Hall.

———. 1991. "Learning from the Outsider Within." In *Beyond Methodology: Feminist Scholarship as Lived Research*, 35–59. Mary Margaret Fonow and Judith A. Cook, eds. Bloomington and Indianapolis: Indiana University Press.

———. 1992. *Black Feminist Thought: Knowledge, Consciousness, and the Politics of Empowerment*. Boston: Unwin Hyman.

———. 2001. "What's Going On? Black Feminist Thought and the Politics of Postmodernism." In *Working in the Ruins: Feminist Poststructural Theory and Methods in Education*, 41–73. Elizabeth A. St. Pierre and Wanda S. Pillow, eds. New York and London: Routledge.

Cooley, Charles Horton. 1902/1965. *Human Nature and Social Order*. New York: Schocken Books.

DeVault, Majorie. 1990. "Talking and Listening to Women's Standpoint: Feminist Strategies for Interviewing Analysis." *Social Problems* 37 (1): 701–721.

———. 1991. *Feeding the Family: The Social Organization of Caring as Gendered Work*. Chicago: University of Chicago Press.

———. 1996. "Talking Back to Sociology: Distinctive Contributions of Feminist Methodology." *Annual Review of Sociology* 22:29–50.

Eichler, Margrit. 1988. *Nonsexist Research Methods: A Practical Guide*. Boston: Unwin.

Ferree, Myra Marx. 1990. "Between Two Worlds: German Feminist Approaches to Working-Class Women and Work." In *Feminist Research Methods: Exemplary Readings in the Social Sciences*, 174–192. Joyce McCarl Nielson, ed. Boulder, CO: Westview Press.

Fetterley, Judith. 1978. *The Resisting Reader: A Feminist Approach to Reading Fiction*. Bloomington: Indiana University Press.

Fonow, Mary Margaret, and Judith A. Cook, eds. 1991. *Beyond Methodology: Feminist Scholarship as Lived Research*. Bloomington and Indianapolis: Indiana University Press.

Gilbert, Kathleen R. 2000. *The Emotional Nature of Qualitative Research*. Boca Raton, FL: CRC Press.

Gilkes, Cheryl Townsend. 1986. "The Roles of the Church and Community Mothers; Ambivalent American Sexism or Fragmented African Familyhood?" *Journal of Feminist Studies in Religion* 2 (1): 41–59.

Gilligan, Carol. 1982. *In a Different Voice: Psychological Theory and Women's Development*. Cambridge, MA: Harvard University Press.

Gluck, Sherma B., and Daphne Patai, eds. 1991. *Women's Words: The Feminist Practice of Oral History*. New York: Routledge.

Goffman, Erving. 1959/1973. *The Presentation of Self in Everyday Life*. Woodstock, NY: Overlook Press.

———. 1963/1986. *Stigma: Notes on the Management of Spoiled Identity*. New York: Simon & Schuster.

Gordon, Deborah, ed. 1988. "Feminism and the Critique of Colonial Discourse." Special issue, *Inscriptions* 3–4:1–26.

Gorelick, Sherry. 1991. "Contradictions of Feminist Methodology." *Gender and Society* 5 (4) December: 459–477.

Graham, Hilary. 1983. "Do Her Answers Fit His Questions? Women and the Survey Method." In *The Public and the Private*, 132–146. Eva Garmarnikow et al., eds. London: Heinemann.

Hacker, Sally L. 1990. "Farming Out the Home: Women and Agribusiness." In *"Doing It the Hard Way": Investigations of Gender and Technology*, 69–88. Dorothy E. Smith and Susan M. Turner, eds. Boston: Unwin Hyman.

Haraway, Donna. 1988. "Situated Knowledges: The Science Question in Feminism and the Privileges of Partial Perspective." *Feminist Studies* 14 (3): 575–599.

Harding, Sandra. 1983. "Why Has the Sex/Gender System Become Visible Only Now?" In *Discovering Reality: Feminist Perspectives on Epistemology, Metaphysics, Methodology, and Philosophy of Science*, 311–322. Sandra Harding and Merill B. Hintikka, eds. Dordrecht, Holland: D. Reidel.

———. 1987. *Feminism and Methodology: Social Science Issues*. Bloomington: Indiana University Press.

———. 1991. *Whose Science? Whose Knowledge?* Ithaca, NY: Cornell University Press.

———, ed. 1993. *The "Racial" Economy of Science*. Bloomington: Indiana University Press.

Hartmann, Heidi L. 1987. "The Family as the Locus of Gender, Class, and Political Struggle." In *Feminism and Methodology: Social Science Issues*, 109–134. Sandra Harding, ed. Bloomington: Indiana University Press.

Herman, Judith, with Lisa Hirshman. 1981. *Father-Daughter Incest*. Cambridge, MA: Harvard University Press.

Hooks, Bell. 1989. *Talking Back: Thinking Feminist, Thinking Black*. Boston: South End Press.

Ingraham, Chrys 1994. "The Heterosexual Imaginary: Feminist Sociology and Theories of Gender." *Social Theory* 12 (2): 203–219.

Irigaray, Luce. 1985a. *This Sex Which is Not One*. Ithaca, NY: Cornell University Press.

———. 1985b. *Speculum of the Other Woman*. Ithaca, NY: Cornell University Press.

Kitzinger, Celia. 1990. "Resisting the Discipline." In *Feminists and Psychological Practice*, 119–186. Erica Burman, ed. London: Sage.

Klein, Renate D. 1983. "How to Do What We Want to Do: Thoughts about Feminist Methodology." In *Theories of Women's Studies*, 88–104. Gloria Bowles and Renate Duelli Klein, eds. London: Routledge & Kegan Paul.

Lerner, Gerder. 1976. "Placing Women in History: A 1975 Perspective." In *Liberating Women's History*, 357–367. Bernice Carroll, ed. Chicago: University of Illinois Press.

MacKinnon, Catharine. 1975. *Sexual Harassment of Working Women: A Case of Sex Discrimination*. New Haven, CT: Yale University Press.

———. 1983. "Feminism, Marxism, Method and the State: An Agenda for Theory." *Signs: Journal of Women in Culture and Society* 515:7.

Mann, Susan A., and Lori R. Kelley. 1997. "Standing at the Crossroads of Modernist Thought: Collins, Smith, and the New Feminist Epistemologies." *Gender and Society* 11 (4) August: 391–408.

Masson, Jeffrey M. 1984. *The Assault on Truth: Freud's Suppression of the Seduction Theory*. New York: Farrar, Straus and Giroux.

———. 1988. *Against Therapy: Emotional Tyranny and the Myth of Psychological Healing*. New York: Atheneum.

Mead, George Herbert. 1934/1967. *Mind, Self, and Society: From the Standpoint of a Social Behaviorist*. Charles W. Morris, ed. Chicago: University of Chicago Press.

Mies, Maria. 1983. "Towards Methodology in Feminist Research." In *Theories of Women's Studies*, 117–139. Gloria Bowles and Renate D. Klein, eds. London: Routledge & Kegan Paul.

Miller, Connie, and Corrinna Treitel. 1991. *Feminist Research Methods: An Annotated Bibliography*. New York: Greenwood Press.

Oakley, Ann. 1981. "Interviewing Women: A Contradiction in Terms." In *Doing Feminist Research*,

30–61. Helen Roberts, ed. London: Routledge & Kegan Paul.

Olesen, Virginia L. 2000. "Feminism and Qualitative Research at and into the Millenium." In *Handbook of Qualitative Research*, 215–256. 2nd ed. Norman K. Denzin and Yvonna S. Lincoln, eds. Thousand Oaks, CA: Sage.

Reinharz, Shulamit. 1979. *On Becoming a Social Scientist*. San Francisco: Jossey-Boss.

———. 1985. "Feminist Distrust: Problems of Content and Context in Sociological Research." In *The Self in Social Inquiry*, 153–172. David N. Berg and Kenwyn K. Smith, eds. Beverly Hills, CA: Sage.

———. 1992. *Feminist Methods in Social Research*. New York: Oxford University Press.

Rollins, Judith. 1985. *Between Women: Domestics and Their Employers*. Philadelphia: Temple University Press.

Romero, Mary. 1992. *Maid in the U.S.A.* London: Routledge.

Smail, Barbara, Judith Shyte, and Alison Kelly. 1982. "Girls into Science and Technology: The First Two Years." *School Science Review* 64:620–630.

Smith, Dorothy E. 1987. *The Everyday World as Problematic: A Feminist Sociology*. Boston: Northeastern University Press.

———. 1990a. *The Conceptual Practices of Power: A Feminist Sociology of Knowledge*. Boston: Northeastern University Press.

———. 1990b. "Editor's Introduction on Sally L. Hacker's Method." In *"Doing It the Hard Way": Investigations of Gender and Technology*, 1–19. Sally L. Hacker, Dorothy E. Smith, and Susan M. Turner, eds. Boston: Unwin Hyman.

———. 1990c. "The Statistics on Women and Mental Illness." In *The Conceptual Practices of Power: A Feminist Sociology of Knowledge*, 107–138. Boston: Northeastern University Press.

Stanley, Liz, and Sue Wise. 1983. "Back into 'the Personal,' or, Our Attempt to Construct 'Feminist Research.'" In *Theories of Women's Studies II*, Chapter 12. Gloria Bowles and Renate D. Klein, eds. London: Routledge and Kegan Paul.

Star, Susan Leigh. 1979. "Strategic Heresy as Scientific Method: Feminism and the Psychology of Consciousness." Paper presented at the American Association for the Advancement of Science, Houston, TX, January 6.

Thompson, Lana, and Vern L. Bullough. 1999. *The Wandering Womb: A Cultural History of Outrageous Beliefs About Woman*. Amherst, NY: Prometheus Books.

Tuana, Nancy. 1988. "The Weaker Seed: The Sexist Bias of Reproductive Theory." *Hypatia* 3 (1) Spring: 35–39.

Walker, Lenore E. 1989. *Terrifying Love: Why Battered Women Kill and How Society Responds*. New York: HarperCollins.

Weitzman, Lenore. 1985. *The Divorce Revolution: The Unexpected Social and Economic Consequences for Women and Children in America*. New York: Free Press.

HISTORICAL ANALYSIS

11

INTRODUCTION

If we become ill, or our parents are going through a divorce, or someone in our family loses a job, we have troubles at a personal level. However, over time, as sociologist C. Wright Mills (1960/2000) pointed out, history and biography intersect. That is, the private troubles that we experience at a microlevel are connected to public issues. In the United States today, there is a growing crisis in health care, both in terms of affordability of and having access to health insurance. The divorce rate has grown so high that in many places half of all marriages do not survive. In addition, as the economy shifted from mostly industrial to mostly postindustrial, pockets of permanent, structural unemployment dot the national map. These are examples of public issues that require historical analysis if we are truly to understand their origins and scope, as well as future trends. In fact, it is no exaggeration to say that without skillful historical analysis we would be deprived of a powerful tool to understand the context that helps us to cope successfully with our private troubles.

Historical analysis is a process calling for multiple methods, both quantitative and qualitative, microlevel as well as macrolevel, and the attention of all the social sciences. In this sense, it cuts against the grain of academic specialization that characterized the twentieth century. It has been a fair assessment of American academic life that the practitioners of the various social science disciplines have had relatively little contact with one another. Sociologists, psychologists, historians, anthropologists, and economists traditionally define the boundaries of their respective fields fairly rigorously. In each discipline, there is a concern with understanding human behavior, but there is also an orthodoxy about the relevant questions for investigation and the methodological techniques and modes of analysis central to the particular area of inquiry. We might think of social life as a giant jigsaw puzzle and envision various investigators working on selected parts of it. There is, in other words, a rather extensive division of labor among the social sciences, brought about by the impossibility of any one discipline being able to attend to the extraordinary number of parts making up the human mosaic.

Each of the social sciences seeks to establish a distinctive **PARADIGM**, or *model*, and to indicate the special problems and issues that are its own. That is how members of an academic field better succeed in affirming their expertise in the minds of others. Sharing a common paradigm makes communication among professionals easier and ensures that there is a body of knowledge used by the members of a discipline. Therefore, there is some consistency to the socialization of new members.

The division of academic labor exists not only between these "kingdoms" but within them as

well. As knowledge grows, specialization within fields becomes more prevalent. Just as has been historically the case in professions like medicine, social scientists have become increasingly specialized. It is common in sociology, for example, for one to develop an expertise in a particular substantive area of investigation – deviance, stratification, large-scale organization, medical sociology, or social change. The specialization is not just in subject matter; there are also theoretical and methodological concentrations. It is now proper to speak of clear boundaries *within* each discipline.

We can view the development of this separatism between and within social sciences in two ways. From one perspective, it is a natural and inevitable consequence of the explosion of knowledge in various fields. From another, it may be, in fact, a weakening of our understanding of the human condition. The artificial distinctions prevent us from developing a comprehensive, whole image of social life. As the new millennium begins, the boundaries dividing each discipline from the others, and even those "silos" separating specialty areas within disciplines, have begun to come down (Klein, 1996). There is increasing recognition that in fact psychology, sociology, history, and economics "pour into" one another. At the very least, the members of one discipline ought not to avoid using the concepts, methods, and modes of analysis of other disciplines when these could contribute to an understanding of a particular problem under investigation.

Nowhere is this trend more apparent than in historical sociology. The inclusion of historical perspectives and methodologies as part of successful social science is not merely a matter of arbitrary choice; it is demanded by the rational acknowledgment that contemporary forms of human behavior all have, by definition, a history.

In his cogent book, *The Rise of Historical Sociology*, Dennis Smith (1992:166) laid out the essential tasks for this genre of methodology:

- Primary exploration of specific historical situations which have wider implications for understanding diversity and change

- Empirical generalizations which draw upon the explorations of others and refer, implicitly or explicitly, to theoretical issues
- Systematic theorizing about processes of historical change, drawing upon the results of historical explorations and empirical generalizations

This ambitious agenda means that researchers will be looking for ways to generalize from single historical incidents to broader patterns of change. They will be using their own and others' work to stimulate the development of social theory. Historical sociology has the potential both to correct historical misconceptions and to broaden the domains of social scientific knowledge (Tilly, 2001:6754). However, to accomplish these worthy goals, its practitioners may have to stretch the boundaries of conventional research methodology.

HISTORY AND CULTURE

Researchers are accustomed to studying social phenomena at one point in time – the present. We ask how a particular institution is operating today or what constitutes deviant behavior in a society today. These are certainly not unreasonable questions, but to answer them only in the form asked may limit our understanding of contemporary events, situations, behaviors, or institutions. "Social forms" do not appear spontaneously and autonomously. Every element of a society – from the individual to the complex organization – has a biography, a life history. We cannot escape the judgment that these elements are a product of their pasts. Moreover, society is constantly in a state of transformation. If we are to expand our understanding of contemporary life, we must look to the transformations through which we have already passed. An example should make our point clear. Let us look at the values held by the members of a society.

Whenever people behave according to their standards of what ought to be done – whenever they act according to what they believe is right, proper, decent, or moral – they are expressing their values. That social scientists have found considerable variation among cultures regarding the central values of their members signals the need for historical analysis. We must think of value orientations as representing a society's long-term response to its total historical situation. Sparta's emphasis on militarism and courage, the high premium placed on youth and strength by Eskimos, the place of the work ethic in American society, cannot be understood apart from the historical and environmental factors that shaped those values. Max Weber (1905/2001), in his brilliant historical analysis of capitalism, traces the origin of that economic form to the Protestant work ethic of Calvinist theology.

We may borrow from the writings of C. Wright Mills (1960/2000) to further our claim for the blending of social and historical analysis. An outspoken critic, Mills expressed discontent with the nonhistorical nature of most social science research of the mid-twentieth century. As he saw it, the failure to view social phenomena in historical perspective was simultaneously a failure to exercise the "sociological imagination." According to Mills, this imagination is reflected in a concern with "problems of biography, of history, and of their intersections within social structures." He states his case this way:

The biographies of men and women, the kinds of individuals they variously become, cannot be understood without reference to the historical structures in which the milieux of their everyday life are organized. Historical transformations carry meanings not only for individual ways of life, but for the very character – the limits and possibilities of the human being.... Whatever else he may be, man is a social and an historical actor who must be understood, if at all, in a close and intricate interplay with social and historical structures. (Mills, 1960/2000:162)

HISTORY AND THE GROWTH OF KNOWLEDGE

In arguing for a more extended use of historical data as a way to better understand contemporary societies, we are not asking researchers to engage in analyses foreign to the tradition of their disciplines. Those writers who have provided us with some of the most important classic theoretical ideas nearly uniformly engaged in historical analysis (Marx, 1867/1992; Durkheim, 1893/1997; de Tocqueville, 1831/2000). Indeed, it was unavoidable for nineteenth-century European scholars because the emergence of modern social science disciplines followed a major historical transformation in the organization of European society. It was the change from peasant agrarian to citified industrial society, a structural upheaval brought about by the French and Industrial revolutions.

Sociology, as an independent, autonomous discipline, arose as certain social themes "called out" for analysis after these two revolutions. The themes of power, wealth, status, alienation, the division of labor, and the nature of community life emerged then and are still important today. Regarding the French Revolution as a catalyst for sociological thought, Robert Nisbet (1966/1993:31) has commented:

The French Revolution was possessed of a suddenness and dramatic intensity. The stirring Declaration of the Rights of Man, the unprecedented nature of the laws that were passed between 1789 and 1795 – *laws touching literally every aspect of the social structure of France* – were sufficient to guarantee to the revolution a kind of millennial character that was to leave it for a whole century the most preoccupying event in French political history. [Italics added.]

The disappearance of the peasant community and the rise of cities caused thinkers to consider the changing basis for social organization. The Industrial Revolution thoroughly altered the condition of labor in society. Karl Marx, still a towering figure in contemporary economics, political science, and sociology, analyzed the developing factory system. His resulting contributions to our understanding of capitalist class structure are, of course, well known. With the growth of technology in large industrial cities, there appeared an extensive and complex system of occupational specialization. This became a theme for the theoretical writings of Emile Durkheim, who, in *The Division of Labor in Society*, examined the changes we have described. Similarly, Sir Henry Maine's (1870) distinction between societies based on *status* relations and those based on *contract* relations;

Ferdinand Tonnies's (1887/1988) conceptualization of *community* and *society*; and Max Weber's discussion of the increasing bureaucratization and rationalization of the modern world (Gerth, 1958/2003) are all rooted in analyses of major social, historical trends. In significant respects, these works reflect the images of history held by their authors. The concepts they generated remain among the major tools for the contemporary study of social change.

Eminent examples of sociologists' use of historical materials and insights include Daniel Bell's (1973/1999) farsighted analysis of the arrival of postindustrial society; Howard Zinn's (2000) critical look at the powerless in American history; Michel Foucault's (1995) examination of the connection between social values as their deepest level and the practice of criminology; Christopher Lasch's (1995) critique of the connection between the appearance of the professional and managerial elite and the decline of democracy; Immanuel Wallerstein's (2000) groundbreaking research on the relationship between the rise of the world capitalist system and social structure; and Anthony Giddens's (2000) study of the social impact of globalization. The work of these and countless other scholars stands as convincing evidence that the broad contours of modern and postmodern society are best seen as part of a moving historical scenario.

To summarize the points made thus far, we may say that to study certain features of society in contemporary isolation severely handicaps our ability to answer two questions: (1) How and why have social forms come to assume their present shape? (2) What shapes are they likely to assume in the future? However, before the case for history and its data and methods is overstated, let it be plain that we are not arguing for a naive **HISTORICAL DETERMINISM**. We would not suppose that every present-day aspect of social life stands in a linear relationship to the past. If we try to *see every feature of life as a function of historically determined events*, we are misusing history.

Neither are we asserting that any research without a historical component is somehow improper. It is fully legitimate to study people's present attitudes, values, beliefs, and behaviors. As we will see in Chapter 12, experimental social psychologists frequently inquire into processes of human behavior such as conformity, aggression, patterns of leadership – many aspects of which can be understood without historical research. It is certainly useful to explain the operation of contemporary large-scale bureaucratic organizations. We need to know how our school systems and mental health programs are functioning; how people adapt to the requirements of such institutions as prisons, hospitals, and homes for the aged; how the present legal system distributes justice; and so on. We are merely suggesting that scientific researchers make use of historical analysis when they believe it could expand their theoretical understanding of whatever they are investigating. Most important, they should not refrain from using historical data merely because the methodologies with which they feel comfortable do not easily equip them to process these data. We must see the worth of adding historical methods to our already established bag of research tools.

Most of the social science methodologies in use today do not easily allow for historical analysis. The questionnaire, for example, while it does permit researchers to ask respondents about their pasts, has its greatest utility in uncovering respondents' present attitudes. Investigators using survey techniques sometimes engage in longitudinal studies, but even when these stretch over many years, they may still be lacking as historical research because the data collected are snapshots of how people behave and feel, or what they believe, at any given point in time. Individuals are not always fully competent or motivated to provide data concerning the evolving social context in which they have lived.

Participant observation does allow the researcher to acquire a sense of process over time in a particular setting, but again the time frame is normally very limited. Experimental research is nearly always restricted to the investigation of behavior at one point in time. Social scientists do, however, use such techniques as content analysis of literature and inspection of insti-

tutional records and personal documents.[1] In these instances, they encounter data sources typical of historical research.

SOURCES OF HISTORICAL DATA

In the remainder of this chapter, we will consider some of the difficulties faced by investigators who choose to base their analyses on personal documents, commercial or confidential records, official government materials, and personal life histories. To evaluate the methodological problems one may expect to encounter in the use of such data, we must consider more fully the issues of reliability and validity they raise.

Primary and Secondary Sources

The central methodological questions researchers ponder when they work with historical data are "How much faith can I place in the evidence? To what extent can I believe the data?" Obviously, the closer we are to the events we describe, the more certain we are of the validity of our data. There is a kind of "hierarchy of credibility" when it comes to believing that we have a correct picture of some event or behavior. If we have seen it ourselves – if we have been an eyewitness to the event – we are most confident that we know what went on. If we did not witness the event but heard a report from an eyewitness, our faith in the picture given is somewhat diminished, but we are still likely to find this firsthand account more credible than secondhand or thirdhand information. As the number of steps between the actual event and our hearing of it increases, our faith in the accuracy of the accounting diminishes. Because historical researchers can rarely be eyewitnesses to events extending a long distance into the past, the adequacy of their data becomes a major concern.

The evaluation of historical data, then, poses special problems of reliability and validity that do not normally confront the researcher who studies contemporary phenomena. A good deal

[1] See Chapter 13 for a discussion of content analysis.

of critical scholarship done by professional historians involves consideration of the validity of data recorded by unseen others. In attending to the distance between data sources and the actual events they describe, we may distinguish between **PRIMARY DATA** and **SECONDARY DATA** (Tilly, 2001). *A primary data source is the written or oral report of an eyewitness*; it must thus have been produced by a contemporary of the events it narrates. Primary sources, then, are tangible materials that provide a description of a historical event and were produced shortly after the event took place. They may take many forms: newspaper accounts, letters, public documents, eyewitness verbal accounts, court decisions, and personal diaries. *Secondary sources, in contrast, borrow the knowledge they contain from other sources*, the evidence contained in them being therefore indirect or hearsay.

Even when social scientists have access to primary data sources, they cannot be certain of their validity. We must recognize that those who produce accounts of events, in any of the possible forms we have named, may do so with their own peculiar perceptions of the situation or with particular ideological or personal-interest perspectives. Journalists, for example, may report events in such a way as to sell the most newspapers. Even a seemingly neutral observer may unwittingly have adopted a position on a particular event. In dealing with any historical record, researchers must be aware that every statement or account is written from a definite perspective and for a specific purpose. There are some records, however, that, by their very nature, we can logically assume to be most accurate. We would expect there to be no intentional deceit or error in stenographic or taped records of courts, political bodies, or committees. Notebooks and other memoranda are also high in credibility because they are intimate and confidential records. When journals and diaries are written spontaneously and intimately, they are valuable historical documents. In other words, those documents that we can assume were written by eyewitness observers with no reason to believe that their accounts would be publicly shared are generally thought of as the least-biased historical data sources.

Using Data versus Generating Data

A major task of historians is to keep the human record straight. Thus, they frequently have a professional investment in establishing facts, for example, by determining the origin or genuineness of a document. In contrast, the social scientist is typically more concerned with using historical data than with generating them. Critical historical scholarship may begin and end with the determination that a particular record is authentic, that a document is still in its original form or wording, or that the purported author of a treatise was competent to write it. Extraordinary effort may be expended in determining when or where a document was written. Historians may thus have to become knowledgeable about such fields as paleography (the science of ancient writing), epigraphy (the science of inscriptions and epigraphs), and philology (the science of ancient languages). However, social researchers who are intent on placing the data in a larger framework would less often be found engaging in these varieties of scholarship.[2]

Another distinction between traditional scientific investigation and historical research involves the scientist's concern with either testing hypotheses developed before data collection or developing theory from collected data. When sociologists or political analysts turn to historical materials, it is usually to reveal conceptual themes that have an application beyond the specific case(s) studied. Historians are often more cautious in their use of data.

Generalizability

The argument has been made that *historical events are spatially and temporally specific, that they are unique and nonrecurring*. Those who support this idea of **HISTORICAL SPECIFICITY** point out that there was only one French Revolution and only one American Revolution. They contend that it is unwise to compare World War I with the War of the Roses, the Vietnam War, or Operation Desert Storm. The supposition

---

[2] In recent decades, historians have made use of statistical tools more customarily employed in such fields as economics and sociology.

underlying this view of the uniqueness of historical events is that the social origins of each event are quite dissimilar.

Let us compare this notion of history with the discipline of sociology. Because it seeks after generalization, sociology is resolutely comparative. Sociologists typically center their investigations on recurrent or institutionalized social phenomena, events that are repeated in a similar form and thereby allow for comparative analysis. Deviance, for example, occurs in every society, and in every culture people are engaged in patterns of social interaction. In every society people can be compared in terms of their religious, ethnic, race, class, and age statuses. Does this mean that unique, historical data are inherently incompatible with the logic of social science inquiry?

History and science, while not identical, are certainly complementary. Events are best understood in terms of their immediate, specific historical contexts. This does not suggest that one outcome of historical analysis ought to be the production of social laws that never vary. On the contrary, one of the values of historical study is to relieve us of our contemporary provincialism. Social scientists sometimes tend to see all of social life as understood by looking at contemporary events. Social scientists sometimes write as if they have uncovered unalterable regularities in patterns of human communication, in the structure of institutions, or in the causes of deviance by investigating their own societies at one point in time. Cross-cultural and historical analyses shake us from this unwarranted faith in the universal truth of much contemporary scientific research. Even if there are few universal historical laws, it is nonetheless possible to use historical data in the search for explanations of contemporary behavior.

Sociologists' use of historical data raises some classic validity questions. Perhaps the attempt to see patterns in historical events that seem to resemble each other is misguided; the causes of these events may be particular to a unique space and time (Tilly, 2001:6754–6755). The potential for invalidity in this case may be lessened if researchers are extremely vigilant in the search for disparities among these events and do not presume that there are always patterns to identify.

Postmodernism and Historical Analysis

Chapters 4, 9, and 10 referred to the influence of the postmodern critique on various research methodologies. As the twenty-first century begins, this questioning of taken-for-granted knowledge has had a similar effect on historical sociology. In some cases, the gap between scientists and nonscientists has been reduced because both historians and nonhistorians are beginning to question not just the quality of their data but its social construction as well.

For example, in examining the "realities" that modern societies take for granted, William G. Roy (2001) studied the historical development of five social constructions: time, space, race, gender, and class. He concludes that much of what we accept as "real" are actually just widely accepted ideas that did not develop inevitably, and that have often caused great damage to individuals throughout history. For instance, people may be assigned to categories, such as intelligence groupings or skin colors, through dominant institutions that have the power to influence the thinking and behavior of others. These categories are then *reified*, or given reality, by being named, accepted, and taught as part of historical/social analysis. Once a social construction is widely accepted as real, it is institutionalized into other areas of life and becomes ever more embedded in the social system.

In describing the history of time, space, race, gender, and class, Roy employs the methodological technique of social criticism. He relies on secondary accounts of history (and others' sociological interpretations of that history), along with comparisons to other, non-Western societies that never developed the same social constructions.

USES OF HISTORY: SOME EXAMPLES

What kinds of research problems warrant, perhaps demand, a historical approach? For purposes of convenience and clarity of organization, we will examine historically based studies in the following categories:

- Attempts to establish long-term cultural trends
- The use of historical case studies to test theoretical ideas
- The use of personal documents and life histories as part of ethnographic reports
- The use of available records to study institutional change

We have two goals in mind as we proceed with a selective review of literature using a historical approach. First, we hope to get a better sense of the place and importance of historical evidence for understanding contemporary social life. Second, we will highlight the methodological problems awaiting the researcher who chooses to consider society in historical perspective. We turn now to social scientists who have endeavored to document long-term processes and regularities in the growth and development of social structures.

Analyzing Evolutionary Trends

Classical writers were never reluctant to propose global theories of change; such theories are in important respects also theories of history. August Comte (1856/1987), who coined the term *sociology* in 1830, is probably most well known for his **EVOLUTIONARY THEORY**, *a theory of gradual changes from one stage to the next*. Comte believed the human mind had passed through three historical stages: the theological, the metaphysical, and the scientific. Each of these stages, Comte thought, grew out of the previous one and would be reflected in the social organization of human life. Another nineteenth-century evolutionary theorist, Herbert Spencer (1873/1996), conceived of society as comparable to any other organism, reasoning that societal and organic growth and change could be understood in the same terms.

The failing of early evolutionary thinkers lay in their inability to explain *why* social change took place. Mere explanation by analogy, as in Spencer's case, did not constitute good scientific analysis. For this reason, Karl Marx is often

considered the first modern theorist of social change because his primary concern was to discover its source. For Marx the answer was to be found in an examination of history, an exercise that in 1848 led him to write in *The Communist Manifesto* (Marx and Engels, 1848/1998:2) that "the history of all hitherto existing society is the history of class struggles." Unlike Comte, Marx saw the evolution of society as rooted not so much in ideas as in material conditions. "Men" made history, Marx insisted, as they transformed these material conditions to their own benefit. For him, history is nothing but the activity of people pursuing their aims. Marx believed that the course of human history would evolve toward the development of a classless society.

An equally comprehensive view of history is to be found in the classic writings of Max Weber (1920/1997). Weber's lifelong concern with the increasing rationality of the modern world is a theme that runs through his discussions of religion, authority relations between people, and especially his analysis of bureaucratic structure. Marx saw revolution leading to a one-class society as the future course of history. Weber's image of history was ever-increasing bureaucratization.

Changes in Urban Life

The works of thinkers such as Weber and Marx are comprehensive and far too complex to analyze within the context of this book. It might be more helpful to turn instead to some research that is more representative of modern sociology. In *A World of Strangers*, Lyn Lofland (1985) tried to answer these questions:

- What is the basis for public social order in cities?
- How is the potentially chaotic world of biographical strangers transformed into a system of predictable social relationships?

Her central thesis is that public urban order is achieved quite differently in modern cities than how it was achieved in preindustrial and early industrial times. The transition has been from a primary *appearential* order to the *spatial* order of present-day cities. "In the pre-industrial city, space was chaotic, appearances were ordered. In the pre-industrial city a man was what he wore. In the modern city a man is where he stands" (Lofland, 1985:82). We need not concern ourselves with her argument per se but rather with the kinds of data she must present to convince us of its correctness.

Clearly, Lofland's is a historical argument. She wants to show us through descriptions of both modern and preindustrial cities that there has, in fact, been a transformation in the ordering of city places. To make the comparison required by her thesis, Lofland must reconstruct a situation that she obviously never experienced. She must create for her reader a picture of life in preindustrial and early industrial cities. Her object in one chapter is, as she puts it, to journey backward in time. Before we think about the threats to the validity of her presentation, we might ask why she chose to frame her analysis of modern cities in historical terms at all. Why didn't she simply present data on contemporary cities and leave it at that?

Historical comparison helps us to better see how our own lives are organized. We tend to take our daily routine for granted and need the "shock" provided by history to see our complacency. Moreover, we should realize that Lofland's book is not just about cities; it is about people's need for order and intelligibility in their lives. It is only through historical comparison that we can see how people have continually adapted to and transformed their environment to produce this order. In a real sense, all knowledge is comparative; here, it is the historical reference point that gives Lofland's analysis its power.

Now, however, we must ask the question always posed when historical data are presented: Can we be sure of their accuracy? As Lofland describes modern cities, we are in a position to judge for ourselves the adequacy of the picture given. We can always ask whether the description closely relates to our own experience. We cannot employ this validity criterion when presented with historical data. We must rely on the author's good judgment in piecing together, largely from secondary sources, an image of life in the earlier cities. As a researcher primar-ily intent on using the preindustrial city as a point of comparison, she cannot invest her energies in the arduous, time-consuming search for primary sources. Her work is a translation of translations. She selectively produces her picture of preindustrial city life from previously written histories. That selectivity raises other questions.

The problem of validity is complicated as soon as the researcher seeks to do more than transmit the historical message as faithfully as possible. Clearly, Lofland was not merely intent on setting the factual record straight. Her sole objective was not simply to create a general picture of the preindustrial city. It was to use that picture for a purpose – to show that the basis for order in that type of city was appearential. To do this, the author had to be selective, emphasizing the portion of the historical record that gave support to her thesis. Those who study contemporary events, through whatever method, will also be selective in their data reporting. For researchers who use secondary historical sources, selectivity is made somewhat more problematic for two reasons: (1) they must draw from the already selective reports of others; and as mentioned earlier (2) their judgment cannot be challenged by our own life experience.

The goal has not been to question Lofland's rendering of history. Rather, her study is a useful example of specifying long-term historical transformations. The reader is urged to examine other works that combine cogent social analysis and a broad sweep of secondary historical data. These sources include Karl Polanyi's (1944/2001) description of the rise and fall of market economies; Barrington Moore's (1966/1993) treatise on the origins or democratic and authoritarian regimes around the world; Samuel P. Huntington's (1993) analysis of the historical origins of democratization in the twentieth century; Richard Sennett's (1992) exploration of human personality and the evolution of contemporary capitalism; David Riesman's (1969/2001) study of changes in American national character; and Robert Samuelson's (1997) account of the reasons that Americans tend to expect so much from their government. Although these treatments of historical change

Guns, Germs, and Steel

In his influential book, Jared Diamond (1999) attempted to determine why some populations of prehistoric man developed into modern societies while others remained distinctly primitive. He traced the development or nondevelopment of agriculture, domesticated livestock, germ immunities, writing, technology, and government and the ways in which these were influenced by differences in geography and climate. Diamond's central premise is that the geography and climate of Eurasia enabled (and, in some sense, required) primitive peoples to emerge from hunter-gathering to organized agriculture. He claims that this shift, rather than racial superiority, enabled Asian and European societies to advance technologically far beyond those of Africa, Polynesia, or the Americas.

For his methodology, Diamond combined insights from anthropology, meteorology, history, geology, and ecology to construct a general analysis of the ways in which geography and climate affected the development of agriculture in Eurasia. He then compared this blueprint with anthropological and climatic histories of a few specific African, American, Polynesian, and Australian societies.

and transformation vary considerably in content, you may, in evaluating them, want to raise some of the same questions as have been asked about Lofland's research.

The Historical Case Study

The issues confronted to this point should be helpful to you in thinking about the use of **HISTORICAL CASE STUDY** materials that *examine in detail one reasonably limited set of historical events* (Vaughan, 1992; Yin, 1994; Gerring, 2007). Rather than documenting trends over time, the case study approach treats every social situation as a laboratory where some aspect of social life can best be studied. The past provides some of our best social laboratories.

A superlative, classic example of a historical case study informed by a theoretical perspective is Kai Erikson's *Wayward Puritans* (1968). Ever since Emile Durkheim put forth the notion that deviance could serve certain useful social functions in a society, researchers have looked for evidence to support that contention. Erikson finds such evidence in seventeenth-century New England. He echoes Durkheim by showing how Puritan society needed its deviants, continually, to reaffirm the norms of propriety. Functional arguments for the importance of deviance are intriguing. They are a novel

way of explaining how certain institutions, if not the society itself, continue to operate. Durkheim maintained, for example, that without sinners a church could not exist. The very existence of sin provides the opportunity for believers to reaffirm the faith that has been offended by the sinner. So, the worst thing that can happen to a church is to completely eliminate sin from the world!

By choosing a specific, dramatic case, Erikson showed how, to the extent that a common morality exists in a society, it comes to depend on its deviants for the maintenance of its social boundaries. These theoretical ideas can be applied to understand the witch hunts in colonial America. Relying most heavily on secondary sources, Erikson described how the "moral entrepreneurs" of early Massachusetts colonial society, in their zeal to maintain religious purity, launched full-scale crusades against alleged Salem witches. Anyone who did not fully identify with Puritanism suffered in these self-conscious attempts to define acceptable behavior in the society.

Although Erikson does not draw these parallels himself, we could say, on the basis of casual historical knowledge, that a number of additional cases might be used as illustrations of the functional view of deviance: McCarthyism of the 1950s (Schrecker, 1994); events leading up to the discriminatory laws against Jews in Nazi Germany (Shirer, 1960/1990); internment of Japanese Americans during World War II (Neiwert, 2005); and antipathy toward the hippies of the mid-1960s (Miller, 1991).

We should be motivated by more than just curiosity about the possible parallels in these historically discrete cases; there is an important methodological point to make. We know that no matter how interesting the researcher's rendering of one historical case, we are compelled to question the representativeness of that case. If, however, investigators can show that their theoretical ideas help to explain a number of cases, two things are accomplished: We are allowed to see underlying dimensions of historical events separated in time; and we have greater faith in the generalizations made from any one case. This positive outcome suggests a strategy for social scientists who see value in using history to test their theoretical ideas. They should be willing to conduct a number of case studies as a way of both understanding what happened in the past and continuing to amplify their theories.

Alternatively, historians might expand their own visions by looking at their data from a social scientific point of view. The difficulty of establishing such a reciprocal relationship is, however, considerable. Note the criticisms leveled at Erikson's research by two writers who found fault with *Wayward Puritans* on two related levels. First, they claimed that because the author began his inquiry with a specific set of theoretical ideas he wished to test, these preconceptions caused him to "misquote and misrepresent in his efforts to make the data conform to his theory" (Nelson and Nelson, 1969:149). Second, they maintained that Erikson used secondary sources too frequently when primary sources were available. They argued that he should have made much more extensive use of sermons, available diaries, and other records and that had he done better history rather than stopping "when he finds a secondary source that tells him what he wants to hear" (p. 150), his analysis and interpretation of the historical case would have been far more effective. We do not consider these criticisms because we want to determine whether they are correct but because

they indicate the kinds of issues for which the social researcher using historical data will likely be held accountable.

Erikson's (1969) reply to his critics was equally interesting. He tried to clarify that his response to the Nelsons ought not to be read as a quarrel between professional historians and social scientists. He admitted quite readily that he had no training in historiography and that if he had mistakes might have been avoided. He also admitted to relying heavily on secondary sources but defended himself by saying that social researchers cannot spend their whole lives becoming intimately acquainted with a particular historical period because their goal is to produce comprehensive generalizations.

Personal Documents

Not all historical research must extend far back in time. Rather, the period of interest may be recent, and the data may be altogether different from government reports and religious edicts. **PERSONAL DOCUMENTS** such as *diaries, letters, and autobiographical statements* have long been used in social research. Perhaps the most well-known classic example of this form of primary data in sociology is William I. Thomas and Florian Znaniecki's study *The Polish Peasant in Europe and America* (1918/1995). In this research, the authors considered a long-standing theoretical problem, namely, how people adapt to new forms of social organization. Polish immigration afforded an excellent opportunity for understanding the modes of adaptation of people transplanted from a largely agrarian culture to a modern industrial one.

The research was based on the letters that immigrants sent to their families in the "old country." Thomas and Znaniecki (1918/1995: 1832) wrote, "We are safe in saying that personal life-records, as complete as possible, constitute the perfect type of sociological material." Acquiring the letters through an advertisement in the newspaper, Thomas and Znaniecki were able to document the nature of the interaction between these persons and their distant families. The data, in effect, provided a continuous history of their New World experience. These letters allowed the researchers to assess dynamics of attitude change, changing relations within primary groups, and development of community life.

Much of the presentation in the two-volume work is thoroughly descriptive. Thomas and Znaniecki appear to have included, in an unedited form, every letter they were able to acquire. This is important because it gives their readers an overall feeling for the data, allowing them to judge the adequacy of the researchers' interpretations. At the same time, we must be skeptical of the data. First, the letters obtained were necessarily selective. The researchers were able to use only those that the self-selected respondents who answered the advertisement saw fit to show them. Second, we must recognize that the authors of these documents may have had some reason for presenting the quality of their experiences in a particular light.[3]

Life History Reports

As part of their effort to see the New World experience from the point of view of the peasants, Thomas and Znaniecki commissioned selected people to record detailed **LIFE HISTORIES** of themselves. In these documents, which read much like novels, the *critical life events responsible for shaping subjects' perspectives* were brought into focus. The life history technique is well represented in the works of Goldman and Brody (2006), Ramos (2002), Sullivan (2001), and Valent and Keneally (2001). Meri Nana-Ama Danquah (2000:1–18) collected a life history account from Nina Barragan, an immigrant from Argentina (see p. 253).

Howard Becker (1978/2006) provided a cogent scientific rationale for the use of life history data. He pointed out that these data are to be clearly distinguished from the more literary autobiography. When we read autobiographies, we do so with the recognition that authors select their material to present a particular image of themselves. We recognize as well that what an author considers as trivial or unimportant and, there-

fore, chooses not to report, may be quite significant for the social scientist. How then does the life history differ? As researchers gather life history reports, they do not simply rely on subjects to determine fully what will be said. Rather, with their particular theoretical interests in mind, they maintain a continuous dialogue with their subjects. Through this dialogue respondents are oriented toward specific kinds of events in their lives; clarification is demanded where ambiguities exist; and, where necessary, the scientist asks for more extensive descriptions of past events. As Dennis Smith (1991:159) has written:

> . . . the historical sociologist can be both involved and detached, relative to the subject of analysis: involved in the sense of empathizing with or entering into the human situations being examined; detached in the sense of being able to discount emotion-laden responses [that] get in the way of clear perception.

Life histories must be used in conjunction with other data sources. If we were to rely solely on a few individual case histories to make our generalizations, criticism of our findings would be justified. Just as we must recognize the extent to which historical events are unique, so also must we suppose an individual's life history to be singular in some respects. As used with other techniques and data sources, however, the life history provides a penetrating, in-depth view of events. It is an extension of the traditional use of "informants" in participant observation research. Used with proper caution, personal documents and life history reports will further our effort to understand the intersection of history, individual biography, and social structure.

The Use of Available Records

As suggested, personal documents and life histories have their limitations as data sources.[4] Although we are able to get an in-depth view of people and events, we usually study only a small number of cases, and the data we acquire are relatively unsystematic. Analysts who wish to comment on the historical experiences of

---

[3] This technique differs from content analysis (see Chapter 13) because there is little or no enumeration of an exhaustive universe or probability sample of letters.

[4] For a more detailed discussion of several of the issues taken up in this section, see Chapter 15.

Doing Archaeology in My America

We entered the U.S. at Miami on August 28, 1944. I was almost nineteen months old, my brother was five. From what I've been told, it was a scorching day, and we were still dressed in our Argentine woolens, including the hats and scarves that my maternal grandmother had knit just before our departure from a cold Buenos Aires. The peeling of layers must have begun in Brazil, continued in Trinidad, and by the time we reached Miami, my mother was carrying a load of heavy garments in her arms. Things went smoothly at immigration, but while we waited for our flight to New York, it seems I managed to create more excitement for my already anxious, exhausted mother. My brother was in charge of walking me around in the airport during our long wait, and on one of our excursions, I spotted a large doll in a display case. The die was cast. Apparently, I could not live without her; she was nearly my size. I threw such a fit of screaming and wailing, refusing to leave the display case, that my mother had no choice but to buy the doll, breaking into one of her two fifty-dollar U.S. bills. This buttery-skinned beauty in a blue gingham pinafore, became my first American friend.

I still have my Argentine passport, issued in Buenos Aires... The photograph is of a cute baby propped on a chair, ribbon in wispy hair... In a certain, clear script, an Argentine bureaucrat has written that I'm blond, with a fair complexion and light eyes. A straight nose – base, narrow. The mouth – medium. The ears – medium. One might easily assume that given my malleable age and outward trappings, becoming an assimilated American could be as easy as apple pie. Yet fate would have that plate just slightly out of my reach, always. As I matured, I came to understand that the development of my identity in the process of becoming American involved the instinctive act of pushing that plate away, as much as pulling it toward me.

[Our] first rented home was... a big, white clapboard house on a hill. We children learned to sleigh and make snowmen, and in the summer, we had a pet duck in our fenced-in yard... We played with our neighbors – their parents were schoolteachers, raised on Iowa farms – and from this family, we learned about America. We watched their mother bake bread and freeze vegetables from the garden... Within a couple of years my parents bought an old Victorian house on a wonderful, tree-lined street. We were no longer visitors, we were here to stay. Iowa City was our new home.

I wonder if most New Americans think their circumstances are unique. Now, in retrospect, I realize how unusual our situation was, although at the time, I didn't think about it. We did not come to a community of people from our homeland, as so many immigrants do. We did not come to a ghetto or an ethnic neighborhood of a large city. We came to a small, Midwestern university town. There were only a handful of Spanish-speaking people, very few from Argentina. We did not come to family that had preceded us. We came alone, and we would remain alone, always... Indeed, independence was our force. It nurtured the strengths of self-sufficiency and commitment to work that our personalities would come to demand. These strengths we carry today. But there were pitfalls. With such a strong emphasis on independence, the concept of belonging to an extended family, or belonging to a community, was virtually nonexistent... We were taught it was best not to depend on others... So we were to exist apart from society...

My growing up became a process of rummaging through what I knew of my parents' history, searching for fragments and relics, doing archaeology in my America...

From Meri Nana-Ama Danquah, ed. 2000. *Becoming American: Personal Essays by First Generation Immigrant Women.* New York: Hyperion.

large groups or population aggregates must, therefore, turn to other data sources. **AVAILABLE RECORDS** have frequently been used by researchers to provide *systematic historical data on large numbers of individuals*. Although social scientists must live with the fact that records are usually not kept with the expectation that they will someday be used for historical investigation, a variety of official documents do exist that make possible the statistical analysis of sociohistorical trends. To get an idea of the types of records available, we may look briefly at the research concerns of those who do demographic analysis.

Demography is the study of population phenomena. Among other issues, demographers seek to document rates of fertility, patterns of immigration and migration, changing food resources in a society, birth rates, and death rates. They may examine trends or changes in these population parameters on many levels: for a selected part of society, for a whole society, for several societies – indeed, even for the world. Obviously, to produce their aggregate population analyses, demographers must rely exclusively on existing records (Swanson and Siegel, 2001).

Although the data are sometimes spotty or incomplete, it is possible to document population trends using such materials as census reports; international migration records; population registers; and records of such vital statistics as disease, birth, and death rates. By looking at population trends historically, demographers have shown consistent relationships between a number of these population characteristics and a society's level of economic development. It is by now a well-established "fact" that as a society becomes more industrialized, people have fewer children. The importance of such a finding for social policy formation needs no elaboration.

Because all their research depends on existing records, demographers have been particularly sensitive to methodological problems. Although censuses, for example, are considered fairly reliable, we know that they will contain certain types of errors. Many people lie about their age or income. In the compilation of any record, some people may be counted twice or omitted altogether. Those responsible for compiling statistics will incorrectly classify some of the cases. For political or ideological reasons, "official" statistics may be altered. Errors may be committed unwittingly in recording data for these statistics. Certain records may have a temporal problem; that is, the statuses of a good number of people will change over time (e.g., marital status, citizenship) and the changes will not be reflected in the records we use. Demographers have taken steps to estimate the degree and direction of these various errors in their data. It is impossible to make aggregate data records error free, but it is possible to be watchful for likely errors in the data and to consider them in assessing the significance of findings.

We have named only a small number of the official record sources employed by the social scientist who wishes to establish statistical trends over time. To those mentioned, we would add the following: voting records; lists of school enrollment; city directories; telephone directories; tax payment records; unemployment figures; sports attendance figures; records of local, state, and national government expenditures; records of police arrests; congressional proceedings; and, of course, codified law. Imagine the kinds of historical trends of potential theoretical significance that could be established using these records. Using telephone directories, it would be conceivable to assess changes in the ethnic composition of an area; records of police arrests may be used to establish how the nature and type of criminal activity have changed over time; the use of voting records to reflect ideological change in the country has been a traditional preoccupation of social scientists.

Example: Changing Attitudes toward Abortion

Studying legalized abortion presents an ideal opportunity to make use of historical methods because the issue combines deeply held religions and political attitudes with changes in medical practice and in the legal environment. When abortion was first legalized in the United States, favorable public discourse was dominated by the women's movement, but a backlash led by religious conservatives and members of the Right to Life Movement altered the political context during the 1980s. Sociologists Jennifer Strickland and Nicholas Danigelis (2002) examined the factors responsible for public attitudes toward legalized abortion in the United States between 1977 and 1996. Although public opinion has changed little on this issue, the authors uncovered shifts in the views of distinct segments of the population. They note (2002:188):

. . . the stability in abortion attitudes may result from counterbalancing shifts in views, rather than stagnation or nonchange. In order to understand the dynamics of attitudinal change, the trends must be disaggregated . . . the segment of the population that is pro-choice in the 1990s may have a markedly different profile from the pro-choice portion of the population in the 1970s.

Using existing data from fifteen *General Social Surveys* conducted by the National Opinion Research Center over a twenty-year period, the authors found that black Americans were becoming more approving of legal abortions, whereas white Americans were becoming less approving. The authors also considered religion as an explanatory variable and found that being Catholic became a weaker predictor of opposition to abortion, whereas Protestant fundamentalism became a stronger predictor. Finally, because the belief in the sanctity of human life is increasing and is associated with opposition to legalized abortion, the authors conclude that the prolife framework for viewing abortion is culturally more influential with the public than is the prochoice framework. However, the data also indicate that beliefs in gender equality and sexual freedom have remained stable, accounting for the absence of broad-based political opposition to abortion (Strickland and Danigelis, 2002:200).

Example: The Persistence of Inequality

Sometimes historical analysis does not focus on a *single* issue over time, as in the previous example but, rather, focuses on drawing out historical patterns from a *variety* of issues.

This approach is well illustrated in Charles Tilly's (1998) book *Durable Inequality*. Although nearly all social relationships involve some level of subordination, Tilly defines a few inequalities that have persisted over time and which affect nearly all human societies. He separates these into pairs (e.g., male/female, aristocrat/plebeian, citizen/foreigner, black/white) and asks how and why these inequalities develop and persist, and how they affect the structure of the societies in which they operate.

Tilly's method of pattern identification employs several case studies that seem to be quite varied but in which the single unifying characteristic is the existence of a relationship of social inequality. His goal is to discover recurring ways in which inequalities are created and sustained. This approach leads him to find common links between the ways in which American mothers feed their children, the monarchical political structure of the Tshiba tribes of Africa, gender differences in construction companies, and the history of the federal prescription-drug program. Tilly offers suggestions for eliminating these durable inequalities, while recognizing that the patterns of history predict that they will persist.

This historical analysis concludes that durable inequalities are dependent on broad differences in types of people, rather than individual differences per se. These inequalities arise because those who control the resources of a society sustain those resources by excluding others from a full share in the rewards. These broad, categorical identifications are institutionalized and enforced as pairs, creating inequality that is durable. Tilly's approach encourages the development of general, macrolevel social theories that expose elements of human nature, whereas the single-issue approach discussed in the first example seems to call for middle-range, or microlevel, explanations of behavior that are more directly tied to the issue being investigated.

HISTORICAL ANALYSIS IN PERSPECTIVE

Charles Tilly (2001:6753) has summarized the value of history for the social sciences by noting that "history contains a record of human successes and failures in dealing with problems persisting into the present." However, although a wide range of social problems may be investigated historically, it is inappropriate to identify a constant and rationalized set of procedures for collecting or processing data from the past. Many of the research methods considered elsewhere in this text can be used in historical analysis, but some (such as content analysis) lend themselves to the task more readily than others (such as experimentation). It is undeniable that a comparative historical perspective helps us see ourselves with greater clarity, as well as the social structures within which we carry out our lives. In recent years, considerable progress has been made in collecting and preserving historical materials, as well as storing and retrieving them on the World Wide Web (McMichael, Rosenzweig, and O'Malley, 1996; Institute of Historical Research, 2003; University of Amsterdam, 2006; A&E, 2007; International Institute of Social History, 2007). These innovations have made historical data more available to the research community and to ordinary citizens than ever before.

As social scientists acquaint themselves more fully with these data sources, they will benefit from discussions with historians about the historiographic methods that will ensure the proper use of the data. Historians, in turn, can profit by considering how social, political, and psychological theories might inform their interpretations of the past. Such a happy rapprochement depends on the willingness of social scientists to risk looking beyond the "conventional wisdoms" produced through the evolution of their respective disciplines.

SUMMARY

Historical analysis is a key starting point for understanding a range of social issues that affect us personally. Social scientists' appreciation of the value of historical data is a most important interdisciplinary goal. Indeed, it is impossible to understand fully contemporary human behavior without some reference to the evolving cultures from which it originates. The motives behind human behavior are revealed through history because culture contains the values, aspirations, and dreams of people, as well as a record of their concrete achievements. The origins of modern social science are found in the attempts of classical writers to wrestle with broad and important historical questions, an important component of the creation of knowledge that may be forgotten in the ahistorical and narrow thrust of much contemporary investigation. It is wise to steer a path between historical determinism, on the one hand, and an unwarranted faith in the universal truth of much of today's scientific research, on the other.

Historical analysis may involve the exploration of specific historical situations or systematic theorizing about processes of change. Sources of historical data include government documents, diaries and personal histories, business records, and official demographic surveys. Many of the data are from secondary, rather than primary, sources. Potential validity problems are created whenever events are not directly observed or when accounts are recorded for purposes other than the researcher's. Difficulties in determining the accuracy of data and in generalizing from information obtained selectively are present in all methods of social research, but historical data pose special problems and are most effectively used when combined with other types of information. Clearly, to maximize validity, historians and social scientists need to combine their efforts.

Countless social problems may be effectively examined via historical analysis, and the number of different uses of historical data is almost as great. Case studies, personal documents, life history reports, and available records are only four sources of what happened in the past, and why.

KEY TERMS

available records
evolutionary theory
historical case study
historical determinism
historical specificity
life history reports

paradigm
personal documents
primary data
secondary data

EXERCISES

1. Create a research project on the September 11, 2001, attack on the World Trade Center. Compare the content and power of personal and secondary source accounts of the attack. Which methodology seems more persuasive to you, and why?

2. Go to the library and read five different newspapers. Choose papers that differ in format and circulation. You might want to include the *Christian Science Monitor*, the *New York Times*, a local newspaper, and your campus newspaper. Describe how these papers differ. Are there variations in how national events are reported? Does each have a distinctive ideological perspective? Speculate on how a historical research report might be affected if the investigator relied on only one of these papers as the data source for a study.

3. As an exercise in realizing the variability in eyewitness accounts, ask several people to give you an account of what went on in a particular meeting or class you did not attend. Write down the accounts immediately after the class or meeting, and interview a few other people a day or two later. In what way(s) do the reports of your informants differ? What are the points of similarity? Did those with whom you spoke immediately after the event give more detailed accounts? What do the "data" lead you to say about the difficulties of relying on only one or a few eyewitness accounts in historical research? What methodological recommendations would you make to increase the validity of information acquired via eyewitness reports?

4. Select a social event that has been analyzed by both a sociologist and an historian. Read their accounts carefully and answer the following questions:

- What types of historical sources are used in the studies? Are they primary or secondary sources?
- Do the reports differ in the types of generalizations the authors attempted to make from their collected data?
- What conclusions might be reached about differences in orientation of sociologists and historians?

5. Perhaps you or some fellow students wrote diaries when you were between ages 12 and 16. If you can find classmates who have saved these personal accounts and who are willing to share them, construct a social history using the diaries as data. What are the strengths and limitations of this source of information?

SUGGESTED READINGS

Readings about the Method

American Sociological Association. 2004. *Homepage of the Comparative and Historical Sociology Section*.

http://www2.asanet.org/sectionchs/.

Contains online articles, a newsletter, and methods bibliography on comparative and historical methods.

Cole, Ardra, and J. Gary Knowles. 2001. *Lives in Context: The Art of Life History Research*. Lanham, MD: Alta Mira Press.

A step-by-step guide through the process of life history research.

Creswell, John W. 1998. *Qualitative Inquiry and Research Design*. Thousand Oaks, CA: Sage.

Creswell compares and contrasts several tools of qualitative historical research, including biographical life history and case studies. Also included are postmodern and feminist approaches.

Fulbrook, Mary. 2002. *Historical Theory: Ways of Imagining the Past*. New York: Routledge.

This is a careful look at historical writing. The author believes that a mixture of facts and social theory is the key to cogent analysis. She argues against postmodernism and the idea that historical narratives are simply inventions imposed on the past.

Hall, John A., and Joseph M. Bryant. 2005. *Historical Methods in the Social Sciences*. London: Sage.

An encyclopedic look at the uses of history in social science analysis, this major reference work contains numerous classic articles and highlights the major debates in the field.

Patai, Daphne, and Sherma B. Gluck, eds. 1991. *Women's Words: The Feminist Practice of Oral History.* New York: Routledge.

This book examines the theoretical, methodological, and practical problems in using oral history as a tool of feminist scholarship.

Sillitoe, Alan. 2002. *Key Issues in Historical and Comparative Sociology.* London: UCL Press.

Various approaches and methods in comparative/historical sociology are reviewed in the context of feudalism and social change in western Europe and the emergence of the modern world.

Stake, Robert E. 1995. *The Art of Case Study Research.* Thousand Oaks, CA: Sage.

A step-by-step guide to setting up a research project based on case studies.

Yow, Valerie R. 2005. *Recording Oral History.* 2nd ed. Lanham, MD: Alta Mira Press.

This volume examines the ethical and legal issues involved in conducting life history interviews and elaborates on community studies, biographies, and family histories.

Readings Illustrating the Method

Allen, Robert, Tommy Bengtsson, and Martin Dribe. 2005. *Living Standards in the Past: New Perspectives on Well-Being in Asia and Europe.* New York: Oxford University Press.

Several scholars compare economic and demographic indicators of well-being in the preindustrial period to answer the question: When did Europe eclipse Asia in living standards?

Astarita, Tommaso. 1999. *Village Justice: Community, Family, and Popular Culture in Early Modern Italy.* Baltimore: Johns Hopkins University Press.

An excellent example of a historic case study, Astarita's work is a social history of an Italian village, including analysis of its economic structures and social hierarchies, family and household life, community justice, sexuality and the role of women, and religion and popular morality.

Castells, Manuel. 2000. *End of Millennium.* 2nd ed. Malden, MA: Blackwell.

A sociological tour de force covering the crisis of the industrial state, the collapse of the Soviet Union, the plight of poor countries, and the unification of Europe.

Collins, Randall. 2000. *Macrohistory: Essays in Sociology of the Long Run.* Stanford, CA: Stanford University Press.

An outstanding collection of essays that demonstrate the variety and uses of historical method. Especially interesting is a contribution on predicting the collapse of the Soviet Union.

Diamond, Jared. 2006. *Collapse: How Societies Choose to Fail or Succeed.* New York: Penguin.

A best-selling author explains why some of the great civilizations of the past collapsed into ruin.

Friedlander, Paul. 2006. *Rock and Roll: A Social History.* 2nd ed. Boulder, CO: Westview.

A social and cultural analysis of rock music.

Frugoni, Chiara. 2005. *A Day in a Medieval City.* Chicago: University of Chicago Press.

A down-to-earth account of daily life in medieval Italy.

Hirsch, Arnold R. 1998. *Making the Second Ghetto: Race and Housing in Chicago 1940–1960.* Chicago: University of Chicago Press.

The author describes the social engineering of post–World War II ghettos by showing how the national urban renewal effort was forged in the context of the racial struggles waged on Chicago's South Side. White ethnic, political, and business interests reacted to the great migration of southern blacks in the 1940s by influencing public policy to segregate the city.

Markoff, John. 1996. *Waves of Democracy: Social Movements and Political Change.* Thousand Oaks, CA: Pine Forge Press.

The author uses the technique of pattern identification to examine several historical periods in which democratic societies have been organized. He attempts to identify the conditions under which popular rule was established and pinpoints the differences between democracies in various historical epochs.

Moore, Barrington. 2000. *Moral Purity and Persecution in History.* Princeton, NJ: Princeton University Press.

This work of social criticism attempts to discover the conditions under which human societies have constructed concepts of moral purity to exclude, punish, reform, or exterminate those who are deemed impure. The development of purity as a concept is traced from its religious origins in the Old Testament to its secular adaptations in the French Revolution

Pritchett, Wendell E. 2002. *Brownsville, Brooklyn: Blacks, Jews, and the Changing Face of the Ghetto.* Chicago: University of Chicago Press.

Pritchett shows how race, ethnicity, culture, and gender have influenced the social history of Brownsville as it evolved from a white, predominantly Jewish, working-class neighborhood to a 75 percent black / 20 percent Puerto Rican neighborhood.

Schrum, Kelly. 2006. *Some Wore Bobby Sox: The Emergence of Teenage Girls' Culture, 1920–1945.* New York: Palgrave.

A lively study of the relationship between the emergent teenage girls' identity and the growth of a market aimed at teenage girls in the decades before World War II.

Street, Paul. 2004. *Empire and Inequality: America and the World Since 9/11.* Boulder, CO: Paradigm.

The author's thesis is that the 9/11 attacks accelerated an already-existing trend toward global hierarchy, inequality, and repression.

Valenze, Deborah. 2006. *The Social Life of Money in the English Past.* New York: Cambridge University Press.

This study looks at the formative period of commercial and financial development in England between 1630 and 1800 in order to analyze the advance of commercial society at the threshold of modern capitalism. It shows how money became involved in relations between people in ways that moved beyond its purely economic functions.

See the references below for additional examples of historical research.

REFERENCES

A&E. 2007. The History Channel.
   http://www.historychannel.com.

Becker, Howard S. 1978/2006. "The Relevance of Life Histories." In *Sociological Methods: A Sourcebook*, 419–428. Norman K. Denzin, ed. New Brunswick, NJ: Transaction.

Bell, Daniel. 1973/1999. *The Coming of Post-Industrial Society: A Venture in Social Forecasting.* New York: Basic Books.

Comte, Auguste. 1856/1987. *The Positive Philosophy.* New York: AMS Press.

Danquah, Meri Nana-Ama, ed. 2000. *Becoming American: Personal Essays by First Generation Immigrant Women.* New York: Hyperion.

Diamond, Jared. 1999. *Guns, Germs, and Steel: The Fates of Human Societies.* New York: W. W. Norton.

Durkheim, Emile. 1893/1997. *The Division of Labor in Society.* New York: Free Press.

Erikson, Kai T. 1968. *Wayward Puritans: A Study in the Sociology of Deviance.* Boston: Allyn & Bacon.

———. 1969. "Response to the Nelsons' 'Case Example.'" *American Sociologist* 1 (2) May: 151–154.

Foucault, Michel. 1995. *Discipline and Punish: The Birth of the Prison.* New York: Vintage.

Gerring, John. 2007. *Case Study Research.* New York: Cambridge University Press.

Gerth, Hans H. 1958/2003. *From Max Weber: Essays in Sociology.* New York: Routledge.

Giddens, Anthony. 2000. *Runaway World: How Globalization Is Reshaping Our Lives.* New York: Routledge.

Goldman, Emma, and Miriam Brody. 2006. *Living My Life.* New York: Penguin.

Huntington, Samuel P. 1993. *The Third Wave: Democratization in the Late Twentieth Century.* Norman: University of Oklahoma Press.

Institute of Historical Research. 2003. *History On-Line.*
   http://www.history.ac.uk/search/welcome.html.

International Institute of Social History. 2007. *World Wide Web Virtual Library: Labor History and Business History.*
   http://www.iisg.nl/~w3vl/.

Klein, Julie Thompson. 1996. *Crossing Boundaries: Knowledge, Disciplinarities, and Interdisciplinarities.* Charlottesville: University Press of Virginia.

Lasch, Christopher. 1995. *The Revolt of the Elites: And the Betrayal of Democracy.* New York: W. W. Norton.

Lofland, Lyn H. 1985. *A World of Strangers: Order and Action in Urban Public Space.* Prospect Heights, IL: Waveland Press.

Maine, Sir Henry. 1870. *Ancient Law.* London: John Murray.

Marx, Karl. 1867/1992. *Capital.* New York: Penguin.

Marx, Karl, and Friedrich Engels. 1848/1998. *The Communist Manifesto.* New York: Signet.

McMichael, Andrew, Roy Rosenzweig, and Michael O'Malley. 1996. *Historians and the Web: A Beginner's Guide.*
    http://www.wku.edu/~andrew.mcmichael/begin.html.

Miller, Timothy. 1991. *The Hippies and American Values.* Knoxville: University of Tennessee Press.

Mills, C. Wright. 1960/2000. *The Sociological Imagination, 40th Anniversary Ed.* New York: Oxford University Press.

Moore, Barrington. 1966/1993. *Social Origins of Dictatorship and Democracy: Lord and Peasant in the Making of the Modern World.* Boston: Beacon Press.

Neiwert, David. 2005. *Strawberry Days: How Internment Destroyed a Japanese American Community.* New York: Palgrave.

Nelson, Ann, and Hart Nelson . 1969. "Problems in the Application of Sociological Method to Historical Data: A Case Example." *American Sociologist* 1 (2) May: 149–151.

Nisbet, Robert A. 1993/1966. *The Sociological Tradition.* New Brunswick, NJ: Transaction.

Polanyi, Karl. 1944/2001. *The Great Transformation: The Political and Economic Origins of Our Time.* 2nd ed. Boston: Beacon Press.

Ramos, Jorge. 2002. *The Other Face of America: Chronicles of the Immigrants Shaping Our Future.* New York: HarperCollins.

Riesman, David, Nathan Glazer, and Reuel Denney. 1969/2001. *The Lonely Crowd, Revised edition: A Study of the Changing American Character.* New Haven, CT: Yale University Press.

Roy, William G. 2001. *Making Societies: The Historical Construction of Our World.* Thousand Oaks, CA: Pine Forge Press.

Samuelson, Robert J. 1997. *The Good Life and Its Discontents: The American Dream in the Age of Entitlement 1945–1995.* New York: Vintage.

Schrecker, Ellen. 1994. *The Age of McCarthyism.* New York: Bedford/St. Martin's Press.

Sennett, Richard. 1992. *The Fall of Public Man.* New York: W. W. Norton.

Shirer, William L. 1960/1990. *The Rise and Fall of the Third Reich: A History of Nazi Germany.* New York: Simon & Schuster.

Smith, Dennis. 1992. *The Rise of Historical Sociology.* Philadelphia: Temple University Press.

Spencer, Herbert. 1873/1996. *The Study of Sociology.* London: Routledge.

Strickland, Jennifer, and Nicholas Danigelis. 2002. "Changing Frameworks in Attitudes Toward Abortion." *Sociological Forum* 17 (2): 187–201.

Sullivan, Zohreh. 2001. *Exiled Memories: Stories of the Iranian Diaspora.* Philadelphia: Temple University Press.

Swanson, David L., and Jacob S. Siegel, eds. 2001. *Methods and Materials of Demography.* New York: Academic Press.

Thomas, William I., and Florian Znaniecki. 1918/1995. *The Polish Peasant in Europe and America: A Classic Work in Immigration History.* Urbana: University of Illinois Press.

Tilly, Charles. 1998. *Durable Inequality.* Berkeley: University of California Press.

———. 2001. "Historical Sociology." In *International Encyclopedia of the Social and Behavioral Sciences,* 6753–6757. Neil Smelser and P. Baltes, eds. New York: Elsevier.

Tocqueville, Alexis de. 1831/2000. *Democracy in America.* Chicago: University of Chicago Press.

Tonnies, Ferdinand. 1887/1988. *Community and Society/Gemeinschaft und Gesellschaft.* New Brunswick, NJ: Transaction.

University of Amsterdam, Sociology Department. 2006. *History and Social Change.*
    http://www.sociosite.net/topics/history.php.

Valent, Paul, and Thomas Keneally. 2002. *Child Survivors of the Holocaust.* New York: Brunner-Routledge.

Vaughan, Diane. 1992. "Theory Elaboration: The Heuristics of Case Analysis." In *What Is a Case?*

Exploring the Foundations of Social Inquiry, 173–202. Charles Ragin and Howard S. Becker, eds. New York: Cambridge University Press.

Wallerstein, Immanuel M. 2000. *The Essential Wallerstein.* New York: New Press.

Weber, Max. 1920/1997. *Theory of Social and Economic Organization.* New York: Free Press.

———. 1905/2001. *The Protestant Ethic and the Spirit of Capitalism.* 3rd ed. Los Angeles: Roxbury.

Yin, Robert K. 1994. *Case Study Research: Design and Methods.* Thousand Oaks, CA: Sage.

Zinn, Howard. 2001. *A People's History of the United States: 1492 to Present.* New York: Harper.

EXPERIMENTAL RESEARCH

12

INTRODUCTION

In this chapter, we consider one of the most deductive of all research techniques, the experiment. As a data collection technique, experimentation seems ultrascripted and not at all spontaneous. However, the elaborate laboratory environment that is prepared in advance in many experiments, and the rigorously practiced research roles assigned to those conducting the experiment, actually require a great deal of research imagination. In this case, the creativity is required at an early stage in research design, long before the research subjects appear in the laboratory to begin the experiment itself.

The idea of an experiment should not be foreign to most of us. We all use loose or incomplete forms of experimentation in our daily lives. Husbands and wives experiment with different ways of preparing food, noting their spouse's reaction to each modification of the prepared dish. Salespersons intent on finding the most persuasive pitch to use in selling a product may systematically test out a number of approaches until they find the one that works best. Teachers experiment with different formats for presenting course material, selecting one that allows students to learn the most. Vacationers in Las Vegas try out many systems at roulette or blackjack, hoping to find the one that will make them winners.

Any time that we systematically manipulate our surroundings and try to assess the effects of these manipulations, we are engaging in an experiment. In all the cases mentioned, actors looked for changes in one or another phenomenon (expressions of pleasure in eating, number of sales made, and so on) after systematically altering some feature of the environment. The presumed purpose of our everyday experimentation is to assert the existence of a **CAUSAL CONNECTION**, or *systematic relationship between two or more variables*.

What, then, distinguishes incomplete experimentation from scientific experimentation? The most basic answer is that most of us typically do not go to the trouble of creating rigorous safeguards to ensure the correctness of the causal relationship suggested by our everyday experiments. Consider the teacher who has been test-ing a number of instructional methods. Suppose that in one class small-group discussion seems to produce the most learning, as measured by a quiz on the material. Should the teacher conclude that the best teaching technique has been uncovered and that small-group discussions should be used in all classes? Are there any kinds of procedural considerations that might cause us to be skeptical about the validity of these findings?

Here are some of the questions we might ask: Isn't it possible that the class responding well to the small-group discussions had better students in the first place and would have learned more regardless of the method used? Might the size of the class have had an effect on the amount learned – independent of the method employed? Might it have made a difference that the teacher's classes met at different times during the day and that, again, independent of the method used, students are more or less attentive during certain school hours? What about the distribution of males and females in the class? Is there any possibility that the gender composition of the class alters the willingness of students to participate in small-group discussions?

To make "safe" causal inferences, we must somehow ensure that factors wholly unrelated to what we presume to be the cause of some phenomenon can be excluded or discounted. In the ideal experimental situation, the only thing that will vary from group to group or situation to situation is the experimental treatment, or manipulation, of the independent variable. Unless the situations studied are similar in all respects other than the presence or absence of an experimental treatment, we cannot be certain that it is indeed the treatment, and not some other difference existing between the groups, that causes certain changes to occur. If we hope to isolate the effects of one or another experimental treatment, we must somehow control for, or rule out, all those factors other than the experimental treatment that could affect the behaviors of those studied. If we want to demonstrate that the variable "small-group discussion" makes a difference in student learning, we must be careful to rule out the effects of class size, gender composition, the time of day the class is taught, and other such factors.

Both scientists and nonscientists are concerned with demonstrating causal connections between various features of the social world. Scientists, however, make every effort to set up their experimental procedures to show clearly that any changes in behavior following an experimental treatment are not contaminated by factors extraneous to, or outside of, that treatment. **EXPERIMENTAL RESEARCH**, therefore, may be defined as *an investigation in which the experimenter manipulates one or more variables under carefully controlled conditions*. The task of scientists is to assess the effects of their experimental manipulation by measuring changes in a specified variable. The key phrase in this definition is that experimental research is conducted under carefully controlled conditions. In this chapter, some of the difficulties involved in achieving such control are considered. Some research problems do not easily submit to pure experimental procedures. However, in order to claim the existence of a causal connection between two or more variables, the degree of control that is indeed possible is the major criterion.

THE ELEMENTS OF TRUE EXPERIMENTATION

Perhaps we can achieve a better picture of how control is exercised and how causality between variables is established by looking at a hypothetical example: an experiment that might be conducted in a social psychologist's laboratory. We will follow the researcher through the process of testing ideas experimentally, and we will offer a rationale for each step in that process. Let us assume that a researcher has a theoretical reason for believing there is a relationship between the degree of anxiety in a group and the cohesiveness of that group. The hypothesis to be tested may be stated as follows:

The greater the anxiety among the members of a group, the greater will be the cohesion of that group.

Independent and Dependent Variables

To determine the experimental procedures needed to test this hypothesis, the researcher must look carefully at its elements. Clearly, the two variables being related in the hypothesis are *anxiety* and *cohesiveness*. The convention in scientific research is to label *the proposed causal variable in a relationship* the **INDEPENDENT VARIABLE** and the *proposed effect of the independent variable* the **DEPENDENT VARIABLE**. In the hypothesis, the researcher has proposed that anxiety causes cohesiveness. So, given our definitions, anxiety is the *independent*, or **TEST VARIABLE**, and cohesiveness is the dependent variable.

Logic demands that to test this hypothesis the researcher must compare at least two groups. The simplest test of the hypothesis would be to compare a low-anxiety group and a high-anxiety group, with the expectation that cohesiveness would be greater in the latter. One of the great strengths of experimental procedure is that the experimenter is in a position to create just the groups needed to test the hypothesis. More explicitly, the experimental researcher may manipulate the independent variable and cause it to vary.

Experimental and Control Groups

The experimenter must think of some way to introduce or produce anxiety in one of the groups to be assembled and compared. In this simplest form of experimentation, where the investigator works with only two groups, the one in which *the independent, or test variable* (in our example, anxiety), *is introduced or manipulated* is called the **EXPERIMENTAL GROUP**; the other, in which *the independent variable is neither introduced nor manipulated*, is called the **CONTROL GROUP**.

How does the experimenter create the two groups, and how exactly is the independent variable manipulated? It is not uncommon for university-associated researchers to advertise in their school newspaper for student volunteers to participate in an experiment. Usually, students who volunteer are paid a nominal sum for their participation.

Later, the possible weaknesses of experimental procedures on human subjects will be discussed. For now, let us note two possible difficulties raised by the recruitment procedure we are outlining here.

First, students represent only one sector of the whole population. They are likely younger and better read, and possibly more intelligent, than the average person in society. If we use only students because of their accessibility, we must recognize that there will be limits to any generalizations made from our experimental findings. It may be that groups more varied in terms of age, ethnicity, and intelligence would behave quite differently from the relatively homogeneous groups of students. Second, our subjects would be SELF-SELECTED, *individuals who choose to participate* in an experiment. This raises another problem of selectivity. Might there be some systematic difference between the types of people willing to participate and those not willing? Researchers must be aware of these factors when they attempt to generalize about group process from their data.

Bearing these problems in mind, let us assume that volunteers have been instructed to sign up some time in advance of the date when the experiment will actually be carried out. Suppose that thirty students have indicated their willingness to participate. Because group size might affect people's behavior, the researcher makes the reasonable decision to have fifteen students in both the experimental and the control groups. The next decision must be to determine which fifteen will be in each group. This decision is absolutely crucial; if improperly made, it could void the results of the experiment. Let us consider the logic of the assignment of the students to the two groups.

What would be wrong with simply assigning the first fifteen names on the list to the experimental group and the last fifteen to the control group? Recall the purpose of the experiment: It is to assess the effects of anxiety on group cohesion. All other variables must be ruled out. We may begin to see why simply splitting the list in half to create the two comparison groups would be an unwise decision. It might be that women, or poor students, or psychology majors have a tendency to sign up for participation in experiments before others. The first fifteen students who sign up might, therefore, differ in important respects from the last fifteen. Because the researcher wants to rule out, or control for, any such systematic differ-

ences, a different procedure must be adopted for assigning subjects to experimental and control groups.

The researcher correctly chooses to make a RANDOM ASSIGNMENT of students to the groups. The laws of statistical probability dictate that the two groups would be neither overrepresented nor underrepresented by individuals with one or another distinctive characteristic. Random selection is, therefore, a key feature of experimental procedure, *allowing the researcher to control effectively for all possible factors extraneous to the specific relationship under investigation*.

Experimental Procedure

The day arrives when the volunteers will show up to participate in the experiment. The research has solved the problem of group assignment and must be prepared to manipulate the independent variable in the experimental group (to somehow create anxiety in that group) and to measure any changes that occur in group cohesiveness. At this point, many variations might be pursued. The following procedure would not be unusual:

1. After assigning individuals to the two groups, the researcher asks the members of each to work together on some reasonably simple problem. The researcher is not interested in their ability to do the assigned problem. The goal is to get people interacting as a group so that certain features of that group interaction can be measured.

2. Before the arrival of the subjects the investigator has determined how to measure cohesiveness, the dependent variable. Although the difficulties of measurement are great and the researcher must be concerned with the reliability and validity of the measures, for simplicity's sake, let us say that cohesiveness is operationalized in terms of the number of times members use "we" to refer to the group as a whole. The researcher might listen to and observe the groups from behind a one-way mirror.

3. After observing each group for a time, the researcher will have arrived at a quantitative measure of cohesiveness for each group before the introduction of the test variable. *Measurement of the dependent variable before the manipulation of the independent variable* is often referred to as a **PRETEST**.

4. The experimenter is now prepared to provide a **STIMULUS** to the experimental group by somehow introducing or raising the level of anxiety in that group. This is the *experimental treatment*. Perhaps, the members of the experimental group might be told that they are not performing as well as they should be on their assigned task and that unless their performances improve, they can expect a reasonably unpleasant punishment. Through such a communication the researcher has presumably increased the level of anxiety in the experimental group and is now in a position to observe any changes in group cohesiveness.

5. The experimenter returns behind the one-way mirror and again assesses the degree of cohesiveness in each group as measured by the frequency of collective group references by the members. *The measure of the dependent variable following the experimental treatment* is often referred to as the **POSTTEST**. Any change in subjects' behaviors or attitudes is established by comparing pretest and posttest measures. The procedure involving these five steps is often called the classic experimental design, or the classic experiment.

Establishing Causality

If, when the researcher compares the pretest and posttest measures of cohesiveness for both the experimental and the control groups, a substantial increase in cohesiveness appears after manipulation of the independent variable in only the experimental group, this may be evidence that the initial hypothesis relating anxiety and cohesiveness is correct. More than that, however, the experimental procedure used allows the researcher to make the even more powerful statement that anxiety is a cause of cohesiveness. Properly executed experimental research allows for collection of the evidence necessary for making causal statements. A review of the hypothetical research we have described will reveal that the investigator has

met the following three criteria for establishing causality between variables:

1. First, the researcher must be able to show that the independent and dependent variables are associated. In other words, any measured change in the independent variable will be accompanied by a measured change in the dependent variable, and vice versa.

2. The idea of causality implies more than simple association, however. It involves, in addition, the direction of the relationship between two variables. It is one thing to say that variables X and Y are related and quite another to say that X caused Y. To establish the more precise direction of causality between two variables, the researcher must show a time sequencing to any measured change in both independent and dependent variables. That is, showing the direction of causality depends on the demonstration that a change in Y clearly *follows* a change in X and not the other way around. The experimental procedure involving the manipulation of an independent variable allows the researcher to illustrate the time sequencing of events. One of the strengths of experimentation is that the researcher frequently controls the timing of events. Any measured change in the dependent variable occurs only after change in the independent variable has been introduced.

3. To establish a causal relationship between two variables, the researcher must show that it is indeed the proposed independent variable, and not some other unknown factor, that is responsible for any measured change in the dependent variable. The experiment that allows for random assignment of subjects to both experimental and control groups ensures that the two groups are not substantially different in important respects. The control over extraneous variables exerted through random assignment allows the researcher to make a very important assertion; namely, that the only difference between the groups studied is that one has not been exposed to the experimental treatment, or stimulus, and the other has.

We have set the stage for further discussion by presenting in some detail, through example, the basic logic and structure of experimental research. We cannot assume, however, that once the minimal conditions for a true experiment are met, researchers can without question establish just how the variables examined in their studies are causally related. As in all the methodologies employed by social scientists, sources of distortion, bias, or error may render invalid the findings produced in a study. We turn, therefore, to a discussion of some of the threats to validity when the classic experimental design is employed.

THREATS TO VALIDITY IN EXPERIMENTAL RESEARCH

Methodologists typically distinguish between threats to internal validity and threats to external validity as they consider sources of distortion in experimental research.[1] When we speak of **INTERNAL VALIDITY**, we are referring to *the ways in which the conduct or process of experimentation itself may affect the results obtained*. Is there anything about the procedures used in conducting an experiment that may distort the "truth value" of the data collected? Remember that the researcher wants to isolate the effects of specific independent variables. Threats to internal validity exist when our ability to see the effect of some independent variable is blurred because the experimental procedure has itself affected subjects' behaviors.

Suppose we have conducted an experiment similar to the one outlined in the preceding section to test the hypothesis that group anxiety produces cohesiveness. If the study takes several hours to complete, and the people in the experimental group spend a great deal of time together waiting for the researcher to perform the measurements, they might get to know each other quite well and become more cohesive as a result. The researcher might indeed find that their cohesiveness increased and attribute this finding to greater anxiety. The conclusion might be incorrect because the design of the experiment allowed another variable affecting cohesiveness (length of time spent together) to intrude. This is a problem of internal validity.

When researchers speak of **EXTERNAL VALIDITY**, they refer to *difficulties in generalizing the*

[1] In our discussion of internal and external validity, we drew on the work of Campbell and Stanley (1963/2005).

findings of experimental research. A frequent criticism of laboratory experiments is that they are artificially constructed situations and that people do not act in the real world as they do in the laboratory. For this reason, generalizations we can make from experimental research are limited (Brannigan, 2004). The external validity question asks whether groups created for purposes of experimentation are sufficiently different from naturally occurring groups that generalization beyond the experimental situation is unwarranted. Before we address this so-called reality problem, let us consider some of the specific obstacles to internal validity in studies using the classic experimental design.

Internal Validity

Internal validity is the sine qua non of experimental research. We must be able to ascertain whether the experimental treatment is, in fact, responsible for any measured changes in a dependent variable. We saw earlier that random assignment of subjects to experimental and control groups ensures, according to the laws of probability, that the groups compared do not differ significantly from one another in their composition. Through random assignment we achieve a degree of control over the range of variables, other than the chosen independent variable, that could be causally related to the dependent variable in our study. We must now examine those factors associated with the experimental procedure itself that cannot be controlled through random assignment.

In all cases, the concern of the researcher is to measure change in some dependent variable after the introduction of a test variable. To assess the change precisely, the researcher must measure the dependent variable at least twice – once before the introduction of the test variable and once after. However, some complications enter into the researcher's assessment of change.

First, the subjects of an experiment may become sensitized to the measurement procedures used. Any initial measurement (pretest) of subjects may reveal to them the interests of the experimenter and affect their responses to the second measurement (the posttest). Suppose researchers want to determine whether a movie showing natural childbirth makes people more or less favorably disposed toward delivery without medication. If the experimenters decide to use the control group/experimental group design and to show the movie (the independent variable) in the experimental group, they would undoubtedly want some initial measure of subjects' attitudes about natural childbirth. But if they ask subjects to fill out an attitude questionnaire on childbirth, the very activity of answering the questions might affect their attitudes. If this occurred, the experimenters would not easily be able to assess the effects of the movie (their independent variable) in changing subjects' attitudes.

Along with the danger of pretest sensitization there may be "maturation" processes that members of either or both groups experience. The subjects of an experiment may be exposed to an event or input from the general experimental environment that is unrelated to the experimental treatment per se but that may nevertheless influence their behaviors and attitudes. We could imagine influential leaders becoming established in a group that has been meeting for even a short time. These leaders could influence the behaviors of other subjects in the study. Another example of maturational effects creating changes in behavior apart from the experimental manipulation is the possibility of subjects becoming bored or fatigued or hungry during the procedure. There are, in other words, a number of factors associated simply with the passage of time that might cause people to change their behavior.

Closely related to the effects of maturation are the potentially confounding effects of history. It could happen, especially in experiments in which there is a reasonable span of time between pretest and posttest measures of the dependent variable, that subjects will learn about an event that has occurred in the society that will influence their attitudes. Campbell and Stanley (1963/2005) cite the example of a 1940 study in which the researcher wanted to assess the effects of Nazi propaganda on students. During the days in which the subjects were reading the propaganda materials, France fell to the Nazis. It is very likely that any changes in student attitudes were more directly a result of this historical event than of the materials they were reading.

In addition to the factors already named, there are occasions when the dependent variable is not measured in exactly the same way in the posttest as in the pretest. There are many experimental studies where observers, scorers, or raters evaluate changes in the dependent variable after some experimental treatment. It could happen that these *people go through a maturational process, become fatigued or bored, and do not, therefore, use exactly the same measurement criteria for the posttest as they did for the pretest.* This problem of MEASUREMENT DECAY is further exacerbated if pretest and posttest measurements are done by altogether different sets of people. It could happen that any measured change in the dependent variable is due to inconsistencies in measurement rather than to the experimental treatment.

Finally, we must mention the possibility that *subjects will drop out of the experiment before it is completed.* EXPERIMENT or SUBJECT MORTALITY will, of course, influence the comparability of the control and experimental groups and will cause researchers to question whether any measured changes in a dependent variable following the experimental treatment might be a function of the changed composition.

The Solomon Four-Group Design

To combat some of the threats to internal validity that we have been considering, investigators have developed elaborations on the classic experiment. To illustrate the ingenuity of researchers who are intent on maximizing internal validity, we will examine a frequently used variation that employs four comparison groups. This procedure has come to be called the Solomon Four-Group Design and takes the form illustrated in Table 12.1.

Up to experimental group 2, this design is identical to the classic experiment. Two additional groups have been added, however, in which no pretest measure of the independent variable is made. What is the rationale for adding experimental group 2 and control group 2?

We begin with the assumption that because individuals have been randomly assigned to

Table 12.1. The Solomon Four-Group Design

	Experimental group 1	Control group 1	Experimental group 2	Control group 2
Pretest conducted	Yes	Yes	No	No
Exposure to test variable	Yes	No	Yes	No
Posttest conducted	Yes	Yes	Yes	Yes

all four groups they do not systematically vary from each other in any important respect. Although no pretest measures are taken in experimental group 2 and control group 2, we can assume, because individuals have been randomly assigned to all four groups, that if a pretest had been given in these groups, the results would not differ substantially from the pretest measures of experimental group 1 and control group 1. We can also assume that the effects of any maturational processes would be the same in all four groups.

Now, let us suppose that the researchers were concerned with the possible sensitizing effects of a pretest measure. Consider the comparison they could make between experimental group 1 and experimental group 2. The only difference between these two groups is that a pretest measure has been conducted in one and not in the other. Therefore, if the pretest has had no effect in changing the individuals' attitudes or behaviors, we would expect that there will be no substantial difference in the posttest measures for these two groups. If there is a substantial posttest measure difference between experimental groups 1 and 2, the researchers can estimate how much influence the pretest has had in producing that change because the only thing distinguishing those two groups is the absence of the pretest in one of them. Moreover, by comparing these experimental groups with control group 1 (pretest done, no experimental treatment), they can assess the effects of their experimental treatment.

What about maturation and history as confounding factors? How can the effects of these two related factors be evaluated? These possible biasing factors can be gauged by means of control group 2. Subjects in control group 2 have experienced neither a pretest nor the experimental treatment. Only a posttest has been done. Any change in control group 2 must, then, be entirely due to maturational processes and not to the effect of the experimental treatment. The pure effect of the experimental treatment can be determined by subtracting the posttest score of control group 2 (effects of maturation) from the posttest score of experimental group 2 (effects of maturation and experimental treatment).

In conclusion, we can see that the elaboration of the classic experimental design to include a larger number of comparison groups allows researchers to determine with much greater accuracy the effects of their stated independent variables. Several design variations are possible. By using a number of groups, researchers can administer several pretests; they can control in a number of ways the timing of events (that is, the timing of the introduction of the test variable); they can sometimes vary the intensity of the test variable in different groups (a researcher interested in the effects of anxiety could, for example, control the degree of anxiety created in groups studied); and they can administer a number of different posttests. While it goes beyond the scope of our discussion to study all these design variations, we can at least understand their purpose. All elaborations on the classical experimental design allow researchers to evaluate more precisely the causal effects of their chosen independent variables.

External Validity

Even when researchers conduct experiments in which they minimize the threats to internal validity, they must still worry about whether they can generalize from their experimental findings. After all, people may not behave in their "natural life situations" as they do when they know that their behaviors are being watched, measured, and evaluated by a scientist. Can we be certain that they conform, react to anxiety, learn how to perform tasks, respond to group leaders, and develop group norms just as they would in situations in which they are not being studied? When we inquire into the correspondence between individuals' behaviors in experimental situations and their "natural world" behaviors, we are raising the question of external validity. If there is no correspondence between the two, it becomes logically dangerous to generalize beyond the experimental situation.

That individuals' behaviors may be altered because they know they are being studied was clearly demonstrated in a famous, classic study of workers (Roethlisberger and Dickson, 1939). *The biasing effect of subjects' knowledge that they are part of a study* has come to be called the **HAWTHORNE EFFECT**, after the name of the factory where the research took place. In the Hawthorne study, researchers set out to investigate factors affecting worker productivity. They manipulated patterns of lighting, monetary incentives for production, patterns of managerial leadership, and so on. The major finding of the study was that regardless of the experimental manipulations employed, the production of workers seemed to improve. One reasonable conclusion from this research is that the workers were pleased to be part of an experiment. They were pleased to receive attention from researchers who expressed an interest in them – and this was the most influential factor affecting productivity. We can, however, be somewhat more specific regarding how subjects' knowledge of their participation in an experiment might cause them to modify their "normal" behaviors.

Modeling Effects

One danger in an experiment is that *subjects may try to behave as they believe the experimenter expects them to behave*. When this occurs, we say an **EXPECTANCY** or **MODELING EFFECT** is operating. Any of us have a need to order and to make intelligible the situations in which we act, and the experimental situation is no exception.

We ought to expect that subjects in an experiment will try to figure out what the experiment is about and what the researchers wish to know. Subjects no doubt have some conception of how people participating in an experiment ought to act; they realize their behaviors are being evaluated and, in most instances, will want to "look good." The problem is compounded by the demonstrated possibility that experimental researchers sometimes unwittingly convey their attitudes and expectations to their subjects, with the result that the subjects conform to those expectations. To combat such a possibility, some experimental designs are double blind. In a **DOUBLE-BLIND EXPERIMENT,** *the researcher conducting the experiment does not know whether subjects are part of the experimental group or the control group*. Thus, medical experimenters, for instance, would not be inclined to expect improvement in certain patients because they would not know which patients had been given a particular drug and which had been given a sugar pill.

Sampling and Generalizability

We mentioned earlier that there are frequently special sampling problems in the conduct of experiments that may also compromise how representative the findings are. More specifically, the subjects of laboratory experiments are often drawn from readily accessible populations. Often, these subjects are students and then only those students who express a willingness to participate. The generalizability of our findings might therefore be threatened by selection processes that favor the inclusion of certain types of subjects and the exclusion of others. Consider the implication of the fact that experimental subjects are often volunteers. Volunteers have been shown to be in higher need of achievement and social approval. Furthermore, they tend to be less well adjusted and have somewhat more unconventional personalities. The problem of generalizability does not belong to the experimental researcher alone. Systematic sample selectivity and expectancy biases must be considered as obstacles to generalization in participant observation and survey research studies as well. In the case of experiments, as we have seen, problems of internal validity can be handled through the use of ingenious experimental designs. There is no such similar logical response to the question of external validity. Satisfaction that the results of our research allow for generalization always demands a leap of faith to some degree. Although we should refrain from claiming a one-to-one relationship between the laboratory situation and the "real world," we should not dismiss the power of the experiment in sensitizing us to important processes of social life. The words of social psychologist Leon Festinger (1971:6) are still worth quoting:

It should be stressed . . . that the problem of application of the results of laboratory experiments to the real-life situation is not solved by a simple extension of the result. Such application requires additional experimentation and study. It is undoubtedly important that the results of laboratory experiments be tested out in real-life situations. Unless this is done the danger of "running dry" or "hitting a dead end" is always present. A continuous interplay between laboratory experiments and studies of real life situations should provide proper perspective, for the results obtained should continually supply new hypotheses for building the theoretical structure and should represent progress in the solution of the problems of application and generalization.

A LABORATORY EXPERIMENT

The selection that follows on pages 273–274 is a summary of an experiment to test the alleviation of women's math anxiety (McIntyre et al., 2005). Heeding Festinger's advice, ask whether the laboratory findings mirror real-life situations, and what might be done to make them more realistic.

This experiment satisfies all of the criteria previously mentioned; that is, the researchers were able to show that the independent and dependent variables are associated; the direction of the relationship is also clear: Exposure to successful role models reduces test anxiety among members of a negatively stereotyped group. Finally, the researchers used a control group as well as systematic comparisons of results from men and women to eliminate the possibility that untested variables accounted for the results they obtained. Notice, however, that there may

be some problems translating the researchers' findings from the laboratory to "real life." The participants were all college students and not necessarily representative of the population as a whole.

The plea for a continuous interplay between experimental procedures and studies of real-life situations provides a useful transition to the rest of this chapter. We have noted that laboratory experiments have the great virtue of letting researchers exercise control over variables extraneous to their research interests. We may suggest that as research is done in the real world – that is, as we try to study people in their natural environments – it becomes more and more difficult to isolate a few variables for investigation. At the same time, we wish to emphasize that it is possible to conduct experiments outside the laboratory situation; it is sometimes possible to have the best of both worlds. Researchers who are legitimately concerned with the artificiality of the laboratory often conduct their experimental inquiries in natural settings. In the next section, some examples of field experiments are examined.

FIELD EXPERIMENTATION

Often the phenomena or processes of interest to social scientists are not easily investigated in an artificial environment. It is difficult to study the development of group culture, consumer behavior, and the effects of mass communication in experimental laboratories. At the same time, sociologists, psychologists, and educators, aware of the many factors that may limit their attempts to establish causal relationships between variables, want to use experimental models whenever possible. This is the primary rationale behind **FIELD EXPERIMENTATION**, *the use of experimental techniques outside the laboratory in a natural setting.*

Not all true field experiments involve large expense. At relatively little cost, Garrity and Degelman (1990) explored the effect of server introduction on tipping in restaurants. In other words, they investigated whether it made a difference whether servers introduced themselves by name (for example, "Hello, my name

The Effects of Role Models on Alleviating Women's Mathematics Stereotype Threat

BACKGROUND

Stereotype threat has been defined as "the social-psychological threat that arises when one is in a situation or doing something for which a negative stereotype about one's group applies." When a situation creates stereotype threat, members of the negatively stereotyped group perform poorly relative to their actual level of competence.

Researchers have discovered techniques that effectively alleviate the performance deficits associated with stereotype threat. These techniques include presenting people with successful role models from their own group. The present experiment tested this premise by varying the number of successful role models used to alleviate women's mathematics stereotype threat. This was accomplished by having subjects read from 0 to 4 biographies of successful women – an architect, lawyer, doctor, or inventor.

PROCEDURE

Two hundred ninety-five college students (209 women and 86 men) participated in mixed-sex groups. Two experimenters were used. The first experimenter informed participants that they would be participating in two separate studies: one to develop stimulus materials for future experiments, and another to standardize quantitative Graduate Record Examination (GRE) items. To be sure that the relevant stereotype had been recently activated for all participants the experimenter explicitly mentioned the stereotype that women perform worse than men on math tests.

The first experimenter then asked participants to read and critique brief essays about successful women that would be used as stimulus materials in future studies. The essays were supposedly abstracted from such popular publications as *Entrepreneur* or *Who's Who*. Participants were randomly assigned to one of five conditions.[2] Participants in the 0 successful women condition read essays that made no mention of successful women [the control group]. In the four experimental conditions participants read a randomly selected 1, 2, 3, or 4 successful women essays.

Then, a second experimenter, a female who had no knowledge of how many biographical essays participants had received, entered to conduct her "unrelated" study. Under the guise of helping to develop and standardize new questions for the GRE, she administered a mathematics test that consisted of 34 difficult quantitative items from sample GRE tests. The experimenter read aloud the usual test instructions that strongly advised against guessing or skipping items. She then gave participants 20 minutes to complete the test. She did not claim to have written the items or to have any special math competence. To the extent that a woman test administrator might have facilitated participant women's performance, it would have done so equally in all conditions. After taking the test, all participants rated their perceptions of the extent that reading the biographical essays led them to conclude that women could do well

---

[2] With random assignment, each specific biography would have a .25 probability of being included in the one biography condition, .5 with two biographies, .75 with three, and 1.0 with four. Thus, if either one specific biography was producing the alleviation, or each additional biography added the same amount of alleviation to the cumulative effect, then we would observe a straight linear pattern of women's test score means, in which, for instance, four biographies work twice as well as two.

at mathematics and made them think that they could do well at mathematics (both on scales from 0 = not at all to 9 = very much). This measure was presented as part of a progressive debriefing, in which no participant guessed that reading the biographies was intended to change his or her test scores.[3]

RESULTS

The primary goal of the present experiment was to examine performance trends for women across these five conditions (0, 1, 2, 3, and 4 role models). However, there were also observed differences between men and women within the five conditions. When both men and women were reminded of the stereotype prior to the math test, but had read no biographies of successful women, women scored .78 standard deviations worse than men.[4] When men and women were both reminded of the stereotype and read 1 biography, women scored .47 standard deviations worse than men; with 2 biographies, women scored .16 standard deviations worse than men; with 3 biographies, women scored .17 standard deviations *better* than men. Finally, with 4 biographies of successful women, women scored .17 standard deviations better than men. When women are reminded of the stereotype and given no information about successful role models, they perform poorly relative to men, but when they are given information about 4 successful women role models, that performance deficit is alleviated.

DISCUSSION

We wanted to answer the question "What trends occur in women's performance under stereotype threat with increasing number of successful women role models?" The answer to this question seemed important from both a theoretical and a practical perspective. Men's performance on the math test did not differ across conditions. After being placed under explicit stereotype threat, however, women who read no biographies of successful women scored worse than men. Women who read a biography of one successful woman scored a little better; women who read biographies of two successful women scored better than that. Women who read biographies of three successful women scored better still (and as well as men), and reading a fourth biography added little compared to reading three. The present results suggest that when women are under mathematics stereotype threat, being more relaxed about potential embarrassment to themselves and to the group, might improve performance.

We can offer only tentative advice to members of negatively stereotyped groups when they approach a threatening situation such as an important standardized test. "The research is at best only preliminary," we might say, "but our initial results lead us to recommend that just before the test, you read three or four brief biographies of other members from your own group who have been successful. One biography probably won't have the full effect, but reading dozens of them is not necessary. Three or four will do."

Adapted with permission from McIntyre et al., 2005. "A Social Impact Trend in the Effects of Role Models on Alleviating Women's Mathematics Stereotype Threat." *Current Research in Social Psychology* 10 (9): 116–136.

---

[3] See Chapter 5, "Research Ethics," for a discussion of debriefing.

[4] See Chapter 18 for an explanation of standard deviation.

is Marilyn") to their customers. Dining parties were randomly assigned to the situation of name introduction or no name introduction. The attempt was made to hold everything else constant. For example, the same 22-year-old female server was employed in more than forty dining parties at Sunday brunches in a California restaurant. By random assignment, half of the dining parties received the name introduction and the other half did not. The results were quite striking and statistically significant. The tipping rate for those who were given the server name introduction was 23.4 percent compared with 15.0 percent for those who did not receive the server name introduction.

This modest example shows that we need not think of the true experiment as possible only in the laboratory situation. We can create a kind of real-life laboratory in some instances. There are situations in the natural world in which it is possible to randomize subjects and to make clear group comparisons. The investigator whose goal is to establish causal relations between variables ought to seek out these situations for natural experimentation whenever possible. Field experiments have wide application in helping to test alternative strategies for improving society with regard to public issues such poverty, inadequate schools, delinquency, or environmental pollution.

Quasi-Field Experiments

We can define the true experiment in terms of three structural elements, or conditions. When these three elements operate simultaneously in research design, they afford researchers maximum control and justification for maximum faith in any causal assertions they make. To qualify as a true experiment, the project must meet the following criteria:

1. It must achieve its results through comparison of at least two groups.

2. It must assign people or subjects to groups randomly.

3. It must be constructed so the researcher has control over, or is able to evaluate, the timing of the experimental treatment.

Although the studies we have described to this point meet the criteria of the true experiment, for practical reasons it is sometimes the case that the problems social scientists wish to investigate can't be researched in a way that satisfies the above criteria. Another strategy, therefore, is to perform **QUASI-EXPERIMENTS**, in which *all the elements of the true experiment are present except for the random assignment of people to groups*. So, quasi-experiments stand in contrast to the true experiment in terms of the degree of control exercised by the researcher over possibly confounding extraneous variables.

A Study of Group Culture

As researchers conduct their inquiries in natural field settings, they often find it either unfeasible or impossible to assign people randomly. Here is an example that will illustrate how and why this is so. Suppose researchers are interested in the formation of group culture.[5] Let us imagine that they have theoretical reason for believing that the development of group culture is enhanced or inhibited by the relative success experienced by a group in realizing its collective goals. More explicitly, they believe that the more successful the group is in realizing collective goals, the more rapid and complete will be the development of a distinctive group culture. Conversely, the failure of a group to realize collective group goals will inhibit the development of group culture.

It would be possible for the researchers to set up their own groups through random assignment of individuals and then somehow to create a situation where these groups would be more or less successful in realizing artificially established goals. It would be possible, in other words, to create the conditions for a true experiment. In this case, however, the researchers have reason to believe that this kind of manipulation might have some distinct drawbacks. They recognize that the theoretical problem they have posed does not easily submit to solution through pure experimental techniques; the researchers see the difficulty of detailing the development of group culture in the short time they would

---

[5] We are indebted to Gary Alan Fine for this example.

be able to observe artificially created laboratory groups. Elaborated cultures simply do not develop in an hour or two, a day or two, or even a week or two.

At the same time, the researchers realize the strength of experimental procedures in establishing causal relationships. They wish at least to approximate a true experimental procedure in testing their hypothesis. They decide, therefore, to look for some naturally occurring situation where they might be able to test their ideas. They are willing to give up some of the rigorous control afforded by true experimental procedure in order to study the phenomenon of interest in a more natural situation. They engage in a trade-off. They know that it is virtually impossible to assess fully all the contemporaneous inputs from a natural environment that could affect behavior. They also know that by choosing to investigate already existent groups in some natural setting they will be unable to assign people to groups randomly; they will have no control over the composition of the groups studied.

To allow them to approximate the conditions of true experimentation, the researchers look for a naturally occurring context with the following characteristics:

1. A situation where they will be able to observe a number of groups from their inception over a long enough time period to see and somehow measure the development of group culture.

2. A situation where, although people have not been strictly assigned to groups randomly, they might expect that the members of the various groups will not vary in any substantial respect.

3. A situation where some groups are successful and others unsuccessful in realizing their collective group goals.

After considering whether there are natural situations where these three theoretically dictated conditions might hold, one of the researchers hits on an idea. Why not study the formation and operation of Little League baseball teams! Here, after all, one can observe a number of groups (teams) over time from the point of their formation. The groups will all be the same size. The age composition of the groups will be the same. Although the researchers will

want to check out the procedure through which individuals are assigned to teams, they have no reason immediately to assume that there will be any gross or systematic variation in the background characteristics of the players from team to team. Finally, the researchers will not have to manipulate the test variable artificially – the relative success the groups experience in realizing their goals – because they can assume that the dominant goal for each group will be to win ball games, and it will naturally occur that some teams will be winners and others losers. As a matter of fact, they will be able to observe teams at a number of points along the continuum of goal realization because the better win/loss record of one team ensures that another team has a worse win/loss record.

More Quasi-Field Experiments

A good example of quasi-experimental research can be seen in the work of Pomeroy, Kiam, and Green (2000), who used a psychoeducational group intervention with male inmates in a large southeastern U.S. metropolitan county jail. The results of their research indicate that their work was successful in improving AIDS knowledge and reducing anxiety, depression, and trauma symptoms among the inmates. Although there were experimental and comparison groups in this study, it was not done as a true experiment because random assignment to the groups did not occur. One factor was that the jail administrators insisted that the participation in the study be voluntary. Assignment to the experimental group was first come, first served, and those initially in a comparison group eventually got the opportunity to participate in another intervention program. Still, the study results showed the positive impact of the program.

Another illustration of quasi-experimental research is McClanahan's (1993) study of how well activity-based as opposed to cognitive-based instructional approaches in wellness courses positively affect student lifestyle behaviors. Pretests and posttests were done on students in courses reflecting the difference between the two approaches. Those in the activity-based course showed more improvement than those students in the cognitive-based course. Random assignment, however, did not occur. Students self-selected the activity-based course. Were these students most motivated to experience positive change in their lifestyle behaviors? Could this explain the change in the dependent variable? This is always a possibility in quasi-experiments where assignment of subjects to the experimental and control groups is not done randomly.

There are a number of other quasi-experimental studies of interest. Leske (1996) investigated whether family members of those undergoing surgery can have their anxiety reduced by progress reports during the surgery. Those who received such reports in person had significantly lower levels of anxiety than others. Kane et al. (1998) studied the effect of a family-planning multimedia campaign in Mali. Greater exposure to the campaign was associated with greater knowledge of contraceptives, more use of contraceptives, and more positive attitudes regarding family planning. Gilmartin (1994) examined the effect of an educational program on myths about rape. The program was more successful with women than with men, as men were less likely to change erroneous ideas as a result of the program. Phillips (1983) explored whether violence in the media encourages an increase in actual violence. His research indicates that in the time period after media presentation of heavyweight fights, homicide rates go up. Finally, another intriguing example of a quasi-experiment appears in the work of Harari, Harari, and White (1985), who looked at the likelihood of men trying to prevent a staged, attempted rape. Of particular interest was whether the males who discovered the staged rapes were by themselves or in a group of two or three males. As might be suspected, the men were less likely to attempt to stop a rape if they were by themselves. Still, the research showed that the majority of men who were by themselves did try to stop the staged attacks.

DEMONSTRATION EXPERIMENTS

We have been looking at how experimental procedures can be employed in real-world situations. As part of our discussion of field experimentation, we distinguished between true experiments and quasi-experiments. In quasi-experiments, researchers are unable to use random assignment procedures in creating experimental and control groups. True and quasi-experiments do not, however, exhaust all the types of research that have been termed experimental. We should like to add to our discussion one other variation. In what we will term DEMONSTRATION EXPERIMENTS, two of the criteria for a true experiment are not met. Demonstration experiments *involve neither group comparison nor random assignment of subjects*. Demonstrations, which may be conducted both in the laboratory and in the field, involve only the introduction of an experimental treatment in some group.

Despite the relative lack of control exercised by the researcher in conducting a demonstration, this variation of the experiment has produced some of the most compelling findings in the social sciences. Stanley Milgram's (1963) study of obedience and authority is an outstanding example of the power of the demonstration to produce dramatic results. Chapter 5 noted Milgram's interest in finding out the effects of authority on the willingness of people to administer punishments to others. Subjects who participated in Milgram's demonstration were told that the object of the research was to better understand how people learn. At the outset, each subject was individually introduced to another person who, it was explained, was simply another volunteer. This second person was a confederate of Milgram's. The real subject was assigned the role of teacher, and Milgram's confederate took the role of student. They were to occupy separate rooms, communicating by use of microphones. The subject taught his student, then tested him. For each wrong answer, the student was to be punished by his teacher. The teacher punished by administering electric shocks, each one stronger than the preceding one. The teacher could only press the shock button, not control the voltage. Milgram stayed in the control room with the teacher.

The procedure was a deception. Milgram's confederate, the student, did not receive any shocks. As the voltage levels began to increase, however, Milgram did turn on a tape recording of a man indicating various degrees of pain, from slight involuntary pained sounds at the beginning to rather lengthy moans as the voltage increased with a succession of "planned" incorrect answers. As the moans became louder and more frequent, and the voltage indicator showed the shocks to be increasingly close to the "extremely dangerous" point, the naive subject would turn to Milgram and show concern, often indicating that he no longer wished to go on with the experiment. Each time, Milgram, who was dressed in an authoritative white lab coat, would simply express his wish for the subject to continue. In each replication of the procedure, well more than 50 percent of the subjects carried the experiment through to the end, administering what they believed to be extremely dangerous shocks to the learner.

An attempt to follow up on the Milgram research on authority is in the work of Brief et al. (1995). They analyzed whether race made a difference if it was suggested as a standard for evaluation in the hiring process by a hypothetical executive high up in an organization. Their experiment compared groups who were encouraged to use race in the selection process with a group that was not encouraged to do so. Brief et al. concluded that the results show the effect of authority much in the same way as Milgram's original research.[6]

Milgram's demonstration experiment suggests that in some situations people are capable of rather extraordinary behavior. Although most of us, if questioned, would say that we would never inflict that kind of pain on another human being, Milgram shows the power of authority in dictating our acts. Despite the nature and possible importance of Milgram's findings for understanding, say, the behavior of soldiers at war, many have questioned the ethical implications of this kind of demonstration.

On the methodological side, the Milgram example can be contrasted with true and quasi-experiments. In these two designs, we find at least two clear comparison groups that experience the experimental treatment differently. Such group comparisons are important because

they help the researcher to pinpoint more precisely the extent of the subjects' change in some behavior or attitude following an experimental treatment. In the case of Milgram's demonstration, people certainly experience an experimental treatment. However, there are no group comparisons to be made in terms of the intensity of treatment given. If there are any differences in the intensity of treatment received, they are controlled by the subject rather than the researcher. The treatment continues, in effect, as long as the subject is willing to continue in the experiment. The demonstration and, therefore, the experimental treatment end when the subject decides he or she will no longer administer shocks to another person. The type of experimental research done by Milgram clearly "demonstrates," highlights, or illustrates certain features, or aspects, of human behavior (the willingness of persons to obey authority) and is highly informative on that level. The demonstration is, however, to be particularly distinguished from the true experiment in the following ways:

- No clear comparison groups that experience different amounts, or intensities, of the same experimental treatment.
- By definition, therefore, there is no random assignment of people to comparison groups. There is no control group.
- There is no clear timing to the experimental treatment because it continues as long as the experiment itself continues.

These procedural or structural characteristics of the demonstration tell us something very important: It cannot be the goal of the demonstration to show causal relations between variables. Causality between variables may be strongly implied by the outcome of demonstrations like Milgram's, but given the structural conditions just outlined, causality cannot be as firmly established as is possible in a true experiment.

A FINAL WORD

A basic criterion used by social scientists in evaluating their methodologies is whether they can assert causal relations between variables. The

---

[6] Note, however, that their research is not an example of a demonstration because they used comparison groups.

certainty of social scientists' claims to causality rests in turn on how successfully they have been able to control those features of the world that could threaten or destroy the causal relationship that they claim exists. The experiment is the most powerful procedure available to us in achieving this control. We may use the true experiment as a baseline against which our other methods may be evaluated. We could rank order our various methods in terms of the amount of control given up in their use.

The matter will not be resolved with such a simple ranking of techniques, however. Social scientists will inevitably have to attach to any of their findings, produced through whatever method, the silent warning that these findings are true "all other things being equal." In short, they must learn to adopt a certain modesty about their research because they must live with the fact that in their investigation of the social world all other things will never really be equal.

Indeed, this chapter on experimentation should help you to appreciate the enormous complexity of the social world. We have seen that the power of the experiment goes furthest in making all other things equal. At the same time, we are forced to acknowledge that even in the most carefully controlled laboratory experiment, we cannot keep potentially contaminating factors out of our findings. No matter how elegantly we achieve an internal consistency in our methods, any methodology is, by its very existence, potentially reactive or biasing.

We should also note again the delicate tension existing between control over extraneous factors in our work and naturalism. As we achieve greater levels of control and as we reduce the possibility of variables unknown to us intruding into our findings, we simultaneously create situations that resemble less and less the social situations in which people normally act. As we strive for naturalism, however, "all other things" become more and more unequal. We are caught in a kind of double bind. We want to strengthen our faith in any causal assertions we make. At the same time, we must be concerned that the variables operating causally in contrived experimental situations may not operate causally as actors carry out their normal daily lives.

SUMMARY

Scientific experimentation is distinguished from everyday manipulation and testing of the environment because researchers create rigorous safeguards to ensure the correctness of the causal relationships suggested by their findings. The most important of these safeguards is to control for, or to rule out, all those factors other than the experimental treatment (independent variable) as influences on the outcome (dependent variable). To accomplish this, experimenters require carefully controlled conditions that are usually present only in the laboratory. In a true experiment, results are achieved through comparison of at least two groups to which subjects have been assigned randomly. The researcher alters the environment for one group (the experimental group) and does not expose the other (the control group) to the test variable. Subsequently, any differences in test scores, behavior, or other measures of the dependent variable may be attributed to the experimental treatment.

The true experiment, if properly conducted, satisfies the minimum criteria for causality, in that independent and dependent variables are shown to be associated, the former precedes the latter in time, and this relationship cannot be explained away by the introduction of other, extraneous variables. However, threats to the validity of experimental research also threaten its ability to establish causal connections among variables. Subjects may react to uncontrolled internal and external stimuli or the experience of being studied. Moreover, unless they are careful, researchers may reveal enough of the rationale behind the experiment, or their own expectations for its outcome, to bias the results. Double-blind experimentation and variations on the classic experimental procedure such as the Solomon Four-Group Design are attempts to improve validity and control.

For some research problems and populations, laboratory experimentation is not feasible, and experiments in the field are possible. Some of these satisfy all the prerequisites for true experiments and many have valuable applications in the selection of appropriate social policies.

However, just as in the laboratory, there are dangers of bias. Quasi-field experiments meet the same requirements, except that people are not randomly assigned to groups. These experiments are useful for the researcher because it is often disruptive to enter a natural setting and create new groups artificially. Hence, the investigator looks for groups and situations already existing in the real world that satisfy experimental conditions. Demonstration experiments are contrasted with true and quasi-experiments in that demonstrations do not contain two clear groups for purposes of comparison. Thus, they cannot establish causality. Nonetheless, they may serve to highlight or illustrate significant patterns of human behavior.

The major limitation of laboratory experiments is that the conditions so carefully controlled for the purpose of establishing causality may be so atypical or artificial that it becomes difficult to generalize from them to the outside world. Field experiments of various kinds have become increasingly popular precisely because of their greater potential for generalizability. In all kinds of experimentation, however, manipulation of subjects' behavior is a necessity, and in most, it is an important part of the research design not to reveal critical details about the study. We must carefully consider the ethics of such deception. Experimentation has aided researchers in pursuit of a human science, but it must also be a humane science.

KEY TERMS

causal connection
control group
demonstration experiment
dependent variable
double-blind experiment
expectancy effect
experiment mortality
experimental group
experimental research
external validity
field experimentation
Hawthorne effect
independent variable
internal validity
measurement decay

modeling effect
posttest
pretest
quasi-experiment
random assignment
self-selected subject
stimulus
subject mortality
test variable

EXERCISES

1. Develop a research topic that could be explored both by a laboratory experiment and a field experiment. How would the research be carried out by both strategies? What are the advantages and disadvantages to doing the research in each way?

2. A long-standing theoretical idea in social psychology is that frustration leads to aggression. Describe the elements of a true laboratory experiment that could be employed to test this relationship. What would be the experimental treatment in your study? How would you measure the independent and dependent variables? How many groups would you study, and why?

3. In many studies, including the experiment on test anxiety described in this chapter, experimenters deceive their subjects. What deceptions did McIntyre et al. (2005) employ? In your opinion, were they justified or not? In the case of Milgram's (1963) experiment on obedience, the deceptions were more serious and potentially harmful; subjects were led to believe that they were administering painful shocks to others. What is your position on the ethicality of experiments like Milgram's? Does it matter how serious the deceptions are?

4. An argument in this chapter has been that in the use of any social science methodology there is a continual tension between control, on the one hand, and naturalism, on the other. Briefly answer the following in terms of this tension:

   a. Describe how maximum control is achieved through the use of experimental procedures.

   b. Make plain the relationship between control and establishing causality between variables.

   c. Indicate why experimental control is achieved at the expense of external validity.

   d. Discuss briefly the value of the *field experiment* in terms of your answers to a, b, and c.

5. A criticism sometimes raised regarding experimental research is that the control group is deprived of something positive that the experimental group receives. Give examples of research situations where this is true and examples where it isn't the case. What can be done to correct the situations where there is a problem?

SUGGESTED READINGS

Readings about the Method

Bickman, Leonard, ed. 2000. *Validity and Social Experimentation*. Thousand Oaks, CA: Sage.

Leading social research methodologists and evaluators address issues of validity, research design, and social experimentation.

Blass, Thomas, ed. 1999. *Obedience to Authority: Current Perspectives on the Milgram Paradigm*. Mahwah, NJ: Lawrence Erlbaum.

A careful analysis of the social significance of Milgram's famous obedience experiments.

Campbell, Donald T., and Julian C. Stanley. 1963/2005. *Experimental and Quasi-experimental Designs for Research*. Boston: Houghton-Mifflin.

In their much-cited book, Campbell and Stanley exhaustively describe the various designs typically used in experimental research and the strengths and limitations of each research design. Although some of the discussion is highly sophisticated, the beginning student should have no trouble following their description of threats to internal and external validity in experimentation.

Lemov, Rebecca. 2005. *World as Laboratory: Experiments with Mice, Mazes, and Men*. New York: Hill and Wang.

The author is an historian and anthropologist whose topic is "'human engineering,' the idea that behavior can be modified through manipulation of the surrounding environment." She views experimentation as the result of an impulse for scientific explanation and control.

Slater, Lauren. 2005. *Opening Skinner's Box: Great Psychological Experiments of the Twentieth Century*. New York: W. W. Norton.

Slater's work is a lively analysis of several famous studies discussed in this text, including Milgram's experiments regarding obedience to authority, Rosenhan's "pseudopatient" study, and Festinger's analysis of cognitive dissonance in a flying-saucer cult.

Readings Illustrating the Method

Abelson, Robert P., et al. 2004. *Experiments with People*. Mahwah, NJ: Lawrence Erlbaum.

This book examines the most important discoveries in social psychology over a forty-year period.

Finckenauer, James O., and Patricia Gavin. 1999. *Scared Straight: The Panacea Phenomenon Revisited*. Prospect Heights, IL: Waveland Press.

The authors evaluate the effect of the Scared Straight program. They discuss the many difficulties in forming experimental and control groups, as well as problems in achieving other requirements of experimental research.

Milgram, Stanley. 1974/2004. *Obedience to Authority: An Experimental View*. New York: Harper.

This original research is a hallmark of twentieth-century social science. Although its findings are shocking and actually changed the way many people view human nature, it is difficult to read in today's environment without considering the ethical critique that Milgram's work helped to inspire.

Roethlisberger, Fritz J., and William J. Dickson. 1939. *Management and the Worker*. Cambridge, MA: Harvard University Press.

This is the original report of the Hawthorne experiments on worker productivity. More recently, a renewed and lively debate has surfaced concerning the validity of the authors' findings. See H. M. Parsons, "What Happened at Hawthorne?" Science 183 (1974): 922–932; and American Sociological Review 43, no. 5 (1978); 44, no. 5 (1979): 995–1005.

Social Psychology Network. 2006. http://www.socialpsychology.org/expts.htm.

This Web site at Wesleyan University contains ninety-five online experiments in which you may participate.

Wextor. 2006.

Wextor is a Web-based tool that lets you quickly design and visualize laboratory experiments and Web-based experiments in a guided step-by-step process. It even delivers a print-ready display of your experimental design. The Web site at the Psychology Institute of the University of Zurich, Switzerland, is http://psych-wextor.unizh.ch/wextor/en/.

REFERENCES

Brannigan, Augustine. 2004. *The Rise and Fall of Social Psychology*. New Brunswick, NJ: Transaction.

Brief, Arthur P., et al. 1995. "Releasing the Beast: A Study of Compliance with Orders to Use Race as a Selection Criterion." *Journal of Social Issues* 51:177–193.

Campbell, Donald T., and Julian C. Stanley. 1963/2005. *Experimental and Quasi-experimental Designs for Research*. Boston: Houghton-Mifflin.

Festinger, Leon. 1971. "Laboratory Experiments." In *Research Methods: Issues and Insights*, 325–330. Billy J. Franklin and Harold W. Osborne, eds. Belmont, CA: Wadsworth.

Garrity, Kimberly, and Douglas Degelman. 1990. "Effect of Server Introduction on Restaurant Tipping." *Journal of Applied Social Psychology* 20:168–172.

Gilmartin, Pat. 1994. "Gender Differences in College Students' Perceptions about Rape: The Results of a Quasi-Experimental Research Design." *Free Inquiry in Creative Sociology* 22:3–12.

Harari, Herbert, Oren Harari, and R. V. White. 1985. "The Reaction to Rape by American Bystanders." *Journal of Social Psychology* 125:653–658.

Kane, Thomas T., et al. 1998. "The Impact of a Family Planning Multimedia Campaign in Bamako, Mali." *Studies in Family Planning* 29:309–323.

Leske, Jane S. 1996. "Intraoperative Progress Reports Decrease Family Members' Anxiety." *AORN Journal* 64:424–435.

McClanahan, Barbara S. 1993. "The Influence of an Undergraduate Wellness Class on Student Lifestyle Behaviors: A Comparison of a Cognitive-Based Course and an Activity-Based Course." *Wellness Perspectives* 9:33–47.

McIntyre, Rusty B., et al. 2005. "A Social Impact Trend in the Effects of Role Models on Alleviating Women's Mathematics Stereotype Threat." *Current Research in Social Psychology* 10 (9): 116–136.

Milgram, Stanley. 1963. "Behavioral Study of Obedience." *Journal of Abnormal and Social Psychology* 67:371–378.

Phillips, David. 1983. "The Impact of Mass Media Violence on U.S. Homicides." *American Sociological Review* 48:560–568.

Pomeroy, Elizabeth C., Risa Kiam, and Diane L. Green. 2000. "Reducing Depression, Anxiety, and Trauma of Male Inmates: An HIV/AIDS Psychoeducational Group Intervention." *Social Work Research* 24:156–168.

Roethlisberger, Fritz J., and William J. Dickson. 1939. *Management and the Worker*. Cambridge, MA: Harvard University Press.

CONTENT ANALYSIS

13

INTRODUCTION

Content analysis is a systematic attempt to examine some form of verbal or image communication such as newspapers, diaries, letters, speeches, movies, or television shows. Usually this communication already exists, and the researcher wants to discover its implications for the study of human behavior. Content analysis can be either inductive or deductive theoretically, but it is primarily quantitative because the examination of communication usually occurs through counting its content. Like other quantitative techniques, the most creative part of the method is concentrated toward the early stages of research design, when the categories to be used for counting have to be defined. In developing their ingenious data collection tools, practitioners of content analysis demonstrate their research imagination.

The analysis of communication content has a long tradition in the social sciences. It has revealed significant information about the values of both communicators and their audiences. This chapter summarizes the major elements of this methodology, offers some examples of its application, and discusses some of the reliability and validity issues that arise for the investigators who use it.

Consider the following example from the work of Simon Davis (1990), who analyzed personal advertisements to see what motivates mate selection. Do men and women differ in the factors seen as important in choosing a partner? Davis pursued this question by looking at the "personals" section in a major daily newspaper. The ads were coded using categories such as attractiveness, physical appeal, sexual interest, picture request, professional occupation, employment, financial status, educational attainment, intelligence, honesty, humor, commitment, and emotional expressiveness. Men and women were compared on the basis of what categories they emphasized in their advertisements. The sex differences revealed in the personal ads showed that men were more likely than women to emphasize physical appearance and attractiveness. Women were more likely than men to emphasize factors involving occupational and financial success. Accordingly, Davis in the title of his research article identified women as "sex objects" and men as "success objects." A conclusion to be drawn from this research is that sexual stereotypes are still alive and well!

Of interest to us methodologically is how Davis went about his research. He did not interview men and women about their attitudes toward the opposite sex. He did not arrange a laboratory study that might reveal how men and women differ in their reactions to some manipulation of an experimental treatment. Furthermore, he did not observe men and women in some social setting to reach a conclusion concerning sex stereotypical behavior. Rather, he pursued his research in an *unobtrusive* manner that is less likely to change the behavior or

attitudes one is interested in exploring. No discernible Hawthorne effect is involved in Davis's work.[1]

AN OVERVIEW OF THE METHOD

Let us look more closely at the process of doing content analysis. Authorities through the years (Holsti, 1969; Berelson, 1971; Weber, 1990; Krippendorf, 2003; Riffe, Lacy, and Fico, 2005) have been consistent in emphasizing that the technique is designed to be objective, that it is systematic and quantitative, and that is considers both manifest and latent content of communication. We will be discussing each of these issues in turn.

Objective Analysis

Other chapters have established that within the social sciences paradigm objectivity is an important criterion in social investigation. Researchers who use content analysis intend to be objective in evaluating the content of communications. How does the ideal of objectivity apply to their work? We can best illustrate the need for objectivity through an example.

Were we to hear people comment about the liberal stance of the editorials in a particular newspaper, we might ask them questions to determine the validity of their assertion. What exactly is their definition of liberalism? Have they read all the editorials in the particular paper or has their reading been selective? How long have they been reading the newspaper? To what other newspapers is this one being implicitly compared? We ask these questions because we know that people may interpret the content of any communication in terms of their own particular needs, interests, biases, or ideologies. In short, our questions might be directed at uncovering the rules that have been used in categorizing and making evaluations of the contents of a particular written document. The essence of objective, scientific content analysis is that researchers make absolutely explicit the rules

---

[1] The process of being researched may change the behavior of the people being studied. See Chapter 12 for a discussion of the Hawthorne effect.

they have used in classifying the content of any communication.

We need not agree with the categories that researchers develop for analyzing the content of materials. Nor need we agree with procedures for placing a unit of communication in one or another category. However, as long as the rules of the game have been spelled out, we can evaluate how conclusions were reached, and we can expect that any researchers who follow those rules, regardless of their own personal values, beliefs, or interests, will document the content of materials in exactly the same way. Content analysis therefore allows researchers using the same procedures to replicate easily the findings of earlier research.

Systematic Analysis

Another characteristic of content analysis is that it is systematic. The idea of systematic procedure adds something to our characterization of objectivity. Suppose we want to compare the editorials in several newspapers. To make a valid comparison, we must systematically use the same procedures in documenting the content of each of the separate papers. In comparing the editorial content of the *New York Times*, the *Chicago Tribune*, the *San Francisco Chronicle*, a small local newspaper, and your college newspaper, it would be contrary to systematic procedure to employ different criteria for each. The variation in the newspapers' size and in the nature of the audience they serve should not matter. When we commit ourselves to a particular strategy for evaluating data, we minimize considerably any personal biases that might intrude in that evaluation. It is by applying criteria systematically to all cases studied that we avoid collecting only data conforming to our theoretical ideas.

Quantitative and Qualitative Analysis

Most content analysis involves quantitative description of human communications. It often employs one of several SYSTEMS OF ENUMERATION for *gauging frequency and intensity*. Perhaps the most common use of content analysis is to detail the *frequency* with which symbols or themes appear in a written document or series of pictures. However, as we will see, those who conduct content analysis are also interested in assessing the *intensity* of particular variables. If we wanted to compare the attitudes of two candidates for office with regard to their position on tax cuts, we could do a content analysis of their speeches. We might choose at the outset to count the number of times each candidate makes positive or negative comments about tax reduction. This relatively simple system of enumeration might be misleading, however. Beyond counting the number of references made, we could devise some set of rules to measure *positive* and *negative* assertions. We can imagine that once the researcher chooses to go beyond measuring simple frequencies, the task of setting up adequate categories becomes more difficult. This is an issue to which we will return.

There are both benefits and risks in the quantification of materials demanded by content analysis. On the positive side, the use of rigorous categories yielding quantitative results allows the researcher to characterize a large volume of materials efficiently. Because the meaning of numbers produced will be clear to any reader, there is no danger that a reader will make impressionistic judgments about the content under investigation. A clear quantitative presentation of the content of materials has another advantage: It can often alert us to themes in those materials that we would otherwise miss.

Nevertheless, as we study content analysis, let us keep in mind that we risk missing the overall sense of a body of communications if we do no more than offer quantitative summaries of their content. Any communication evokes a feeling, an overall impression, or a sense that cannot be captured simply by counting the frequency with which certain items appear. We might say that any communication is going to be more that the sum of its parts. Therefore, we would claim, as we have done elsewhere in this book, that qualitative and quantitative techniques must be used in conjunction with one another.[2]

---

[2] See Mayring (2000) for examples of qualitative content analysis.

Manifest and Latent Content

Content analysis deals most effectively with the
MANIFEST CONTENT of communication, that
is, with *what explicitly appears in a text*. As a
systematic procedure, content analysis is highly
reliable when researchers restrict their activity to
documenting the elements, symbols, or themes
that may be enumerated in a communication.
By contrast, the LATENT CONTENT, or *meanings
implied by the written content that do not actually appear in the text*, is more difficult to discern.
If a group of researchers is assigned the task of
"reading between the lines" of a book, continually interpreting the latent impression given off
by the manifest, written symbols, there are likely
to be numerous disagreements among them. It is
easier, and more reliable, to count specific negative adjectives applied to members of an ethnic
group in a novel than it is to definitively characterize a variety of situations described in the
novel as being examples of prejudiced behavior.
To use content analysis to gauge the latent, or
implied meaning, of a communication requires
that researchers be trained extensively and that
pretesting be done to ensure that they are making their judgments from common premises.
To maximize reliability, interpretation of data
should not be made as communication content
is being enumerated, but at a later stage when
the investigators can focus all of their attention
on assessing what patterns appear in the data.

How then does our initial example (Davis,
1990) measure up regarding these characteristics of content analysis? We know the rules
that were applied in his analysis of personal
advertisements. Attributes such as attractiveness, educational attainment, physical appeal,
and employment were explicitly stated and
used. This fulfills the objectivity criterion. We
conclude from Davis's article that his coding
was done consistently on all the advertisements
included in his sample. Therefore, his study was
systematic. It also appears that his study was
a quantitative analysis of the manifest content
of the personal ads. Here, he provided us with
data on the frequencies with which men and
women emphasized different desired attributes.
In this case, the ads were not lengthy or complex enough to be a fruitful source of latent
communication.

APPLICATIONS OF CONTENT ANALYSIS

Now that we have an overview of content analysis, let us examine more examples of research
employing it. Note the data sources used and
the different questions and research goals that
frequently motivate the analyses.

Social scientists have examined the content of
an enormous variety of materials. Newspapers,
periodicals, personal documents such as letters
and diaries, novels, recorded speeches, children's books, songs, billboards, sociology textbooks, obituary notices, medical records, suicide notes, e-mail and voice mail messages, and
Web pages are among the communications that
have been studied. In addition, researchers have
analyzed the content of such diverse media as
inscriptions and images on works of art and television and radio programming.

Whether the data sources are written, visual,
or verbal (or some combination), nearly all
communications research has been guided by
some aspect of the question, "Who says what
to whom and with what effect?" The concern of
the researcher may be to analyze the content of
the message to understand the motives, goals,
intentions, or values of its author or source. Or,
the investigation may center on the communication itself to determine how the content sheds
light on larger social phenomena. Finally, the
goal may be to assess the effects of communications on particular audiences. We can order our
discussion of some exemplary content analysis
studies in terms of these research goals.

Inferences to the Source
of Communications

Often the concern of content analysis is to infer
from themes uncovered in a communication
the characteristics of the people or institutions
responsible for creating it. These studies are
based on the apparently reasonable assumption
that attitudes, values, and beliefs are revealed
in symbolic communications. On the basis of
this assumption, researchers have analyzed a

A Content Analysis of Video Games

(Drawn from television coverage, WCVB, Boston)

Thompson and Haninger (2001) analyzed the depiction of violence, sex, alcohol, tobacco, and drugs in fifty-five E-rated video games sold for one or more of the four leading home gaming consoles: Dreamcast, Nintendo, PlayStation, and PlayStation 2. The researchers initiated the study because there had been no comprehensive examination of the content of video games available to children despite their popularity as a form of entertainment. It is estimated that 70 percent of youths under 19 have at least one game console in their home and 30 percent have at least one game in their bedrooms.

The ratings on computer games are supposed to make it easy for parents to keep inappropriate content away from their children. The "E" rating is similar to the "G" rating for movies, but the researchers found that "many E-rated games do involve violence, killing, and the use of weapons in the course of normal play. No games provide messages about not using violence, and some reward or require violence and the destruction of objects." Sixty-four percent of the games involved intentional violence that lasted about a third of the total time the user played the game. In 60 percent of the games, the player had to injure other characters in order to advance. "Action and shooting games led to the largest numbers of deaths from violent acts, and we found a significant correlation between the proportion of violent game play and the number of deaths per minute of play," the authors wrote.

The power of content analysis is revealed in this study because the findings may be immediately useful in a social policy context. On the basis of their results, the authors recommended that parents should be more aware of the genre of games their children are using and should participate actively in selecting them. The researchers also suggested that pediatricians should ask children about their exposure to video games, then tell parents about it. They recommended that the medical and public health communities play an active role in informing parents about the content in video games.

variety of documents ranging from diaries to public speeches and suicide notes.

In one classic study (Paige, 1966), the personal letters of widow Jenny Cosgrove were examined to better understand certain features of personality structure. Although clinicians were able to provide insight into specific features of the series of letters written by Jenny to her son, the statistical data produced through content analysis revealed patterns that even a careful reading missed. The analysis, done with a computer, helped to uncover important themes centering on Jenny's conception of herself, her son, her job, and her attitudes toward death. In similar studies, suicide notes have been examined to understand the consciousness of people willing to take their own lives. Ogilvie, Stone, and Schneidman (1966) were able to develop a set of categories for analysis sophisticated enough to permit them to distinguish actual from simulated suicide notes. Later, Bourgoin (1995) studied prison suicide through notes left behind and related his findings to Emile Durkheim's theory of suicide.

Patterson (1994) carried out a content analysis of presidential campaign stories in major newspapers and magazines to determine how the leading candidates were characterized. This example suggests another strength of content analysis. It provides the opportunity to study individuals or groups generally inaccessible to social scientists. Elites are one such group.

Observing the daily activities of many powerful individuals or even to interview them personally is nearly impossible. Content analysis partially remedies this problem because we can analyze only the communications that people consider to be fit for public consumption.

There is something else to consider in inferring the intentions or values of communication sources. A number of studies have been directed at understanding how the political, economic, or social interests of the originating person or institution affect the content and accuracy of communications. One illustration is the content analysis conducted by Gordy and Pritchard(1995) that examined social studies textbooks to see how American slavery and Reconstruction issues were presented at the fifth-grade level. The authors concluded that the students receive only a partial and sanitized version of this important part of American history because the perspective of people of color is generally omitted from these texts. Another interesting illustration of the accuracy issue is Oliver's (1994) content analysis of "reality-based" police shows to see how crime, race, and aggression were presented. One finding was that violent crime was overrepresented in the programs. In a similar vein, Wysocki and Harrison (1991) explored the extent to which popular magazines geared toward children and adolescents adequately informed young people about AIDS. Their conclusion was that these magazines were not presenting enough factual information about the disease.

Many communications have been analyzed to demonstrate that the coverage of events, phenomena, or social processes may be seen as a function of personal or institutionally based ideological interests. A good illustration of this genre can be seen in a study of how the intifada and the Gulf War were covered on U.S. and Israeli television. Liebes (1992) concludes from a content analysis of television news coverage that objectivity and balance were compromised by the journalist's role as a citizen with a particular position regarding the conflict. The "other side" became demonized, and the faults of the country with which a journalist identified were downplayed. The role of ideology is also seen in a study of the connection between economic conditions and media treatment of criminals and crime (Barlow, Barlow, and Chiricos, 1995). The researchers found that when the economy is weak (e.g., if unemployment is high) the media images of criminals and crime worsen. When economic conditions are more favorable, criminal behavior is not presented so negatively. Why is this the case? Barlow et al. maintain that the reason is ideological. They argue that the media presents crime in a manner that supports powerful institutions in our capitalist society. Related to this argument is the research by Welch and Fenwick (1997) that, once again on the basis of content analysis, shows how the media rely on law enforcement officials to define crime and thereby support the dominant ideology. These are interesting works because they begin to show how institutional, economic, or political factors can affect the production and distribution of information in society.

Inferences to Populations: Communication Content and Social Values

We may distinguish another type of content analysis, in which the purpose is to infer from the data the values of the populations or audiences reached by communications. These investigations trace the connection between media content and general social values.

A classic study in this vein is *Achieving Society* (McClelland, 1967/1985) that examines the relationship between a society's rate of economic development and the emphasis it places on achievement values. By correlating achievement themes in 1,300 children's stories from nearly every country in the world with such indicators of economic growth as increases in coal and electricity consumption, the author was able to show a greater concern with achievement values in societies with higher rates of economic growth. McClelland also demonstrated that a number of additional communications sources may be used to study value changes historically. He used such literary forms as poems, epigrams, legends, tales, and the writings of major authors to measure achievement motivation in societies extending back to ancient Greece.

Analyzing *The Daily Show* II

Students conducted a content analysis of *The Daily Show* (*TDS*) with Jon Stewart, a leading television source for mock news (that is, news that parodies both the form and content of traditional news). The analysis was inspired by recent findings that many Americans – particularly younger ones – use political comedy shows such as *TDS* to get political news, and that those who watch *TDS* appear to be better informed than those who do not, all else being equal.

The analysis included 222 stories from the 52 new episodes that ran from January 4 to April 19, 2005. Here are some of the key findings:

1. More than half of the stories (56%) addressed political topics. Also, around half (53%) included at least one joke targeting a political figure; 35% included a sound bite from at least one such figure. The show targeted a wide range of politicians. Not surprisingly, however, President George W. Bush was the most frequent joke target (13% of all stories included humor at his expense) as well as the most frequent sound bite source.

2. Of the stories that addressed politics, half included a public policy theme. One could take this finding as evidence that *TDS* offers a substantial amount of issue-based coverage. The war in Iraq and Social Security were among the most frequently covered issues.

3. Almost half of all stories (46%) covered international news in some way. Again, the show's coverage of what it called "Mess-O-Potamia" led the way. Many of the world news stories came as part of a regular feature, the International Pamphlet.

4. Fifteen percent of the stories covered topics having to do with the news media. Virtually identical percentages of stories targeted the news media with jokes and included sound bites from news media figures.

5. Around one in four stories addressed celebrity/entertainment news; a similar proportion targeted celebrities or entertainers with jokes. Only one in ten, however, included sound bites from celebrities or entertainers.

6. *The Daily Show* relied heavily on the traditional news media for video footage, with 41 percent of all stories including clips from network or cable news shows.

7. Half of the 52 guests could be labeled "serious" guests: that is, they were politicians, current or former government officials, news media figures, or authors of books about public affairs topics.

Adapted from Brewer (2005).

Prevalent social values have also been explored in more recent studies using content analysis concerning violence (Wurtzel and Lometti, 1984); sexual explicitness in the media (Bogaert, Turkovich, and Hafe, 1993); how poverty is perceived (Pritchard, 1993); women's views of presidential candidates (Danowski and Lind, 2001); the value placed on consumption of alcohol (Pendleton, Smith, and Roberts, 1991); and how cigars have made a comeback in popularity (Wenger, Malone, and Bero, 2001).

The concern of this genre of content analysis need not be to document society-wide values; specific groups or subcultures may also be examined. For example, many studies have been conducted to discover how men and women are perceived and valued at different stages of the life cycle. Evans et al. (1991) analyzed teen magazines, including *Sassy*, *Seventeen*, and *Young Miss*, to uncover gender-related messages in adolescent life. A major pattern uncovered was a focus on how women can physically attract men. A later analysis of *Seventeen* magazine by Schlenker, Caron, and Halterman (1998) indicates little change in values in response to the feminist movement during the period 1945–1995. In a similar vein, a study of the main characters in magazine fiction designed for female readers (Peirce, 1997) identifies women's problems primarily as romantic. Even college textbooks in courses on human sexuality and marriage and the family continue traditional sex role messages for women, according to the research of Low and Sherrard (1999).

The content analyses relating to men also suggest a continuation of stereotypical sex role expectations. Evans and Kimberly (2000) explore this issue in their well-titled article "No Sissy Boys Here." They found that books used in elementary schools portray males as competitive and aggressive. Craig (1992) concluded that television commercials tended to present men in the traditional, dominant role. Finally, Zimmerman, Holm, and Haddock (2001) describe a similar trend in their content analysis of self-help literature, where most of the best-selling books were found to encourage men and women to conform to traditional gender socialization.

Another group addressed in content analysis research has been the African American population. Martin Gilens (1996) explored American perceptions of the connection between race and poverty as seen through the media of television and news magazines. These media, according to Gilens's analysis, present the poor as considerably more "black" than is the case in reality. For example, at the time of the study, 29 percent of the poor in America were African Americans, whereas 62 percent of the poor were black in news magazine pictures. This research shows how the negative stereotype of black poverty reflects the perception of the American population at large. To some extent, what Gilens found, namely, the exaggeration of how many blacks are poor, is a continuation of the negative way blacks have been portrayed historically in America. Mellinger (1992) analyzed postcards showing African Americans from 1893 to 1917 and concluded that the cards frequently presented them as the "other-as-beast." In other words, they were seen as inferior to whites both in intellectual and physical terms.

In the studies previously considered, the focus is less on the characteristics of those who produce communications than on how the themes contained in them reflect either comprehensive societal values or the values of specific segments of the population. We acknowledge that some considerable leaps of inference are demanded in these studies, which means that we must weigh very carefully the validity of the interpretations made. Can we know with any certainty that the content of postcards really does reflect the values of the larger culture or that the content of reality-based television programs reflects the ideals of a segment of people in society? The greater the number of independent sources showing essentially the same findings, the firmer will be our faith in any interpretive assertions made.

Evaluating the Effects of Communications

The research described to this point is concerned almost exclusively with the themes found within the materials studied. However, a significant body of research on the *effects* of communications considers the circumstances under which people are persuaded and whether they tend to avoid communications that run contrary to their preexisting attitudes. In effects-oriented research the specific analysis of content is only a part, albeit a significant one, of the total research effort.

Many examples of content analysis examine the effects of communications. Hong (1992) documented a nineteenth-century version of the "red scare," a successful negative stereotyping of anarchism that occurred in mainstream American magazines during the period 1880–1903. Crouch and Damphousse (1992) discovered a similarly effective campaign against satanism in major U.S. newspapers during the 1980s. In another study, Alperstein (1990) showed the latent effect of television advertising by measuring the degree to which the wording of the ads becomes part of our everyday language and verbal expression. Williams (1989) performed a content analysis of *TV Guide* that focused on how advertisements for television programs emphasize sex and violence. The author concluded that the more violence appeared in the ads, the more highly rated the programs.

One of the earliest studies designed to assess the effects of communications shows us the utility of combining content analysis with other methodological techniques. In Herbert Blumer's (1970) examination of the relationship between exposure to movies and people's conduct, a sample of people kept diaries in which they were asked to record their attitudes, feelings, reactions, sentiments, and values concerning the themes, characters, or behaviors in the movies they watched. Researchers analyzed the content of these diaries to determine how various types of people reacted to the medium. Blumer later conducted personal interviews with his subjects to establish still further the effects of the movies.

We are all familiar with the ongoing debate in the social sciences on whether violence depicted in the mass media causes people to display violence and aggression. The research evidence is mixed. After doing content analysis to measure the extent of violence portrayed in comic books and other media, Wertham (1996) indicated that a sample of children who had committed violent or criminal acts had more exposure to high-violence materials than a comparative sample of "normal" children. Other researchers, however, have suggested that violent and aggressive material is usually chosen by people who do not engage in such behavior. Most recently, the link between violence in the media and violent behavior has been affirmed by Villani (2001), who reviewed the relevant literature over a ten-year period.

In these studies, it is a major methodological problem to determine whether the communications actually *cause* certain behaviors or whether they simply reflect people's previously held attitudes, behaviors, or dispositions. Debate continues around the issue. In the late 1990s, for example, there were those who argued that news reports of shootings in high schools around the country were instrumental in pro-

voking additional copycat incidents (Volz, 1999). We can surmise that if there is any relationship between news reports of violence and further crime, it is not a simple one. Perhaps the issue turns on *how* such activity is presented in the news. The validity of this hunch could be tested by analyzing the content and style of news presentations in cities that experienced violence in schools and in those that did not. Such a historical study might help to clarify the relationship between media presentations and their effects on audiences.

PERFORMING CONTENT ANALYSIS

The general overview provided thus far cannot fully express the complexities of content analysis when actually applied to a research problem. The manner of its application will vary somewhat, depending on the topic for research. It is nonetheless possible to describe the types of decisions and judgments that need to be made in the process of any content analysis investigation. One way to do this is to consider how social scientists might plan and carry out a specific study. We will imagine, therefore, a group of researchers with a general interest in investigating changing women's roles in the United States. Their first task is to specify the research problem.

Specification of the Research Problem

Concerning the sex roles of men and women in American society over the past thirty years, we know that some studies (cited previously) suggest that attitudes have not changed much. However, let us assume that our researchers begin by asking: Has the women's movement had any effect in altering images and stereotypes of the female role? From that general question flow a number of other, more specific, questions. Have there been any changes in the kinds of activities thought proper for men and women? Have there been any changes in the kinds of occupations thought appropriate for men and women? Are females pictured in more egalitarian relationships with men today than they were in the past?

As the researchers continue to spell out these and similar questions, they begin to consider how their focus ought to be narrowed so that they can actually begin to collect data. Let us imagine they decide that one way to focus their problem would be to study changes in the kinds of gender images that children perceive. One rationale for such a choice might be that, if women's roles really change, there have to be corresponding basic alterations in the gender role socialization of children. The theoretical literature on socialization has convinced researchers that gender roles are learned and become deeply ingrained during childhood.

Once the problem has been specified theoretically to consider only the images and stereotypes taught to young children about female roles, the attention of the researchers logically turns to the kinds of data sources that can be used to assess any changes in the content of socialization over time. We can imagine several options. It would be possible to consider how males and females are portrayed to children in such mass media sources as television or movies. One could, for example, do a content analysis of such children's shows as *Sesame Street* or *Teletubbies* and compare them over time. After considering all the means by which they could study socialization changes, the researchers decide to restrict their data source to children's books for several good reasons. First, there is considerable precedent in the literature for using children's books to establish social trends (McClelland, 1967/1985). A second and more pragmatic reason is that children's books are easily accessible. The researchers might also decide that the use of children's books provides the opportunity for more rigorous comparative analysis than other data sources. If they choose to, they can compare books that are a particular length, they can limit their analysis to works of fiction, and so on. Having specified the problem to this point, the investigators must begin to think about how they will use the chosen data source to answer their research question:

Has the women's movement had any effect on the female stereotypes or images found in children's books?

We can see that there are many procedural decisions still to be made. The first of these is to determine just how the children's books will be sampled.

Sampling Items

The stated problem demands a research design that compares past and current books. At a minimum, two samples of books are required: one sample from before the beginning of the women's movement and another from contemporary books. Assuming it is historically accurate that the women's movement began in the mid-1960s, the researchers could choose to sample books published each year from about 1960 (four or five years before the emergence of the movement) to the present. If there have been any changes in sex role images, such a sampling design would allow the investigators to say more precisely just when these changes began to take place. If they have the money and staff to sample materials in this way, they might be in a position to make some elegant theoretical statements concerning the length of time before a movement begins to have any noticeable effect in changing the content of published materials. To simplify our analysis somewhat, however, we will assume that the researchers choose to compare two samples of books. One sample will be taken from books published in the three years immediately before the emergence of the women's movement. The second sample will be composed of books published during the past three years.

Even if the researchers opt for this relatively simple design, their sampling problems are not resolved. After all, there are literally thousands of children's books published each year. Sampling is, in the case of content analysis, nearly always a multistage process. Once researchers make some preliminary determination of the **UNIVERSE**, or *totality of materials applicable to their problem* (in our case, all children's books), they are still left with many more materials than are manageable. In most content analysis investigations it would be literally impossible to analyze all the items applicable to the problem. Our investigators might, therefore, restrict their attention to only those schoolbooks used in grades 1 and 2. If asked why, they could argue (1) that children are likely to become most intimately acquainted with the books they use in school and (2) that children in the early grades are at a formative age when sex role socialization will have its greatest impact.

If, after having made this decision, the researchers still feel that the universe is unmanageably large, they would likely consider analyzing only those books used in a particular area of the country, a single city, or perhaps even one school district. They must recognize, however, that as they restrict the universe of books, they also restrict the generalizability of their findings.[3]

Once the universe is clearly determined, the final items for analysis might be drawn in a number of ways. If the total number of items is small, they may all be included in the final study. Our researchers, however, decide that it would be unfeasible, given resources and staffing, to analyze more than 100 books, 50 in each of their two samples. It might be possible for them to construct their two samples by choosing the 100 books at random. Simple random sampling can be used, however, only if all the appropriate items that it is possible to include in the sample can be clearly identified.

Sometimes simple random sampling is not possible because one cannot identify all the elements of the universe or because such a sampling procedure does not meet the demands of the research problem. Our researchers might decide, for example, that all children's books do not have an equal influence because some are more widely read than others. Consequently, they would fashion a sampling procedure to put them in contact with those books likely to have greatest influence because they are the most widely circulated. Were they to make this decision, they might use judges or experts to help them determine the most useful books for their research problem. They could consult with a number of primary school teachers or publishing company representatives who would be asked to submit lists of the most frequently used books. If possible, this information could be supplemented with school records of books ordered. It might even be reasonable to tabulate the books most frequently checked out of school libraries. The wisest course might be to combine the procedures mentioned. However this is accomplished, we can assume that the researchers now have in hand the 100 books that will be the basis for their analysis.

At this point, the investigators must decide which aspects of gender image they wish to measure and how that measurement shall be done. Will they consider the images portrayed in each book as a whole? Will they code the images portrayed in particular stories within each book? Will they code the images presented in the books paragraph by paragraph? Sentence by sentence? Might it be possible, indeed, to code specific words (for example, adjectives) related to female images in the books?

Two decisions must be made at this juncture: (1) Which dimensions of female role image are going to be assessed? Which categories, in other words, should guide the coding of the data? (2) What exactly ought to be the UNIT OF ANALYSIS (specifically, *what will be generalized from*) in the study (words, sentences, paragraphs, stories, the book as a whole)? In any content analysis, these decisions must be made in terms of the research questions, hypotheses, and theoretical ideas guiding the study, as well as the peculiarities of the data source used. There are, however, some general methodological considerations that ought to guide both of these interrelated decisions. We will say a few words about units of analysis and then consider in greater detail the problems of category construction.

Choosing the Unit of Analysis

In our earlier discussion of the kinds of research conducted using content analysis, we saw that the *specific unit of content tabulated*, or the RECORDING UNIT, can vary considerably. In some studies, researchers will tabulate the simplest content unit constituting any communication – the *single word*. One way researchers

---

[3] This issue, and other key principles of sampling, are discussed in Chapter 6.

studying female role images could proceed would be by coding every adjective used to describe males and females in the books examined. They could create procedural rules for classifying each of the adjectives attached to gender. The choice of the single word, or symbol, as the unit of analysis has some advantages. The primary benefit is that coders must make relatively few judgments in classifying this recording unit and, in the usual case, make few inferences about its meaning. Instructions can be so explicit that virtually all decisions about proper coding are made ahead of time. Coders could be told, for example, that every time they see the adjective "aggressive" it is to be classified in category X. The researchers could even provide the coders with an exhaustive list of adjectives, with directions concerning the category into which each should be coded. As coders confront each adjective in the textual material, they simply consult this prepared coding list and are, therefore, relieved of any interpretive decisions. The use of this simplest unit thus has the advantage of increasing reliability.

However, the materials to be analyzed, the variables of interest to the researchers, the hypotheses to be tested, and the theories to be evaluated may make the single word an inappropriate unit of analysis. Researchers may need to work with more comprehensive units – such as the content of sentences, paragraphs, or chapters, or the entire item (a whole book, a whole film, a whole newspaper). Using any of these units, categories will be devised to tabulate the themes, types of people or characters, or types of behaviors represented.

As researchers move to the analysis of more comprehensive units with the idea of extracting specific themes from them, the coding task becomes more complicated. Unlike the situation in which coders can simply consult a list to determine exactly how a particular word ought to be categorized, the analysis of themes in sentences, paragraphs, or whole books cannot be achieved by reference to comprehensive coding rules; interpretive judgments are an integral part of these analyses.

Category Construction

The most critical step in content analysis is the construction of the categories that will direct the coding of the content. In the construction of categories, the researchers indicate just how they will classify the materials being investigated. If the categories are to be successful, they must bear a close relationship to the problem as originally stated. They must faithfully reflect the major theoretical concepts on which the study is based.

Procedurally, researchers normally begin to construct coding categories by exhaustively listing all aspects or dimensions of the phenomenon being investigated. In our research example, the types of behaviors, themes, ideas, or symbols on this preliminary, tentative listing might include power in interaction, personality characteristics, expressed occupational aspirations, leisure-time activities, sexual divisions of labor, types of children's play activities, the number of males and females appearing in the items, and the type of dress of male and female characters.

As the researchers continue to list the dimensions of gender role image, they will find it necessary to specify subdivisions within each broad category they propose. They could, for example, elaborate the interactional power dimension mentioned above by distinguishing whether females are pictured in subordinate, egalitarian, or superordinate power positions when in interaction with males. As the researchers continue to refine their categories, they will likely consider, at the same time, the procedural rules that will guide the classification of unit contents into one or another of the proposed categories. Coders might be provided rules of the following sort for classifying each instance of male/female power interaction:

1. Each time a female is pictured interacting with a male, classify the female as in a subordinate power position if she is asking the male for advice of any kind.

2. If the male and female are pictured as talking approximately the same amount and neither

Female Role Position	Pre-movement Books (N=50)		Current Books (N=50)	
Subordinate	Number of Cases	%	Number of Cases	%
Egalitarian	Number of Cases	%	Number of Cases	%
Superordinate	Number of Cases	%	Number of Cases	%
	Total	100 %	Total	100 %

Figure 13.1. Changing images of female/male power relations.

is giving advice to the other, classify this as an instance of an egalitarian role relationship.

3. If the male is asking the female for advice, classify this as an instance of the female in a superordinate power position.

Researchers also frequently find it useful to imagine just how their collected data will eventually be arranged in tabular form. If, in their final report, they are to have a section on "changing images of female/male power relations" (see Figure 13.1), and if the principles for constructing categories are well laid out and unambiguous, those responsible for coding content data will achieve a high degree of consistency or reliability.

Before finally committing themselves to particular coding categories, researchers will normally conduct a pretest. They will ask a number of people to code the same body of data independently. If they find little consistency in the classification of the data, they will have to rework the categories. Researchers typically find it useful to put coders through a short training program on the use of the categories. Coding reliability must be high if we are to have any faith in the accuracy of the final data tabulations.

It should be apparent that every single case of male/female interaction noted in the books studied should fit into one of the categories proposed. Categories are **EXHAUSTIVE** when *every specimen of data or every case under investigation will fit into at least one of the categories developed*. They must be reconstructed if certain types of data necessary for testing research hypotheses cannot be coded.

It is often difficult, in fact, to create categories that are completely exhaustive. Unexpected or one-of-a-kind units may turn up that do not

clearly fit into one of the categories developed at the outset of the study. In much the same way, the criterion of **MUTUAL EXCLUSIVITY**, *keeping categories pure and separate from one another*, is often harder to maintain in practice than to state in theory. To the extent that any symbolic communication will allow for a number of interpretations, it could potentially fit into more than one coding category. The safest assertion to make is that high reliability in any content analysis is dependent on the production of clear, rule-guided categories.

The fewer the number of decisions, interpretations, or judgments coders must make as they classify data, the greater will be the overall reliability of the study. This general rule has implications for the number of categories researchers may wish to use in their studies. The coding task will generally become more complicated as the number of categories increases. Theoretically, the number of categories that can be used in a study is limitless. In the example we have been using, the researchers simply classified male/female interactions into one of three power categories – female subordinate, female equal, female superordinate. They might decide, however, that it would be theoretically useful to know not only the power positions most frequently experienced by females but also the particular contexts of these relations. Are females shown more frequently in subordinate positions when in the work world than when engaged in leisure activities? In male/female interactions in leisure activities, are females more often subordinate in sports than in other games? They might, therefore, choose to elaborate their categories to include this context variable. By doing so, they will be able to make many more comparisons of different features of the data in their final analysis. In sum, as the number of categories used in a study increases, researchers provide themselves on the opportunity for more extensive analysis of their data, but they may do so at the expense of the accuracy or reliability of the data coded.

We have been assuming that researchers using content analysis are concerned only with tabulating how often or how frequently themes appear in a given communication. There are, however, occasions when researchers will consider it theoretically appropriate to determine as well the *intensity* or degree of a theme or variable in the communications studied. We will look at a brief example to illustrate how the decision to measure the intensity of variables in content analysis necessarily complicates the coding task.

Suppose our sex role researchers feel that an important theme for analysis in the children's books is females' expression of dissatisfaction with their expected roles. It then follows that one coding task will be to identify and tabulate each instance where a female is shown expressing dissatisfaction. Beyond that, however, the researchers want to know the intensity of the dissatisfaction females are shown to express. Once this decision is taken, the number of judgments that coders must make as they seek to classify the contents of a unit will at least double. The coder must first decide whether the theme of dissatisfaction is present. Once the theme is determined to be present, the coder must employ another set of rules to rate the degree of its intensity. Coders may be provided rules for placing instances of expressed dissatisfaction into ordinal categories (for example, high dissatisfaction, medium dissatisfaction, or low dissatisfaction).

Our example on the issue of intensity shows that content analysis need not be limited to the simple tabulation of word or theme frequencies. It is possible to develop more sophisticated measures but with a cost. As the number of categories and coding rules increases, the analysis of data becomes much more time consuming, the number of interpretive judgments we ask coders to make increases substantially, and the consequent decrease in coding reliability is possible.

When researchers have defined their problem, decided on their unit of analysis, created coding categories, and made explicit the rules for classifying data, they have completed the major technical steps for their investigation. By now, you may infer that the actual tabulation of data is likely to be laborious and tedious. A significant number of classification errors inevitably result simply because coding is often a fatiguing job. The problem of fatigue and boredom is greater, of course, with large samples of items for analysis. In cases where the number of items makes hand tabulation of data nearly impossible, researchers use computer programs designed explicitly for coding in content analysis.

COMPUTER-ASSISTED CONTENT ANALYSIS

We suggested earlier that as the unit of analysis becomes larger and more comprehensive, coders must make a greater number of interpretive judgments about the meaning of the content before a particular unit can be assigned to a category. Human beings can recognize meanings by reading complete phrases, sentences, or paragraphs in a text. As we read textual material, we do not split up a sentence or paragraph into its component parts. We do not separate out nouns, adjectives, and the like. Rather, we consider the communications read as a whole, as a single meaningful picture. Human beings are, in other words, capable of high levels of symbolic abstraction. In studies where researchers must make subtle decisions about thematic meaning in a communication, computers can be helpful but within certain limits.

Computers will, for example, perform with unerring accuracy any coding task in which the classification rules are unambiguous. This logic may be used to find the authorship of anonymous writings by looking at vocabulary or patterns of words, so long as these are specified by the researcher (Tankard, 2001). Such was the case in a study to determine the authorship of several of the unsigned Federalist papers (Mosteller and Wallace, 1964). The researchers first looked at the known writings of the three authors – Hamilton, Madison, and Jay – and tabulated the frequency with which each of the authors used 265 key words. They then programmed a computer to tabulate the frequencies of these words in the twelve papers of unknown authorship. The data produced clearly suggested Madison as the author of those papers.

The first widely used computer programs for content analysis were developed by Philip Stone and his colleagues (1966); revised versions of the *General Inquirer* system are still in use today and provide a set of computer procedures for tabulating a variety of textual characteristics (Stone, 1997). In addition, many of the same software packages that are useful in the analysis of qualitative data from field studies[4] may also aid the researcher who wants to do content analysis. Berg (2001) identifies and discusses a number of different kinds of programs such as text retrievers, code-and-retrieve programs, and code-based theory builders. Text retrievers perform the basic function of finding all cases of a particular phrase or word. Code-and-retrieve programs such as *Ethnograph* will split the text into groups, give codes to them, and show these coded groups. Code-based theory builders such as *HyperResearch* and *NUD*IST* can code and retrieve but also help in developing theoretical connections between concepts which have been coded.

The *Diction* software program can process an unlimited number of texts using a 10,000-word search corpus. It processes sixty passages (30,000 words) per minute. Perhaps more significant than its speed, however, is its capacity to determine the "tone" of a verbal message. It searches texts for some relatively subtle characteristics:

- Certainty – language indicating resoluteness, inflexibility, and completeness
- Activity – language featuring movement, change, the implementation of ideas and the avoidance of inertia
- Optimism – language endorsing some person, group, concept or event

- Commonality – language highlighting the agreed-upon values of a group and rejecting idiosyncratic modes of engagement
- Realism – language describing tangible, immediate, recognizable matters that affect people's everyday lives

Diction also produces comprehensive written reports about the texts it processes and writes its results to numeric files for later statistical analysis.

While there is no doubt that significant progress has been made in computer-assisted content analysis (West, 2001), it is Berg's assessment that we are still at a relatively early stage in the use of computers for this purpose. He argues that with any content analysis program the researcher still must figure out the theoretical meaning of what is uncovered. As he states, "Creating an apparatus that can simultaneously present the findings and describe their analytic importance would require perfection of artificial computer intelligence – a step into the future at least several decades away" (Berg, 2001:263).

As more social scientists see the potential of computers for making the coding of content data easier, we would expect a continued development of increasingly sophisticated computer programs (Neuendorf, 2006). However, we must emphasize that a computer is only a tool. It is valueless without the sound theoretical reasoning of the social scientist, who must choose meaningful problems, determine the materials to be used for analysis, construct categories that reflect the theoretical issues at hand, and finally make sense of the collected data.

THE TECHNIQUE IN PERSPECTIVE

One of the most significant strengths of content analysis is that it is a thoroughly **UNOBTRUSIVE METHOD** because *the subjects of investigation are not directly questioned or observed*. Nearly all the data collection techniques employed by social scientists necessitate a direct involvement with subjects. This is certainly so in survey, experimental, and participant observation research. However, content analysis, which makes use of available materials, eliminates a

[4] See Chapter 9.

source of troublesome bias that threatens our research (Lee, 2000). We do not have to bother with the potential response biases of subjects who are influenced by the presence of an investigator or by the knowledge that they are participating in a study. In this respect, the "nonreactive" nature of content analysis may complement the more obtrusive methods discussed elsewhere in this book.

While content analysis may serve as the central method in an investigation, it can also be used to test preliminary ideas, hypotheses, hunches, or theories before a more complete investigation. By conducting a pilot study through the content analysis of a few selected communication sources, researchers may generate hypotheses and discover important variables. The findings of such initial research may then guide further work where perhaps surveys or participant observation become the primary data collection methods. Although content analysis is a powerful tool for evaluating personal or social values, investigators may want to employ intensive interviewing, survey research, or direct observation to check the validity of inferences made from the communication sources used in a study. This is especially likely when the specific goal of the research is to evaluate the effects of communications. Indeed, if the test of a causal relationship is the goal of a particular research project, content analysis cannot test such a relationship; a rigorous experiment would be the ideal means to do so.

Content analysis is an adaptable research method. It is an economical and time-efficient procedure. It sometimes becomes the central technique in historical research concerned either with a particular period or with longitudinal trends over considerable time periods. One is usually limited to communications already made. (Of course, these may not exist for a given research topic.) Content analysis also makes possible a variety of cross-cultural studies that would likely be unfeasible using other methods. In addition, because of the availability of data sources (as shown in our hypothetical example) and the relative simplicity of the mechanics involved, students with little research experience can readily make use of the method. Content analysis will often be a productive research strategy when our interests lead us to inquire into the values, ideologies, sentiments, or beliefs motivating behavior in society.

SUMMARY

Words and phrases are valuable sources of social science data. The primary intent of content analysis is to uncover themes in these sources of communication that represent an entire culture, a specific group of people, or the life of an individual. In some studies, the discovery of these themes may be accomplished through tabulation of specific words. Alternatively, the thematic content in sentences, paragraphs, or perhaps an entire essay or book may be uncovered. Regardless of the particular unit of analysis employed, the underlying goal of the research remains constant: to find logic in the identified themes so that the characteristics of authors or their audiences may be better understood.

Realization of this central goal rests on the objective and systematic collection and processing of data. Strict rules for categorizing the content of communication must be adopted and followed. Categories for the classification of data must reflect the major theoretical concepts being used in a given study. The validity of the judgments made about the values, motives, beliefs, or ideologies of individuals, populations, and societies depends on the nature of the theoretical categories. Two basic requirements are that categories be mutually exclusive and exhaustive to minimize problems of reliability in coding. Of course, even the most complete and valid set of categories is useless without proper sampling procedures.

Increasingly, the time-consuming and intricate routine of data processing in content analysis has been taken over by computers. At present, computers are superb at enumerating content but less reliable in assessing its contextual meaning. Content analysis has a bright future as an unobtrusive technique that eliminates respondent bias and that has wide practical application in all of the social sciences. There are some potential difficulties in the method, threats to the reliability of its coding procedures and to the validity of its categories for classifying data, but these are readily recognized and are being addressed continually.

KEY TERMS

exhaustive categories
latent content
manifest content
mutually exclusive categories
recording unit
systems of enumeration
unit of analysis
universe
unobtrusive method

EXERCISES

1. Carry out a study replicating the work of Simon Davis (1990) described at the beginning of this chapter. Choose a major newspaper that runs personal advertisements and analyze them according to the categories used by Davis.

2. Do different communications sources "make" news? Answer this question by comparing coverage in a major newspaper and in a neighborhood newspaper on any political, social, or economic event that has been in the news recently. It will probably be best to restrict your content analysis to one week's reporting and analysis of the event in the respective newspapers. Decide on the features of the coverage you will document (for example, column space devoted to the event, the kinds of details reported, the position taken by the paper on the event). Be sure to include in your brief report some description of the categories constructed for analyzing the reports and the unit of analysis used. Speculate from your collected data on the values of the audiences served by the two newspapers. If you expected a difference in coverage between the papers but found none, try to explain this result.

3. According to many social analysts, racism is still a major social problem in America, if not the number one social problem. Decide how you might study this problem by using content analysis. Be sure to cover the major issues with respect to performing content analysis.

4. Several observers, including those in the antiglobalization movement, have criticized the role of corporations in society. How would you use content analysis to study how society views corporations? What categories of analysis would be appropriate?

5. Watch television from seven o'clock in the evening until midnight. Do a content analysis of all the commercials you see, according to the explanation given in each for buying the product or service being offered. It will help you to devise your categories in advance. Try to think of at least five mutually exclusive reasons for buying a product or using a service (quality, price, etc.). After you have collected your data, draw some inferences about the preferences and motivations of the viewing public. How do the advertisers see the public to whom they are trying to appeal?

SUGGESTED READINGS

Readings about the Method

Berg, Bruce L. 2001. *Qualitative Research Methods for the Social Sciences*. Needham Heights, MA: Allyn & Bacon.

Gives a thorough introduction to content analysis as a methodological technique with an extensive discussion of how to conduct it.

Krippendorff, Klaus. 2003. *Content Analysis: An Introduction to Its Methodology*. 2nd ed. Thousand Oaks, CA: Sage.

An authoritative source on the history and core principles of content analysis as well as a guide to analyzing texts, images, and voices.

Neuendorf, Kimberly A. 2001. *The Content Analysis Guidebook*. Thousand Oaks, CA: Sage.

A comprehensive, step-by-step guide to the method.

Roberts, Carl, ed. 1997. *Text Analysis for the Social Sciences*. Mahwah, NJ: Lawrence Erlbaum.

A good introductory source for content analysis and the use of the computer.

West, Mark D. 2001. *Theory, Method, and Practice in Computer Content Analysis*. Westport, CT: Ablex.

This book covers the history of computer-assisted content analysis by reviewing the theories that underlie development of state-of-the-art software packages. There are also sections devoted to applications in the fields of education, evaluation research, and psychology, as well as predictions for the future of computers in content analysis.

Readings Illustrating the Method

Barlow, Melissa Hickman, David Barlow, and Theodore G. Chiricos. 1995. "Economic Conditions and Ideologies of Crime in the Media: A Content Analysis of Crime News." *Crime and Delinquency* 41:3–19.

The authors use content analysis to show that the way crime and criminal behavior are presented in the media is affected by overall economic conditions in society.

Davis, Simon. 1990. "Men as Success Objects and Women as Sex Objects: A Study of Personal Advertisements." *Sex Roles* 23:43–50.

Davis presents a straightforward example of how a topic that might seem somewhat unapproachable by other research methods can be tackled by the relatively unobtrusive method of content analysis.

Gilens, Martin. 1996. "Race and Poverty in America: Public Misperceptions and the American News Media." *Public Opinion Quarterly* 60:515–541.

Gilens uses content analysis to explore the proposition that U.S. news media exaggerate African American poverty in a manner that contributes to a negative stereotype.

Gordy, Laurie L., and Alice Pritchard. 1995. "Redirecting Our Voyage through History: A Content Analysis of Social Studies Textbooks." *Urban Education* 30:195–218.

This study analyzes thematic material derived from textbooks used in American schools to understand the ideas emphasized in the educational system.

Leavy, Patricia. 2000. "Feminist Content Analysis and Representative Characters." *Qualitative Report* 5 (1–2) May.
http://www.nova.edu/ssss/QR/QR5-1/leavy.html.

*A representative character is a focal point from which to begin to discuss the larger social-cultural-political landscape of a specified time and place; the selected character must be analyzed in the **multiple forms** in which it is pre-*sented/represented. In this case, the author studied the television character Ally McBeal.

Mayring, Philipp. 2000. "Qualitative Content Analysis." *Forum: Qualitative Social Research* 1 (2) June.
http://www.qualitative-research.net/fqs-texte/2-00/2-00mayring-e.htm.

Most content analysis is quantitative in nature, but this Web site presents examples of using the technique qualitatively, in which coding categories are developed inductively as the research progresses.

McClelland, David C. 1967/1985. *Achieving Society.* New York: Free Press.

This classic study employs content analysis of children's stories around the world to identify how strongly the value of achievement is emphasized in different countries.

Pettinari, Catherine Johnson, ed. 1997. *Task, Talk and Text in the Operating Room: A Study in Medical Discourse.* Westport, CT: Ablex.

This study uses hospital operating room notes to analyze surgery and medical record keeping. The author makes use of content analysis of speech and documents to compare what is said around the operating table with what eventually appears in the patient's record.

West, Mark D., ed. 2001. *Applications of Computer Content Analysis.* Westport, CT: Ablex.

This volume contains examples of "best practice" in contemporary computer content analysis. Research is presented by scholars in political science, natural resource management, mass communication, marketing, and education. Two very engaging pieces concern the content analysis of voice mail and of pharmacist–patient interactions.

Resources

Center for Media and Public Affairs (CMPA). 2006.
http://www.cmpa.com/.

The CMPA is a nonpartisan research and educational organization that conducts scientific studies of the news and entertainment media. Their Web site contains links to a variety of media studies using content analysis.

General Inquirer. n.d.

The home page for the General Inquirer tool mentioned in this chapter is http://www.wjh.harvard.edu/~inquirer/.

Klein, Harald. 2003. "Text Analysis Info Page." http://www.intext.de/eindex.html.

A good Web site with an emphasis on text analysis. It contains a bibliography as well as a bulletin board for conferences and new developments in the field.

Neuendorf, Kimberly A. 2006. *The Content Analysis Guidebook Online.* http://academic.csuohio.edu/kneuendorf/content/.

This Web site has links to other content analysis software sites.

Oregon Social Learning Center (OSLC). 2006. http://www.oslc.org/.

The OSLC is a nonprofit research center that helps children and parents cope with aggressive and oppositional behaviors. They have developed codes to assess the interactions of parents, children, and therapists. Over the past fifteen years, nearly 3,000 children and families have been observed. The Web site explains the coding of the information from these interactions, as well as how the "coders" are trained.

QSR International. 2005. http://www.qsr.com.au/.

This Web site contains information about the NUD*IST software program mentioned in this chapter.

ResearchWare, Inc. 2007. http://www.researchware.com/.

This Web site contains information about the HyperResearch software program mentioned in this chapter.

REFERENCES

Alperstein, Neil M. 1990. "The Verbal Content of TV Advertising and Its Circulation in Everyday Life." *Journal of Advertising* 19:15–22.

Barlow, Melissa Hickman, David Barlow, and Theodore G. Chiricos. 1995. "Economic Conditions and Ideologies of Crime in the Media: A Content Analysis of Crime News." *Crime and Delinquency* 41:3–19.

Berelson, Bernard. 1971. *Content Analysis in Communication Research.* New York: Macmillan.

Berg, Bruce L. 2001. *Qualitative Research Methods for the Social Sciences.* Needham Heights, MA: Allyn & Bacon.

Blumer, Herbert. 1970. *Movies, Delinquency, and Crime.* North Stratford, NH: Ayer.

Bogaert, Anthony F., D. A. Turkovich, and C. L. Hafer. 1993. "A Content Analysis of Playboy Centerfolds from 1953 through 1990: Changes in Explicitness, Objectification, and Model's Age." *Journal of Sex Research* 30:135–139.

Bourgoin, Nicolas. 1995. "Suicide in Prison: Some Elements of a Strategic Analysis." *Cahiers Internationaux de Sociologie* 98:59–105.

Brewer, Paul. 2005. "Analyzing the Daily Show II." *Public Brewery Blog.* August 2. http://publicbrewery.blogspot.com/2005/08/analyzing-daily-show-ii.html.

Craig, Stephen R. 1992. "The Effect of Television Part on Gender Portrayals in Television Commercials: A Content Analysis." *Sex Roles* 26:197–211.

Crouch, Ben M., and Kelly R. Damphousse. 1992. "Newspapers and the Antisatanism Movement: A Content Analysis." *Sociological Spectrum* 12:1–20.

Danowski, James A., and Rebecca Ann Lind. 2001. "Linking Gender Language in News about Presidential Candidates to Gender Gaps in Politics: A Time-Series Analysis of the 1996 Campaign." In *Applications of Computer Content Analysis*, 87–102. Mark D. West, ed. Westport, CT: Ablex.

Davis, Simon. 1990. "Men as Success Objects and Women as Sex Objects: A Study of Personal Advertisements." *Sex Roles* 23:43–50.

Evans, Ellis D., et al. 1991. "A Content Analysis of Contemporary Teen Magazines for Adolescent Females." *Youth and Society* 23:99–120.

Evans, Lorraine, and Kimberly Davis. 2000. "No Sissy Boys Here: A Content Analysis of the Representative Masculinity in Elementary School Reading Textbooks." *Sex Roles* 42:255–270.

Gilens, Martin. 1996. "Race and Poverty in America: Public Misperceptions and the American News Media." *Public Opinion Quarterly* 60:515–541.

Gordy, Laurie L., and Alice Pritchard. 1995. "Redirecting Our Voyage through History: A Content

Analysis of Social Studies Textbooks." *Urban Education* 30:195–218.

Holsti, Ole R. 1969. *Content Analysis for the Social Sciences and Humanities*. Reading, MA: Addison-Wesley.

Hong, Nathaniel. 1992. "Constructing the Anarchist Beast in American Periodical Literature." *Critical Studies in Mass Communication* 9:110–130.

Krippendorff, Klaus. 2003. *Content Analysis: An Introduction to Its Methodology*. 2nd ed. Thousand Oaks, CA: Sage.

Lee, Raymond M. 2000. *Unobtrusive Methods in Social Research*. Buckingham, UK: Open University Press.

Liebes, Tamar. 1991. "Our War/Their War: Comparing the Intifadeh and the Gulf War on U.S. and Israeli Television." *Critical Studies in Mass Communications* 9:44–55.

Low, Jason, and Peter Sherrard. 1999. "Portrayal of Women in Sexuality and Marriage and Family Textbooks: A Content Analysis of Photographs from the 1970s to the 1990s." *Sex Roles* 40:309–318.

Mayring, Philipp. 2000. "Qualitative Content Analysis." *Forum: Qualitative Social Research* 1 (2) June. http://www.qualitative-research.net/fqs-texte/2-00/2-00mayring-e.htm.

McClelland, David C. 1967/1985. *Achieving Society*. New York: Free Press.

Mellinger, Wayne Martin. 1992. "Postcards from the Edge of the Color Line: Images of African Americans in Popular Culture, 1893–1917." *Symbolic Interaction* 15:413–433.

Mosteller, Frederick, and David L. Wallace. 1964. *Inference and Disputed Authorship: The Federalist*. Reading, MA: Addison-Wesley.

Neuendorf, Kimberly A. 2007. *The Content Analysis Guidebook Online*. http://academic.csuohio.edu/kneuendorf/content/.

Ogilvie, Daniel M., Philip J. Stone, and Edwin Schneidman. 1966. "Some Characteristics of Genuine versus Simulated Suicide Notes." In *The General Inquirer: A Computer Approach to Content Analysis in the Behavioral Sciences*, 527–535. Philip Stone et al., eds. Cambridge, MA: MIT Press.

Oliver, Mary Beth. 1994. "Portrayals of Crime, Race, and Aggression in 'Reality-Based' Police Shows: A Content Analysis." *Journal of Broadcasting and Electronic Media* 38:179–192.

Paige, Jeffrey M. 1966. "Letters from Jenny: An Approach to the Clinical Analysis of Personality Structure by Computer." In *The General Inquirer: A Computer Approach to Content Analysis in the Behavioral Sciences*, 431–451. Philip Stone et al., eds. Cambridge, MA: MIT Press.

Patterson, Thomas E. 1994. *Out of Order*. New York: Vintage.

Peirce, Kate. 1997. "Women's Magazine Fiction: A Content Analysis of the Roles, Attributes, and Occupations of Main Characters." *Sex Roles* 37:581–593.

Pendleton, Laura, L., Christopher Smith, and John L. Roberts. 1991. "Drinking on Television: A Content Analysis of Recent Alcohol Portrayal." *British Journal of Addiction* 86:769–774.

Pritchard, Alice M. 1990. "A Common Format for Poverty: A Content Analysis of Social Problems Textbooks." *Teaching Sociology* 21:42–49.

Riffe, Daniel, Stephen Lacy, and Frederick G. Fico. 2005. *Analyzing Media Messages: Using Quantitative Content Analysis in Research*. Mahwah, NJ: Lawrence Erlbaum.

Schlenker, Jennifer A., Sandra L. Caron, and William A. Halterman. 1998. "A Feminist Analysis of *Seventeen* Magazine: A Content Analysis from 1945–1995." *Sex Roles* 38:135–149.

Stone, Philip J. 1997. "Thematic Text Analysis: New Agendas for Analyzing Text Content." In *Text Analysis for the Social Sciences*, 35–54. Carl Roberts, ed. Mahwah, NJ: Lawrence Erlbaum.

Stone, Philip, et al., eds. 1966. *The General Inquirer: A Computer Approach to Content Analysis in the Behavioral Sciences*. Cambridge, MA: MIT Press.

Tankard, James W., Jr. 2001. "Using the Computer to Identify Unknown Authors." In *Applications of Computer Content Analysis*, 51–64. Mark D. West, ed. Westport, CT: Ablex.

Thompson, Kimberly M., and Kevin Haninger. 2001. "Violence in E-Rated Video Games." *Journal of the American Medical Association* 286:591–598.

Villani, Susan. 2001. "Impact of Media on Children and Adolescents: A 10-Year Review of the

Research." *Journal of the American Academy of Child and Adolescent Psychiatry* 40:392–401.

Volz, Joe. 1999. "Media Distorts the Truth about Violence in School." *Monitor Online* 30 (9) October. http://www.apa.org/monitor/oct99/cf2.html.

Weber, Robert P. 1990. *Basic Content Analysis*. 2nd ed. Beverly Hills, CA: Sage.

Welch, Michael, and Melissa Fenwick. 2001. "Primary Definitions of Crime and Moral Panic: A Content Analysis of Experts' Quotes in Feature Newspaper Articles on Crime." *Journal of Research in Crime and Delinquency* 34:474–495.

Wenger, Lynn, Ruth Malone, and Lisa Bero. 2001. "The Cigar Revival and the Popular Press: A Content Analysis, 1987–1997." *American Journal of Public Health* 91:288–291.

Wertham, Frederick. 1996. *Seduction of the Innocent*. New York: Amereon.

West, Mark D., ed. 2001. *Theory, Method, and Practice in Computer Content Analysis*. Greenwich, CT: Ablex.

Williams, Gilbert A. 1989. "Enticing Viewers: Sex and Violence in *TV Guide* Program Advertisements." *Journalism Quarterly* 66:970–973.

Wurtzel, Alan, and Guy Lometti. 1984. "Researching Television Violence." *Society* 21:22–30.

Wysocki, Diane Kolas, and Rebecca Harrison. 1991. "AIDS and the Media: A Look at How Periodicals Influence Children and Teenagers in Their Knowledge of AIDS." *Journal of Health Education* 22:20–23.

Zimmerman, Toni Schindler, Kristen E. Holm, and Shelley A. Haddock. 2001. "A Decade of Advice for Women and Men in the Best-Selling Self-Help Literature." *Family Relations* 50:122–134.

AGGREGATE DATA ANALYSIS

14

INTRODUCTION

Social scientists want to understand the behavior of individuals and how this behavior is affected by membership in social groups. Many of the methodologies we have discussed in earlier chapters (for instance, survey research, experimentation, participant observation) are used to examine peoples' attitudes, beliefs, and values. If we want to discover why people vote as they do, exhibit prejudice, or engage in criminal behavior, we often proceed by interviewing or observing an appropriate sample of individuals. We try to show the distinctive characteristics of people who engage in these behaviors by taking individuals as the **UNITS OF ANALYSIS**, that is, *the source of the data from which we are able to make generalizations.*

However, individuals are not always the focus of social research. We may want to understand the nature, character, and dynamics of social structures, as well. We frequently wish to compare institutions according to some attribute. Social scientists sometimes take as their unit of analysis such organizations as universities, business corporations, prisons, or hospitals. As we will see, much investigation is also concerned with *geographical*, or **AREAL GROUPINGS**, of people. We might be interested in comparing rates of suicide in various countries. Although it is true that individuals are responsible for taking their own lives, the focus of our research need not be on the particular or separate motives, beliefs, or personal life conditions of these individuals. Rather, it may be directed at understanding the characteristics of societies where, relatively speaking, large or small numbers of persons commit suicide. With many research problems, data on individuals are used primarily to arrive at a comprehensive characterization of social structures as a whole. Making this shift in emphasis is an exercise in the research imagination.

Whenever we combine information about the *behaviors, attitudes, or other attributes of individuals to represent statistically some social unit comprising those people*, we are using AGGREGATE DATA. These social *units will vary in size and comprehensiveness*. Researchers might, for example, study the same phenomenon at progressively higher LEVELS OF AGGREGATION. They might investigate how rates of mental illness vary in different neighborhoods, then combine, or aggregate, these data to examine mental illness rates in entire cities. Information from various cities, in turn, could be aggregated to generate data on counties, and so forth. As a logical extension of this aggregation process, researchers could compare countries concerning their mental illness rates.

The procedure of combining, or aggregating, information on individuals to produce an overall group rating should not be unfamiliar to us. College administrators may boast in their public relations literature that students' average verbal Scholastic Aptitude Test score is over 650. This one score is used to characterize the whole student body and is produced by combining data on each student in the school. In much the same way, we make judgments about society's condition and the quality of our own lives using "official statistics" computed by aggregating data on individuals. These statistics, we should note, are often the basis for the creation of social policy.

Some people are willing to measure the morality of a society in terms of suicide statistics, rates of divorce, or church attendance. Politicians promise us that if elected they will institute programs to reduce the frequency of crime in our major cities. We weigh our economic futures by monitoring unemployment statistics. Ecologists and environmentalists ask us to consider seriously the implications of population growth rates. Comparisons are often made between cities, counties, states, and nations in terms of

juvenile delinquency, infant mortality, literacy, average income, and migration. Clearly, aggregate data make up a significant portion of the information that both professionals and non-professionals need to assess social, economic, and political behavior in relative terms.

Our goal in this chapter is to discuss some of the methodological issues raised when aggregate data are used in research. Among the questions that will occupy our attention are: How do researchers decide on the appropriate unit of analysis in their studies? How closely do the rates reflected in aggregate data approximate the true extent of the phenomenon studied? Do crime rates, for example, really tell us how much criminal activity actually exists? Can we ever make statements about individuals from aggregate data? If we find, for example, that rates of delinquency are highest in areas where the divorce rate is highest, can we then infer that family disorganization causes specific individuals to engage in delinquent behaviors? Under what conditions might it be misleading to characterize an institution by summing up the characteristics of the people composing it? Are there situations where the whole is more than, less than, or at least different from the sum of its parts? Are there any differences in the nature of the information obtained as we move from one level of aggregation to another?

Before we tackle some of these issues, let us consider some applications of aggregate data analysis.

APPLICATIONS OF AGGREGATE DATA ANALYSIS

Aggregate data analysis is not restricted to one or a few areas of social science inquiry. Those studying such diverse subjects as deviance, stratification, race relations, urban life, large-scale organizations, occupations and professions, and mass communications will frequently formulate research problems that require aggregate data analysis; however, there are certain topics for investigation where it is nearly always necessary. All demographic analyses of population trends rely on official statistics already aggregated. A good deal of research in urban sociology makes use of census data collected periodically by the federal government. Criminologists must rely heavily on available crime statistics. Social scientists have progressed in developing indicators for evaluating the "social well-being" of nations. In this research, aggregate statistics are used for assessing changes in such social rates as poverty, public safety, health, and employment.

Because of the extraordinary range of applications for aggregate data analysis, we must be selective in our discussion. We have chosen to examine some research problems that call for extensive, if not exclusive, use of aggregate data analysis and that also highlight the methodological problems connected with its use. We will treat, in turn, studies employing census materials and crime statistics, as well as research devoted to the development of social indicators and the forecasting of future social trends.

Using Census Materials to Study Race Relations

Suppose we had the idea that major changes in the structure and composition of American cities had occurred over the past seventy-five years. We theorize that the growth of suburbs has affected the age, ethnic, racial, and income characteristics of city dwellers. We want to test the hypothesis that large cities are increasingly inhabited by younger, lower-income minority groups, especially blacks, Hispanics, and Asians. Consider the kind of data we need to test this hypothesis. We need information on the attributes of people in each major city, collected periodically and regularly over a long time period. Aggregate census statistics are indispensable to social scientists because they contain precisely the kind of demographic data often used to characterize the population attributes of distinctive territorial groupings of people.

The data available in census reports refer to other territorial groupings besides cities, some less and some more comprehensive. A *territorial grouping, or geographical unit, that may include fewer than a hundred households* is called a CENSUS BLOCK. Traditionally, however, social scientists have made greater use of aggregate

census data reported for a somewhat broader areal unit called the CENSUS TRACT. Although bigger than the census block, the census tract is still *a relatively small area generally containing a population of between 1,500 and 8,000 persons.*[1] Each city is divided into a number of census tracts. Although there is certainly an arbitrary component to the specification of census tract areas, they are reasonably uniform in terms of population and size. Social scientists sometimes want to compare geographically defined social structures larger than census blocks, census tracts, or cities. Census data can be obtained to characterize counties, states, areas of the country, and the nation as a whole. Moreover, nearly all nations maintain census records, and this makes it possible to engage in CROSS-CULTURAL COMPARISONS *from one country to another.*

The population characteristics mentioned earlier (age, race, ethnicity, and income) are only a few of those collected and reported in census statistics. Among other aggregate data reported for each of the territorial levels mentioned are the following: place of birth, occupational level, educational attainment, marital status, and family size. Without the data contained in census reports, much social investigation would be impossible. On a simple, descriptive level, we could not determine with any accuracy how different groups (ethnic, racial, class, etc.) are distributed geographically throughout cities. We could not determine rates of urban population growth and decline. We could not easily assess income differences among city groups. Nor could we specify the relationships between such variables as population growth and economic development or residential location and occupational status.

Race relations are an important issue in American society. As a nation of immigrants, the success of America depends in no small part on how well it integrates its various racial and ethnic communities. Historically, the census has provided important insights about the progress of this integration. Yet, as desirable as it may be, obtaining an accurate account of the racial and

---

[1] For more information, see U.S. Census Bureau (2000).

ethnic mix of the American population is a serious and, perhaps, increasing challenge for the U.S. Census Bureau. Despite the efforts of the Census Bureau, some minority groups may be systematically undercounted. However, part of the difficulty facing the bureau's racial and ethnic counts is due to the intermixing of the American population, which obscures racial and ethnic identities (Skerry, 2000:3). To accommodate this blurring of the race and ethnic boundaries, census respondents can now choose more than one category when describing their racial or ethnic status. Despite these difficulties, the census remains an essential source of data for analyzing the state of race relations in the United States. As examples of research relying on the aggregate data provided in census reports, we will review four studies that have employed census data to investigate race relations. We will review in some detail a classic study from the 1960s and follow that with brief reviews of three more recent studies.

For our first study, Karl and Alma Taeuber's (1966) classic and still influential study of one of our most difficult social problems will be examined: racial residential segregation in American cities. In their research, the authors used census data to investigate various aspects of segregation in United States' metropolitan areas, focusing on 1940 through 1960. The Taeubers reasoned that if race made absolutely no difference in determining where a person chose to live, or was allowed to live, then no area of a city would be all black or all white. If, for example, blacks constituted 25 percent of a city's population, it would be expected that in each city block examined they would comprise 25 percent of the residents. Similarly, if blacks made up 50 percent of a city's population, it would be expected that one of every two households would be black. These assumptions would hold only if there were absolutely no residential segregation.

To compare one metropolitan area with another, the authors devised an index of housing segregation, ranging from 0 to 100. If a city had no racial segregation, it could theoretically be assigned a score of zero. However, if each block examined were all black or all white, the index

score would be 100.[2] Using census materials to compute a segregation index for 207 cities, the Taeubers were able to show convincingly that "a high degree of residential segregation is universal in American cities" (1966:2). For all areas examined, the lowest index was 60.4 and the highest was 98.1, with half the cities having values above 87.8 and one-fourth above 91.7.[3]

Presenting all the findings in this study is not possible in a short review. However, by beginning with census data and processing them, the authors were able to present (1) comparisons in residential segregation between areas of the country, (2) statistics on changes in segregation rates for cities and areas of the country between 1940 and 1960, (3) data on the economic and social characteristics of black residential areas, (4) an analysis of the factors involved in the flight of whites as blacks move into an area, and (5) data describing the economic characteristics of blacks in racially mixed census tracts.

The wide-ranging information reported in this study was valuable for two related reasons. First, the descriptive aggregate rates of segregation for separate cities and areas of the country allowed us to see exactly the parameters of the problems we faced. The data presented in this study certainly laid to rest the stereotype held by many that segregation was primarily a Southern problem. Second, by uncovering the patterns of racial segregation in this country, the study provided policy makers with some of the information necessary to formulate an intelligent social policy response.

In the years since the publication of the Taeubers' study a number of federal, state and local laws and regulations were passed to guarantee the fair availability of housing to all citizens. Minorities secured court-protected rights to live in the neighborhoods they chose. During

---

[2] For a discussion of the major issues in index construction, see Chapter 17.

[3] As long as race is correlated with income, it would be possible for there to be differences in the distribution of the races even if there were no racial discrimination in the allocation of residence. The evidence, however, indicates that economic factors "cannot account for more than a small portion of observed levels of racial residential segregation" (Taeuber and Taeuber, 1966:2).

this same period, the racial demographics of the American population have changed significantly. The Hispanic and Asian populations of the United States have more than doubled their share of the total population. In response to these legal and demographic changes and other social and cultural factors as well, the dynamics of racial segregation have changed in the United States. As it did for the Taeubers' study, census data continues to be vital to understanding the dimensions of residential racial patterns and race relations. For example, among the many studies using census data, Glaeser and Vigdor (2001) show that while racial segregation remains strong in some older metropolitan areas, it is much lower in many small cities and some of the faster-growing areas of the nation in the West and South. Also, Hwang and Murdock (1998) used census data to examine whether black populations grew faster in suburbs with larger or smaller existing black populations. Taylor (1998) used census-level data with *General Social Survey* data in a multilevel model[4] to determine how whites' racial prejudice varies with the size of the local black population.

Available sources of aggregate data such as censuses are indeed valuable, but we must also recognize the limitations and methodological problems involved in the use of such "official" statistics. Certain errors may creep into the aggregate data with which we often work. First, there may be **ERRORS OF COVERAGE**. Inevitably, *counting mistakes will be made in the original collection of data* from individuals. Some people are invariably missed and therefore not represented in the aggregate figures compiled, and some may be counted twice. (Those who work frequently with census materials suggest that coverage errors result much more often in undercounts than in overcounts.)

Second, there will be unavoidable **CLASSIFICATION ERRORS**. Census data, collected every ten years, are obtained using self-administered questionnaires delivered through the mail or by enumerators hired to conduct personal interviews. As would be the case in evaluating the quality of any data collected via questionnaire, we know that *respondents will lie about certain issues*. People may want to "look good" in their own eyes and in the eyes of the interviewer and consequently give false information about such items as their education, income, and occupational levels. Common sense would lead us to expect that the direction of the error will be toward the higher education, income, and occupational categories. It is always possible, further, that people will not understand the questions asked by census enumerators or that those collecting the data will themselves make systematic classification errors. Mistakes may occur in the final processing, tabulating, or aggregating of the data collected on millions of people.

The researcher using census data may face other problems. As indicated in our review of the Taeubers' research, investigators frequently want to compare changes over time in particular areal units. We might be interested in how the income distributions for particular towns have varied over a fifty-year period. Unfortunately, town boundaries may expand during the ten intervening years between census tabulations, making the desired comparison difficult. For researchers who wish to make cross-cultural comparisons using census data, there will be other problems: certain types of data collected in one country may not be collected in another; data for certain countries may be incomplete; there may be special cultural factors in a society that induce individuals to misrepresent themselves; ideology or politics might affect the way that statistics are reported; the individuals' categories used for classifying (say, by education or income) will vary from country to country and again hinder comparative analysis.[5]

Some types of problems we have been discussing with reference to census data are more strongly highlighted when we consider other official statistics that social scientists frequently employ in their research. To extend our

---

[4] Multilevel models allow researchers to combine individual level data, such as survey data, with aggregated data that may have been measured for census blocks, states, universities, and so on.

[5] For a discussion of some of the problems encountered in comparative research using aggregate data, see Chapter 14.

comments on the possible errors contaminating available aggregate data – errors that, in turn, may lead us to false conclusions and inferences – we will consider briefly some of the methodological dilemmas of those who rely on official crime statistics.

Estimated Rates and True Rates: The Case of Crime Statistics

Of all the aggregate data available to social scientists, official crime rate statistics may be among the most unreliable. Although the problems with using these figures may be especially severe, they are nevertheless the types of difficulties that we must cope with when we use any aggregate data previously prepared by others. Because of a variety of errors in the compilation of any data, there will always be a discrepancy between the **REPORTED RATE** of some phenomenon and the **TRUE** (or *actual*) **RATE.** We would do well to consider just how great this discrepancy is likely to be in the data we use.

In the United States, two major indices are used to measure national crime levels and trends. The FBI's Uniform Crime Reports (UCR) record crime reported by victims to local police departments as well as unreported crimes that are known to the police. The UCR measures most types of crime, but the major section primarily focuses on seven types of serious crime against individuals, businesses, governments, and other organizations. The Bureau of Justice Statistics' National Crime Victim Survey (NCVS) uses survey responses to count crime committed against persons over 12 years old or their households.[6] As indicators of national crime trends, these two indices serve to complement one another. More serious crimes are likely to be counted in the UCR whereas less serious crimes are more likely to be counted in the NCVS (Steffensmeier and Harer, 1999:257). When considered jointly, these two indices generally provide a good indication of the direction of crime in the United States.

---

[6] A new system, the National Incident Based Reporting System (NIBRS), collects far more data about crime than does the UCR. It is slowly being implemented across the United States. For more information, see http://www.icpsr.umich.edu/NACJD/NIBRS/.

Despite the efforts of the U.S. Justice Department and law enforcement officials around the country to develop accurate crime accounting measures, it is quite likely that crime statistics do not provide an accurate accounting of the *amount* of crime in the United States. We know that there are many more crimes committed than appear in official statistics. The number of crimes known to the police is always substantially smaller than the total actually committed. The statistics do not accurately reflect the commission of crimes that are rarely reported by victims, such as rape, or the commission of many types of white-collar crime, such as fraud or embezzlement where the victims are unaware of the crime committed against them. Indeed, it can be argued that under current crime reporting measures the true extent of white-collar crime is unknown (Barnett, 2002). Contributing to the suspicion about the validity of crime statistics is the knowledge that the tabulation may vary with local police policies, court policies, and public opinion. Crime rates vary widely because local administrators may interpret the law differently. If we were to treat the statistics at face value, we might believe that there is more crime in one community than another, when in fact the difference may simply be a result of the methods used in compiling the statistics. If law enforcement officials began systematically to arrest people for vagrancy, prostitution, or drug dealing, where they had previously been lenient toward these crimes, it would be incorrect to conclude that there had been a substantial upsurge in the crime rate. Because of political pressure from government leaders or citizens' groups, police officials may periodically "crack down" on certain kinds of activities. However, we could imagine officials not reporting in their records all the crimes they know occur in their areas so that it will appear that they are succeeding in keeping the crime rate down. Such biasing factors affecting the reporting and maintenance of statistics make the study of changing rates of crime very difficult. We cannot easily know whether differences from year to year in a given jurisdiction are real.

Some have argued that crime rate statistics are badly flawed because police officials may not enforce the law the same way in each community they serve. Blacks are much more likely than whites to be arrested for the same behaviors or that middle- or upper-class youngsters are likely to only be warned by local police when engaging in behaviors that would lead to the arrest of adolescents in working-class areas.

The factors mentioned, taken together, conspire to make the validity of statistical crime rates highly questionable. It has not been our intention, however, merely to comment on one substantive area of social investigation. Crime statistics stand as a convenient example to raise a larger point. Whenever we use aggregate data already compiled by others, we need to be skeptical about the extent to which the rates presented reflect the actual volume of behaviors, events, or demographic attributes in the groups studied.

Development of Social Indicators

A country cannot chart its own progress, change, or growth by looking at the behavior or life conditions of only a few individuals. Aggregate analysis is required if we wish to develop yardsticks for evaluating the social state and well-being of a nation. Just as economists have charted trends using such economic indicators as gross national product, median family income, and unemployment rate, so too have social scientists developed **SOCIAL INDICATORS**.[7] Social indicators are *used to measure change in such conditions as poverty, public safety, education, health, and housing*. They are also used to produce knowledge that will be useful in social planning and the formulation of public policy. Such information can be of help in determining where our money, programs, and general efforts at creating social change are most needed. Social indicators are generally presented as **TIME SERIES DATA**; this makes it possible to *chart changes over time*. Not all time-series statistics would be classified as social indicators. Typically, social indicators are quantitative aggregate measures "used to

monitor the social system, helping to identify changes and to guide intervention to alter the course of social change" (Ferriss, 1988:601).

The widespread use of social indicators is relatively recent. Some work was done in the 1930s, but the effort did not really mature until the mid-1960s. Some who do social indicators research focus on the production of longitudinal statistics, documenting trends in various aspects of the quality of social life. Others apply these statistics to the study of social mobility, to changes in the female occupational structure, to changes in degree of racial segregation, and so on – that is, to studies based on social indicator trend data.

Suppose we were to ask the question: Is the health status of the United States improving? We might turn to a source such as the Centers for Disease Control and Prevention's National Health Statistics Web site, www.cdc.gov/nchs, which makes statistics available for a variety of health measures. Among the statistics available at this site are life expectancy at birth (by sex and race), death rates (by age, sex, race, and cause of death), infant mortality rates, teenage pregnancy rates, and physician office visits. Some of the statistics are available as time series over many decades, whereas others are available for shorter periods. To answer our research question, we might decide to limit ourselves to a particular aspect of health status, or we might attempt to combine many measures.

Our discussion of social indicators may be used as a platform for thinking about the implications of the level of aggregation on which we carry out our research. Social indicators typically represent rates for a whole nation or society, but what information is gained or lost as the level of aggregation becomes more comprehensive? To answer this question, it is best to start with a concrete example. As previously mentioned, one social indicator of health at the national level of aggregation is average life expectancy. This indicator will tell us of changes, up to the present, in the average life expectancy of individuals at birth. Let us look at Figure 14.1 for some actual data on life expectancy rates broken down by sex and race for the United States during the 1929– 1996 period.

---

[7] Presentation of social indicators is always in the form of aggregate data, but it is sometimes the case that the information was obtained from a nonaggregate source, such as survey research data.

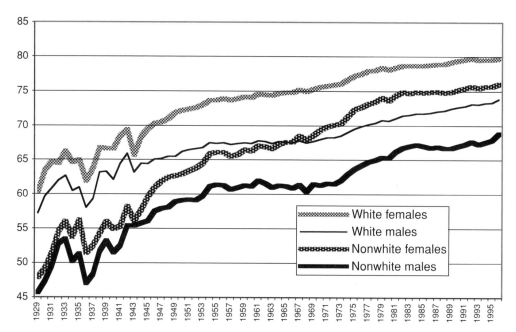

Figure 14.1. U.S. life expectancy at birth by race and sex, 1929–1996. *Source:* Anderson (1998).

These data indicate that average life expectancies were quite variable during the 1930s and early 1940s as the United States faced the shocks of the Great Depression, the Dust Bowl, World War II, and diseases such as poliomyelitis. By the mid-1940s life expectancy for the four identified groups began to increase and has continued to do so. We should note the substantial differences between men and women and the even more startling variation between white men and women and nonwhite men. White women can expect to live longer than white men. Nonwhite women can expect to live longer than nonwhite men. For much of the period, white men could expect to live longer than both nonwhite men and women. Only since about 1965 has the average life expectancy of nonwhite women surpassed white men's. As recently as 1968 white women could expect to live about fifteen years longer than nonwhite men, a gap that closed to about eleven years by 1996.

As we consider these figures on life expectancy, consider this basic question: What potentially important information is unavailable to us, given that the data are presented on the national level of aggregation? Imagine that we are administrators responsible for the allocation of monies to various health improvement programs around the country. We would say that these national figures are interesting but that they do not tell the whole story. We might comment that the national statistics do not allow us to see variations between areas of the country (West, Midwest, Northeast, etc.) in life expectancy rates. It could be that life expectancy rates are quite high in one area but relatively low in another. If we knew this to be so, we would have a better idea of where to allocate available funds.

It is possible to rework the available data so that we can see differences between areas of the country in life expectancy rates. This process is called DISAGGREGATION – *taking an existing unit of data and breaking it into finer or less comprehensive units.* By disaggregating the national data into regions, we would have more information because it would be possible for us to see differences that were masked in the national-level data. Even then, however, we might not be altogether satisfied because individual states can vary widely in life expectancy rates. If we could see such variations, it would further enhance our decision making; we would give more money to programs in the states with lower life expectancy rates. Because the data aggregated at the regional level do not provide us information on separate states, we could ask that the data be further disaggregated to this less comprehensive unit.

With the available data from the fifty states, we might have the idea that life expectancy rates will still vary for different cities. At this point, we have to accept that the data are becoming somewhat unwieldy. We have gone from one rate (the national level) to five or six rates (regions of the country) to fifty rates (states), and we must now recognize that disaggregation to the city level would mean looking at several hundred separate rates. An important point is made from our example of information gained and lost as we aggregate and disaggregate data. Each time researchers move to a higher level of aggregation, they lose information about levels immediately below. At the same time, there is an efficiency to the statistics on higher levels of aggregation. At the national level, we need deal with only one rate; at the state level, it increases to fifty rates, and so forth, until it would be literally impossible to manage or interpret the extraordinary amount of data at lower levels of aggregation.

There is, then, no easy answer to the question: At what aggregate level ought a researcher to carry out analysis? We want to maximize both information and efficiency. In some cases, however, there is little choice in the matter. We simply must work at the level for which available statistics have already been aggregated. This is so when we make use of census data. Here we are limited by the geographical units for which census data are reported. In other words, whenever available statistics are used, they can always be aggregated to higher levels but not disaggregated to levels lower than the one presented in the available data. Where researchers do have a number of options relative to level of aggregation in a study, their choice must be made in terms of the research goals and theories guiding the investigation.

Forecasting

Social indicators, we have noted, allow researchers to evaluate changes in the condition of a nation over time, from some point in the past to the present. It is a somewhat different task to forecast adequately future trends in a society. We know that it is important for planning purposes to estimate with some accuracy what the population will be in the United States in fifty years or more. It is vital to know what our energy needs and natural resources will be in the future. We might also want to know whether welfare caseloads will increase or decrease or whether there will be significant changes in employment opportunities. Typically, those who do such social forecasting must rely on aggregate data. Forecasting is often done by looking at aggregate trends in the factors of interest (birth rates, welfare expenditures, and so on) from some point in the past to the present. If we assume that the rates of increase or decrease that we see will not change substantially, we can estimate future trends or growth.

DEMOGRAPHERS (*those who study population trends*) are quite capable of making short-term population forecasts, for example, about the number of persons of a certain age group who are likely to survive for a certain period.[8] For longer periods however, forecasting population can pose serious challenges. Suppose we wanted to forecast long-term population trends in a certain country. We would need to look at historical data to try to glean some kind of pattern that could be used to make our forecast. Clearly, we would not simply look at regular increases or decreases of the birth rate; total population growth is a function of several variables, and birth rates alone would not provide enough data for us to make an adequate forecast. To estimate future population growth, we would have to take into account such additional factors as national death and migration rates and the factors that influence birth, death, and migration rates. To demonstrate the kinds of issues population forecasters face, we will look at data for Sweden made available by Statistics Sweden.[9] Swedish national and local governments have kept good records of population changes for more than two centuries. We will look at data from 1800 to 2001. Ordinarily, demographers would not need

---

[8] For information about such short-term forecasts, see Siegal (2002) or Smith, Tayman, and Swanson (2001).

[9] The English language Statistics Sweden home page is http://www.scb.se/default__2154.asp.

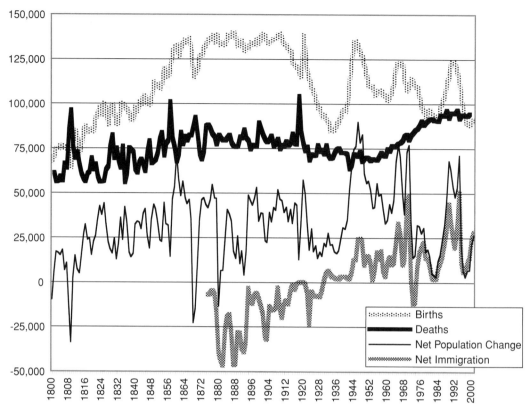

Figure 14.2. Swedish births, deaths, new immigration, and net population change, 1800–2001. *Source:* Statistics Sweden. http://www.scb.se/templates/tableOrChart__26047.asp.

such a long data series to make their forecast, but as we examine data for this period, we will be able to see an important trend in Swedish population growth that not only makes predicting population difficult but also has worldwide implications.

The three major components of population change are births, deaths, and migration. Figure 14.2 is a chart of data of the actual number of births and deaths in Sweden as well as the net migration amount and net population change.

We can see in this particular case that the number of births, the level of net immigration, and the net change in population have varied widely in the nineteenth and twentieth centuries. The raw numbers in this chart are useful to give us an initial idea of the scope of population changes in Sweden. From the data presented, it is clear that births rose markedly during the nineteenth century, while number of deaths appears less variable and became fairly

constant in the 1990s. The total population of Sweden generally increased during this period because births greatly exceeded deaths for most of the period and because more people immigrated to Sweden after 1933 than emigrated from it. Births dropped by nearly a third between 1990 and 2001, resulting in the number of deaths in each of the years between 1996 and 2001 exceeding the number of births. Indeed, without immigration during the 1996–2001 period, the population of Sweden would have declined.

The variability of the number of births, deaths, and migrants indicates the kinds of challenges faced by demographers in trying to forecast future population levels. However, forecasters generally move beyond raw data to examine the rates of change of various population components in complex models, as well as the factors that influence those rates. For example, they use total birth or death rates or the rates of childbirth for subgroups such as women between the ages

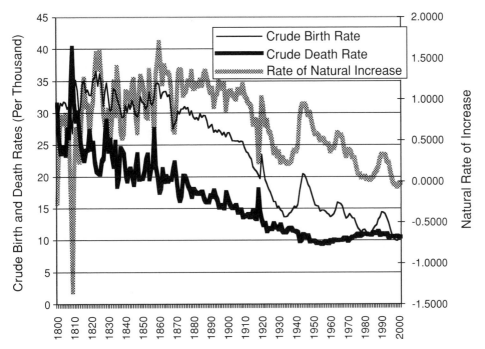

Figure 14.3. Swedish crude birth and death rates and rate of natural increase, 1800–2001. *Source:* Statistics Sweden. http://www.scb.se/templates/tableOrChart__26047.asp.

of 20 and 30. Because the goal here is simply to show the kinds of challenges that social forecasters face, the discussion will be limited to crude birth and death rates and the rate of natural increase for the national population.[10] Figure 14.3 displays the crude birth and crude death rates for Sweden for the years 1800–2001 (left axis) as well as the annual natural rate of increase of the population (right axis). In this chart, we get a clearer picture of the demographic changes in Swedish population over the past 200 years. Beginning around 1830, the death rate of the Swedish population began a steady decline. In contrast, birth rates remained high until about 1870, resulting in strong population growth. The birth rate then began to decline,

but generally remained higher than the death rate until the late 1990s, so that population change from natural increase continued to be positive until 1996. After 1996, the Swedish death rate exceeded the birth rate. The small increase in population in Sweden after 1996 was due to immigration.

The demographic experience of Sweden over that past two centuries depicted in Figure 14.3 is characteristic of what demographers call the **DEMOGRAPHIC TRANSITION**. *After remaining relatively stable because of simultaneously high birth and death rates, national populations begin a rapid increase* as death rates decline (because of improvements in health and standard of living) and birth rates remain stable (Jones and Douglas, 1997:3). Eventually, birth rates fall as cultural values change and population stabilizes or grows only slowly. Emigration restrained population increases in Sweden during the nineteenth and early twentieth centuries, but otherwise that nation closely followed the demographic transition.

Although there is a great deal of variability in the pace and timing of birth and death rate declines, with the exception of certain

[10] Crude birth and death rates are measured as the number of events per thousand population. To calculate these rates, the numbers of births and deaths are totaled at the end of the year. Because the national population count changes continuously during the year, the population at the midpoint of the year is often used in determining the "per thousand population" part of the ratio. Natural increase is the difference between births and deaths. The rate of natural increase is the rate (expressed as a percentage) at which a population grows because of births and deaths. It differs from the total population growth rate because it does not include migration.

sub-Saharan African countries, most of the world's nations appear to be progressing through the stages described in demographic transition theory. The scourge of AIDS has sharply increased death rates in some African countries to the point that some may experience population decline during the first decade of the twenty-first century. Otherwise, even most fast-growing Third World nations are experiencing significant birth rate and death rate declines. And, most Western nations have already experienced the kinds of birth rate and death rate declines represented by the democratic transition concept. Indeed, birth and death rates have fallen so low in a number of Western nations that they have already begun to experience what has been called the "second demographic transition," a decline of birth rates to the point of population decline, perhaps even rapid population decline. Italy and Spain, for example, have fertility rates (the number of children per woman) of 1.3 and 1.2, respectively.[11]

Phenomena such as the demographic transition and the second demographic transition make it difficult to project national or world population levels far into the future. We simply do not know whether various national birth rates will continue to decline, whether they might stabilize, or even increase in response to yet unforeseen economic or cultural transformations. Also, it is impossible to predict accurately death or migration rates far into the future. We do not know what diseases may yet plague the world's population or what medical advances may benefit it. We cannot know how migration rates may change in response to various climatological, military, or social forces. We may wish to project population trends into the future, but we must acknowledge that unpredictable rate changes seriously hinder clear predictions. That is why demographers do not make flat predictions about future population growth rates. Instead, they talk about ranges of growth or decline that are based on a number of forecasts; and each forecast rests on a different assumption about future fertility or death rates or migration

levels. The demographer may say, "If the fertility rate is 2.5 births per woman, we can expect the population to grow this way; if the rate is 2.0 births, population growth will assume a different direction," and so forth. In other words, demographers will not make a once-and-for-all prediction but rather will lay out a number of scenarios based on alternative assumptions about key rates. Although we cannot know for certain which of the several assumptions is correct, we can still extract important information from the kind of research we have been describing. We might find that for the lowest plausible estimate of future fertility, the population will double during the next thirty years; that is, we can be sure that at the very least the population will grow to a certain size within this specified time.

The problems that we face in forecasting long-term population changes are typical of the challenges encountered in virtually all social forecasting. Whenever we make predictions about future events, we base our estimates on assumptions about how relevant factors will affect our forecasts. The further out we carry our forecasts, the less confidence we can have that our assumptions will hold. Whenever we try to make projections of social events, we must try to anticipate changes in all the factors that may influence our prediction and include those potential changes in our analysis. Informed social planning and public policy is dependent on information of this kind.

FALLACIES IN THE INTERPRETATION OF AGGREGATE DATA

We have provided examples of aggregate data analysis and pondered some of the questions and problems faced by researchers who do it. They must worry about errors in the available data with which they work. In some cases, aggregate rates are poor estimates of true rates. Researchers must also be certain that the data describing each of the units they compare have been collected according to the same criteria. Even if we could assume ideal research conditions where none of these problems existed, it would still be possible to commit certain logical errors in making inferences from aggregate data.

[11] Replacement level fertility rate is the number of children the average woman must have to maintain a stable population (leaving out migration issues). It is generally held to be about 2.1 to account for childhood mortality.

Methodologists have pointed out a number of fallacies that may trap researchers as they try to interpret information. In nearly all cases where such logical errors occur, data have been collected at one level of aggregation (say, at the individual or small-group level), but the researcher has tried to use the data to make statements about phenomena at a different level. Keeping in mind that the level of aggregation influences the specific interpretations one can make, let us examine two common errors of inference, the ecological fallacy and the atomistic fallacy.

The Ecological Fallacy

Although in some instances the relationships between aggregate data variables are of direct interest to social scientists, more commonly researchers hope to use aggregate data to infer individual behavior. ECOLOGICAL INFERENCE is the name given to *efforts to infer individual behavior from aggregate data*. Unfortunately, using aggregate data to infer individual behavior can be problematic, so we must be wary about *employing data collected from and about groups in order to make inferences to individuals*. The ECOLOGICAL FALLACY involves making such an illegitimate shift of inference. Suppose that a jury is deciding a case and after much deliberation reports to the judge that it cannot as a group decide the guilt or innocence of the defendant. The jury is hung; as a group, it is undecided. Although the jury is composed of twelve individuals, we can refer to the group as a whole (this is essentially what we do when we aggregate data). We can say that the jury is undecided.

Now to the important point: Can we move from our statement that the jury is undecided to say that individual jurors are undecided? Certainly not! Indeed, it may very well be that none of the twelve jurors is undecided; they are simply individually decided in different directions. The conceptual, logical point to be made here is that one cannot properly make inferences about individuals in groups on the basis of data about the group as a whole. To do so is to commit the aggregative, or ecological, fallacy. Let us proceed from our simple example to one suggested by Robinson (1950) in his influential article about the dangers of using ecological corre-

lations (correlations from aggregate data using averages or rates) to make generalizations about individuals.[12]

Robinson knew that the individual level correlation between persons being foreign born and being illiterate for the U.S. population as a whole was .118, suggesting, relative to the native-born United States population, a weak but positive association between those variables.[13] However, when he used data from the 1930 census aggregated at the state level, Robinson found dramatically different results. The state level correlation between the percent foreign born and illiteracy was .526, suggesting that foreign-born individuals were less likely to be illiterate than native-born Americans. How could the results be so different? One reason ecological correlations may differ from individual correlations is that ecological correlations may overlook important contextual information. In Robinson's analysis, the important context was the total literacy rates of the particular states where the foreign born tended to live. As Freedman (2001:4028) points out, Robinson found a fairly strong negative correlation between percent foreign-born and percent illiterate because the foreign-born tended to live in states with relatively high literacy rates. In Robinson's correlation analysis, the relatively high literacy rates of the native born overcame the relatively high illiteracy rates of the foreign born.

Given the same logic presented here, we cannot say that because there is, for example, a high correlation between the percentage of divorced persons in a particular area and rates of juvenile delinquency in that area, that family disorganization is more generally and inevitably linked to delinquency. In the cases we have mentioned, it might immediately seem reasonable to make inferences about individuals from aggregate data, but there is a grave danger in doing so.

---

[12] Robinson's article, which has been cited more than 800 times (King, 1997:6), had an important impact on social research. Although he was not the first to draw attention to the problem, he is widely credited with alerting the social science community to the dangers of inferring individual behavior from aggregate data. While he did not use the term "ecological fallacy" in his article, the term later became associated with the problem that he described.

[13] For a discussion of correlation, see Chapter 18.

The most important idea that the ecological fallacy alerts us to is that the level on which we conduct our analysis must, where possible, correspond to the level of the units referred to in our hypotheses and at issue in our theories. If the conceptual model focuses on the differences between individuals, we should attempt to secure individual-level data. If we are certain that the data level used in a study corresponds to the units of analysis referred to in our hypotheses and theoretical constructs, we can be confident we have avoided the ecological fallacy.

Because aggregate data are often the only data available to researchers attempting to understand individual behavior, a number of methodological approaches have been developed that attempt to address the ecological inference problem. It is beyond the scope of this chapter to discuss the particulars of these methods, but research indicates that they are not generally reliable (Cleave and Brown, 1995). King (1997) has proposed a strategy for inferring individual behavior from aggregate data. While he acknowledges that his is "*a* solution, rather than *the* solution" (p. 17), King's work is an elaborate and comprehensive effort. As Firebaugh (2001:4026) points out, the value of King's solution for this previously intractable problem will be determined as it is applied by the social science research community.

The Atomistic Fallacy

The ecological fallacy can be committed in reverse – to make incorrect statements about groups on the basis of data from individuals. When we *try to test hypotheses about groups when we have only individual-level data*, we risk committing what has been called the ATOM-ISTIC FALLACY.

Suppose we had in mind the hypothesis that there is a relationship between rates of residential mobility in cities and rates of mental illness. More specifically, we believe that the higher the rates of residential mobility, the greater the incidence of mental illness. This hypothesis refers to the characteristics of cities as social systems. It is not an hypothesis about differences between individuals. Consider now the inferential error

we would make if we were mistakenly to test this group-level hypothesis with individual-level data.

We might begin the research by collecting data on individuals. We could do this by getting the names of all people in a particular city who were committed to mental hospitals within the last year. We might then interview these people or check records to determine how many times they had moved (a measure of residential mobility) during the five years before entering the hospital. We might find that the people studied move very infrequently and therefore conclude that our original hypothesis – that high rates of residential mobility will be strongly related to mental illness rates – is incorrect. We will have rejected a hypothesis about spatial groupings or structural units by examining data from individuals. Will we have properly rejected our original hypothesis, or will we have committed a logical error of inference?

It could be that the individuals who become mentally ill in cities are precisely those who are left behind when their friends move out of the immediate neighborhood. There is, in other words, a structural effect operating. The likelihood of individuals becoming mentally ill may not be a function of what they themselves do but of what is happening around them. Indeed, it could be that there is quite a strong relationship between rates of residential mobility in cities and rates of mental illness, which has not been seen because our researcher looked only at individual-level data. The researcher has simply assumed that what the individuals studied do is sufficient data on which to characterize the social groupings of which they are a part.

Whether we commit the ecological or the atomistic fallacy, the underlying reason for the mistake remains the same. We have, in both cases, committed what Galtung (1967) called "the fallacy of the wrong level."

SUMMARY

When we combine data on individuals to represent some social unit comprising these people statistically, we are using aggregate data. The possible levels of aggregation vary considerably, from relatively small census tracts to cities, states, and nations. The proper use of aggregate data involves taking these entities as units of analysis in order to make generalizations about the character of social structures.

Aggregate data analysis has wide application in the social sciences, for example, in demography, criminology, and urban planning. It is also useful in studies that compare neighborhoods, counties, or countries, as well as those that assess trends in poverty, health, education, and public safety. Census data are particularly helpful, but in working with them, errors of coverage, classification, and processing typical of all existing data are liable to occur. We know that the reported rates in crime statistics vary considerably from the true incidence of crime within a population and that criteria for data collection differ according to jurisdiction. We must recognize that aggregate data offer only an estimate of the group characteristics of interest to us. We need to take this into account as we interpret the information collected.

Researchers must conduct their investigations on the aggregate level for which data are available. Further, the level of aggregation at which they carry out their analysis affects the nature of the generalizations they can make. In devising social indicators (yardsticks for measuring the well-being of large groups of people), important information regarding differences between units at lower levels of aggregation may be lost or unavailable. This principle applies also to another application of group data – forecasting trends. We must be careful not to assume that the aggregate data variables we have available are the most important ones for determining future events. We may be able to forecast events such as future population growth, but such forecasts are subject to the same potential validity errors as is standard aggregate data analysis.

Finally, we must avoid mixing levels of aggregation by making inferences about individual behaviors from group data (the ecological fallacy) and by drawing conclusions about groups from individual data (the atomistic fallacy). The better we know the potential flaws or biases in dealing with specific kinds of data, the more likely we are to avoid these errors and thus improve the quality of our findings.

KEY TERMS

aggregate data
areal groupings
atomistic fallacy
census block
census tract
classification error
cross-cultural comparison
demographer
demographic transition
disaggregation
ecological fallacy
ecological inference
error of coverage
reported vs. true rate
social indicator
time-series data
unit of analysis

EXERCISES

1. Examine the extent to which your college has changed over the past twenty years. You might be interested in looking at one or more of the following variables: average college board scores of entering freshmen, the proportion of persons majoring in the natural sciences, the winning percentage of the school football team, or the percentage of seniors graduating with honors. What other variables interest you? Choose two variables for which you can obtain data for each of the past twenty years. After constructing tables presenting your collected data, try to offer an explanation of any changes discovered.

2. There is a hypothesis that individuals who come from homes where parents are divorced are more likely to commit delinquent acts than individuals who come from two-parent homes. Could you test this hypothesis by comparing delinquency rates in city areas with high and low divorce rates? Why not? Explain the kind of fallacy you might be committing if you use these suggested data. What kind of data would you need to test your hypothesis?

3. Suppose you get into a discussion with someone who points out that the average life expectancy rate in the United States as of 2005 was 77.6 years. Imagine the person uses this national-level social indicator to argue that all Americans experience very good health. Would you accept his or her judgment based on this one national-level statistic? In what ways might differences between segments of the American population in life expectancy be masked at the national level of aggregation? What additional information can be gained by disaggregating, if possible, these national-level data? What would be the advantages and disadvantages of looking at data for a number of different aggregate levels?

4. Using data from the World Bank's *World Development Indicators* (available in many libraries or at http://www.worldbank.org/data/) collect birth and death rates for the most recent year available for three countries from each of the following regions: Africa, Asia, Europe, North America, and South America. For the year for which you obtained data, what do birth and death rates tell you about the rate of natural increase for each of the countries that you selected? In general, do birth and death rates differ by region? If yes, how do they differ? Do birth and death statistics provide sufficient information for you to know how total population changed for your countries? If not, what other information would you need to calculate total population change?

5. Working alone or with another student in your class, collect data to show whether there is any association between the percentage of population that is nonwhite and the crime rates in cities. Collect data for both variables on ten cities of your choice. The percentage of nonwhite persons in each case can be determined using available census materials (e.g., http://www.census.gov). An overall crime rate for the same cities can be obtained from the most recent edition of the *Uniform Crime Reports* for the United States (see, e.g., http://www.fbi.gov/ucr/ucr.htm). Arrange your data in a table or graph to visually identify any association between the variables. What trends are you able to note in your data? Is there a positive relationship between the two variables (i.e., does the crime rate increase as the percentage of nonwhite persons in the population increases)? If you do find a positive relationship, can you draw the inference that nonwhite persons are more likely to commit crimes than white persons? Why? Why not?

SUGGESTED READINGS AND SOURCES

Readings about the Method

Ferriss, Abbott L. 1988. "The Uses of Social Indicators." *Social Forces* 66:601–617.

Social indicators are important tools in the analysis of social progress. With a focus on their use in the United States, this article discusses how social indicators can be used to monitor and forecast social trends, facilitate resource allocation, and identify social needs.

Hanusjek, Eric A., John Jackson, and John Kain. 1974. "Model Specification, Use of Aggregate Data, and the Ecological Correlation Fallacy." *Political Methodology* 1:89–107.

An advanced look at the ecological fallacy. The authors see it less as a problem of logic and more as a statistical issue.

King, Gary 1997. *A Solution to the Ecological Inference Problem: Reconstructing Individual Behavior from Aggregate Data*. Princeton, NJ: Princeton University Press.

In his first chapter, King offers a good nontechnical introduction to the general issues of ecological inference.

Kreft, Ita G. G., and Jan de Leeuw. 1998. *Introducing Multilevel Modeling*. Thousand Oaks, CA: Sage.

This book provides a general and nontechnical introduction to the theory and application of multilevel models.

National Research Council. 2000. *Beyond Six Billion: Forecasting the World's Population*. Panel on Population Projections. John Bongaarts and Rodolpho A. Bulatao, eds. Washington, DC: National Academy Press.

This book examines the accuracy of population forecasts, the factors that influence them, and how they can be improved. It includes an analysis of recent trends and research issues for the three components of population growth, fertility, mortality, and migration.

Robinson, W. S. 1950. "Ecological Correlations and the Behavior of Individuals." *American Sociological Review* 15:351–357.

The nature of the ecological fallacy is described in this classic, often cited, and still relevant article. It is not difficult to follow Robinson's argument, and the data presented show that it is fallacious to assume that properties associated at the group level are also associated at the individual level.

Siegal, Jacob S. 2002. *Applied Demography: Applications to Business, Government, Law, and Public Policy.* San Diego, CA: Academic Press.

This textbook is a detailed presentation of the way demography can be applied to a wide range of policy and business issues, including health care, Social Security, labor force changes, and marketing strategies.

Smith, Stanley K., Jeff Tayman, and David A. Swanson. 2001. *State and Local Population Projections: Methodology and Analysis.* New York: Kluwer Academic/Plenum.

This impressive book focuses on the methodology and analysis of projecting state and local populations. It provides a solid introduction to the components of population change and the fundamentals of population analysis including data resources.

Readings Illustrating the Method

Blumstein, Alfred, Frederick P. Rivara, and Richard Rosenfeld. 2000. "The Rise and Decline of Homicide – and Why." *Annual Review of Public Health* 21:505–541.

This article examines the trends in homicide from the middle 1980s through the early 1990s. Much of the discussion is augmented with charts based on aggregate data.

Esping-Andersen, Gøsta. 1999. *Social Foundations of Postindustrial Economies.* New York: Oxford University Press.

The author uses aggregate data to examine welfare issues in the emerging postindustrial economies and the dilemmas different types of welfare regimes face in addressing them.

Franklin, Donna L. 1997. *Ensuring Inequality: the Structural Transformation of the African-American Family.* New York: Oxford University Press.

This book includes aggregate data in an analysis of the history and current status of the African American family. It examines the effects of slavery, sharecropping, the northern migration, social and economic change, and government policies on the relations between black men and women and their consequences for family formation.

Goldstein, Joshua R., and Catherine T. Kenney. 2001. "Marriage Delayed or Marriage Forgone? New Cohort Forecasts of First Marriage for U.S. Women." *American Sociological Review* 66:506–519.

Marriage rates have declined in the United States in recent decades. This article examines whether cohabitation is replacing marriage as a social institution. Using data from the Current Population Survey it presents forecasts of marriage rates by race and education of women from different birth cohorts. There is little evidence to indicate a general moving away from marriage among American women.

Pampel, Fred C. 2001. *The Institutional Context of Population Change: Patterns of Fertility and Mortality across High-Income Nations.* Chicago: University of Chicago Press.

A cohort is a group of people sharing one or more demographic traits, for example, persons born in the 1950s, who are followed over time. This book examines the way public policies, particularly public benefit programs, mediate the effect of cohort size and female labor force participation on fertility, suicide, and homicide in high-income nations.

Putnam, Robert D. 2001. *Bowling Alone: The Collapse and Revival of American Community.* New York: Simon & Schuster.

In this influential book, Putnam uses aggregate data from commercial sources, government agencies, and private organizations to examine the decline in civic engagement in American society.

South, Scott J., and Steven F. Messner. 2000. "Crime and Demography: Multiple Linkages, Reciprocal Relations." *Annual Review of Sociology* 26:83–106.

This article reviews a vast literature linking two frequent subjects of aggregate data analysis, crime and demography. It reviews not only the widely studied role of demographic variables in explaining crime but also the less well-studied relationship between crime and demography.

Wu, Lawrence L., and Barbara Wolfe, eds. 2000. *Out of Wedlock: Causes and Consequences of Nonmarital Fertility.* New York: Russell Sage Foundation.

The rapid increase in out-of-wedlock childbirth has been one of the most prominent changes in family structure in the West over the past half-century. This book looks at the trends in nonmarital childbearing, the public policy implications of this increasing phenomenon, and the consequences for children and adults.

Data Sites on the Web

A number of sources on the Web offer data and information about aggregate data analysis. Some sites such as the United Nations, the World Bank, the Organization for Economic Cooperation and Development, the Population Reference Bureau, and the U.S. Census Bureau offer their own data, while others have links to data sources or other useful Web sites.

Data on the Net. 2006. University of California, San Diego.

http://3stages.org/idata/.

This site offers information and links to hundreds of "Internet sites of numeric social science statistical data, data catalogs, data libraries, social science gateways, addresses and more." Many of the sites offer downloadable aggregate data.

Documents Center. 2006. University of Michigan.

http://www.lib.umich.edu/govdocs/.

This site offers links to Web sites of international agencies, many of which provide aggregate data. Especially useful are "Statistical Resources on the Web," http://www.lib.umich.edu/govdocs/stats.html *and "International Agencies and Information on the Web,"* http://www.lib.umich.edu/govdocs/intl.html.

Inter-University Consortium for Political and Social Research (ICPSR). 2006. University of Michigan.

http://www.icpsr.umich.edu/index.html.

This site maintains an archive of social science data. Much of it is limited to member organizations or available for a fee, but some, including international crime data, is available free of charge. The ICPSR Web site also contains valuable links to other social science research sites.

Lewis Mumford Center for Comparative Urban and Regional Research. 2002. University at Albany.

http://mumford.albany.edu/census/.

This site contains information and data about the racial and ethnic composition of American cities.

National Center for Health Statistics. 2006. Centers for Disease Control and Prevention.

http://www.cdc.gov/nchs/default.htm.

This site provides health data and links to health-related Web sites.

Organization for Economic Cooperation and Development (OECD). 2006.

http://www.oecd.org/.

An excellent source of statistical data on OECD ("first world") countries.

Population Reference Bureau. 2006.

http://www.prb.org/.

This comprehensive directory of population-related Web sites not only provides data but also links to many other valuable data and informational population sites.

Social Science Information Gateway. 2005. "Demography" page.

http://www.sosig.ac.uk/roads/subject-listing/World/demog.html.

This site contains links to many useful demography Web sites.

Stat Cat. 2005. Yale University.

http://ssrs.yale.edu/statcat/Welcome.do;jsessionid=D43C8FC38005F75F9DD26DC919457541.

This site does not provide data directly but has links to many sites with downloadable data, including many aggregate data sites.

United Nations' Web Site. 2006.

http://www.un.org/english/.

The site contains links to U.N. data and other resources.

U.S. Census Bureau. 2006. Home Page.

http://www.census.gov.

This Web site is a gateway to its vast collection of data on the U.S. population.

World Bank. 2006. Data and Statistics Page.

http://worldbank.org/data/databytopic/databytopic.html.

This site offers data from its own publication, World Development Indicators, or links to sites with data.

REFERENCES

Anderson, Robert, N. 1998. *National Vital Statistics Reports*, 47 (13). Centers for Disease Control and Prevention. Hyattsville, MD: National Vital Statistics Center.

Barnett, Cynthia. 2002. "The Measurement of White-Collar Crime Using Uniform Crime Reporting (UCR) Data." Washington, DC: U.S. Dept of Justice, Federal Bureau of Investigation, Criminal Justice Information Services Division.
www.fbi.gov/ucr/whitecollarforweb.pdf.

Cleave, N., and P. J. Brown. 1995. "Evaluation of Methods for Ecological Inference." *Journal of the Royal Statistical Society* 158:55–72.

Ferriss, Abbott L. 1988. "The Uses of Social Indicators." *Social Forces* 66:601–617.

Firebaugh, Glenn. 2001. "Ecological Fallacy, Statistics of." In *Encyclopedia of the Social and Behavioral Sciences*, 6:4023–4026. Neil Smelser and Robert B. Bates, eds. New York: Elsevier.

Freedman, David A. 2001. "Ecological Inference." *Encyclopedia of the Social and Behavioral Sciences*, 6:4026–4030. In Neil Smelser and Robert B. Bates, eds. New York: Elsevier.

Galtung, Johan. 1967. *Theory and Methods of Social Research*. New York: Columbia University Press.

Glaeser, Edward L., and Jacob L. Vigdor. 2001. "Racial Segregation in the 2000 Census: Promising News."
http://www.brook.edu/dybdocroot/es/urban/census/glaeser.pdf.

Hwang, Sean-Shong, and Steve H. Murdock. 1998. "Racial Attraction or Racial Avoidance in American Suburbs." *Social Forces* 77:541–566.

Jones, Gavin W., and R. M. Douglas. 1997. "Introduction." In *The Continuing Demographic Transition*, 1–12. G. W. Jones, R. M. Douglas, J. C. Caldwell, and R. M. D'Souza, eds. Oxford: Clarendon Press.

King, Gary. 1997. *A Solution to the Ecological Inference Problem: Reconstructing Individual Behavior from Aggregate Data*. Princeton, NJ: Princeton University Press.

Robinson, W. S. 1950. "Ecological Correlations and the Behavior of Individuals." *American Sociological Review* 15:351–357.

Siegal, Jacob S. 2002. *Applied Demography: Applications to Business, Government, Law, and Public Policy*. San Diego, CA: Academic Press.

Skerry, Peter. 2000. *Counting on the Census? Race, Group Identity, and the Evasion of Politics*. Washington, DC: Brookings Institution.

Smith, Stanley K., Jeff Tayman, and David A. Swanson. 2001. *State and Local Population Projections: Methodology and Analysis*. New York: Kluwer Academic/Plenum.

Steffensmeier, Darrell, and Miles D. Harer. 1999. "Making Sense of Recent U.S. Crime Trends, 1980 to 1996/1998: Age Composition Effects and Other Explanations." *Journal of Research in Crime and Delinquency* 36:235–274.

Taeuber, Karl E., and Alma F. Taeuber. 1966. *Negroes in Cities: Residential Segregation and Neighborhood Change*. Chicago: Aldine de Gruyter.

Taylor, Marylee C. 1998. "How White Attitudes Vary with the Local Racial Composition of Local Populations: Numbers Count." *American Sociological Review* 63:512–535.

United Nations Population Division. 2002. "Fertility Levels and Trends in Countries with Intermediate Levels of Fertility." Population Division, Department of Economic and Social Affairs, United Nations Secretariat, New York, 11–14.
www.un.org/esa/population/publications/completingfertility/FFPSPOPDIVpaper.PDF>.

U.S. Census Bureau. 2000. "Census Tracts and Block Numbering Areas."
http://www.census.gov/geo/www/cen_tract.html.

COMPARATIVE RESEARCH
METHODS

15

INTRODUCTION

In contrast to the chapters on survey research, experimentation, or content analysis that described a distinct set of skills, in this chapter, a variety of comparative research techniques are discussed. What makes a study comparative is not the particular techniques employed but the theoretical orientation and the sources of data. All the tools of the social scientist, including historical analysis, fieldwork, surveys, and aggregate data analysis, can be used to achieve the goals of comparative research. So, there is plenty of room for the research imagination in the choice of data collection strategies. There is a wide divide between quantitative and qualitative approaches in comparative work. Most studies are either exclusively qualitative (e.g., individual case studies of a small number of countries) or exclusively quantitative, most often using many cases and a cross-national focus (Ragin, 1991:7). Ideally, increasing numbers of studies in the future will use both traditions, as the skills, tools, and quality of data in comparative research continue to improve.[1]

In almost all social research, we look at how social processes vary and are experienced in different settings to develop our knowledge of the causes and effects of human behavior. This holds true if we are trying to explain the behavior of nations or individuals. So, it may then seem redundant to include a chapter in this book specifically dedicated to comparative research methods when all the other methods discussed are ultimately comparative. Indeed, it is fair to say that all studies that attempt theoretical analysis or classification of social phenomena by examining similarities or differences are comparative (Jary and Jary, 1991:71). Typically, however, academic tradition assigns the term "comparative research," or **COMPARATIVE SOCIOLOGY,** to *studies that include two or more nations or cultures.*

The idea that comparative work is a distinct category of research is not universally accepted (Nowak, 1989:37; Øyen, 1990:10). Some prac-

titioners believe that the issues and problems faced by comparativists are not substantially different from those confronted in all areas of social research. A precise definition is elusive, but for our purposes, we can consider comparative research to include studies that are cross-cultural, cross-national, or cross-historical[2] as well as case studies that are implicitly comparative[3] (Nowak, 1989:35).

In this chapter, the principal advantages of using comparative data will be outlined. We can use it to improve the validity of our generalizations. In addition, some research questions simply cannot be answered except through comparative analysis. Researchers who employ data from societies other than their own have to confront a host of potential pitfalls. These will be examined as various applications of the comparative method are illustrated.

A Brief History

Comparative social research has a long history. Herodotus (495–424 BC) was one of the first to use systematic observation across societies as a basis for generalizing about human behavior. Many of the topics he considered in his *Nine Books of History* would today be classified as anthropology, political science, or sociology. At one point, he compared the Egyptians with the Lacedaemonians with respect to interaction between young men and their elders. In both societies, when they met on the street, the young men gave way to their elders by stepping aside, and when an elder came into the room, the young men rose from their seats. In *The Peloponnesian War*, Thucydides (460–400 BC) made a number of cross-societal comparisons. He pointed out that Sparta controlled its allies by establishing oligarchies to rule them; in contrast, Athens tended to focus on exacting tribute from its allies. Aristotle (384–322 BC) collected and analyzed data on 158 political constitutions. His concern with cross-societal

---

[1] Comparative Qualitative Analysis (QCA), an example of combining both approaches, is found in Ragin (1998).

[2] Cross-historical studies examine a society at different times. See, for example, Marsh (1998).

[3] Comparative studies may examine a single society but make reference, at least implicitly, to another society or a theoretically ideal type society. See Ragin (1987:4).

similarities and differences in governments, and particularly in constitutions, is extensively documented in *Politics*.[4]

The comparative method as practiced today may be traced most directly to the work of Herbert Spencer (1873/2001) and other nineteenth-century evolutionists. The proponents of **EVOLUTIONARY THEORY** viewed society as *passing through a series of stages*. Evidence from existing primitive societies could be used to make inferences about what more advanced societies were like at earlier stages in their evolution. Karl Marx (1848/2001) also drew heavily on comparative historical data. One example is his discussion of the various epochs characterized by differences in the "modes of production," ranging from primitive communism, to ancient society (slavery), to feudal society (serfdom), and finally to modern capitalism (wage labor).

Following World War I, there appeared much criticism of the evolutionist perspective, with a consequent movement away from cross-cultural analysis. The revival of the method is due, in part, to the work of George Murdock (1937), who was interested in the relationship between kinship structure and other aspects of culture. He based his analysis on a sample of 230 (predominantly primitive) societies drawn from around the world. After 1945, improvements in transportation and communications, as well as the more assertive role of the United States in world affairs, produced new generations of comparativists, not only in anthropology but also in sociology, political science, and psychology. Some of these researchers analyzed the industrial democracies of Western Europe and North America. Others concentrated on the centrally planned economies of the communist bloc. Beginning in the early 1960s, the developing and newly independent countries of Asia, Africa, and Latin America became a third major focus for comparative investigation.

As a result of the renewed interest in comparative research, the number of such studies has continued to increase since the 1960s. Major journals in sociology and political science regularly include qualitative and quantitative cross-national research. There has been a surge in historical-comparative work and in case studies of important social events. Books and articles focus on population, social stratification, growth of state structures, criminology, education, and many other topics.

One very important factor in the growing emphasis on quantitative comparative research has been the explosion in data available for such work. Organizations such as the United Nations and the Organization for Economic Cooperation and Development (OECD) produce volumes of data concerning the social, political, and economic affairs of their member nations, and those data are often readily available to researchers. Also, international projects such as the World Values Survey (2003) have distributed high-quality data to comparative researchers.

WHY DO COMPARATIVE RESEARCH?

Among the many benefits of these trends over the past sixty years has been the accumulation of a rich storehouse of information about social and political structures and the process of personality formation in foreign cultures. Two more enduring benefits of the growing contemporary interest in comparative social science are its value in creating and testing new theory and in confirming, challenging, or qualifying existing theory.

Testing and Qualifying Existing Theories

Social scientists have long been curious about the ways social institutions and structures influence economic performance in capitalist countries. Max Weber, for instance, was keenly interested in how cultural and political factors influenced the development of capitalism in the West (Weber and Swedberg, 1999; Weber and Kilburn, 2001). In recent years, a number of investigators have examined government's impact on economic growth in a single country or across groups of countries. They have focused on the relationship between the size of government, as measured by public spending, and

---

[4] This historical summary draws on Warwick and Osherson (1973:3–6).

economic growth over varying periods of time. Other studies have looked at the role institutional factors such as government bureaucracies have played in economic growth, but these studies have often been limited to just one or a few nations. From a Weberian perspective, strong and stable bureaucracies may promote growth in a variety of ways, for example, by providing reliable information to investors and resolving trade disputes. Given the dominance of capitalism as the organizing principle of national economies and the emphasis Weber attached to the relationship between strong bureaucracies and economic growth, the idea that bureaucratic government could facilitate growth should be of interest to researchers. But, until recently, a reliable cross-national measure of the strength of bureaucracies has prevented a consequent analysis of their economic influence.

Inspired by Weber's theories, Evans and Rauch (1999) created an innovative data set to examine the effects of "bureaucratic authority structures" on economic growth in a large group of developing countries from 1970 to 1990. To create their Weberianness Scale, they recruited experts who were knowledgeable about the nature of government bureaucracies in each of the countries covered by the study. Each expert was then asked ten questions about the role of the government agencies in the economy and the nature of the bureaucracy. One of the questions aimed to measure the importance of the government agencies in "generating economic policy." The remaining questions tried to capture whether bureaucratic hiring and promotion was based on merit, whether the jobs were prestigious, well paid and durable, and whether bribes were an important part of salary. Evans and Rauch found a strong positive association between their Weberianness Scale and economic performance in their selected countries for the 1970–1990 period. Their study confirmed a theoretical idea that Weber proposed nearly a century ago, that is, that "state bureaucracies characterized by meritocratic recruitment and predictable, rewarding career-ladders are associated with higher growth rates" (1999:749). The Evans and Rauch study demonstrates the value of comparative research for testing existing theory. Often

researchers test theory on only a single case or culture. However, when we test theory on data from many nations, we are more likely to have confidence in the results *and* the theory.

Where Rauch and Evans's work confirms a long-standing social theory, a study by de Soysa and Oneal (1999) challenges one. Economists and sociologists have viewed the value of foreign economic investment to developing countries differently. Where economists have viewed foreign investment as a useful stimulant to economic development (Rostow, 1991), an important group of sociologists, dependency theorists, has argued that foreign investment, through multinational corporations, is a net drain on the resources of developing countries (So, 1990). Dependency theory lost much of its political appeal during the 1980s and 1990s as many political leaders in underdeveloped nations embraced capitalism as the path to economic development. Still, academic debates about the merits of dependency theory have continued. In their study of the effects of foreign direct investment on the developing countries, de Soysa and Oneal employ recently released data in an effort to resolve the ongoing debate. Contrary to the work of dependency theorists, the authors find that foreign direct investment is valuable as a source of economic growth, more valuable dollar for dollar than direct investment from within nations.

To see how a comparative study can qualify or identify exceptions to a theory, consider a study by Kelley and De Graf (1997). They examined how a nation's religious environment influences the beliefs of its citizens. Do citizens in nations with national religious cultures differ in the intensity and nature of their religious beliefs from citizens of secular nations? To explore this issue, the authors used survey data from the International Social Survey Programme (ISSP) for nearly 18,000 respondents from fifteen countries. Among their notable findings are the positive effects of a nation's religious environment on the beliefs of its citizens. In addition, they found that the strength of a nation's religious beliefs and the influence of family vary in devout and secular nations. However, the author's test of modernization theory revealed the study's most important conclusion. As Kelly and De Graf point out, modernity theory generally holds that as nations prosper their citizens will become less religious. However, some theorists contend that the United States is an exception to this general rule, being simultaneously a very prosperous nation and one that is also strongly religious. The Kelly and De Graf analysis finds that modernity theory is confirmed when the United States respondents are absent from the analysis, but the results are reversed when the United States respondents are included. Their analysis demonstrates the value of testing theory cross-nationally or cross-culturally and the usefulness of comparative research in helping researchers qualify existing theory.

Testing Theory Cross-Culturally

One of the most noteworthy strengths of the comparative method is that it can be used to test the generalizability of a finding that is based on data from one society. It is not at all uncommon for propositions to be stated as if they applied to all societies, but such propositions have often not been actually tested cross-societally. An example of research that was undertaken to examine whether results from one society are replicated in a second is the Diekmann and Englehardt (1999) study of intergenerational divorce in Germany. The "transmission hypothesis" states that marriage partners are more likely to experience divorce if their parents were divorced than if their parents were not divorced. In line with previous research, Diekmann and Englehardt suggest a number of intervening social, economic, and psychological factors that may account for the increased likelihood of divorce if the transmission hypothesis holds. Previous research has confirmed the transmission hypothesis in the United States. Diekmann and Englehardt examine recent German data to determine whether the transmission hypothesis holds in a country outside North America. Their results confirm the transmission hypothesis for Germany. Children from divorced families were much more likely to divorce than were children from families where a divorce did not occur.

We know from earlier chapters that replication is a fundamental aspect of the scientific enterprise. Studies are most typically replicated in the same society, but it is often of great value to be able to replicate a finding across several societies. When we turn to comparative data to test the generalizability of a finding based on one society, we can argue that the original finding has been replicated if it is sustained for the other societies we consider. A good example of work that has initially been undertaken in one culture and then tested in other cultures is the effort by Kohn and Schooler (1969) to test the effect of social stratification, or the place individuals have in the social structure, on psychological functioning. In their original study, conducted in the United States, the authors found that social stratification had a pronounced effect on the values held by men. In general, social class influenced the way men viewed themselves and the desirability of self-direction, with men of higher social standing valuing self-direction more than men of lower standing. Educational experience and occupational positions were found to be especially important in determining class-based values because education influences intellectual flexibility, and occupational position determines the capability for self-direction.

To determine whether social stratification had similar effects in socialist and non-Western societies, replications of the Kohn and Schooler study were carried out in Poland (Slomczynski, Miller, and Kohn, 1981) and Japan (Naoi and Schooler, 1981). Those studies found that for Polish and Japanese workers the importance of social class was similar to the United States. The occupational self-direction that often accompanies work in higher social positions led to an appreciation for self-direction in other aspects of workers' lives.

Specifying the Conditions under Which Theory Applies

When we use comparative data to test findings cross-culturally, we sometimes discover that the results for the original society will be supported in some settings but not in others. If we can find some characteristic that differentiates those societies within which the original relationship holds from those in which it does not, we will have specified the conditions under which the original relationship exists. This is another strength of the comparative method.

The specification of theory is illustrated by the classic Lipset et al. (1954) study of voter participation in the United States and in various European cities. The research focused on the rate of participation of the working class in relation to that of the middle class. A higher rate of turnout for middle-class voters than for working-class voters was found in the United States. This pattern was confirmed in Great Britain but was reversed in some Austrian and German cities. When the investigators looked more closely at these cities, they found that the labor movement there had created a network for indoctrination of workers; such networks were less developed in Great Britain and in the United States. The research of Lipset et al. had thus identified the condition under which the relationship originally found for one country held true for others, and the condition under which it failed to hold true.

For some purposes, it is useful to make comparisons between societies that are similar in many respects. For other purposes, it is useful to select societies that are as different as possible. Shin and Hytrek (2000) studied the phenomenon of capitalist development and its connection to divergent patterns of conflict resolution. The authors selected two countries with marked differences, South Korea and Costa Rica. Although both nations have experienced forms of capitalist development, Korea has a historically authoritarian system and Costa Rica a historically democratic one. Differing patterns of dependent development produced, in the case of Korea, a strong state that was able to dictate class formation, and in Costa Rica, a more simultaneous process of state and class formation. As Shin and Hytrek (2002:474) noted:

The contrasting patterns of state and class formation and balance of power between the two . . . led to contrasting form(s) of conflict resolution. In Korea, conflict resolution took the forms of both repression and accommodation, while in Costa Rica, it was primarily accommodating . . . In Korea the state took the initiative in resolving conflicts and con-

structed a social base for its authoritarian system. In contrast, the Costa Rican state tended to mediate conflict among contending social classes . . . The contrasting forms and nature of conflict resolution, then, was responsible for the emergence of authoritarian and social democratic systems, respectively.

When our objective is to argue for the generalizability of a relationship between two variables, such as capitalist economic development and democratic conflict resolution, the case is strongest when it can be shown to be consistent across a very diverse range of societies. However, the strategy of selecting for comparison societies that have minimal differences between them helps to isolate just those variables that might be relevant to an explanation of the divergent systems of the two countries.

Discovering the Relationships among Macrolevel Variables

Another strength of the comparative method is that it allows us to test theories that specify as variables **MACROLEVEL** structures or behaviors – that is, *characteristics of entire societies*. If a theory states that the political or economic structure of a country has a causal impact on the way in which income and wealth are distributed, we encounter problems in attempting to verify this proposition on the basis of data from that one country alone. It is not possible to assess the impact of a variable such as economic structure, which is a constant for any one nation. However, if we compare income inequality in several societies with different types of economies, we will be in a position to draw some conclusions about the impact of economic structure on the distribution of wealth. In general, it is not possible to obtain a quantitative estimate of the effect of any society-wide characteristic on the basis of data from just one country. However, if we base our study on several societies and select them in such a way that there is variation in the macrolevel characteristic of interest to us, it is possible to estimate the effect of this variable.

This use of comparative data is well illustrated in the work of Gustafsson and Johansson (1999) who constructed a model to account for changes in income inequality, or the distribution of income, in industrialized countries.

Their study continues a long-standing interest among economists and sociologists in modeling income inequality within and between nations. Among the variables of interest to the investigators were the size of the industrial sector of the economy, the strength of labor unions, and the size of government. By basing their study on data from sixteen countries, they were able to make some quantitative estimates of the causal impact of these characteristics on the extent of income inequality within those nations. However, because they limited their analysis to industrialized counties, we would not assume the same variables would affect income distribution in developing nations.

RELIABILITY AND VALIDITY ISSUES

There are many strong reasons for doing comparative research. Yet, there are also a number of obstacles facing those who use cross-cultural data. We face many of these difficulties when research is conducted in one society, but in the context of comparative research, they are even more problematic.

Most of the research methods considered in preceding chapters may be used comparatively, but some are employed more extensively than others. Much cross-national research has been done using survey techniques, but comparative experimentation is still quite rare. In this section, the four most frequently used methods of data collection in comparative research are discussed: ethnographic fieldwork, historical analysis, survey research, and aggregate data analysis. Two other methods – experimentation and content analysis – are briefly reviewed. Some ways in which these six research methods have been used comparatively will be illustrated. In addition, problems that must be confronted when using each method in a comparative context are outlined. Some of these difficulties are unique to a specific technique; others tend to appear in all forms of comparative research.

Fieldwork

Anthropologists and, to a lesser extent, sociologists have carried out studies of other cultures using observational techniques. Typically, an anthropologist goes to live with a people in a distant land, such as villagers in Nepal (McHugh, 2001), for an extended time and then writes an **ETHNOGRAPHY** based on this fieldwork. The ethnography *describes the society's organizations, kinship system, language, religious beliefs*, and so forth. Is such a work an example of comparative research if it is based on only one society? Although the research report describes only one setting, there is a sense in which it is comparative. The anthropologist is almost always from a different society, and consequently there will often be some explicit, and always many implicit, contrasts with that society.

We can raise a similar question about much of the *social and political research carried out in a single foreign country* (often referred to as **AREA STUDIES**). Ball and Hooker (1999) investigated the practice of British parents "co-sleeping" with their young children. Previous research had indicated that parents sleep with their babies in much of the world, but there has been little research published about these sleep arrangements in Britain. Although the Ball and Hooker study was based on the sleep patterns of parents and newborns in one area of England, the authors' choice of issues for emphasis was unavoidably informed by published results of sleep patterns in other nations and cultures. We do not seek to resolve the debate about whether all ethnographic reports and other single-society area studies should be considered de facto comparative. Some unquestionably fit the label better than others. However, when data from several area studies or ethnographies are combined, the product is unquestionably an example of comparative research. For example, LeTendre's (2000) comparison of the way adolescence is constructed in American and Japanese middle schools is a clear example of comparative research. Through his fieldwork, he explored the cultural and institutional assumptions about adolescence in those nations and the way those assumptions shape the adolescent experience in middle schools.

Ethnographic data depend heavily on the observations, judgments, and interpretations of the small number of social scientists (often only one) conducting the research. It is, for example, a common practice among anthropologists to develop a certain territoriality about the group they have studied. The same anthropologist may return to a community several times over the years; it is uncommon for another person to study exactly the same community. When independent studies are made of the same setting, the observations and conclusions can be quite inconsistent. In 1930, Robert Redfield published *Tepoztlan: A Mexican Village*, which was based on his personal observations. Having observed a great deal of harmony and cooperation among the people, he stressed in his report the positive aspects of "folk" life as opposed to "modern" life in the community. Oscar Lewis (1951) later went to the identical town; he presented his description in *Life in a Mexican Village*. He drew an almost totally opposite portrait, including reports of discord among villagers and a description of interpersonal relationships more characteristic of the negative stereotype of the city dweller who fears even the next-door neighbors.

How could their widely divergent findings differ? It could be that one of these researchers was an unusually poor observer, although a more likely explanation is that each one expected to find different things and behaved differently in the research setting. The range of community life to which each investigator was exposed was not identical; their experiences probably overlapped only partially. Examples such as this cast doubt on the reliability of comparative ethnographies. As noted in Chapter 9, studies based on fieldwork data are difficult to replicate, even more so when they have occurred in exotic settings. Moreover, the traditional strength of the ethnographic technique, the validity that comes from a lengthy stay in a particular setting and from participant observation, may be mitigated or compromised in comparative work. The investigator may be dealing with an unfamiliar language and culture. As a result, the investigator may not realize that he or she is misinterpreting events or being fed inaccurate information by respondents who resent the intrusion or who do not understand, or mistakenly believe that they *do* understand, what the researcher wants to know.

Ethnographic Data Files

In 1938, George Murdock initiated a major attempt to codify and rationalize comparative field data in the Human Relations Area Files (HRAF, 2006). The database was compiled from observational ethnographic reports by anthropologists and sociologists prepared for more than 300 societies. These ethnographies have been organized into a set of categories, which is described in the *Outline of Cultural Materials* (Murdock et al., 1987); there are more than 700 such categories, including infant feeding, childbirth, independence training, cosmology, and suicide.[5]

Numerous studies have been based on these data. One example is Divale's (1999) article on the development of numerical counting systems. Using data from sixty-nine cultural groups, he examined the relationship between the development of counting systems and climatic variability. Cultures that experience predictable climate variations often have to store and manage food for periods of scarcity. Divale found that cultures that experienced climate change were more likely to have developed counting systems.

The HRAF files have proved to be a valuable source of information for cross-cultural research. In view of their importance, a few of the major problems that must be faced by those who choose to work with this source and with less elaborate databases must be considered. One of the most common difficulties is that the researcher's categories do not correspond to the ethnographic data classifications. If we are lucky, it is possible to find the relevant material by looking under two or three existing categories or by shifting to a more general heading. However, there are always some issues for which the standard categories are inappropriate. In such instances, we run the risk of missing information that is actually available in the file.

In using older ethnographic data files, recognize that past generations of scholars assumed

---

[5] The data are available on both CD-ROM and by subscription through the World Wide Web. See http://www.yale.edu/hraf/ for an introduction to cross-cultural research using the Human Relations Area Files.

ethnicity to be a fixed trait based on ancestry (Geertz, 1973). In contrast, more recent work treats ethnicity as an outcome of a process of social classification (Bourdieu, 1991:221; Jenkins, 1994:202). This means that ethnic categories are nowadays presumed to be more fluid, so that caution is required when accessing data categorized with ethnic labels.

Another issue that all users of ethnographic data files must face is the selection of a unit of analysis. Some reports may describe a nation, others a tribe or society, but by far, the most common are ethnographic descriptions of a specific community within a tribe or a society. This fairly small unit of analysis reflects the emphasis in the ethnographic work that anthropologists have done over the past century. The Oromo, for example, are among the most numerous peoples of Africa. Most of them live in Ethiopia, but a smaller number live in Kenya. In his book, *Being Oromo in Kenya*, Mario Aguilar (1998) reports on a segment of Oromo society, the Waso Boorana; he did not conduct a systematic analysis of all those who call themselves Oromo. The anthropologist will generally be explicit about whether a hamlet, subtribe, or an entire society is being studied, but the researcher must track down such information to ensure consistency, or equivalence, in the level of the cases on file.[6]

Sampling is one of the most difficult exercises confronting those who choose to use resources such as the HRAF files. The major problem is in deciding which communities, tribes, societies, or cultures are sufficiently distinct as to represent independent observations. Anthropologists are debating the criteria for defining a society or a culture; we could not hope, in this brief discussion, to present, let alone resolve, the debate. One area of disagreement has to do with the considerable overlap between tribes regarding language and other cultural aspects. This diffusion of culture makes it more reasonable to talk about criteria for measuring the *degree*

of independence between societies, rather than to look for criteria to measure complete independence. This *problem of lack of independence between units* is referred to as GALTON'S PROBLEM; Sir Francis Galton was the first to raise the issue in 1889. What appears to be a large number of societies in which the researcher's hypothesis is supported may actually turn out to be duplicate observations of one society. To date, there has been no adequate mechanism for solving Galton's Problem although several methods have been proposed.[7]

Although many methodological problems await those who work with the HRAF files, these are minor when contrasted with the difficulties in trying to collect the relevant data for twenty-five, fifty, or seventy-five societies each time we want to carry out a comprehensive, comparative ethnographic study. The existence of these data files makes possible the testing of a variety of hypotheses that could not be tested without them.

Historical-Comparative Research

Historical-comparative research has a long tradition in sociology,[8] beginning with the founding fathers of the field. However, for much of the twentieth century, there was relatively little such work in North American sociology. That situation has changed dramatically since the 1960s as comparative sociologists have regularly undertaken and reported research using historical methods. In this section, we describe some of the strengths and limitations of historical-comparative research and discuss some recent studies that employ the method.

Social scientists often seek to understand the causes of social events or phenomena.[9] One way to accomplish this task might be to collect data on a large number of cases and conduct

---

[6] Sometimes restricting the study to nation-states solves the issue of consistency in the level of the unit of analysis, but even this strategy has its problems. Some nation-states have a population of less than 100,000 persons, which for many purposes would be more equivalent to one state in a larger nation such as the United States.

[7] Research difficulties associated with Galton's Problem are not limited to analyses of tribal or preindustrial societies; they may be even more severe in advanced societies. The adaptation of attitudes, programs, policies, and many other social practices are likely to be influenced as much by external factors as they are by internal ones (Goldthorpe, 1997).

[8] Refer to Chapter 11 for a discussion of historical method.

[9] The discussion in this section is drawn, in part, from Ragin (1987:1–52).

a statistical analysis to determine the factors associated with various outcomes. Often the goals or design of research projects argue against the use of variable-based quantitative analysis when doing comparative research. One reason is that historical-comparative researchers are often interested in determining the complex set of events that have produced certain social outcomes such as political or economic change. For example, consider the difference between a research project that aims to measure the influence of women's labor force participation on government spending in a group of developed countries (Huber and Stephens, 2000) and one that aims to explain the evolution toward democracy in Central American nations with coffee-based economies. An attempt to model the first project quantitatively would be relatively straightforward, both theoretically and methodologically, and data would be readily available. Attempts to model the second project quantitatively would be more problematic because there are too few cases to allow quantitative analysis. In addition, and perhaps more important, the complexity of the process would be lost in a quantitative analysis.

This is the problem that Jeffrey Paige (1997) faced in his highly regarded study, *Coffee and Power: Revolution and the Rise of Democracy in Central America*.[10] He analyzed the evolution toward democracy in three Central American countries: El Salvador, Costa Rica, and Nicaragua. Using interviews and historical sources, he traced the influence of ruling elites in these countries in the political development from authoritarianism to democracy. Wealth and power in all three countries were significantly based on the growth and exportation of coffee. Paige showed how the varying influence of the coffee elites resulted in different paths to democracy.

Another well-received book using historical-comparative research is Anthony Marx's *Mak-*

ing Race and Nation: A Comparison of South Africa, the United States, and Brazil (1998).[11] Marx began his study in an attempt to understand the problem of race in the twentieth century. He contrasted race relations in the United States, South Africa, and Brazil. Through historical analysis, he shows how government policies in those nations have established realities of race relations that have an enduring legacy.

The works of Jeffery Paige and Anthony Marx demonstrate the value and the process of the historical method in comparative research. Generally, historical-comparative researchers undertake their analysis to determine the cause of social events (e.g., revolution) or the change in institutions (e.g., educational systems) or organizations (e.g., labor unions). They use a variety of historical materials to identify the complex of conditions that yield social outcomes and expose relationships previously unseen. Yet, as with other comparative research methods, historical researchers face a number of obstacles.[12] The availability, quality, and representativeness of their data may be uncertain. They are vulnerable to claims that the cases they have selected are not truly comparable. They have to make certain that the nations or cultural units under study share the macrosociological traits being studied. Public and private records may have been established and preserved because they served a particular interest and may not accurately reflect social realities as a whole in any given time period. And seemingly similar concepts (e.g., property rights) may have different meanings in different cultures. Finally, comparative researchers have to be watchful that Galton's Problem may affect their research. Nations or cultures may acquire or experience certain social events not because they have evolved to them but, rather, because they have adopted them after having seen them succeed in other nations.

---

[10] Paige received an honorable mention for the 1998 Barrington Moore Prize for the best book published in 1996–1997 in the area of comparative and historical sociology, awarded by the Comparative and Historical Sociology Section of the American Sociological Association.

[11] Marx won the 2000 Barrington Moore Prize by the Comparative and Historical Sociology Section of the American Sociological Association.

[12] The following argument draws from Borgatta and Borgatta (1992:263–264) and Goldthorpe (1997).

COMPARATIVE SURVEY RESEARCH

The dramatic increase in the number of cross-national surveys has been a major factor in the rise of quantitative comparative research. The communications revolution and the establishment of a number of repositories for comparative survey data have made possible a growing collaboration between international researchers (Kluegel, Mason, and Wegener, 1995:2; Arts and Halman, 1999:4). One of the largest of these, the Roper Public Opinion Center, has stored data from several thousand survey research studies conducted in almost seventy countries. Such *repositories* (referred to as **DATA BANKS**) can be very useful to those interested in the secondary analysis of survey research data to undertake comparative research.

One of the most ambitious comparative projects to date has been the World Values Survey. This international collaborative effort has conducted research on the values, attitudes, and opinions of citizens in sixty-five countries in four waves beginning in 1981.[13] In one of the many studies based on World Values Survey data, Inglehart and Baker (2000) examined whether economic changes are associated with major changes in cultural values. They found that, in general, developed nations have value systems that are markedly different from those of less developed nations. As economic development increases, citizens become increasingly secular, less concerned with survival issues, and more concerned with self-expression. They also become more tolerant of people of different nationalities and ways of life living among them. However, the effects of economic development are not absolute. Cultural history also influences attitudes and values. For example, historically Catholic nations have more traditional values than do Confucian nations even when the Catholic nations are similarly industrialized.

Some of the methodological problems that confront those who seek to carry out compara-

tive survey research relate to conceptual equivalence, measurement equivalence, sampling, and interviewing. Each will be examined in turn.

Conceptual and Measurement Equivalence

CONCEPTUAL EQUIVALENCE is central to all cross-societal research; *the concepts used must be similarly meaningful in all the cultures being compared.* Some concepts – such as "unemployment," "bureaucracy," and "civil service" – have meaning in some societies but not in others. Obviously, we cannot attempt comparison between one society in which a concept does have meaning and another in which it does not. However, social scientists often find themselves working with such variables as "individual modernity," "achievement motivation," "fatalism," and "alienation"; it is most difficult to say with certainty that these have *no* meaning in a particular setting. We are much more likely to conclude that a construct such as achievement motivation has a very different meaning in two given societies or to conclude that it is much less important in one of those societies. Perhaps the goals toward which achievement motivation is directed are widely divergent, even antithetical, across the societies being compared. The same comparison applies to the idea of alienation. We must know each society to comprehend the forms that alienation takes. We must then determine an appropriate way to define and measure it in each setting.

Equivalence in definition can be very difficult to achieve. We know that there may be some variation from one society to another with respect to the specific components of a concept. It makes no sense to use a concept that has not been adjusted to take cultural context into consideration, but we can never be sure that the adjustment has been done in such a way that the resulting measure is equivalent across the societies being compared.

The problem of **MEASUREMENT EQUIVALENCE**, that is, of *operationalizing theoretical concepts in such a way that the resulting measures are comparable across all societies* being considered, must be confronted by all

---

[13] See the World Values Survey Web site http://wvs.isr.umich.edu/ for updated information about recent surveys, methodology, and the availability of the research for secondary analysis.

comparative researchers. Suppose our theory calls for a measure of upper-class membership. Clearly, the criteria for membership in the highest social class vary from one society to another. The variety of possible criteria makes constructing equivalent measures difficult. Let us assume for the sake of the present discussion that one criterion that is important for each of the societies being considered is a family's assets. We select one society and determine that the most appropriate lower limit for upper-class membership is assets in excess of $100,000. For that society, only 1 percent of the population is classified as "upper class." Now, suppose we want to construct an equivalent measure of upper-class membership for a second society, which is at a substantially higher level of economic development. If we again used the figure of $100,000, it would result in 20 percent of the population being classified as upper class. If, alternatively, we propose a different criterion, such as $500,000, we would again restrict the upper class to 1 percent of the population. In effect, we are shaping the criterion for upper-class membership: We are making it a family's net worth rather than, say, what some given amount of money can buy or how long the money has been in the family.

So far we have considered only one criterion for upper-class membership. The task becomes even more complicated as we attempt to introduce other criteria, such as occupation, education, and annual income. Our goal is simply to obtain a measure of upper-class membership that is equivalent across each of the societies being considered. In the process, we must confront choices between alternative dimensions of equivalence. We can get more equivalence in one respect but at a cost of reduced equivalence in another. For this reason, regardless of how careful we are in constructing our measure of upper-class membership, we will be vulnerable to the criticism that our indicator shows a lack of comparability.

Although the problem of measurement equivalence will never be entirely resolved, a number of techniques have been developed to manage it. Suppose we want to measure a concept such as "fatalism" for respondents in several coun-

tries. Typically, we would start with an English version of the questionnaire and then translate it into each of the local languages needed. But how can we be sure that we have not lost something important in the translation? One strategy that has been developed for coping with this problem is **BACK TRANSLATION**. *First, we have one bilingual person translate the questionnaire from English into the language of the society we are considering. Then, we have a second bilingual person, who has no knowledge of the original English version, translate the questionnaire back into English*. Then, the original version and the back translation can be compared. When there are major discrepancies, the questionnaire is rewritten and the process is repeated.

We now turn to a strategy for formulating survey questions that is sometimes used when the goal is to obtain equivalent measures of abstract psychological concepts such as "alienation." Typically, alienation is measured using an index constructed by combining the answers for several individual attitudinal questions.[14] The researcher often writes a set of general questions that do not refer to a specific cultural context, assuming that if the wording is sufficiently abstract, the resulting measure will be equivalent across cultures. A criticism of such measures is that many respondents either do not understand these abstract questions or interpret them in ways that the researcher has not anticipated. One way to deal with this problem is to base the measure instead on questions that are very concrete and have been tailored to each cultural context; that is, the actual situation described in the questions will differ from one society to another. However, we will still be faced with the possibility that these questions may not yield a measure that is in all ways comparable across each of the societies studied. To resolve this dilemma, we can combine the two approaches. For each society being considered, we write two types of questionnaire items. One set attempts to measure the concept of interest – in this example, alienation – in general terms. The second set of questions prepared for each

---

[14] The construction of indexes is explained thoroughly in Chapter 17.

society attempts to assess the same concept by using terminology or scenarios specific to that society.

Comparative Sampling and Interviewing

The quality of survey research depends in large measure on the quality of the sampling. For this reason, efforts to obtain equivalent samples receive considerable attention in comparative studies. Most wealthy nations have experienced survey research organizations, but these exist in only a few less-developed nations. Therefore, significant variability may occur in the quality of the sampling from one country to another; this is particularly true if different investigators have set up studies independently.

There are a variety of ways in which sampling issues arise in comparative survey research. One important decision is the selection of countries to be included. Given the expense of such an investigation, it is unusual to survey more than five or six countries if primary data are being collected;[15] studies based on secondary analysis can extend the number of countries. It is common for the researcher's prior experience to have some bearing on the final selection of settings, which has obvious implications for the representativeness of the countries selected. With awareness of cost considerations, the researcher sometimes restricts the study to a specific community or region of each nation being included; national samples are typically much more expensive to administer. Another factor that can influence the quality of the sample is the nonresponse rate, which can vary considerably from one culture to another.

Interviewing is another area in which problems may arise in comparative survey research. The pollster or interviewer is not an ordinary part of a person's life in most societies. The interview situation is a strange and frightening experience for many people. When this is compounded by differences in dress, status, and manner (and possibly in native language) between surveyor and subject, the validity of the

results obtained can be seriously questioned. The interviewer is often a stranger and is sometimes suspected of being a government agent. When such fears are present, we can expect less than candid responses on a number of issues, including political alienation, degree of support for the government, and personal income.

For many reasons, it is often necessary to conduct an interview in the presence of a third party. Women, for example, require a chaperone in some societies. The presence of a third party can be positive in the sense that the person may help keep the respondent honest or prompt the respondent to remember required information, but the effect is more typically to reduce the validity of responses given. The presence of others may force the respondent to give culturally approved answers; it may also keep the subject from openly discussing personal matters.

A final factor that can affect the interview situation is **COURTESY BIAS**. This phenomenon occurs when *respondents provide information that they feel will please the interviewer* or that they feel is befitting to people of their status. There is some evidence that the direction of courtesy bias differs from country to country. It has been observed that Japanese humility has resulted in an understatement of personal achievement, class position, and income level; in other countries, respondents have exaggerated their wealth and social position in response to survey questions (Mitchell, 1968).

Secondary Data Analysis

There are many data repositories from survey research conducted in countries around the world. As with the Human Relations Area Files, these data banks make possible the testing of a variety of hypotheses that would otherwise be difficult to test. They provide comparative survey research data to many investigators who could not otherwise afford to obtain them. However, those who seek to carry out a secondary analysis using these data banks may encounter some significant problems. One is that there is occasionally a lack of documentation of the various sources of irregularity in the original study, particularly in the area of sampling. The

---

[15] The World Values Survey and International Social Survey Programme are important exceptions.

quality of the data varies considerably, but it is often hard to assess based on the information provided.

Other difficulties can occur in measurement equivalence. Typically, the researcher will be attempting to compare the results for several countries, each of which may measure concepts in a somewhat different way. There are serious problems of equivalence with respect to such variables as occupation and income. In the case of foreign-language questionnaires, we are occasionally able to check an English version to verify that the same questions have been asked, but we know from our earlier discussion that it is dangerous to assume that nothing was lost or changed in the process of translation into the relevant local language.

These are only some of the obstacles we face if we choose to engage in secondary analysis of comparative survey data. In briefly, some of the others are variation in the training of interviewers and in the quality of their supervision, variation in nonresponse rates and in ways of coping with these, and specific national events that may have produced a temporary shift of opinion on certain issues. These obstacles are in most cases extensions of similar problems that occur when a survey is carried out in one society, but they can be even more troublesome in the context of comparative research. Much the same argument can be made about the use of national-level aggregate statistics, a topic to which we now turn. Many of these statistics are based on survey data and thus are subject to some of the same sources of bias.

THE NATION AS A UNIT OF AGGREGATION

Aggregate data analysis can be carried out at a variety of levels.[16] In the present discussion, we are concerned with data for which the unit of aggregation is the nation. Major sources of such data are the World Bank, through publications such as the *World Development Report* (2006); the Organization for Economic

Cooperation and Development (OECD); and the United Nations, through its various publications such as the *Demographic Yearbook* and the *Statistical Yearbook* and through its specialized agencies such as the International Labor Office. Many social science programs have been devised to collect various types of aggregate statistics and to organize them in a form permitting comparisons among nations. The National Bureau of Economic Research is an example of such a long-standing project in the field of economics. Data are gathered on national income, economic development, and economic stability.

Our social theories sometimes specify structural characteristics of nations as independent variables: the political structures (for example, representative democracy vs. totalitarianism) or the economic structures (for instance, capitalism vs. communism) are acknowledged to be important determinants of a range of social phenomena within a nation. Such factors cannot be used in an analysis based on one country because they are constant for that country. When we shift to the nation as the unit of analysis, these factors can be included as variables as long as there are differences between countries with respect to them. These variables are not based on aggregate data, but they can be used along with other variables that are (for example, infant mortality rate, percentage illiterate, percentage older than age 65). Informative studies have been conducted that combine national-level aggregate statistics with measures of structural characteristics of nations.

Two Examples

Income inequality, both between and within nations, has received considerable attention from social scientists. An analysis by Gustafson and Johansson (1999) used aggregate data to study the way income inequality varies over time within nations by looking at data from sixteen industrialized countries. The authors examined which of the following five factors was most responsible for determining income inequality:

• The industrialization level of the economy

[16] Recall from the discussion in Chapter 14 the aggregate data on one level, such as the nation, are obtained by combining data for units at a lower level of aggregation such as the state or the individual.

- The amount of international trade conducted by a nation
- Economic growth
- Population changes
- The size of government

As their dependent variable, they used the Gini coefficient, a common measure that enables us to compare the distribution of income across all countries. They concluded that several factors affect distribution of income, such as the changes in the size of the industrial sector of the economy, importation of goods from developing nations, the size of government, the strength of labor unions, and the percentage of the population younger than 15 years old.

The size of government has grown remarkably in wealthy nations over the past fifty years. Spending on social programs, particularly social transfer programs, has been responsible for much of this increase. Given the implications of government spending for economic growth and income inequality (as the Gustafson and Johansson study indicated), social scientists have devoted considerable attention to determining the factors responsible for it. Huber and Stephens (2000) expand on studies examining the growth of transfer payments by exploring the factors responsible for variations in non-transfer welfare state programs such as health and education. They conclude that high levels of women's labor force participation and Christian democratic and social democratic government are strongly associated with the public delivery of welfare state services. Other topics have also been investigated using techniques similar to those of Gustafson and Johansson and Huber and Stephens. For example, researchers have studied income inequality between nations (Firebaugh, 1999), the long-term effects of foreign investment on economic growth (Kentor, 1998), and age patterns of suicide and homicide rates in affluent nations (Pampel and Williamson, 2001).

Warning: Use with Care

Aggregate data analysis using secondary survey data or public records is an attractive research strategy for several reasons. First, ethical problems are minimized because the face-to-face contact of fieldwork or conducting primary surveys is avoided. Another favorable aspect of comparative aggregate analysis is that the data can generally be obtained easily; they are often as close as the nearest major library. Although the cost of obtaining primary data of this sort would be prohibitive, the fee for available secondary data is usually nominal. In recent years, the number of countries for which these data are collected has been increasing, as has the quality and comprehensiveness of the information. It is likely that the number of such studies will continue to increase. For this reason among others, it is important that we keep in mind some of the potential pitfalls of using comparative aggregate data.

The United Nations, which is a major source of data, has very little control over the quality of the data provided by member nations. For some countries, the data are quite reliable, but for others, they are poor.[17] To further complicate matters, there is usually little documentation with which we could judge the quality of the data for individual countries. In general, there is a tendency for the reliability of the data to rise with the level of economic development. Because collection and evaluation of such information are expensive and require skilled personnel, the more industrialized countries are better equipped to do them.

One of the most serious problems is that the categories used in collecting aggregate data vary from one country to another. There is little uniformity in the definition of such basic concepts as unemployment, family size, family income, literacy, and cause of death. Take, for example, the definition of "literacy." Most nations define it as "the ability to read and write," but some countries define it simply as "the ability to write." There is also considerable variation in the minimal level of reading and writing required of those classified as literate. Another factor in literacy rates is the section of the population for which literacy is determined; most countries

[17] When a regional office is faced with a demand for data that it is incapable of collecting, it may find ingenious ways of fabricating the desired information.

base estimates on the population older than age 15, but some countries select a different age criterion.

As a second example, we can consider statistics on cause of death. Death sometimes results from more than one factor; in such situations, the recording of the *one* primary cause can be quite misleading. Moreover, in some countries, a single death may be classified under any of several possible categories. Suicide is one cause of death for which the definition varies from one country to another. Even when the definition is the same, there is a potential lack of comparability in the statistics because of variation in the willingness to use the category of suicide; there are often other categories, such as drug overdose or automobile accident, under which a death might be classified (Atkinson, 1978).

Another source of error in statistics provided to the United Nations and other international organizations is distortion of data for political purposes. A country might decide to slant the economic figures so that it appears more stable economically than it actually is. This distortion may occur in order to attract foreign investment capital, or for internal political purposes. Representation in the national assembly may be based on population estimates provided by a national census. Such data sometimes are intentionally inflated for certain regions of the country in an effort to obtain more seats in the assembly for those regions.

The aggregate data provided to the United Nations by its member states are not collected with the idea of social research in mind.[18] The researcher who attempts to use secondary data collected for entirely different purposes runs the risk making the data into something they are not. There is a fine line between the creative use and the misuse of such data. It is common for the researcher to find that the exact data called for by theory are simply not available. One response is to select *one or more available variables as indicators* or PROXIES for the variable of actual theoretical interest. If the proxy selected is too different from the theoretical variable, the results obtained will be useless. Another related problem is that some researchers start with the variables for which aggregate data are available and then attempt to construct a theory that justifies using these variables. All too often, the result is a very weak theory and a study without theoretical merit.

OTHER COMPARATIVE TECHNIQUES

So far we have discussed four categories of comparative analysis: ethnographic, historical, survey, and aggregate. Although these approaches account for a substantial proportion of the comparative studies that have been done in recent years, other techniques – such as content analysis and experimental approaches – are also used. The examples to which we now turn illustrate these alternative approaches.

In their "Cross-Cultural Study of Political Advertising in the United States and Korea," Tak, Kaid, and Lee (1997) examined the way political advertising reflected underlying cultural values in the United States and Korea. They completed a content analysis of political advertising placed in major newspapers and on television for recent presidential campaigns in those nations. Their findings that the advertisements reflected deep cultural orientations suggest that political advertising is a good indicator of cultural values.

In a classic cross-national example of an experiment, Stanley Milgram (1961) investigated differences between countries with respect to conformity behavior. He adapted for the purpose Solomon Asch's (1952) study of conformity in small groups. In the original experiment, six students were shown several lines of different lengths. Each student was then asked to judge the relative length of these lines. The group was set up so that the students who were actually confederates of the experimenter would speak first and give what was clearly an incorrect answer. Asch found that in response to this group pressure a very high percentage of the experimental subjects conformed to the obviously incorrect judgments of others.

In Milgram's adaptation, subjects made judgments as to the length of auditory signals (tones).

---

[18] Governments have many reasons for collecting aggregate statistics. Planning for the future, assessing the needs of the population, and administering existing governmental programs are just a few of these. Data that satisfy these needs do not always have relevance for social science research.

The other members of the listening group were simulated rather than actually being present; that is, the experimental subject went into one booth and was led to believe that the people they heard talking over his earphones were in the other booths, but in reality they were only hearing their voices on a tape recording. Milgram conducted his experiment in both Oslo and Paris. He ran several variations on the basic design, but in all of them he consistently found (1) a tendency for a substantial percentage of the subjects to conform to the group pressure – a replication of Asch's findings – and (2) a consistent trend for the Norwegian subjects to conform more frequently than the French subjects.

When we use content analysis or experimentation comparatively, we face methodological issues that are unique to each of these approaches. At the same time, we encounter other difficulties that are generically comparative, in defining units of analysis, selecting samples cross-nationally, and in attempting to establish conceptual and measurement equivalence. As indicated, one long-standing debate is whether there is a body of procedures properly identified as the "comparative method" or whether it is more appropriate to consider comparative research merely as a specific application of a variety of techniques such as survey research and experimentation. To the extent that there is a common set of problems with which comparativists must cope, it is legitimate to conclude that in spite of the many forms it takes, the comparative method is a separate entity in social science, requiring its own special expertise and exposing researchers who use it to many similar experiences.

SUMMARY

In recent decades, the number of comparative research studies published in the social sciences, particularly in sociology, has increased substantially. Given that the goal of social science is to make universal generalizations, this increase is not surprising. In this chapter, we have considered many benefits of comparative analysis, as well as some of the obstacles to making valid and reliable comparisons across national boundaries.

Comparative social science has a unique role in extending and qualifying existing theory in psychology, political science, and sociology. Data from one society may be tested in another, and the specific circumstances under which existing theory applies may be uncovered. Replications of studies in other cultures are useful because they make us aware of those aspects of our behavior that are unique to our culture, and of those that are found in most, or all, settings. Much of our theorizing is a product of a given cultural context. Comparative research forces us to realize the limitations of theories that are often accepted uncritically or thought to be universally applicable. As social problems become truly worldwide, and as improvements in communication make possible increased contact and mutual education of peoples, the need for methodological techniques to analyze macrolevel variables increases. Because social structures are typically constant in one country, it is impossible to gauge their impact without recourse to cross-national data.

It is possible to use a variety of data-gathering methods comparatively. Much fieldwork in foreign countries is implicitly comparative, even when it does not specifically mention the United States or its institutions. The major problem in using cross-national ethnographic data is the singular nature of these data. The experiences of fieldworkers may not be similar enough for reliable comparison. The categories used for description and analysis, even in similar settings, are likely to differ. To help resolve these and other difficulties, files of ethnographic data have been created, which combine reports from hundreds of countries and regions. These files are a boon to research, but it is sometimes difficult to find a workable unit of analysis and sampling procedure.

Secondary databases of survey research suffer from similar problems, and in addition serious validity questions must be raised regarding the use of survey instruments cross-culturally. Equivalence of measurement and meaning must be established. Sampling procedures are often not as sophisticated as are required for reliable results. The survey interview, a cultural institution in the Western world, may provoke bewilderment or hostility in other settings. A variety of techniques have been employed to reduce the Western bias of comparative surveys to improve their reliability and validity.

Another popular technique for comparative analysis is the use of aggregate data. Although official statistics can be unreliable, this method has great promise, particularly when statistics are combined with national-level structural variables to explain differences between nations. Care must be taken to avoid the temptation to use such data merely because they are available or because they are assumed to be reliable. This pitfall of research leads to studies that are theoretically weak and even sometimes useless.

Because these and a variety of other techniques have been used comparatively, there is a tendency to see cross-national research as just another specific application of the methodological tools that have been described in other chapters. Because comparative social science in all disciplines requires common skills of researchers, a case may be made that the "comparative method" deserves attention as a separate social science interest and specialty.

KEY TERMS

area studies
back translation
comparative sociology
conceptual equivalence
courtesy bias
data banks
ethnography
evolutionary theory
Galton's Problem
macrolevel variable
measurement equivalence
proxy variable

EXERCISES

1. Select two or three anthropology studies that have sections on child rearing, marriage practices, or any other topic in which you are interested. Reading just those sections that deal with the topic you are investigating, compare the reports in terms of their degree of thoroughness and completeness. In what way do the practices in these societies differ? How are they similar? Are there any social phenomena that are discussed in only one of the reports? Can you conclusively determine that their absence in the other report(s) is not the result of the failure of the observer to either record or observe their occurrence? What reasons can you give to support your answer?

2. Using one of the publications of aggregate international statistics mentioned in the text, such as the *Demographic Yearbook* of the United Nations, select a small sample of societies (five to ten). Choose an abstract characteristic such as industrialization or modernization and select a series of indicators for that dimension, for example, statistics on production, gross national product, type of industry, and distribution of the workforce. Are statistics available on every indicator you selected for each society in your sample? How do these societies compare with one another on each of the selected indicators? What can be said about each society in terms of the overall problem being explored? What solution can you offer to include the societies that did not have information available on every indicator in your comparative analysis?

3. As a class project, work in groups of five to compose a questionnaire on some general topic to be administered cross-culturally. Select a topic that is broad and has universal reference, such as attitudes toward education, marriage practices, or rural versus urban life. The questionnaire should be short and written in a format that will make it easy to administer it to people from other countries. Administer the questionnaire to a sample of native-born students and foreign students. What are the results? Were the questions equally relevant to both groups of students? Were there any difficulties experienced in administering the questionnaire? Were some questions embarrassing to the foreign students? Why?

4. Consider a research area that you would like to pursue by comparative international research. What countries would you examine? Why? What type of comparative approach would you use to study this problem? What factors would be important to consider in selecting a particular approach?

5. Consider a recent issue in the news that you believe may be reported by the press differently in

the United States and England. Do a content analysis of the *New York Times* and the *London Times* (recent issues are available in many libraries and on the World Wide Web) to determine if those papers cover the issue differently. If coverage is different, describe in what way it is so, and construct a theory to explain the difference.

SUGGESTED READINGS AND SOURCES

Readings about the Method

Dogan, Mattei, and Dominique Pelassy. 2001. *How to Compare Nations: Strategies in Comparative Politics*. Chatham, NJ: Seven Bridges Press.

This accessible book introduces important concepts in the strategy of comparative political research. It includes clear discussions of analytical concepts such as political culture, social class, and political socialization.

Kohn, Melvin, ed. 1989. *Cross-National Research in Sociology*. Newbury Park, CA: Sage.

Many of the chapters in this book are reports or interpretations of cross-national research, but part 1 is primarily of theoretical or methodological interest. Stefan Nowak writes about the role that cross-national research plays in the development of social theory.

Ragin, Charles C. 1981. *The Comparative Method: Moving Beyond Qualitative and Quantitative Strategies*. Berkeley and Los Angeles: University of California Press.

This is an important and frequently cited work in the methodology of comparative social research.

Ragin, Charles C. 1998. "The Logic of Qualitative Comparative Analysis." *International Review of Social History* 43 (suppl. 6) December: 105–124.

This article discusses differences between qualitative and quantitative comparative research and presents qualitative comparative analysis (QCA), a research approach incorporating elements of each. QCA provides a framework for cross-case comparison using Boolean algebra to identify patterns of similarity and difference.

Sica, Alan, ed. 2005. *Comparative Methods in the Social Sciences*. Thousand Oaks, CA: Sage.

This multivolume work is an encyclopedia of articles and book chapters on comparative analysis.

The selections include explanations of how to do it in a reliable and creative way.

Readings Illustrating the Method

Arts, Wil, and Loek Halman, eds. 1999. *New Directions in Quantitative Comparative Sociology*. Boston: Brill.

This book presents papers that are theoretically and methodologically rigorous. Three of the papers use aggregate data to look at income equality and social justice; the others use social survey data from the International Social Survey Programme and the European and World Values Survey.

Foner, Nancy. 2005. *In A New Land: A Comparative View Of Immigration*. New York: New York University Press.

This book is a model of interdisciplinary comparative method. Foner contrasts immigrants to America with their counterparts a century ago, as well as with others who immigrate to destinations in Europe.

Inglehart, Ronald. 1997. *Modernization and Postmodernization: Cultural, Economic, and Political Change in 43 Societies*. Princeton, NJ: Princeton University Press.

Using data from the World Values Survey, Inglehart analyzes the political and cultural changes that accompany economic development.

Iversen, Torben. 2005. *Capitalism, Democracy, and Welfare*. New York: Cambridge University Press.

This is a comparative analysis of the welfare state and the problems of employment and social protection in the political economies of highly industrialized democracies.

Johnson, Roberta Ann. 2004. *The Struggle against Corruption: A Comparative Study*. New York: Palgrave Macmillan.

An excellent comparative study of the causes and cures for corruption in politics, administration and business, with data from four countries: the United States, Israel, Russia, and India.

LeTendre, Gerald K. 2000. *Learning to Be Adolescent: Growing up in U.S. and Japanese Middle Schools*. New Haven, CT: Yale University Press.

Social institutions often reflect deeply held cultural understandings of the populations they serve. LeTendre's book reports his ethnographic study of the way cultural understandings of adolescence shape the middle-school experience of students in Japan and the United States.

Sachs, Jeffrey. 2005. *The End of Poverty: Economic Possibilities for Our Time.* New York: Penguin.

The author offers a variety of case studies, details small-scale projects that have worked, and analyzes large amounts of comparative data. His provocative argument is that wealthy nations can make modest sacrifices in order to lift the 1 billion poorest individuals around the world out of poverty.

Sarat, Austin, and Christian Boulanger, eds. 2005. *The Cultural Lives of Capital Punishment: Comparative Perspectives.* Stanford, CA: Stanford University Press.

This book examines the dynamics of the death penalty in Mexico, the United States, Poland, Kyrgyzstan, India, Israel, Palestine, Japan, China, Singapore, and South Korea.

Sasaki, Masamichi, ed. 1998. *Values and Attitudes across Nations and Time.* Boston: Brill.

This volume contains nine comparative studies of values and attitudes. An illuminating article by Alex Inkeles and Herbert Leiderman discusses the process of developing a cross-national scale for measuring the psychosocial maturity of adolescents.

Sieber, Sam. 2005. *Second-Rate Nation: From the American Dream to the American Myth.* Boulder, CO: Paradigm.

Using extensive comparative evidence, the author shows that the United States lags behind many other nations in health care, education, crime, civil liberties, environmental protection, and race relations.

Svallfors, Stefan. 2006. *The Moral Economy of Class: Class and Attitudes in Comparative Perspective.* Stanford, CA: Stanford University Press.

The author builds on data from large-scale comparative surveys to paint a picture of class differences among the United States, Britain, Germany, and Sweden.

Williamson, John B., and Fred C. Pampel. 1993. *Old-Age Security in Comparative Perspective.* New York: Oxford University Press.

Few comparative research studies attempt to balance quantitative and qualitative analysis. In this study of growth of public pension benefits in nine nations, the authors offer both case studies and quantitative analysis.

Each issue of the journal *Cross-Cultural Research* sponsored by the Human Relations Area Files project, offers a number of papers demonstrating cross-cultural and cross-national research. One of the strengths of this journal is that it publishes both qualitative and quantitative papers using a variety of research methods.

Data for Comparative Research

In this chapter, the Human Relations Area Files as a data resource for ethnographic research was discussed. Here other sources of data for comparative researchers are suggested. A good place to begin a search for comparative data is with a social sciences librarian or computer database manager at your college. They are generally knowledgeable about resources available on campus, including databases. In addition, for aggregate data resources, please consult the Web site list at the end of Chapter 14.

American Sociological Association (ASA). 2005. http://www2.asanet.org/sectionchs/.

The "Research Tools" link on the Web site of the Comparative and Historical Sociology Section of the ASA provides references to university and special collections that may be useful to the historical researcher as well as links to document collections and other helpful Web sites.

Data on the Net 2006. University of California, San Diego. http://odwin.ucsd.edu/idata.

This site offers information and links to hundreds of "Internet sites of numeric social science statistical data, data catalogs, data libraries, social science gateways, addresses and more." Many of the sites offer downloadable cross-national data.

Documents Center. 2006. University of Michigan. http://www.lib.umich.edu/govdocs/.

This site offers links to Web sites of international agencies, many of which provide cross-national data. Especially useful are "Statistical Resources on the Web," http://www.lib.umich.edu/govdocs/stats.html, and "International Agencies and Information on the Web," http://www.lib.umich.edu/govdocs/intl.html.

Inter-University Consortium for Political & Social Research (ICPSR). 2006. University of Michigan. http://www.icpsr.umich.edu/index.html.

This site maintains an archive of social science data. Much of it is limited to member organizations or available for a fee, but some, including international crime data, is available free of charge. The ICPSR Web site also contains valuable links to other social science research sites.

Luxembourg Income Study (LIS). 2006.

http://www.lisproject.org/.

This is a twenty-five nation research project collecting household income, expenditures, and demographic income. Data are free to citizens of member countries. Users do not acquire the data but submit jobs through e-mail to LIS.

The Roper Center. 2004. University of Connecticut. Roper

http://www.ropercenter.uconn.edu/.

Roper maintains a large archive of survey studies that are available to researchers for a fee.

REFERENCES

Aguilar, Mario I. 1998. *Being Oromo in Kenya.* Lawrenceville, NJ: Africa World Press.

Arts, Wil, and Loek Halman. 1999. "New Directions in Quantitative Comparative Sociology: An Introduction." In *New Directions in Quantitative Comparative Sociology*, 1–12. Wil Arts and Loek Halman, eds. Boston: Brill.

Asch, Solomon. 1952. *Social Psychology.* Englewood Cliffs, NJ: Prentice Hall.

Atkinson, J. Maxwell. 1978. *Discovering Suicide: Studies in the Social Organization of Sudden Death.* Pittsburgh: University of Pittsburgh Press.

Ball, Helen L., and Elaine Hooker. 1999. "Where Will the Baby Sleep? Attitudes and Practices of New and Experienced Parents Regarding Cosleeping and Their Newborn Infants." *American Anthropologist* 101:143–154.

Borgatta, Edgar F., and Marie Borgatta. 1992. *Encyclopedia of Sociology.* Vol. 1. New York: Macmillan.

Bourdieu, Pierre. 1991. *Language and Symbolic Power.* Cambridge, MA: Harvard University Press.

de Soysa, Indra, and John R. Oneal. 1999. "Boon or Bane? Reassessing the Productivity of Foreign Direct Investment." *American Sociological Review* 64:766–782.

Diekmann, Andreas, and Henriette Englehardt. 1999. "The Social Inheritance of Divorce: Effects of Parent's Family Type in Postwar Germany." *American Sociological Review* 64:783–793.

Divale, William. 1999. "Climactic Instability, Food Storage, and the Development of Numerical Counting Systems: A Cross-Cultural Study." *Cross-Cultural Research* 33:341–368.

Evans, Peter, and James E. Rauch. 1999. "Bureaucracy and Growth: A Cross-National Analysis of the Effects of 'Weberian' State Structures on Economic Growth." *American Sociological Review* 64:748–765.

Firebaugh, Glenn. 1999. "Empirics of World Income Inequality." *American Journal of Sociology* 104:1597–1630.

Geertz, Clifford. 1973. *The Interpretation of Cultures.* New York: Basic Books.

Goldthorpe, John. 1997. "Current Issues in Comparative Macrosociology: A Debate on Methodological Issues." *Comparative Social Research* 16:1–26.

Gustafsson, Björn, and Mats Johansson. 1999. "In Search of Smoking Guns: What Makes Income Inequality Vary Over Time in Different Countries?" *American Sociological Review* 64:585–605.

Huber, Evelyne, and John D. Stephens. 2000. "Partisan Governance, Women's Employment, and the Social Democratic Service State." *American Sociological Review* 65:323–342.

Human Relations Area Files (HRAF). 2006. Home page.

http://www.yale.edu/hraf/.

Inglehart, Ronald, and Wayne E. Baker. 2000. "Modernization, Cultural Change, and the Persistence of Traditional Values." *American Sociological Review* 65:19–51.

Jary, Davie, and Julian Jary. 1991. *The Harper-Collins Dictionary of Sociology.* New York: Harper.

Jenkins, Richard. 1994. "Rethinking Ethnicity: Identity, Categorization, and Power." *Ethnic and Racial Studies* 17:198–227.

Kelley, Jonathan, and Nan Dirk De Graaf. 1997. "National Context, Parental Socialization, and

Religious Belief: Results from 15 Nations." *American Sociological Review* 62:639–659.

Kentor, Jeffrey. 1998. "The Long-Term Effects of Foreign Investment Dependence on Economic Growth, 1940–1990." *American Journal of Sociology* 103:1024–1046.

Kluegel, James R., David S. Mason, and Bernd Wegener. 1995. "The International Social Justice Project." In *Social Justice and Political Change. Public Opinion in Capitalist and Post-Communist States*, 1–14. James R. Kluegel, David S. Mason, and Bernd Wegener, eds. New York: Aldine de Gruyter.

Kohn, Melvin, and Carmi Schooler. 1969. "Class, Occupation and Orientation." *American Sociological Review* 34:659–678.

LeTendre, Gerald K. 2000. *Learning to Be Adolescent: Growing Up in U.S. and Japanese Middle Schools*. New Haven, CT: Yale University Press.

Lewis, Oscar. 1951. *Life in a Mexican Village*. Urbana: University of Illinois Press.

Lipset, Seymour M., et al. 1954. "The Psychology of Voting: An Analysis of Political Behavior." In *Handbook of Social Psychology*, 1124–1175. Gardner Lindzey, ed. Reading, MA: Addison-Wesley.

Marsh, Robert M. 1998. "Gender and Pay in Taiwan: Men's Attitudes in 1963 and 1991." *International Journal of Comparative Sociology* 39 (1): 115–137.

Marx, Anthony W. 1998. *Making Race and Nation: A Comparison of South Africa, the United States, and Brazil*. Cambridge, MA: Harvard University Press.

Marx, Karl. 1848/2001. *Collected Works of Karl Marx*. New York: International Publishers.

McHugh, Ernestine. 2001. *Love and Honor in the Himalayas: Coming to Know Another Culture*. Philadelphia: University of Pennsylvania Press.

Milgram, Stanley. 1961. "Nationality and Conformity." *Scientific American* 205 (December): 45–51.

Mitchell, Robert E. 1968. "Survey Materials Collected in Developing Countries: Obstacles to Comparison." In *Comparative Research across Cultures and Nations*, 210–239. Stein Rokkan, ed. The Hague: Mouton.

Murdock, George P. 1937. "Correlations of Matrilineal and Patrilineal Institutions." In *Studies in the Science of Society*, 445–470. George P. Murdock, ed. New Haven, CT: Yale University Press.

Murdock, George P., et al. 1987. *Outline of Cultural Materials*. 5th ed. New Haven, CT: Human Relations Area Files.

Naoi Atushi, and Carmi Schooler. 1979. "Occupational Conditions and Psychological Functioning in Japan. *American Journal of Sociology* 9:729–752.

Nowak, Stefan. 1989. "Comparative Studies and Social Theory." In *Cross-National Research in Sociology*, 34–56. Melvin Kohn, ed. Newbury Park, CA: Sage.

Øyen, Else. 1990. "The Imperfection of Comparisons." In *Comparative Methodology: Theory and Practice in Social Research*, 1–18. Elsie Øyen, ed. Newbury Park, CA: Sage.

Paige, Jeffery. 1997. *Coffee and Power: Revolution and the Rise of Democracy in Central America*. Cambridge, MA: Harvard University Press.

Pampel, Fred C., and John B. Williamson. 2001. "Age Patterns of Suicide and Homicide Mortality Rates in High Income Nations." *Social Forces* 80 (1): 251–282.

Ragin, Charles C. 1987. *The Comparative Method: Moving Beyond Qualitative and Quantitative Strategies*. Berkeley and Los Angeles: University of California Press.

———. 1991. "Introduction: The Problems of Balancing Discourse on Cases and Variables in Comparative Social Science." *International Journal of Comparative Sociology* 32 (1–2) January–April: 1–8.

———. 1998. "The Logic of Qualitative Comparative Analysis." *International Review of Social History* 43 (suppl. 6) December: 105–124.

Redfield, Robert. 1930/1973. *Tepoztlan: A Mexican Village*. Chicago: University of Chicago Press.

Rostow, Walt W. 1991. *The Stages of Economic Growth: A Non-Communist Manifesto*. 3rd ed. New York: Cambridge University Press.

Shin, Gi-Wook, and Gary Hytrek. 2000. "Social Origins of Authoritarianism and Democracy: A Comparative Study of South Korea And Costa Rica."
http://www.sscnet.ucla.edu/soc/groups/ccsa/shin.PDF. Center for Comparative Social Analysis, University of California at Los Angeles.

Shin, Gi-Wook, and Gary Hytrek. 2002. "Social Conflict and Regime Formation: A Comparative Study of South Korea and Costa Rica." *International Sociology* 17 (4): 459–480.

Slomczynski, Kazmierz M., Joanne Miller, and Melvin L. Kohn. 1981. "Stratification Work and Values: A Polish-United States Comparison." *American Sociological Review* 46:720–744.

So, Alvin Y. 1990. *Social Change and Development: Modernization, Dependency and World-Systems Theory*. Newbury Park, CA: Sage.

Spencer, Herbert. 1873/2001. *The Principles of Sociology*. New Brunswick, NJ: Transaction.

Tak, Jinyoung, Lynda L. Kaid, and Soobum Lee. 1997. "Cross-Cultural Study of Political Advertising in the United States and Korea." *Communication Research* 24:413–430.

Warwick, Donald P., and Samuel Osherson, eds. 1973. *Comparative Research Methods*. Englewood Cliffs, NJ: Prentice Hall.

Weber, Max, and Stephen Kalberg, eds. 2001. *The Protestant Ethic and the Spirit of Capitalism*. Chicago: Fitzroy Dearborn.

Weber, Max, and Richard Swedberg, eds. 1999. *Essays in Economic Sociology*. Princeton, NJ: Princeton University Press.

World Bank, ed. 2006. *World Development Report 2006: Equity and Development*. New York: Oxford University Press.

World Values Survey. 2003. http://wvs.isr.umich.edu/.

EVALUATION RESEARCH

16

Figure 16.1. New York pedestrian safety cone.

INTRODUCTION

Evaluation research is designed to solve practical problems for individuals and groups. It accomplishes this goal by assessing the need for, and evaluating the ongoing functioning of, a variety of projects and organizations in the worlds of for-profit business, nonprofit community agencies, and government. Often, evaluation research measures the effectiveness of a program or initiative by comparing its original goals with its subsequent, actual accomplishments. The findings from this comparison are then used to determine the value of the program and perhaps how to change it in the future. Evaluation research makes use of a variety of methods of data collection including interviewing, surveying, and experimentation. However, all of these techniques are applied in a real-world setting. Indeed, it is an example of **APPLIED SOCIAL RESEARCH**, a problem-solving effort that has *taken social investigation out of the ivory tower of academic endeavor and into real-world set-*

tings. This chapter will highlight the problems that have arisen as this transition occurs.

An Example: Pedestrian Safety

The major components of evaluation research are illustrated in the following example. The Federal Highway Administration commissioned a four-year study (Huang et al., 2000) to find out which type of motorist warning signs produce the safest conditions at pedestrian crosswalks.[1] Noting that many drivers do not slow down at intersections even when they are legally required to do so, the researchers wondered whether signage directed at motorists would improve pedestrian safety, and further, which

---

[1] Prior research showed that 32 percent of vehicle/pedestrian accidents occur at intersections and that 40 percent of these accidents happen at uncontrolled intersections where there are no stop signs or lights. In fact, the number of accidents at locations where crosswalks are painted on the street is actually much higher than at locations where no painting has been done because pedestrians experience a false sense of security walking within the white lines.

Figure 16.2. Seattle crosswalk sign.

type of sign would be most effective in getting motorists to yield for pedestrians. Prior research conducted over a thirty-year period was inconclusive, so they decided to test the relative merits of three different designs: (1) the New York pedestrian safety cones (Figure 16.1), (2) the Seattle crosswalk sign (Figure 16.2), and (3) the Tucson overhead pedestrian regulatory signs (Figure 16.3).

The New York safety cones are about three feet high and are placed in the middle of the crosswalk. Each cone is fitted with a safety sign: "STATE LAW – YIELD TO PEDESTRIANS IN YOUR HALF OF ROAD." Pedestrian safety cones are the least costly of the three signs tested (about $150 each). The sign evaluated in Seattle consisted of the word "CROSSWALK" in black letters on a yellow background. The cost of one of these

Figure 16.3. Tucson overhead pedestrian regulatory signs.

signs ranges from $1,000 to $4,000. The Tucson overhead regulatory signs are activated by a pedestrian push button. The message "STOP FOR PEDESTRIAN IN CROSSWALK" starts to flash immediately on both overhead and side-mounted signs after the button is pushed. These signs cost about $60,000 per site.

To arrive at a baseline measure of safety at unsigned crosswalks, the researchers carefully monitored driver and pedestrian behavior at eleven locations in four different states at various daylight hours. They then performed a systematic comparison of results before and after the signs were installed. A video camera was used to collect data at all locations. It recorded the behavior of pedestrians in the crosswalk and in the vicinity of the intersections, as well as whether approaching motorists stopped or slowed down for pedestrians. The videotapes were subsequently watched, and pedestrian and motorist behaviors were coded for use in analysis. The coding categories included:

1. Pedestrians for whom motorists yielded
2. Motorists who yielded to pedestrians
3. Pedestrians who ran, aborted, or hesitated
4. Pedestrians who crossed in the crosswalk

The results from this evaluation showed that all three designs improved pedestrian safety by increasing the number of pedestrians for whom motorists yield. The overhead CROSSWALK sign in Seattle had better results in getting motorists to yield to pedestrians than the regulatory signs in Tucson and New York State. However, of the treatments that were evaluated, pedestrian safety cones were most likely to cause motorists to *stop* for pedestrians.

This evaluation design was a field experiment.[2] Because of the real-life, natural setting in which research was conducted, it was subject to some limitations. The three devices were used in different cities and under significantly different conditions. Ideally, a larger number of locations would have been used and data would have been collected on a more continuous basis to more accurately represent conditions at each site. Additional hours of data collection would

have taken place at locations with low pedestrian activity (Huang et al., 2000).

This Federal Highway Administration research contains the three elements that, when they occur together, define a problem-solving effort as evaluation research. First, the effort must occur in a *real-world setting*. In evaluation research, the focus is on practical applied problems that may or may not be relevant to the more general theoretical issues that often concern academic social science researchers. Second, evaluation research must involve a program design aimed at improving the life situation of a specified group of people. In this case, the affected populations were motorists and pedestrians in urban areas of the United States. Third, provisions must be made for an evaluation of the program's success. Although the researchers recognized some of the real-world limitations of their findings, they clearly established the relative advantages of each of the three different types of signage.

The Social Significance of Evaluation Research

Since the 1930s, both the public and private sectors of American society have begun numerous programs to eliminate some negative condition, or to create some positive condition, affecting people's lives. For instance, since the 1960s the federal government has initiated various programs that have had the ultimate goal of reducing poverty. Other programs have been established in the areas of corrections, mental health, and population policy. Scientific evaluation research grew as the need arose to measure the degree to which such improvement-oriented programs have achieved what they set out to achieve.

- Does the "privatizing" of public agencies lead to greater demand for public services?
- Does standardized testing really improve students' performance in school?
- Does increasing the penalty for violation of a law really deter potential criminals?
- Is it more effective to target AIDS prevention programs to high-risk populations, or to the general public?

---

[2] See Chapter 12 for a full explanation of field experimentation.

Each of these questions and countless others may be examined through evaluation research. Today, findings that question a common wisdom, particularly when based on compelling evaluation evidence, can be effective for changing public policy decisions (Light, 2001). Which programs should be altered, and in what way? Which programs should be eliminated?

The need to determine the effectiveness of these initiatives is not just inspired by the desire to improve the quality of our organizations and our work. Financial pressures on taxpayers, voluntary associations, and businesses create a demand for efficient use of resources. Increasingly, the results of evaluation research are used as measures to improve **ACCOUNTABILITY**. *If practitioners can cite data from evaluation research to demonstrate the effectiveness of their programs, then the initiatives may not be cut or denied support.*

We might well ask how evaluation research differs, if at all, from nonevaluation research. Ideally, the same basic steps of the research process should be followed for each. Special problems are associated with the attempt to do rigorous evaluation research. Weiss (1998) notes the distinction between evaluation research and **BASIC RESEARCH**. Whereas the latter is typically *focused on the gathering of general information in the testing of hypotheses or adding to knowledge* in some systematic way, evaluation research is typically focused on the immediate, practical use of knowledge. This means that the needs of those sponsoring evaluation research can shape both the choice of research problem and methodology employed (Rossi, Lipsey, and Freeman, 2004). Executives, administrators, and employees who fear that negative findings might lead to the termination of their work may develop strategies to conceal negative information. There may be difficulty in getting a representative sample if those *not* sampled are thereby deprived of gaining something positive from the program. There is constant pressure to cut corners in determining sample size, the conceptual depth of questions asked in surveys and interviews, and the sheer time allocated for data analysis. To meet these challenges, the skilled evaluator will need to employ a considerable amount of research imagination. We will con-

sider these issues later in some detail, but for now let us begin by exploring the two main types of evaluation research and the evaluator's role.

THE EVALUATOR'S ROLE

The evaluator's avowed purpose may be **FORMATIVE** (*trying to improve the program*) or **SUMMATIVE** (*rendering a judgment regarding the program's mission and/or effectiveness*) (Chambers, 1994; Posavac and Carey, 1997:14). In each of these two general roles, the evaluator typically asks a different range of research questions and uses a distinctive methodological toolkit.

Formative Evaluation

In formative research there are three major questions:

- What is the definition and scope of the problem or issue?

To answer this question the researcher works together with clients to elicit ideas, for example, by using focus groups or stakeholder analysis.[3] Conceptualizing methods, such as brainstorming or creating visual maps of ideas and their connections to each other (Deshler, 1990), are often employed in this type of exercise.

- Who needs the program, how great is the need, how big or serious is it?

To answer these questions a **NEEDS ASSESSMENT** – a *comprehensive evaluation of the demand for some new program or service* – is performed. Need assessments typically rely on existing data sources, surveys, and in-depth interviews.

- How is the program being run, and how can program delivery be improved?

These questions are answered via **PROCESS EVALUATION**, which *investigates the actual implementation of a program*, including possible alternative delivery procedures. Some of the methods appropriate to process evaluation

---

[3] See the sections on "Focus Groups" and "Sampling" in this chapter.

are multivariate statistics and causal modeling,[4] simulation and gaming techniques, and the
examination of organizational flowcharts and
project schedules as well as the lines of authority
in decision making. Management information
systems are an ideal source of data for process
evaluation.

Summative Evaluation

In summative evaluation there are two major
questions:

- What is the effectiveness of the program?

To answer this question one may select observational methods, or perform statistical correlations to demonstrate whether desired effects
occurred. Quasi-experimental and experimental designs can establish whether observed
effects can reasonably be attributed to the intervention and not to other sources[5] (Trochim,
2002).

- What is the net impact of the program?

IMPACT EVALUATION is typically *more detailed and covers a longer time period than just
measuring program effectiveness*. It looks at both
intended and unintended consequences of the
whole program. For example, we might measure
the effectiveness of placing some high school
juniors in an "honors track" by testing whether
they achieve higher scores on a standardized test
of mathematics. However, in a more thorough
impact evaluation, we would ask whether the
tracking of these high school mathematics students favorably influenced their performance
in college-level math courses. Or, we might ask
whether students not placed in the highest track
suffered a loss of self-esteem as an unintended
consequence (Loveless, 1999).

Other types of summative evaluation, cost-
effectiveness and **COST-BENEFIT ANALYSIS**,
*address questions of efficiency by standardizing
outcomes in terms of their dollar costs* and values
(Boardman et al., 2000; Trochim, 2002).

---

[4] See Chapter 18 for coverage of these methodologies.
[5] Observational, correlation, and experimental techniques
are explained in Chapters 9, 18, and 12, respectively.

Resistance to the Evaluation: Outsiders and Insiders

Whether the evaluator's role is primarily formative or summative, resistance to his or her
presence or approach may develop. One reason for conflict is that investigators and program personnel are not in a naturally cooperative situation. Many researchers are at least
somewhat concerned with the relationship of
the study's findings to the growth of knowledge
in a particular academic discipline. Program
personnel, however, may have a more nuts-and-
bolts attitude. The academic training of some
researchers encourages a more detached and
analytical posture, whereas program personnel
may be more sensitive to the issue of servicing
people's needs right now. Closely associated with
these potential personality conflicts are differences in the respective roles. Program personnel
are usually committed to the policies and strategies currently in use, whereas the researcher
is in the position of asking how effective these
strategies are. Indeed, it is likely that evaluation
researchers are always viewed with some skepticism and often as a threat. The personnel see
the researcher as taking time and money from
the program while offering a possibly negative
report in return. Furthermore, they may perceive the researcher as unfavorably judging their
work, competence, and personalities. They may
be uncertain regarding the criteria being used
for making judgments or suspicious concerning the "real" motives of the evaluator. These
conflicts of interest are compounded when the
investigator is not actually hired by the agency
or program concerned but by the government or
another supervisory body.

Social scientists who do evaluation research
are usually hired from outside an organization that is in the process of developing its
own assessment plan or has constituted its own
task force to work on solving a problem. The
researcher is retained as an "expert" to assist
in the implementation of the assessment or to
help reach a solution. In this situation, the outsider must be sensitive to the way in which the
problem has been defined and the preexisting
efforts to solve it. Failure to approach these tasks

in the spirit of collaboration can easily produce a sense of suspicion and hostility toward the outsider. Careful inquires should be made about the perceived causes of the problem and the rationale for the evaluation plan. To be most effective, these inquiries should be posed not only to the most senior decision makers in the organization but also to a variety of people at all levels. Here, the outsider's role resembles the participant-as-observer in fieldwork.[6] Even if the evaluator is using quantitative methods to collect data, the principles of effective rapport that apply to qualitative fieldwork nonetheless apply. Without basic trust and mutual understanding of the purpose of the intervention, even the best evaluation research design will fail.

An increasing number of evaluation research exercises are not being conducted by outsider "experts," but *by regular employees of organizations* hired to perform **IN-HOUSE RESEARCH** (Gill and Johnson, 2002). Self-study for the purpose of solving problems or assessing program effectiveness may be more economical than hiring outside consultants, especially if these employees are not full-time evaluators. Insiders are generally more knowledgeable about the functioning of the program being investigated. However, these individuals face a special set of constraints: (1) they may be less well trained than professional researchers; (2) they may be less likely to "push back" when cost-cutting serves as an incentive to do "quick and dirty" research with inadequate sampling or analysis; and (3) their scientific objectivity may be threatened to a greater extent than outsiders because, as regular employees, they may be only too aware of hidden agendas. Sometimes the real purpose of conducting an in-house study is to provide evidence that senior management's pet project is a success; in this situation, to design a study that may show it to be a failure may put one's own position at risk.

Let us examine the tensions inherent in the outsider's and insider's evaluator roles by looking at a large corporation that has launched a program to publicize what it is doing to hire and retain more female executives and wants the initiative evaluated. Is the organization sincerely interested in adding significant numbers of qualified women and acknowledging its own part in creating the problem or is it merely trying to convince the public that it is doing something valuable by showcasing a few, token female hires to bolster its own image? It is precisely this kind of focusing that is needed at the outset of the evaluation for the researcher to be able to decide whether the project is desirable from a personal and ethical point of view.

If the answer is that problems of hiring discrimination against women are actually being ignored, the outsider as evaluator may expose the initiative for what it is and recommend a more effective strategy that, in the long term, would lead to the hiring of more women. For example, to sensitize male executives to the overall issue, a teaching team composed of a psychologist, a sociologist, an American historian, and an economist – all with special knowledge in the area of women's studies – could be contracted to organize and conduct intensive seminars on the topic of inclusion. Alternatively, if the evaluation is being sponsored by an unsympathetic corporation, a potential evaluator may choose not to participate at all rather than become part of a deceptive public relations campaign. An insider taking the role of an evaluator, and who wants to be a "team player," may have less freedom to select research approaches and make recommendations.

As the twenty-first century begins, an effort is under way to develop some alternative evaluator roles that can avoid or reduce tensions such as these by decentering the evaluator as "expert." These new roles encourage the active participation of those being evaluated in *all* aspects of the work, including the planning of the engagement, data collection, the process of making recommendations and implementing them. The impetus for this innovation in evaluation research comes from the same source as the feminist and postmodern critiques of conventional research methodology:[7]

The argument for involving evaluators more closely with program people (and other interested parties)

---

[6] See Chapter 9 for a full explanation of this role.

[7] Refer to Chapter 10 for a review of these critiques.

has a philosophical basis in...multiple perspectives and multiple realities...Truth is contingent and conditional. People in different locations in the social system construe knowledge...in markedly different ways, each of them legitimate and worthy. Evaluation should not privilege one set of beliefs over others. (Weiss, 1998:100–101)

Innovative techniques have been developed that have the effect of democratizing the evaluation process. In business organizations, for example, self-assessments (Porter and Tanner, 1998; Carden, 2000) associated with total quality management are popular. These approaches systematize the process of evaluation from the top of the organization to the bottom. They do have the advantage of eliminating or reducing defensiveness in reaction to the outside evaluator or even to a formally recognized internal one. However, from a scientific point of view, they are lacking the perspective of the neutral observer. Self-assessments approach the canon of objectivity via internal consensus rather than externally validated standards for behavior.

Two other innovative approaches to evaluation, action research (Stringer, 1999) and outcome mapping (Earl et al., 2001), are reviewed on pages 366–367. Using these techniques, the evaluator acts primarily as a **FACILITATOR**, that is, *a person who helps members of the organization to maximize the value of the evaluation for themselves*. In that role, the evaluator helps to empower those being evaluated to identify their strengths and vulnerabilities and to think of themselves as competent to solve the problems they are confronting.

EVALUATION RESEARCH PROCESS

In the discussion that follows, we offer a general outline of how evaluation research is done. In actual practice, there are usually some deviations from this outline. It would be wisest to think of it as a checklist of important points to consider as a creative process unfolds, rather than as a fixed list to be followed at all costs. The first stage in the process is the identification and specification of the research problem, including the choice of program or organization for study. A second broad phase in the evaluation process is the development of a plan for the conduct of research. Next, the research design is implemented. Finally, the results are prepared for decision making. In some evaluation engagements, the researcher makes use of the findings in a consultant's role, actually advising, and sometimes participating with, relevant decision makers.

Formulation of the Problem

Typically, before evaluation researchers arrive on the scene, the organizations that require their services have identified a problem that needs solving. It may be an internal issue or one involving the work of the organization in the wider community. Examples of internal issues include inefficient staffing, low employee morale, the launching of a new framework for determining salaries and benefits, or the opening of a new division or branch location. External issues might be the development of a new membership campaign, a proposal to partner or merge with another organization, or simply the assessment of how effective delivery of services or products has been.

The research problem may, or may not, be identical to the problem that the ongoing program or initiative was created to solve. For instance, a community-based organization may have been created to address the issues of poor-quality schools, juvenile delinquency, or teenage pregnancy. That does not necessarily mean that the evaluation researcher has been engaged to help them directly to solve any of these social problems. Similarly, most businesses exist to make a profit, but the evaluation researcher need not be an expert on "bottom-line" results if she or he is asked to help with human resources or community relations initiatives. Indeed, nowadays organizations of many kinds, social service agencies, government bureaus and major corporations, all use evaluation research to improve the performance of their leadership and their responsiveness to the public's concerns. Carol Weiss makes a useful distinction between process evaluation and outcome evaluation. The latter is designed to measure the extent to which goals have been achieved or whether anything has been achieved. The former is designed to measure "what goes on inside the program ... participant enrollment, activities offered, actions taken, staff practices, and client actions" (Weiss, 1998:32).

Identifying the research problem in evaluation research is not always a straightforward matter. Programs may have unclear goals or the goals may have shifted over time. Sometimes initiatives may have both short- and long-term effects, and care must be taken to measure both. Moreover, it is possible for a program to produce immediate positive results but ultimately fail because *the theory underlying the formulation of the problem was faulty*. An example of such **THEORY FAILURE** might be a training program that succeeds in producing competent building tradespeople but does not result in the participants' finding employment, as had been expected (Finsterbusch and Motz, 1980).

Suchman (1967:39–41)[8] provided a guideline of questions to be considered as the research problem is being identified:

1. *What* is the nature of the content of the program's objective(s)? Is it interested in changing knowledge, attitudes, or behavior? Is it concerned with producing exposure, awareness, interest, or action?

2. *Who* is the target of the program? At which groups in the population is the program aimed?

3. *When* is the desired change to take place? Are the decision makers seeking an immediate effect, or are they gradually building toward some postponed effect?

4. Are the objectives unitary or multiple? Is the program aimed at a single change or at a series of changes?

The box on page 358 shows how these considerations might shape our evaluation of the corporate seminars on inclusion and how we could measure whether or not the seminars were really effective in reducing hiring discrimination against women.

Because the research problem in evaluation research is not always directly related to the manifest mission of the organization, identify-ing just what needs to be done may require some preliminary investigation. Sometimes an educated guess has to be made to determine what decision makers really want to find out. The people running the organization are not themselves always paying for the research (which is typically the case when government is evaluating vendor agencies, for example). If program executives are unclear about how the program should be evaluated, researchers often must reconstruct the original objectives of the program, especially if these have changed since its inception.

It is not always to the advantage of either the researcher or the organization to recruit evaluators after the general problem has already been selected, the issue narrowed down, or the specific evaluation strategy chosen because these decisions, once made, may be difficult to revise. It is generally more helpful to offer advice to individuals and groups who are not fully committed to particular strategies. Sometimes, what people *say* they need to have studied and evaluated is difficult or impossible to investigate, given potential problems of bias or lack of time and resources.

Let us assume that the ideal situation exists; the evaluation researcher is consulted from the outset. The first aim should be to narrow down the research problem in such a way that the evaluation is indeed measuring the right variables. For example, if an organization is trying to combat discrimination against women, the researcher must decide what kind of discrimination to focus on – discrimination in employment? Discrimination in compensation? The answer will depend on how the organization has allocated its efforts. Suppose it is determined that discrimination in employment has been its main concern. Once again, is it discrimination in hiring or in promotion? Without knowing the answers to these questions, it will be difficult to design a research instrument that is effective. A concrete and manageable evaluation plan always involves an informed judgment concerning the actual functioning of the organization, its history, and the broader context in which it operates. For this reason, standard cookie-cutter evaluations that use a one-size-fits-all method of collecting data are usually

[8] Reprinted with permission from Edward A. Suchman. 1967. *Evaluative Research: Principles and Practice in Public Service and Social Action Programs.* New York: Russell Sage.

Evaluation Research Process in Action

The objective is to diminish the prejudiced behavior of businessmen in the area of job promotions for women. Any seminar program would most likely seek to inform businessmen of certain facts about the condition of contemporary women in America and the ways in which institutional sexism operates. Hopefully, this would lead to a reduction of prejudiced attitudes about women who work. The final goal would be for the businessmen to change their attitudes and to reduce prejudiced behavior with respect to job promotions for women.

Who Is the Target Population?

The target of the program would be male administrators in the business world who make decisions about job promotions for women. But which ones? The decision might ultimately be reached to concentrate on one or two large branches of the corporation sponsoring the research.

Impact Timing

The question of timing of the changes might be handled by agreeing that it is desirable for change to occur in both the short term and the long run. Some significantly different behavior in the area of job promotions might be expected from businessmen who had been exposed to consciousness-raising seminars over a period of six months to a year. More dramatic changes would probably be expected over a longer period of time.

Manifest and Latent Impacts

The changes created by any program are rarely unitary. We have already agreed that any program would most likely have the purpose of changing knowledge, attitudes, and behavior about job discrimination toward women. It is also likely that such a program would not be concerned solely with changes in the area of job promotions. There would probably also be interest in diminishing discriminatory behavior toward women in the day-to-day work process. Furthermore, thought should be given to the *unintended effects*, as well as to the stated objectives of any program. Strategies for change carry the potential for **LATENT CONSEQUENCES**, which may or may not work against the original rationale for intervention. In this example, improving promotion chances for women in the firm may in fact have a negative effect on the hiring of new female employees at relatively high positions. This possibility should be recognized early on so that it may be addressed.

less effective than a research plan based on collaboration and inquiry between researcher and the people in the organization under review.

Research Design

Assuming that the issues involved in the formulation of the problem are addressed, the next task will be to develop a design that tests the effectiveness of the specified program. This design is essentially the game plan that the researcher spells out in detail before data collection commences. The basic elements of research design are the same for both nonevaluation and evaluation research. What we will consider here is their particular relevance for evaluation research.

Experimentation would seem to be an ideal model for evaluation research because its design isolates the influence of variables associated with the operation of the program being evaluated. However, other methodological approaches can be quite appropriate. For example,

Rossi et al. (2004) rank several possible techniques for data collection from "soft" to "hard" in the following way: program administrators' narrative reports concerning the program (least desired), program audits based on the qualitative judgments of outside observers, correlational designs in which statistical controls are used, quasi-experiments with impure control groups, and controlled experiments (most desired). Rossi and his associates argue that it is valid to use nonexperimental designs to see whether a particular program creates a large impact. If they do not reveal such an impact, it is unlikely that harder approaches will. If significant results do appear in research using the softer techniques, it is appropriate to pursue evaluation by more quantitative means.

Under certain circumstances qualitative techniques (such as observational fieldwork) are the most valid approaches to evaluation. Patton (2002) lists a variety of situations in which qualitative methods are the preferred choice, including

- Programs that emphasize individualized outcomes, rather than those affecting large numbers of people in common
- The need for detailed, in-depth information about individual cases
- The need for information about the nuances of program *quality*, not just "levels, amounts, and quantities of program activity" (Patton, 2002:41)
- Environments where the administration of quantitative, standardized tests or measures will be obtrusive
- Environments where no believable and valid standardized instruments are available
- Environments where qualitative inquiry can uncover latent or unintended consequences of program operation

Another context where fieldwork and other qualitative methods greatly improve the validity of evaluation research is one in which the statistics to be used in experimental design are problematic. If the difference between the control group and the experimental group is to be measured using inflated, or falsified figures, the evaluation is doomed. Often, the only way to discover whether an agency or organization is

supplying the evaluator with reliable data is to learn how the data are produced and for what purpose; fieldwork is an effective way of doing this.

The amount of records, reports, and other documentary evidence that is required in most evaluations of welfare and other human services delivery programs has ballooned in recent years. One result of this trend has been an increase in the number of personnel whose duties relate directly to the collection and processing of information. Although this monitoring is potentially beneficial to social research, there is also a danger that the statistics are conveying an inaccurate impression of the need for programs or the level of their performance. As the box on page 360 shows, observational research provides a way of checking on and improving the validity of such data.

Sources of Data

After the general game plan for program evaluation has been chosen, procedures are devised for the collection of data, sampling, and measurement of variables. It is important not to exclude any potential sources of evidence that a program is either succeeding or failing. The following is a list of sources proposed by Weiss (1998):

- Clinical examinations
- Diary records
- Documents (minutes of board meetings, newspaper accounts of policy actions, transcripts of trials)
- Financial records
- Government statistics
- Institutional records
- Interviews
- Observations
- Physical evidence
- Questionnaires
- Ratings (by peers, staff, experts)
- Tests (of information, interpretation, skills, application of knowledge): projective tests; psychometric tests (of attitudes, values, personality preferences, norms, beliefs); and situational tests (presenting the respondent with simulated life situations)

Bogus Statistics

John Johnson (1975:44–45) researched the welfare bureaucracy, specifically Child Welfare Services. The following remarks from supervisors and social workers have a direct bearing on the statistics generated by the welfare system:

"I think, really though, that the paperwork mill has become a disaster. I can't even keep up with it myself anymore. Half the time I'm not sure what I've just signed."

"We really don't have any idea of what we're doing. . . . But we never say so publicly, of course. . . . Yeah, the [classification] forms are always neat; it's always this or that, and it's never in between."

"It isn't what you actually do that makes a goddam bit of difference around here, but only what you appear to be doing. That's where it's at, just the numbers. They just say what you want 'em to say."

Some of these sources overlap with one another. Nevertheless, it is plain that there are many alternatives. The selection of a combination of data sources may be appropriate for a given evaluation study. There is usually a connection between the general research approach and the data source. If one wishes to approximate a controlled experiment, for example, the usual data sources are observation, interviews, and questionnaires.

Sampling

Probability sampling is generally preferred for selecting people from a target population of sufficient size,[9] but it is often not possible in evaluation research. It is more likely that a sample will be composed of self-selected volunteers. In such cases, allowances and corrections must be made for the possible bias in the sample. A problem often encountered is pressure on the sample selection process from clients who want to ensure that the maximum number of people who have been favorably affected by their program are included (see box on p. 361). Another potential difficulty is the attrition of members over time from the groups being studied in a field experiment design, which can result in a loss of representativeness. To deal with these problems, the evaluator needs to emphasize the scientific demands of the research process.

In many cases, an adequate sampling frame composed of individuals affected by the program being evaluated does not exist. If probability sampling is ruled out, a quota sample plan can be substituted. One useful way to construct this plan is to make a list of relevant **STAKE-HOLDERS** (Guba and Lincoln, 1989; Waddock, 2001) – various categories of *individuals and groups who make up the organization's client base and its collaborative partners and suppliers in the community*, as well as opinion leaders who would be in a position to evaluate the program from a greater distance. A stakeholder list for a business organization might include the following:

- Customers
- Employees
- Other businesses, including competitors and vendors
- State and local government officials – both appointed and elected – especially those responsible for regulating the business
- Nongovernmental or nonprofit organizations – especially those who have received corporate contributions from the business
- Education and religious leaders
- Executives from print and broadcast media responsible for covering business

By establishing numerical quotas from each category, the stakeholder list can serve as a guide for selecting the respondents to be interviewed.

[9] Refer to Chapter 6 for a discussion of sampling plans.

"Don't Go There!"

One of your authors was evaluating the corporate citizenship program of a company located in a large midwestern city. The firm was very proud of its initiative in a formerly rundown neighborhood surrounding its plant, where it had provided low-interest loans to homeowners so that the undesirable area could be cleaned up. The client and the researcher drove for several blocks, admiring the newly painted facades of the homes and the flower boxes brimming with new plantings. As part of the evaluation research design, we agreed to sample the opinions of these homeowners concerning the commitment of the company to the community. At one point, the researcher noticed several blocks of untouched, slum housing. "Let's take a look over there," he said. The client replied, "Oh, you don't want to go there. Those houses haven't been done yet. I don't want you to include those blocks in the sample."

It is often helpful for the evaluator to consult with key decision makers in the organization being studied, so that some of their suggestions for stakeholders are included in the sample. Care must be taken, however, that the interviewees are not merely **CHEERLEADERS**, *reliable acquaintances of the sponsors of the study*, or "star clients" who have been positively affected by the program more than most people. To reduce bias, the evaluator can also ask the client for the names of their most vocal or influential critics and include them in the sample as well.

FOCUS GROUPS

A **FOCUS GROUP** is *a small (six to ten person) collection of individuals brought together for a one to two hour discussion of some issue, idea, product, or program* (Morgan, 1997). The focus group technique has become increasingly popular in part because of the sampling difficulties previously outlined. That is, participants are chosen for their special expertise, experience, or interest, and they agree to volunteer (sometimes in exchange for a small stipend). Thus, their conversation can be a source of highly informed data not otherwise available in evaluation research. Focus groups may be comprised of the clients of a nonprofit agency, the consumers of a new product or service, decision makers within an organization, or community leaders. These groups are also widely used in market and medical research, and in other inves-

tigations where qualified, motivated individuals are difficult to locate using more conventional sampling procedures.

The role of the moderator, or convener, of a focus group is to be as unobtrusive as possible, albeit while maintaining an overall sense of control over the topics for discussion and the pacing of the conversation. Typically, the moderator will thank everyone for attending and remind them of the purpose of the meeting. Next, participants are asked to introduce themselves to the group. Then, the convener will ask a series of general stimulus questions designed to encourage contributions from group members.[10] The moderator intervenes only when a particular subject seems to have been exhausted, when a few members of the group appear to be dominating the discussion, or when restating the conclusions of the group would be useful. Otherwise, participants experience focus groups as moving ahead without much formal hierarchy or rigid agenda. A reduced or more passive role for the moderator is preferred because of the desire to elicit interaction among group members, which may be stifled if they are looking to the moderator for inspiration or approval.

Compared with other qualitative methodologies, focus groups have a number of advantages that may contribute to a successful evaluation exercise. There are fewer problems of access and rapport than in participant observation. In

---

[10] A good rule of thumb is to prepare about six questions per hour of group meeting time.

contrast to in-depth interviewing, focus groups are less time consuming and typically place less emphasis on the interviewer's views and more on the respondents' (Krueger and Casey, 2000). Perhaps the most important benefit of focus groups is that the give-and-take among participants fosters reflection on other people's ideas. This reflection may uncover core issues for further examination or help the leaders of an organization to prioritize decisions. Focus group data may be sound or video-recorded and later analyzed in the same manner as data from intensive interviews or fieldwork.

Drawbacks of the focus group technique include sampling bias and expectancy effects. Because of the small size of the groups and the necessity of using volunteers, participants are not broadly representative of any population. Validity of focus group findings is therefore heavily dependent on the authenticity of participants' prior experience and their willingness to be frank. However, because the purpose for convening the group is part of the pitch used to attract participants and to keep their conversation on track, the process is open to the same expectancy or modeling effects often noted in experiments. Respondents may conform to the expectations of the sponsors of the research because of their desire to fit in or to be helpful to them.

Because focus groups have the potential of giving a voice to underrepresented populations, there has been increasing interest in using this technique in academic social science research (Ryan and Destefano, 2000). For example, focus group data may be used effectively in the early stages of research to help determine the subject matter and wording of survey questions. This is one instance where methodology long utilized in evaluation research has had influence in more mainstream applications.

MEASUREMENT AND VARIABLES

A fundamental part of all social scientific research is the development of reliable and valid measures of variables. This is only possible in evaluation research if a program has clearly and explicitly defined goals. Otherwise, the evalua-

tor will find it impossible to gauge success or failure. Consider the following dialogue between a researcher and the administrator of a job training program:

RESEARCHER: What are the goals of your program?

ADMINISTRATOR: We seek to teach our students the kind of knowledge that will be useful to them wherever they go in life.

Clearly, this answer is too general for purposes of measurement in research because it does not suggest specific variables.

RESEARCHER: Could you give me more details?

ADMINISTRATOR: Certainly. We take juvenile delinquents and turn them into productive, contributing, self-supporting citizens.

This is a more useful answer because the researcher may begin to have an idea how to measure *productivity*. However, the goals of the program can be expressed even more concretely.

RESEARCHER: In what sense do you mean, "contributing citizens"?

ADMINISTRATOR: Well, the program is designed to teach each boy a skill, to help him get a job, to follow his progress in the job to see how he's doing and to provide advice and support where needed.

Here we have four explicit goals that can be measured effectively. Have participants learned a skill? Have they obtained employment? Have they adapted well to work routine? And, has the program provided effective counseling?

ONE-SHOT AND BEFORE-AND-AFTER STUDIES

There are many possible overall strategies for evaluating a program. One technique is *to study a group of people from the target population after it has been exposed to a program that has caused some change*. This approach is called the ONE-SHOT STUDY. In our earlier example, a group of businessmen who attended the seminars on inclusion would be examined to see whether their knowledge, attitudes, and behavior toward women had changed in a nondiscriminatory direction. There are some obvious difficulties with this approach. One is that there is no **BASE-LINE MEASUREMENT** – no *assessment of the knowledge, attitudes, and behavior* of the businessmen toward women *before their exposure* to the seminars. What are the findings of such a study to be compared with? One way out of this dilemma is to ask the participants of programs, after the fact, about their prior knowledge, attitudes, and behavior. One of the many potential sources of error here is the inaccuracy generated by the fallibility of the human memory.

An alternative technique is *to study a group of people both before and after exposure to a particular program*. This circumvents many of the problems of the one-shot study. **BEFORE-AND-AFTER** studies, however, suffer from another potential flaw. Suppose that positive findings (a change in the direction in which the program is aiming) emerge from such a study. These findings could be explained by experiences other than participation in a given program. Returning to our example, a group of businessmen could show changes in the direction of nondiscrimination toward women. We may ask whether these findings could have been produced by the men having had their consciousness raised through people they had met who were strong feminists, perhaps even their own daughters! What is needed to avoid this difficulty is some means of taking such extraneous factors into account. (It should be apparent that the one-shot study also suffers from this deficiency.) The **CONTROLLED EXPERIMENT** *provides such a check on unaccounted-for variables* and is therefore considered to be an ideal research approach for evaluation research.

EXPERIMENTATION AND EVALUATION

There are many different kinds of controlled experiments. The simplest for purposes of evaluation research is set up in the following way: We select a number of people from the target population (when possible, we would want to use probability sampling). Our goal is to create two groups as nearly alike as possible. The usual way to do this is through the *random assign-ment of half of the selected people to one group and half to the other group* (the technical term for this process is **RANDOMIZATION**). The key aspect to experimentation is that one group, the experimental group, participates in the program under consideration whereas the second group, the control group, does not.[11]

Measurements of the desired goals and outcomes of the program are made both before and after the program is up and running to see whether the program produces the desired changes. This is done for both the experimental group and the control group. The measurements should show no difference between the two groups before the program commences. If the program is effective, the "after" measurements should show that the experimental group has experienced a change in the desired direction that is significantly greater than any change registered for the control group. The "after" measurement for the control group is the means by which we take into account any of the extraneous or outside factors related to the desired outcome of the program that may be occurring for both the experimental and the control groups. If we subtract the change experienced by the control group from the change evidenced in the experimental group, the result is a measure of the program's impact.

A controlled experiment is clearly superior to either a one-shot study or a before-and-after study. The control group in an experiment eliminates the possible interpretation that extraneous factors are not accounted for in the one-shot and before-and-after approaches. The "before" measurement in an experiment provides the baseline that is lacking in the one-shot study. Yet, with all these advantages, controlled experiments are used less frequently in evaluation research than we might think. The reason for this is that there are a number of problems involved in experimental evaluation research.

---

[11] For a more detailed discussion of experimental designs, see Chapter 12. In that chapter, we describe the "true experiment" in which subjects are randomly assigned to either the control or the experimental group. We also discuss the quasi-experiment in which a control group is used but without random assignment of subjects. Both the true experiment and the quasi-experiment are forms of what we refer to in this chapter as the *controlled experiment*.

A general source of resistance to using the controlled experiment is that the research on the effectiveness of a particular program is often considered to be secondary to the program itself. The prime concern of the sponsoring organization and its administrators is the successful operation of the program, not the research. This means that the more ideal conditions under which an experiment can be conducted in a laboratory usually cannot be duplicated. Most administrators are reluctant to allow a research approach that makes it possible for any members of the target population to be excluded from the services or influence of the program. However, the random assignment of people from the target population to experimental and control groups requires this exclusion. In our example, it may be difficult to exclude a control group of male executives responsible for hiring from attending the inclusion seminars. After all, the purpose of the experiment is to see if they will continue to discriminate – not a desirable outcome for any organization. Moreover, because the corporation is not a pure laboratory setting, it may be impossible to prevent executives from learning about the new hiring initiative and the experiment; they may conform to the new set of expectations whether or not they have attended the seminars.

One possible solution to this dilemma is to compare self-selected people in one group that participates in a social program voluntarily and another group that has decided not to participate. If the two groups are similar in important background variables, and if differences emerge between them after the program is completed, there is some justification in attributing the differences to the impact of the program. Even if both these conditions are satisfied, there is still the gnawing question of whether the selectivity involved has operated in such a way as to make the two groups actually nonequivalent. However, the use of somewhat nonequivalent groups is better than having no comparison group at all.

Another strategy is to shift the emphasis from testing the effectiveness of one program to examining the effectiveness of alternative programs. What is involved here is a variation of the simple controlled experiment where different groups are exposed to different programs. The issue of control groups not having the opportunity to share in the benefits of a program disappears, as should some of the resistance of program administrators. An example of this solution in our hypothetical example would be to compare the relative merits of three types of consciousness-raising seminars. Note that a pure control group (participating in no program) is not included in this research approach. If a pure control group is added to the groups that are exposed to different programs, some of the resistance to experimentation is likely to reappear.

A third solution to the difficulties involved in employing the controlled experiment in evaluation research is perhaps the most obvious: randomly assign members of the target population to the experimental and control groups in such a way that it will not meet with resistance. If, for example, there are not enough funds to allow all interested people in the target population to participate in a program, a random basis for selection may be possible. The sponsoring organization may be promised that people who are not selected initially may be able to participate in a program at a later time. In the meantime, these people can function as a control group for the people who are selected first. Such situations do not always occur. The evaluation researcher is usually forced to accept some form of compromise with the desired goal of a controlled experiment.

DIFFICULTIES IN IMPLEMENTING RESEARCH DESIGN

If administrators understand and agree with how goals are to be measured at the beginning of a study, they are more likely to be persuaded of the validity of the findings at its conclusion. From the point of view of the researcher, however, it is unfortunate that a detailed and explicit statement of program objectives is often difficult to obtain. One obvious reason is that the more specific are the stated goals of an organization, the more accountable it must be for their accomplishment. Administrators may have a vested interest in deflecting criticism of their own performance by being vague about the objectives of their agency or program. A second reason is that to obtain funding or authorization in the first place, a social program may have only the most general mandate or statement of purpose. One consequence of the political process, whether in government or in the politics of smaller organizations, is that specific proposals that might provoke disagreement are often whittled down or softened. Therefore, programs that do receive the go-ahead are sometimes so non-controversial in purpose that they are difficult to criticize or evaluate in practice.

This is certainly an instance where the administrator may be at odds with the researcher, who is attempting to carry out a **GOAL-BASED EVALUATION**. The social scientist typically wants to *express the objectives of an organization in terms specific enough to permit the organization's behavior to be measured*; the administrator may simply want the program or agency to remain in operation. One argument the researcher may use to encourage greater specification of program goals is that if evaluation measures are vague, critics can claim that it was not the program itself that succeeded but, rather, an invalid measure that produced the positive results.

An alternative strategy that reduces the potential for distrust between a researcher and program personnel is the so-called **GOAL-FREE EVALUATION** (Scriven, 2000). Proponents of this model believe that information should be gathered that reflects a array of actual program accomplishments in response to general social needs, and that *data collection must not be confined solely to the more narrow and specific list of goals* that may appear in a program's official statement of purpose. A program is then judged according to its observed effect on the setting in which it functions, and there are no a priori restrictions on the range of data to be obtained. If conducted with skill, goal-free evaluation may reduce the anxiety of administrators that their organizations are "on trial." At the same time, important, unanticipated benefits of program operation may be uncovered and assessed. Our discussion of data collection and measurement highlights the fact that the realities of the setting under investigation often make it difficult to

do evaluation research exactly as one may have been taught to do it.

We have noted that researching the effectiveness of a program is often considered by administrators and program personnel to be secondary to the implementation of the program. There are obvious conflicts between the two goals. It is common to find a **SHIFTING PROGRAM**, *one that is not executed in a perfectly predictable manner*. It is not unusual for strategies dealing with the problem area to be altered as a result of the decisions of program administrators. Program personnel may change through the resignation of staff members. Participants may drop out, and others may join the program while it is in progress. How is the evaluation researcher supposed to cope with such difficulties and still adequately evaluate how successful a program is in attaining its objectives?

Some concrete suggestions for dealing with these issues have been offered by Weiss (1998):

1. Take frequent periodic measures of program effect (for example, monthly assessments in programs of education, training, therapy), rather than limiting collection of outcome data to one point in time.

2. Encourage a clear transition from one program approach to another. If changes are going to be made, try to see that A is done for a set period, then B, then C.

3. Clarify the assumptions and procedures of each phase and classify them systematically.

4. Keep careful records of the persons who participated in each phase. Rather than lumping all participants together, analyze outcomes in terms of the phase(s) of the program in which each person participated.

A traditional solution to relational problems between researcher and personnel is to clarify role definitions and lines of authority. This solution entails spelling out the role expectations of all parties before the beginning of the program so that it is known who makes which decisions and what channels of appeal exist. A different, more innovative design is to involve program personnel in developing strategies for the evaluation, so they will better understand the nature of the research (Fetterman, 2000; Stake, 2004; Fetterman and Wandersman, 2005). A more participatory approach may reduce their uneasiness about why so many questions must be asked; they may become more committed to the research if they contribute to its implementation.

ACTION RESEARCH

One way of dealing with the fears and suspicions of program personnel is to design an **ACTION RESEARCH** evaluation in which *the focus is on providing feedback as the program progresses.* Here the idea is to offer suggestions for improvement along the way, rather than making one final *pro or con* judgment. One advantage of such a focus is that personnel can see the benefits to the program and get some evidence that the research is of value to them. Another advantage is that the results are more likely to be put to use. Action research is a qualitative, consultative methodology for addressing these concerns. It has had wide application in studies of hospitals and clinics (Morton-Cooper, 2000), governmental organizations (Greenwood and Levin, 1998), and schools (Anderson, Herr, and Nihlen, 2007).

Stringer (1999) characterizes action research as:

- Rigorously empirical and reflective
- Engaging people who have traditionally been called "subjects" as participants in the research process
- Resulting in some practical outcome related to the work of the participants

Although he claims that action research has moved away from the conventional rules of the research game, such as generalizability, objectivity, reliability, and validity, these considerations have not disappeared altogether. When it is done well, action research pays scrupulous attention to validity. The role of the participants is to answer the researcher's constant queries: "This is what I believe is occurring in your organization; is that correct?" "This is what I understand to be the basis for your decision

making; is that right?" Action research is thus a combination of data collection and consulting that combines continuous, internal validation and a client focus. (See the box on p. 367.)

The key to successful action research is to begin not with predetermined categories or standards for evaluation but instead to find out where the organization stands. The researcher then becomes a catalyst who helps people analyze their own situation by encouraging them to develop measures for evaluating performance that have meaning for the participants. To be accepted in the role of catalyst or facilitator, the researcher must obtain the trust of those being evaluated. Trust is typically increased by treating people as colleagues, rather than as research subjects, and by establishing a continuing presence in the research setting, akin to the role of complete participant in field research.[12] This research role requires patience, being an attentive listener, and avoiding the appearance of partisanship.

Of course, even when it is well executed and successful from the viewpoint of those being helped, action research is open to the critique that its conclusions are biased because the evaluator's ideas have become so commingled with those of participants that an objective viewpoint is impossible. However, advocates of action research assert that the loss of the true "outsider's" viewpoint is more than compensated for by the participants' sense of self-reflection and their respect for the measures of their own performance (Guijt, 2000). Often, having experienced the benefits of action research, clients develop "an ongoing interest in evaluation as a mechanism for learning and organization building" (Carden, 2000:189).

OUTCOME MAPPING

Another genre of participatory evaluation is called **OUTCOME MAPPING**. *With the aid of facilitators, program staff and project participants focus on changes in their own behavior, relationships, and activities when planning strategies,*

[12] See Chapter 9 for a review of this research role.

An Action Research Approach to Interviewing

Dick (1997) offers the following account of interview strategy in action research. Note the open-ended nature of the concepts and categories that emerge from the initial interviews, and the continual revalidation of ideas and contradictions initially discovered.[13]

A colleague and I were approached by a staff member in the training and development unit of an organization. We were asked if we would evaluate a project-based training program which the unit had set up...Each of us first carried out one interview with a different informant...To begin the interview proper, we said "Tell me about [the program]." We then used attentive listening, and other verbal and non-verbal signs of attention, to keep our informant talking for about 45 minutes...During the interview we listened for important themes. *At the end of each interview we asked our informant to summarize their interview for us.* We mentally compared their summary to our recollection of the themes, as a check.

After each pair of interviews, [my colleague] and I met to compare results. We made particular note of any themes mentioned by both informants. (In the later interviews we also noted themes mentioned by only one of the two informants, but which had come up in earlier interviews.) Here is an important feature of the technique...*For each theme identified, we developed probe questions to explore the theme further in later interviews...we actively sought out exceptions to apparent agreements, and explanations for apparent disagreements.*

All interviews began in the same open-ended way. We wanted to ensure that the information we collected was contributed freely by the informants. We didn't want it to be determined by the questions we asked. As the series of interviews progressed, the probes increased in number and detail. *In other words, we allowed the data, and the interpretations placed upon it by our informants, to lead us deeper into the study.*

monitoring performance, or documenting outcomes. The outcomes of a program are expressed in terms of changes in the behaviors of its **BOUNDARY PARTNERS** – "*individuals, groups, and organizations with whom the program interacts directly* and with whom the program anticipates opportunities for influence" (Earl et al., 2001:1). The interventions applied by a program are assessed in relation to changes in what its "boundary partners" do. Outcome mapping therefore represents a refinement of the goal-free evaluation approach mentioned earlier, a strategy designed to identify latent effects of program functioning. Moreover, as program staff identifies boundary partners and discusses a wide range of expectations for their behavior, the evaluation is transformed into a planning and monitoring exercise. After the facilitator com-

pletes the engagement, the influence of the exercise is assessed through the program staff's continued use of the blueprint of desired boundary partner actions and relationships to guide future action.

Outcome mapping also discourages the defensiveness associated with goal-based, conventional evaluation. One practitioner, an experienced facilitator, explains its influence on the participants:

The intended "impact" of the program is [seen as] its guiding light and directional beacon, not the yardstick against which [the program] is measured...feedback on performance concentrates on improving rather than on proving, on understanding rather than on reporting, on creating knowledge rather than on taking credit. (Smutylo, 2001:7)

Thus, the evaluator has become more of a colleague and less of a judge, reducing the threat associated with standard evaluation techniques.

---

[13] Italics are added to emphasize the distinctive features of action research.

UTILIZATION OF RESULTS FOR DECISION MAKING

We have noted that action research, outcome mapping, self-assessments, and other forms of innovative, participatory evaluation have been developed to reduce the potential skepticism of those being evaluated. If successful, these techniques will also increase the likelihood that the results of the evaluation will actually be used to improve the program under scrutiny. When we assess the effect of more traditional evaluation research on future decisions in organizations, we discover a basic problem: The organization may react negatively to the research conclusion. It may either resist implementing the recommendations of the researcher or use the findings selectively for its own purposes. Suchman (1967:143)[14] pointed out that an organization that is responsible for a particular program may misuse evaluation research in the following ways:

1. **EYEWASH**: *an attempt to justify a weak or bad program by deliberately selecting only those aspects that "look good."* The objective of the evaluation is limited to those parts of the program that appear successful.

2. **WHITEWASH**: *an attempt to cover up program failure or errors by avoiding any objective appraisal.* A favorite device here is to solicit "testimonials" that divert attention from the failure.

3. **POSTURE**: *an attempt to use evaluation as a "gesture" of objectivity and to assume the pose of "scientific" research.* This "looks good" to the public and is a sign of "professional" status.

4. **POSTPONEMENT**: *an attempt to delay needed action by pretending to seek the "facts."* Evaluative research takes time and, hopefully, the storm will blow over by the time the study is completed.

What is common to all these responses is the effort of an organization to manipulate evaluation research for its own interests. Researchers must always be on their guard against the possibility of being co-opted as a "servant of power." They must be concerned about this possibility

from their first contact with a particular evaluation research situation until the entire process is completed. If it appears that any of the suggested manipulations are being planned or executed, researchers should attempt to correct the situation or disassociate themselves from the specific research enterprise.

Another possible negative reaction to the results of evaluation research is that the organization whose program has been found lacking will disregard unfavorable findings. Let us consider the following list of rationalizations (Ward and Kassebaum, 1972:302) used by professionals in the field of corrections:

- The therapeutic relationships examined or the impact of the program is "too subtle to measure with statistics."
- The presence of outsiders "disturbs the normal conduct of the program" or the group or the session.
- "Even though they may come back to prison, they are better or happier or more emotionally stable people for having participated in the program."
- "The effects of the program can only be measured in the long run, not just during the first six months or year after release."
- "The program or the techniques is OK but it is not designed for this particular individual."
- "The reason that the program failed is that it wasn't extensive enough or long enough or applied by the right people."
- "The program is worth it if it saved one man."

It is probably sensible to expect such rationalizations from people and organizations whose programs are subjected to criticism as a result of evaluation research. One commonly offered solution to this problem is for investigators to shift their attention away from determining whether a specific social program should be totally accepted or totally rejected. Standard evaluation research is much more likely to be well received if its concern is to examine the relative merits of different programs sponsored by the same organization or if its emphasis is

---

[14] Reprinted with permission from Edward A. Suchman. 1967. *Evaluation Research: Principles and Practice in Public Service and Social Action Programs.* New York: Russell Sage. Bold italics and capitalization added.

to examine possible modifications in any given program.

Another potential obstacle to the proper use of results from evaluation research is the relationship between the researcher and the sponsors. Most researchers are primarily oriented toward the academic community for acceptance of their efforts. Rewards are more frequently reaped via publication than through taking extra time to carefully interpret the research results for decision makers. In addition, evaluation researchers are often encouraged by those who hire them to say nothing or to stay uninvolved in the application of results.

It is unfortunate that so much of what passes for evaluation research is based on faulty premises or improper investigative procedures. When two authors rated a sample of evaluation research, they found that less than one-fourth of the studies met even the most elementary scientific criteria (Gordon and Morse, 1975). The investigators discovered that most of the competent research had reported a negative evaluation of a program. Moreover, the most rigorous standards of research tended to be employed by evaluators who were outsiders, that is, not officially connected with the agency or program being evaluated. These data have important implications for using research findings. Favorable evaluations may be, in effect, little more than sophisticated public relations tactics. Negative conclusions may be suppressed or attributed to irresolvable differences of values and opinion between the academics who do research and the personnel who work in the programs being studied.

A conservative interpretation of the scientific canon of objectivity can lead one to the position that researchers should not become involved in advocating any particular use of their findings. In evaluation research, this position has become more difficult to sustain as organizations have become more adept in suppressing negative findings that would discredit them. The participatory evaluation approaches summarized in this chapter do indeed expose the researcher to the risk of bias, as it is construed in traditional social science. However, nowadays many evaluators, including those who consider themselves

social scientists, are willing to accept that risk in return for increasing the likelihood that they will be supplied with authentic, valid data and that their conclusions will be respected and acted on more readily (Deutscher, 1999). To fail to take an active role in pressing for the constructive application of one's findings is to relegate much evaluation research to a graveyard of useless or misleading information. Those who follow up their work to see that it is correctly and completely reported and that it is used for the solution of human problems contribute to the overall quality of evaluation research and to the relevance of science for society.

SUMMARY

Evaluation research is designed to solve real problems. It assesses the need for, and evaluates the ongoing functioning of, various projects and organizations. It uses several methods of data collection, including interviewing, surveying, and experimentation. However, all of these techniques are applied in a real-world setting and are aimed at improving the life situation of a specified group of people. In most cases, the original goals of an agency or organization are compared with its subsequent, actual accomplishments, but more innovative evaluation approaches use goal-free analyses that capture the latent functions of programs and their stakeholder connections with the wider community.

Evaluation research makes scientific methodology and data collection techniques directly relevant to social life. However, problems typically occur in implementing even the most thorough study design. These include the following:

- The organization that hires the evaluation researcher may perceive the problem for investigation quite differently from the way it is perceived by the evaluator. The organization may not be bound by the same ethical principles.
- The purpose of the study, from the sponsor's point of view, may not be to present a scientifically valid picture of what transpires in the organization. Motives for evaluation

research that are potentially opposed to science include the mechanical and uninspired satisfaction of red tape requirements for program monitoring or the desire to depict a program in the most favorable light, regardless of the evidence.

- Any program may have unintended, hidden consequences that may or may not negate its original purpose. These must be accounted for in an effective study design; yet, they are often difficult to discover, particularly in the short run.
- It is often difficult to sample effectively or to maintain other necessary procedures of controlled experimentation because program administrators are typically more interested in getting on with their work than in producing a rigorous study.
- The data supplied by an organization for purposes of evaluation may be unreliable.

It is possible to anticipate and correct some of these problems by encouraging program administrators to be as specific as possible in identifying their goals and the rationale behind them; by using observational and other qualitative techniques to check on the validity of data provided by the organization under study; and by using quasi-experimental designs that take into account actual conditions in the field. It is important to remain as flexible as possible, both in choosing data collection strategies and in deciding what the sources of the data will be. In many cases, however, these tactics are less than completely successful. The overall scientific quality of evaluation research remains low because of the many methodological problems that must be addressed and because of the relationship between researchers and program personnel, which is often less than fully cooperative.

To improve the scientific quality of evaluation research, as well as its usefulness in solving human problems, researchers should exercise their responsibility to see that their work is fully and fairly reported by the sponsors and that improper use of research results is brought to light. Some alternative evaluation designs have been developed to avoid or reduce defensiveness on the part of those being evaluated. These designs – including action research, self-assessment, and outcome mapping – encourage the active participation of those being evaluated in all aspects of the work, including the planning of the engagement, data collection, the process of making recommendations, and implementing them. In doing so, they stretch the limits of objectivity in traditional social science.

KEY TERMS

accountability
action research
applied social research
baseline measurement
basic research
before-and-after study
boundary partners
cheerleaders
controlled experiment
cost-benefit analysis
eyewash
facilitator
focus group
formative evaluation
goal-based evaluation
goal-free evaluation
impact analysis
in-house research
latent consequences
needs assessment
one-shot study
outcome mapping
process evaluation
randomization
shifting program
stakeholders
summative evaluation
theory failure
whitewash

EXERCISES

1. By yourself or with another student, choose a group active in your college or community and, using any methodology you wish, design a study to evaluate its effectiveness.

2. By yourself or with another student, choose a group active in your college or community and, assuming that you have designed a study to evaluate its effectiveness, approach the leaders of the group in order to secure their cooperation.

What sources of tension do you perceive? How do your own ideas concerning the study differ from those of the leaders of the group?

3. Design an experiment or field experiment to evaluate the effectiveness of one of the following:

- Student advisement at your college or university
- Changes in your campus dining menus
- The manner in which dormitory rooms are assigned
- The scheduling of extracurricular activities

As part of your design, set up control and experimental groups, and tell how you would actually select people to be in those groups. Elaborate on how the design you have chosen would control for outside events or extraneous factors that you believe could influence the results.

4. Using a qualitative methodology, evaluate the effectiveness of one of the following:

- Student advisement at your college or university
- Changes in your campus dining menus
- The manner in which dormitory rooms are assigned
- The scheduling of extracurricular activities

5. Evaluate one of the following by arranging and conducting a focus group of six or seven people:

- Student advisement at your college or university
- Changes in your campus dining menus
- The manner in which dormitory rooms are assigned
- The scheduling of extracurricular activities

SUGGESTED READINGS

Readings and Sources about the Method

Action Research Resources. 2004. http://www.scu.edu.au/schools/gcm/ar/arhome.html.

This site contains various resources on action research theory and practice.

Davidson, E. Jane. 2005. *Evaluation Methodology Basics.* Thousand Oaks, CA: Sage.

A step-by-step guide for doing an actual evaluation.

Earl, Sarah, et al. 2001. *Outcome Mapping: Building Learning and Reflection into Development Programs.* Ottawa: IDRC.

Provides a guide to creating an outcome mapping workshop.

Krueger, Richard A., and Mary Anne Casey. 2000. *Focus Groups: A Practical Guide for Applied Research.* 3rd ed. Thousand Oaks, CA: Sage.

A detailed, step-by-step roadmap of how to design, prepare for, implement, analyze, and report on focus groups.

McNiff, Jean, ed. 2006. *Action Research in Organizations.* New York: Routledge.

This text shows how action research can be used to promote management and organizational improvement.

Mertler, Craig. 2005. *Teachers as Researchers in the Classroom.* Thousand Oaks, CA: Sage.

A guide for teachers who wish to conduct research in their own classrooms.

Murray, P. J. 1997. "Using Virtual Focus Groups in Qualitative Research." *Qualitative Health Research* 7 (4): 542–549.

A discussion of the manner in which the online focus group is facilitated using the Internet, including its advantages and disadvantages.

Orr, Larry L. 1998. *Social Experiments.* Thousand Oaks, CA: Sage.

An authoritative source on the design of experiments to evaluate public programs.

Patton, Michael Quinn. 1997. *Utilization-Focused Evaluation: The New Century Text.* 3rd ed. Thousand Oaks, CA: Sage.

This volume provides a thoughtful discussion of qualitative evaluation issues by a leading practitioner and contains a good discussion of goal-free evaluation.

Patton, Michael Quinn. 2002. *Qualitative Research and Evaluation Methods.* 3rd ed. Thousand Oaks, CA: Sage.

A complete explication of the role of fieldwork data collection techniques in the process of evaluation research. This book describes the particular strengths of qualitative methods for making evaluations and gives examples from actual studies.

Preskill, Hallie, and Darlene Russ-Eft. 2004. *Building Evaluation Capacity.* Thousand Oaks, CA: Sage.

This volume offers seventy-two activities for learning how to design and conduct evaluations, including building and sustaining support from those being evaluated.

Rossi, Peter H., Mark W. Lipsey, and Howard E. Freeman. 2004. *Evaluation: A Systematic Approach.* 3rd ed. Thousand Oaks, CA: Sage.

> *This book summarizes a broad range of evaluation approaches and is particularly strong on the development of evaluation questions.*

Soriano, Fernando I. 1995. *Conducting Needs Assessments: A Multidisciplinary Approach.* Thousand Oaks, CA: Sage.

> *A guide to the development and implementation of needs assessments.*

Stewart, David W., Prem N. Shamdasani, and Dennis W. Rook. 2006. *Focus Groups: Theory and Practice.* Thousand Oaks, CA: Sage.

> *A systematic examination of the design, conduct, and interpretation of focus group discussions.*

Weiss, Carol H. 1998. *Evaluation: Methods for Studying Programs and Policies.* 2nd ed. Upper Saddle River, NJ: Prentice Hall.

> *This is a sophisticated introduction that does not use excessively technical jargon. The heart of the text is concerned with how one would design a piece of evaluation research. There are also useful discussions of the ethical issues involved in evaluation.*

Readings Illustrating the Method

Armstrong, Gaylene S. 2001. *Private vs. Public Operation of Juvenile Correctional Facilities.* New York: LFB.

> *A systematic comparison of the incarceration environments of public and private prisons.*

Ellsworth, Jeanne, and Lynda J. Ames, eds. 1998. *Critical Perspectives on Project Head Start: Revisioning the Hope and Challenge.* Albany, NY: SUNY Press.

> *A series of evaluations of Project Head Start in several communities.*

Friedlander, Daniel, and Gary Burtles. 1996. *Five Years After: The Long-Term Effects of Welfare-To-Work Programs.* New York: Russell Sage.

> *Evaluation research on the impacts of the controversial legislation requiring welfare recipients to work.*

Greenberg, David H., and Mark Shroder. 1997. *Digest of Social Experiments.* 2nd ed. Washington, DC: Urban Institute Press.

> *An encyclopedia of evaluations of government programs.*

Kaplan, Edward Harris, and Ron Brookmeyer, eds. 2001. *Quantitative Evaluation of HIV Prevention Programs.* New Haven, CT: Yale University Press.

> *A comprehensive review of programs designed to solve an urgent social problem.*

Reason, Peter, and Hilary Bradbury, eds. 2001. *Handbook of Action Research.* Thousand Oaks, CA: Sage.

> *A variety of action research projects in diverse settings are described.*

Rossi, Peter Henry. 1998. *Feeding the Poor: Assessing Federal Food Aid.* Washington, DC: AEI Press.

> *Rossi examines five federal food programs to assess their effectiveness.*

Skarupski, Kimberly. 2005. "Outcomes Evaluation of the Long Distance Dads (LDD) Program." *Research in Review* 8 (2) September: 2–10.

> *This evaluation research was conducted for the Pennsylvania Commission on Crime and Delinquency. The report contains a description of the LDD initiative as well as a summary of the methods used in the research. Thousands of evaluation studies are published online each year. This example is available at the National Institute of Corrections Web site http://nicic.org/BrowseTheLibrary/Topic160.htm.*

The journals *Evaluation* and *Evaluation Review* contain examples of evaluation research in such areas as education, health care, and criminal justice.

REFERENCES

Anderson, Gary L., Kathryn G. Herr, and Ann Nihlen. 2007. *Studying Your Own School: An Educator's Guide to Practitioner Action Research.* Thousand Oaks, CA: Corwin Press.

Boardman, Anthony E., et al., eds. 2000. *Cost-Benefit Analysis: Concepts and Practice.* 2nd ed. Upper Saddle River, NJ: Prentice Hall.

Carden, Fred. 2000. "Giving Evaluation Away: Challenges in a Learning-based Approach to Institutional Assessment." In *Learning from Change: Issues and Experiences in Participatory Monitoring and Evaluation,* 176–185. Marisol Estrella et al., eds. Ottawa: IDRC.

Chambers, Fred. 1994. "Removing the Confusion about Formative and Summative Evaluation." *Evaluation and Program Planning* 17:9–12.

Deshler, Donald. 1990. "Conceptual Mapping: Drawing Charts of the Mind." In *Fostering Critical Reflection in Adulthood*, 336–353. Jack Mezirow, ed. San Francisco: Jossey-Bass.

Deutscher, Irwin. 1999. *Making a Difference: The Practice of Sociology*. New Brunswick, NJ: Transaction.

Dick, Bob. 1997. "Case Study 1: An Evaluation of an Action Learning Program."
http://www.scu.edu.au/schools/gcm/ar/arp/case1.html.

Earl, Sarah, et al. 2001. *Outcome Mapping: Building Learning and Reflection into Development Programs*. Ottawa: IDRC.

Fetterman, David M. 2000. *Foundations of Empowerment Evaluation*. Thousand Oaks, CA: Sage.

Fetterman, David M., and Abraham Wandersman. 2005. *Empowerment Evaluation Principles in Practice*. New York: Guilford Press.

Finsterbusch, Kurt, and Annabelle Bender Motz. 1980. *Social Research for Policy Decisions*. Belmont, CA: Wadsworth.

Gill, John, and Phil Johnson. 2002. *Research Methods for Managers*. 3rd ed. Thousand Oaks, CA: Sage.

Gordon, Gerald, and Edward V. Morse. 1975. "Evaluation Research." In *Annual Review of Sociology*, 339–361. Vol. 1. Alex Inkeles et al., eds. New York: Free Press.

Greenwood, Davydd J., and Morten Levin. 1998. *Introduction to Action Research: Social Research for Social Change*. Thousand Oaks, CA: Sage.

Guba, Egon, and Yvonne Lincoln. 1989. *Fourth Generation Evaluation*. Thousand Oaks, CA: Sage.

Guijt, Irene. 2000. "Methodological Issues in Participatory Monitoring and Evaluation." In *Learning from Change: Issues and Experiences in Participatory Monitoring and Evaluation*, 201–216. Marisol Estrella et al., eds. Ottawa: IDRC.

Huang, Herman, et al. 2000. "The Effects of Innovative Pedestrian Signs at Unsignalized Locations: A Tale of Three Treatments." Report No. FHWA-RD-00–098. U.S. Federal Highway Administration.

Johnson, John M. 1975. *Doing Field Research*. New York: Free Press.

Krueger, Richard A., and Mary Anne Casey. 2000. *Focus Groups: A Practical Guide for Applied Research*. Thousand Oaks, CA: Sage.

Light, Richard J., ed. 2001. *Evaluation Findings that Surprise*. San Francisco: Jossey-Bass.

Loveless, Tom. 1999. *The Tracking Wars: State Reform Meets School Policy*. Washington, DC: Brookings Institution.

Morgan, David L. 1997. *Focus Groups as Qualitative Research*. 2nd ed. Newbury Park, CA: Sage.

Morton-Cooper, Alison. 2000. *Action Research in Health Care*. Malden, MA: Blackwell.

Patton, Michael Quinn. 2002. *Qualitative Research and Evaluation Methods*. 3rd ed. Thousand Oaks, CA: Sage.

Porter, Les, and Steve Tanner. 1998. *Assessing Business Excellence: A Guide to Self-Assessment*. Woburn, MA: Butterworth-Heineman.

Posavac, Emil J., and Raymond G. Carey. 1997. *Program Evaluation: Methods and Case Studies*. 5th ed. Upper Saddle River, NJ: Prentice Hall.

Rossi, Peter H., Mark W. Lipsey, and Howard E. Freeman. 2004. *Evaluation: A Systematic Approach*. 6th ed. Thousand Oaks, CA: Sage.

Ryan, Katherine E., and Lizanne Destefano, eds. 2000. *Evaluation as a Democratic Process: Promoting Inclusion, Dialogue, and Deliberation*. San Francisco: Jossey-Bass.

Scriven, Michael. 2000. *Evaluation Thesaurus*. 4th ed. Thousand Oaks, CA: Sage.

Smutylo, Terry. 2001. "Crouching Impact, Hidden Attribution: Overcoming Threats to Learning in Development Programs." Draft Background Paper No. 3. Block Island Workshop on Across Portfolio Learning, IDRC.

Stake, Robert E. 2004. *Standards-Based and Responsive Evaluation*. Thousand Oaks, CA: Sage.

Stringer, Ernest T. 1999. *Action Research*. 2nd ed. Thousand Oaks, CA: Corwin Press.

Suchman, Edward A. 1967. *Evaluative Research: Principles and Practice in Public Service and Social Action Programs*. New York: Russell Sage.

Trochim, William M. K. 2002. "Evaluation Research." In *Research Methods Knowledge Base*. Ithaca, NY: Cornell University.
http://trochim.cornell.edu/kb/evaluation.htm.

Waddock, Sandra A. 2001. *Leading Corporate Citizens*. Columbus, OH: Irwin/McGraw-Hill.

Ward, David, and Gene Kassebaum. 1972. "On Biting the Hand That Feeds: Some Implications of Sociological Evaluations of Correctional Effective-ness." In *Evaluating Action Programs*, 300–310. Carol Weiss, ed. Boston: Allyn & Bacon.

Weiss, Carol H. 1998. *Evaluation: Methods for Studying Programs and Policies.* 2nd ed. Upper Saddle River, NJ: Prentice Hall.

17

INDEXES AND SCALES

INTRODUCTION

This chapter is about the measurement of complex behaviors and attitudes. We know from earlier discussions that many of the variables that researchers manipulate are complex; for example, a number of separate mental and physical operations are required to produce the attitude of prejudice as well as discriminatory behavior, or the attitude of religiosity as well as pious behavior. Indexing and scaling are techniques for measuring these and other complex phenomena in social science.

Before some concrete examples are presented and the logic of index and scale construction is explained, it will be helpful to recall the basic principles of measurement outlined in Chapter 4 and the illustrations of questionnaire items in Chapter 7. An important way to increase both the reliability and the validity of abstract constructs – such as "happiness," "alienation," "tolerance," and "anxiety" – is to operationalize them by using **MULTIPLE INDICATORS** of the same phenomenon. *A number of survey questions may be combined to assess the strength of a particular variable*, the degree to which it is present, or its intensity. This idea will be explored in more detail.

Indexes and scales are devices for creating a single **COMPOSITE MEASURE** of behavior and attitudes out of *a number of related indicators*. Thus, they are particularly useful for summarizing complicated activities and orientations such as human mental capacity and people's perceptions, interests, and intentions. An index composed of several items elicits a greater range of responses than does a single question and therefore may reflect a more comprehensive and accurate picture of the respondent. To discover how liberal a person is politically, we may elicit an opinion on defense spending or gun control alone, but if we create an *index* of "liberalism" containing, say, twenty-five items, with topics including abortion, race relations, nuclear power, and so forth, we will obtain a much more complete impression of the person's political attitudes. We will also have greatly reduced the chances that the responses given to one or two questions were a fluke or atypical of the person's positions on most issues.

As explained in Chapter 4, an **INDEX SCORE** is obtained *by assigning numbers to the answers given*, in relation to the presence or absence of the variable under investigation. If we have decided that a "liberal" is someone who approves of a woman's right to choose, increased aid to public education, and reduced military expenditures, then these responses might each be assigned a score of 1, and the opposite answers may each receive a score of zero. Because indexes and scales can convert a wide variety of qualitative variables to ordinal measures, they make possible a ranking of each respondent, relative to others. In our example, the liberals will have higher index scores than the moderates or conservatives; the higher the score, the more liberal the respondent.

The index score makes comparison easier, but it is also useful for purposes of **DATA REDUCTION**; that is, it *expresses a wide range of data in abbreviated, numerical form*. This is important not only for the measurement of attitudes but also for gauging the behavior of large organizations that are composed of many subunits. Consider the problem of assessing the performance of the New York Stock Exchange, with thousands of firms represented, on any given day. Information concerning the stock market is vital for graphing trends, for measuring business cycles, or for tracing the impact of government decisions and international events on investors' behavior. Yet, it is far too cumbersome to use figures for every firm on the stock exchange to achieve these goals. Furthermore, many stocks are inactive because they are not traded in large quantities or because their firms are not located in volatile sectors of the economy. Assessing economic trends by looking at these firms might cause an observer to underestimate an upward or downward direction in the market as a whole. The solution is the development of composite measures of the market, for example, Standard & Poor's Index or the Dow Jones Industrial Average.[1] These measures are obtained by looking at the behavior of carefully selected stocks of varying

---

[1] The Web site for Standard & Poor's is http://www.spglobal.com/index.html; Dow Jones may be accessed at http://www.dj.com/. Both sites offer information on the construction of their indexes.

degrees of volatility and in different sectors of the economy.

The stock market example helps to illustrate a final, important point about indexes and scales. On a given day, the Dow Jones index may go down, while Standard & Poor's may go up or remain the same because each is composed of different indicators. The value and overall representativeness of each measure depend on the validity of item selection for each index (in this case, the choice of business firms). Later we will discuss the validation of indexes and scales. For now, let us recall that there is always the danger of information loss when numbers are substituted for qualitative impressions or when relatively few numbers are taken to represent many. An index will be meaningless if its indicators are invalid. A composite measure of political liberalism, stock market behavior, or any other phenomenon must be judged on the quality of the items that contribute to it. Index scores may appear precise, but they will not be accurate if they are quantifying misinformation. Steps can be taken to maximize validity, enabling the researcher to use scales and indexes with confidence to reduce data to a manageable size, to increase the range and accuracy of measurement, and to compare people's complex behavior and attitudes. Indeed, the development of valid and reliable indexes and scales is one of the primary goals of the research imagination.

An Example: The Consumer Price Index

Now that we have outlined the major benefits and potential problems of composite measures in social science, let us examine one that affects all of us in the real world. The Consumer Price Index (CPI), devised by the U.S. Bureau of Labor Statistics, has appeared in various forms continuously since 1913. Its history and composition, as well as its many uses, demonstrate how research methodology may influence public policy and meet national needs for reliable information. Indeed, largely because of the publicity that the CPI receives through the media as well as from government and labor movement officials, economics has become dinner-table conversation in millions of homes across the country.

The CPI compares the cost of a market basket of goods and services each month with its cost in prior months or years. *The point in time to which today's prices are compared* is called the BASE PERIOD. As this chapter is being written, the base period for the CPI is 1982–1984 (U.S. Bureau of Labor Statistics [USBLS], 2006). This means that the cost of today's market basket is measured in 1982–1984 dollars (1983 = 100). In December 2006, for example, the CPI was 201.8; that is, the same combination of goods and services that cost $100.00 in 1983 cost $210.80 twenty-three years later. The CPI covers more than 200 categories, arranged into eight major groups. Here are some examples:

- Food and beverages (breakfast cereal, milk, coffee, chicken, wine, full-service meals, and snacks)
- Housing (rent of primary residence, owners' equivalent rent, fuel oil, bedroom furniture)
- Apparel (men's shirts and sweaters, women's dresses, jewelry)
- Transportation (new vehicles, airline fares, gasoline, motor vehicle insurance)
- Medical care (prescription drugs and medical supplies, physicians' services, eyeglasses and eye care, hospital services)
- Recreation (television, cable television, pets and pet products, sports equipment, admission to sporting events)
- Education and communication (college tuition, postage, telephone services, computer software and accessories)
- Other goods and services (tobacco and smoking products, haircuts and other personal services, funeral expenses) (USBLS, 2006).

CPI scores are widely used by government and the public. The CPI measures price changes and is therefore an index of inflation during times of rising prices; it serves as an indicator of the success or failure of government attempts to control inflation; and it has an influence on income payments to pensioners, welfare recipients, and more than 2 million workers whose salaries are pegged to the CPI. When the index rises, government payments to more than 80 million people increase automatically. Changes in the CPI also affect the cost of school lunches for 26.7 million children. Even the operational definition of poverty changes as the CPI changes, as the official federal poverty line is kept current in relation to the index.

You can imagine that great care must be taken both in selecting the items for the CPI and in determining what prices people are paying for them. If the cost of specific goods (such as caviar and champagne) is increasing, but few consumers buy these items regularly, it may be unwise to include them in the index. If items were sampled at unusually expensive stores of a sort that only a small percentage of the buying public patronizes, the overall index score will be unrealistically inflated. Because it has such important policy applications, the reliability and validity of the CPI are even more crucial than for most composite measures. Because of the vast sums of money involved, a small error in calculating the CPI could lead to the misdirection of millions of dollars. It is doubtful that any index or scale you would be called on to devise would involve such responsibility. Nonetheless, as we examine how indexes are put together, scored, and validated, it is important to recognize that any one of a series of seemingly minor research decisions could have subsequent, major consequences.

INDEX CONSTRUCTION

Item Selection

An index is a device for "adding the unaddable" (Simon, 1978:258). Everyone knows you cannot add apples and oranges; yet, that is precisely what the CPI does. It reduces the various commodities to what they have in common: their cost. Similarly, an index of "liberalism" may bring together opinions on various social issues by boiling them down conceptually to positions on a common spectrum of political ideas. To guide the researcher in what is often a sensitive and time-consuming procedure, several basic criteria for item selection are used: face validity, unidimensionality, achieving conceptual balance among the index items, and establishing a statistical relationship among them.

Face Validity

Let us say that we want to devise a composite measure of "authoritarianism" in a number of families, such that we could rank them on a continuum such as the one in Figure 17.1. To position a given family on the continuum, we would have to assign it an index score; the more authoritarian, the further to the right it would be placed. But to produce the index score, we need to create specific indicators of the concept.

At this point we must ask: What are the major aspects and components of "authoritarianism in the family"? Clearly, it is a complex constellation of behaviors and attitudes, some directly observable by an outsider and some that only become apparent by getting to know the context of family life. Adorno, Frenkel-Brunswik, and Levinson (1950/1993) defined the authoritarian personality syndrome as comprising several variables, including aggression, superstition and stereotyping, power and toughness, destructiveness, and cynicism. In this case, we might develop indicators from the following three general **DOMAINS,** or *components*, of authoritarianism: *physical, moral,* and *political.* These are summarized in Table 17.1.

These indicators, which could be operationalized through intensive interviews, questionnaires, or psychological tests of personality, have **FACE VALIDITY.** They are *logically related to the overall concept being measured.* This is the most elementary criterion for item selection but an important one. An infinite number of variables do not seem to be logically related to authoritarianism at all (for example, whether a family

Non-Authoritarian	Occasionally Authoritarian	Authoritarian	Extremely Authoritarian
0	1	2	3

Figure 17.1. Authoritarianism continuum.

Table 17.1. Domains and Indicators of the Concept "Authoritarian Family"

Domain	Indicators
Physical	Family members show signs of bodily abuse – bruises, cuts, burns, etc. They report that these injuries have been inflicted by others in the family.
Moral	Family members of all ages maintain inflexible attitudes toward "right" and "wrong" behavior. There is a high degree of intolerance for weakness and error, and family members manifest considerable guilt for failure to live up to expectations.
Political	The family is run in a highly autocratic manner. The head(s) of the household rarely consult(s) with others before announcing decisions or priorities with regard to family finances, the home routine, or outside activities. Little or no open opposition to or appeal from these decisions is tolerated.

member was born on a Wednesday, the city in which a family is located, the color of their living room). These may immediately be excluded from consideration as index items.

Unidimensionality

An index may contain a set of questions designed to tap different domains of a concept, but it is important to remember that just one construct, albeit a complex one, is being measured. Indexes must have **UNIDIMENSIONALITY** in that they must *adhere to one topic only*. It may be the case that there is much boisterous vocal behavior (loud talking, yelling, etc.) in a highly authoritarian family, but this could also be the case in a democratic household where family members were spirited in defending their points of view. If we include such evidence as part of an index of "authoritarianism," we risk losing unidimensionality; we could instead be measuring "argumentativeness."

Achieving Conceptual Balance

Item selection for composite measurement is an exercise in sampling. The researcher needs to select relatively few items: those that will reflect most efficiently the full *range* and *variability* of consumer prices, political attitudes, or any other phenomena present among the universe being examined. The **CONTENT VALIDITY** of an index is established by ensuring that *a representative sampling of all possible components of the concept has been achieved*. The concept we are measuring has to be operationally defined; then, index items that reflect a balance among the various aspects of this operational definition should be included. If we define "authoritarianism" as a physical, moral, and political phenomenon – each domain being of about equal importance within the context of the family – then we need indicators of each of these three components in about equal proportions in the index. So, if the index contains thirty items or questions, ten might be designed to obtain evidence in each of its domains.

Statistical Relationship among Items

The last major criterion for the selection of items in an index is that they be statistically related to on another. If a composite measure is truly unidimensional, then each respondent's answers will be consistent. Let us examine how to verify a statistical relationship between and among items in a nontechnical way.[2]

Table 17.2 depicts an index of "self-efficacy," which is used in research on school-aged children. Bandura (1986:391) defines the construct as "people's judgments of their capabilities to

---

[2] In practice, the techniques of bivariate and multivariate analysis are frequently used for this purpose. See Chapters 18 and 19.

Table 17.2. A Composite Measure of "Self-Efficacy"

Talent Items

1. I am a good science student.
2. Sometimes I think an assignment is easy when the other kids think it is hard.
3. I am a good social studies student.
4. I am one of the best students in my class.
5. My teacher thinks I am smart.
6. I am a good math student.
7. I usually understand my homework assignments.
8. I could get the best grades in class if I tried hard enough.
9. I am a good reading student.
10. It is not hard for me to get good grades in school.
11. I am smart.
12. When the teacher asks a question I usually know the answer even if the other kids don't.

Context Items

13. I would get better grades if my teacher liked me better.*
14. I will graduate from high school.
15. Adults who have good jobs probably were good students when they were kids.
16. When I am old enough I will go to college.
17. No one cares if I do well in school.*
18. What I learn in school is not important.*
19. It does not matter if I do well in school.*
20. Kids who get better grades than I do get more help from the teacher than I do.*
21. I will quit school as soon as I can.*
22. It is important to go to high school.

Effort Items

23. I work hard in school.
24. Most of my classmates work harder on their homework than I do.
25. I always get good grades when I try hard.
26. I usually do not get good grades in math because it is too hard.*

---

*Denotes absence of self-efficacy.
From Jerry Jinks and Vicky Morgan. 1999. "Children's Perceived Academic Self-Efficacy: An Inventory Scale." *Clearing House* 72, no. 4 (April): 224–230. Reprinted with permission of the Helen Dwight Reid Educational Foundation. Published by Heldref Publication, 1319 Eighteenth St., NW, Washington, DC 20036-1802. Copyright © 1999.

organize and execute courses of action required to attain designated types of performances." He maintains that it is concerned "not with the skills one has but with the judgments of what one can do with whatever skills one possesses." Notice that seven of the twenty-six items (those marked with an asterisk) denote an absence of self-efficacy and thus are to be scored in reverse. The students ranking highest in self-efficacy would therefore answer statements 13, 17, 18, 19, 20, 21, and 26 in the negative and the remaining items in the affirmative. The twenty-six items in the index are distributed over the three domains of the concept as operationally defined: students' perception of their own talent, their sense of managing the context of school, and their reflections on their own motivation.

To establish a statistical relationship among the twenty-six items, we could record the percentage of respondents who answered "no" to statements 2 and 4, and those who answered "yes" to statements 7 and 8, and so forth. If, for example, 85 percent of those who gave a negative answer to item 7 also gave a negative answer to item 11, we may say that a strong, positive statistical relationship exists between these two items.

In a good composite measure, all items will correlate highly with one another. We should be wary of those that correlate poorly. In our example, suppose that only 10 percent of respondents who answered "yes" to statement 2 ("Sometimes I think an assignment is easy when the other kids think it is hard.") also answered item 5 ("My teacher thinks I am smart.") in the affirmative. This should warn us that the scale may not be unidimensional. Perhaps respondents do not perceive themselves as doing well in school without a great deal of effort, or perhaps they believe that their teacher's perception of them would change if she knew how hard they had to work to master the material. In order to determine whether perceived reputation among teachers is really an integral part of the total idea of "self-efficacy," we might sample other populations, and if our findings are repeated, the item that correlates poorly should be discarded.

Another principle in establishing statistical relationships between and among index items is that every question asked should add something to the evaluation of each respondent. In our attempt to achieve unidimensionality, we must be careful that we do not simply repeat the same question again and again in different items, using synonyms or different ways of phrasing the identical ideas. In Table 17.2, for example, is it really necessary to ask about students' performance in four separate subjects: science, math, social studies, and reading? To ensure the usefulness of each item, there is usually a *pretest* phase of index construction, in which statements or questions are tried and discarded. In addition, there is frequently a *retest* phase, in which the index items that appear to be unidimensional for one population are used to elicit data from another population. Sophisticated computer programs can assess the correlation between index items. The time and effort are indeed worth it because composite measures that are painstakingly perfected have the widest applicability. Some IQ tests and various psychological measures of personality and aptitude have been used for decades with only minor modifications because the initial research that helped to devise them was so thorough.

INDEX SCORING

As intricate and sensitive as item selection may be, it is only part of the process of index construction. Four critical decisions must also be made regarding the scoring of a composite measure once the items are selected. These are (1) determining the range of response categories, (2) deciding how to assign numbers to responses and what the range of scores will be, (3) deciding whether responses to all items will be weighted equally, and (4) coping with missing data. Let us look at each of these issues.

The Range and Numbering of Response Categories

When determining the appropriate response categories for a composite measure, we need to keep in mind the general principles for creating answer formats explained in Chapter 7. Categories must be *exhaustive, mutually exclusive*, and *clear*. Various index scoring formats are commonly used in social research. In its simplest form, a positive answer (one indicating the presence of the variable under investigation) might be assigned a score of 1, and a negative answer, a score of zero. However, as the range of possible answers increases, more intricate numbering schemes are called for. In the **FORCED-RANKING** technique, *respondents are asked to arrange a fixed set of items in order of importance*. For instance, a researcher may instruct respondents to assign the numbers 1–6 (1 being most important) to each of the following characteristics of an "ideal date":

Physically attractive

Financially stable

Has a sense of humor

Is kind to me

Wears fashionable clothes

Shares values in common with me

The advantage of this format is that each of the items may be ranked against the others. Although we can determine whether a respondent thinks that physical attractiveness in the abstract sense is more important than a sense of humor, or vice versa, the forced-ranking format does not enable us to discover the importance of each item for the respondents in a personal sense. Perhaps the value ranked most important is still not very meaningful for them.

RATIO SCALING is a technique for dealing with this dilemma. It is *a response format that uses a fixed set of items but that allows the subject some autonomy* in scaling. In a study of the "stigma," or negative image, attached to various forms of public aid to the poor, Williamson (1974) employed such a ratio scale. A list of social programs was prepared and shown to each respondent. The list included the following forms of public assistance:

Aid to Families with Dependent Children (AFDC)

Aid to the permanently and totally disabled

General relief

Guaranteed annual income

Head Start

Old-age assistance

Public housing

Social Security

Unemployment compensation

Unemployment compensation, a program with which most respondents were familiar, was assigned a score of 100 because it proved to be relatively acceptable in a pretest. Subjects were then asked to rate the amount of stigma associated with being a recipient of each of the other kinds of aid, relative to that associated with unemployment compensation. A respondent scored a particular program 50 if it had half the stigma; 300 if it had three times the stigma, and so on. To make sure that subjects understood this ratio-scaling system, they were given practice exercises as part of the interview.

Perhaps the most common type of response format for composite measures is the LIKERT SCALING technique. Examples of two survey items together with Likert response options appear in Table 17.3. These formats offer a wider range of response alternatives than do simple summated ratings, but they *display ordinal response categories that can then be assigned a score*. In an index of teacher quality, one of the statements in Table 17.3 might be used. The response "strongly agree" could be given a score of 5, "agree" a score of 4, and so on. This technique elicits a great deal of information

---

Table 17.3. Likert Response Formats

Overall, I would rate the quality of the instruction I have received in this course as:

___ Excellent	___ Excellent	___ Above Average
___ Good	___ Good	___ Average
___ Fair	___ Average	___ Below Average
___ Poor	___ Fair	
	___ Poor	

I would recommend that others take this course.

___ Strongly Agree	___ Strongly Agree	___ Agree
___ Agree Somewhat	___ Agree	___ No Opinion or Don't Know
___ Disagree Somewhat	___ Neither Agree or Disagree	___ Disagree
___ Strongly Disagree	___ Disagree	
	___ Strongly Disagree	

Adapted from Philliber (1980).

A Depression Screening Test

Online psychological tests have become increasingly popular. This instrument, developed by a physician at New York University Department of Psychiatry, is actually a very reliable composite measure of the concept "depression." Note that the questions are operationalizations of both physiological and social relations indicators of the concept. All items are answered in Likert-type format:

A. Never

B. Rarely

C. Sometimes

D. Very often

E. Most of the time

Are You Depressed? FOR MORE THAN TWO WEEKS . . .

1. Do you feel sad, blue, unhappy or "down in the dumps"?

2. Do you feel tired, having little energy, unable to concentrate?

3. Do you feel uneasy, restless or irritable?

4. Do you have trouble sleeping or eating (too little or too much)?

5. Do you feel that you are not enjoying the activities that you used to?

6. Do you feel that you lost interest in sex or are experiencing sexual difficulties?

7. Do you feel that it takes you longer than before to make decisions or that you are unable to concentrate?

8. Do you feel inadequate, like a failure or that nobody likes you anymore?

9. Do you feel guilty without a rational reason, or put yourself down?

10. Do you feel that things always go or will go wrong no matter how hard you try?

Reproduced with permission from Waguih William IsHak, MD. 2005. *ODST: Online Depression Screening Test*. New York University Department of Psychiatry. http://www.med.nyu.edu/psych/screens/depres.html.

because people will make relative judgments more readily than absolute ones.

Usually, Likert response formats contain between three and seven alternatives. More choices might be confusing to subjects and also probably futile because there is a limit to the subtleties of opinion that people have, or think they have. The number of categories for responses should always reflect as closely as possible the estimated or expected variation in the answers given. The choice of answer format can be difficult. If the range of answers is too restricted, information loss may result; on the other hand, generating a large number of response options

that are not chosen does not usually add much to what we know about the respondents.

Another commonly used arrangement for response categories is the SEMANTIC DIFFERENTIAL, which *relies on opposing adjectives to serve as a stimulus for rating*. Table 17.4 provides some examples taken from hypothetical research on a soft drink. Numbers may be assigned to each of the boxes to produce an overall score.

Weighting of Index Items

In scoring strategies that use SUMMATED RATINGS, *each index item contributes equally to the*

Table 17.4. The Semantic Differential

"Please give us your impression of Yum-Yum Cola by placing an 'X' in the appropriate box between each pair of words":

Up-To-Date					Old-Fashioned
In the Mainstream					On the Edge
Original					Like All the Others
Exciting					Boring
Expensive					Cheap

overall score. In the indexes of political attitudes, self-efficacy, authoritarianism, and depression that we have thus far used as examples, the various questions asked may be designed to tap different domains of the concepts, but no one component is deemed to be more important than the rest. Similarly, the forced-ranking, ratio-scaling, and Likert-type formats may score various response options differently, but each item in the index has an equal chance of contributing to the total. However, sometimes *some questions or parts of the composite measure are judged to be worth more than others.* In such cases, WEIGHT-ING of index items is desirable.

The judgment for the assignment of weights is made by the researcher, based on theory or on prior estimates of the behavior that the index is designed to measure. The CPI, mentioned earlier in this chapter, is actually a weighted index; more than 30,000 individuals and families provide expenditure information for use in determining the relative importance, or weight, of the market basket categories in the CPI index structure (USBLS, 2006).

If we were creating an index of socioeconomic status, we might include indicators of three major components: respondents' income, occupational position, and education. Suppose that income was thought to be more important than the other variables. We could score the income indicators so that they would count double. Table 17.5 compares a three-item-weighted index with an unweighted index. As the result of weighting, the variable "income" receives a greater proportion of the total score.

Coping with Missing Data

Missing data are a problem common to all social research, especially large surveys, but the problem is particularly critical in the development of composite measures that have wide application but depend on a one-shot observation. To see how researchers deal with incomplete data, let us return to the example of the Consumer Price Index. For each of more than 200 categories of goods and services, the U.S. Bureau of Labor Statistics uses statistical procedures

Table 17.5. Comparison of Two Scoring Procedures for Three Indicators of Socioeconomic Status

Summated Ratings Index		Weighted Index	
	Score Range		Score Range
Income	1–5	Income	2–10
Occupation	1–5	Occupation	1–5
Education	1–5	Education	1–5
Total Score Range	3–15	Total Score Range	4–20

to choose samples of several hundred specific items within selected business establishments frequented by consumers. These samples, containing about 80,000 items each month, represent the thousands of varieties available in the marketplace. For example, "in a given supermarket, the Bureau may choose a plastic bag of golden delicious apples, U.S. extra fancy grade, weighing 4.4 pounds to represent the 'Apples' category" (USBLS, 2006).

Enumerators visit or contact by telephone about 23,000 retail and service outlets as part of the nationwide data collection process. What do these researchers do when they attempt to price an item, such as skimmed milk in quart containers, and find that it is missing from the dairy compartment? In such cases, the CPI enumerators adopt the principle of **IMPUTATION**, or *making inferences*. They ascribe to missing sample items the change in price for groups of goods and services presumed to have similar price movements. It would be impractical to wait until the next milk delivery or to return to the store again and again in hopes of finding the specific sample item, given the expense and intricate scheduling of data collection involved in the research.

Imputation is just one of the strategies that have been devised to manage the problem of missing data. Another is to *infer* the respondent's answer. Suppose a person is asked whether he or she belongs to any of ten voluntary organizations on a list, and the person answers "yes" to the Rotary Club and the Junior Chamber of Commerce, leaving blank the negative options for the other organizations. In such a case, it is proper to assume that membership is limited to those groups for which an affirmative response was given.

An additional tactic used for index items where there is a range of scores – say, from 1 to 5 – is to count missing data as the midpoint score of 3. This approach is particularly helpful when the midpoint signifies "neutral" or "unsure." In a summated-rating index, a similar procedure is often followed, wherein the missing score is assigned as the equivalent of the average of the other scores, so that if an index contains ten items and the scores for nine of them average .78, then the missing tenth item is given a score of .78

as well. In other words, the value of what is *not* observed is based on the value of what *is* observed.

INDEX VALIDATION

The rigorous concern with reliability and validity that is a guiding principle of all science is an integral part of the construction of indexes. Many composite measures are developed over a period of months or years by eliminating the less reliable and valid index items and replacing them with better ones. A variety of analytic techniques exist to assess the worth of each question or indicator and its contribution to the total index score. These techniques are of two types: those *internal* to the measure itself and those that are *external*.[3]

Internal Validation

If questions and indicators have been carefully selected initially to meet the criteria of face validity and statistical relatedness, the result is likely to be both a valid index (which measures what it is supposed to measure) and a reliable one (which may be used in replicated studies with consistent results). Often, researchers attempt to establish **INTERNAL VALIDITY** – *demonstrating how appropriate their choice of items was* by performing statistical tests on a particular composite measure after data have been collected.

This process of internal validation is accomplished through **ITEM ANALYSIS**, in which *the effects of each of the many parts of an index are assessed*. In **ITEM-TO-SCALE CORRELATION**, for instance, *the results for each statement or question are compared with those for the entire instrument*. For each person from whom data are collected, scores on individual questions should conform to the overall score. *The extent to which this conformity occurs* when an instrument is administered to a sample or series of samples is reflected by an item-to-scale **RELIABILITY COEFFICIENT**.[4] *The consistency of results*

---

[3] See Chapter 4 for a general discussion of validity, reliability, and systematic measurement error.

[4] Perhaps the most common reliability coefficient is called alpha (Spector, 1992). It is expressed in scores from .01 to .99; the higher the coefficient, the greater the reliability of index items. If data are dichotomous, that is, if there are only

obtained when an index is used repeatedly is referred to as **STABILITY**. The item-to-scale reliability coefficient may be used to assess stability from one administration of a test to the next.

Another type of item analysis is the **SPLIT-HALF CORRELATION**. Here, *all the items in the instrument are divided into two groups* (say, by selecting odd- and even-numbered questions). The comparison of the scores from these two subscales is then reported as a split-half reliability coefficient.[5] This coefficient shows the extent to which each of the two halves measures the same thing (Litwin, 1995). It can also be used to determine the stability of responses to tests over time. Another use of the split-half correlation is to assess the effectiveness of a revision of a previously employed data collection instrument. Scores for the "established" half are compared with scores for the "new" half that is being considered for adoption (Spector, 1992).

These and other procedures for assessing internal validity are quite sophisticated, but they are not sufficient to prove that researchers have in fact done what they set out to do. Reliability coefficients may be quite high even when **ITEM-TO-ITEM CORRELATIONS** (i.e., *comparisons among items*) are low, showing that although a measure may be stable, this does not necessarily imply that it is unidimensional. To establish definitively the validity of a composite measure, some outside source of information about identical or related variables must be consulted.

External Validation

The most common form of **EXTERNAL VALIDATION** involves the creation of a composite measure by carving out of a portion of the items in a questionnaire. Then, *the results for this measure are compared with answers from the other portion of the instrument that was not included in the index being validated*. However, the information against which an index is checked is not necessarily contained in subsets

of the same questionnaire. To measure women's fear of rape, two researchers, Charlene Senn and Katalin Dzinas (1996), developed a thirty-six-item scale that they administered to a sample of 167 female university and college students. To maximize external validity, they gave the students both an additional background questionnaire and a separate survey about their sexual experience. The answers to all of the items in the three instruments, taken together, painted a coherent, composite picture of the "fear of rape." Discovering the extent to which this sort of coherence is present is the goal of external validation.

The Consumer Price Index market basket, mentioned earlier, is an example of a composite measure that is subjected to extensive external validation. It is developed from detailed expenditure information provided by 5,000 families and individuals who are interviewed about what they actually buy. To maximize validity, another 5,000 families keep diaries listing everything they purchase during a two-week period. Yet another sample (of about 16,800 families each year) serves as the basis for a Point-of-Purchase Survey that identifies the *places* where households obtain various types of goods and services (USBLS, 2005).

A word of caution is in order. Suppose that an outside source of information correlates poorly with a particular composite measure of a related phenomenon. Does this necessarily mean that the index is poor? The answer is that it does not. Researchers are often faced with a dilemma in this regard because it is as difficult to establish the validity and reliability of the outside measure as it is to evaluate the quality of the index itself. Perhaps the index, or scale, is valid, but the external validator is poor! This dilemma underscores the researcher's obligation to be ever vigilant in the selection of measures.

THE SCALING OF RESPONSES

We have thus far considered only those indexes for which there is an accumulation of the scores assigned to individual attributes. There is another type of composite measure in social science that is created by assigning different scores to behaviors and attitudes according to

---

two response alternatives, alpha is equivalent to the reliability coefficient KR-20, another commonly used measure for assessing reliability.
[5] The most common such measure is the Spearman-Brown coefficient.

Table 17.6. Measure of Tolerance for Homosexuals

Item	Occupation	(check one)	
		Proper	Not proper
1	Bricklayer	—	—
2	Primary school teacher	—	—
3	Stage performer	—	—
4	Law enforcement officer	—	—
5	Dishwasher	—	—
6	Interior designer	—	—
7	Insurance salesperson	—	—
8	Corporate executive	—	—
9	Telephone operator	—	—
10	President of the United States	—	—

"Proper" = 1
"Not proper" = 0

the part each plays in a *pattern* of attributes. In this section, these two measurement strategies are compared.

If we were interested in gauging people's tolerance of homosexuals, we might devise a series of questions such as those in Table 17.6 asking respondents to say whether it was proper for a gay man or woman to work in a number of occupations. If we scored an affirmative response to each item as 1, we could compare index scores for a sample of respondents. The more occupations deemed appropriate for homosexuals, the more tolerant the subject.

As we have noted in discussing numerous, similar illustrations, this is a useful measuring strategy, and it is commonly employed in social science. It does have certain drawbacks, however. Two respondents for whom the same total index score is obtained may in fact have divergent patterns of response. A person who replied affirmatively to items 1, 3, 5, 7, and 9 only would net the identical overall score as a person who replied affirmatively only to items 2, 4, 6, 8, and 10. Thus, there is considerable information loss connected with this indexing procedure. Similar total scores can mask the real differences among respondents' attitudes. Another shortcoming of this indexing technique is its failure to gauge the *intensity* of subjects' feelings. Perhaps in a particular respondent's view certain occupations

are just barely unacceptable, whereas others are completely out of the question. Because each item contributes to the total score in equal proportion, we have no way of judging the degree of conviction with which a given attitude is held.[6]

Measuring Intensity and Response Patterns

The terms *indexing* and *scaling* are often used interchangeably, but for the sake of convenience, we will refer to the scoring of *patterns of response* as "scaling." Scaling enables the different total scores obtained on a composite measure to reflect the varying intensity of respondents' feelings. In addition, it ensures that divergent patterns of response will be reflected in divergent total scores. To accomplish these aims, the researcher arranges index items in a logical order for the purpose of analysis, such that the most intense or powerful indicators

---

[6] We could use a more sophisticated answer format such as Likert alternatives (Strongly agree . . . Strongly disagree), but this approach measures a respondent's intensity of feeling for each item separately, not comparatively among items. The Likert format assumes that each item has approximately equal intensity. If we used the ratio-scaling technique, we would learn the *relative* importance of each item to the respondent but not the *absolute* value of any one item.

Table 17.7. Scaled Measure of Tolerance for Homosexuals

Item	Occupation	(check one) Proper	Not proper
1	President of the United States	—	—
2	Primary school teacher	—	—
3	Law enforcement officer	—	—
4	Corporate executive	—	—
5	Insurance salesperson	—	—
6	Stage performer	—	—
7	Interior designer	—	—
8	Dishwasher	—	—
9	Telephone operator	—	—
10	Bricklayer	—	—

gradually give way to the less powerful ones. Table 17.7 shows how the items in Table 17.6 might be scaled.

In Table 17.7, the occupations have been arranged to reflect reasonably expected intensity of feeling. A person who would not object to an actor or actress being a known homosexual (item 6) may be expected to accept items 7 through 10 as "proper." Similarly, most respondents who would find it acceptable that a primary schoolteacher (item 2) be a homosexual would likely accept a homosexual as a police officer (item 3) or an executive (item 4). A respondent who is completely tolerant of homosexuals would answer in the affirmative to ten items. A moderately tolerant individual might find all occupations acceptable except the top two or three. A highly intolerant respondent whose prejudice against homosexuals was extreme might find even items 9 and 10 (representing occupations that are relatively remote from the public) nonetheless unacceptable.

The scoring of a scaled sequence of index items is a type of weighting that always follows their assumed intensity structure. The "hardest" or most potent measure of a variable (in this case, tolerance of homosexuals) is scored the highest, followed by the remainder in descending order. In our example, because there are ten items, we might want to give the affirmative response to item 1 a score of 10, to item 2 a score of 9, to item 3 a score of 8, and so on. The total score thus reflects a pattern of answers, not just the sum of individual responses.

Some Well-Known Scaling Techniques

As examples of the actual application of the logic of scaling, we will consider three important measures: the Bogardus Social Distance Scale, Thurstone scaling, and the Guttman scale.

THE BOGARDUS SOCIAL DISTANCE SCALE. There are many variations on this measure of the **SOCIAL DISTANCE** that respondents perceive *between themselves and members of different social categories* (nationalities, racial groups, deviants, etc.). The Bogardus Social Distance Scale, for example, is weighted according to the type of interaction that the subject is willing to engage in with members of a group or of different groups (see Figure 17.2). The logic of the increment in intensity is the perceived threat to respondents of each situation described by the scale items.

Theoretically, an individual who would readily accept a member of another ethnic group as a relative would have no objection to working alongside that person or to that person's becoming an American citizen. Because scores for each item vary with its potency, we can tell *which* relationships a respondent is willing to

1. Remember to give your *first feeling reaction* in every case.
2. Give your reactions to each nationality as a group. Do not give your reactions to the best or the worst members that you have known, but think of the picture or stereotype that you have of the whole group.
3. Put a cross in as many of the boxes as your feelings dictate.

Scoring Weights	Category	Mexicans	Vietnamese	Nigerians	Syrians
7	Close kinship by marriage				
6	In my club as personal friends				
5	On my street as neighbors				
4	Working alongside me in my occupation				
3	As citizens in my country				
2	As visitors only to my country				
1	Would exclude from my country				

Figure 17.2. A Bogardus Social Distance Scale. Adapted from Bogardus (1959).

accept by knowing *how many* relationships were acceptable and the total scale score.[7] Therefore, the Bogardus scaling technique is an effective means of data reduction.

Although social distance scales appear to have reliability and validity, a possible objection to their use is that the response categories are not, in reality, equally distant from each other, although the numbers assigned to each category (1, 2, 3, 4, etc.) are. The Bogardus scale is scored as if it were an interval measurement; yet, the distances between items are unknown and are likely to differ. For example, the distance between marrying a person and having him or her as a neighbor seems greater than the distance between having someone as a neighbor and knowing him or her only casually.

THURSTONE SCALING. The Thurstone scaling technique is an attempt to cope with the problem of making an ordinal series of numbers fit phenomena that are more difficult to arrange intuitively than is social distance. Louis L. Thurstone created a **DIFFERENTIAL SCALE**, in which

the relative positions of the many indicators of a single variable are determined from the ratings or rankings produced by a panel of judges. The issue of distance between each indicator is resolved by constructing the scale in such a way that the intervals appear equal.[8]

There are four basic steps in Thurstone scaling. First, the researcher makes a list of the possible indicators for the variable under investigation. Sometimes the list is in the form of attitude statements (possibly as many as 100 or 200). Then, a large number of evaluators, perhaps hundreds, are asked to classify these indicators by scoring them independently, according to how well they measure the variable. There may be as many as eleven or more scoring categories, ranging from "extremely powerful" indicator of the phenomenon being examined to "barely related." If sexism were being measured, one judge might find the statement: "Women should think of their children before thinking about a career" to be a potent indicator and assign it a score of 9 or 10 out of a possible 11. Another evaluator might see the statement as denoting less sexism and assign it a score of 5 or 6.

---

[7] If a subject reacting to Mexicans as a group achieves a score of 15, and we know that five categories have been checked, then we know automatically which categories they are (the bottom five) because the only combination of five numbers totaling 15 is 1, 2, 3, 4, and 5.

[8] By contrast, most other scales in social science, including those reviewed in this chapter, are ordinal rather than interval.

Next, the scale value of each indicator is determined by calculating the average score obtained for each. Indicators on which there is too little consensus are eliminated. Finally, the specific indicators that will be used to measure the variable are chosen from among those that fall along the scale from one extreme to the other. These indicators may later be incorporated in a questionnaire or other data-gathering instrument.

The Thurstone scaling technique is ingenious in that random errors in rating the indicators tend to cancel one another out when a large number of independent judgments are made. The result is a valid set of components for each complex variable being measured. Unfortunately, the four-step procedure is quite time consuming and expensive, so that actual examples of research using Thurstone scaling are rare. Its major utility is for illustrating the logic of scale construction.

GUTTMAN SCALING. Like the other scaling techniques we have discussed, the procedure developed by Guttman (1950) relies on the fact that some indicators are more vivid or powerful reflectors of a variable than are others. However, in Guttman scaling, both respondents and index items are ranked, according to the actual answers given. As a result, we may verify that items already scaled have been ranked correctly for a given population. Alternatively, or in addition, Guttman scaling may be used to rank responses to indexes that were originally scored using summated ratings.

To show the logic of the technique, let us assume a variation on the Bogardus Social Distance Scale, in which twelve subjects are asked to respond "yes" or "no" to a series of four items:[9]

A. I would marry an ex-convict.

B. I would have an ex-convict for a friend.

C. It would be acceptable for an ex-convict to live on my street.

---

[9] It is possible to use Guttman scaling when more than two response alternatives are provided, but the procedure is more complex.

D. It would be acceptable for an ex-convict to live in my community.

Each affirmative response will receive a score of 1; each negative response will receive a score of zero. Table 17.8 shows how the data, once collected, could be summarized. The item score is the sum of all positive responses for each item. The respondent score is the sum of all positive responses for each respondent.

The next step in the procedure is to construct a **SCALOGRAM**, *a table formed by rearranging the data to reflect the ranks of respondent scores together with item scores.*[10] The scalogram in Table 17.9 tells us the degree to which the social distance scale we used reflects the actual intensity of attitudes among the twelve respondents. It also shows us the extent to which knowledge of a respondent's score helps us to discover the patterning of answers that contributed to it.

If we look at the extent of variation in the patterns that produced each respondent score, we may select the one pattern for which each score is the best predictor. The most frequent (in this case, the only) pattern that produced a respondent score of 4 is 1, 1, 1, 1. Thus, if we use the respondent score alone to predict the actual responses for respondents 11 and 5, we would make no errors. Similarly, a respondent score of 3 predicts an answer pattern of 1, 1, 1, 0, with no errors; a score of 2 predicts the pattern 1, 1, 0, 0, with no errors; a score of zero, of course, predicts the pattern 0, 0, 0, 0, with no errors.

The answers from subjects who obtained a score of 1 are harder to analyze. In this case, the respondent score 1 is a mixed type. Respondents 2, 3, and 9 show the pattern 1, 0, 0, 0; therefore, if we use the score of 1 to predict their answers, we will make no errors. However, respondent 8 shows a pattern in which the score of 1 was obtained by the sequence 0, 0, 0, 1. Therefore, if we used the most frequent response

---

[10] The process of Guttman scaling analysis is often more intricate than this example, which is meant only to be illustrative. Many more index items and a much larger sample are typically employed in actual data collection; a computer program is used to create the Guttman scalogram in such cases.

Table 17.8. Scores on Four Attitude Items, by Item and Respondent

Respondent	Item A	Item B	Item C	Item D	Respondent Score
1	1	0	0	1	= 2
2	0	0	0	1	= 1
3	0	0	0	1	= 1
4	0	0	0	0	= 0
5	1	1	1	1	= 4
6	1	1	0	1	= 3
7	1	1	0	1	= 3
8	0	0	1	0	= 1
9	0	0	0	1	= 1
10	1	0	0	1	= 2
11	1	1	1	1	= 4
12	1	1	0	1	= 3
Item Score	7	5	3	10	

pattern for score 1 to predict the exact answers of respondent 8, we would make *two* errors (the replies to items C and D would not match our prediction).

This scalogram analysis shows that we were able to make forty-eight separate predictions (12 respondents × 4 items) and that by taking the most frequent pattern of answers for each respondent score as a guide, we would make two errors. *The relationship between predictions and errors* is called the **COEFFICIENT OF REPRO-DUCIBILITY** and is expressed in the following formula:

$$\text{Coefficient of reproducibility} = \frac{\text{correct predictions}}{\text{total predictions}}$$

or, in our example: $\frac{46}{48} = .96$ or 96%

In social research, a Guttman scale is acceptable if its coefficient of reproducibility exceeds

Table 17.9. Scalogram of Four Attitude Items

Respondent	Item D	Item A	Item B	Item C	Respondent Score
11	1	1	1	1	= 4
5	1	1	1	1	= 4
6	1	1	1	0	= 3
7	1	1	1	0	= 3
12	1	1	1	0	= 3
1	1	1	0	0	= 2
10	1	1	0	0	= 2
2	1	0	0	0	= 1
3	1	0	0	0	= 1
9	1	0	0	0	= 1
8	0	0	0	1	= 1
4	0	0	0	0	= 0
Item Score	10	7	5	3	

90 percent. Over 95 percent is considered excellent.

Barring errors of prediction, there is only one way to obtain each Guttman scale score. Therefore, the coefficient of reproducibility measures the extent to which the total score is an accurate data-reduction device. Like any measuring tool, this one must be used with care. There is no guarantee that valid indicators have been selected for inclusion in a Guttman scale. Indeed, the coefficient of reproducibility may be high; yet, the possibility remains that the items or questions do not really measure the variable of interest. Moreover, **SCALABILITY**, *the extent to which a set of items may be arranged according to a logical order of intensity*, is sample dependent. The identical set of questions may result in two different coefficients of reproducibility when scaled for different groups of respondents. So, the Guttman scaling technique is not a way to devise once-and-for-all, reliable measures, but a tool for analyzing the answers given by a particular group of respondents.

Not all measures are necessarily as sample dependent as are Guttman scales, but there is the unfortunate tendency to regard some frequently used indexes of complex variables as being "etched in stone" because their reliability coefficients are high or because their predictive validity seems to have been proved over the years. In fact, researchers should pay careful and continuous attention to *the circumstances (time, place, and population) for which composite measures were originally validated*, or **STANDARDIZED**.

STANDARDIZATION OF COMPOSITE MEASURES

Previous sections of this chapter have amply demonstrated the usefulness of composite measures, especially when they are asked to do no more than they were designed to do. This final section adds to our discussion in Chapter 4 by emphasizing once again the problematic nature of the search for "truth" in social science and the impossibility of knowing which specific measuring tool is best without also knowing the purpose of the research for which that tool is to be used. As our example of the Consumer Price Index shows, it is possible for measures to become dated and therefore to be less than fully useful or downright misleading, unless they are periodically revised to account for demographic trends. Even Thurstone scaling, which attempts to maximize validity of measurement via a lengthy and elaborate procedure, can result in biased research findings if the judges who rank the indicators, or scale items, are not typical of the population about which the research seeks to generalize.

To illustrate the notion that the process of index standardization may influence research findings every bit as much as the specific questions asked of respondents or the types of observation made during data collection, let us consider the example of international research on poverty. In 2003, American gross domestic product per capita was $36,924. In Ghana, a struggling West African nation, the corresponding figure was $354 (United Nations, 2006). By this measure alone, Ghana is obviously much poorer than the United States. Three hundred fifty-four dollars would pay only a small portion of one *month's* expenses for most Americans! However, poverty is a complex concept that involves more than personal income or the general health of the national economy. Costs of labor, rent, medical care, and most foodstuffs are much lower in Ghana, and it is possible that many millions of people are relatively comfortable there while earning only a small fraction of what they would need to just to survive in the United States. If we are trying to identify that portion of the population of Ghana that is "middle class," we would find that all but the wealthiest Ghanaian families are "poor" *by American standards*. Many people in the Ghanaian "middle class" would not have access to a telephone, indoor plumbing, or a washing machine, obvious indicators of middle-class status in the United States. Clearly, it does not make scientific sense to use the same yardstick for assessing poverty in the United States that we use for Ghana. Ironically, in this case, a measure standardized for the United States would inflate absolute poverty figures and deflate estimates of middle-class status, if applied in a much poorer country.

Scholars have argued that effective international poverty assessment should rely on a combination of measures aside from income, including purchasing power and unsatisfied basic needs (Allen and Thomas, 2000). Clearly, the assessment of poverty needs to be expressed in *relative* terms.

It is wrong to suggest that poverty can be considered in terms of an absolute standard that can be applied to all countries at all times, independent of the social structure and the level of development...A threshold of poverty cannot be defined in a vacuum, but only in relation to a particular society on a particular date. (Atkinson and Hills, 1998)

However, international researchers are left with the challenge of developing universal measures for poverty because they want to know how great the need is for goods and services in every country so that global programs of aid and technical assistance may be prioritized. Is it possible to develop such a standardized measuring tool? Two promising approaches to this problem are the "sectorial gaps" technique and identifying the poverty line in each country (Social Watch, 2001). Both of these strategies begin by taking individual nations as the units of analysis.

The sectorial gaps technique uses data from individual countries to define minimum needs in several areas, for example:

- educational level of adults
- school attendance of minors
- literacy
- access to electricity
- access to water and sewage services
- safe housing
- household furniture and equipment
- free time for recreation
- food
- clothing, shoes, and personal care
- personal and household hygiene
- transportation and basic communications

It then calculates the proportion of the population whose needs are unsatisfied for each of these variables. In this approach, the number of poor identified depends on the number of basic needs chosen, so it becomes important that countries agree on the list of needs.

The poverty-line approach defines a basic food basket for each country, calculates its cost, and divides the portion of spending devoted to food into the total cost of satisfying basic needs. The goal for each country is to determine that portion of the population falling below "the poverty line."

The Politics of Measurement

An important lesson to be learned from this example is that researchers need to investigate the purpose of measures that they adapt for their own use. To maximize validity, it is clear that measures of complex phenomena such as poverty should be standardized in as similar a setting as possible to the settings in which they are to be applied. The significance of this example, however, goes beyond the social scientist's search for valid knowledge. It has potential political implications as well.

Suppose a United Nations official or other world leader wanted to justify spending a large amount of money to eliminate global poverty. Which research tool would be preferable, a measure of absolute poverty standardized in the United States or a measure of relative poverty standardized after collecting data from a large number of individual countries? How may we answer this question to the leader's satisfaction, and to our own, keeping in mind the canon of objectivity in science? Does it matter which measuring tool is more accurate if people's living conditions could actually be improved more by using a less valid measure? It is at this point that the goals of politics and science may be in conflict.

Social scientists, having created immensely beneficial composite measures, must not misuse them or allow them to be misused. In the United States, analysts who have the power to change the elements in the Consumer Price Index should not let themselves be influenced by politicians or special interests. In fact, each time the basis for computing the CPI has been altered in recent years, labor union leaders and representatives of the elderly and others on fixed incomes have greeted the changes with considerable concern. Can we really expect them to be as vigilant about the scientific quest for reliability and validity as they are about the potential reduction of income that tinkering with the index could bring?

SUMMARY

Indexing and scaling are techniques for measuring complex phenomena in social science. They create a single, composite measure of behavior and attitudes out of several related indicators. Index items are then scored or assigned numbers to enable us to compare respondents and to provide a means of reducing data. Any composite measure is only as good as the validity of the items measured. For this reason, much attention is given to the composition of indexes and scales; researchers pretest and retest them in an attempt to eliminate items that are not unidimensional or that do not relate well enough to one another statistically. Every item in a composite measure should add something to our ability to understand respondents, so items that nearly duplicate one another are also removed or altered.

Composite measures can be scored in many ways such as summated ratings, forced rankings, and ratio scaling. Perhaps the most commonly used in situations where it is desirable to offer a range of responses for each question is the Likert format. Each of these ways of categorizing answers differs with regard to the number of options given and the respondents' autonomy in answering. They share the attribute that each item has an equal chance of contributing to the overall score of the composite measure, unless the index items are weighted.

Weighting is desirable in some indexing exercises, but it is essential in scaling because the purpose is to gauge the intensity of subjects' feelings and to be able to reflect patterns of response in composite measure scores. Three important scaling techniques are the Bogardus Social Distance Scale, the Thurstone scale, and the Guttman scale. These measures may be efficient ways of reducing data because the scale score implies more than does a summated rating. Guttman scaling techniques rank respondents as well as scale items, resulting in a mechanism for measuring how efficiently the scale score predicts actual responses.

As sophisticated as some scaling procedures are, they do not guarantee validity. Both the reliability and validity of composite measures are checked internally (by comparing responses to the separate items in the measure) and externally (by comparing responses to some outside source of information on a similar or related variable). Despite this continued effort, composite measures are sometimes used inappropriately. Researchers may not be sufficiently aware of the specific environment for which the measure was standardized and may engage in unwarranted extension of a scale beyond its limits. Because the results using different composite measures may vary significantly, it is possible for the measurement process to be subverted for political or pecuniary motives. The researcher must be aware of these possibilities and work to minimize them.

KEY TERMS

base period
coefficient of reproducibility
composite measure
content validity
data reduction
differential scale
domains
external validation
face validity
forced ranking
imputation
index score
internal validity
item analysis
item-to-item correlation
item-to-scale correlation
Likert scaling
multiple indicators
ratio scaling
reliability coefficient
scalability
scalogram
social distance scale
split-half correlation
stability

standardized measure
summated ratings
unidimensionality
weighting

EXERCISES

1. Select one of the following complex concepts – "love," "leadership," or "jealousy" – and develop a list of its various aspects or components. Operationalize each component that you have identified by creating an appropriate statement or question for inclusion in an index.

2. Develop a ten-item scale designed to measure alcoholism, and specify the scale items in increasing order of intensity or potency.

3. A researcher wants to develop an index of occupational prestige in the United States by asking respondents to rank ten selected occupations, but the specific occupational categories need to be chosen. Suppose you were assisting this researcher. If you could pick only ten occupational titles as a sample of the full range of jobs in America, which ones would you select? Make such a list and give the reasons for your choices.

4. Participate with your class in a Thurstone-type rating of indicators. Some students should be responsible for devising the list of indicators, and a larger group should be the judges. Some suggested variables for investigations are "sex appeal," "patriotism," and "racism." What major differences, if any, appear in the rankings made by the evaluators? What do the ranking patterns reveal about the group of judges and about the difficulty of achieving validity in social science measurement?

5. Think of a concept that might be operationalized and scaled with the Guttman technique. Create five scale items and administer them to five respondents. You may wish to refer to the tables of contents of Robinson, Shaver, and Wrightsman (1990) and Robinson, Shaver, and Wrightsman (1999) for inspiration. Summarize your findings in a format similar to that used in Table 17.9. Did the items scale as you expected they would?

SUGGESTED READINGS AND SOURCES

DeVellis, Robert F. 2003. *Scale Development: Theory and Applications*. Newbury Park, CA: Sage.

This volume is designed to help the researcher to develop original, reliable, and valid instruments for measurement.

Gorden, Raymond L. 1997. *Unidimensional Scaling of Social Variable: Concepts and Procedures*. New York: Free Press.

Another excellent source on scale construction.

Kinsey Institute. 2006. *Kinsey's Heterosexual-Homosexual Rating Scale*. Bloomington, IN. http://www.indiana.edu/~kinsey/research/ak-hhscale.html.

This Web site contains scale items for assessing sexual orientation, together with a bibliography.

McIver, John, and Edward G. Carmines. 1981. *Unidimensional Scaling*. Beverly Hills, CA: Sage.

This book provides an introduction to the fundamentals of scaling theory and construction. The authors present an overview and comparative analysis of such techniques as Thurstone scaling, Likert scaling, and Guttman scaling.

Miller, Delbert, ed. 1991. *Handbook of Research Design and Social Measurement*. 35th ed. Newbury Park, CA: Sage.

This book abounds with examples and suggestions for the application of composite measures.

Netemeyer, Richard G., William O. Bearden, and Subhash Sharma. 2003. *Scaling Procedures: Issues and Applications*. Thousand Oaks, CA: Sage.

This book covers the fundamentals of scaling theory and provides numerous examples.

Robinson, John P., Phillip R. Shaver, and Lawrence S. Wrightsman. 1990. *Measures of Personality and Social Psychological Attitudes*. New York: Academic Press.

This volume is packed with illustrations of composite measures of variables such as life satisfaction, self-esteem, authoritarianism, and religious attitudes. For each measure cited, a summary of the rationale for its use is given, as well as the results of tests of validity and reliability and additional topical references.

Robinson, John P., Phillip R. Shaver, and Lawrence S. Wrightsman. 1999. *Measures of Political Attitudes*. New York: Academic Press.

Similar in format to Robinson, Shaver, and Wrightsman (1990), this volume covers measures of public reaction to political issues, liberalism and conservatism, racial and ethnic attitudes, and orientation toward the political process.

Senn, Charlene Y., and Karalin Dzinas. 1996. "Measuring Fear of Rape: A New Scale." *Canadian Journal of Behavioural Science* 28:141–144.

In addition to empirical findings, this article presents the thirty-six scale items used to measure the fear of rape. The authors supply detailed information about sampling procedures and strategies for assuring construct validity. They summarize procedures for maximizing both internal and external validity.

ShrinkTank. 2005.

http://www.shrinktank.com/testing.htm.

This Web site contains links to dozens of popular psychological tests and measures, including self-diagnostic scales and indexes.

Spector, Paul. 1992. *Summated Rating Scale Construction: An Introduction.* Newbury Park, CA: Sage.

Aimed at helping researchers construct more effective summated rating scales, Spector's book shows how to determine the number of items necessary, the appropriate amount of response categories, the most productive wording of items, how to sort good items from bad, and how to validate a scale.

REFERENCES

Adorno, Theodor W., Else Frenkel-Brunswik, and Daniel J. Levinson. 1950/1993. *The Authoritarian Personality.* New York: W. W. Norton.

Allen, Tim, and Alan Thomas, eds. 2000. *Poverty and Development: Into the 21st Century.* New York: Oxford University Press.

Atkinson, Tony, and John Hills. 1998. "Exclusion, Employment and Opportunity." CASE Paper 4. London School of Economics.

Bandura, Albert. 1986. *Social Foundations of Thought and Action: A Social Cognitive Theory.* Englewood Cliffs, NJ: Prentice Hall.

Bogardus, Emory S. 1959. *Social Distance.* Yellow Springs, OH: Antioch Press.

Guttman, Louis. 1950. "The Basis for Scalogram Analysis." In *Measurement and Prediction*, 60–90. Samuel A. Stouffer et al., eds. Princeton, NJ: Princeton University Press.

IsHak, Waguih William, MD. 2005. *ODST: Online Depression Screening Test.* New York University Department of Psychiatry.

http://www.med.nyu.edu/psych/screens/depres.html.

Jinks, Jerry, and Vicky Morgan. 1999. "Children's Perceived Academic Self-Efficacy: An Inventory Scale." *Clearing House* 72 (4) April: 224–230.

Litwin, Mark S. 1995. *How to Measure Survey Reliability and Validity.* Thousand Oaks, CA: Sage.

Philliber, Susan G. 1980. *Social Research: Guides to a Decision-Making Process.* Itasca, IL: Peacock.

Robinson, John P., Phillip R. Shaver, and Lawrence S. Wrightsman. 1990. *Measures of Personality and Social Psychological Attitudes.* New York: Academic Press.

Robinson, John P., Phillip R. Shaver, and Lawrence S. Wrightsman. 1999. *Measures of Political Attitudes.* New York: Academic Press.

Senn, Charlene Y., and Karalin Dzinas. 1996. "Measuring Fear of Rape: A New Scale." *Canadian Journal of Behavioural Science* 28:141–144.

Simon, Julian L. 1978. *Basic Research Methods in Social Science.* 2nd ed. New York: Random House.

Social Watch. 2001. *The Dimensions of Poverty.* Montevideo, Uruguay: Instituto del Tercer Mundo.

http://www.socialwatch.org/en/informeImpreso/tablaDeContenidos1997.htm.

Spector, Paul. 1992. *Summated Rating Scale Construction: An Introduction.* Newbury Park, CA: Sage.

United Nations. 2006. *Social Indicators Home Page.* United Nations Statistics Division.

http://unstats.un.org/unsd/demographic/products/socind/.

U.S. Bureau of Labor Statistics (USBLS). 2006.

http://www.bls.gov/home.htm.

Williamson, John B. 1974. "The Stigma of Public Dependency: A Comparison of Alternative Forms of Public Aid to the Poor." *Social Problems* 22 (2) December: 213–228.

BASIC STATISTICAL ANALYSIS

18

INTRODUCTION

The last two chapters of this book cover the field of statistics, from a basic introduction through multivariate analysis.[1] Social scientists

---

[1] The treatment of these issues is designed to complement the material presented in several earlier chapters concerning measurement, sampling, survey research, content analysis, aggregate data analysis, and scaling. For more detailed treatment, please refer to the suggested readings at the conclusion of Chapters 18 and 19.

regularly encounter quantitative data that have been summarized and presented in statistical form. They find statistics in almost everything they read, from articles in popular newspapers and magazines to scholarly journals. Published reports of the results of quantitative research usually include charts, diagrams, graphs, and tables. To evaluate such work, it is essential to develop a thorough understanding of statistical procedures, including the assumptions

Table 18.1. Marginals for the Variable "Religion"

"What is your present religious affiliation?"

Category	Frequencies	Percentages	Adjusted percentages
Protestant	720	48	60
Catholic	360	24	30
Jewish	120	8	10
Other/none	180	12	–
Missing data	120	8	–
TOTAL	1,500	100%	100%

and limitations underlying each technique. The purpose of this chapter is to outline the basic procedures, ideas, and issues associated with the analysis of quantitative data.

UNIVARIATE ANALYSIS

A distinction is often made between **DESCRIPTIVE RESEARCH**, which *highlights the outstanding characteristics of a sample, or of the population from which the sample was drawn*, and **EXPLANATORY RESEARCH,** which *concentrates on cause–effect connections* among those characteristics. In practice, most quantitative studies involve elements of both description and explanation, beginning with a descriptive statistical summary of the data and progressing toward testing hypotheses and causal relationships. Descriptive analysis typically involves consideration of *one variable at a time* rather than the relationship between two or more variables. For this reason, it is often referred to as **UNIVARIATE ANALYSIS.**

Marginals

Suppose we were to draw a representative state sample of 1,500 people for a study of the characteristics of people who belong to different religions. We might want to start by looking at the proportion of the sample belonging to each of the major religions. Responses to the question, "What is your present religious affiliation?" are placed in four categories: "Protestant," "Catholic," "Jewish," and "Other or none," a residual category for all those who

either belong to a group that is numerically small in the state being considered or who profess atheism. A table that presents the **FREQUENCY DISTRIBUTION** (*count of cases*) and *the percentage distribution (proportion of all cases) for each response category associated with the variable* is referred to as a table of **MARGINALS.** Table 18.1 presents marginals for the variable "religion."

Notice that percentages are computed twice in Table 18.1, and the results depend on which cases we take to represent the whole, or 100 percent. The first row indicates that the sample included 720 Protestants, who make up 48 percent of the total of 1,500 persons surveyed. If the researcher were interested only in making comparisons among the major religious groups, the 180 persons who indicated that they belong to no religious group or to a small one, and the 120 persons who refuse to disclose their religion, could be excluded from subsequent analysis. This would leave 1,200 cases; the third column, labeled **ADJUSTED PERCENTAGES**, presents the *recomputed figures* for this working sample. Hence, the 720 Protestants constitute 48 percent (720/1,500) of all persons polled, but they constitute 60 percent (720/1,200) of the cases to be analyzed. Percentages are routinely adjusted in this way whenever the researcher intends to exclude missing data (or responses not considered appropriate) from the analysis.

The data presented in Table 18.1 can also be summarized graphically. In Figure 18.1, the adjusted percentages are presented in the form of a **BAR GRAPH**; in Figure 18.2, they are presented in the form of a **PIE DIAGRAM**. Although they convey somewhat less information than the table from which they were extracted, these alternative ways of presenting the same data can often be useful in highlighting some especially important point.

Marginals are particularly useful for summarizing the responses of a large sample to a question that has only a few response categories – such as race, religion, or gender. But, what if we were to construct marginals for variables such as "years of education" or "income"?

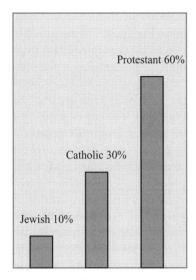

Figure 18.1. Bar graph for data in Table 18.1.

The number of possible response categories for these variables can be so unwieldy that the marginals table no longer presents a succinct summary. One solution to this problem is the use of summary statistics that measure important characteristics of the distribution. Measures of central tendency and measures of variability are useful for this purpose.

Central Tendency and Levels of Measurement

MEASURES OF CENTRAL TENDENCY are *statistics used to represent an average or typical respondent*. The actual statistic used to repre-

sent the average depends on the level of measurement that has been reached for the characteristic being considered. As will be recalled from the discussion in Chapter 4, we can distinguish between four levels of measurement: nominal, ordinal, interval, and ratio.

For a *nominal-level variable* such as sex, race, or religion we must be able to classify all our respondents into a set of categories that are mutually exclusive and exhaustive. It must be possible to find a category that each respondent in the sample will fit into (the categories must be exhaustive), and no respondent should be able to fit into more than one of the categories (they must be mutually exclusive). The variable "religion," considered in Table 18.1, meets both of these criteria.

An *ordinal-level variable* shares the properties of a nominal-level variable (i.e., the categories must be mutually exclusive and exhaustive), but the categories must also be ranked, that is, put into some order of progression, such as from high to low, or from very strong to very weak. Each category represents more of the variable's characteristic than the next-lower category, but we cannot measure the distance between categories. In Table 18.2 on page 400, we can say that persons in category 1 favor handgun control more than persons in any other category. Nevertheless, we cannot say they favor handgun control twice as much as persons in category 2 or three times as much as persons in category 3. Nor can we say that the difference in sentiments between persons in categories 1 and 2 is equal to the difference in sentiments between persons in categories 2 and 3 because the distance between categories is subjective and unknown.

An *interval-level variable* has all the properties of an ordinal-level variable, but it has the additional capacity to measure the distance between categories. An example is temperature measured in degrees Fahrenheit. A *ratio-level variable* has all the properties of an interval-level variable and also has a zero point that represents the total absence of whatever the variable measures (0 years of education,

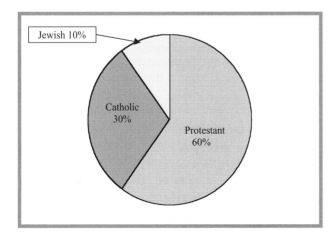

Figure 18.2. Pie diagram for the data in Table 18.1.

Table 18.2. Marginals for an Ordinal Level Variable

"The private ownership of handguns should be made illegal."

Category	Frequency	Percentage
1. Agree strongly	400	40
2. Agree	250	25
3. Disagree	150	15
4. Disagree strongly	200	20
TOTAL	1,000	100%

0 dollars of income, and so on). By contrast, a reading of 0 degrees Fahrenheit does not represent a total absence of temperature. For most social science research, the distinction between interval and ratio measures is not important because most statistical procedures require only an interval-level measure.

At the nominal level of measurement, the only appropriate measure of central tendency is the **MODE**, defined as *the category of a variable with the largest number of cases in it.* In Table 18.1, the mode is the Protestant category, with 48 percent of the respondents. The modal category, though it is the most typical response in the sample, does not necessarily contain a majority of the cases. For this reason, and because there is no reason to consider cases in any other categories to be near or similar to cases in the modal category, the mode is a very weak indicator of central tendency.

For variables that reach the ordinal level of measurement, there is a stronger measure of central tendency, the **MEDIAN**. The median is the category in which the middle observation falls; it is *the point in the distribution where half of the cases have less and the other half of the cases have more of the characteristics being measured* than does the median. For the following set of numbers – 7, 3, 5, 17, 2, 20, 17, 5, 3, 17, 14 – the median is 7 because it is the value that falls in the middle of the distribution. For the data in Table 18.2, we would start at either end of the distribution and count to the 500th person. Because

this person would be found in the "agree" category, this becomes the median for the variable. The mode can also be determined and used, but the mode and the median do not necessarily coincide. The median is generally considered a better measure of central tendency than the mode because it takes into consideration the order that exists between response categories.

For interval-level and ratio-level variables, the **MEAN** can be used as a measure of central tendency. The mean is simply *the arithmetic average* – the sum of all observations divided by the total number of observations. Table 18.3 presents the computation of the mean for the set of numbers cited earlier and a comparison of this measure to the median and the mode. The mean is often used with such variables as income, years of schooling completed, and age. The more closely the mean, median, and mode correspond when they are all computed for the same variable, the more confident you can be of having found a value that is typical or average. In Table 18.3, the wide divergence among these three statistics indicates a distribution of observations that fails to converge on any central point.

For interval and ratio levels of measurement it is always possible to compute both the median and the mode in addition to the mean. The mode, however, is rarely used with interval-level data, but the median is used, particularly when the researcher wants to de-emphasize the effect of a few extremely high or extremely low observations. The mean can be very strongly influenced by even one observation at a very high or low value; in this sense the mean is less stable than the median. For the set of numbers 1, 5, 7, 12, 275, the mean is 60, and the median is 7. If we have any reason to believe that there might be an error in the one extremely high observation, or if we know it to be an accurate but **DEVIANT CASE** (*an extremely unusual observation* that should not be allowed to influence the computation of an average value), then the median would be a more appropriate measure of central tendency than the mean.

The measures of central tendency that we have considered can be used to describe the average or typical respondent, but they tell us

Table 18.3. Computation of Mean, Median, and Mode for a Set of Eleven Observations

Observations: 7 3 5 17 2 20 17 5 3 17 14

Mode = most frequent value = 17

Median = middle of the distribution = 7

Distribution of scores from lowest to highest:

2 3 3 5 5 7 14 17 17 17 20
                  ↑   ↑
              median   mode

$$Mean = \frac{sum\ of\ all\ observations}{number\ of\ observations}$$

$$= \frac{2+3+3+5+5+7+14+17+17+17+20}{1}$$

$$= \frac{110}{11}$$

$$= 10$$

Mode: 17 Median: 7 Mean: 10

nothing about the degree of **DISPERSION** or *variability* of the data around this average or central point. Table 18.4 presents two sets of observations that have identical means and medians but that are dispersed in quite different ways. Distribution B is much more dispersed than distribution A. We can get some idea of the degree of variability in a distribution by simply examining its marginals, but we often need a more concise way to compute and summarize this variability. For this purpose, a number of statistics have been developed that measure variability.

Measures of Variability

There are no generally accepted measures of variability for either nominal-level or ordinal-level variables. In this section, we will consider the *range, standard deviation, and vari-*

ance, each of which is an appropriate **MEASURE OF VARIABILITY** for data at the interval-level or ratio-level of measurement.

The **RANGE** is the simplest measure of variability: *It is the difference between the largest and the smallest observations* in the sample. If in a sample of 1,000 respondents the lowest reported income is $1,500 and the highest is $76,500, then the range is $75,000. The range is very easy to compute and to understand. It is, however, highly unstable because it is based on extreme observations at each end of the distribution.

The **STANDARD DEVIATION** is the most frequently used measure of variability and is based on *calculating how far each individual observation (X_1) deviates from the mean $\overline{X}$.* The formula for the standard deviation is

$$\text{Standard Deviation} = s = \sqrt{\frac{\sum(X_1 - \overline{X})^2}{N}}$$

where X_1 = a score on variable,

$\overline{X}$ = the mean for all scores on variable X,

N = the number of observations.

To compute the standard deviation, first compute the mean, and then subtract this mean from each individual observation. Next, square the results of each of these individual subtractions, and then add all these squares together. Divide the total sum of the squares by N, the number of observations, and take the square root of the resulting quotient. Table 18.5 illustrates these steps in computing the standard deviation for a set of observations from a sample of five cases.

Table 18.4. Central Tendency in Two Distributions with Differing Degrees of Variability

Distribution A	8	8	9	9	10	10	10	11	11	12	12
	Mean: 10					Median: 10					
Distribution B	1	2	2	4	8	10	13	16	16	18	20
	Mean: 10					Median: 10					

Table 18.5. The Computation of the Standard Deviation

The following computations give the standard deviation for the five observations of the variable X: 0, 50, 100, 140, 200

Observed value (X_1)	Deviation from sample mean ($X_1 - \overline{X}$)	Square of deviation from sample mean ($X_1 - \overline{X})^2$
0	−100	10,000
50	−50	2,500
100	0	0
150	50	2,500
200	100	10,000

N = Sample size = 5

$$\overline{X} = \text{mean} = \frac{\sum X_1}{N} = \frac{(0 + 50 + 100 + 150 + 200)}{5} = 100$$

$$\text{Standard Deviation} = s = \sqrt{\frac{\sum(X_1 - \overline{X})^2}{N}}$$

$$= \sqrt{\frac{(10{,}000 + 2{,}500 + 0 + 2{,}500 + 10{,}000)}{5}}$$

$$= \sqrt{5{,}000}$$

$$= 70.71$$

The squaring of deviations from the mean gives a heavy emphasis to the larger (more extreme) deviations from the mean. To check this point in Table 18.5, compare the relative magnitudes of the values in the ($X_1 - \overline{X}$) column to those in the ($X_1 - \overline{X})^2$ column. A small standard deviation indicates that the observations tend to cluster closely around the mean; a large standard deviation indicates a great deal of dispersion in the data, with relatively few observations close to the mean. Hence, when the standard deviation is small, the mean can be interpreted as a fairly accurate description of most respondents in the sample. To better understand this important relationship between the mean and the standard deviation, you might find it helpful to compute for yourself the standard deviations for each of the two sets of observations presented in Table 18.4.

Although the standard deviation is somewhat more complicated than other measures of dispersion, and more difficult to calculate, it is used frequently because it has a special meaning in relation to the NORMAL CURVE (see Figure 18.3) and hence also in relation to variables whose distributions approximate the normal curve.

When plotted, some variables, such as SAT (Scholastic Aptitude Test) or IQ scores, closely approximate the normal curve's distribution – with *most cases falling close to the mean and the more extreme scores tapering off and becoming less common as we move farther and farther from the mean value.* This tendency to approximate a normal distribution is true of a wide variety of variables used in social research, such as years of education and various political attitudes. Errors in sampling also tend to be normally distributed. When a variable is distributed normally, we can use its mean and standard deviation directly to determine what proportion of all observations fall within a specified distance of the mean.

As we see in Figure 18.3, for the normal curve, approximately 68 percent of all observations fall within one standard deviation on

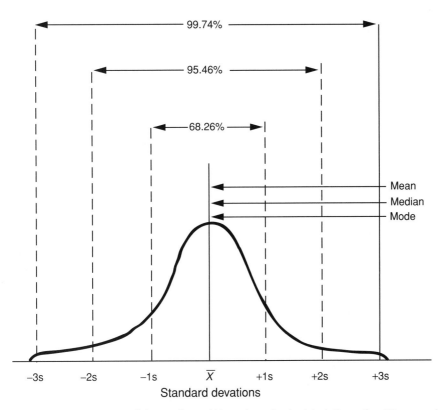

Figure 18.3. Percentages of observations within various standard deviation units of the mean for the normal curve.

either side of the mean; approximately 95 percent fall within two standard deviations; and approximately 99 percent fall within three standard deviations on either side of the mean. If we know that the mean of a distribution is 100 and the standard deviation is 15, then 68 percent of the cases will be between 85 (100 − 15) and 115 (100 + 15); 95 percent of the cases will fall between 70 (100 − 30) and 130 (100 + 30); and 99 percent will be between 55 (100 − 45) and 145 (100 + 45). This property of the normal curve (and of variables or statistics that we can assume are normally distributed) allows us to specify the chance (probability) of any score deviating from the mean by a given magnitude. Another noteworthy property of the normal distribution that can be seen in Figure 18.3 is that the mean, median, and mode all coincide. You will recall that the procedure for determining the standard deviation requires us to take the square root as our last step. Omitting this last step produces a third measure of variability, referred to as the **VARIANCE**, which *is equal to the square of the standard deviation*:

$$\text{Variance} = s^2 = \frac{\sum (X_1 - \overline{X})^2}{N}$$

The standard deviation is used more extensively than the variance in descriptive analysis because of its special relationship to the normal curve. Variance, however, becomes very important in more complex statistical procedures, such as correlation and regression, which are based upon an analysis of the variance.

Grouping and Recoding Data

Many variables, especially those measured at the interval or ratio levels, have a large number of categories. In a large sample of adults whose ages range from 21 to 95, it is conceivable that scores on the age variable might fall into

Table 18.6. A Categorization of the Income Variable

Income category	Frequency	Percentage
$0–$10,000	50	5
$10,001–$20,000	300	30
$20,001–$45,000	400	40
$45,001–$60,000	200	20
More than $60,000	50	5
TOTAL	1,000	100%

more than seventy different categories. When this happens, it is inconvenient to present the data as a set of marginals without first consolidating groups (ranges) of values into broad categories. With a variable such as income, if we had no such broad categories and instead recorded each individual's exact income, we might end up with as many different values as we had persons in the sample. Although for some purposes such accuracy and precision in measurement might be very desirable, it is not a strategy that lends itself to summary presentation of the data. To present data concisely in tables, we need to use a grouping scheme for such variables. Table 18.6 shows one possible categorization of the income variable.

Every scheme for grouping data has to conform to the needs of the research project, keeping in mind how the data will later be used. When an interval-level or ratio-level variable is being coded, a grouping scheme can be devised and built directly into the coding process. When devising your coding scheme, remember that the more categories you allow for a variable, the more precise your measurements will be; however, the fewer categories you use, the easier it will be to present the data in a table. Often, however, computer programs such as SPSS (Statistical Package for the Social Sciences) allow you to take data that were originally coded into a very large number of categories and easily reduce them to a more manageable form, thereby achieving both precision and convenience.[2] You can then put your data into differ-

ent forms according to the needs of the various phases of your analysis.

When we take a ratio-level variable such as income and categorize its values as we have done in Table 18.6, what level of measurement can we now assume for the newly recoded variable?

In going from uncollapsed income data to the summary categories presented in this table, we have lost information. In sacrificing precision for convenience, we are always giving up information, and this happens every time we collapse the categories of a variable. As a result, what was a ratio-level variable is now only an ordinal-level variable. Why? Because the difference in income between respondents in adjacent income categories in Table 18.6 might be $4, $40, $400, or any amount ranging between $1 and $10,000 or $15,000. Whenever an interval-level or ratio-level variable is categorized into ranges, the resulting variable drops to the ordinal level of measurement.

Marginals, measures of central tendency, and measures of variability are the main tools of univariate analysis. Marginals provide a great deal of descriptive information, but for some purposes it is useful to summarize this information more concisely, using measures of central tendency and variability. Such measures give us an idea of what the average case of respondent is like and how similar other cases or respondents are to the average. Although some quantitative studies stop with univariate analysis, seeking only to describe the characteristics of their samples, most studies go beyond this to look at the interrelationships among the variables examined.

BIVARIATE ANALYSIS

BIVARIATE ANALYSIS refers to any presentation of data in which an *attempt is made to relate two variables to one another*. Table 18.6 presented data only for the variable "income," describing what proportion of a sample of 1,000 persons fit into each of several income categories. After we have examined this overall income distribution, it would seem reasonable to divide the sample into distinct subgroups whose income distributions we suspect will be different from the

---

[2] For an introduction to SPSS, see Field (2000) as well as Bryman and Cramer (2001).

Table 18.7. A Bivariate Frequency Distribution of Income by Race

Income category	White	Nonwhite	TOTAL
$0–$10,000	20	30	50
$10,001–$20,000	180	120	300
$20,001–$45,000	300	100	400
$45,001–$60,000	155	45	200
More than $60,000	45	5	50
TOTAL	700	300	1,000

attention is drawn to the way in which race affects income. If the two distributions were nearly identical, then we might conclude that race does not affect income (for the population from which our sample was drawn). However, the two distributions in Table 18.7 appear to be quite different, so we have preliminary evidence that race is an important factor affecting a person's income. Because the sample of whites in Table 18.7 is much larger than the sample of nonwhites, it is difficult to compare the two distributions. Such comparisons are much easier to make when we convert these frequencies into percentages, as is done in Table 18.8 on page 406.

overall figures of Table 18.6 and also different from one another. We might divide the sample into women and men and compare each group's income distributions. Alternatively, we might divide the sample into three religious groups – Protestants, Catholics, and Jews – to compare them with respect to income. Table 18.7 illustrates this technique; the sample is divided into whites and nonwhites.

Cross-Tabulation

Table 18.7 is an example of a technique called **CROSS-TABULATION**, on which most bivariate analysis is based. In cross-tabulation *the categories of two variables are used simultaneously to define subgroups* into which the total sample is divided. A table (cross-tabulation) is made up of all possible combinations of the categories of one variable with the categories of the other variable. This provides us with a more elaborate description of the data by transforming the univariate frequency distribution of Table 18.6 into the bivariate frequency distribution of Table 18.7, and to this extent cross-tabulation serves the purposes of purely descriptive research. We can now describe separately the income distribution for whites and for nonwhites.

Bivariate analysis, however, has important uses besides making descriptions more elaborate. Cross-tabulations allow comparisons to be made between subgroups within the sample, and when such comparisons are made, the relationship between one variable and another begins to emerge. By comparing the income distribution for whites to that for nonwhites, our

Computing Percentages for Cross-Tabulations

The simplest form of explanatory research involves testing for the existence of a relationship, or association, between an independent variable and a dependent variable.[3] In this case, it is logical to consider race the independent variable affecting income, the dependent variable. As Table 18.8 illustrates, percentages are computed by considering the categories of the independent variable one at a time. Starting with whites, for example, divide the frequency in each income subcategory ($0 to $5,000, $5,001 to $10,000, and so forth) by the total number of whites (700). Follow the same procedure for each category of the independent variable until you have computed an appropriate percentage for each cell in the table. The end result allows direct comparisons between the percentage of whites and the percentage of nonwhites in each income category.

In a cross-tabulation there are several possible ways to compute percentages, and each method of calculation serves a different analytical

---

[3] Sometimes it is appropriate to characterize this relationship as "causal"; that is, the independent variable causes the dependent variable. However, it is often more appropriate to note that the two variables are "associated," or statistically related.

Table 18.8. A Cross-Tabulation of Income by Race, with Frequencies and Column Percentages

Income category	White	Nonwhite	TOTAL
$0–$10,000	3% (20)*	10% (30)	5% (50)
$10,001–$20,000	26% (180)	40% (120)	30% (300)
$20,001–$45,000	43% (300)	33% (100)	40% (400)
$45,001–$60,000	22% (155)	15% (45)	20% (200)
More than $60,000	6% (45)	2% (5)	5% (50)
TOTAL	100% (700)	100% (300)	100% (1,000)

*Numbers in parentheses represent the number of cases.

purpose. Percentages may be calculated *across* ROW totals, *down* COLUMN totals, or in other ways; the manner in which they are calculated defines and restricts the statements and comparisons that can legitimately be based on the percentages. It follows, therefore, that you should never compute percentages in a cross-tabulation until you are certain that the direction in which they are computed is suited to your research questions and the comparisons you need to make.

Reexamine Table 18.8, and see how the percentages were calculated. Noticing, for example, that there are twenty whites with incomes of $10,000 or less, we could have calculated across the row that 40 percent (20 of 50) of all the persons with incomes of $10,000 or less are white. Instead, we calculate down the column that 3 percent (20 of 700) of all whites have incomes of $10,000 or less. The difference between these two statements is a crucial one that exposes the essential logic of computing percentages. Percentages must be computed in a way that allows us to make intergroup comparisons that are unaffected by differences in the sizes of the groups. To state that 40 percent of the persons with incomes less than $10,000 are white and that 60 percent are nonwhite is to make an almost meaningless comparison between whites and nonwhites, because the percentages are mainly a function of the larger number of whites in the sample. It is far more useful, in this context, to state that only 3 percent of whites in contrast to 10 percent of nonwhites have incomes of $10,000 or less.

Using column percentages throughout the table to compare whites against nonwhites systematically with respect to their incomes, a general pattern becomes clear. Whites are more likely than nonwhites to be in high-income categories; conversely, nonwhites are more often found in low-income categories. Half of all nonwhites (50%) but less than a third of whites (29%) have incomes of $20,000 or less. We conclude, therefore, that the independent variable "race" does indeed affect "income" – with a substantial income advantage accruing to whites. The cross-tabulation has shifted our focus away from either race or income individually; we are now squarely confronted with the relationship between the two variables.

Measures of Association

Cross-tabulations are a useful and compact way to illustrate relationships between variables, but they require that the variables be expressed in only a few categories. As the number of categories for each variable increases, the size of the resulting table increases geometrically. The larger the table, the more difficult it is to interpret. Should the table exceed, say, twenty-five cells, it will likely not be as easy to see the pattern of relationship between variables. One solution is to group data using recoding, thereby reducing the number of categories so that the cross-tabulations remain manageable. Unfortunately, as we saw earlier, data reduction by grouping inevitably diminishes the amount of information by sacrificing precise measurement

Table 18.9. Cross-Tabulation of Grade Point Average in College by Verbal SAT Scores

	Verbal SAT scores			
	Low (below 400)	Moderate (400–600)	High (above 600)	TOTAL
Grade-point average				
High (above 3.3)	10% (25)	25% (125)	60% (150)	30% (300)
Moderate (2.5–3.3)	40% (100)	55% (275)	30% (75)	45% (450)
Low (below 2.5)	50% (125)	20% (100)	10% (25)	25% (250)
TOTAL	100% (250)	100% (500)	100% (250)	100% (1000)

for the sake of convenience. Happily, there is another solution to the problem of large tables.

CORRELATION. Suppose we have data from a large sample of college graduates on their verbal SAT scores before college entry and on their grade-point averages during college. We would like to know whether the SAT scores (the independent variable) are correlated with grade-point averages (the dependent variable). One way to test for an association between these two variables might be to reduce each variable to only three categories (low scores, moderate scores, and high scores) and then to cross-tabulate them, as in Table 18.9. The results show a fairly clear pattern: Persons with high SAT scores tend to do well in college, whereas those with low SAT scores tend to do poorly. Sixty percent of those with SAT scores above 600 achieved a college grade-point average of over 3.3, whereas only 10 percent of those whose SAT scores were below 400 achieved as well.

CORRELATIONS are complex computations that *measure the degree of association between two variables*, using exact scores instead of rough categories. The computation produces a single number, called a **CORRELATION COEFFICIENT**, which *summarizes the relationship*. A coefficient of 0.0 means that the independent variable's value does not help us to predict or explain anything about the dependent variable. At the other extreme a coefficient of either +1.0 or −1.0 signifies a perfect correlation

between the two variables: If we know someone's score on the independent variable, we can exactly predict their score on the dependent variable. To illustrate the correlation between SAT scores and grades, we will graph the data from Table 18.9, using exact scores instead of summary categories. The type of graph depicted in Figure 18.4 on page 408, in which *each case is plotted according to its values on the independent and the dependent variable*, is called a **SCATTERGRAM**. Note the similarities between Table 18.9 and Figure 18.4, which present the same data in different ways.

One way to think of the correlation coefficient is in terns of the relationship between a set of data points and a line that has been drawn through these points in such a way as to minimize the sum of the square of the distances between each point and the line. The closer the points fall to this line, the higher the correlation. The Pearson correlation coefficient (r) will be positive if the line through the points slopes upward as we move to the right (as in Figure 18.4), that is, if the values of the dependent variable get larger as the values of the independent variable increase. Conversely, the coefficient will be negative (ranging from 0.0−1.0) if the line through these data points slopes downward as we move to the right, indicating that as the values of the independent variable increase, the values of the dependent variable decrease. Figure 18.4 illustrates a strong positive correlation ($r = +.70$).

The scattergrams in Figure 18.5 on page 409 illustrate several alternative relationships

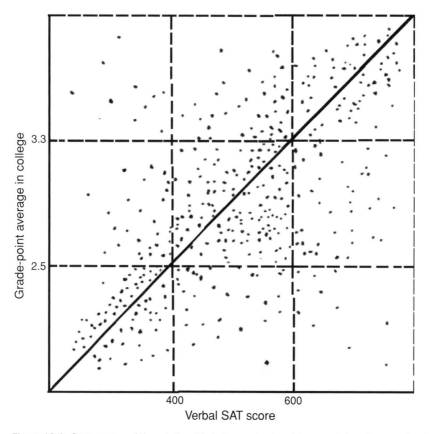

Figure 18.4. Scattergram of the relationship between grade-point average in college and verbal SAT score.

between the independent variable X and the dependent variable Y. The following observations can be made based on the information in Figure 18.5:

A. The data for this scattergram illustrate a moderately strong positive correlation that would be approximately .60. You will note that in this scattergram, as in most of the others, the X values increase from left to right, that is, from L (low) to H (high), and the Y values increase from bottom to top (also from low to high). As with all positive correlations, there is a tendency for the Y values to increase as the X values increase.

B. Here all the data points fall along a straight line; this is what happens when there is a perfect positive correlation between X and Y ($r = 1.00$). The correlation is perfect only in the sense that it represents the upper limit for the correlation coefficient. In actual social research applications, we do not get correlations of 1.00 unless we have somehow managed to correlate a variable with itself.

C. Here there is no relationship between X and Y ($r = .00$).

D. Here there is a weak positive correlation ($r = +.20$) between X and Y.

E. Here there is a very strong positive correlation ($r = +.90$).

F. Here there is a perfect negative correlation ($r = 1.00$). Note that for a negative correlation Y decreases as X increases.

G. Here there is a strong negative correlation ($r = -.90$). An example of a negative correlation would be the relationship between cigarette consumption (X) and life expectancy (Y). As cigarette consumption increases, life expectancy decreases. (Undoubtedly, the actual correlation between these two variables is weaker than $-.90$.)

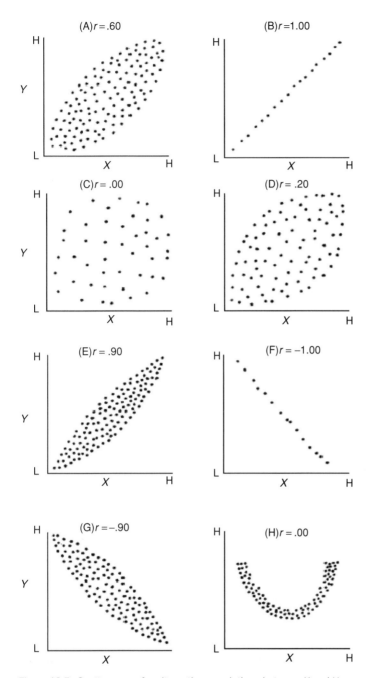

Figure 18.5. Scattergrams for alternative correlations between *X* and *Y*.

H. Here there is a strong **NONLINLAR RELA-TIONSHIP** between *X* and *Y* ($r = .00$); that is, *the data do not fall along a straight line*. It is not appropriate to use the correlation coefficient to summarize this relationship. The low correlation masks a strong, but nonlinear relationship.

Other Measures of Association

The correlation coefficient, *r*, is a statistic designed to measure the strength of association between two interval-level or ratio-level variables. When one (or both) of the variables whose strength of association you are testing fails to reach at least the interval level, some measure of association other than r should be used (although many researchers violate this rule and apply r to ordinal-level data). Alternative coefficients have been designed to suit almost any situation, and they are described in most statistics texts. Although all of these coefficients appear at first to be similar in form to r and to one another, each is calculated in a different way, and each needs to be interpreted with great caution.

Not all coefficients vary between -1.0 and $+1.0$; some never take negative values, and others never reach either $+1.0$ or -1.0. A number of coefficients cannot distinguish between a positive and a negative association. In general, the varying methods of calculation make it impossible to compare one coefficient directly with any other coefficient; each must be interpreted according to its own standards.[4] It is thus imperative that the researcher become thoroughly familiar with the purposes of, and the calculations behind, any coefficient before using it.

STATISTICAL CONTROL

Bivariate procedures allow us to assess the impact of one variable on another by using measures of association or by constructing a **TWO-WAY TABLE** (*a cross-tabulation involving two variables*). These procedures are adequate for relatively simple relationships between variables, but many problems that we wish to analyze involve more complex relationships. Table 18.8 presented hypothetical data on the relationship between race and income, but the two-way table does not explain this relationship. In an effort to increase our understanding of this relationship, we might want to consider a series of **TEST FACTORS** such as age, education, years of experience, type of occupation, area of residence, and union membership *to see what effect each has on the association between race and income*.

Testing the effects of outside influences on the original, bivariate relationship is referred to as "introducing statistical controls," and it is

Table 18.10. The Bivariate Relationship Between Female Literacy and Urbanization

		Urbanization	
		High	Low
Female Literacy	High	82% (82)	18% (18)
	Low	18% (18)	82% (82)
	TOTAL	100% (100)	100% (100)

accomplished by extending the basic principles of cross-tabulation and correlation. The following example illustrates how statistical control can be brought about by introducing a third variable in a cross-tabulation.

Suppose that for a sample of 200 countries we were to find the two-way (bivariate) relationship between the variables level of female literacy and level of urbanization that is reported in Table 18.10. The table presents a surprisingly strong association between the level of urbanization and level of female literacy. Eighty-two percent of the countries with high urbanization have high female literacy, whereas only 18 percent of the countries with low urbanization have a high female literacy level.

The Elaboration Paradigm

The **ELABORATION PARADIGM** is *a set of procedures for introducing a* **CONTROL VARIABLE** *(or test factor) into a cross-tabulation and analyzing the causal relationships* in the resulting *three-way table*, called a **CONTINGENCY TABLE**.[5] We refer to the process of introducing a third variable as *controlling* for the variable because it results in a series of subtables for each of which

---

[4] It is risky to compare the results of one study reporting an association of .40 to the results of a second study reporting an association of .60 using a different measure.

[5] Paul Lazarsfeld originally did much of the work on the paradigm. For an early treatment of the work, see Kendall and Lazarsfeld (1950).

Table 18.11. The Relationship between Female Literacy and Urbanization Controlling for Gross National Product: An Example of Explanation

GNP

		High GNP Countries		Low GNP Countries	
		Urbanization		Urbanization	
		High	Low	High	Low
Female Literacy	High	90% (81)	90% (9)	10% (1)	10% (9)
	Low	10% (9)	10% (1)	90% (9)	90% (81)
	TOTAL	100% (90)	100% (10)	100% (10)	100% (90)
		(Subtable 1)		(Subtable 2)	

the third variable takes a constant value (i.e., its value is controlled instead of being allowed to vary, as in most tables).

The control variable takes on different values for each subtable, but within any single subtable its value remains constant. Table 18.11 reexamines the relationship between *urbanization* and *female literacy* while controlling for the effects of a third contingency, or variable, *gross national product* (GNP*).* Two subtables are generated, one for each value of the control variable.

The elaboration paradigm is simply an organized approach to analyzing what happens to the relationship between two variables when a third variable is controlled. The three major categories of elaboration are explanation, interpretation, and specification. Table 18.11 is an example of explanation, the type of elaboration we will consider first.

EXPLANATION. We may suspect that Table 18.10 presents a **SPURIOUS RELATIONSHIP** because we suspect (rightly or wrongly) that urbanization does not cause increases in female literacy. To demonstrate that the relationship is spurious, we must show that *it can be accounted for through some other variable*, that is (1) causally

before both female literacy rate and urbanization and (2) related to both female literacy and urbanization. If we are successful in locating a control variable that meets these two conditions and also *makes the original, bivariate relationship substantially decrease or disappear*, we will have carried out the form of elaboration known as **EXPLANATION.**

We may test a series of control variables in an attempt to show that the relationship between female literacy rate and urbanization is spurious. Table 18.11 presents one of these tests. If the original relationship is spurious, then it will disappear in the subtables. Recall that the original table (Table 18.10) showed high female literacy levels associated with high levels of urbanization and low female literacy levels with low urbanization levels. Subtable 1 of Table 18.11, which comprises all countries whose gross national product is high, shows no such association; low female literacy levels are found in 10 percent of countries with high levels of GNP, irrespective of the level of urbanization. Similarly, subtable 2 (all countries with low levels of GNP) shows a 90 percent likelihood of low female literacy rates, irrespective of the level of urbanization. So, because the urbanization variable

Table 18.12. The Bivariate Relationship between Abortion Attitude and Size of Birthplace

		Size of Birthplace	
		Town	City
Attitude Toward Abortion	No	82% (410)	18% (90)
	Yes	18% (90)	82% (410)
	TOTAL	100% (500)	100% (500)

that, in turn, affects the dependent variable. Table 18.13 on page 413 illustrates the effects of an intervening variable.

Searching for an intervening variable that might qualify the relationship between abortion attitude and size of birthplace (Table 18.12), one might hypothesize that towns and cities promote very different kinds of political and social ideologies, which in turn might account for the city/town differences in abortion attitudes. In effect, people born in towns are more likely to be conservative than are people born in cities, and conservatives are more likely than liberals to oppose abortion. In Table 18.13 there are no longer any differences in abortion attitudes between town people and city people in either subtable; all town/city differences have been accounted for by subdividing the sample into conservatives and liberals. Hence, we have successfully interpreted the relationship by locating an intervening variable.

Compare Table 18.11 with Table 18.13. The results have the same statistical form; that is, the introduction of a control variable makes the original relationship disappear. Hence, the difference between explanation and interpretation rests in the underlying logic, not in the statistics. We now turn to a third form of elaboration, referred to as **SPECIFICATION**, in which *the objective is not to make the original relationship disappear but, rather, to specify the conditions under which the strength of the original relationship varies in intensity*

becomes irrelevant when we control for gross national product, the original bivariate association of Table 18.10 has been explained.

INTERPRETATION. Table 18.12, a cross-tabulation of the relationship between attitudes toward abortion and size of one's birthplace, suggests that persons from cities are much more likely (82%) to endorse the right of women to obtain an abortion than are persons from towns (18%). Suppose, as in the previous example, we try to explain away the relationship but fail to discover any control variable that meets both requirements (i.e., associated with and causally prior to both original variables). When explanation fails to reduce such a nonobvious relationship between two variables, the possibility still exists that we can uncover a third factor to help clarify the chain of circumstances that connects the two variables to one another. **INTERPRETATION**, the second part of the elaboration paradigm, is *the search for a control variable (Z) that causally intervenes between the independent variable (X) and the dependent variable (Y).* Figure 18.6 on page 413 diagrams the differences between explanation and interpretation as they modify the original relationship between the independent and dependent variables.

An **INTERVENING VARIABLE** *must be related to both the independent and the dependent variable, and it must be plausible to think of it as somehow a result of the independent variable*

SPECIFICATION. Table 18.14 on page 414 reexamines the relationship between size of birthplace and attitudes toward abortion while controlling for a third variable, the region of the country in which a person was born. Here the original relationship changes (compare with Table 18.12) but does not disappear; instead, it takes on a different form from one subtable to the next. The original relationship disappears for persons born in the South, where town and city people show identical attitudes toward abortion; it

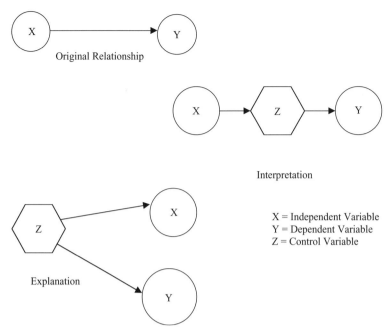

Figure 18.6. Models illustrating the distinction between explanation and interpretation.

remains strong in the West, where town people are more likely than city people to oppose abortion (86 percent vs. 21 percent); and it intensifies in the North, where differences between town and city people regarding abortion attitudes are most pronounced (89% vs. 0% oppose abortion). Introducing a control variable has enabled us to analyze the relationship between size of

Table 18.13. The Relationship between Abortion Attitude and Size of Birthplace Controlling for Political Ideology: An Example of Interpetation

"Should it be possible for a woman to obtain an abortion on demand?"

Political Ideology

	Conservative			Liberal	
	Size of Birthplace			*Size of Birthplace*	
	Town	City		Town	City
No	90% (405)	90% (45)		10% (5)	10% (45)
Yes	10% (45)	10% (5)		90% (45)	90% (405)
TOTAL	100% (450)	100% (50)		100% (50)	100% (450)
	(Subtable 1)			(Subtable 2)	

Table 18.14. The Relationship between Abortion Attitudes and Size of Birthplace, Controlling for Region of Birthplace: An Example of Specification

"Should it be possible for a woman to obtain an abortion on demand?"

Region of Birthplace

	South			West			North	
	Size of Birthplace			Size of Birthplace			Size of Birthplace	
	Town	City		Town	City		Town	City
No	50% (40)	50% (40)	No	86% (160)	21% (50)	No	89% (210)	0% (0)
Yes	50% (40)	50% (40)	Yes	14% (25)	79% (190)	Yes	11% (25)	100% (180)
TOTAL	100% (80)	100% (80)	TOTAL	100% (185)	100% (240)	TOTAL	100% (235)	100% (180)
	(Subtable 1)			(Subtable 2)			(Subtable 3)	

birthplace and attitude toward abortion more precisely, pinpointing the circumstances under which the association holds. This is an example of specification.

The use of a control variable for specification of a relationship, as in Table 18.14, may produce fundamentally different relationships in different subtables. Town persons might favor abortion more than city persons in one region, and yet the opposite might be true in another area. When this occurs, there is good reason to suspect that other, undiscovered factors are affecting the relationship. A specification that results in such markedly different subtables is an invitation to pursue the analysis further, as the following case illustrates.

SUPPRESSOR VARIABLES. Suppose we have a table in which no relationship appears, even though we had good reason to expect to find an association. In Table 18.14, the data for the West and the North indicate a strong association between size of birthplace and abortion attitude; yet, the association disappears in data for the South. Why? It is possible that some hidden third factor is *suppressing* the true relationship between the two original variables. Such a factor is referred to as a **SUPPRESSOR VARIABLE** because it *hides the actual relationship until it is controlled.*

Table 18.15 reanalyzes this data for the South, controlling for another variable, percentage of persons in the community who are black. Whereas the original data showed no relationship between size of birthplace and abortion attitude, these two subtables each show strong (but opposite) associations. Subtable 1 shows data that are consistent with the overall findings presented in Table 18.14, while subtable 2 isolates the deviant cases. When the two subtables are combined, as they were in subtable 1 of Table 18.14, the relationship is no longer discernible.

The data we have presented in this discussion of various methods of elaboration (Tables 18.10 to 18.15) are hypothetical and exaggerated to illustrate points of analysis. In actual research, relationships are seldom so strong, nor are distinctions between types of elaboration so clear. However, the logic that underlies these idealized

Table 18.15. A Three-Way Table Illustrating the Effect of Introducing a Suppressor Variable

"Should it be possible for a woman to obtain an abortion on demand?"

Percent Black in Community of Birth
For Respondents Born in South

	High				Low	
	Size of Birthplace				Size of Birthplace	
	Town	City			Town	City
No	100% (40)	0% (0)			0% (0)	100% (40)
Yes	0% (0)	100% (40)			100% (40)	0% (0)
TOTAL	100% (40)	100% (40)		TOTAL	100% (40)	100% (40)
	(Subtable 1)				(Subtable 2)	

examples shows the range of possibilities for analysis that you will encounter in real research, and a thorough knowledge of these classifications will serve as a useful guide. For the sake of simplicity we have developed elaboration around dichotomies – variables with only two values. The same logic applies to more complex alternatives (when using variables with, say, four or five categories), but when tables get larger, the elaboration soon become unwieldy. Indeed, it is often desirable to control for the effects of more than one variable, but we find ourselves confronted with the same practical difficulty. Just as correlation analysis was introduced to solve the analogous problem for two-variable tables with many cells, a technique called *partial correlation* exists to aid in the analysis if there is a need to introduce control variables when working with interval level data.

Partial Correlation

Earlier in this chapter we discussed the correlation coefficient as a measure of association between two variables. There is also a **MULTIVARIATE** (*more than two variable*) form of

this measure, referred to as **PARTIAL CORRELATION**.[6] It may be used to analyze more than two variables in many ways similar to the bivariate contingency-table elaboration previously discussed. The partial correlation between variable X_1 and variable X_2 controlling for X_3 is designated symbolically as "$r_{12.3}$," and conceptually it can be thought of as the mean of the correlations between X_1 and X_2 for each of the scattergrams that would result if a separate scattergram were plotted between X_1 and X_2 for each value of X_3. It is a measure of the average correlation between X_1 and X_2 when X_3 is controlled. It has the same range and interpretation as the two-variable (Pearson) correlation.

Suppose we are presented with a correlation between X_1 and X_2 that we suspect is spurious. To check for this possibility, we introduce several control variables that are causally prior to both X_1 and X_2. Eventually, we hit on a causally prior

---

[6] When data are analyzed one variable at a time, it is called "univariate analysis." When we consider the relationship between two variables, we call it "bivariate analysis." When we consider the relationship between two variables controlling for the effects of one or more other variables, we call it "multivariate analysis." See Chapter 19.

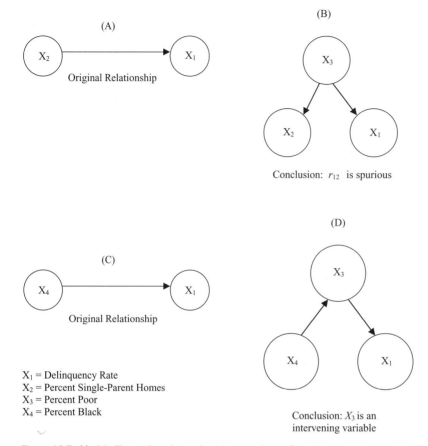

Figure 18.7. Models illustrating alternative interpretations of partial correlation results.

control variable X_3 for which the partial correlation drops to zero (or nearly zero). In so doing, we have demonstrated that the original relationship was spurious.

To be more concrete, suppose we are doing a study in which the census tract is the unit of analysis (a census tract is an area made up of a cluster of blocks and includes approximately 3,000 residents). Suppose that we find a high correlation ($r_{12} = .60$) between our measure of "delinquency rate" (X_1) and "percent single-parent homes" (X_2).[7] If we suspect that this correlation is spurious, we might attempt to locate a causally prior control variable that can account for this relationship. Suppose we eventually hit on the variable "percent poor" (X_3). When X_3 is controlled for, the partial correlation turns out to be very

close to zero ($r_{12.3} = .05$). Because of this evidence, we would conclude that the original correlation ($r_{12} = .60$) was spurious. This outcome is illustrated in Figure 18.7. There is a very close parallel between what we have done here and the form of elaboration we earlier referred to as "explanation."

Suppose we are presented with a strong correlation ($r_{14} = .60$) between the variable "percent black" (X_4) and "delinquency rate" (X_4). As part of our analysis of this relationship, we might decide to search for possible variables that intervene between percent black and delinquency rate. Suppose we eventually try the variable "percent poor" (X_3) and find that when this variable is controlled, the partial correlation is much below the original correlation. With such results we would conclude that percent poor is an intervening variable between percent black and delinquency rate. This outcome

---

[7] What we are referring to here as r_{12} is the same (Pearson) correlation we referred to earlier in the chapter as r where we omitted subscripts.

is illustrated in diagram D of Figure 18.7 The parallel between this example and the form of contingency-table elaboration referred to as "interpretation" should be evident.

Thus far we have considered only examples in which one control variable is introduced. It is possible to control for several variables simultaneously, using higher-order partial correlations. Thus we may compare the partial correlation between X_1 and X_2 controlling for X_3, X_4, X_5, X_6, ($r_{12.3456}$). In partial-correlation analysis, the Pearson correlation is often referred to as the ZERO-ORDER CORRELATION *to distinguish it from a first-order partial correlation (for example,* $r_{12.3}$*), a second-order partial correlation (for example,* $r_{12.34}$*), and other, higher order partial correlations* in which the order of the partial correlation corresponds to the number of variables being controlled.

An advantage of partial correlation as a statistical technique, relative to contingency-table analysis, is that the controlling operation is based on statistical adjustments of the scores for the original two variables rather than on the construction of physically separated subtables. Partial correlation is very useful when the investigator wants to control simultaneously for several factors, particularly if the sample is relatively small. In contrast, attempts to control for several variables simultaneously in contingency-table analysis become awkward because some of the partial tables end up with few, if any, respondents.

This advantage of partial correlation analysis also has its costs. A major disadvantage is the loss of information about variation in the strength of the relationship between the original two variables for the various categories of the control variable. The strength of the relationship may fluctuate considerably for the different categories of the control variable. If we were to construct separate scattergrams (and compile separate zero-order correlations) for the same data, we would be able to see this fluctuation. However, with partial-correlation analysis, all we get is one summary number that averages the relationship for the various subcategories. If these fluctuations are of no interest to us, or if there is very little fluctuation in the strength of the rela-

tionship for the various categories of the control variable, then this loss of information is not a major problem. The contingency-table alternative to partial correlation also involves a loss of information – albeit in a different form; that is, information is lost when interval-level variables are recoded into a relatively small number of categories for tabular analysis.

SUMMARY

This chapter has presented some of the most commonly used techniques of basic quantitative analysis. Univariate analysis is a description of the characteristics of a set of scores (measures) for a single variable. For variables with a small number of categories, univariate analysis usually begins with a presentation of the distribution of scores. For interval level variables with many categories, summary univariate statistics exist that are designed to estimate two major characteristics of the variable's distribution – its central tendency and its dispersion. To decide what summary statistics are most applicable in any situation, one must first determine the variable's level of measurement.

Bivariate statistics are useful for analyzing the relationship between two variables. The simplest and most easily understood form of bivariate analysis is the cross-tabulation. Because cross-tabulations usually involve comparisons of unequally sized subgroups, figures must be converted into percentages before proper comparisons can be made. Because percentages can be computed either across row totals or down column totals in a cross-tabulation, great care must be taken to specify the logic of the group comparisons you wish to make before deciding how to compute percentages.

When there are a large number of categories for one or both of the variables being considered, it is often convenient to summarize the relationship in terms of one or more of the standard measures of association. The one most commonly used is the Pearson correlation coefficient, but there are many other measures of association. Some are most appropriate for interval-level data, some for ordinal-level data, and some for nominal-level data.

Bivariate associations can be further analyzed using statistical procedures that are extensions of correlation analysis and cross-tabulation analysis. The technique of cross-tabular analysis that involves the introduction of a third control variable is referred to as the elaboration paradigm. Correlation with statistical controls is referred to as partial correlation; it follows a logic that is very similar to that in the elaboration paradigm.

KEY TERMS

adjusted percentage
bar graph
bivariate analysis
column
contingency table
control variable
correlation
correlation coefficient
cross-tabulation
descriptive research
deviant case
dispersion
elaboration paradigm
explanation
explanatory research
frequency distribution
interpretation
intervening variable
marginals
mean
measure of central tendency
measure of variability
median
mode
multivariate analysis
nonlinear relationship
normal curve
partial correlation
pie diagram
range
row
specification
spurious relationship
standard deviation
suppressor variable
test factor
two-way table

univariate analysis
variance
zero-order correlation

EXERCISES

1. Compute the mean, the median, and the mode for the following set of numbers:
   5, 10, 6, 5, 10, 1, 4, 10, 7, 5, 10, 3, 5, 8, 10, 10.

2. Compute the standard deviation for the set of numbers in exercise 1.

3. Using the SPSS data set of female and male respondents in the 1998 *General Social Survey*, available at http://webapp.icpsr.umich.edu/GSS/, calculate the mean, median, mode, and standard deviation for the variable, "mother's education" (MAEDUC).

4. In Table 18.1, the largest category includes only 48 percent of the sample. Is it possible for the modal category to include less than 50 percent of the sample? What is the smallest percentage of the sample that a category can include and still be classified as the mode?

5. Use the Internet to find an article or document that discusses the existence of a statistically spurious relationship. Write down the Web address of the report and briefly summarize why the given relationship is spurious.

6. On the basis of the data presented in Tables 18.12 and 18.13, would you conclude that the original relationship between size of birthplace and attitude toward abortion was spurious? Explain.

7. Compute percentages across the rows of Table 18.7, and then use these percentages to discuss the data in the table. Now compare these percentages with those in Table 18.8. Which set of percentages is more useful? Explain.

8. Using the data presented in Table 18.11, construct the tables you would need to demonstrate that the control variable is related to both of the variables in the original table (Table 18.10).

9. Using the data presented in Table 18.13, construct the tables you would need to show that the control variable is related to both of the variables in the original table (Table 18.12).

10. There is a partial-correlation equivalent of "explanation" as the term is used in the elaboration paradigm. There is also an equivalent of "interpretation." Explain why there is no partial-correlation equivalent of "specification."

SUGGESTED READINGS

Best, Joel. 2001. *Damned Lies and Statistics: Untangling Numbers from the Media, Politicians, and Activists*. Berkeley: University of California Press.

This book is a very simple introduction to descriptive statistics. Its objective is to sensitize the reader to the various ways in which statistics are used in the mass media and other popular sources of information to mislead the audience.

Coolidge, Frederick L. 2006. *Statistics: A Gentle Introduction*. Thousand Oaks, CA: Sage.

An easy-to-understand primer on basic statistical concepts.

Keller, Dana K. 2006. *The Tao of Statistics*. Thousand Oaks, CA: Sage.

This is a nonmathematical introduction, explaining what statistics mean, minus the actual computations.

Levin, Jack, and James Alan Fox. 2006. *Elementary Statistics in Social Research*. Boston: Allyn & Bacon.

Step-by-step illustrations of the procedures mentioned in this chapter, and much more.

Moore, David S. 2000. *Statistics: Concepts and Controversies*. 4th ed. New York: W. H. Freeman.

A very clearly written introduction to descriptive and inductive statistics for the undergraduate social science major. The book deals with such topics as measures of centrality, measures of dispersion, correlation analysis, probability theory, sampling, and measurement accuracy. Moore also alerts us to how statistics can be used in a deceptive manner.

REFERENCES

Bryman, Alan, and Duncan Cramer. 2000. *Quantitative Data Analysis for SPSS 10 Release for Windows*. New York: Routledge.

Field, Andy. 2000. *Discovering Statistics Using SPSS for Windows: Advanced Techniques for the Beginners*. London: Sage.

Kendall, Patricia L., and Paul F. Lazarsfeld. 1950. "Problems of Survey Analysis." In *Continuities in Social Research: Studies in the Scope and Method of the American Soldier*, 133–196. Robert K. Merton and Paul F. Lazarsfeld, eds. Glencoe, IL: Free Press.

MULTIVARIATE ANALYSIS AND STATISTICAL SIGNIFICANCE

19

INTRODUCTION

The first part of this chapter introduces regression analysis, one of the most widely used multivariate statistical techniques. Although a comprehensive treatment of this topic is beyond the scope of a first course in research methods, a brief introduction to regression analysis is essential because it appears so frequently in quantitative social research literature. The aim of the present discussion is to give the reader a basic overview and some suggestions for further reading. One reason that regression analysis is so widely used is that it lends itself to causal modeling. Although there are many types of causal modeling, we discuss path analysis here because it is one of the most commonly used types.

The second section of this chapter covers statistical inference. Social researchers use tests of

This chapter may be difficult without a prior course in statistics.

significance to make inferences about a population (or universe) based on the evidence obtained from a sample selected from that population. Many social researchers put a great deal of confidence in these tests of significance, and it is important that both researchers and consumers of social research understand their uses and misuses. Although they can help researchers to answer legitimately a wide range of questions, tests of significance simply cannot answer some questions.

MULTIVARIATE ANALYSIS

Regression Analysis

LINEAR REGRESSION is a statistical procedure *used to estimate the amount of change in a dependent variable that can be expected for a given change in an independent variable*. We will begin by considering **SIMPLE REGRESSION**,

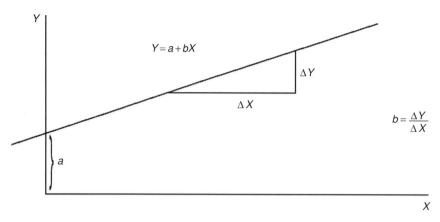

Figure 19.1. The equation for a straight line.

which *involves one dependent variable and one independent variable* (or predictor). We will then consider **MULTIPLE REGRESSION**, which *involves one dependent variable and two or more predictors*. Recall from elementary algebra that the equation for a straight line is

$$Y = a + bX.$$

Figure 19.1 is an illustration of the interpretation of the constants a and b in this equation. We find that a is the value Y takes when X is equal to zero. It is referred to as the *Y-intercept* because it is the value of Y at the point where the straight line crosses the Y-axis. The constant b is equal to the slope of this line. If we move an arbitrary distance along the line described by this equation, recording the amount that Y has changed (call it Y) and the amount X has changed (call it X), and then divide the change in Y by the change in X, the result is the slope of the line (i.e., $b = Y/X$).

In this example from elementary algebra, the Y values refer to points along the straight line defined by the equation $Y = a + bX$. This formula does not account for any Y values that do not fall on this line. For any arbitrary value of X, we can find the corresponding Y value that satisfies the equation by locating the Y value on the straight line that falls directly over the specified X value (i.e., we would determine that point at which a line constructed perpendicular to the X-axis from the specified X value intersects the straight line given by the equation $Y = a + bX$).

Simple regression is a procedure for fitting a straight line to a set of points in a scattergram, as illustrated in Figure 19.2. The regression line is that line through the set of points for which the sum of the squares of the deviations from the line is a minimum. These deviations are shown in Figure 19.2. For any line other than the regression line through the same set of points, the sum of the squares of the deviations is greater.

The major distinction between the regression line equation and the basic algebra linear equation is that in regression values of Y rarely fall along the actual line, whereas in basic algebra values of Y always fall along the line. By constructing a vertical line from each observed Y value to the regression line, as illustrated in Figure 19.2, we can locate a set of $\hat{Y}$ (called Y-predicted) values that do fall along the regression line. Thus, the equation for the regression line becomes

$$\hat{Y} = a + bX.$$

Suppose that Y is "annual income" and that X is "years of education." In simple regression, the *slope* (b) is referred to as the **REGRESSION COEFFICIENT**. If the regression coefficient has a value of 500, we would estimate that for a one-year increase in level of education there would be a $500 increase in annual income. In general, the regression coefficient gives the number of units of change in Y (in whatever units Y is measured) that can be expected for a one-unit change in X (in whatever units X is measured).

In regression analysis, it is important to distinguish between the actual Y values that do not fall on the regression line and the corresponding $\hat{Y}$ values that we would estimate based on

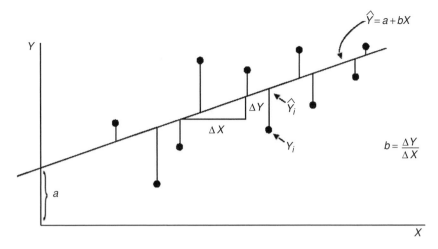

Figure 19.2. Fitting a least squares regression line to a set of points in a scattergram.

a given respondent's X value. The discrepancy between the actual Y value and the estimated $\hat{Y}$ value represents prediction error. When the Y values tend to cluster very close to the regression line, $\hat{Y}$ and Y values will be very similar, and the error in prediction will be low. However, when the Y values tend to deviate markedly from the regression line, the Y and $\hat{Y}$ values will be quite different, and the error in prediction will be high.

Multiple regression is an extension of simple regression: Instead of one predictor, we include two or more predictors in a single regression equation. When there are four predictors, the equation is as follows:

$$\hat{Y} = a + b_1 x_1 + b_2 x_2, + b_3 x_3 + b_4 x_4.$$

The b values in multiple regression are referred to as partial-regression coefficients.[1] These coefficients give the change in the dependent variable (in whatever units the dependent variable is measured) that we would estimate for a one-unit change in the specified predictor (in whatever units the predictor is measured).

The **MULTIPLE CORRELATION COEFFICIENT** (R) is *used to summarize the accuracy of our prediction equation.*[2] Recall that the difference between Y and $\hat{Y}$ represents error in our prediction. If we have selected a set of predictors that yield accurate estimates of Y, then the difference between Y and $\hat{Y}$ values will be small, and the multiple correlation will be high. If, however, we have selected a set of predictors that yields poor estimates of Y, then the difference between $\hat{Y}$ and Y values will tend to be larger, and the multiple correlation will be low. The multiple correlation ranges from .00 (when the independent variables in no way help to predict Y) to 1.00 (when the independent variables predict Y with complete accuracy). The multiple-correlation coefficient squared (R^2) gives the proportion of the variance in the dependent variable that is accounted for by the set of predictors included in the regression equation. If $R = .50$, then $R^2 = .25$; we would conclude that the predictors being considered account for 25 percent of the variance in the dependent variable.

Let us assume that our goal is to predict the grade-point average for 1,000 seniors who have just graduated from college. Suppose we decide to use the following four predictors: high

[1] It is equal to the Pearson correlation between Y and the $\hat{Y}$ values. The b values are referred to as partial-regression coefficients because they are estimates of the change in the dependent variable that is estimated for a one-unit change in the specified predictor after we statistically control for the effects of the other predictors in the equation.

[2] The subscripted version of the multiple-correlation coefficient is designated symbolically as "$R_{1.2345}$" where the subscript 1 refers to the dependent variable X_1 and the subscripts 2, 3, 4, and 5 refer to the predictors X_2, X_3, X_4, and X_5. There will be as many numbers following the period in the subscript as there are predictors. The notation system has been changed here so that the dependent variable referred to in the test as Y is referred to here as X_1. For the subscripted multiple-correlation coefficient, as for several other multivariate statistics (e.g., the partial-correlation coefficient), the notion is simpler if we refer to our variables as X_1, X_2, X_3, and so on, rather than as Y, X_1, and X_2.

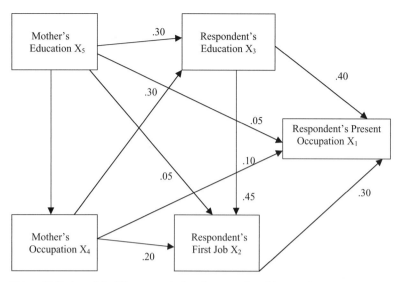

Figure 19.3. A model of the process of socioeconomic achievement.

school grade-point average (X_1), mother's education (X_2), verbal SAT (Scholastic Aptitude Test) score (X_3), and mother's occupational status (X_4). These variables are all measured in different units; consequently, we cannot make direct comparisons among these partial-regression coefficients (b_1, b_2, b_3, and b_4) to determine their relative strength as predictors of grade-point average.

Fortunately, there is a way to manage this problem. It calls for computing **STANDARDIZED PARTIAL-REGRESSION COEFFICIENTS** (these coefficients are commonly referred to as **BETA WEIGHTS**) for each of these predictors. The beta weight *is a partial-regression coefficient that has been adjusted in such a way that the unit of measure does not influence its value*. All units are changed to standard deviation units. Thus, when a beta weight equals .50, our interpretation is that there will be a .50 standard deviation change in the dependent variable (grade-point average) for a 1 standard deviation change in the specified predictor. Because each of the coefficients is now stated in standard deviation units, it is possible to compare the relative strength of each predictor.

The statistic referred to earlier as the partial-regression coefficient is also called the **UNSTANDARDIZED PARTIAL-REGRESSION COEFFICIENT**. As we recall, *this statistic indicates how many units the dependent variable*

is estimated to change (in whatever units it is measured) *for a one-unit change in the independent variable* (in whatever units it is measured). For this reason, the units in which the variables are measured make a difference. If income were one of our predictors, we would have a choice of units for measuring it. We might decide on yen, dollars, or lire. Depending on which units we selected, we would get a different unstandardized partial-regression coefficient for income. However, because the *standardized* partial-regression coefficient is not influenced by the unit of measurement, it would be the same for each of these three alternatives.

Path Analysis

Now that we have considered multiple regression, it is appropriate to discuss **PATH ANALYSIS**, *a form of causal modeling based on multiple regression*. Path analysis can be viewed as a procedure for presenting the results of a series of multiple regressions, or as a procedure for doing causal modeling with multiple regression. To be more concrete, we will consider a model of socioeconomic achievement.

The model in Figure 19.3 includes four predictors and the "respondent's present occupation," which is the main dependent variable. The arrows in the model specify a seemingly plausible causal order among these variables before looking at the data. The selection of predictors and the assumed causal ordering among these predictors is based on prior theory, past research, and common sense. In the present model, we assume that "mother's education" (x_5) influences "mother's occupation" (x_4), that "mother's education" and "mother's occupation" influence "respondent's education" (x_3), that all three influence "respondent's first job" (x_2), and that all four influence "respondent's present occupation" (x_1). This model is then used to set up a series of multiple-regression equations. In this case, four separate equations would be called for, one for each variable in the model that is used as a dependent variable. (Any variable that has an arrow coming toward it is being used as a dependent variable.) For equation (1), "respondent's present occupation" is the dependent variable, and it is predicted by the other four variables. In equation (2), "respondent's first job" is the dependent variable, and it is predicted by the three variables in the model that are causally prior to it. In equation (3), "respondent's education" is the dependent variable, and it is predicted by the two variables that are causally prior. Finally, in equation (4), "mother's occupation" is the dependent variable, and it is predicted by the one variable, "mother's education," that is causally prior to it. These four equations may be summarized as follows:

$$\hat{X}_1 = a_1 + b_1 x_1 + b_2 x_2 + b_3 x_3 + b_4 x_4 \quad (1)$$

$$\hat{X}_2 = a_2 + b_1 x_1 + b_2 x_2 + b_3 x_3 \quad (2)$$

$$\hat{X}_3 = a_3 + b_1 x_1 + b_2 x_2 \quad (3)$$

$$\hat{X}_4 = a_4 + b_1 x_1 \quad (4)$$

These equations yield a set of unstandardized partial-regression coefficients that are sometimes used in path analysis, but it is more common to use the corresponding standardized partial-regression coefficients, or beta weights. *In path analysis, the beta weights are called* PATH COEFFICIENTS and are often presented along the corresponding arrows as we have done in Figure 19.3. The path coefficient for the so-

called direct effect of "respondent's education" on "respondent's present occupation" is .40; that is, for every increase of 1 standard deviation in "respondent's education," we would estimate an increase of .40 standard deviation in the score for "respondent's present occupation." On the basis of the path coefficients in Figure 19.3, we would conclude that the direct effect of "respondent's education" on "respondent's first job" (.45) is much greater than is the direct effect of "mother's education" on "respondent's first job" (.05). It is also possible to use path analysis to estimate the indirect effect of one variable on another through an intervening variable, by multiplying the appropriate path coefficients.[3]

Because of space limitations, the presentation of path analysis has been simplified in many ways. We have not discussed residual paths or the decomposition of the total relationship between variables into causal and noncausal components. We have only briefly touched on the decomposition of the causal component into direct and indirect components.[4]

Other Multivariate Techniques

Although this chapter focuses on multiple regression as an important example of the logic of multivariate analysis, researchers have a range of multivariate techniques from which to select.

Many of these techniques are similar to multiple regression in that they involve one dependent variable and two or more predictors, but do not necessarily require both the independent and dependent variables to be interval level. Techniques such as logistic regression and discriminant analysis involve a nominal-level dependent variable; n-way ANOVA (*analysis of variance*) and ANCOVA (*analysis of covariance*) involve mostly nominal-level independent variables. Survival or failure analysis is used when

---

[3] In Figure 19.3, we may obtain the indirect effect of "respondent's education" on "respondent's present occupation," which occurs through the intervening variable, "respondent's first job." We multiply the direct effect of X_3 on X_2 (which is .45) by the direct effect of X_2 on X_1 (which is .30) and obtain an indirect effect of X_3 on X_1, through the intervening variable X_2, equal to .135, which we might round to .14.

[4] For a more complete introduction to path models, see Ullman (2001).

the dependent variable is the time until an event, such as getting married or getting divorced, occurs. These techniques, along with many others, seek to predict the values of the dependent variable based on the independent variables. Other multivariate techniques do not explicitly deal with independent and dependent variables. For instance, log-linear analysis examines the association between three or more nominal-level variables. Other techniques, such as cluster analysis and factor analysis, look for clusters of related cases or variables.[5]

STATISTICAL INFERENCE

In quantitative research, we are rarely interested in our sample per se. Rather, we want to generalize about a larger population based on what we know about the sample drawn from it. When our goal is simply to describe the characteristics of the sample or to describe the relationship between variables for the sample, we engage in descriptive statistical analysis. However, we often want to infer characteristics of the population based on a sample's characteristics or make inferences about the relationship between variables in the population based on the relationship between these variables in the sample. When we want *to infer population characteristics based on information from a sample*, we engage in **STATISTICAL INFERENCE**. Tests of significance are often used as a basis for statistical inference.

Tests of Statistical Significance

TESTS OF SIGNIFICANCE are widely used in both descriptive and explanatory research. Researchers often use these tests to help decide, based on the relationship between two variables in a sample, *whether to infer a relationship between these variables in the population from which the sample was drawn*. Suppose we interview a representative cross section of a local community and find that the sample estimate of the mean income for Republican respondents is $70,000, whereas the sample estimate of

the mean income for Democratic respondents is $45,000. On the basis of this evidence, we know that there is a difference in mean income between Republicans and Democrats for the sample. We are probably more interested, however, in knowing whether we can infer from this that there is a tendency in the community as a whole for Republicans to have higher incomes than do Democrats.

Estimates based on a sample rarely correspond to the exact value for the population. As we learned in Chapter 6, probability theory assures us that there will be **SAMPLING ERROR** (*the deviation of the mean for our sample from the true population mean*) in our estimates of the mean; that is, sample estimates will fluctuate around the true population value. Because some sample estimates will be too high and others will be too low, we do not know whether our estimate of $70,000 is above or below the actual mean income of Republicans in the community. The mean income for Democrats might be higher than the mean income for Republicans. This would be the case if, owing to sampling error, the sample estimate for Republican respondents overstates their actual income in the community by $15,000 and the sample estimate for Democratic respondents understates their actual income by $11,000. In that case, the actual population mean for Republicans would be $55,000, whereas the actual mean for Democrats would be $56,000.

Suppose that before looking at our data, we have the idea that in the community the mean income for Republicans is higher than the mean income for Democrats. How might we test this research hypothesis? As a first step, we might compute the mean incomes for Republicans ($70,000) and Democrats ($45,000) in our sample. Nevertheless, our hypothesis refers to the community, not to our sample. We can ask how likely it is that we would find a difference as great that in our sample as the result of sampling error alone, if the population mean incomes of Republicans and Democrats were equal. More generally, whenever we want to test the hypothesis that one group is different from another, we can ask whether the difference found in the sample could be expected on the basis of sampling error (chance) alone. To this end, we formulate

---

[5] See Mertler and Vannatta (2001) for introductions to most of these techniques.

what is referred to as a **NULL HYPOTHESIS** *that there is indeed no difference*. Our null hypothesis in this case is that in the community the mean income of Republicans is equal to the mean income of Democrats.

Along with the null hypothesis, we always formulate a research hypothesis. In the preceding example, we specified a **DIRECTIONAL HYPOTHESIS**, that is, that the mean income of Republicans is higher than the mean income of Democrats. Sometimes we do not specify a direction in our research hypothesis. A **NONDIRECTIONAL HYPOTHESIS** appropriate to the example would be that the mean income for Republicans is not equal to that for Democrats. The income for Republicans could be either higher or lower than that for Democrats and still be consistent with this nondirectional research hypothesis. When our research hypothesis is directional, we use what is referred to as **ONE-TAILED TESTS OF SIGNIFICANCE** because we have *specified the nature of the relationship between variables in our hypothesis*. When our research hypothesis is nondirectional, we use **TWO-TAILED TESTS OF SIGNIFICANCE** because *we have not specified the nature of the relationship*.[6]

When carrying out a significance test, we always specify a **SIGNIFICANCE LEVEL**. It is a common practice to select in advance one of the conventional significance levels, such as .05, .01, or .001. These levels refer to there being a 5 percent, 1 percent, and .1 percent *probability*, respectively, *of getting a relationship as strong as that in our sample when there is in fact no relationship between the variables in the population*. If, for example, we select the .05 level, this says that we are going to classify the difference in means as statistically significant if there are fewer than 5 chances in 100 that the difference is due to sampling error alone. Suppose we carry out a test of significance on the difference between the mean incomes of Republicans and Democrats for our sample. If the difference is significant at the .05 level, we refer to the relationship as being **STATISTICALLY SIGNIFICANT**; that

is, *we reject the null hypothesis* that the incomes of Republicans and Democrats are equal for the community. However, we realize that we could be wrong. We realize that there are 5 chances in 100 that a difference as great as that found in our sample could have resulted from sampling error alone. Although we have decided to classify the difference in income as statistically significant, it is still possible that the incomes for Republicans and Democrats in the community are equal.

What if we had carried out a test of significance and found that we were not able to reject the null hypothesis that the mean incomes for Republicans and Democrats are exactly equal? Does this mean that we accept the null hypothesis and conclude that the incomes are identical? No, we do not. There is a difference between failing to *reject* the null hypothesis and actually *accepting* it. It is very unlikely that the mean income for Republicans will be exactly equal to the mean income for Democrats even if we have failed to reject the null hypothesis. There is a distinction between the conclusion that the difference in means found in our sample could result from chance (sampling error) alone if the population means were exactly equal and the conclusion that the population means are identical.

A test of significance is a procedure for deciding how likely it is that the relationship we have found in the sample is due to sampling error when there is no relationship between variables in the population. It cannot be used to prove that there actually is a relationship in the population. In addition, it cannot prove that there actually is no relationship in the population. A test of significance can be used only to indicate how likely we would be to obtain the relationship we find in the sample if there were no relationship in the population.

The *t*-**TEST** *is a test of significance that we use when we are interested in comparing the means for two samples or two categories of the same sample*. The null hypothesis for a *t*-test is that the population means are equal (and therefore, in the example above, that the mean incomes for the Democrats and Republicans are equal). When we want *to compare the means for more than two groups in the same test of significance*, we use the *F*-**TEST**. The null hypothesis for the *F*-test is that the means for all the groups being

---

[6] The rationale for the names "one-tailed" and "two-tailed" tests of significance is too technical for present treatment; a full discussion of the issue may be found in any introductory statistics text.

compared are equal (for example, the means for the Democrats, Independents, and Republican incomes). The research hypothesis for the *F*-test is that the means are not equal; there is no directional (one-tailed) option when more than two groups are being considered.

Tests of significance are often used in contingency table analysis. *The test most often used with contingency tables, when at least one of the variables concerned is at the nominal level*, is the **CHI-SQUARE**(χ^2). The null hypothesis for the chi-square test is that there is no relationship between the two variables in the table; that is, the respondents are distributed among the table cells as would be expected by chance.

The **PEARSON CORRELATION COEFFICIENT** (*r*), *a well-used measure of association*, can be tested for statistical significance. The null hypothesis here is that the correlation between the two variables in the population is zero. If we have grounds for predicting the direction of the correlation, we choose an alternative research hypothesis that states that there is a positive or negative correlation between the variables and we use a one-tailed test. If we do not have a prior hypothesis as to the direction of the correlation, the research hypothesis states that in the population the correlation between the two variables is not equal to zero, and we use a two-tailed test. In this case, if the correlation proves to be statistically significant, we accept the research hypothesis that the correlation in the population is not zero. Note that the significance test does *not* say the correlation in the population is equal to the correlation for the sample. In fact, it says nothing about the actual strength of the correlation in the population. More generally, the strength of a correlation and the statistical significance of a correlation are conceptually independent. In general, for a given sample size, correlation that are statistically significant will tend to be larger than correlations that are not. However, with a large enough sample, a weak correlation will be statistically significant; and with a small enough sample, a strong correlation will not be statistically significant.

The reason that the same-strength correlation is more likely to be classified as statistically significant if it is based on a larger sample is that there is less sampling error for a large sample.

If we were to draw a sample of 5 to estimate the mean income for a community, our estimate would tend to be less accurate than if it were based on a sample of 500. In general, a sample statistic based on a larger sample will more closely approximate the corresponding population parameter than will the same statistic based on a smaller sample.[7] Thus, a nonzero correlation based on a large sample is less likely to be due to chance than is the same correlation based on a smaller sample. The same logic applies to all measures of association. For a given strength of association, the larger the sample size, the more likely it is that the association will prove to be statistically significant.[8]

The Misuse of Tests of Significance

Social scientists have debated a great deal about the use of tests of significance. Of particular concern is the evidence that such tests are frequently used in situations for which the requirements underlying the test have not been met. Some argue that the problem has been made worse by pressure from journal editors and reviewers who encourage the use of such tests, despite the violation of the assumptions that underlie them. Others argue that tests of significance do have their uses even when these assumptions are not completely satisfied.

All tests of significance require a probability sample, and most assume a simple random sample. However, it is common to find tests used in studies where there is not even a remote approximation to a simple random sample. Most social research is based on cluster, quota, or accidental samples, for which the error is much greater than in a simple random sample. This failing can lead to inflated estimates of statistical significance.

A related problem is the use of tests of significance when the researcher is working with the entire population. Suppose we are using state-level data, and we find a correlation of .30 between "median income" and "level of state educational expenditures." Suppose also that we are working with data for all fifty states. In such

---

[7] For a complete discussion of the logic of probability sampling, see Chapter 6.
[8] See Ritchey (2000) for a brief discussion of statistical power.

a situation, our sample ($N = 50$) *is* the population, and so it is inappropriate to compute a test of statistical significance. If the correlation between these variable is .30, then .30 is the correlation in the population, and it is meaningless to compute a test of significance to test the null hypothesis that in the population the correlation is zero. In short, if we already have the population, there is no need to make the inferences that tests of significance are designed to help us make.

Researchers sometimes use a test of significance to generalize beyond the population from which the sample was drawn. Suppose we have a simple random sample of the seniors at a college, and we find that the Jews in the sample are more likely to support gun control than the Catholics. If this difference turns out to be statistically significant, we can generalize to all the seniors at the college. It might seem plausible that a similar trend would hold for seniors at other colleges, for all college students, or for the adult population in general. However, we have no grounds for making such a generalization based on the data we have.

Statistical significance is often confused with **SUBSTANTIVE SIGNIFICANCE**, that is, *whether some piece of data is important to us*. It is common for researchers to suggest that a finding is important *because* it is statistically significant. While it is generally reasonable to discount findings that are *not* statistically significant, statistical significance per se does not make a relationship important. We can often find statistically significant relationships between variables that are causally unrelated, variables that are alternative measures of the same thing (for instance, the relationship between age and year of birth), and variables that are sociologically uninteresting (such as the relationship between weight and waist measurement). There can also be relationships based on very large samples that are statistically significant but so weak as to be substantively unimportant. A correlation can be very close to zero (even .01) and still be statistically significant if the sample size is large enough.

Another misuse of significance tests is illustrated by researchers who compute a very large number of tests and then prepare research reports based only on the statistically significant relationships. Such researchers are capitalizing on sampling error and may prepare an entire report around a set of correlations that could not be replicated. Suppose a researcher computes 1,000 correlation coefficients and tests each for statistical significance. Even if all of these correlations in the population are zero, we would expect on the basis of sampling error that 50 (or 5 of every 100) of these correlations would be significant at the .05 level. Thus, if the researcher looks through the 1,000 correlations and bases the report on the 50 or so that are statistically significant, the findings reported run a risk of being highly unreliable. Most of these correlations will have resulted from sampling error alone. For this reason, it will not be possible to replicate the findings of the study.

There are different tests of significance for various types of data. Some tests are appropriate for nominal-level data, some are appropriate for ordinal-level data, and still others are appropriate for interval- and ratio-level data. A common error is to use a test of significance appropriate for interval-level data when the data are only ordinal level. A typical example of this error is the computation of a test of significance for a Pearson correlation between two ordinal-level variables.

SUMMARY

Regression is one of the most commonly used statistical procedures in social research. In simple regression analysis, we consider only two variables, one dependent variable and one independent variable (the predictor). The regression line is the line through the set of data points being considered that minimizes the sum of the square of the deviations from the line. For any other line through this same set of points, the sum is greater.

Multiple regression, an extension of simple regression to include two or more predictors, is the most widely used form of regression analysis. The coefficients that result when we do multiple regression are called *partial-regression coefficients*, or *unstandardized partial-regression coefficients*. These specify the number of units of difference in the dependent variable we would estimate for a one-unit difference in the predictor being considered when we statistically control all the other predictors in the equation. For some purposes, such as path analysis, it is useful to obtain a set of standardized partial-regression coefficients, which are called beta weights in the context of multiple-regression analysis, and path coefficients in the context of path analysis. The beta weight gives the number of standard deviations difference in the dependent variable we would estimate for a one standard deviation unit difference in the predictor being considered. When using beta weights, it is possible to compare the "effects" of the various predictors because they are all being measured in the same standard deviation units.

Tests of statistical significance are extensively used in explanatory research. A test of significance cannot be used to prove that there actually is a relationship in the population or that there actually is no relationship in the population. Such a test can, however, be used to indicate how likely we are to obtain the relationship we find in the sample, if there is no relationship in the population. Tests of significance are used incorrectly by many social researchers. One of the most common errors is the use of such tests when there are flagrant violations of the assumption of a simple random sample. In such situations, levels of statistical significance are often greatly inflated. They are also inflated when the researcher uses a test that assumes interval-level data on measures that are ordinal. Another error is explicitly or implicitly to convey the impression that statistically significant relationships are substantively significant when in fact they are not. When the sample is large, a very weak relationship, one that may account for less than 1 percent of the variance, may turn out to be statistically significant.

KEY TERMS

beta weight
chi-square
directional research hypothesis
F-test
linear regression
multiple regression
multiple-correlation
nondirectional research hypothesis
null hypothesis
one-tailed test of significance
partial-regression coefficient
path analysis
path coefficient
Pearson correlation coefficient
regression coefficient
sampling error
significance level
simple regression
standardized partial-regression coefficient
statistical inference
statistical significance
substantive significance
t-test
two-tailed test of significance
unstandardized partial-regression coefficient

EXERCISES

1. If we consider a simple regression in which the dependent variable is "monthly income measured in yen" and the predictor is "time at work measured in hours," what would be the units for the regression coefficient? If the numerical value of the regression coefficient were to be 1,000, how much of a difference in income would we expect between two persons who differ by six hours with respect to hours worked?

2. Consider a multiple regression in which X_1, is the dependent variable, with X_2, and X_3, as predictors. That is, where $X_1 = a + b_2x_2 + b_3x_3$. Assume also that

$X_1 = $ monthly income in dollars

$X_2 = $ time worked in hours

$X_3 = $ years of education completed

a. Set up the appropriate regression equation for the above example. Be sure to use subscripts for the partial-regression coefficients.

b. If you wanted to compare the relative strength of time worked (X_2) and years of education completed (X_3,) as predictors, which would you use – the unstandardized partial-regression coefficients or the standardized partial-regression coefficients? Defend your choice.

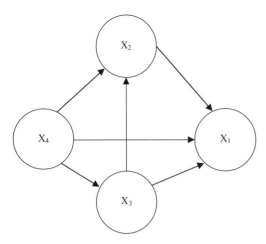

Figure 19.4. Comparing path coefficients.

c. If we are considering an equation based on unstandardized partial-regression coefficients, how much of a difference in X_1 would we estimate for a one-unit difference in X_2? If we are considering an equation based on standardized partial-regression coefficients, how much of a difference in X_1 values would we estimate for a one-unit difference in X_2? Assume that $b_2 = 1,000$ and $b_3 = 50,000$ and that the corresponding standardized coefficients are .63 and .47.

3. Construct the series of regression equations that would be used to estimate the path coefficients in Figure 19.4. Would you prefer to use the unstandardized partial-regression coefficients or the standardized partial-regression coefficients to estimate the path coefficients? Defend your choice.

4. In what ways is a standardized partial-regression coefficient similar to a partial-correlation coefficient? In what ways is it different?

5. For the path model in Figure 19.5, compare the direct effect of X_3 on X_1 with the indirect effect of X_3

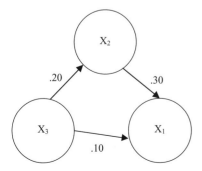

Figure 19.5. Comparing direct and indirect effects.

on X_1 through the intervening variable X_2. Which is larger?

6. Using a data set provided by your instructor, perform some basic statistical tests, such as one-tailed and two-tailed t-tests and one-way ANOVAs.

7. From the section on the misuse of tests of significance, we know that sometimes people incorrectly generalize results from one population to another. Using the SPSS data sets of female and male respondents in the 1998 *General Social Survey*, available at http://webapp.icpsr.umich.edu/GSS/, run the same regression analysis using each data set. Use respondent's education (EDUC) as the dependent variable, and mother's education (MAEDUC), father's education (PAEDUC), and age of respondent (AGE) as independent variables. How are the results similar or different for men and for women?

SUGGESTED READINGS

Kuh, George D. 2006. *The National Survey of Student Engagement: Conceptual Framework and Overview of Psychometric Properties*. Indiana University.

> *This Web site* http://nsse.iub.edu/redirect.cfm?target *contains data from, and description of, a regression analysis performed on American college students. In surveys, students are asked to report the frequency with which they engage in dozens of activities that represent good educational practice, such as using the institution's human resources, curricular programs, and other opportunities for learning and development that the college provides. Additional items assess the amount of reading and writing students did during the current school year, the number of hours per week they devoted to schoolwork, extracurricular activities, employment, and family matters.*

Levin, Jack, and James Alan Fox. 2006. *Elementary Statistics in Social Research*. Boston: Allyn & Bacon.

> *This book is an introduction to descriptive statistics, hypothesis testing, one-tailed and two-tailed tests, and significance tests such as analysis of variance, chi-square tests, correlation, and simple regression.*

Mertler, Craig A., and Rachel A. Vannatta. 2001. *Advanced and Multivariate Statistical Methods:*

Practical Application and Interpretation. Los Angeles: Pryrczak.

> *This text introduces a range of multivariate statistics, including analysis of variance and covariance, multivariate analysis of variance and covariance, multiple regression, path analysis, factor analysis, discriminant analysis, and logistic regression. Instructions for these techniques using SPSS for Windows are included, along with suggestions for interpreting the SPSS output.*

Ritchey, Ferris. 2000. *The Statistical Imagination: Elementary Statistics for the Social Sciences.* Boston: McGraw-Hill.

> *This is another introduction to basic statistics that includes more treatment of "statistical fallacies" such as treating sample estimates as if they were true of the population and assuming that point estimates are true of the population.*

Spicer, John. 2004. *Making Sense of Multivariate Data Analysis.* Thousand Oaks, CA: Sage.

> *This book offers an introduction to the approaches to data discussed in this chapter.*

Tabachnick, Barbara G., and Linda S. Fidell. 2001. *Using Multivariate Statistics.* 4th ed. Boston: Allyn & Bacon.

> *An alternative to Mertler and Vannatta (2001) that provides a more in-depth treatment of techniques such as multiple regression, canonical correlation, analysis of variance and covariance, loglinear analysis, discriminant function analysis, logistic regression, factor analysis, and structural equation modeling.*

REFERENCES

Mertler, Craig A., and Rachel A. Vannatta. 2001. *Advanced and Multivariate Statistical Methods: Practical Application and Interpretation.* Los Angeles: Pryrczak.

Ritchey, Ferris. 2000. *The Statistical Imagination: Elementary Statistics for the Social Sciences.* Boston: McGraw-Hill.

Ullman, Jodie B. 2001. "Structural Equation Modeling." In *Using Multivariate Statistics*, 653–771. 4th ed. Barbara G. Tabachnick and Linda S. Fidell, eds. Boston: Allyn & Bacon.

EPILOGUE: THE VALUE AND LIMITS OF SOCIAL SCIENCE KNOWLEDGE

By now you have spent many hours reading about social investigation. You have been introduced to a new vocabulary of key terms and have become familiar with the search for "objectivity," reliability, and validity. You have examined some of the ethical dilemmas of research. It is now time to take stock of what you have learned.

A CRITICAL PERSPECTIVE

Although this textbook may have increased your awareness of research methodology, you may not be pursuing a career in the social sciences. Many of you will never carry out your own research outside the context of a college classroom. Does this mean that the knowledge of methods is of no use to you? To the contrary, the same criteria used to evaluate social science research equip you to consider critically the wide range of assertions about social life that all of us read and hear daily. Knowledge of the obstacles to a sure understanding of society should enable you to develop a healthy skepticism toward the generalizations offered in the mass media, in literature, and in informal conversation.

Of course, we all make sense of our individual and collective experiences by making generalizations about the world. But it is important to realize that individuals are, in some measure, limited by the boundaries of their own experience. Our knowledge of social life emerges from the distinctive social positions we occupy, and our "realities" are constrained by our own life situations. Because our private understandings of social life are generated from a limited data database, a continuing task of social science investigation is to uncover those features of life that lie hidden beneath the veneer of accepted social knowledge about the world. In some instances, our investigations will cause us thoroughly to reject commonly held images or stereotypes. In other cases, our research will lead us to modify those images in important ways. The promise of the social sciences is to let us go beyond our own realities so that we might be freed to view the world from unfamiliar perspectives, to discover how our assumptions may blind us to the way the world is operating. Therefore, a major goal of social science investigation must be precisely to debunk the validity of long-standing truisms.

Methodologies serve the function of helping us become strangers to that which is normally familiar to us. They act as safeguards in that they force us to question what we usually do not. We want to maximize the likelihood of seeing how and why our individual understandings of the world may be dramatically incorrect. It is when we accomplish this end that research fulfills the promise for which methodologies were invented.

THE IMPORTANCE OF THE RULES OF INVESTIGATION

Researchers want to say at the conclusion of their investigation: "We have employed every precaution feasible to ensure that our findings are correct." As bodies of procedural rules, social science methodologies are designed to cause researchers continually to ask themselves: "What might we do to be even more certain of our findings?" Your knowledge of methods, then, should make you critical of the accuracy and validity of research. You should now be able to look at any study and quarrel with it, question its possible errors, and ask how the research might have been done more convincingly.

Have the researchers employed the method(s) most appropriate to their research problem? Have proper sampling procedures been used? Have necessary steps been taken to reduce bias and error in the findings? Have they taken care to use the most precise measurement procedures feasible? Is there any question about the validity of the presented findings? Might the researchers have shown greater sensitivity to the ethical issues raised by their research? Are statements of cause and effect warranted by the data collected and the methods used? Have investigators remained true to their data in making their interpretations and inferences? If the researchers are frank about how their own assumptions, ideologies, or interests may have affected the findings they present, is that admission more useful than harmful? You should be able to address each of these questions.

SCIENCE AS A BLUEPRINT; IMAGINATION AS INSPIRATION

As important as the rules of investigation are, following them is not enough! *Both* precise, rigorous data collection and artful, creative, imaginative interpretation are essential to the testing of theories about human behavior, as well as the formulation of public policy and developing plans for social change. We have referred to social investigation as a craft as well as a science. We hope you are convinced that there is not a contradiction in the use of these two descriptions of the research process. We have focused on many methodological techniques, but we should not forget that mastering them is an important but first step in reaching the broader goal of satisfying one's own intellectual curiosity. The importance of social science, after all, lies primarily in producing knowledge that matters to each of us.

One way to think about the various methods we have described and analyzed is that they are creative inventions. Each technique is designed to collect certain types of data about the world. Each raises one set of research issues more than another, and each has its own strengths and weaknesses. That social scientists have seen the need to invent the number of methods covered in this book confirms the judgment that social life is enormously complicated. We cannot use the same tools to investigate historical trends as we would use to understand contemporary attitudes and beliefs. Our grasp of basic processes of social interaction depends on techniques of inquiry different from those we would use to compare social values cross-culturally. Observational tools do us little good if our research goal is to forecast world population growth.

The methods with which you are now acquainted vary along a number of dimensions. Some are best employed to study people in their natural settings; others allow researchers in a laboratory to exert maximum control over variables outside of their immediate research interests. If we wish to assess attitudes, we choose certain methods, but we need other techniques if we wish to catalogue people's behaviors directly. The methods described vary in degree of obtrusiveness. Some, such as survey research, are highly obtrusive; others, such as content analysis, are unobtrusive. One technique lets us systematically study large numbers of people, while another best helps to capture the flavor of behavior in small groups. We choose our procedures according to whether we seek breadth or depth in our investigation. Sometimes we need quantitative renderings of social phenomena, and other times we need more qualitative images. We can test hypotheses with some methods. Others are better suited to the discovery of theory.

The differences mentioned are revealing. They support the idea that we must indeed use our imagination – that we cannot adopt uniform procedures to deal with the quite varied problems that are legitimately part of social investigation.

TOLERANCE FOR AMBIGUITY: LIMITS TO POSITIVISM?

Scientists are not happy with explanations of events or situations that rely on guesswork or casual observation. We must acknowledge, however, that methodological rigor will not easily and inevitably yield unquestionable, universal, or unalterable findings about social life. Knowledge is limited. We must be candid about these limits and consider why it is impossible to produce more certain findings. Why, if knowledge is cumulative, do social scientists continue to argue the validity of theoretical propositions produced, in some cases, two centuries ago? Why haven't social scientists discovered laws about society, as natural scientists have done for the physical world? How is it that we seem unable to predict events any distance into the future? Natural scientists, it might be pointed out, can predict certain phenomena (for example, eclipses) years in advance.

Unflattering comparisons can be made between the nature of physical and social scientific discoveries. The discovery of DNA's molecular structure is a convenient example. After reading Watson and Crick's findings, scientists uniformly agreed that the researchers had found the structure of DNA. There was no question that one of the mysteries of life had been solved. Scientists did not say, "Perhaps this is the structure of DNA" or that Watson and Crick's description of the DNA molecule "seems plausible" or that their data "generally seem to confirm" their picture of the structure as correct. In comparison, social scientists can rarely establish the absolute truth of their findings or interpretations.

Over the past thirty years, there has appeared a mounting criticism of social scientific research. The critics are correct in their assertion that social scientific knowledge does not have a high cumulativeness to it. It is not easy to make accurate predictions about future social life; many events take us by surprise. How many social scientists accurately forecast the civil rights activity of the 1950s, the urban riots of the mid-1960s, the women's rights activity of the 1970s, the rise of neoconservatism in the 1980s, or the threat posed by international terrorism as the twenty-first century began? Indeed, we frequently seem to be in the business of trying to explain why something happened *after* its occurrence.

It is also true that social scientists disagree about the theories used to explain a body of data to a much greater extent than do natural scientists. A casual search will find frequent debates in the literature about the causes of deviance, poverty, prejudice, and many other puzzling phenomena. One can, as well, easily find studies where findings directly contradict one another or where the same variables are measured in thoroughly different ways. Critics who deconstruct this process have connected these differences to the social positioning and different experiences of researchers. They question whether there is really any such thing as true objectivity. Researchers are pioneering a more value-charged and experiential view of social life through various postpositivist techniques.

We must, however, ask whether social scientists should apologetically bow their heads and merely promise to try harder in the future? Certainly, progress can be made in further refining methodological techniques. However, it is appropriate to point out that the social world and the physical world are really two different subjects. The structure of a DNA molecule remains constant, which is not true of social structures. It may be more appropriate for natural scientists to claim that they have discovered absolute truths, but it would certainly be unwise to assert that social truths are absolute. Human beings are continuously rearranging their social worlds. We simply do not respond in completely predictable ways to the situations in which we find ourselves. Unlike atoms, molecules, or stable elements of the physical universe, people think, construct meanings, and interpret the behaviors of others.

Individuals possess a certain plasticity that allows them to respond creatively to their environments. The meanings of events, people, objects, and institutions can change over time. Values and attitudes change. Behaviors once thought taboo become incorporated into our routine of legitimate or conventional activities. We create new social forms if they seem better able to meet our needs. We participate in unpredictable fads of our own making. In short, human activity and hence the social world are continually in a state of process, a state of production. It is human beings' unparalleled capacity for adaptation that makes any generalization produced by social scientists time specific.

It is for these reasons that social scientists must be prepared to use their imagination, to alter their research theories and their methods, just as people alter other views and perceptions of the world. The emergence of cultural globalization, the outbreak of AIDS, and unpredicted changes in the international economic structure have transformed the face of societies. Theories, methods, and explanations must reflect the nature of the objects with which they deal. If the world is continually changing, theoretical constructs must also change. Explanation, in this sense, never ends.

All positivistic research methods are employed to realize a common goal –providing complete, honest, reliable, valid, objective descriptions or explanations of social phenomena. We can and must produce good, complete contemporary explanations. We can with a high degree of certainty and accuracy say, on the basis of our carefully collected data, this is the way the world is operating now; these are people's attitudes, beliefs, ideologies; and these are the behavioral consequences of their present constructions of the world. In positivistic social science, we may seem to overstress such issues as objectivity, reliability, and validity, but it is only because these are yardsticks against which our knowledge may be judged. To be a social scientist, you must reconcile yourself to the hard reality that you will never be able to say that you fully and completely know why human beings act as they do or that your findings have universal applicability. You can say, however, that you have been imaginative and creative, that you have honestly tried to assess the validity of knowledge at every step in its production. These, indeed, are the ultimate principles of successful research.

SOLVING SOCIAL PROBLEMS: DATA AND DEMOCRACY

We have been careful to suggest the limits of social science knowledge. However, we should not be overly modest about the significance of our work. Research can be profoundly liberating by letting us see how social forces shape our identities and life situations and how we are influenced by the institutions with which we live. Close examination of the social world informs us about the delicate balance between social order and personal freedom existing in a society. It serves to raise our consciousness about the constant interplay between individuals and social structures. The knowledge and insight provided by social scientists have direct implications for

collective action. Those groups in any society that are oppressed socially or economically will be better able to alter their situations once they correctly perceive how that oppression has been accomplished.

On a more concrete level, social scientists have successfully questioned long-standing beliefs about the poor, demonstrated the faulty character of racial stereotypes, uncovered the informal structure of bureaucratic organizations, and caused us to better understand the behaviors and attitudes of segments of the population with whom we might rarely come into contact. When they use their research imagination to expose such life constancies as the allocation, distribution, and use of power in a society, and varieties of social interaction, group formation, and patterns of deviance, researchers are talking about processes that touch us all. The clarity and insight that social scientists gain about such processes can be only as good as the data that are the basis for their explanation. Methodologies ensure that the data from which the understanding of society is inferred are as valid as possible.

Why is all this important? Why must we worry about the data from which we draw our generalizations about social life? All decision making, all policy formulation, must proceed from some knowledge base, not just the decisions that we make privately but also, and perhaps more importantly, the decisions often made for us. The excellence of our schools, the livability of our cities, the effectiveness of programs developed to reduce crime, to respond to terrorism and natural disasters must be grounded in some conception of how and why people behave as they do. Social scientists proceed with the belief that it is possible to avoid creating social policy with information or knowledge that is merely intuitive or developed with inadequate data. Is punishment a deterrent to antisocial behavior? Does the physical deterioration of an area lead to family disorganization? To what extent is education related to future occupational success? Does integration raise the academic achievement levels of minority students? These are the types of questions to which clear answers can be provided. These are also the kinds of questions to which we apply our research imagination as we work to develop plans for creating beneficial change in a society.

The dangers of using intuition, common sense, or what appears to be the obvious to answer questions like those posed above are very great. Time and again enormous amounts of money and energy have been invested in programs that were bound to fail because they were based on faulty knowledge. Planners, for example, have torn up areas of cities because they incorrectly believed there to be an obvious relationship between the physical appearance of an area and social disorganization. Our prison system reflects the faultiness of another "obvious" assumption – that if people are severely punished, they will cease to engage in antisocial behavior. In other words, as long as common sense is frequently shown to be neither common nor necessarily sensible, social scientists will have a crucial task to perform.

Today, we face extraordinary problems in our society and throughout the world. Social scientific knowledge alone will not solve these problems, but we have no hope of forging solutions without a sensitive and deep understanding of how people relate to one another in the social structures and institutions of their own making.

A PRECODED QUESTIONNAIRE

SOCIAL AND POLITICAL PRIORITIES: A SURVEY

Identification Number _____   (1) _____

Please answer all questions in this survey to the best of your ability. Remember there are no right or wrong answers or opinions; in all cases, we just want to hear your own, personal opinion!

In most cases, you can answer the question simply by circling the response that is true for you or that comes closest to your own opinion. Feel free to write in comments or explanations whenever you feel it is necessary.

1. There are a number of problems facing this country, none of which can be solved easily or inexpensively. The following is a list of some of those problems. Please consider each problem carefully, and then indicate whether, in your opinion, the government is presently spending too much, too little, or about the right amount to deal with the problem:

   a. To protect and improve the environment, the government is
      spending   (2) _____
      (1) Too much
      (2) About the right amount
      (3) Too little
      (4) Not enough information to answer

   b. To protect and improve the nation's health, the government is
      spending   (3) _____
      (1) Too much
      (2) About the right amount
      (3) Too little
      (4) Not enough information to answer

   c. To solve the problems of big cities, the government is spending   (4) _____
      (1) Too much
      (2) About the right amount
      (3) Too little
      (4) Not enough information to answer

   d. To lower the crime rate, the government is spending   (5) _____
      (1) Too much
      (2) About the right amount
      (3) Too little
      (4) Not enough information to answer

   e. To deal with drug addiction, the government is spending   (6) _____
      (1) Too much
      (2) About the right amount

439

       (3) Too little
       (4) Not enough information to answer

f.   To improve the nation's educational system, the government is
     spending   (7) _____
       (1) Too much
       (2) About the right amount
       (3) Too little
       (4) Not enough information to answer

g.   To provide adequate assistance to the poor, the government is
     spending   (8) _____
       (1) Too much
       (2) About the right amount
       (3) Too little
       (4) Not enough information to answer

h.   To reduce unemployment and improve working conditions, the
     government is spending   (9) _____
       (1) Too much
       (2) About the right amount
       (3) Too little
       (4) Not enough information to answer

i.   To meet the needs of the nation's elderly citizens, the government is
     spending   (10) _____
       (1) Too much
       (2) About the right amount
       (3) Too little
       (4) Not enough information to answer

The following items of personal information are needed and will be used only
for statistical purposes. We would appreciate it if you would tell us the following
about yourself:

What is your year of birth? _____   (11) _____
What is your gender?   (12) _____
(please circle the correct answer)

1.   Male
2.   Female

What is the highest year of school that you completed?
(please circle the correct answer)

- No formal schooling
- 1st grade
- 2nd grade
- 3rd grade
- 4th grade
- 5th grade
- 6th grade
- 7th grade
- 8th grade
- 9th grade
- 10th grade

- 11th grade
- 12th grade
- 1 year of college
- 2 years of college
- 3 years of college
- 4 years of college
- 5 years of college
- 6 years of college
- 7 years of college
- 8 years of college
- More than 8 years of college

Source: Adapted from Davis, James A., Tom W. Smith, and Peter V. Marsden. 2005. *General Social Surveys, 1972–2004 Cumulative File.* ICPSR04295-v1. Chicago: National Opinion Research Center.

EXCERPT FROM A CODEBOOK

CONTENTS OF LINE NO. 1

Question Number	Column Location	Question Wording and Response Codes
—	1	IDENTIFICATION NUMBER
1		There are a number of problems facing this country, none of which can be solved easily or inexpensively. The following is a list of some of those problems. Please consider each problem carefully, and then indicate whether, in your opinion, the government is presently spending too much, too little, or about the right amount to deal with the problem:
1a	2	Improving and protecting the environment 　　Too much 　　About the right amount 　　Too little 　　Not informed enough to answer 　　Missing data
1b	3	Improving and protecting the nation's health 　　(same response codes as in 1a)
1c	4	Solving the problems of big cities 　　(same response codes as in 1a)
1d	5	Lowering the crime rate 　　(same response codes as in 1a)
1e	6	Dealing with problems created by drug addiction 　　(same response codes as in 1a)
1f	7	Improving the nation's educational system 　　(same response codes as in 1a)
1g	8	Providing adequate assistance to the poor 　　(same response codes as in 1a)
1h	9	Reducing unemployment and improving working conditions 　　(same response codes as in 1a)
1i	10	Meeting the needs of the nation's elderly citizens 　　(same response codes as in 1a)

The following items of personal information are needed and will be used only for statistical purposes. We would appreciate it if you would tell us the following about yourself:

2	11	Year of birth 　　(code the four digit year exactly)
3	12	Gender 　　Male 　　Female 　　Missing data

Question Number	Column Location	Question Wording and Response Codes
4	13	The highest year of school that you completed

Code as follows:

00	no formal schooling
1	1st grade
2	2nd grade
3	3rd grade
4	4th grade
5	5th grade
6	6th grade
7	7th grade
8	8th grade
9	9th grade
10	10th grade
11	11th grade
12	12th grade
13	1 year of college
14	2 years of college
15	3 years of college
16	4 years of college
17	5 years of college
18	6 years of college
19	7 years of college
20	8 years of college
21	more than 8 years of college

AUTHOR INDEX

SUBJECT INDEX